THE NEXT FRONTIER

Y0-BRD-104

Recent Titles in

STUDIES IN CRIME AND PUBLIC POLICY

Michael Tonry and Norval Morris, General Editors

THE NEXT FRONTIER

National Development, Political Change,

and the Death Penalty in Asia

David T. Johnson

Franklin E. Zimring

OXFORD

UNIVERSITY PRESS

2009

OXFORD
UNIVERSITY PRESS

Oxford University Press, Inc., publishes works that further
Oxford University's objective of excellence
in research, scholarship, and education.

Oxford   New York
Auckland   Cape Town   Dar es Salaam   Hong Kong   Karachi
Kuala Lumpur   Madrid   Melbourne   Mexico City   Nairobi
New Delhi   Shanghai   Taipei   Toronto

With offices in
Argentina   Austria   Brazil   Chile   Czech Republic   France   Greece
Guatemala   Hungary   Italy   Japan   Poland   Portugal   Singapore
South Korea   Switzerland   Thailand   Turkey   Ukraine   Vietnam

Published by Oxford University Press, Inc.
198 Madison Avenue, New York, New York 10016

www.oup.com

Oxford is a registered trademark of Oxford University Press

Library of Congress Cataloging-in-Publication Data
Johnson, David T. (David Ted), 1960–
The next frontier : national development, political change, and the death penalty in
Asia / David T. Johnson, Franklin E. Zimring.
p.   cm. — (Studies in crime and public policy)
Includes bibliographical references and index.
ISBN 978-0-19-533740-2; 978-0-19-538245-7 (pbk.)
1. Capital punishment—Asia.   2. Capital punishment—Asia—Case studies.
I. Zimring, Franklin E.   II. Title.
HV8699.A78J63 2009
364.66095—dc22   2008019677

9 8 7 6 5 4 3 2 1

Printed in the United States of America
on acid-free paper

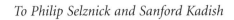

To Philip Selznick and Sanford Kadish

Foreword

KIM DAE JUNG

Far from being an "Asian value," the practice of capital punishment is inconsistent with the main currents of philosophical and religious thought in Asia. There are teachings left by many religious leaders that human life should be sacred as the supreme value and never be taken without good reason. Confucianism preaches that people should be served like heaven, and Confucius pursued benevolence as the indisputable sublime virtue of human beings in which forgiveness is the essence. Buddhism sees the omnipresence of the Buddha's power in every direction, meaning that the dignity of all forms of life and human rights are the most invaluable things in earth, heaven, and the universe. In Hinduism, *ahimsa* or the principle of noninjury bars the killing or injuring of living beings, including even small bugs. Islam also points out that human rights and people's lives hold supreme value. And Donghak (Eastern Learning), a homegrown religion in Korea, stresses that all persons contain divinity; there is "Heaven in Humanity."

All of these religions are rooted in Asia and have respected and protected human rights and living beings as their most exalted values. This is what our enlightened predecessors have taught and what we can relate to in our objective of abandoning capital punishment. The Christian community in Asia has also been teaching the profound belief that human beings are sons and daughters of God, requiring people to respect human lives with divinity.

Apart from these holy words, there are solid and earthly reasons not to take people's lives by the very hands of people, even if the killing is conducted in the name of government authority, law, and justice.

First of all, people, by nature, have both angel and evil in their inmost recess. If the evil from within rises and overwhelms you, you may commit a heavy crime deserving of the death penalty. But if the angel wins in the fight with evil, you can overpower the evil and regain the essence of goodness. There are countless cases of desperate criminals on death row regaining their goodness and doing much good to others. Capital punishment, which deprives people of the chance to be reformed, must not be conducted.

Second, there are many cases of wrongful conviction. Imagine how many innocent people around the world have lost their precious lives in wrongfully conducted trials and how tragic it is. Even when judges are given absolute authority to pass judgment over crimes, they should not put people to an irrevocable sentence of death. I say "irrevocable" because once a sentence is executed, the lost life cannot be brought back even if he or she is later found to be wrongfully convicted. For this reason, the death penalty should be replaced by life imprisonment.

Third, the death penalty in many cases has been misused for political retaliation, which is still happening throughout the world. Since its founding in 1948, Korea has seen more than 900 death row inmates executed (not including persons executed by court martial during the Korean War). Some of them were opposition party leaders and young democratic activists killed in legally disguised political retribution. When the "April 3rd Communist Uprising" occurred in 1948 on Jeju Island, the biggest southern island of Korea, approximately 320 innocent civilians were sentenced to death in military trials on ungrounded charges of being communist sympathizers and put to death. I was also sentenced to death in 1980 on charges of sedition and conspiracy, and barely avoided execution. Later, all of these cases were retried and the convicted were found to be innocent after all. Koreans who watched these tragedies feel heartbreaking sadness and bitter sorrow for those sacrificed on false charges. How can they be brought back to life after being killed? Capital punishment should be ended once and for all in order to prevent such irreversible and fatal political retaliation.

Fourth, whether the death penalty is retained in law or practice is one of the prime indicators of the level of democratization and civilization of a country. European nations have abandoned capital punishment across the board. But the number of abolitionist countries in Asia is still limited. Democratization has occurred or is proceeding in many Asian countries, during which respect for human rights often takes center stage. And respect for human rights culminates in the abrogation of the death penalty in law. The decision to eliminate death sentences will open a road leading to a truly democratic and civilized community.

Finally, according to United Nations surveys, countries with capital punishment do not experience obvious downward trends in homicide. If the death penalty is found to be little effective in reducing fatal crime rates, why do countries have to retain the system of taking sacred lives? It would be better to replace the death penalty with life imprisonment, as I stated before.

Opposition to the abolition of capital punishment is still strong in Korea. While in office from 1998 to 2003 as president of the Republic of Korea, I did not order a single execution and commuted the sentences of 13 out of 52 death row inmates. I did try to commute the death sentences of more inmates but to little avail because of the obstinate resistance of the related government officers, who were arguing for the legal authority of the fatal sentences. My nonexecution practice was succeeded by the following government of President Roh Moo Hyun, and this resulted in nonexecution for ten consecutive years in Korea, which means that the country rose to the rank of a de facto abolitionist nation. Not only governments, but Korea's National Assembly also played a part in this endeavor. The majority of lawmakers formally presented a bill calling for abolition of the death penalty, whose passage was thwarted by the opposition of conservative forces. But such efforts have not been discouraged. The noble quest in the National Assembly and among Koreans more generally will continue until capital punishment is officially abolished.

This is an important and valuable book. Professors Johnson and Zimring show the political essence of the death penalty in Asia and suggest political reform as the mechanism to end execution in the region. I pay tribute to their endeavor, and I sincerely hope that their work will serve as guidance to the abolition of the death penalty in Asia.

15th President of South Korea and Nobel Peace Prize Laureate
Seoul, Korea
July 2008

The debate in the UN General Assembly over capital punishment in the fall of 2007 was not a direct clash on the merits of state killing as a criminal punishment but rather a contest between two views of the jurisprudential character of the death penalty in the modern world. Proponents of a nonbinding resolution calling for a moratorium on state executions regarded the execution of criminal offenders as a human rights problem that requires a universal limit on governmental power applicable to all civilized nations. Opponents of the resolution argued for national autonomy in decisions about death as a punishment, claiming that whether to execute serious criminal offenders is a question of which sanctions are necessary and effective, a matter best left to sovereign nations to settle for themselves. The UN resolution passed, with 104 in favor, 54 opposed, and 29 abstentions, but the ultimate issue—whether state executions should be forbidden by general human rights principles or permitted to nations that wish to conduct them—is far from resolved. Over half of the world's nearly 200 nations have abolished the death penalty, and another 44 have stopped executing in practice, but the large majority of the world's population lives in countries where executions are still allowed, and death as a criminal punishment is inflicted thousands of times each year. Will this change?

We launched this study because we believe Asia is the next frontier in the two-century debate about state execution as a criminal punishment. There are at least two compelling reasons to concentrate on capital punishment in Asia. First, Asia will be hugely important for the worldwide future of the death penalty because 60 percent of the earth's population resides in the region and because it is where more than 90 percent of the world's executions have taken place in recent years. What happens in Asia in the coming decades will reveal whether the campaign against state killing that has gained momentum since World War II is a global phenomenon. The nations of Asia are also an important laboratory for learning about the major influences on death penalty policy and the impact of policy changes on society and government. Most knowledge of capital punishment and penal policy comes from the study of a few developed nations in the West—especially the United States—over a relatively short period of time. Are the themes and influences that are prominent in Western history also significant in Asia? And are there elements in the culture or politics of Asia that alter the prospects for reducing capital punishment or the appropriate tactics for trying to end it?

This study consists of three unequal parts. Part I introduces the topic and provides a short summary of what is known about the law and practice of capital punishment in Asia. The next part—the bulk of the book—is devoted to a series of detailed case studies of Asian nations. Five are profiled in part II, and seven others are discussed in the appendixes. Part III discusses the lessons learned from the Asian case studies and explores the course of capital punishment in Asia's future.

Despite huge variations in death penalty practice throughout Asia, two general patterns suggest a tendency toward reduced use of execution and increased ambivalence about the appropriateness of the punishment. First, even in most of the Asian nations that retain death as a criminal sanction, its use is rare and has little or no importance for crime control. In fact, the most common situation in Asian nations with death penalties in their statute books is very low use, a pattern we call "inertial retention." Since there are no strong reasons for such nations to perform executions, they avoid them. At the same time, they do not abolish the ultimate penalty because there are few strong incentives for doing so.

The second death penalty trend among Asian nations is toward fewer executions over time. In the mid-1990s, about half the nations in the region had executions in any given year, but by 2006 the proportion had declined to about one-third. The most dramatic declines occurred in the rapidly developing democracies of South Korea and Taiwan, but declines have also occurred in nations such as India and Malaysia. Until quite recently, this general pattern of decline was counterbalanced by persistently high numbers of executions in the People's Republic of China, but chapter 7 reports that even China seems to be joining the downward trend—as does Singapore, long one of the most aggressive executing states in Asia and the world.

Despite all this downward momentum, there are still far more executions in Asia than in any other region of the world. Only three or four Asian nations execute with any frequency, but they probably account for more than 90 percent of all the judicial executions that have occurred so far in the 21st century. Is that because these countries are set apart from the rest of the world by history or culture? Probably not. It is authoritarian government rather than Confucian or Asian culture that separates the high-execution nations of China, Singapore, Vietnam, and North Korea from the rest of the nations in the region and from most of the countries on earth. The states in Asia that use execution most aggressively do not differ from neighboring nations in culture, religion, or public opinion so much as in the choices made by those with the power to govern.

There is a natural affinity between executions and authoritarian ideology because authoritarian governments are little concerned with limiting their own powers. But at the same time, there are few practical benefits for hard-line governments that employ execution as a criminal sanction for street criminals and drug sellers. The modern prison does incapacitate, and the legal protections demanded by a world increasingly suspicious of death penalties almost always make capital punishment more expensive than protracted imprisonment. The one comparative advantage of an active execution policy is that it facilitates the suppression of political opposition during periods of political uncertainty and instability. The continued existence of a prominent political enemy, even if imprisoned, threatens any government system. The utility of execution as a political tool may be one reason authoritarian governments hold fast to capital punishment long after other governments have given up on it.

Regarding the future of capital punishment in Asia, the biggest issues have to do with when rather than whether capital punishment will cease. The long-term trends that undermine and stigmatize state executions in the West are occurring in Asia, too. And when development and plural democracy take root in Asia, the decline of execution as a punishment usually comes sooner rather than later. Conversely, when authoritarian governments persevere with capital punishment, progress in restraining the volume of executions depends more on external pressure than on domestic initiatives. The good news about the potential role of international norms and external pressures in inhibiting death penalties is that there are no great benefits to a modern state in executing common criminals and therefore no large material costs to ending the practice. Capital punishment is not an issue like air or water pollution in which compliance with international norms carries significant costs for the domestic economy. The pace toward ending the death penalty is slow more because the incentives to cease execution are weak than because the costs of abolition are high.

Could we be envisioning this encouraging conclusion through rose-colored glasses? Our normative commitment to abolishing capital punishment has clearly informed many of the judgments in this book, but we have tried not to let it distort our analysis. A desire to end the death penalty tempered by a rigorous empirical realism is a more constructive approach to the subject than would be preaching to the converted or proselytizing the lost. That has been the ambition of this book.

Acknowledgments

This research benefited from a wide variety of material and intellectual resources. Material support came from the Criminal Justice Research Program of the University of California at Berkeley's Boalt Hall School of Law, the Center for Japanese Studies and the Research Relations Fund of the University of Hawaii, a Fulbright Senior Researcher grant to Johnson (in 2003–2004), a University of California Pacific Rim Research grant to Zimring and Johnson (in 2005–2006), and a Center for Global Partnership/Japan Foundation grant to Johnson (in 2006–2007).

The Center for Global Partnership also supported meetings in Berkeley and Honolulu between the authors of this book and four outside experts who reviewed late drafts. Roger Hood, the dean of international death penalty studies, conducted a comprehensive tutorial in Berkeley in November 2007, and the next draft was read by Jerome Cohen, Tom Ginsburg, and Koichi Hamai and discussed at a meeting in Honolulu in January 2008. Whatever flaws remain, the result of these two review processes is a much improved manuscript.

We also received valuable advice and instruction from many readers of chapter drafts, including Bob Berring, Chen Xingliang, Richard Chiang, Byung-Sun Cho, Laura Desfor Edles, Laurel Fletcher, Jonathan Goldberg-Hiller, Bill Hebenton, Margaret Lewis, Liang Genlin, Fort Fu-Te Liao, Stanley Lubman, Robert Luoling, Satoru Shinomiya, Jaw-Perng Wang, Wang Yunhai, and Zhang Ning, whose seminal study of the political origins of China's death penalty exceptionalism influenced chapter 7. More broadly, this project has been built on the accumulated work of two generations of scholarship in Asian studies, comparative law and society, and capital punishment.

Four student researchers at Berkeley provided essential services during this venture. Jiang Su helped with all manner of PRC puzzles in addition to summarizing the death penalty positions taken in the recent presidential campaigns in South Korea and Taiwan. Aaron Blumenthal was our statistical jack-of-all-trades. Parichart Munsgool did research on the death penalty in Thailand. And Alexandra Yin translated several Chinese sources.

The fiscal, physical, and editorial organization of this project involved many persons as well. Chief among them are James Cook of Oxford University Press, who was the editorial leader from start to finish; Toni Mendicino at UC-Berkeley, who produced, shaped, and sheltered the manuscript; David Anderson at Boalt Hall; and Karen Chin at Berkeley's Institute for Legal Research and Kim Kaapana and Linda Fong of the University of Hawaii's Department of Sociology, who shared responsibility for a complicated set of geographical and administrative arrangements. We thank them all.

We brought insufficient sophistication and knowledge to the case studies that make up the core of this book, so in writing each chapter in part II we had to rely on the goodwill and expertise of a large body of specialists. Johnson's institutional host in Japan in recent years has been Waseda University, where professors Satoru Shinomiya and Takashi Takano provided introductions, instruction, and inspiration. The chapter on the Philippines was made possible through the networking efforts of Arlie Tagayuna of New Mexico Highlands University and the generous cooperation of Cookie Diokno of the Free Legal Assistance Group in Manila. In China, the Peking University Law School played host to Johnson three times and to Zimring once. Professors Chen Xingliang and Liang Genlin—and their multitalented protégé Jiang Su—provided all kinds of primary assistance. In Taiwan, Fort Fu-Te Liao's work on capital punishment laid a solid foundation for the study that appears here, and in South Korea, death penalty essays by Byung-Sun Cho provided much valuable information for our own inquiries.

We also thank and acknowledge the help we have received from the following people, organized by case study.

For Japan: Byung-Ho An, Shigemitsu Dando, Thomas Ellis, Eric Feldman, Michael H. Fox and the Japan Death Penalty Information Center, Taku Fukada, Ryuji and Sayuri Furukawa, Yuki Furuta, Akio Harada, Masaharu Harada, Takashi Hirose, Nobuto Hosaka, Futaba Igarashi, Tatsuya Inagawa, Kenjiro Ishii, Shinichi Ishizuka, Koichi Kikuta, Kentaro Kitagawa, Tetsuya Kobayashi, Charles Lane, David Leheny, Koya Matsuo, Sakae Menda, Tamaki Mitsui, Setsuo Miyazawa, Yasutomo Morigiwa, Takeko Mukai, Takeyoshi Nakamichi, Reiko Oshima, Kaori Sakagami, Masako and Ayumi Sato, Yoshitaka Seki, Sachio Shimomura, Morikazu Taguchi, Maiko Tagusari, Akiko Takada, Takashi Takano, Takao Tanase, Fumio Tejima, Shigeki Todani, Isa Tsujimoto, Wang Yunhai, Jiro Yada, Misaki Yagishita, Jiro Yamamoto, Terutoshi Yamashita, and the leader of Japan's anti–death penalty movement, Yoshihiro Yasuda.

For the Philippines: Teresita Ang See, Daisy Buenaventura, Randolf David, Max M. de Mesa, Rodolfo de los Santos Diamante, Dolly and Myrna, Roilo Golez, Richard Gordon, Grace Gorospe-Jamon, Seema Kandelia, Lydia Labong, Edcel Lagman, Frumencio A. Lagustan, Liza Lim, Precy Miranda, Aquilino Pimentel Jr., Emma Porio, Fidel Ramos, Jessica Reyes-Cantos, Amparita S. Sta. Maria, Richie LL. Supan, Lorenzo Tanada, and a variety of people at the Free Legal Assistance Group, the Coalition against the Death Penalty, and the Catholic Bishops Conference of the Philippines.

For South Korea: Chang-Ho Ahn, Gun-Ho Cho, Kuk Cho, Kyoon-Seok Cho, Sang-Chul Cho, Sung-Wook Cho, Sang-Myoung Choung, Kang-Jin Chun, Ki-Heung Chun, Chul-Ho Han, Cheol-Kyu Hwang, Jun-Hee Jang, Chan-Soo Jung, Jang-Hyun Jung, Hee-Jun Kim, Hee-Kwan Kim, Jong-Ryal Kim, Seung-Kew Kim, Sung-Ho Kim, Yong-Chul Kim, Young-Min Kim, Hong-Sook Lee, Jun-Sik Lee, Keun-Woong Lee, Young-Ryeol Lee, Dong-Ki Li, Nae-Hyun Lim, Kyung-Sik Min, Sang-Ok Park, Woo-Jung Shim, Hyun-Ho Shin, Roh-Myung Sun, Jae-Min Wee, and Yoo-Ihn Tae, the parliamentarian who helped lead South Korea's abolitionist movement after his own exit from death row.

For Taiwan: John C. Chen, Kenneth H. C. Chiu, Wen-Ting Hsieh, Mab Huang, Remington Huang, Robert Hung, Sam-Rong Hwang, Chia-Wen Lee, Hope Lee, Mengbin Lee, Hsinyi Lin, John-Paul Lin, Shing-I Liu, Edmund Ryden, Dan-Ho Wen, Chih-Kuang Wu, Lydia Yu-Yeh Wang, and other people at the Taiwan Alliance to End the Death Penalty and Fu Jen Catholic University.

For China: Borge Bakken, Cai Guanhong, Dan Wei, Fang Peng, Roland Gao, Gu Xiao Rong, Jian Xu, Li Ruisheng, Nicola Macbean, Seio Nakajima, Ouyang Yujing, Randall Peerenboom, Qu Xinjiu, Su Xinghe, Susan Trevaskes, Wang Baoming, Wang Mu, Wang Ping, Wang Yunhai, Wu Biguang, Xie Ping, Xu Yibei, Yang Jianhong, Yang Jinguo, Yao Jianlong, Yi Yanyou, Yu Gaizhi, Yuan Guan, Zhang Jialing, Zhang Jing, Zhang Peitian, Zhao Wenzhuo, Zheng Jianjun, Zhou Changjun, scholars at the Academy of Social Sciences in Shanghai and the Academy of Social Sciences in Beijing, and officials at Yancheng Prison in Hebei Province.

For help with the India appendix we thank Bikram Jeet Batra, Pratiksha Baxi, Upendra Baxi, Kiran Bedi, Tom Clifford, Rajeev Dhavan, Navroz Dubash, Sima Gulati, Sankaran Krishna, Nitya Ramakrishna, Usha Ramanathan, Amita Singh, Manoj and Sanjiv, and all the guys at Jorbagh 27. For assistance with the Vietnam appendix we thank Penelope Faulkner of the Vietnam Committee on Human Rights, and for help with the Singapore appendix we thank David Garland and Michael Hor. For general instruction and advice about capital punishment and related matters we thank Kent Anderson, Christian Boulanger, Richard Dieter, Malcolm Feeley, Daniel Foote, Tim Goodwin (author of the immensely helpful Asia Death Penalty Blog), Peter Grabosky, David Greenberg, Michael McCann, Michael Radelet, Austin Sarat, Hugh Selby, Jonathan Simon, Michael Tonry, Mark Tracy, Valerie West, and Ryoko Yamamoto.

David Johnson thanks Adrienne Birch for providing the best kind of human companionship, and Taka, Scooby, and Bei for providing companionship of the canine kind. In the late 17th century, Japan's Tokugawa Tsunayoshi issued the infamous "Laws of Compassion," which required his subjects to treat dogs (and other animals) humanely and punished some violators with death. Although Johnson's affection for dogs does not reach the "Dog Shogun's" level, it is still considerable, and it has often required more than the usual patience from the other human in that household. For that and many other things, he is grateful.

A final debt we are happy to acknowledge is to the architects of the program that brought each of us to Berkeley in the 1980s and that was the origin of our later collaboration. The doctoral program in jurisprudence and social policy was created through the inspiration and efforts of Philip Selznick and Sanford Kadish. If work of the kind reported in these pages has value to scholarship and policy, much of the credit should go to those who built the program that made it possible.

Contents

Issues and Methods

Part I of this book introduces the substantive subject of our study by describing the range of death penalty policies that can be found in contemporary Asia and comparing them with policies elsewhere in the world. Chapter 1 summarizes the recent history of capital punishment in Western nations and highlights some unanswered questions about the nature and limits of the anti–death penalty movement that has been gaining support and political attention in Europe and elsewhere. Chapter 2 profiles the varieties of death penalty policy in Asia at the turn of the 21st century, discusses trends over time in the incidence and prevalence of executions in Asian nations, and compares patterns in Asia with those in other parts of the world. Chapter 2 also discusses the case study method that is used in part II and explains why we selected certain nations for sustained analysis.

Asia and the Future of Capital Punishment

The central premise of this book is that Asia is the next important frontier for policy debate and legal change with respect to capital punishment. This introductory chapter explains why this is a critical time for the death penalty in Asia and why Asia will be so significant in determining the future course of the death penalty worldwide. In our first section, we provide a short review of the history of death penalty policy since the end of World War II. The focus is western Europe, which has been the center of a two-stage change in death penalty practice and theory: first capital punishment was abolished, and then the stated reasons for concern about state execution were transformed from criminal justice questions into basic principles about limiting the power of governments to ignore the interests of any of their citizens. In our second section, we outline some unanswered questions about the death penalty, and the most fundamental open question is how far the Europe-led campaign to end execution will go. The final section of this chapter shows why Asia is a critical proving ground for theories about capital punishment and for claims about the future of death as a criminal sanction.

■ The Postwar Pattern

The last half of the 20th century was a remarkably active period for changes in policy toward state execution as a criminal punishment and for new views as to why death should not be available as a government punishment. The campaign to end execution started in western Europe with the publication of Cesare Beccaria's *On Crimes and Punishments* in 1764 and then made slow and uneven progress for more than a century (Banner 2002:91). Executions had probably declined in many nations even before Beccaria, and they continued their downward trend for most of the 19th century. But by 1900 only one small city-state— San Marino (in 1865)—had abolished the death penalty for all crimes, as had three states in the United States and two South American nations—Venezuela in 1863 and Costa Rica in 1877 (Hood 2002; Zimring 2003).

The first decades of the 20th century saw continued pressure for abolition in several U.S. states and in western Europe, but World War I and its aftermath ended the abolitionist era in the United States and produced in much of Europe political changes as unfriendly to limitations of state power as history has yet witnessed. The Russian Revolution and its aftermath led to decades of Stalinism in the Soviet Union. The rise of Mussolini in Italy during the 1920s was followed by the ascension of the Nazi regime in Germany in 1933 and of repressive governments in other nations and by a world war of unprecedented violence.

The rise of totalitarian governments and World War II represented a major setback for the abolition of state execution. Governments of the hard right and hard left are united in their opposition to limits on government power in both theory and practice, so the formal reinstatement of the death penalty in Italy under Mussolini reflected a central element of his regime's theory of the state. The expansion of state execution as a tool of government during the second quarter of the 20th century was certainly vast but also difficult to measure. In the Stalinist 1930s and in Germany's Holocaust era, a variety of types of state killing were less formal and less "legal" than traditional execution but still central to the exercise of state power. When a person's status is the basis for killing, is that in any sense an execution for a *crime*? Can it be called *capital punishment*?

It is impossible to know how the cataclysmic events of the 1930s and 1940s affected the later history of capital punishment in western Europe. We would need a "control group," a Europe that did not suffer through the events of those decades, to determine whether the nations of western Europe would still have abolished the death penalty and redefined capital punishment as a human rights issue. But what we do know is that the half century after World War II produced three related transformations in European policy toward capital punishment. First, in the decades after 1945 the nations of western Europe abolished the death penalty as a criminal sanction. The first abolitions took place in the nations that lost the war—Italy, Germany, and Austria—and then other nations such as Great Britain, Spain, and France followed suit. The last European nation to abolish was France (in 1981), and the last execution in western Europe was the death by guillotine in 1977 of a Tunisian agricultural worker convicted of murder (Zimring 2003:16).

After the last major power in western Europe had abolished its death penalty, the nations of Europe collectively transformed the issue of capital punishment from a question of criminal justice policy into an issue of human rights and limits on government. This second step was a major change from the each-country-makes-its-own-decisions pattern that had prevailed in international law and practice prior to the 1980s. "Protocol No. 6" to the European Convention on Human Rights was ratified in 1983, only two years after the French abolished capital punishment. The Protocol announced that for all nations subject to this Convention, "The death penalty shall be abolished. No one shall be condemned to such penalty or executed." The technical scope of this provision was limited to those nations subject to the European Convention, but the impact of the new standard was much broader because it defined a minimum political standard for governments that excluded capital punishment as a legitimate tool of the state. This general principle acknowledged no national limits. In this sense, the governments of western Europe put themselves in the business of exporting the abolition of capital punishment immediately after the last of their members had abolished it. While the European Convention on Human Rights was politically limited to a single continent, the general principle that Europe announced knew no territorial boundaries. In effect, the nations of western Europe had assigned themselves and each other the mission of eliminating capital punishment in the modern world.

What were the circumstances in which these death penalty changes occurred? By 1980, Amnesty International had begun to publish periodic reports on death penalty policy and practice, building its estimates from UN reports and from information collected by its associates around the world. The 1980 report divided nations into three categories: those that retained the death penalty, those that had abolished it "for all crimes," and those that had abolished it "for ordinary crimes only," reserving it as a possible sentence for treason or for crimes under military law.

Figure 1.1 depicts the distribution of nations by category in the Amnesty report for 1980. It shows that 200 years after the campaign for abolition started, more than three-quarters of all nations still retained the death penalty (130 out of 167 nations). Conversely, only 22 percent of countries had abolished the death penalty as of 1980–12 percent for all crimes, and another 10 percent for ordinary offenses.

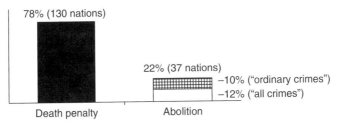

Figure 1.1
Death penalty policy as of 1980 in 167 nations
Source: Amnesty International.

But there are two respects in which the simple division of nations into abolition and retention categories understates the progress away from state execution that had taken place by 1980. In the first place, figure 1.1 only indicates whether a state retained a capital sanction on its statute books, not how often executions occurred. The elimination of the law was often the last step in a process that began with declining rates of execution and only culminated in formal legal change decades later. By 1980, the executioner had ceased to be an important part of state crime control in most of the nations that retained capital punishment in their statute books, with executions occurring infrequently and only for offenses of high seriousness and notoriety. In 1980, for example, the United States had three-quarters of a million persons in prisons and jails but fewer than 25 executions. The great majority of the 130 nations that retained the death penalty in 1980 did not use it often.

The second reason the simple sorting of nations into two death penalty categories understates the extent of change is that by 1980 the most developed nations were clustered in the abolition category. Of the most developed nations, only France, Japan, and the United States still retained capital punishment in 1980, and France would abolish the following year. To the extent that developed nations tend to be leaders in political development—as appears to be true (Friedman 2005)—the clustering of developed nations suggests that the trend toward abolition might have spread rapidly after 1980 even without the European shift to a human rights perspective and Europe's new emphasis on exporting abolition to the rest of the world.

Despite these qualifications, the pace of change in worldwide capital punishment policy during the two decades after 1980 has to be called striking. Figure 1.2 presents the number of nations classified in the two abolitionist categories by Amnesty International at six points in time between 1980 and 2006. Between 1980 and 2006, the number of nations that abolished the death

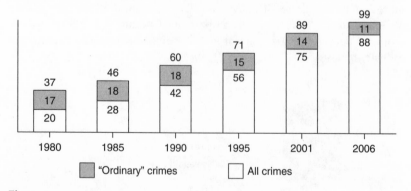

Figure 1.2

Prevalence of death penalty abolition in the world, 1980–2006

Note: "'Ordinary' crimes" means abolitionist for "ordinary" crimes only and "all crimes" means abolitionist for all crimes. *Source*: Amnesty International (various years).

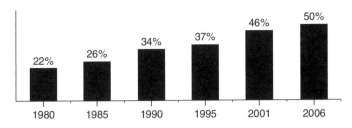

Figure 1.3

Percentage of all nations that abolished capital punishment, 1980–2006 (for all crimes and for "ordinary" crimes)

Source: Amnesty International (various years).

penalty grew from 37 to 99, a 168 percent increase. More nations abolished capital punishment in the quarter century after 1980 than in the two centuries before. Figure 1.3 tells the same story in a different way, by displaying the percentage of nations classified as abolitionist between 1980 and 2006. The percentage of nations with formal abolition more than doubled after 1981, from 22 percent to 50 percent, indicating that the steep rise in abolitionist market share persists when controls are made for the new political units that emerged late in the 20th century.

By 2001, Amnesty International was able to claim that the majority of nations no longer executed because 20 nations were classified as "abolitionist de facto" (defined as not executing for at least 10 years because of an explicit moratorium policy) in addition to the 89 nations that had formally abolished. By the end of 2006, the abolition of capital punishment had been transformed from a policy adopted by a small minority of nations into one embraced by a majority. And adding the 32 "de facto" jurisdictions that Amnesty had identified as of 2007 pushed the total of nonexecuting nations to some two-thirds of all the nations in the world.

The pace of change in the recent past has been impressive, and this dynamic pattern invites inquiry about what future developments can be expected, the probable pace of change, and the degree to which global changes in death penalty policy reflect changing conceptions of capital punishment.

■ Open Questions

The unprecedented pace of change in death penalty policy over the past quarter century generates a number of open questions about where events are heading, the nature and scope of influences on future policy, and the extent to which the death penalty is an issue connected to criminal justice institutions and operations at the national level. The most important questions concern how far the international campaign to end executions will go—and how fast. The goal of the Europeans and increasingly of transnational organizations is total abolition, although how important this goal is in the current priorities of organizations such as the European Union, the executive of the UN, and the International Criminal Court is difficult to judge at present or predict for the future. The pace of formal abolition has been averaging well over 1 percent of nonabolition nations per year since 1980, and one method of projection would be a straight-line continuation of current patterns for the foreseeable future, a guess that would estimate the end of the death penalty worldwide around the middle of the 21st century. But this methodology ignores much that is known about the selective pattern of abolition and retention in the 20th century. The leadership of those developed nations pushing an abolitionist agenda might accelerate the trends toward comprehensive abolition once 60 percent or some other tipping point of abolition is achieved. But the reverse pattern, a slow-down, may also be possible. The nations closest to Europe and under the most substantial European influence have already been recruited to the abolitionist camp. The self-selected nations that have held out against abolition to date may also be a harder sell in the future, as Leon Radzinowicz predicted when he said that "most of the countries likely to embrace the abolitionist cause have by now done so" (Radzinowicz 1999:293).

So rather than a linear extrapolation from the past, the best way to examine the course ahead is to analyze the circumstances, power, and priorities of those nations in the half of the world that have not yet changed their death penalty policies. As the next section shows, this requires close attention to the nations of Asia. The region accounts for 60 percent of the world's population, about three-quarters of the people who live in nations that still execute, and more than 90 percent of all current executions. Although many Asian nations seldom execute and do not depend on capital punishment for crime control, at least two nations in the region—China and Singapore—have an operational system of capital punishment that is a significant part of their approach to criminal deterrence. Will this make it more difficult to extend abolition in the region?

A second open question is the extent to which the push toward abolition in recent decades is mainly a European influence and concern, and what impact European distinctiveness might have on the prospects for change in a region as distant in geography and economy as any in the modern world can be. Research on policy diffusion suggests that the adoption of liberal practices tends to be highly clustered both temporally and spatially, with the process typically involving two main mechanisms: adaptation to an environment in which the benefits of adoption have increased, and learning about the benefits of adopting from those who adopted earlier (Simmons and Elkins 2004; Elkins and Simmons 2005). There is no doubt that western Europe has been the epicenter for reform of capital punishment, but it is important to distinguish between the origins of the current abolitionist movement and the breadth of its appeal. It is also important to distinguish the material inducements for change in European death penalty policies from the political and normative appeal of the human rights frame that has been used in Europe's campaign against capital punishment (Bae 2007). Europe has been the center of abolition activity on the world stage for the past quarter century, but that does not imply any necessary limit to the appeals it has used or the principles that inform them (Yorke 2006–2007). The material inducements that motivated the newly liberated nations of central Europe to reject the death penalty in the 1990s seem unique to the region (Zimring 2003:35). But the appeal of cultural and political arguments that originate in Europe may not be limited to Western audiences. To what extent does the rhetoric of human rights and limits on government generate support in developed nations and in nations with developmental ambitions in other parts of the world?

If the resonance of human rights appeals in non-Western settings is not yet known, there is also the possibility that particular features of non-Western governments may make the abolition of capital punishment more difficult. One issue is the general organization of political systems. Totalitarian governmental structures are by definition allergic to limits on state power, but totalitarian regimes have largely disappeared in recent years. What about authoritarian governments with diminished respect for individual liberty and a strong emphasis on social order? Are these regimes also likely to soften with time and international pressure? If not, is there not an inherent tension between the central premise of authoritarian government—the primacy of state power—and the primary assumption of the abolition movement, and would this not inspire the resistance of authoritarian regimes to limits on their power to punish? If authoritarian governments are inclined to take a stand against abolition, then the future of the anti-death penalty crusade may depend on the prospects for political liberalization in places like Singapore and China. If, on the other hand, authoritarian governments do not hold fast to a limitless power to punish, then they could give up state execution without changing other elements of their character, and the movement to abolish capital punishment need not bump into bigger questions about the character and power of modern governments.

Another open question encountered in the drive to achieve comprehensive abolition is whether the few nations that use the death penalty as a significant part of their criminal justice systems resist abolition with special force. If they do, then the anti–death penalty movement will require larger incentives and greater resources to accomplish its end. With the possible exception of Germany in 1949, every government that made the transition from a death penalty in the law books to abolition of capital punishment in the second half of the 20th century did so at practically no pecuniary cost and without the need to refashion their systems of criminal justice and crime control. This could only be the case because executions had ceased to play an important role in crime control long before abolition. During the prelude to abolition, the death penalty was a potent symbol in France, Great Britain, Canada, and Australia, but it was a puny part of the machinery for controlling crime. When nations switch from a seldom used symbolic death penalty to a criminal justice system with no capital punishment, it is almost universally true that they save money and legal resources.

But what of nations that put practical emphasis on execution for crime control and punishment? We know of only three or four countries with broadly threatened and applied capital sanctions—China, Singapore, Vietnam, and perhaps North Korea—but one of them is the world's largest! China is only a single entry in the 197-nation scorecard for recording death penalty status, but estimates since the 1990s suggest it probably accounted for more than 90 percent of executions worldwide during that period. Such estimates must be qualified, of course, because the number of executions in contemporary China remains a state secret, but China's annual total is by all plausible accounts in the thousands, and it probably was upward of 10,000 during the peak years of recent "strike hard" campaigns. The dominance of China in the worldwide execution count is a function of its huge size and its distinctive willingness to consider execution a primary part of criminal justice. In the Asian region, only tiny Singapore generates a comparable rate of executions per population unit, and in the rest of the world only a handful of nations are even close (Hood 2001:336; Hood 2002:92; Hood and Hoyle 2008:149).

In operational death penalty systems such as China's, eliminating capital punishment requires finding alternative punishments at the top of the seriousness scale and confronting concerns about the government's ability to control violence without executions. It is hardly rational when Japanese citizens worry that the reduction of annual executions in their country from four to zero might unleash a wave of violent crime. But in China, there is reason to wonder what a good safety and security substitute would be for 8,000 executions a year. Near the end of a worldwide abolition campaign, the anti–death penalty movement must ultimately confront a few countries in which executions possess practical importance for crime control, and a life without parole (LWOP) substitute is not necessarily an attractive solution (Appleton and Grover 2007). It is by no means obvious that overcoming the national will of a nation like China will prove as uncomplicated as ending much lower levels of state execution in places such as Greece, Turkey, and Russia.

It is also unclear whether the human rights themes that have played an important role in the abolition campaign in Europe, the Commonwealth nations, and South Africa will capture the support of elites in and out of government in Asia. Does the human rights appeal mean the same thing to adolescents in Asia as it does in Prague or Budapest? And if the substantive meaning of the human rights frame is much the same in different regions and cultures, are human rights values as important to citizens in places without the particular history and priorities of Europe? Or will young persons in China and India place greater relative weight on security and prosperity than on political liberty and limits on government power?

Closely related to the effects of human rights arguments is the peculiar status of capital punishment in Europe and the Commonwealth nations at the turn of the 21st century. To borrow a phrase from the U.S. Supreme Court, "death is different" from other criminal punishments in its severity, its finality, and what it implies about the relationship between citizens and the state (see *Woodson v. North Carolina*, 1976; *Ford v. Wainwright*, 1986). While the finality of state execution had always set death apart from other punishments such as prison and probation, the singular political status of the capital sanction was a

European innovation of the late 20th century. To see the presence or absence of execution as a central aspect of the relationship between government and its citizens is a distinctive and important change in outlook. But is it a Western or a more general phenomenon?

■ Asian Answers to Open Questions

Our review of the open questions about the present circumstances and future course of death penalty policy has convinced us that Asia is the next frontier for study of the death penalty in both theory and practice. The practical point does not require the analytic apparatus of the previous section, for if the abolition of capital punishment is to become the worldwide pattern, the majority of unfinished business will have to occur in what is now the regional capital of capital punishment. And if abolition does not spread throughout Asia, or if the Asian pattern of change differs from what has been observed in other places, then learning about the Asian differences will provide a new basis for interpreting the death penalty changes that occurred in the Western world in previous decades. Everything we learn about Asia can help us better understand not only the future of death penalty policy but the meaning of major developments elsewhere in the world. Is death "different" just in the West or in the rest of the world as well? One key test is Asia. Are human rights concerns an inevitable part of death penalty discourse or are they merely or mostly a European trend? An important test is Asia. Do governments agree to end executions only when the penalty has lapsed into disuse and obsolescence? Must abolition of capital punishment await the decline of authoritarian governments or will the executioner be retired by hard-line regimes even before more organic change occurs? If these are interesting questions (and we believe they are), then a study of capital punishment in Asia is an essential undertaking.

Two Myths

There are, however, two mistakes to avoid when focusing on this regional environment: the myth of Asian unity, and the myth of Asian separation. There is a wide diversity of culture, government, and policy across the Asian continent—in many respects, as much variation within Asia as there is worldwide. We do not focus on Asia on the assumption that there are shared characteristics that constitute a single "Asian view" or "Asian policy" with respect to capital punishment (or anything else for that matter).[1] Indeed, one

---

1. Some analysts say that while there may be Asian Americans in the United States, "there are no Asians in Asia, only people with national identities, such as Chinese, Japanese, Korean, Indian, Vietnamese, and Filipino" (Takaki 1998:502). Others believe "Asia is simply too enormous . . . and too diverse to serve as a very meaningful label" (Holcombe 2006:9).

important difference between death penalty policy in Europe and in Asia is the much wider variety of policies that can be found in the latter region. With a single exception (Belarus, which has executed every year since gaining independence in 1991), Europe is now an execution-free zone. By contrast, the only unity we assume in policy and practice across Asia is the near absence of scholarly study of capital punishment in this region (but see Tsujimoto and Tsujimoto 1993; Wang 2005; Suzuki 2007; Tomiya 2008). And what makes Asia particularly valuable for death penalty scholarship is the diversity of perspective and policy that can be found there.

We also do not expect to find that Asian policies stand completely apart from Western and international influences. We live in an era in which the term "globalization" has become a well-worn cliché, regardless of the policy or topic discussed. But behind this cliché is the fundamental truth that humans now live on a smaller and more intensely interactive planet. The distance between Europe and Asia in culture and economy may not be very large in the first decade of the 21st century, but the degree of separation is still as substantial as one is likely to find. There is more cultural and economic autonomy in Asia than in Africa, and more geographic separation between Asia and Europe than between Europe and the Middle East. We study Asia not because we believe there is no international influence but in order to assess its texture and extent. With the sole exception of the United States, the major powers on the Pacific Rim are as freestanding from European concepts and pressures as any other place on earth.[2] So one focus of this book is not some chimerical unity or

---

The concept of "Asia" *is* ambiguous and contradictory, and historically speaking it only gained real currency in the 18th century when a vision of a distinctive "Western civilization," descended from ancient Greece and fundamentally different from the Oriental Other, began to be imagined. But "Asia" is useful in several respects, including as an arena in which West-centric views can be identified, analyzed, compared, and critiqued. Following the trends of globalization and regionalization, the idea of "Asia" has also been "revived" in recent years in a wide variety of economic, political, and cultural fields (Hui 2007; Emmott 2008; Mahbubani 2008).

2. There is also the converse question of Asia's influence on the rest of the world, both with respect to capital punishment and in other policy spheres (Marks 2006). Looking backward, Asia played a major role in the making of modernity, even if the standard Eurocentric narrative assumes that the "rise of the West" is the story of the coming of the modern world and posits endogenous European developments as the key cause of modernity (Landes 1998; Stark 2005). In recent years, alternative narratives have emerged that draw on scholarship about Asia, Africa, and the New World and claim that these parts of the world played a key role in the rise of modernity (Pomeranz 2000; Hobson 2004; Marks 2007). Looking forward, the influence of Asian countries is likely to grow substantially—and not just in economics (Shambaugh 2005; Kynge 2007; Meredith 2007; Pyle 2007; Emmott 2008; Mahbubani 2008). Among other things, Asia is home to four of the world's eight declared nuclear-weapons powers.

autonomy in Asian death penalty policy but rather the relationship of variations in policy in Asia to other elements of culture and government. Our aim, in short, is to describe and explain some of the diversity in Asian death penalties by relating Asian policies and practices to other social facts inside and outside the region.

Varieties of Capital Punishment in Contemporary Asia

Chapter 1 argued that studying the death penalty in Asia is a critical part of understanding capital punishment in the modern world. This chapter extends the analysis by profiling the great variety of death penalty policies in Asia and by outlining the research strategy employed in the chapters that follow. In the first and second sections, we provide an overview of the varieties of death penalty policy found in contemporary Asia by examining the region first cross-sectionally and then temporally. We then present our case study methodology and explain our selection of five nations in East and Southeast Asia as the central subjects of this book.

■ A Cross-sectional Approach

Figure 2.1 uses the capital punishment categories employed by Amnesty International to depict some of the variety in death penalty policy among governments in contemporary Asia. The 29 Asian jurisdictions divide into 13 with both legal retention of the death penalty and at least one execution in the previous ten years, and 16 with either formal abolition or "de facto" abolition status (more than ten years without execution). In constructing this profile, we accept the view that the military junta of Myanmar has ceased conducting judicial executions (Hood and Hoyle 2008:88), but we reject similar assertions from North Korea (see appendix A), and we classify the jurisdictions of Hong

Figure 2.1

Status of the death penalty in 29 Asian jurisdictions as of January 2008

Abolition for all crimes: Australia (abolished in 1985), Bhutan (2004), Cambodia (1989), East Timor (1999), Hong Kong (1993), Macao, Nepal (1997), New Zealand (1989), the Philippines (2006). *De facto abolition*: Brunei Darussalam (last execution 1957), Laos (1989), Maldives (1952), Myanmar (1989), Papua New Guinea (1950), South Korea (1997), Sri Lanka (1976). *Retention*: Bangladesh, China, India, Indonesia, Japan, Malaysia, Mongolia, North Korea, Pakistan, Singapore, Taiwan, Thailand, Vietnam. *Note*: The Special Administrative Regions of Hong Kong and Macao do not have capital punishment, but offenders can be executed in the PRC through the process of "rendition" (see appendix B). *Sources*: Hood 1989; Hood 1996; Hood 2002; Amnesty International 2006b.

Kong and Macao separately from the PRC (see appendix B).[1] We also define "Asia" in a way that includes Australia and New Zealand as well as Papua New Guinea (Hood 2002:43,45), which obtained formal independence from Australia in 1975 and has not carried out any judicial executions since 1950 despite persistently high levels of lethal violence (Salak 2001). Our definition of Asia excludes five countries in what some analysts call "Central Asia": Kazakhstan, Kyrgyzstan, Tajikistan, Turkmenistan, and Uzbekistan.[2] These nations all retained capital punishment at the time they gained their independence following the breakup of the Soviet Union in 1991, and all but Kazakhstan (which is 47 percent Muslim) are Muslim-majority. But as of January 2008, Turkmenistan (1999), Kyrgyzstan (2006), and Uzbekistan (2008) had completely abolished the death penalty, Kazakhstan had abolished it (in 2007) for all crimes except terrorist killings, and Tajikistan had introduced a moratorium on executions in 2004 and was "expected to abolish capital

1. Hong Kong and Macao are reported separately because the death penalty was abolished in both places before they became Special Administrative Regions (SARs) of the PRC, and because the PRC has agreed to respect their death penalty decisions under its "one country, two systems" policy (see appendix B).

2. Some definitions of "Central Asia" also include the Muslim-majority nations of Afghanistan and Iran (see, for example, the Web site for the Asia Society, www.asiasource. org), but we regard them as parts of the Middle East (as does Roger Hood; see Hood 2002:37).

punishment shortly" (Abdymen 2008).[3] Moreover, of these five nations, only Uzbekistan has carried out any judicial executions in recent years, leading Amnesty International to call it the "last executioner" in Central Asia, and even before Uzbekistan abolished on the first day of 2008, no death sentences had been issued in that country since 2004 ("Uzbekistan" 2005; Abdymen 2007a; Abdymen 2007b; Halperin 2007; "Uzbek Senate" 2007).[4] Including Central Asia in our analysis, therefore, would result in a cross-sectional profile of the Asian region that is slightly more abolitionist than what is depicted in figure 2.1.[5] Our definition of Asia also excludes 18 Pacific Island countries that have abolished the death penalty in law or practice (their total population is less than three million),[6] as well as 19 nations in what some analysts call "Western Asia" but we prefer to treat as parts of the Middle East and other regions.[7]

The almost 50-50 split in figure 2.1 does not reflect the actual balance of death penalty policy in Asia because all of the major population centers in the region remain retentionist. Indeed, approximately 95 percent of the residents

3. Belarus is the only ex-Soviet republic that maintains an active death penalty. From the time it gained independence in 1991 through 2008, Belarus has carried out executions every year. The peak year was 1998, with 47 executions in a population of less than 10 million. In June 2008, the country's prosecutor general declared that Belarus would eventually abolish capital punishment, noting that the penalty is only a "temporary measure" (Klomegah 2008).

4. The secretive regime of Turkmenistan became the first country in Central Asia to abolish the death penalty when despotic leader Saparmurat Niyazov decided to abandon it in 1999. Kyrgyzstan removed capital punishment from its criminal code in June 2007. Kazakhstan put a moratorium in place in 2003 and then all but abolished the death penalty in May 2007 with constitutional amendments that banned the taking of life. Uzbekistan abolished in January 2008, though it remains "a repressive country where law means little, rights are relative and torture is endemic" (Tavernise 2008). And Tajikistan instituted a moratorium on executions in 2004. These developments led Gulnara Kaliakbarova, Penal Reform International's Director for Central Asia, to conclude that "in reality the death penalty has been abolished in four of [the five] countries" in the region (Abdymen 2007a).

5. Roger Hood's analysis of capital punishment in the world treats these conceivably "Central Asian" nations as parts of "Eastern Europe and the Former Soviet Union" (Hood 2002:33).

6. The 18 Pacific Island countries that have abolished are American Samoa, Cook Islands, Federated States of Micronesia, Federated States of Midway Islands, Fiji, French Polynesia, Guam, Kiribati, Marshall Islands, Nauru, New Caledonia, Northern Mariana Islands, Palau, Pitcairn Islands, Solomon Islands, Tonga, Tuvalu, and Vanuatu (see the Asia Society Web site, www.asiasource.org).

7. As of May 2007, the Wikipedia entry for "Asia" defined "Western Asia" as made up of the following places: Armenia, Azerbaijan, Bahrain, Cyprus, Gaza, Georgia, Iraq, Israel, Jordan, Kuwait, Lebanon, Oman, Qatar, Saudi Arabia, Syria, Turkey, United Arab Emirates, West Bank, and Yemen (see http://en.wikipedia.org/wiki/Asia). We follow Hood (2002) and others (Anckar 2004; Hood and Hoyle 2008) in regarding these jurisdictions as located outside the "Asia" region.

of Asia live in jurisdictions that continue to use capital punishment. But the impression of uniformity that comes from classifying such a high proportion of the region's population as living in executing states breaks down when attention is paid to the character of capital punishment policy. Consider Asia's two most populous nations: India and China. Both are "retentionist" in the Amnesty International sense, and neither provides precise or transparent statistics on execution activity, but best estimates suggest that India, with a population of 1.1 billion, executed only one person in the ten years between 1998 and 2007, for an annual rate per million persons that is about 1/3,000th that for the United States in 1996–2000 (see appendix F). China, by contrast, with 1.3 billion in population, has carried out at least 2,000 and perhaps more than 10,000 executions per year in recent years, a rate of execution per million (at the high end of the Chinese estimate) that is at least 50,000 times that of India (Nathan and Gilley 2003:218; Zhang 2005a; "Execution Appeals" 2006).[8] A 50,000-to-1 difference in execution rate is a difference in degree so vast that it is also a difference in kind.

Rates of execution are not the only dramatic differences to be found among Asian nations lumped together in the same death penalty category, for many retentionist nations have gone long periods of time without execution. Among populous nations with discretionary nonexecution interludes one can count Japan (1989–1992), the Philippines (1994–1998 and 2001–2006), Thailand (1988–1995 and 2004–2006), India (1999–2003 and 2005–2007), Indonesia (1949–1973 and 1996–2000), Malaysia (1969–1980, 1997–2000, and 2003–2005), and Bangladesh (1989–1992 and 1998–2001). Thus, at least 7 of the 13 retentionist nations in Asia have had protracted periods without execution. Both the suspension of executions (as in South Korea since 1998) and sharp reductions in execution volume (as in Taiwan since 1990) are sometimes intended as a transitional stage on the road to abolition (B. Cho 2008; Liao 2008).[9] In China, too, there is discussion of a "kill less and kill carefully" policy as the first step on the road to ultimate abolition (Chen 2006c:430; see chapter 7), although current rates of execution are so high and the nation is

8. After India's most recent execution (in August 2004), unnamed government officials were quoted as saying that in over fifty years of independence, the nation had executed only 55 persons, but the Indian organization People's Union for Democratic Rights discovered government documents that indicated more than 1,600 executions had occurred in one decade alone (1954–1963), for an annual rate per million population (0.39) that was almost 4,000 times higher than the rate (0.0001) for 1998–2007. Although executions in India have declined markedly over the last several decades and in recent years as well (only one person was executed between 1998 and 2007), India's death row has expanded from 110 persons in 2001 to 333 in 2003 and to 563 in 2004 (see appendix F).

9. Moratoria and steep reductions in execution are sometimes intended as transitional stages on the way to abolition, but the evidence from around the world shows that "the road to abolition need no longer be a long or arduous one," and there are "many routes by which it can be achieved" (Hood 2007:23).

so large that even steep declines would leave the PRC with world-leading execution volumes.

At the highest levels of execution in Asia, by contrast, we find retentionist nations that rely on capital punishment for crime control and a level of usage long absent from nations in the developed West. In particular, China and Singapore carry out executions so aggressively that there are some categories of crime for which execution is a frequently used criminal sanction rather than a one-in-a-thousand penalty of chiefly symbolic importance. Some China-watchers even believe that execution may be a cost-effective alternative to long terms of imprisonment (Macbean and Li 2003:40; various Chinese scholars and legal professionals, interviews by Johnson, June 2007).[10] There is arguably more of a contrast between nations that use execution to practical effect and low-use countries such as Japan, India, and Indonesia than between states with death penalties in their statute books and those without. In some cases, the huge differences within the retentionist category reflect different stages of evolving death penalty policy. South Korea and Taiwan had much higher rates of execution a generation ago than in recent years, and the decline in the former has been so great and so sustained that South Korea now belongs in the abolitionist de facto category. But in other cases, such as Japan, execution rates have been low for decades.

Nations with large Islamic populations are in the retentionist category in Asia, as they are in the Middle East, but in Asia, which is home to more than 65 percent of the world's Muslim population, they are concentrated at the low-execution-rate end of that category. Several Asian nations with large Islamic populations have recently gone long periods without executions, including Indonesia, Malaysia, and Bangladesh. In Indonesia, the most populous Muslim-majority country in the world, there were at least 91 persons on death row as of 2007, but in the preceding two decades there had been fewer than 50 executions (Hands Off Cain 2007; Hood and Hoyle 2008:95).[11] In Malaysia, which had some 300 persons on death row in 2007, and which former prime minister Mahathir Mohamad deemed "in reality already Islamic" (even if not officially an Islamic state) because in his view it fulfills fundamental teachings of Islam, there were only 12 executions in the first eight years of the new millennium, a major decline from an average of more than ten executions per year for the previous four decades (Kuppusamy 2007a; Kuppusamy 2007b; see

10. In the United States, "the evidence clearly shows that capital punishment systems . . . are always more expensive than punishment systems without capital punishment because 'super due process' is required in the former but not in the latter" (Bohm 2003c:592).

11. Many of the 300 or so persons on Malaysia's death row are Indonesians who have been convicted of trafficking cannabis (Kuppusamy 2007a). Some observers wrongly regard Indonesia—with the world's fourth largest population and the largest Muslim population of any country (170 million out of more than 200 million people identify themselves as Muslim)—as the "largest Islamic country on earth," but it is a secular republic, not an Islamic state.

also Hands Off Cain 2002). And in Bangladesh, the execution rate in 1997–2005 was only 1/20th the rate in the United States and less than 1/100th the rate in Texas (Mash 2007). Most of these Muslim-majority, low-execution nations have governments with secular rather than religious orientations, but the tiny nation of Brunei Darussalam has combined an Islamic theocratic regime with no executions for the past half century.[12] And within Asia, a high concentration of Islamic population is *not* found in those nations—China, Singapore, and Vietnam—that have the highest levels of execution.[13]

Most of the completely abolitionist states in Asia are not plausible candidates to predict the motivation and method for abolition in other Asian nations, largely because of their close historical connections to European

12. In the Maldives, where the sultanate was abolished by national referendum in 1968, there have been no executions since 1952 (Hood 2002:248).

13. The only Muslim-majority nation in Asia with high execution rates is Pakistan, and there the rate varies considerably from year to year. According to the director of the Human Rights Commission of Pakistan, the country carried out 18 executions in 2003, 21 in 2004, 52 in 2005, 83 in 2006, and 134 in 2007. This makes Pakistan (along with Japan) one of only two Asian nations where executions have clearly increased in the most recent years. Yet decline may be on the horizon. Following Benazir Bhutto's assassination in December 2007, Prime Minister Yousuf Raza Gilani (from the same Pakistan People's Party that Bhutto had led) announced that his government was recommending that President Pervez Musharraf commute all death sentences to life imprisonment as part of a birthday tribute to the slain PPP leader (Subramanian 2008). However that recommendation is handled, even in high-rate years Pakistan's execution rate is lower than the execution rates in China and Singapore. In 2006, for example, Pakistan's rate was 0.5 executions per million population, which is seven times higher than the rate calculated by Roger Hood (0.07) for the period 1996–2000 but less than one-tenth the rates in China and Singapore over the same five-year interval (Hood 2002:92).

Pakistani ambivalence about capital punishment seems evident in the huge gap between the volume of executions and the size of death row (a similar gap exists in Thailand). In 2007, for example, there were 7,400 prisoners on Pakistan's death row—6,985 in the province of Punjab alone—which means this one country was home to more than one-quarter of all the condemned inmates in the world (International Federation for Human Rights and Human Rights Commission of Pakistan 2007:16; see also human rights researcher Mark Warren's estimated death row populations at www3.sympatico.ca/aiwarren/global.htm). Even in the high-rate execution year of 2007, Pakistan executed only 1.8 percent of its death row inmates. The Islamic system of *diyat*, whereby money is paid as compensation to the family of the victim in exchange for leniency, is one reason few condemned persons get executed. In 2007, the "blood money" amount was often the equivalent of $20,000 (Ebrahim 2007). This class dimension of Pakistani capital punishment is most evident when a wealthy person is indicted for killing a poor one, for "the abject conditions of the poor person's family make it all but impossible for them to refuse blood money, and once they do, the crime itself is effectively eradicated" (Zakaria 2007). It is unsurprising, therefore, that the vast majority of people on Pakistan's death row are destitute, though they may have wealthier (and unorthodox) allies. Some Pakistani prison superintendents who oppose capital punishment spend considerable time and energy trying to raise diyat funds for the condemned (Ebrahim 2007).

culture and governmental influence. Abolitions in Australia, New Zealand, Hong Kong, and Macao were closely linked to English and Portuguese governmental initiatives (Engel 1977; Richards 2002; appendix B).[14] By contrast, the patterns of de facto abolition and the long pauses in executions in several larger and more autonomous Asian nations seem more appropriate models of discourse and method for other Asian states. Taiwan may be a better model for future debates in China and Mongolia than Hong Kong is, and the moratoria on executions in South Korea and Sri Lanka may be better models for stepping away from capital punishment in Asia than are the stories of Australia, New Zealand, and Macao. If these hunches are right, then this could be encouraging news for abolitionists because the Taiwan and South Korea developments are not only recent, they also suggest that the death penalty can be deemphasized independent of direct European influence.

Estimating Execution Frequency

While not foolproof, the classification of Asian nations into different legal categories of death penalty policy is a relatively straightforward task. Only authoritarian regimes with extremely unreliable data—like North Korea—present serious problems. But estimating the execution rates of Asian governments is a more difficult task, and large and inescapable uncertainties cloud our results. First, the number of executions varies over time, so any annual total is a snapshot that may be out of date before the ink is dry on the report. Second, many nations do not report execution statistics (China, Vietnam, North Korea, India, Pakistan), and at least the first two of those nations consider execution statistics a state secret. Where official statistics are not available, unofficial estimates must come from nongovernmental organizations (NGOs) such as Amnesty International or Hands Off Cain, both of which have a special interest in promoting human rights and restricting executions. One result is that unofficial estimates can be unreliable. In the

14. Most of the countries of the world that are now independent used to be colonies, and "the two most important colonial powers were Britain and France" (Anckar 2004:75). In general, the British allowed native populations to participate in administration more extensively than the French did, giving rise to the view that "democracy has a better breeding ground in former British colonies than elsewhere" (76). However, a comparative study of capital punishment in the world concludes that countries without any colonial past make markedly less use of the death penalty than do countries that were once British or French colonies, and "former British and French colonies make use of the death penalty to an equal extent" (87). It is also striking that as of 2000, all five of the former Portuguese colonies had abandoned capital punishment—including Macao (see appendix B). Portugal itself abolished the death penalty for ordinary crimes in 1867, and the last known execution in that country occurred in 1849 (Hood 2002:250). Of the 75 countries that had completely abolished the death penalty as of December 2001, only four ceased executing earlier than Portugal: San Marino (1468), Iceland (1830), Cape Verde (1835), and Monaco (1847).

case of Amnesty International, for example, estimates are made by relying on information received about specific executions, chiefly from foreign and domestic news agencies, so the numbers produced tend to err on the low side, in some places by a very large margin. Chapter 7 argues that the true annual total of executions in China in recent years may well be three to ten times higher than the Amnesty estimates, depending on the year.

Despite these problems, it is still important to provide information about executions when describing national death penalty policies. Table 2.1 classifies 14 Asian nations that retained the death penalty as of 2006 by their execution rates in calendar year 2000. The retentionist nation of North Korea is omitted because decent information is unavailable (see appendix A). We use the execution rate estimates for the year 2000 to place these retentionist nations into four policy classifications. At the high end, an annual rate of execution of over one per million population is deemed to be an *operational* death penalty system because at that level, judicial executions are a recurrent and important part of the criminal justice system. In 2000, there were at least two such Asian nations: China and Singapore.[15] The range of estimates of executions in China is vast—2,000 to 15,000 per year—but even the lowest estimate puts the PRC well within this operational category. Taking a midpoint of 8,000 executions for 2000 yields a Chinese execution rate of 6.3 per million. The city-state of Singapore carried out 21 executions in 2000, giving it an execution rate of 5.2 per million, which is not an unusually high total for this small country (see appendix E).

The next highest category reported in table 2.1 is a rate higher than one execution per 10 million population per year but less than one per million. Countries in this category have an *exceptional* execution rate because at this level, execution is not a standard punishment for any class of offense, it is reserved for exceptional cases. In homicide cases, for example, most murderers are not executed; only the ones who committed an aggravated killing are set apart for execution instead of receiving the more standard punishment of imprisonment. Two nations seemed to meet these criteria in 2000: Taiwan, with an execution rate of 0.77 per million, and Vietnam, where the NGO guess (probably low) was 12 executions for a population of 79 million, yielding an execution rate of 0.15 per million.

The next category is the *nominal*, where the minimum execution rate is one per 25 million. Two Asian nations exceeded that level in 2000 while also falling below one execution per 10 million: Malaysia (0.092) and Pakistan (0.04). The term "nominal" implies that rates of execution this low are not so much a function of variations in the rates of different types of crime as they are a result of governmental decisions about how many executions it is appropriate to conduct.

15. As explained in appendixes A and C, the data-poor nations of North Korea and Vietnam may also have had "operational" execution rates in 2000.

Table 2.1

Varieties of execution policy among retentionist nations in Asia, by execution rate in 2000

Operational	Exceptional	Nominal	Symbolic	
More than 1 execution per 1,000,000 population	More than 1 execution per 10,000,000 population	More than 1 execution per 25,000,000 population	Less than 1 execution per 25,000,000 population	No executions
China: 6.3 per million, execution range is 2,000–15,000, use estimate of 8,000 executions for population of 1,269,000,000

Singapore: 5.2 per million, 21 executions, 4,037,000 population | Taiwan: 0.77 per million, 17 executions, 22,151,000 population

Vietnam: 0.152 per million, 12 executions, 79,000,000 population | Malaysia: 0.092 per million, 2 executions, 21,793,000 population

Pakistan: 0.04 per million, 6 executions, 146,000,000 population | Thailand: 0.032 per million, 2 executions, 61,231,000 population

Philippines: 0.01 per million, 1 execution, 76,500,000 population

Japan: 0.024 per million, 3 executions, 126,550,000 population | Bangladesh: 130,407,000 population

India: 1,014,004,000 population

Indonesia: 224,138,000 population

Mongolia: 2,601,000 population

South Korea: 47,471,000 population |

Sources: Amnesty International and official rates from reporting nations.

The fourth category is the *symbolic:* execution of less than one person per 25 million. Three nations with some executions during 2000 belonged in this category—Thailand (0.032), Japan (0.024), and the Philippines (0.01)—together with five nations that did not execute at all that year: Bangladesh, India, Indonesia, Mongolia, and South Korea.

Despite the uncertainties associated with estimating execution rates, two features of table 2.1 deserve special attention. The first is the bottom-heavy nature of the distribution of countries. More than half the Asian nations that retained capital punishment in 2006 were in the bottom category of execution frequency at the turn of the 21st century. And these are not small nations: the median population of symbolic death penalty nations is more than 100 million, and the mean is more than 200 million. Yet eight of the nations that retained capital punishment produced a total of only six executions in a population exceeding 1.7 billion, for a collective execution rate that was less than 2 percent of a typical rate in the United States (Hood 2002:92). Even among the Asian nations that retain capital punishment, a greater number carried out zero executions in 2000 (five) than used execution at a rate exceeding one per million (two). This bias toward the bottom end of the execution scale is found in Muslim-majority nations (Indonesia and Bangladesh), in non-Muslim nations (Japan, South Korea, Thailand, and India), and in East, South, and Southeast Asia. Indeed, the tendency for retentionist nations to produce low execution rates seems to hold true for all parts of the region.

A second feature of table 2.1 is that large differences in rates separate clusters of states throughout the distribution of death penalty states. We call this phenomenon "lumpiness." The two operational death penalty nations—China and Singapore—have execution rates close to each other (6.3 and 5.2 per million, respectively), but the lowest of these two nations has a rate almost seven times higher than the highest of the two nations in the next category (Taiwan), and the average rate for China and Singapore (5.75 per million) is more than 12 times the average rate for the two states in the next highest category (0.46 per million). This sharp drop-off continues when the two "exceptional" states (Taiwan and Vietnam, with an annual rate average of 0.46) are compared to the rates of execution in the two "nominal" states (annual rate average of 0.066); the high pair has an average rate seven times higher than the low pair. In short, there is little continuity in the distribution of execution rates among Asian nations. These large differences in execution rates between categories provide some margin of error for our classifications, which we need, given the guesses one has to make for nations such as China and Vietnam. In order for China to fall into the "exceptional" category, its rate would have to be even lower than the rate generated by the extremely conservative count of 1,457 made by Amnesty International in 2000.

One aspect of the lumpy distribution of Asian retentionist nations is the extraordinary influence of Chinese executions on the regional total. If China's execution total is estimated to be 8,000 for the year 2000, then this one nation, with 43 percent of the population of Asian states that retain the death penalty, carried out more than 99 percent of the region's executions.[16] The dominant role played by Chinese executions illustrates the value that execution rate estimates add to formal categories such as "retention" by measuring a policy's intensity. Execution rates in places like Singapore and the PRC are not merely different in degree from the bulk of other Asian nations that retain the ultimate sanction, they are different in kind.

16. The total volume of executions summarized in table 2.1 is 8,064, and 8,000/8,064 = 99.2 percent.

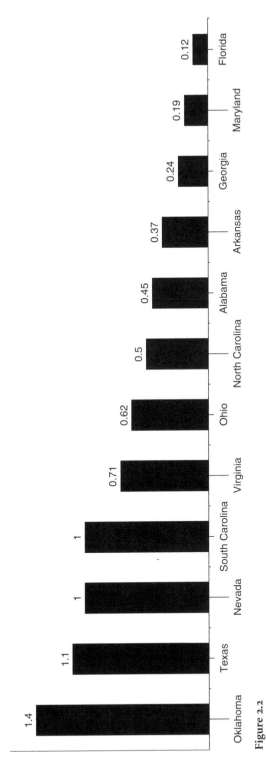

Figure 2.2

Execution rates per million population in the United States for states that had executions, 2004

Sources: U.S. Census Bureau 2001; U.S. Department of Justice, Bureau of Justice Statistics 2006.

The extreme differences in intensity of execution policy described in table 2.1 are also a basis for doubting that any common regional, cultural, religious, or historical factor is the major determinant of contemporary capital punishment policy. Even among Asia's retentionist nations, there are simply too many discontinuities in execution policy to allow for a dominant regional trend. Singapore and the PRC may resemble each other, but they are too far removed from the policies of most of their Asian neighbors to be explained by any unitary theory of Asian values or difference (Kim 1994; Bell 2000).

To compare the lumpy quality of the Asian distribution with variations in execution rates in the United States, we computed the per capita rate of executions for the 12 American states that carried out executions in 2004. See figure 2.2. The execution rates for the U.S. states show a steady downward progression from highest to lowest, with no state that has an execution rate as high as double that of the next highest state. By contrast, the nine executing jurisdictions in Asia have five situations where one step up in execution more than doubles the rate. Similarly, the mean difference between each U.S. state and the next highest state is 25 percent, while the mean difference in the Asian comparisons is more than 150 percent. America is notorious for having large state-to-state differences in execution rates, especially between northern and southern states (Zimring 2003:73), yet the differences between Asian nations that execute are on average more than six times higher. Even if we remove the two highest rate Asian jurisdictions (China and Singapore) from table 2.1, the average gap between nations in ascending order of execution remains well above 100 percent, which is still four times the U.S. variance. Of course, differences in population and data quality must be taken into account in this comparison, but the huge differences in Asia do seem to be a distinctive feature of that region.

■ A Temporal Approach

The primary method of organizing Asian data in the previous section was cross-sectional, and it showed that the region has a higher incidence of death sentences and executions than do other parts of the world. For abolitionists, the pattern over time should be more encouraging (though the data on trends over time are not good) because for Asian nations without strong ties to Western democracies, most of the visible reductions in executions have been recent, as have most of the publicly reported discussions of abolition. Indeed, 11 of the 13 known cases of suspended executions for multiyear periods (three years or more) in Asia's retentionist jurisdictions occurred after 1987.[17]

17. The 13 known cases of discretionary execution moratoria for multiyear periods are South Korea (no executions from 1998 to 2007), Bangladesh (1989–1992 and 1998–2001),

Of course, one reason the known cases of suspension are clustered in the recent past is the poor quality of information on executions over time in much, if not most, of Asia. What we do not know about trends in execution over time in China could fill several books (Macbean and Li 2003:32; Ho 2005:274; Zhang 2005a:2), and temporal data are not much better for some other Asian countries (Hood 2002:43; Hood and Hoyle 2008:84). It is quite possible that executions have increased over time in the PRC and, if they have, then the worldwide volume of executions may not have decreased. But it is also possible that executions have declined over time in China. We do not know, and if other researchers do they apparently have not written about it.

Long-term trends in other major Asian nations can be identified, and the number of executions is down in most of them, including Japan, South Korea, Taiwan, the Philippines, Indonesia, India, Malaysia, and probably Bangladesh.[18] But students of policy who demand reliable footnotes would not be happy with the factual evidence supporting some of these suppositions.[19]

On the other hand, while the general trajectory of executions seems downward, the recent history of Asia also shows several reversals of death penalty policy. Most of the suspensions of execution mentioned earlier in this section were followed by resumptions. In the Philippines, for example, what looked very much like a prelude to abolition—a 12-year pause between 1987 and 1998—was followed by six executions in 1999 and one more in 2000 (Tagayuna 2004:16).[20] In Western nations, the resumption of executions after long suspensions was uncommon (Zimring and Hawkins 1986:3; Zimring 2003:17), but

---

Indonesia (1949–1973 and 1996–2000), Japan (1989–1992), Malaysia (1969–1980, 1997–2000, and 2003–2005), the Philippines (1994–1998 and 2001–2006), and Thailand (1988–1995 and 2004–2006).

18. In Singapore, too, executions seem to have declined in recent years (see appendix E).

19. Capital punishment is only one type of "state killing," and the discussion here is limited to judicial (vs. extrajudicial) executions. De facto abolition in a state such as Myanmar (1989–2007) illustrates the possibility that states that suspend judicial executions may remain vigorous killing states. The same can be said of Thailand, where police summarily killed more than 3,000 suspected drug dealers in 2003 (see appendix D), India (see appendix F), and the Philippines, where despite no executions from January 2000 until the nation's second abolition in June 2006, extrajudicial killings occurred on a large scale and frequently were carried out by members of the police and military (Amnesty International 2006e). For a more detailed discussion of the relationships between judicial and extrajudicial killing, see appendix G.

20. There were no executions in the Philippines for ten years before the first abolition in 1987, and there were no executions for six years before the second abolition occurred in 2006. Thus, in the 30 years between 1977 and 2006, judicial executions occurred in only two of them: 1999 and 2000. See chapter 4.

this may not be as true in Asia (or the United States).[21] Moreover, some of our generalizations about patterns in this part of the world may be vulnerable because of data problems of epic proportions. Good historical accounts of death penalty practice in Asia can be difficult to construct, but they are no less necessary for that reason. One reason part II stresses the case study of individual nations is our hope that sustained analysis of particular cases will generate previously unavailable information about long-term trends in Asia.

Incidence versus Prevalence of Asian Executions

Is it possible to make any rigorous comparisons of trends over time in Asian execution policy? At least one limited comparison can be done with existing data: a count of the number of governments that have executed each year over the past decade. After showing why this measure is available, we will present data on trends since the mid-1990s.

In theory, two different measures of execution could provide data on trends over time in Asia. The first is the *incidence* of executions. An analysis of incidence would entail measuring the Asian per capita rate of execution each year and the trend up or down over time. The second measure is the *prevalence* of executions in Asia, by which we mean the number of nations that carry out executions in any given year and the trend over time in the proportion of all Asian nations that use executions.

Two aspects of criminal justice in China make the incidence of executions in Asia an impossible statistic to obtain and also a poor indicator of national policy in the Asian region as a whole. To start with, nobody can measure the number of executions in Asia because more than 95 percent of all executions (and probably more than 99 percent) take place in China, where reliable data on executions cannot be obtained. Without a good measure of Chinese executions, the Asian total is unknowable. Simple arithmetic helps make the point: if Chinese executions were to increase from (say) 8,000 in 2000 to 8,000 plus 1 percent in 2001, and if every other nation in Asia stopped executing entirely, the total number of executions in Asia would *increase*. Conversely, if Chinese executions dropped 3 percent and executions everywhere else in Asia tripled from their totals in the year 2000, then the total volume of executions in Asia would *decrease*. Without good information on Chinese executions, there is no way to know whether modest changes in Chinese capital punishment might be overwhelming big changes elsewhere in Asia. It is also true that with China's huge impact on regional totals, even reliable data on the number of executions in Asia would not be a good measure of policy trends for Asian

---

21. "The number of American jurisdictions that have abolished the death penalty, only to restore it a few years later, is only slightly smaller than the number that have abolished it once and for all" (Bedau 2004:24).

governments. If 95 or 99 percent of all executions occur in the PRC, then variations in the regional execution rate really only reveal what is happening in Asia's largest country.

On the other hand, taking a census of how many Asian nations execute each year in order to determine the national prevalence rate of executions does provide some indication of national policy trends. In this measure, each nation gets only one vote, so any general pattern cannot be dominated by one or two countries.

Figure 2.3 shows, for each year since 1995, the count of executing nations in Asia, based on Amnesty International's estimates. The incidence estimates (how many executions each year) provided by Amnesty tend to be low, especially for countries with nontransparent political systems, but there is no reason to doubt the accuracy of Amnesty's prevalence judgments where executions are concerned. Indeed, any inaccuracies that do exist would probably be underestimates of the number of nations that have performed executions. Since we believe such underestimates are more frequent in earlier years than in recent ones (because news coverage of capital punishment has improved), figure 2.3 may understate the trends in prevalence over time. The individual nations counted in the tabulations for figure 2.3 pop in and out of the listings, but the trend over time is downward. The highest recorded totals are for 1996 and 1997, the second and third years in the series, while the lowest two totals are for 2006 and 2005 (tied with 2000 and 1998). Similarly, the three-year average in the mid-1990s is 16 executing nations per year, while the three-year total at the end of this series is 11, a decline of five nations (about 30 percent) in only a decade. In short, Asia experienced a marked decline in execution prevalence during the most recent 12-year period for which data are available.

One other finding from this prevalence study merits mention. The smallest number of nations with reported executions in figure 2.3 was ten in 2006, but only half of the ten that executed that year also carried out executions in each of the previous 11 years. During this 12-year period, China, Singapore, Vietnam, Pakistan, and Japan were the only nations that consistently appeared on Amnesty International's annual execution scorecard. If there is a "hard core" of executing countries in Asia, it may be closer to five than to ten.

We invented the national prevalence measure to test for regional trends not overwhelmed by the abundance of Chinese executions. There is also value in using this measure outside Asia to see what it reveals about other regions that use capital punishment. Figure 2.4 shows execution prevalence for nations in the Middle East and Africa for the same years covered in the Asian profile, again relying on Amnesty International's estimates.[22] The contrast between the

22. In addition to Asia, the Middle East, and Africa, the 13 countries of the Caribbean make up a fourth region of the world that remains largely retentionist. Their combined population is about five million, and only two—Haiti and the Dominican Republic—were classified by Amnesty International as abolitionist in 2007 (see Miethe, Lu, and Deibert 2005:117; A. Johnson

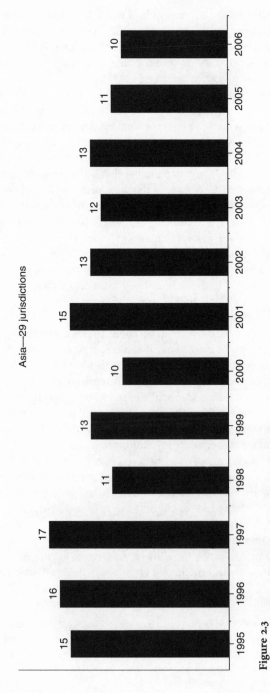

Asia—29 jurisdictions

Figure 2.3
Prevalence of nations using execution in Asia, 1995–2006
Source: Amnesty International (various years).

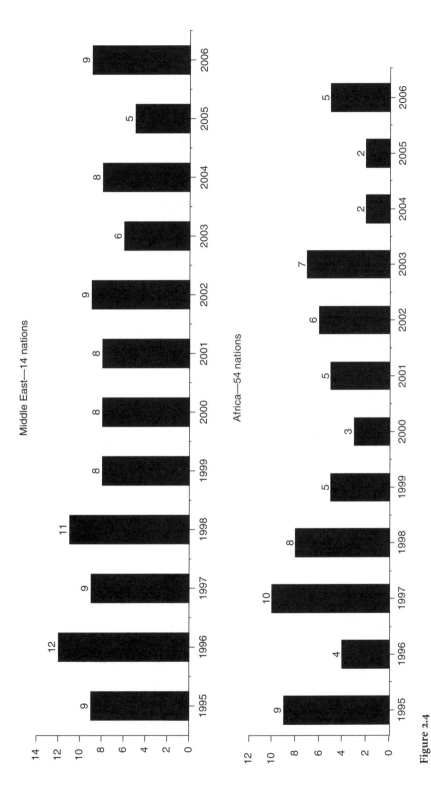

Figure 2.4

Prevalence of nations using execution in the Middle East and Africa, 1995–2006

Source: Amnesty International (various years).

Middle East and Africa is clear, and the pattern in Asia seems closer to that observed in Africa over time. Africa starts with a lower prevalence of execution: nine countries carried out executions in 2005. And though Africa's annual totals are volatile, the trend over time is downward, from an average of eight nations per year at the beginning of the period to three per year in the three-year period from 2004 to 2006. The return to five nations in 2006 is not consistent with this overall pattern but does not on its own reverse the longer-term trend. Even with a prevalence of five, the rate of execution in 2006 was less than 10 percent of the total number of 54 nations in Africa south of the Sahara.

There are three respects in which the prevalence of executions in the Middle East differs from that in Africa and Asia and is best considered trendless over this 12-year period. First, there is little variance or volatility in the number of executing nations, ranging only between 5 and 12 in this period, a close to 2-to-1 ratio compared to 5-to-1 for Africa. Second, there is not much evidence of change over time in the Middle East. The number of executing nations in 2006 and 2004 is indistinguishable from the annual totals in 1995, 1997, and the period from 1999 to 2002. The only indications of any downward trend are the six-nation entry for 2003 and the five-nation entry for 2005, but the return to nine executing nations in 2006 suggests that the drops in 2003 and 2005 are not a strong sign of declining use of execution in the region. Third, the nine executing nations in 2006 are nearly two-thirds of the 14 nations in the Middle East region, a rate almost seven times higher than the African prevalence rate for the same year.

In sum, the evidence of declining use of execution over time in Asia parallels the trend in Africa but not in the Middle East. And with 10 of its 29 jurisdictions executing in 2006, Asia is midway between the prevalence rates for the Middle

---

2008). Per capita, the death row population in the Caribbean is about four times that of the United States, but executions are relatively rare events (Burnham 2005). The largest death row populations are in Jamaica and Trinidad and Tobago, but in Jamaica there have been no executions since 1988, while Trinidad and Tobago has carried out no executions since nine persons were hanged in June 1999—the nation's first executions since 1994 (Amnesty International 2002b; see also Roberts 1999). Executions in the Caribbean declined markedly following a 1993 ruling in a Jamaican case by the Judicial Committee of the Privy Council, which held that delays of more than five years between capital convictions and executions constituted cruel and unusual punishment (*Pratt & Morgan v. Attorney General of Jamaica*). In Trinidad and Tobago, where the homicide rate of 30 per 100,000 population is five times the rate in the United States and 19 times the rate in England and Wales, "the penalty for all types of murder, whatever the circumstances, is death" (Hood and Seemungal 2006). By contrast, the death penalty is not mandatory for murder in China. Even in Trinidad and Tobago, the certainty of conviction for murder is so low (about 1 in 20) that a mandatory death penalty is not an effective deterrent to homicide. The existence of a mandatory death penalty for murder in Trinidad and Tobago is itself probably one of the causes of the country's low murder conviction rate (Hood and Seemungal 2006). For the classic account of how mandatory death penalties were avoided in 18th-century England, see Hay (1975).

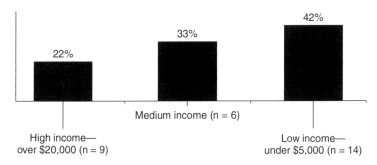

Figure 2.5
Percentage of Asian nations with executions in 2006, by GDP per capita adjusted for purchasing power
Sources: Amnesty International (various years); International Monetary Fund.

East and Africa. In all three regions, the use of prevalence counts seems an accurate and reasonably sensitive way to measure patterns over time.[23]

One further feature of the prevalence comparisons concerns the impact of economic status on death penalty policy. Asia is the site of two apparent exceptions—Japan and Singapore—to the theory that economic development is associated with rejection of capital punishment (Anckar 2004:44; Greenberg and West 2008:331). But are they really exceptions to a rule, or is Asia a place where the conventional wisdom does not apply? Figure 2.5 uses data from the International Monetary Fund (which measures gross domestic product corrected for purchasing power) to group the 29 jurisdictions profiled in figure 2.1 into three income categories: high income (9 nations with over $20,000 per head), medium income (6 nations with between $5,000 and $20,000 per head), and low income (14 nations with under $5,000 per head).

23. A study of "cross-national variability in capital punishment" worldwide has documented the legal status of the death penalty on the basis of Amnesty International reports for 2003 (Miethe, Lu, and Deibert 2005:117). In this account of legal prevalence at one point in time, 13 of the 14 countries in the Middle East retained capital punishment (the sole exception was Israel), as did 11 of 13 countries in the Caribbean (85 percent) and 41 of 52 countries in Africa (79 percent). In Asia, which was defined as including six "Central Asian" nations that we have excluded (Afghanistan, Kazakhstan, Kyrgyzstan, Tajikistan, Turkmenistan, and Uzbekistan) and excluding five jurisdictions we have included (Hong Kong, Macao, Australia, New Zealand, and Papua New Guinea), 25 out of 30 countries legally retained the death penalty (83 percent). In this study, therefore, Asia was the third most retentionist region, behind the Middle East and the Caribbean and just ahead of Africa. The same study indicates that in regional terms, the legal status of capital punishment has a largely bipolar distribution, with at least 79 percent of the countries in the four "retentionist regions" mentioned earlier retaining the death penalty but only 4 to 33 percent of countries retaining it in the five "abolitionist regions" of Europe (4 percent), South America (17 percent), Oceania (20 percent), Central America (29 percent), and North America (33 percent).

Jurisdictions at all three economic levels in figure 2.5 both use execution and refrain from using it, but the higher income jurisdictions are about half as likely to have executed as the lower income jurisdictions (22 percent vs. 42 percent). A similar contrast occurs when comparing long-term trends; two-thirds of the high-income Asian nations have either abolished the death penalty or have not executed in over ten years, compared to just under half of all low-income ones. Thus, the tendency for high income to be associated with less capital punishment is found in Asia even though it is far short of an iron law.[24]

Some Recent Developments

Another method of assessing recent influences on capital punishment policy is to use the same categories of classification that were used in table 2.1 for the year 2000 to examine executions in Asian death penalty retention states in 2007. Table 2.2 provides this information for the 13 nations in Asia with death penalty statutes still in force. North Korea is absent from both this and the previous table because it claims it has stopped executing and because good information is unavailable, and the Philippines is excluded from the 2007 table because it abolished the death penalty in 2006.

The most recent data show both significant increases for some nations (Japan and Pakistan) and significant decreases for others (Taiwan, Singapore, and Malaysia), but the overall trend is toward a lower prevalence of executions (nine nations in 2000 vs. seven in 2007) and a lower incidence of executions (only one nation is in the highest use category in 2007 vs. two—China and Singapore—in 2000, and four nations moved to a lower usage classification in 2007—including the Philippines—compared with two nations moving to higher usage). China remained in the top execution category in 2007, but the rate there was down as well. Yet the data in table 2.2 also show that change in death penalty policy is not a one-way street, for Japan and Pakistan are both large countries with significant recent surges in executions. Nonetheless, half the Asian nations that had death penalties in 2000 performed no executions in 2007, including the nations that had the third and fifth highest rates in 2000 (Taiwan and Malaysia, respectively).

24. Of the nine Asian jurisdictions that have abolished capital punishment for all crimes, four are low income (Bhutan, Cambodia, East Timor, and Nepal) and one more—the Philippines—is barely middle income. In this death penalty category, only Australia, New Zealand, Hong Kong, and Macao can be called high-income jurisdictions. Of the seven Asian jurisdictions in the de facto abolition category, two (Brunei and South Korea) are high income, two (Sri Lanka and the Maldives) are middle income, and three (Laos, Myanmar, and Papua New Guinea) are low income. In total, therefore, of the 16 abolitionist nations in figure 2.1, six are high income, three are middle income, and seven are low income.

Table 2.2

Varieties of execution policy among retentionist nations in Asia, by execution rate in 2007

Operational	Exceptional	Nominal	Symbolic	
More than 1 execution per 1,000,000 population	More than 1 execution per 10,000,000 population	More than 1 execution per 25,000,000 population	Less than 1 execution per 25,000,000 population	No executions
China: 4.7 per million, execution range is 2,000–15,000; use estimate of 6,000 executions for population of 1,269,000,000	Pakistan: 0.8 per million, 135 executions, 164,000,000 population	Japan: 0.024 per million, 3 executions, 126,550,000 population	Bangladesh: 0.04 per million, 6 executions, 150,500,000 population	India: 1,014,004,000 population
	Singapore: 0.45 per million, 2 executions, 4,000,000 population		Indonesia: 0.004 per million, 1 execution, 235,000,000 population	Thailand: 65,000,000 population
				South Korea: 47,471,000 population
	Vietnam: 0.29 per million, 25 executions, 85,000,000 population			Malaysia: 24,821,000 population
				Taiwan: 23,000,000 population
				Mongolia: 2,875,000 population

■ Research Plan

How best to study death penalty policy in Asia with limited data and resources? This section discusses four core features of our research plan: (1) the focus on East Asia; (2) the regional comparison method; (3) the reliance on national-level case studies of capital punishment in social and political context; and (4) the selection of five sites as the subjects for our main case studies.

Why East Asia?

Because Asia is such a vast and diverse area and because the authors have limited resources and life spans, a focus was necessary in order to conduct this study of the death penalty in the region. In our view, the argument for concentrating on the jurisdictions of East Asia is compelling.[25] East Asia has a huge population; its 1.5 billion residents are 25 percent of the world's population, 40 percent of the population of Asia, and twice the population of Europe. East Asia also has a wide variety of political systems and levels of development and a deserved reputation as the subregion of Asia with the most dynamic economic development in addition to rapid rates of social and political change. At present, the East Asian jurisdictions of South Korea and Taiwan have per capita GDPs that are 3 to 12 times higher than those prevailing in four of the core countries of Southeast Asia: Indonesia, Malaysia, Thailand, and the Philippines. Fifty years ago, the difference in GDP was negligible (Studwell 2007:192). The development of East Asia in the intervening half century is a global power shift with few historical precedents (Arrighi, Hamashita, and Selden 2003; Shambaugh 2005; Dent 2008).[26] Indeed, the most important long-term trend in world affairs may well be the ongoing shift of economic and political power to this part of the world (Emmott 2008; Mahbubani 2008). As previous researchers have recognized, there are many good reasons to make this rising region the focus of study for social and political phenomena ranging from industrialization (Vogel 1991), commerce (Katzenstein et al. 2000), democratization (Diamond and Plattner 1998), the rule of law (Peerenboom 2004), and human rights (Christie and Roy 2001; Neary 2002; Hashimoto

25. "East Asia" has been defined geographically and culturally. Geographically, this subregion covers some 12 million square kilometers, about 28 percent of the Asian continent and about 15 percent larger than all of Europe. The following political entities are commonly seen as geographically located in East Asia: the PRC (including the Special Administrative Regions of Hong Kong and Macao), Taiwan, Japan, North Korea, South Korea, and Mongolia. This book includes long or short case studies of all of these jurisdictions except Mongolia (for which death penalty information is scarce but where there have been "cautious moves in the abolitionist direction"; see Hood 2002:46). In cultural terms, East Asia is often regarded as comprised of those societies that have long been part of China's cultural sphere, including the "Chinese societies" of the PRC (with Hong Kong and Macao), Taiwan, and Singapore (Buruma 2001a), in addition to Japan, the two Koreas, Mongolia, and Vietnam (see www.asiasource.org; http://en.wikipedia.org/wiki/East_Asia). This book includes long or short case studies of the death penalty in all of these East Asian places except Mongolia. In some classification schemes, the Philippines (our chapter 4) and Singapore (appendix E) are considered parts of "Southeast Asia" (see www.asiasource.org). For an excellent account of the "East Asian model" of national development in its various incarnations, see Peerenboom (2007:31–33). And for an insightful interpretation of why East Asian models of national development have "worked better" than Southeast Asian models, see journalist Joe Studwell's *Asian Godfathers* (2007), describing the families who dominate the economies of Singapore, Malaysia, Thailand, Indonesia, and the Philippines (as well as Hong Kong). The last chapter of Studwell's book is titled "Finale: The Politics, Stupid."

26. Harvard historian Andrew Gordon believes the "economic advances in Japan during the 1950s, in South Korea during the 1960s, and in China during the 1980s, together rank as the most significant development in the economic history of the 20th century" (Gordon 2007).

2003) to education (Mok 2006), ideology (Best 2007), women's status (Lee and Clark 2000), and fast food (Watson 2006).[27]

In addition to these general reasons for focusing on East Asia, there are at least two aspects of capital punishment in the region that demand sustained attention. The first is the high volume of executions. As mentioned, the PRC has probably carried out more than 90 percent of all the judicial executions in the world since the early 1980s. Moreover, Singapore frequently has had rates of execution that rival China's (Hood 2002:92); Vietnam's execution rate sometimes seems to approach or exceed the 1.0 threshold for an "operational" death penalty system (see appendix C); Taiwan had extremely high rates of execution into the 1990s (Liao 2008); and both Koreas are currently ruled by leaders who lived in high execution periods (B. Cho 2008). Thus, Asia has been home to many aggressive killing states, but when one nation is responsible for nine-tenths or more of the world's executions, it will play an outsized role in determining future world trends. For this reason, China is a compulsory stop on any tour of capital punishment in the world, and it is the most important case study in this book even though information limitations significantly restrict the death penalty questions that can be confidently answered.

The second distinguishing feature of East Asia as a death penalty focus is the variation in policy across countries and over time. Every policy type to be found in Asia can be found in East Asia, and there have been very substantial changes over time. South Korea carried out many executions during and after the Korean War, but as of this writing it is in the 11th year of a moratorium on hanging. Similarly, Taiwan had a rate of executions not far removed from the PRC in the 1950s and 1960s but "the other China" performed no executions at all in 2006 and 2007. One feature of these variations in death penalty policy over time and cross-sectionally is the absence of colonial influences to explain them. In the first part of this chapter we saw that some of the variation in Asian death penalty policy relates to colonial histories and connections to

27. For a summary of human rights in 12 Asian jurisdictions (plus France and the United States), see Peerenboom and colleagues (2006). Like East Asia, Southeast Asia—the core of which consists of the five original members of ASEAN (Singapore, Malaysia, Thailand, Indonesia, and the Philippines)—is an extremely diverse region that has experienced rapid economic, political, and social change. Unlike the economies of East Asia, however, the economies of these Southeast Asian nations are dominated by a small group of billionaire families. In 1996, for example, the year before the start of the "Asian financial crisis" that turned this region upside down, Southeast Asia was home to 8 of the 25 richest individuals in the world—and to none of the world's 500 largest corporations (Studwell 2007:xii). Five other states—Vietnam, Cambodia, Laos, Myanmar, and Brunei—sometimes describe themselves as Southeast Asian, but they return an economic product little more than half that of Singapore (xi). Throughout Southeast Asia, "a failure by politicians to enforce regulatory norms" has contributed to the extraordinary concentration of wealth in so few hands, and some analysts believe that without fundamental political change, the region may "find itself stuck on a Latin American highway" (114,180).

Western powers. Australia and New Zealand are the most obvious cases of tradition-driven differences in death penalty policy, but this kind of outside influence can directly explain only two small enclaves of East Asian abolition: Hong Kong (British influence) and Macao (Portuguese). The Philippines' long colonial and cultural linkage with Spain influenced death penalty policy in the 20th century and had indirect effects on its abolition in 2006, but much of the variation elsewhere in East Asia has no clear links to outside influences of that kind. Comparing China and Taiwan in 2007, or South Korea and Japan, there seem to be no clear historical or cultural cleavages that could explain the large differences in death penalty policy that have emerged in recent years.[28] This, too, makes East Asia a fascinating setting for comparative study.

Why a Regional Focus?

There is also value in bringing a regional perspective to the study of individual nations within East Asia because claims of cultural and political exceptionalism are made in the death penalty discourses of practically every nation. China can only be compared with itself because of its unique cultural, historical, and political circumstances. Japan is singular and peculiar. The Koreas are beyond comparison with other nations because of the current division between north and south. Taiwan is exceptional because it is excluded from the UN and because its leaders must act in the shadow of the Chinese giant to their west. And so on. Some of these claims of uniqueness have elements of truth, but all are overstated. The best way to test the degree to which particular claims of national exceptionalism can explain differences in death penalty policy is to compare the circumstances, policies, and practices of different nations in the same region.

Although no comparison is perfect, it does seem more sensible to compare conditions in Japan with those in South Korea than to compare Japan with Canada or South Korea with South Carolina. There are sufficient similarities in the histories, cultures, and economies of the East Asian nations to enable comparisons between them that will generate insights about how and why policies differ and how much room for change is permitted by their shared and diverse conditions. But of course there are also large differences between some of these nations. The Philippines, for instance, does not closely resemble Japan or China on any important political or cultural dimension. Nevertheless, careful comparisons within the region are a promising method for assessing how culture, history, and national development shape death penalty policy. The recent histories of some East Asian nations—South Korea and Taiwan

28. In Southeast Asia, for example, France had a big influence in what today are called Vietnam, Cambodia, and Laos, but Vietnam now has one of the highest execution rates in all of Asia, while Cambodia has completely abolished the death penalty, and Laos has not carried out judicial executions since 1989.

especially—may also provide clues to the likely direction of death penalty policy in other Asian nations in the years to come.

The use of a regional approach to explore changes in death penalty policy is not unprecedented. Franklin Zimring's study of Europe employed a regional focus to explore the post–World War II path to abolition in the western and eastern parts of that region and the subsequent transformation of the death penalty from a criminal justice into a human rights issue (Zimring 2003:16; see also Puhar 2003). But there have been relatively few attempts to shrink the frame of analysis from global aggregations (Anckar 2004; Greenberg and West 2008; Neumayer 2008) to a scope that locates the experiences of individual nations within a meaningful regional context. Roger Hood's global reports have used regional frames for some comparative purposes (Hood 1989; Hood 1996; Hood 2001; Hood 2002; Hood 2007; Hood and Hoyle 2008), and regional studies have been done of the death penalty in Africa (Yorke 2003; Aya, Christou, and Raymond 2005; Yorke 2005; Chenwi 2007) and the Caribbean (Amnesty International 2002b; Knowles 2004; Burnham 2005), but for the most part, extant studies of capital punishment focus on the death penalty either worldwide or at a national level (but see Tsujimoto and Tsujimoto 1993; Suzuki 2007; Tomiya 2008).

The focus of this book on East Asia means that the countries we have chosen for in-depth analysis and the totality of the patterns thereby revealed make up an incomplete portrait of the larger Asia region. In particular, the national experiences of the area to the west and south of East Asia—home to nearly two billion people—are not subject to much scrutiny in this book. Portraits of capital punishment in countries such as Indonesia, Sri Lanka, Pakistan, Bangladesh, and accounts of capital punishment in the Central Asian states spun off from the former Soviet Union, fall largely outside our focus. We hope that this book will inspire others to fill the gaps and answer the questions that our strategic choices leave open.[29]

Case Studies in Comparative Context

The bulk of the research reported in this book is a series of national-level case studies in death penalty policy over time. Previous accounts of cross-national variability in capital punishment have concluded that there are "substantial context-specific effects" and that "future research should be better able to isolate the particular sociopolitical factors" that explain death penalty variation if it employs "comparative historical methods" (Miethe, Lu, and Deibert

---

29. As we have done for several of the case studies in this book, students of capital punishment in the understudied nations of Asia will often have to assume the risk of data shortages and unreliability. As the American judge Benjamin Cardozo said in his classic discussion of the dangers of a different sport, "May the timorous stay at home" (*Murphy v. Steeplechase Amusement Co.*, 250 N.Y. 479).

2005:115,128).[30] To a large extent, that is what we have tried to do here. Since context is central to understanding what the death penalty is and what it will become, so are case studies (Flybjerg 2001:9).[31]

For each nation profiled in part II, we have tried to provide some social and political history as a context for understanding the current status of death penalty policy and for exploring the possibilities for future change. Each analysis focuses on a single country, but each case study was constructed by self-consciously comparing the nation under review with other countries that have been the subjects of study. Constructing the profiles of five East Asian nations therefore created the opportunity to generate comparative insights. In this way, the case studies that constitute the core of this project not only expand the number of countries for which detailed accounts exist, they also enrich our understanding of each national history by employing a regional framework for analysis.

These strategic advantages have come at a price. There exist several long and good books on the history of the death penalty in individual nations (Evans 1996; Banner 2002; Turrell 2004), but obviously we had to sacrifice some degree of scholarly thoroughness in order to produce five national studies. The limited space available for each case study is only one of many limitations on information that shaped this volume. Decent data on crime and criminal justice are unevenly distributed across the countries of East Asia, and some nations (such as China) with little reliable information on key questions (such as executions) are nonetheless essential subjects for study. Another constraint was linguistic. Since we can only read literature in English and Japanese (which was enough for the chapters on Japan and the Philippines), we commissioned English summaries of some Chinese-language publications in addition to relying on the accounts provided to us by Korean, Chinese, and Taiwanese scholars. Although their help has been indispensable, this study is still constrained by our own language limitations.

30. The same account that reached these conclusions identified no fewer than 20 different "profiles" of sociopolitical factors that are associated with abolitionist and retentionist legal practices (Miethe, Lu, and Deibert 2005:125). The existence of that many discrete clusters of death penalty countries strongly suggests that context is essential—and so are case studies.

31. Even one of the most ambitious variable-driven comparative accounts of capital punishment acknowledges that statistical analyses cannot provide convincing evidence of the "determinants" of the death penalty (Anckar 2004:102–121). In that study's search for "regional patterns," the data requirements of regression analysis caused the author to fold the countries of the Middle East and Oceania into Asia in order to make the mathematical model work (122). To us that seems a classic case of the methodological tail wagging the substantive dog. For similar quantitative studies of the death penalty worldwide, see Greenberg and West (2008) and Neumayer (2008). For an excellent discussion of the need to incorporate more sociohistorical context into cross-national criminological studies, see Stamatel (2006). And for an insightful account of the power, dangers, and distinctiveness of case-oriented comparative methods, see Ragin (1987).

Selecting Five Nations

Once the decision was made to concentrate on East Asia, five nations became prime candidates for case study: China, Japan, South Korea, Taiwan, and the Philippines. If China, as both the largest nation on earth and by far the most frequent executioner, is the sine qua non for deep analysis of the death penalty in Asia, it is also one of the most difficult places on earth to gather reliable data. A second obvious candidate for sustained study is Japan, the most fully developed nation in Asia, with the world's second largest per capita economy. Japan is also the only developed nation other than the United States that retains capital punishment and continues to conduct executions. Moreover, at a time when executions are decreasing in the United States and the UN has passed a resolution calling for a worldwide moratorium, the volume of death sentences in Japan continues to rise and Japanese hangmen are becoming busier (Shikei Haishi Henshu Iinkai 2006).

The third compulsory candidate for study is South Korea, a smaller nation than Japan and one in which rapid economic, political, and cultural development has occurred more recently. When South Korea's moratorium on executions passed the ten-year milestone in December 2007, the nation became Asia's newest de facto abolitionist jurisdiction, even though execution had been widely used there just a generation ago. More significantly, South Korea is a potential leader of other nations in the region, a rival to Japan for cultural and political respect and, perhaps, an Asian vanguard on death penalty issues.

Our other two case studies are of Taiwan and the Philippines. Taiwan's population of 23 million has experienced rapid economic development and political change in recent decades but the nation is in some ways constrained by its closeness to the Chinese mainland. At the same time, Taiwan has self-consciously tried to distinguish its politics and government from those in China. Reliable historical data on the death penalty in Taiwan are difficult to obtain, but it does seem clear that in less than a generation Taiwan has moved from extremely high rates of execution to no executions at all in the two most recent years—2006 and 2007—for which information is available.

Finally, in contrast to Japan, South Korea, and Taiwan, the Philippines stands out as a less developed nation that abolished capital punishment in the late 1980s, reintroduced it several years later, and then abolished it again in 2006. The Philippines is thus striking in that it abolished the death penalty at a relatively early stage of development, and it is also interesting and important because of its complicated and contentious history of death penalty instability.

The aim of each case study is to provide a history of the evolution of death penalty policy, an empirical profile of capital punishment in the political and criminal justice systems, and an analysis of the factors that may influence future policy on death as a criminal sanction. The five nations include two democracies—Japan and the Philippines—with very different death penalty policies; two rapidly developing nations now in the later stages of building democratic institutions after long periods of rapid economic growth under authoritarian regimes—South Korea and Taiwan; and the authoritarian and communist PRC. The first six appendixes—abbreviated accounts that supplement the main case study analyses—cover two communist governments with high execution rates and limited data availability, Vietnam and North Korea; three small jurisdictions with unusual death penalty policies, Singapore, Hong Kong, and Macao; and two large nations to the south, Thailand and India. The data and detail in the appendixes are far less substantial than those in the full case studies, but the conclusions reported in chapters 8 and 9 are based on observations from all of these profiles.

Even with appendixes that test a publisher's patience, the materials in this book fall far short of a comprehensive account of capital punishment in Asia. Among other deficiencies, our report on India gives a small fraction of the attention that interesting and important nation deserves, and two other large nations—Indonesia and Pakistan—are only mentioned in passing in this book.

One of our main aims is to provide a framework of theory and questions for wider as well as deeper study of the death penalty in Asia. The methods we use and the explanations we discuss are intended to inspire better data collection, more rigorous testing and development of theory, and close examination of other national experiences in the region and the world. The greatest compliment that could be paid to our effort is the production of scholarship that will render this book obsolete.

National Profiles

The main aim of this book is to examine developments in death penalty policy on a regional basis, but each of the five chapters in this part is devoted to an analysis of capital punishment in a single Asian jurisdiction. These studies locate death penalty policy and discourse in the history, politics, and culture of the places we have selected for sustained analysis: Japan, the Philippines, South Korea, Taiwan, and the PRC. Supplemental materials on North Korea, Hong Kong and Macao, Vietnam, Thailand, Singapore, and India are presented in the appendixes, as is an exploration of the relationships between judicial and extrajudicial killing.

Individually, these case studies explore the role capital punishment plays in a variety of Asian contexts. Collectively, the profiles and appendixes reveal some of the common themes and significant differences in Asian death penalty policies and provide the foundation for our discussion of Asian patterns and trends in part III of this book. In these ways, our case studies are intended both to have stand-alone value and to supply an inductive basis for our concluding analysis of regional patterns.

3

Development without Abolition
Japan in the 21st Century

The death penalty system in Japan has clearly entered a new
stage. An era of overproduction of death sentences and reckless
executions has arrived.

—Taku Fukada, *You, Too, Will Be Forced to Issue a Death
Sentence* (2007)

[Minister of Justice Kunio] Hatoyama, 59, said he visited the
graves of his grandfather and father, former prime minister
and foreign minister, respectively, to calm his mind before signing
death warrants. "I can't sleep for several days between signing the
orders and executions. I'm alone with no help as the justice
minister has nobody to consult with" on death warrants, he said.

—"Japan's Grim Reaper Defends Record Executions" (2008)

■ A Tale of Two Christmases: 1951 and 2006

On Christmas Day 1951, penniless farmhand Sakae Menda, who would later
become Japan's most well-known death row graduate and one of the country's
leading death penalty abolitionists, had his death sentence finalized by the
Japanese Supreme Court. The previous year he had been convicted of a double
homicide and sentenced to death by a panel of three judges in the Kumamoto
District Court. In 1983, after spending 33 years on death row, Menda was
exonerated of the murders in what would become the first of four death
penalty retrial acquittals that occurred in Japan during the 1980s (Foote
1992b:25). All of the wrongful convictions were rooted in coerced confessions
(Foote 1993). Menda was denied food, water, and sleep and was beaten with
bamboo sticks while hung upside down from the ceiling.

Menda lived on death row for 12,410 days in a 55-square-foot, unheated,
solitary cell that was lit day and night and monitored constantly. His parents
disowned him after he was condemned, and a Buddhist prison chaplain
exhorted him to accept his fate, maintaining that if he did not assent to
what had been decided in a previous life, Menda's parents, siblings, and friends
would not be saved (McNeill and Mason 2007). Menda responded by con-
verting to Christianity. Over the course of 33 years, Menda watched dozens of
death row inmates get escorted or dragged to the gallows an hour or two after
being told their time had come (Menda 2004:137). Some shouted to the

inmates left behind, "I will go first and will be waiting for you." After he was exonerated, Menda observed that waiting to die in such circumstances "is a kind of torture, worse than death itself" (quoted in McNeill and Mason 2007).

Following his release in 1983—after 80 judges had heard his case and three decades of struggle—54-year-old Sakae Menda received 7,000 yen for each day he was wrongly imprisoned—a total of 90 million yen ($750,000). He gave half to a group that campaigns to end capital punishment. But financial compensation did little to curb Menda's hatred for the police, the judiciary, and what he calls "Japan's feudal attitude toward justice and democracy" (McNeill and Mason 2007). Despite high hopes for abolition that emerged as exonerations accumulated in the 1980s (Johnson 2006c:263) and a 40-month moratorium on executions (from November 1989 to March 1993) that came on their heels, Menda believes the system that tore his life apart remains "unchanged," and he is pessimistic about the prospects for abolition because "the concept of human rights is not engrained in our history" (quoted in McNeill and Mason 2007).

On Christmas morning 2006—55 years to the day after Menda's death sentence was finalized—the prospects for abolition in Japan did not look good. Four convicted murderers were hanged that day: two in Tokyo, one in Osaka, and one in Hiroshima. These men were the first persons to be executed in Japan since September 2005 (19 more would be hanged in the subsequent 18 months). At the time of execution their ages were 77, 75, 64, and 44. Their average age of 65 was four years higher than the average age of the 97 persons then on death row, and the average time that had elapsed since their capital crimes were committed was 23 years.[1] There was no advance notice to the families of the condemned or their victims prior to these executions, while the condemned themselves received about one hour's notice. To discourage unexcused absences, members of the execution team were told on execution day. In many respects, this was the same execution protocol that was employed while Sakae Menda was on death row, though the wait was substantially longer than what was average in the 1950s and 1960s (Johnson 2006a). Indeed, since these condemned men spent an average of 11 years on death row with a finalized death sentence, the average number of mornings in which they woke up wondering "Will this day be my last?" was about 4,000 (Amnesty International 2006f; Sakagami 2008).

Seventy-five-year-old Yoshio Fujinami stopped wondering when he was pushed to the gallows in a wheelchair on that Christmas morning. Before he was hanged, Fujinami scribbled a note to his supporters that said in part, "I cannot walk by myself, I am ill, and yet you still kill such a person. I should be the last person executed" (Forum 90, 2007; Sieg 2007). Fujinami had been

1. As of April 2007, there were 97 men and 5 women on Japanese death rows, and several seemed to be clinically insane, "driven there by the burden of solitary confinement" and the stress of not knowing when they would be hanged (McNeill and Mason 2007).

sentenced to death for killing two of his ex-wife's brothers after they prevented him from meeting his estranged wife. His defense argued that he snapped because he was addicted to methamphetamines. The oldest offender, 77-year-old Yoshimitsu Akiyama, also went to the newly refurbished execution chamber in Tokyo after eating Christmas breakfast. Partially blind and struggling to walk, he had to be helped to the gallows by prison guards. Akiyama was sentenced to die for beating a company president to death with a baseball bat in 1975 and then stealing $80,000 in cash from the victim before burying his body on a farm. (The two men hanged in Osaka and Hiroshima had killed three and four people, respectively.) At the time of their executions, Akiyama and Fujinami were in the process of appealing for retrials. About half of Japan's death row inmates claim they are not guilty of all or some of the charges for which they have been condemned (McNeill and Mason 2007). The day after the Christmas executions, the Nagoya High Court stipulated (in a separate case) that retrials are permitted only when newly discovered evidence is deemed sufficient to prove the innocence of a convict. A defense lawyer in that case denounced the decision as a "guilty until proven innocent" approach to potential miscarriages of justice and said it was "tantamount to the suicide of Japan's judicial system" (Suzuki 2007).

Japan and the United States are the only major industrialized nations that retain capital punishment. In the United States, Yuletide executions would probably be considered perverse, but in Japan the Christmas hangings reflected a distinctively Japanese context,[2] though some commentators, including a former British ambassador to Japan, did contend that the timing was "a deliberate affront to Christians" (Cortazzi 2007). Several conditions made conducting at least one execution in 2006 an imperative for the prosecutors in the Ministry of Justice who select condemned persons for hanging and present their choices to the minister of justice for formal authorization. To start with, Japan's death row had nearly doubled in size, from 56 in 2003 to 97 on Christmas Eve 2006. The so-called mass production of death sentences (*shikei hanketsu o ryosan suru*) by prosecutors and courts is part of a larger pattern of increased harshness (*genbatsuka*) in Japanese criminal justice during the decade that followed the subway gas attacks by Aum Shinrikyo in 1995 (Miyazawa 2008). In addition, officials in the Ministry of Justice said they felt "a sense of crisis" as the death row population approached 100, arguing that the basis for the whole system of capital punishment would be called into question if death sentences were not carried out as provided

---

2. Christmas in Japan is almost exclusively a commercial event, not a sacred occasion, and unless it is a Sunday it remains a day for work and school. Since New Year's is a much bigger event, many Japanese businesses make December 28 the last working day of the year before an extended holiday. In addition, the emperor's birthday falls on December 23, and some government officials said it would be imprudent to carry out executions before that national holiday even though executions did take place during the week before the emperor's birthday in 1995, 1996, and 1999.

by law.[3] Most important, prosecutors in the ministry are determined to ensure that at least one execution occurs in every calendar year so as to forestall the kind of momentum that led to the 40-month moratorium on executions in 1989–1993.[4] Jinen Nagase, the minister of justice who signed the execution orders for the Christmas hangings in 2006, was appointed to his post largely because he supported capital punishment and could be counted on to sign execution warrants. His predecessor, Seiken Sugiura, a lawyer and former Buddhist priest, refused to sign execution orders during his year in office, despite persistent pressure from his subordinates in the ministry.[5] Nagase's authorization of executions reflected the strong sentiment among prosecutors in his ministry that "a year with zero executions must absolutely be avoided."[6]

Whether the minister of justice will sign execution orders has been "a core issue" in the politics of capital punishment in postwar Japan (Schmidt 2002:62).[7] Indeed, there has been recurrent conflict over this question even within the conservative party that has ruled Japan almost uninterruptedly since 1955. It is from the ranks of this inaptly named Liberal Democratic Party (LDP) that most ministers have come, and scholars have identified three

3. The next executions that occurred in Japan—three persons were hanged on the eve of Japan's Golden Week holiday in April 2007—were also justified as necessary in order to keep the death row population below 100.

4. During this moratorium, four successive ministers of justice declined to sign any death warrants (Hara 1997). One of them was Megumu Sato, a former Buddhist priest who led the ministry from 1990 to 1991. In 1997, he told a newspaper that when ministry officials asked him to sign execution orders for two condemned men, "I took an entire week to read the papers. I returned the papers and said that I would not sign them. Even if executions are legally allowed, we should not take life away" (quoted in Lane 2004). Different ministers of justice seem to approach executions with different levels of seriousness. Hideo Usui, who served as minister from 1999 to 2000, says he "didn't take long to read [the documents he received]. I think I reached a conclusion by the end of the day.... Signing itself is very important. But not more important than other things a Minister has to do" (quoted in Lane 2004).

5. On Sugiura's first day as minister of justice in 2005, he said, "I'll never sign any execution order. It's because of my religious and philosophical views. I think the death penalty will eventually be abolished." Following a backlash from prosecutors, he retracted his statement the very next day, saying it was "an expression of my feelings as an individual and was not spoken in relation to the conducting of the duties and responsibilities of a Justice Minister who must oversee the legal system." Despite continued pressure from prosecutors in his ministry, Sugiura refused to sign any execution orders during his subsequent 11 months in office, a stand that disturbed many of his subordinates (Hongo 2006).

6. Quoted in *Asahi Shimbun*, December 25, 2006. When Nagase was appointed minister, he stressed that he was "ready to sign death penalty orders" because "rulings by the courts must not be ignored" (Hongo 2006).

7. During the 32 years that Sadamichi Hirasawa lived with a finalized sentence of death, 33 different justice ministers decided not to sign his execution order (Hirano 2006). Hirasawa died in prison of pneumonia in 1987. He was 95 (Schreiber 1996:54).

distinct types. First are the "hawks" and "sheriffs," who have no personal scruples about capital punishment and freely sign execution orders in the pursuit of social stability. One "sheriff" who signed 26 execution orders in 1970 told a subordinate, "I have run out of execution orders. Bring it to me when another one is ready" (quoted in Schmidt 2002:65). On the other end of the spectrum are the "doves" and "samaritans" who are reluctant to sign execution orders for personal or religious reasons. These include Megumu Sato (1990–1991), Seiken Sugiura (2005–2006), and Bunzo Akama. Akama, who served as minister for a year in 1967–1968, signed no execution orders, and when he was presented with one for the first time he reportedly said, "What?...You idiot! I won't do something like that! I don't care what the [other ministers of justice] do, but I won't do this" (quoted in Schmidt 2002:63). Between the sheriffs and the samaritans are the "servants" of the law, consisting of the majority of "dutiful" ministers who try to separate their personal views and emotions from their official duties and who sign execution orders because they believe the law requires it. In addition to Jinen Nagase, the minister who authorized the Christmas executions in 2006, the two ministers who broke Japan's moratorium in 1993 (Masaharu Gotoda and Akira Mikazuki) were "servants" of this kind. Both said they supported the eventual abolition of capital punishment in Japan, and both invoked the authority of law to explain and justify their actions (Schmidt 2002:62–73; Ambler 2006:9–10).[8]

This chapter traces the development of Japan's death penalty policy in order to arrive at a historically informed understanding of how contemporary policy-makers came to believe that at least one execution should occur each year and in order to discern why conflict persists around death penalty issues. In the first half of the chapter we describe and explain key capital punishment developments during four periods of Japanese history: the de facto abolition of the death penalty in premodern Japan; the dramatic decline of executions during the Meiji restoration of the late 19th century; the retention of capital punishment during the American-led occupation of Japan after the Pacific war; and the steady decrease in executions in the first four decades following the occupation. Sakae Menda's view notwithstanding, there was significant change in Japan's death penalty after his own occupation-era conviction. In the fifth section, we show that change is ongoing by examining the causes and consequences of the resurgence of capital punishment since the Aum Shinri-kyo gas attacks of 1995. The two concluding sections identify lessons from Japanese history and explore alternative futures for the death penalty in Asia's most developed nation.

---

8. This typology also reflects the disagreements among Japanese scholars and legal professionals about whether the minister of justice has an obligation to sign execution orders (Fukuda 2002; Schmidt 2002). Whatever the legal answers, the existential truth is that at least some ministers have exercised "bad faith" by acting as though signing is necessary when in fact it is voluntary (see Berger 1963:143).

This case study of Japan's death penalty provides evidence that one does not really understand an issue until one knows its history. Many academic and journalistic discussions of the death penalty in Japan assume or argue that policy and practice are mainly responsive to domestic needs and developments. The timing, direction, and details of Japan's capital punishment policy are distinctively Japanese, but this chapter shows that international influences have strongly shaped Japan's death penalty for 150 years. We believe external forces may prove decisive in the years to come.

■ **Abolition and Severity in Premodern Japan**

Although traditional Japanese conceptions of "offense and retribution" differ from their counterparts in Judeo-Christian cultures, death has been such a central sanction throughout Japanese history that some students of the subject believe "the history of punishment [in Japan] is the history of the death penalty" (Sansom 1978; Schmidt 2002:9; Williams 2003). The early history of Japan also displays wild swings in death penalty policy, from three and a half centuries of nonuse that began nearly 1,000 years before any hint of reform in Western systems of capital punishment, to executions on a grand scale and by methods as gory as any the world has seen. By the end of the Tokugawa era (1600–1867), which closed Japan's premodern period, the shogunate and its subordinate warlords were still executing over 1,000 persons per year, even though some horrifying methods of execution and torture had disappeared and punishments had been gradually systematized and standardized in different parts of the country (Murano 1992:53; Botsman 2005:14).[9]

In Japan as in many other nations, the death penalty had religious roots (Domikova-Hashimoto 1996:84; see Camus 1960:222; Banner 2002). For political offenses, for example, it was the sacred person of the emperor who personally handed down the ultimate punishment (Williams 2003:87,165). Until the fourth century, when Chinese concepts of punishment began to influence Japan, law and morality were inseparable normative spheres, and perpetrators of many kinds were publicly executed through ritualistic displays of violence designed to reestablish order, dramatize community disapproval, and celebrate the sovereign's authority (Murano 1992:40). The executioners in the premodern period were members of the Mononobe clan, one of the most powerful families of that era (Williams 2003:88), but by the beginning of the Tokugawa period the executioner's role was carried out by outcasts—"leather-workers," "polluted ones," and other "despised groups"—so as to help the

9. Despite perceptions to the contrary, political violence has been common in Japanese history (Maruko 2003).

ruling warrior caste "project and protect their image of benevolence" (Botsman 2005:54).[10]

The history of capital punishment in Japan "took an unprecedented turn" toward leniency during the Heian period, which lasted from 794 to 1185 C.E. (Schmidt 2002:10). Although Chinese influences continued to shape Japanese institutions in general and the criminal law in particular, many of the cruel methods of execution practiced in China (more than 200 different ones) were not adopted in Japan during this era. On the eve of the Heian period, Japan employed only two forms of execution: hanging and decapitation (Schmidt 2002:10). Moreover, two periods of de facto abolition occurred in prefeudal Japan, and both were largely inspired by the teachings of Buddhism, which had been introduced into the country in 538 C.E. First, Emperor Shomu, a devout Buddhist who had converted after hearing a sermon, declared himself a servant of "the three treasures" (Buddha, the Buddhist teachings, and the Buddhist community) and went on to prohibit capital punishment after he became emperor when his aunt abdicated the throne in 724 C.E. (Horigan 1996:271,283; Amnesty International 2006f). He ruled for 25 years. In 810 C.E., a second abolitionist era began that would last until the Hogen-no-Ran rebellion of 1156 inaugurated "one of the most cruel and blood-thirsty periods in Japanese history" (Schmidt 2002:12). With only "a few exceptions," this moratorium on executions lasted almost 350 years. Although theories about its causes "vary widely" (11), it seems to have been enabled by two main conditions: the peace Japan enjoyed during the Heian period, and the flourishing of Buddhism in that era (Dando 2000:493). Instead of execution, offenders were routinely exiled or given lesser sanctions such as flogging.

Some Japanese are "proud" of the "remarkable fact" of abolition in their premodern history (Dando 2000:493), but there appear to be at least three other examples of abolition in Asia that long preceded Cesare Beccaria's 1764 *Essay on Crime and Punishments*, which is generally considered "the first work

---

10. Handling the dead in Tokugawa Japan was also considered a source of "pollution" (*kegare*) to be avoided by respectable people. In contemporary Japan, the secrecy that surrounds executions has sometimes been justified as being "in the executioner's interest" (Johnson 2006c:265), and a significant proportion of the death penalty literature concerns the executioner's plight. The Japanese interest in what the death penalty does *to* them, not just for them, was also evident in classes taught by an American professor at a university in Osaka. When he asked students to decide whether their "ideal" criminal justice system would include capital punishment, a stark contrast consistently emerged: none of the foreign students considered its effect on the executioners, while all of the Japanese students did (Johnson 2006a:94). For accounts by former Japanese prison guards of what it is like to participate in executions, see Sakamoto (2003) and McNeill and Mason (2007). And for a moving short story about a Japanese prison official who is haunted by his experience after volunteering to assist at a hanging in order to earn extra days off for his honeymoon, see Yoshimura (1989) and *Kyuka*, the 2008 film based on that short story, directed by Hajime Kadoi.

to present a rigorous, sustained attack on the utility and legitimacy of the death penalty" in the Western world (Banner 2002:91).[11] As in Japan, these other Asian examples were significantly "inspired by Buddhism" (Horigan 2001:106; Schmidt 2002:11). What they collectively suggest is that abolition in Asia is not merely a recent policy position or a Western imposition; it has native origins as well.

During the seven centuries of samurai rule that followed the resumption of executions in 12th-century Japan—from the beginning of the Kamakura period until the end of the Tokugawa—capital punishment again became a common criminal sanction (Schmidt 2002:12).[12] Most crimes, from larceny to homicide, were punishable by death, and execution methods became increasingly cruel, eventually embracing the full variety of barbarity that existed in Chinese laws, including boiling, burning, being torn apart by oxen, being flayed alive, being buried alive, being thrown from a cliff, spearing, sawing, crucifixion, hanging, being tied upside down to a cross set in a tidal flat to cause slow drowning by the incoming tide, and several methods of beheading (Ono 1963; Schmidt 2002:14; Botsman 2005:201). After beheading, the severed head was often impaled (with nails) on a special gibbet measuring four feet long and three and a half feet high, usually for a period of two nights and three days. At night, a wooden bucket was placed over the head "to prevent scavengers from nibbling on it" (Schreiber 2001:46). Self-inflicted capital punishment through disembowelment (*seppuku* or *hara-kiri*) was reserved for the warrior class and usually was executed in prison or in the offender's home in the presence of an official (Sato 1994:105).

Throughout this period, the law provided different punishments for similar crimes, depending on the social status of the offender and the victim (Botsman 2005:59). In many cases, executions were elaborately staged in order to simultaneously degrade the offender and celebrate the sovereignty of the ruling

11. In India, Emperor Ashoka fostered "a golden age of Buddhism" in the 2nd century B.C.E., and one part of his emphasis on nonviolence (*ahimsa*) was a policy that greatly restricted the use of capital punishment. In the Korean kingdom of Baekje, where Buddhism also played a major role, King Beop (599–600 C.E.) banned the execution of humans and the killing of animals. And in the 16th century, Mongol king Altan Khan decreed that prisoners of war and other captives should not be executed, largely because of the influence of a Tibetan monk named Sonam Gyatso (1543–1588), who later was designated "Dalai Lama" (Horigan 2001:103).

12. Reliable data for the number of executions in the Tokugawa period apparently do not exist, but "over a period of two centuries" the figure 200,000 "is commonly given for the number of people executed" at Kotsukappara Keijo, one of the main execution grounds in what is today called Tokyo (Schreiber 2001:53). There were, of course, many other execution grounds outside Tokyo. The lords of small domains could not sentence people to death without the central government's permission, but large domains generally used the death penalty "with confidence, regardless of their relations with the Tokugawa house" (Botsman 2005:82).

elites. Even after restrictions were placed on public gatherings at the execution grounds (the bans began in 1620), condemned men and women were still paraded in public places before their executions, and their corpses were left staked or hanging as "signposts" afterward. For those burned at the stake, death did not always mark the end of the punishment. Once the prisoner's life was extinguished, so, too, were the main flames. Torches then were used "to concentrate fire on the genitals of male bodies and breasts of female ones, as well as on the nose, in order to produce a grotesque stump of humanity for the explicit purpose of display" (19). As this example suggests, the death penalty in feudal Japan was more than just one penal technique among many; it was the "base point" from which other punishments were defined. Japanese officials used a variety of means to intensify the penalty and create "degrees of death." In 1600, when the Tokugawa period started and Englishmen sailed into Japan searching for gold and trade, they were alarmed and appalled by the corpses they encountered along the Tokaido road connecting Tokyo to Kyoto. They were the remains of crucified criminals, and the diary of one English captain describes corpses that had been hewn "into pieces as small as a man's hand" by the swords of passersby (Milton 2003:180). In some cases the practice, called *tameshi-giri* ("practice cutting"), was even performed on live prisoners. Testing swords in this manner was one way Tokugawa executioners supplemented their income, and one industrious head-chopper is said to have "tried out new blades on more than 6000 corpses" (Schreiber 2001:49). Another source of extra income came from removing victims' livers, drying them, grinding them into pellets, and selling the resultant product as a remedy for people with diseases such as tuberculosis (52).

Japan's so-called Christian century started in 1549, when the Basque Jesuit Francis Xavier landed in Kagoshima, and it ended with the Shimabara rebellion in the late 1630s. By 1640, "most of the nation's 300,000 [Christian] converts had been killed" (Hoffman 2007a),[13] and the shogun had expelled all foreigners from the country except for a small group of Dutchmen who were confined to an island off the coast of Nagasaki.[14] Over the next 230 years

---

13. The Christians who were not killed were "driven so deep underground that scarcely a trace of their existence was to surface for 250 years" (Hoffman 2007a). Engelbert Kaempfer, one of the few foreigners still living in Japan early in the 18th century, called the country's anti-Christian movement "the most cruel persecution and torture of Christians ever witnessed on this globe" (quoted in Hoffman 2007a). Today less than 1 percent of Japanese are practicing Christians, and some observers believe Japan's resistance to Christianity "even exceeds the resistance often seen in the Islamic world" (Hoffman 2007b).

14. The Dutch became uniquely privileged among European traders because they were willing, as the Spanish and Portuguese were not, to trample on a crucifix or an image of the Virgin Mary, which was Tokugawa Japan's test for foreigners wanting to do business (Fernandez-Armesto 2006). This was also a method for determining who was guilty of the capital crime of being a Christian. People who refused to tread on the objects were recognized as Christians and killed.

of Tokugawa history, thousands more Christians were publicly tortured and killed by agents of a government that feared their "destabilizing" influence (Johnston 1966:8).[15] Some executioners were eager. In 1716, Yamamoto Tsunetomo, the author of the *Hagakure* (one of Japan's most famous works of samurai thought), said that he found beheading "an extremely good feeling. To think that it is unnerving is a symptom of cowardice," and went on to note that "everyone [every samurai], by the time they were fourteen or fifteen, was ordered to do a beheading without fail" (quoted in Schreiber 2001:48). But orders were unnecessary for many samurai, because they possessed legal authority to summarily execute commoners who violated Tokugawa Japan's elaborate rules of social decorum (Westney 1987).

Executions declined during the 18th century, but since criminals could only be punished after a confession, coercion was institutionalized as a means of obtaining the requisite evidence—much as in medieval Europe (Langbein 1978; Schmidt 2002:18). Moreover, while legal orders were publicized, the public was told little about punishments out of fear that too much knowledge might encourage the calculators. Many of those punishments were still administered in public, and this along with their elaborate cruelty served the purpose of general deterrence, in addition to demonstrating and celebrating the sovereignty of the ruling authorities (Botsman 2005:25). As in 18th-century England (Hay 1975), the severity of punishment in Tokugawa Japan generated little public protest because the frequent use of pardons and other acts of mercy helped protect the shogun's image of benevolence. Samurai authorities protected their image by having outcastes take responsibility for physically administering punishments, thus associating penal cruelty with the acts of "nonhumans" (Botsman 2005:50). These and related strategies of benevolence helped cultivate popular consent for a system whose primary pillar was the death penalty.

■ Meiji Decline: 1868 to 1911

In the 18th century, Japanese critics emerged who advocated reducing the scope and scale of capital punishment and reforming other "brutal" penal practices (Botsman 2005:85–114). They had little effect. The critical break with tradition only occurred after Japan ended its self-imposed isolation and opened itself to engage with the West following Commodore Matthew Perry's

---

15. The next section shows that the steep decline of the death penalty in Meiji Japan was caused by the opening of the country to the outside world and by its adaptation to international expectations. Midori Wakakuwa's (2005) award-winning study of the torture and execution of Christians in 17th-century Nagasaki argues the converse, that the Tokugawa excesses occurred "because Japan turned its back on the world and shut itself off, thereby tragically falling behind the modern Western European world" (quoted in "Martyrdoms" 2007).

mission to force this opening in 1853. It was a radical rupture with the past even though "right up until the final days of the Tokugawa period, significant change to the old system of criminal justice seemed only a distant possibility" (Botsman 2005:142). By 1900, torture was forbidden, a new penal code was enacted, decision-making was centralized, the modern prison was born, and hanging was the only method of execution.[16] For our purposes, the most striking changes parallel the shifts that occurred during the decline of capital punishment in Western nations from the 17th century onward (Garland 2005:355; see also Botsman 2005:115–200). In both Meiji Japan and Western countries the following developments occurred:

1. Reduction in the range of capital offenses and eligible offenders
2. Abolition of aggravated death sentences
3. Removal of executions from the public gaze
4. Adoption of technologies designed to speed death and reduce pain
5. Emergence of a normative discourse challenging capital punishment
6. Appearance of divisions in public attitudes toward the penalty's propriety
7. Development of more formalized legal procedures and safeguards
8. Decline in the frequency of executions[17]

The steep decline in executions in Meiji Japan is especially notable (see fig. 3.1). Writing at the same time as the Meiji transformation unfolded, Victor Hugo, the French author and advocate of abolition, said that "the scaffold is the only edifice which revolutions do not demolish" (quoted in "Punishment" 2007). The Meiji restoration "proved to be a revolutionary event" in many ways (Pyle 2006:397), and if Japan's scaffolds were not demolished by this externally induced "revolution from above" (Keene 2002), traffic to them did

---

16. As in the United States (Denno 2003), one proximate cause of the change in Japan's execution method was a botched execution. In 1879, a Tokyo executioner carried out Japan's "last officially sanctioned decapitation of a woman," but at the critical moment she moved, and the executioner "failed to dispatch her on the first two swings" (Schreiber 2001:52). In 1881, the same executioner performed his last beheadings (he had been 12 years old at the time his first job was finished), and by 1882 all executions had to be carried out inside prison grounds, where guards and other state officials were the only persons permitted to be present (Johnson 2006a:79). A journalist's eyewitness account of a mass beheading (seven men, one woman) in 1873 reports that "there was a dense crowd of Japanese present, including many women and even children." They ate, smoked, and chattered "the whole time," and some laughed "just as if they were at a theatre" (Schreiber 2001:55).

17. According to Garland, the final stage in the decline of capital punishment in Western nations is "the movement to partial then complete abolition, first *de facto*, then *de jure*" (Garland 2005:355). Roger Hood has challenged this view, arguing that it is "too tidy a story" to account for the variety of paths that countries have traveled to abolition (Hood 2007), but in any event the United States and Japan have experienced the first eight dimensions of decline without going through the ninth (abolition) as many of their developed counterparts in Europe did.

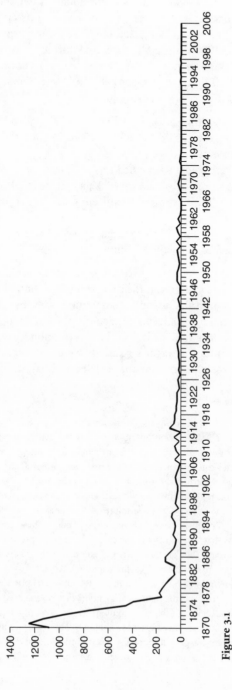

Figure 3.1

Executions in Japan, 1870–2006

Source: Murano 1992:53.

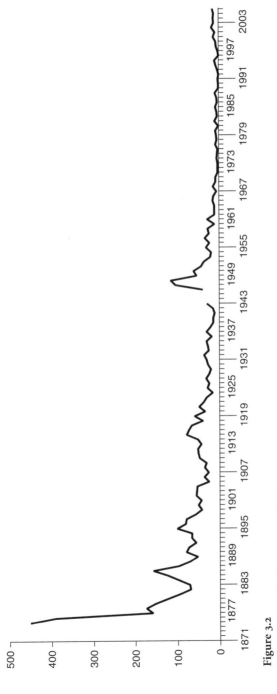

Figure 3.2

District court death sentences in Japan, 1875–2006

Source: Dando 2000:458.

slow remarkably. From 1870 to 1872 (the first years for which decent data exist), executions averaged 1,151 per year.[18] By contrast, executions averaged only 36 a year during 1897–1899. Per capita, therefore, Meiji Japan experienced a 97 percent decrease in less than 30 years (Murano 1992:53). We know of no other nation in which executions dropped so far so fast during a non-postwar period.[19] The decline in death sentences was almost as steep. Between 1875 and 1879, Japanese district courts issued an average of 266 death sentences each year. Between 1895 and 1899, that average fell to 73 per year—a 73 percent drop in only 20 years (Dando 2000:458).[20] (See fig. 3.2.)

In comparative perspective, the Meiji rate of 32.4 executions per million in 1872 is about five times higher than the execution rates in contemporary Singapore and China, the most active executing states in Asia (and the world) at the turn of the 21st century (Hood 2002:92; Nathan and Gilley 2003:217–218). Moreover, the Meiji rate of 0.78 executions per million at the turn of the 20th century was 25 percent lower than the per capita execution rate in the United States at the same point in time ("Executions in the U.S." 2007). In fact, while executions in Japan dropped from more than 1,000 per year to less than 40 per year between 1870 and 1900, executions in the United States were rising and continued to rise until reaching a peak of nearly 200 executions a year (1.5 executions per million) in the mid-1930s. Japan's transition from instrumental to symbolic capital punishment occurred both *earlier* and *faster* than the parallel transition in the United States.[21]

What explains the radical break between Tokugawa and Meiji penality and the urgency with which death penalty reform was pursued in the early Meiji

18. By comparison, England and Wales executed an average of seven persons per year over the same three-year period (1870–1872), which is just 0.6 percent of the Japanese average. Executions declined much earlier and more gradually in Britain than in Japan (see Richard Clark's Web site at www.richardclark32.btinternet.co.uk/contents.html). Tudor England, with a population barely in excess of five million, hanged about 70,000 people over a four-decade period in the late 15th and early 16th centuries, for an annual per capita rate of about 350 executions per million people (Abramsky 2007:xvii). During the decade 1820–1830, England executed only 797 people, for a per capita rate of 6.9 per million. Thus, it took England about two centuries to achieve the same percentage decline as Japan achieved in less than 30 years.

19. One of Meiji Japan's closest European competitors was 18th-century Burgundy (in present-day France), where use of the death penalty declined from 13 to 14.5 percent of all criminal condemnations in the first half of the century to under 5 percent between 1770 and 1789—a 60–65 percent drop. One major cause of this decrease was the Parliament of Burgundy, which stopped ordering torture to obtain confessions (Hunt 2007:245).

20. Improvements in defense lawyering do not help explain the sharp declines in death sentences and executions early in the Meiji period, not least because defense lawyers did not appear on the scene until 1880. Before then, district court death sentences had already dropped dramatically, from 452 in 1875 to 125 in 1880—a 72 percent drop in five years (Dando 2000:458).

21. In historical perspective, the American era most analogous to Japan's Meiji decline may be the postwar period in which executions fell from a peak of more than 150 a year in the 1940s to zero executions during the moratorium that lasted from 1967 to 1977 ("Executions in the U.S." 2007).

years? More precisely, why was the frequency of execution at the turn of the 20th century less than one-30th the initial Meiji level? The core of the answer to these questions is that the Meiji revolution in punishment occurred because of Japan's need to earn the recognition and respect of "the civilized world" that was then colonizing Asia.[22] After Commodore Perry's armada opened Japan to the outside world in 1853, the Western powers imposed treaties granting their own citizens special rights to immunity and leniency in Japanese criminal cases. Although the main purpose of these "unequal treaties" was to ensure that Western commercial interests enjoyed favorable conditions of trade (through contract, customs, and tariff clauses), they also functioned to uphold "the standards of modern 'civilization' in a thoroughly alien environment" by linking economic concerns to questions of Japan's "barbaric" punishments (Botsman 2005:140). As long as these "extraterritoriality" provisions remained in place, it proved impossible for Japan to revise other aspects of the treaties. Hence, revising the treaties—and reforming Japanese penality—became imperative not only for economic reasons but also because it helped Japan escape the inferior status it had been assigned in the imperialist world order (115–140). Here, as on many other occasions in its modern history, Japan was "invented" through its encounters with the West (Buruma 2003), and the most active agents of invention were Japanese leaders who were then, and still are today, highly sensitive to changes in Japan's external environment (Pyle 2007).

Although international influences were the main cause of the decline in capital punishment, domestic considerations also shaped the Meiji reforms. In particular, reducing the harshness of Tokugawa punishments[23] helped buttress the emperor's reputation as a "benevolent" ruler,[24] and requiring that the emperor approve all death sentences helped centralize his authority (Botsman 2005:142).[25] Nonetheless, the transnational nature of the main transformative forces in Meiji Japan is a sharp contrast to "the narcissism of the national death penalty debates" that preceded the decline of capital punishment in

22. As subsequent chapters show, similar concerns about international "recognition and respect" help explain the dramatic execution declines that have already occurred in democratic South Korea and Taiwan, and the apparently large execution decrease that seems to be starting in the PRC. See chapters 5, 6, and 7.

23. As in the West (Foucault 1977), penal reform in Meiji Japan resulted in punishments that focused more on the soul than the body, and they therefore appeared more humane. In some respects, however, such as the "discipline" of prison labor that often resulted in a slow, drawn-out dying, Meiji penal practices were as cruel as the more elaborate theatres of punishment that prevailed in the Tokugawa period (Botsman 2005:179).

24. Although penal reforms helped Emperor Meiji maintain his benevolent image, when it came to capital punishment he sometimes opposed more liberal officials in the Ministry of Justice (Keene 2002:345).

25. For a moving account of one woman's "reflections on the way to the gallows" at the end of the Meiji era, see Hane (1988:51–74). The woman, an anarchist named Sugako Kanno who plotted to assassinate the emperor because he was "the chief person responsible for the

the developed nations of western Europe (Zimring 2003:24). In this respect, the forces that produced the Meiji decline of capital punishment resemble the western European pressures that led to the decline of the death penalty in central Europe—"the fastest and most complete regional abolition in history" (Zimring 2003:35). The diffusion of death penalty reforms and sensibilities across national boundaries is hardly a recent development.

■ Occupation Effects: 1945–1952

If the Meiji transformation of capital punishment was largely a result of Japan's interactions with the West, the occupation of Japan (1945–1952) after the Pacific war further demonstrates how much of Japan's death penalty policy has been "invented" through its encounters with Western nations—especially the United States.

For the American officials—in particular General Douglas MacArthur, the supreme commander of the Allied Powers—who governed Japan during the occupation, "demilitarizing and democratizing" this supposedly pagan, "Oriental" society was unequivocally "a Christian mission" (Dower 1999:23). The main premise of these officials' governance was Japan's acquiescence to America's overwhelming authority, and that authority helped forge two central features of Japan's postwar death penalty policy: the retention of capital punishment, and a policy of secrecy that is taken to extremes seldom seen in other nations (Johnson 2006a:81).

Why was capital punishment retained? Occupation authorities could have abolished the death penalty in postwar Japan, and their decision not to do so was neither natural nor inevitable. In Italy, Germany, Spain, Romania, the Philippines, and many other nations, the fall of an authoritarian regime was the "precipitating circumstance" for abolition (Zimring 2003:23). The Occupation's "democratizing" agenda *was* highly ambitious: the downsizing of the emperor from "god" to mere "symbol of the State and of the unity of the people," the renunciation of war, the creation of due process rights, and the establishment of the principle of equality of the sexes, of the Diet as the highest organ of state power, of the power of judicial review, of land redistribution, and so on. But the abolition of capital punishment was nowhere on that agenda, partly because American officials were determined to put "war

---

exploitation of the people economically" (56), was hanged on January 24, 1911, the day after 11 male codefendants were executed at the same Tokyo gallows. Kanno's trial was closed to the public, but newspaper reports from the period reveal that executions then were far less secretive than they became in the postwar period (57). On the whole, executions of women were uncommon in Meiji Japan. In 1873 and 1874, for example, 44 women were executed, compared with 1,676 men—a 1-to-38 ratio (Murano 1990:208). By comparison, in 1990–2006 the ratio of executed women to executed men in the world was estimated to be 1 to 166 (see www.richard.clark32.btinternet.co.uk/women.html).

criminals" to death in the Tokyo War Crimes Trial (Eiji 2002). In the end, 25 defendants were convicted at the "main" Tokyo trial, of whom seven were hanged, including former prime minister and war minister Hideki Tojo, who after the imposition of his death sentence said "this trial was a political trial. It was only victors' justice." Much subsequent scholarship agrees with his assessment (Minear 1971; Maga 1980; Brackman 1988; Dower 1999; Bix 2000).[26]

Although the Tokyo War Crimes Trial was flawed in many ways (Johnson 2006a:82–84), the most prominent problem was that Emperor Hirohito was nowhere to be found in the indictments—and not because he lacked culpability. Hirohito was "a man of strong will and real authority" who "bore enormous responsibility for the consequences of his actions in each of his many roles" (Bix 2005). If anyone deserved to be in the Tokyo dock, this would seem to be the man (Dower 1999:277). However, the United States made a calculated decision to preserve the person and the institution of the emperor out of the belief that their continuation would facilitate governing postwar Japan and out of fear that trying and executing Hirohito might create lasting resentment among the Japanese (Totani 2008). In some respects, this decision to separate Hirohito from the other military leaders proved effective, for postwar Japan is much freer, richer, and more egalitarian than imperial Japan ever was. On the other hand, because Hirohito's role in the war was never seriously investigated, justice was rendered so arbitrary that the Tokyo trial has been called "an exercise in revenge," "a white man's tribunal," and "the worst hypocrisy in recorded history" (Dower 1999:469).

The retention of the death penalty in contemporary Japan is not only the first key consequence of the Occupation, it also distinguishes Japan's occupation from the parallel occupation of Germany. Four situational contrasts help explain this difference in outcomes (Johnson 2006c:274).[27] First, the United States was the sole occupying authority in Japan, while Germany was occupied by a combination of American, French, British, and Russian officials. Although all four occupiers of Germany began as "firm adherents of the death penalty," the British eventually insisted that "judicial hangings should

26. What was called the "main" Tokyo War Crimes Trial was actually one of many. Altogether, about 5,700 Japanese were tried on "war crimes" charges in a variety of legal forums, and at least 920 were executed. By country, the number of war-crime death sentences imposed on Japanese "war criminals" was as follows: Dutch, 236; British, 223; Australian, 153; Chinese, 149; American, 140; French, 26; and Filipino, 17. In addition, "the Soviets may have executed as many as three thousand Japanese as war criminals, following summary proceedings" (Dower 1999:447,449). As for "self-inflicted capital punishment" (Black 1983), more than 500 Japanese military officers committed suicide soon after Japan's surrender. For an argument that the Tokyo War Crimes Trial was not "victors' justice" but rather reflected the sound application of the legal principles established at Nuremberg, see Totani (2008).

27. Capital punishment was excluded from the West German Constitution of 1949. In East Germany, executions ceased in 1981, and the death penalty was formally abolished in 1987 (Evans 1996).

no longer be carried out" (Evans 1996:741,789). Second, Occupation officials in Germany delegated more authority to local citizens than American officials did during the first few years of occupied Japan (before U.S. policy "reversed course" to emphasize its cold war interests instead of democratization and demilitarization), in part because American, French, and British officials believed the new priorities of resisting communism and fighting the cold war required giving German inhabitants of the western zones more responsibility for their own affairs (786). As "the task of prosecuting German war criminals was gradually passed over to the Germans themselves" (756), a motive for abolition emerged in elite German circles: "the Nazi past left no other option" (Whaley 1996:9). This belief connects to the third and most obvious situational difference distinguishing the two occupations: Japan had no counterpart to the German death camps that killed millions, a fact which also figured large in postabolition conversations about whether to reintroduce capital punishment in West Germany after its 1949 abolition (Evans 1996:803). Finally, Japan's new postwar constitution was not only American-made, it also was promulgated in 1947, two years before Germany's new constitution took effect (Dower 1999:346). The German constitution was a more autonomous creation, at least in part because it came at a point in time when the occupying powers had ceded more control to German citizens than they had to Japanese citizens at a parallel stage of constitutional reform.

In addition to the retention of capital punishment, the U.S. occupation's other death penalty legacy in Japan was the secrecy and silence that have characterized capital punishment in the postwar period. Aspects of this policy include the following. There is no prior notification of execution to the condemned or to anyone except a handful of government officials. No private persons are allowed to attend the gallows. The condemned are not free to choose abolitionist spiritual advisors. Inmates on death row are "socially executed" through strict prohibitions on meetings and correspondence. Executions are often scheduled when Parliament is not in session in order to minimize the possibility of protest and debate. Condemned inmates are selected for execution on the basis not of longevity on death row but of other ill-defined criteria. Death penalty documents and information are denied to reporters and researchers. And the Japanese government is often unwilling to cooperate with foreign visitors or sign international treaties and protocols related to capital punishment (Johnson 2005; Johnson 2006a; Johnson 2006c). If transparency and accountability are two hallmarks of a healthy democracy, then the secrecy and silence that surround capital punishment in Japan seem decidedly undemocratic.[28]

28. As explained later in this chapter, justice minister Kunio Hatoyama deviated from the policy of death penalty secrecy when his ministry started disclosing the names of the condemned and the details of their crimes in December 2007, but critics condemned Hatoyama for failing to disclose sufficient information and for doing so only after executions had already been carried out (Hongo 2007; Makino 2007).

Some aspects of this secrecy policy originated in the Occupation (Johnson 2006a:87). For instance, the record of the Tokyo trial proceedings was "buried" after the trial ended; not even the majority judgment was made readily accessible (Dower 1999:454). This effort to control information has an obvious affinity with the secrecy that surrounds capital punishment in contemporary Japan, but the legacies of the Occupation's policy of "censored democracy" are broader than that. The U.S. occupation's censorship bureaucracy, 6,000 persons strong, extended to most aspects of public expression in occupied Japan, including public justification or defense of any of the defendants at the Tokyo trial (412). Only after the American authorities left in 1952 did it become possible to discuss such forbidden subjects. By then, seven years of "censored democracy" had helped construct a postwar political consciousness that to this day remains inclined to "acquiesce to overweening power," "conform to a dictated consensus," and accept authority "fatalistically" (439). Though these habits of the heart have come to be considered peculiarly Japanese, they are in important respects legacies of the Occupation (440). Thus, in addition to the retention of capital punishment, what America bequeathed—a postwar political consciousness that seems comfortable with the silences dictated by "censored democracy"—helps explain why Japan's subsequent death penalty policy encountered little organized resistance. In these ways, part of Japan's contemporary policy of capital punishment fits the label "made in the U.S.A."

■ Postwar Decline: 1945–1993

Historians often emphasize the "transwar continuities" that characterize Japanese society before and after the Pacific war of 1931–1945. Indeed, "the linkages and influences are apparent almost everywhere one looks," including capital punishment (Dower 1990:50). Not only was the death penalty retained despite sweeping Occupation reforms, the policy of secrecy born in the Meiji period took deeper root as a result of the American interregnum. One also sees transwar continuity in Japan's execution rates. During the decade preceding the Pacific war (1920–1929), Japan averaged 24.1 executions per year, and the first full decade after that war ended (1950–1959) averaged 24.6 executions per year. Even controlling for the increase in population during this 30-year interval, Japan's execution rate changed little.[29]

However, the decline of executions that started in the Meiji period resumed in the 1960s and continued until the end of a moratorium that lasted from 1989 to 1993. As table 3.1 shows, Japan's annual average number of executions

29. Although executions varied little from the 1920s through the 1950s, death sentences spiked to more than 100 per year during the disorder that followed Japan's surrender in 1945 (Dower 1999:97). By the end of the occupation, death sentences had returned to their prewar level (Schmidt 2002:37).

dropped from 24.6 in the 1950s to 1.5 in the 1980s—a 94 percent decline. Similarly, Japan's per capita execution rate fell from 0.37 per million in 1950 to just 0.009 in 1989—a 98 percent drop.[30] By the end of the 1980s Japan had become, along with India and Indonesia, one of the world's least frequent users of death as a criminal sanction among retentionist nations (Hood 2002:92). As for death sentences, the annual number fell below 20 after 1960 and below ten only a decade later (Schmidt 2002:38), while the percentage of potentially capital cases resulting in a death sentence (*shikei gaitozai ni tai suru isshin shikei*) declined from 5.38 percent in 1948–1950 to 0.32 percent in 1971–1975 (Murano 1992:63). Much of this decline was due to the near disappearance of capital convictions for robbery-homicide. From 1948 to 1950, 136 death sentences were imposed for robbery-homicide, accounting for 58 percent of all death sentences, while from 1972 to 1974 there were only three such sentences, accounting for 23 percent of the total (Murano 1992:64). The number of death row inmates (with finalized sentences) also declined in the postwar period, from 70 in 1965 to 26 in 1980 (Schmidt 2002:38).[31] Finally, the average delay between finalization of a death sentence and execution lengthened substantially, from 34 months for persons executed in 1957–1961 to 91 months for persons executed in 1982–1989 and 100 months for persons executed in 1993–2004 (Schmidt 2002:59; Shikei Haishi Henshu Iinkai 2006:269–278). The increased delay in carrying out death sentences seemed to reflect increased ambivalence in Japanese society and in the Japanese procuracy about using the ultimate punishment. Unlike the United States, however, where there is also extensive delay, the delay in Japan has generated little "resentment and frustration" among the general public and cannot be attributed to federalism, the demands of due process, or lengthy appeals (Zimring 2003:78). Since Japan's moratorium ended in 1993 until executions started to increase in 2007–2008, it took more than eight years, on the average, to perform an execution even after all legal appeals were exhausted and even though the Code of Criminal

---

30. Executive clemency does not help explain the decline of executions in postwar Japan. Since 1954, the Japanese cabinet has not issued a single pardon to a condemned prisoner, while the National Offenders Rehabilitation Commission only granted single amnesties in 1965, 1970, and 1975 (Lane 2004). As in the United States, in Japan there has been a radical decline in the use of executive power to stop executions in the postwar period, even though mercy and leniency remain much more conspicuous at other stages of Japan's criminal process than they do in America (see Sarat 2005; see also Foote 1992a; Johnson 2002a).

31. One dimension of the postwar decline in death sentences was the disappearance of capital convictions for the crime of patricide. In 1973, the Supreme Court's *Aizawa* decision reversed the position it had adopted in 1950 upholding the constitutionality of article 200 of the Penal Code that provided only life imprisonment or a death sentence for killing a lineal ascendant. Although the Penal Code was not amended until 1995, article 200 was never again invoked by a prosecutor after the *Aizawa* decision (Beer and Maki 2002:154). The law on the books followed the law in action; for years before *Aizawa* the number of death sentences imposed for patricide had already declined substantially (Murano 1992:57).

Table 3.1
Executions in Japan by decade, 1870–2006

Decade	Annual execution average
1870–1879	650.0
1880–1889	85.2
1890–1899	50.9
1900–1909	31.0
1910–1919	46.9
1920–1929	24.1
1930–1939	19.6
1940–1949	19.5
1950–1959	24.6
1960–1969	13.2
1970–1979	9.4
1980–1989	1.5
1990–1999	3.6
2000–2006	2.1

Sources: Murano 1992:53; Shikei Haishi Henshu Iinkai 2005:141.

Procedure requires that executions occur within six months of the finalization of the sentence.[32]

The context of Japan's postwar decline in capital punishment has four principal features: economic growth, democratization, a steep drop in homicides, and a rapid rise in the number of nations abolishing the death penalty. Penal events and institutions are frequently overdetermined in the sense that they have a variety of complementary (rather than competing) causes (Garland 1990:280). The Japanese decrease in capital punishment from 1945 to 1995 is overdetermined in this way.[33]

32. That there is seldom an execution within the prescribed period is partly because many condemned inmates repeatedly request pardon or retrial, but a bigger cause seems to be the Ministry of Justice's own ambivalence about conducting executions (Ministry of Justice officials, interviews by Johnson, March–April 2004).

33. One institution not directly responsible for Japan's postwar decline in capital punishment is the Supreme Court. In 1948, the Court gave voice to the ideological tensions at the heart of the controversy over capital punishment. "Human life is precious," it said. And "the life of a single person is worth more than the entire world." But in a decision holding that capital punishment is not unconstitutionally cruel, the Court went on to conclude that the death penalty "through its power of intimidation, provides general deterrence; the execution of death sentences eliminates a certain form of social evil; and in these ways the death penalty seeks to protect society. Moreover, the death penalty gives priority to a collective view of morality over an individual view of morality." Similarly, in 1961 the Court held that hanging does not violate the postwar constitution's ban on "cruel" punishments. This was the first and only time the Court has considered a form of execution first adopted in 1873 (Lane

First, the postwar Japanese economy experienced "spectacular success" (Lincoln 1990:191). In 1945, Japan's gross national product (GNP) was only half of what it had been when the Showa era opened in 1926, but by the end of Showa in 1989 Japan was a great economic power, poised, as one analyst put it, "to overtake the U.S. by the year 2000" (Fingleton 1995). Although this prediction proved wrong—Japan's economy performed poorly during the 1990s—the nation's rapid economic growth during the first four decades of the postwar period affected death penalty policy and practice in at least two ways: (1) declining levels of economic stress helped reduce homicide substantially and thereby decreased the supply of potentially capital cases (Roberts and LaFree 2004:202), and (2) rising standards of living not only brought concrete improvements in how individuals lived but also shaped the "moral character" of Japanese society and of key death penalty decision-makers in the procuracy, the judiciary, and the Ministry of Justice (Friedman 2005:4).

2005a:41). In a 1983 case involving defendant Norio Nagayama, who shot and killed four victims in 1968 while a 19-year-old juvenile (the age of majority is 20 in Japan) and who became a best-selling author before his execution in 1997, the Supreme Court quashed the life sentence imposed by the Tokyo High Court and issued what it called "clear criteria" for distinguishing who deserves death instead of some lesser sentence. In their concrete application, however, the Court's guidelines "remain extremely ambiguous" (Schmidt 2002:55).

On the whole, death sentence dissents are rare in Japan's appellate courts because the conservative politicians who have ruled in the postwar period seem to exclude abolitionist judges from the highest benches and because, more generally, appellate courts tend to be "deferential in the extreme" to the executive and legislative branches of government (Ramseyer and Rasmusen 2003:63). In addition, Supreme Court justices in Japan serve only a short time on the Court (the mandatory retirement age is 70, and most justices join the Court in their early sixties), and they encounter relatively few cases in which actual innocence is an issue. In the United States, by contrast, the Supreme Court justices who have changed course on the death penalty—and there have been many—tend to do so after decades of exposure on the bench to the reality of innocent people facing execution. In the words of Erwin Chemerinsky, innocence issues have "had a profound effect" on many American Supreme Court justices (quoted in Lithwick 2007). The most prominent death penalty "dissenter" on Japan's Supreme Court probably was Justice Masao Ono, who expressed reservations about capital punishment in a 1993 opinion in State v. Hasegawa in which he voted with the majority to uphold a sentence of death (Johnson 2006a:108). And in 2007, nearly 40 years after Norimichi Kumamoto agreed with two more senior judges to impose a death sentence on Iwao Hakamada—despite having prepared a 360-page document describing the reasons supporting the defendant's innocence—this now-retired judge publicly announced that the evidence against Hakamada "did not make sense" ("Boxer" 2007). Hakamada has remained on death row since Kumamoto and his two colleagues on the Shizuoka District Court sentenced him to death in 1968. In addition to considerable evidence of his innocence, there is substantial evidence that he has lost his mind during his four decades on death row. Although judges in Japan have seldom displayed anti–death penalty impulses, there was some "progressive activism" by the appellate judiciary in its postconviction review of death sentences in the 1980s (Foote 1993:462). It did not last long (Suzuki 2007).

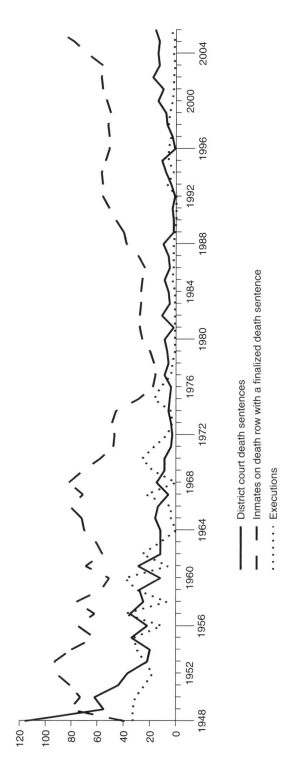

Figure 3.3

Death sentences, death row populations, and executions in Japan, 1948–2006

Source: Shikei Haishi Henshu Iinkai (various years).

District court death sentences

Inmates on death row with a finalized death sentence

Executions

Second, the main story about development during the last few decades throughout the developing world has been the "parallel advance of economic growth and political democracy" (Friedman 2005:9). In Japan, too, postwar economic development helped produce a "stable political democracy" (Curtis 1999:ix). The global trend away from capital punishment is generally contingent on the spread of democracy (Anckar 2004; Greenberg and West 2008; Neumayer 2008). In Japan as well, the development of democracy corresponded to a steady decline in both death sentences and executions (see fig. 3.3).

Third, Japan's homicide rate in 1990 was less than one-third what it was in 1955 (Johnson 2006b; Johnson 2008b).[34] Although the death penalty in Japan can be imposed on offenders for any of 17 offenses (Amnesty International 2006f), in practice it is only homicide offenders who now are sentenced to death. One result is that Japan's extraordinary homicide drop has sharply reduced the number of cases that prosecutors could charge as capital.

Finally, although the Japanese government has been reluctant to sign international treaties and protocols that would limit its use of capital punishment, the growth of an international human rights movement and political pressure from international institutions—and from European governments and organs especially—have had a braking effect on Japanese officials' propensity to convert death sentences into executions, much as they have in other national contexts (Hood 2001:337; Bae 2007). As chapter 2 explained, the binary categories so often used in comparative studies of capital punishment—a nation either has it and uses it or does not—can obscure important changes in death penalty practice. Japan is one example: it remained retentionist throughout the postwar period, even though its per capita execution rate dropped by more than 90 percent. And India is another: while remaining retentionist, executions in the world's largest democracy fell from an average of 140 per year in the 1950s to only 2 to 3 per year in the 1980s and 1990s (see appendix F).

The decline of capital punishment in postwar Japan culminated in an unofficial 40-month moratorium on executions that lasted from November 1989 until March 1993. During this period, four successive ministers of justice refused to sign (or had no opportunity to sign) the requisite death warrants. Despite no significant public opposition to the moratorium, it ended when a new minister of justice, Masaharu Gotoda, signed warrants authorizing the hanging of three condemned men, all on the same March morning. Eight

34. The "vanishing killer" in postwar Japan is largely young and male. When the postwar homicide decline started in 1955, there were 23 murderers for every 100,000 men aged 20 to 24. Since 1990, the corresponding number has hovered around two. Thus, this age-specific homicide rate dropped to less than one-tenth its previous level, and the homicide decline for Japanese males aged 25 to 29 is almost as steep (Hasegawa 2003).

months later, under a different minister—a former law professor at Tokyo University—four more men were executed, making 1993 the year with the most executions since 1976, when 12 persons were executed. In his memoirs, Gotoda called capital punishment an "insoluble problem" while providing three reasons for authorizing executions: his obligation as minister of justice to "protect law and order," the thorough process of case "review and consultation" (*kessai*) that officials in the ministry engage in before selecting persons for execution, and "public support" for the death penalty (Gotoda 1998:268). Whatever his reasons, the resumption of executions surprised many Japanese, including abolitionists who believed the moratorium was the prelude to inevitable abolition (Yasuda 2004:18). As the next section shows, the moratorium actually was followed by a resurgence of capital punishment.

■ Resurgence: 1993–?

While Japan moved away from capital punishment during the postwar period, the United States, the only other developed democracy that retained the death penalty, traveled "in the opposite direction," with executions rising from zero per year from 1968 to 1976 to an average of 80 per year from 1997 to 1999 (Foote 1993:369). As of this writing, the United States and Japan continue to move in opposite directions, but only because both have reversed course. While Japan's death penalty accelerated in the new millennium, American capital punishment was "experiencing a period of consistent decline for the first time in twenty-five years" (Prejean 2005:224). The causes of the American decline—death sentences that remained at about 300 a year during the 1990s dropped 60 percent by 2006, and executions fell from a peak of 98 in 1999 to 53 in 2006—include a steep drop in the homicide rate, the spread of LWOP sentencing alternatives to death, improved legal representation for capital defendants, Supreme Court decisions forbidding the imposition of death sentences on minors or the mentally retarded, and a variety of appellate court opinions finding legal flaws in the procedures and protocols for lethal injection, which is practically the only way executions can occur in the United States (Lewis 2006). Japan has experienced none of these changes. Yet the most important cause of decline in American capital punishment appears to be revelations of wrongful convictions, which have produced public and jury skepticism about the reliability of verdicts and have made prosecutors more cautious about when to seek a capital sentence (Lewis 2006). Between 1973 and 2006, 123 people in 25 American states were released from death row with evidence of their innocence, and between 1989 and 2006, more than 190 convicted felons were exonerated by DNA testing, at least 12 of them in capital cases (Garrett 2008).

Japan has not experienced a wrongful conviction revolution even though four convicted murderers were exonerated and released from the nation's death rows during the 1980s (Foote 1992b).[35] These men had spent 27 to 34 years under a sentence of death (all had been convicted in the 1950s), and their wrongful convictions all resulted from false confessions and from prosecutors' nondisclosure of evidence to the defense—problems that continue to plague Japanese criminal justice to this day (Johnson 2002a:243). People on both sides of Japan's death penalty divide believe it is no accident that the nation's 40-month moratorium began after these miscarriages were exposed. The exonerations not only embarrassed Japanese prosecutors, who sincerely believe that miscarriages of justice are all but impossible in their system; they stimulated considerable soul-searching and led to numerous proposals for reform—few of which have been enacted (Foote 1992b; Mori 2008).[36] Nevertheless, as of 1993, the best study of this subject concluded that with respect to collateral review of capital convictions, "there seems little doubt an innocent individual would prefer Japan's retrial system" over what was then available in the United States (Foote 1993:520).

A decade later there are doubts in abundance. There have been no death penalty retrials in Japan since Masao Akabori was exonerated in 1989, and DNA analysis, though frequently used to help the state convict, has not been used to obtain a postconviction exoneration in any criminal case.[37] There probably are fewer "actually innocent" persons on Japanese death rows (and in Japanese prisons) than there are in America, in part because Japanese prosecutors are generally more cautious about charging cases than their American counterparts (Johnson 2002a:238). On the other hand, since the death row exonerations of the 1980s, Japanese prosecutors have tightened their control over the evidence needed by the defense to challenge capital convictions, and Japanese courts have become increasingly reluctant to open the door to retrial (Akiyama 2002; Kitani 2004). The result is a paralyzed system for collateral review of capital convictions.[38]

35. In addition to the four death row exonerations, five other convicted murderers received retrials between 1975 and 1990, and three of them were exonerated (Schreiber 1996:57). Of the 35 persons executed in Japan in 1981–1996, at least eight claimed to be innocent of some or all of the crimes for which they had been condemned [Forum 90, 2007]). In 2006, Amnesty International (2006f) said it had "received reports" that eight death row inmates were innocent.

36. In the midst of the soul-searching stimulated by the four death penalty retrial acquittals, Japan's abolitionist movement gained strength and coalesced into an umbrella organization known as Forum 90, which has a membership of more than 5,000 and an active core of about 50 (Johnson 2006a:96).

37. By contrast, in 2001–2006, 12 convicted felons were exonerated by DNA testing in Dallas County, Texas, more than occurred anywhere else in America except the entire states of New York and Illinois, and 12 more than have occurred in Japan since America's first DNA exoneration in 1989 (Blumenthal 2007).

38. As mentioned at this chapter's start, the Nagoya High Court made a decision in 2006 that "legitimizes the refusal to grant a retrial unless the defense team first proves the defendant

Besides the disappearance of death penalty retrials, the resurgence of capital punishment in contemporary Japan has several leading indicators. To start with, there has been a rebound in executions since the 1980s, with the annual average falling from 9.4 in the 1970s to 1.5 in the 1980s before rising to 3.6 in the 1990s and 3.0 in 2000–2007. The nine executions in 2007 were the largest yearly total since 1976, and there were ten more executions in the first six months of 2008. Thus, in the 18 months between Christmas 2006 and June 2008, 23 persons were hanged—eight more than the total number executed during the entire decade of the 1980s. Following the first executions of 2008, some members of Parliament lashed out at the Ministry of Justice for being too aggressive. But Kunio Hatoyama, the minister of justice at the time, was in no mood to slow down. Indeed, he tried to make it easier to execute. One proposal was to scrap the rule requiring the minister's approval for executions because "no one wants to put his signature on an execution order" ("Remove Justice Minister" 2007). Toward this end, Hatoyama established a "study group" in his ministry to determine whether a more "automatic and objective" procedure for execution could be implemented. He wanted to "carry out executions in a methodical manner"—"automatically" and "like a conveyor belt"—rather than thinking about the timing of executions or the intervals between them, as most previous ministers had done ("Executions" 2007; "Three Japanese" 2008).[39] This proposal produced "shockwaves of criticism" in some quarters (Murakami 2007), and Shizuka Kamei, the chairman of the Diet Members League for the Abolition of the Death Penalty, even said Hatoyama "doesn't have the qualifications to be a Justice Minister or the qualification to be human" ("Justice Minister" 2007). Some months later, Japan's newspaper of record (the *Asahi Shimbun*) published a poem calling Hatoyama "the grim reaper" (*shinigami*). Through it all, Hatoyama insisted he was merely trying to bring current execution practice into conformity with the law, which requires that the justice minister sign an execution order within

---

is innocent" (Suzuki 2007). If the Supreme Court affirms it, this line of reasoning will make it even more difficult to rectify wrongful convictions.

39. For more detailed remarks on the death penalty by Justice Minister Hatoyama, see his interview with *Shukan Asahi* (Fox 2007; Hatoyama 2007). He said that "those who most dread dealing with the death penalty are the administrators in the Ministry of Justice," and he noted that his efforts to discuss it more openly were "like opening a Pandora's Box or breaking a taboo." As we stress in this chapter, Hatoyama also acknowledged that the frequency of executions in Japan changes "according to the attitude of the minister in office," a pattern many people consider "strange." Hatoyama wants to reduce this inconsistency by leaving execution decisions up to "a professional body." Among other things, Hatoyama contends that "Western nations" are "moving toward the abolition of the death penalty" because they have "a conception of the value of life [that] is weaker than the Japanese." Some analysts believe Hatoyama's many public statements on capital punishment are calculated to advance his own political career (Makino 2007).

six months after a death sentence has been finalized—a far cry from the usual wait of five years or more ("Openness" 2007). Hatoyama's second proposal was to make the execution process more "tranquil" for the condemned, perhaps by replacing hanging with an alternative method such as lethal injection (in countries such as the United States and China, one function of lethal injection reforms has been to legitimize executions by making them seem "kindler and gentler"). Finally, starting with the three men who were hanged in December 2007,[40] Hatoyama broke with the Ministry of Justice's long-standing policy of secrecy by ordering his subordinates to disclose to the public the names of the condemned and the details of their crimes. Critics rebuked Hatoyama for failing to disclose sufficient information—Why this person? Why now? Was the condemned even sane at the time of execution?—and for only providing information after the hangings had already occurred, but the ministry's policy of increased "openness" reflected two recent changes in Japanese law: the trend toward greater information disclosure in government (Johnson 2006c), and the approaching advent of Japan's lay judge system (*saiban-in seido*), which will begin adjudicating capital cases in May 2009 (Anderson and Nolan 2004; Takayama 2006; Foote 2007; Goto 2008). At the same time, there appeared to be three motivations for the new disclosure policy that could be more directly linked to the recent surge in executions: foreign and domestic criticism of Japan's opaque execution process, the need to give greater consideration to the desires of crime victims and their bereaved families, and the belief that more disclosure would generate greater public support for executions ("Japan Finally Names" 2007; Makino 2007).

The increase in Japanese death sentences has been more substantial than the rise in executions. After remaining relatively flat through the 1980s, at an average of six "first instance trial death sentences" (*isshin shikei hanketsu*) per year, the average dropped to 3.6 a year during the first half of the 1990s before rebounding to six a year in the second half of that decade and then more than doubling to an average of 14 per year for the period 2000–2004. There were more death sentences in the first five years of Japan's 21st century than in the previous 13 years combined, and the number of death sentences (18) in the peak year of 2002 was the same as during the first five years of the 1990s. In 2007, courts at all levels handed down or upheld the highest number of death sentences since 1980, the earliest year for which comparable data are available ("Forty-six Sentenced" 2008). As one Japanese judge has noted,

40. At the time they were hanged, the condemned men were 74, 65, 63, 47, 42, and 37 years old, and their average age was 55. After 74-year-old Noboru Ikemoto was executed in December 2007 for three murders he committed 22 years earlier during a dispute with his neighbors over litter on his property, Louise Arbour, the UN high commissioner for human rights, said, "It is difficult to see what legitimate purpose is served by carrying out such executions of the elderly. At the very least, on humanitarian grounds, I would urge Japan to refrain from such action" ("UN Condemns" 2007).

"the threshold for the death penalty has been lowered" ("Punishment That Hurts" 2007; Takamura 2008).[41]

As death sentences have increased, Japan's death row has expanded accordingly, from 26 persons with a finalized death sentence in 1985 to 54 in 1995, to 97 at the time of the Christmas executions of 2006, to 106 at the end of 2007 (Schmidt 2002:38; "Forty-six Sentenced" 2008). In polls conducted by the prime minister's office, public support for capital punishment reached a postwar high of 81 percent in 2005, compared with the postwar low of 56.9 percent in 1975 and 66.5 percent support in 1989, the year of Japan's last death row exoneration (Schmidt 2002:165–166; "Support" 2005).[42] In a survey conducted in 2006, only 6 percent of Japanese respondents said the death penalty should be abolished—a much lower level of opposition to capital punishment than is found in parallel polls in the United States and South Korea (Hamai 2008:116). Public support for the death penalty and the overflowing death row are both frequently invoked by Japanese leaders as reasons to continue conducting executions and to accelerate their pace (Shikei Haishi Henshu Iinkai 2007).

In addition to these numerical measures of death penalty resurgence, there are at least three more qualitative signs of capital punishment's comeback in contemporary Japan. First, prosecutors have adopted a more aggressive policy for charging cases as capital (Japan has no mandatory death penalty laws) and for appealing nondeath sentences in potentially capital cases. Former prosecutor general Akio Harada's claim that Japanese "prosecutors wherever possible avoid requesting death" is neither true on its own terms nor as true today as it was in the early 1990s (Lane 2004:9). In recent years, prosecutors have sought a sentence of death in numerous cases they would not have considered capital in the past—cases involving single victims, defendants who are minors, and prosecutors' own appeals of noncapital sentences (Miyazawa 2006). In one 2003 trial, "a Tokyo prosecutor made his case for a death sentence by handing a judge a petition signed by 76,000 people" (Lane 2005b). The prosecutor more than any other actor controls the course of capital punishment in Japan, for the prosecutor controls both the inputs into the system, that is, which cases to charge as capital, and its outputs—which cases to present to the minister of justice for the signing that authorizes hanging. The more aggressive pursuit of

41. Before the death penalty threshold was lowered, Japanese judges imposed sentences of death in 55 percent of the cases in which prosecutors sought it (in trial courts in 1974–1988). By comparison, American juries impose about the same percentage after state-level convictions in which the death sentence is an option, though they impose it in only about one-third of federal capital trials ("Shikei no Genzai" 1990:248; Benac 2006).

42. The last years of double-digit executions in Japan were 1975 (n = 17) and 1976 (n = 12); from 1977 to 1992 executions varied from zero to four a year. The execution decline after 1976 corresponded with a decline in public support for capital punishment (Schmidt 2002:165–166). Whether the softening of support helped *cause* the fall in executions has not, to our knowledge, been a subject of serious study.

capital punishment that Japanese prosecutors began in the last half of the 1990s is therefore notable.[43]

Second, Japan's trial courts have become more willing to impose death as a criminal sanction, and its appellate courts have become more inclined to uphold sentences of death. The Supreme Court is an important part of this trend, "finalizing" (*kakutei suru*) as many death sentences in 2004 (n = 13) as it did in the previous five years combined (Shikei Haishi Henshu Iinkai 2005:141). Thirty years before, the Supreme Court "led the way in reexamining capital punishment," and its *Shiratori* and *Saitakawa* retrial rulings of the 1970s still stand as the progressive peak of Japan's capital jurisprudence (Foote 1993:440).[44] For Japanese abolitionists, one jurisprudential nadir was reached in 1999 when the Supreme Court overturned the life sentence of a man convicted of robbery and murder, the first time since 1983 it had recommended that a life sentence be replaced with death (Lane 2005b). This was widely regarded as a sign that the Court endorsed the acceleration of capital justice.

Finally, the resurgence of capital punishment in contemporary Japan is evident in the Japanese media's increasingly enthusiastic support for capital charges, capital convictions, and executions (Hamai 2008; Miyazawa 2008). Even *Asahi Shimbun*, Japan's most liberal national newspaper, now publishes editorials arguing that the death penalty is "unavoidable" and "inevitable" in certain cases. More broadly, news stories and editorials in the print and electronic media routinely focus on the heinousness of homicide offenses, the needs of victims and survivors, and the appropriateness of capital punishment (Harada 2004; Kawai 2004:47; Hamai and Ellis 2006). This is very different from the way the death penalty was reported after executions resumed in 1993 (Domikova-Hashimoto 1996; Yamaguchi 2004; Hamai and Ellis 2008; Miyazawa 2008; Mori 2008).

There are three complementary explanations of the resurgence of Japan's death penalty. The first and simplest is that the revival of capital punishment is one part of a larger trend toward increasingly severe punishments (*genbatsuka*)

---

43. Another sign of prosecutors' increased aggressiveness is the increased speed with which condemned inmates are hanged after finalization of sentence. From 1993 through 1999, every execution took at least seven years, but from 2000 through 2005, only 1 of 12 executions had that much delay (and the average delay was 5.5 years). One notorious killer (Mamoru Takuma, who abandoned his appeals and said he wanted to die) was hanged in 2004 only one year after he was convicted—the speediest Japanese execution in decades (Shikei Haishi Henshu Iinkai 2006:278).

44. On the surface, the Supreme Court's retrial decisions were a rare instance of "progressive activism" by Japan's judiciary (Foote 1993:462), but they had an unprogressive effect on Japanese prosecutors in the Ministry of Justice, who stopped giving advance notice of execution to the condemned in order (death penalty opponents say) to "break the inmate's will" and "discourage extended appeals" (Lane 2005a:39). This episode in Japan's death penalty jurisprudence illustrates the truth that abolitionists everywhere should be careful what reform they wish for because they just might get it (Haines 1996:22,149).

in Japanese criminal justice (Miyazawa 2008). Not only did death sentences double between 1995 and 2005, other criminal sentences became harsher as well, with the number of lifers in Japanese prisons rising from less than 300 in the early 1990s to almost 1,400 in 2006, and the percentage of inmates with a sentence of two years or less falling from 80 percent in 1985 to less than 60 percent in 2004 (Hamai and Ellis 2006).[45] More generally, while Japan's national population remained flat, its prison population rose 80 percent, from 38,000 in 1994 to nearly 70,000 in 2004. Similarly, in the early years of the new millennium the Japanese police force expanded for the first time in decades and its style of policing became markedly more aggressive. In the lawmaking sphere, Japan's various legislatures—especially the National Diet—criminalized more conduct, made statutory sanctions more severe, and expanded criminal liability. Some analysts even wonder whether Japan is starting to develop a "culture of control" of the kind David Garland (2001) identified in the United States and the United Kingdom (Johnson 2007b).

The second way of explaining Japan's death penalty resurgence identifies specific causes of both the revival of capital punishment and of the "get tougher" trend of which it is one part. Although a variety of forces have shaped these developments—official crime rates have risen;[46] citizens believe public safety has deteriorated;[47] and the needs and claims of crime victims and survivors receive much more attention than they used to[48]—the influence of

45. As the number of lifers has almost quintupled, parole for them has plummeted (Hamai 2008).

46. From 1999 to 2004, the number of "incidents" reported to and recorded by the Japanese police increased from 343,663 to 1,800,670 (Hamai and Ellis 2008). Though not all of these incidents are "criminal," Japan's official crime rates increased as well. However, the homicide rate has remained stable since 1990 (at the lowest national level in the world) after dropping continuously for the previous 35 years (Johnson 2007a). For many other offense categories, there are reasons to believe that the rise in Japan's official crime rate is more apparent than real (Kawai 2004; Johnson 2007a).

47. A national survey in 2004 found that 94 percent of eligible Japanese voters believed "public safety has deteriorated in recent years," and another poll in the same year revealed that more than half of adults said Japan is no longer "a safe and secure nation" (Johnson 2007a). Even if Japan's crime rise reflects changes in official behavior more than changes in criminal conduct (Kawai 2004; Johnson 2007a), the public's subjective perception of the security situation (*taikan chian*) is an important social fact in its own right (Miyazawa 2008). As sociologist W. I. Thomas noted, when "people define situations as real, they are real in their consequences." The Tokyo subway attacks had large effects on Japanese definitions of the security situation (Shikei Haishi Henshu Iinkai 2005) and on media representations of it (Shikei Haishi Henshu Iinkai 2006).

48. Since the Tokyo subway attacks, much new legislation has been passed in an attempt to better satisfy the financial and emotional needs of victims and to give victims and survivors more rights to participate in the criminal process (Miyazawa 2006). One expression of this movement is the fact that since the mid-1990s, capital punishment has increasingly come to be construed as a means of serving victims' needs, especially by satisfying their

specific events on the hardening of Japan's penal policy has been considerable (Johnson 2007b). Most important, the March 1995 sarin gas attacks in the Tokyo subways killed 12, injured 5,500, and scared millions who were accustomed to believing that they lived in "the safest country among the developed democracies" (Bayley 1991:169; Kaplan and Marshall 1996; Murakami 2000). With the Tokyo subway attacks, the unthinkable happened: a major urban transit system became the target of a terrorist attack. Soon afterward, "Japanese views and perceptions suddenly and completely changed" to reflect a new and profound sense of the nation's vulnerability (Yasuda 2004:47). These attacks have even been called "Japan's 9/11" because of the powerful effects they have had on public perceptions and government confidence (Yoshida and Ito 2006).

Three such effects are fundamental: citizens' concern about their own security, government anxiety about its own potency, and the state's felt need to "make muscles" in response to the first two effects.[49] Capital punishment has become one way the Japanese state tries to reassure citizens by demonstrating its responsiveness to their concerns (Nagata 2005). In this way, the Tokyo subway attacks and other high-profile homicide cases—the beheading of a child in Kobe in 1997, the murder of a pregnant woman and her baby daughter in Hikari in 1999, a massacre at an Osaka elementary school in 2001—have provided motivation and opportunity for the Japanese state to "govern through crime" (Simon 2007; Hikari-shi Jiken Bengodan 2008; Miyazawa 2008). As for the Tokyo subway attacks' other effects on the death penalty, they were "a watershed event" that made it more difficult to appeal for abolition or for additional restraints on using death as a criminal sanction (Lane 2005b; Shikei Haishi Henshu Iinkai 2006). In specific case terms, of the 50 death sentences issued by Japanese trial courts in 1999–2002, nine were imposed on Aum Shinrikyo conspirators. By the time Aum Shinrikyo founder and guru Shoko Asahara's death sentence was finalized in September 2006, Japanese courts had imposed capital sentences on 13 of the 189 Aum Shinrikyo

---

desire for retribution (Shikei Haishi Henshu Iinkai 2005:18). As in the United States, the reframing of capital punishment in these terms turns attention away from state killing and gives "the horrifying process of human execution a positive impact that many citizens can identify with" (Zimring 2003:62). At the same time, framing the death penalty as "for victims" links the symbolism of contemporary capital punishment with a long Japanese tradition of victim and survivor participation in punishment decision-making (Botsman 2005:42). If supporters of the death penalty in Japan imported this frame from the United States, they did so at least partly because of the affinities it has with elements of their own tradition (Glenn 2004).

49. As one of Japan's most important contemporary novelists sees it, the Tokyo subway attacks in March 1995 and the Kobe earthquake two months earlier "are two of the gravest tragedies in Japan's postwar history. It is no exaggeration to say that there was a marked change in the Japanese consciousness 'before' and 'after' these events....They ushered in a period of critical inquiry into the very roots of the Japanese state" (Murakami 2000:237).

members who had been indicted (Hongo and Wijers-Hasegawa 2006). Thus, a significant slice—perhaps 20 percent—of the recent resurgence in Japanese death sentences can be attributed to the Japanese government's direct response to Aum Shinrikyo's attacks on it. But in broader terms, a more significant cause of the resurgence has been the attacks' indirect effects on the public mood and on government confidence.

The third and final way of explaining the resurgence is through comparison to the revival of capital punishment that occurred in the United States from 1972 to 1999. This approach helps highlight what is distinctive and what is shared in these national experiences. In both countries, public anxiety about crime was one key part of the context, as was a shift from framing the death penalty as a question about state power to reframing it as a matter of satisfying victims. Similarly, in both countries, the media's preoccupation with crime helped make "moral panics" an almost everyday occurrence, thereby stimulating public demand that the state do more to solve law-and-order problems.

Despite these similarities, the differences between the American and Japanese revivals are striking. In the United States, the Supreme Court's *Furman* decision in 1972 (finding the capital sentencing process unconstitutionally "cruel and unusual" because jurors had unrestricted discretion) sparked a backlash by state governments outraged by what they deemed an unjustified act of judicial activism. In Japan, by contrast, the judiciary has been at most a supporting actor. More important, regional influences were the most powerful factor in the revival of death sentences and executions in the United States, with southern states leading the charge to roll back the Court's ruling (Zimring and Hawkins 1986:x,38). In Japan, there are long-standing regional differences in the propensity to use capital punishment (with jurisdictions around Tokyo more likely to employ it than jurisdictions elsewhere), but they are not nearly as large as the regional differences in the United States, and they have little effect on those in the procuracy, the Ministry of Justice, and the Supreme Court who make the ultimate decisions about who deserves a death sentence and who will be executed. In this sense, the resurgence of capital punishment in contemporary Japan has been more driven by elites than was the more populist revival that began in the United States some two decades earlier. The most significant contrast between the systems of capital punishment in the world's only two developed democracies that still regularly use it is that there is much more concentrated central control over key death penalty decisions in Japan than in the United States.[50] The specific emphasis on capital

50. Many Japanese officials and abolitionists believe their country uses capital punishment more rarely and more carefully than does the United States, and some analysts think this is the most critical death penalty difference between the two nations. But the belief that Japan's rate is lower is not well grounded. It is true that, per capita, Japan's rate of execution is about seven times lower than that of the United States and more than 30 times lower than the high-rate American states of Texas, Oklahoma, and Virginia. And from 1977 to July 2004, Harris County (Houston), Texas, had more executions (73) than did all of Japan (66). These

punishment that followed the Tokyo subway attacks came from governing elites, not the Japanese public. One of the key dimensions of the "repetitive pattern" of abolition in the developed world has been "leadership from the front"—that is, abolition movements that are led by political elites despite majority support for the death penalty among the general public (Zimring 2003:22). As subsequent chapters on the Philippines, South Korea, and Taiwan show, that phenomenon is being replicated in developed and developing Asia. But the case of Japan illustrates how political "leadership from the front" can also characterize accelerations of capital punishment.

■ History Lessons

We have described centuries of development in the Japanese death penalty not only because there is a rich historical record for this nation but also because capital punishment in contemporary Japan is "Japanese" in the sense that it reflects that society's distinctive arrangements of law, politics, and culture. Compared to capital punishment in the United States, for example, the Japanese way of capital punishment exhibits several distinctive traits, including centralized decision-making, small variation between geographic regions, little constitutionalization of the capital process and little emphasis on the principles or practices of adversarial legalism, low salience of racial and class issues, informal, bureaucratic control over the charge and execution processes, a surplus of secrecy and silence and a concomitant shortage of transparency and accountability (especially in the posttrial stages), and a low level of cultural conflict around death penalty issues (see Garland 2005:369).

But if capital punishment in Japan is distinctively Japanese, our historical overview shows that international influences have often been critical. If there had been no Buddhism to import in the premodern period, there would have been no 350-year moratorium, and if there had been no Chinese influence after executions resumed, medieval Japan's execution methods would not have involved

---

facts notwithstanding, people who are condemned and executed are not randomly selected for death, they are drawn, for the most part, from a larger pool of potentially capital cases. In Japan and the United States, these pools consist entirely of homicide crimes, and when the size of the pools is taken into account, the probability of a known murderer being sentenced to death in Japan in recent years (1.33 percent for 1994 to 2003, and 1.96 percent for 2000 to 2003) was about what it was in California and Virginia (Johnson 2006a:106). In 2007, when Japan had 14 first-instance death sentences and the United States had 110, the ratio of homicides to death sentences in Japan was about three times higher than that in the United States—approximately 50 to 1 in Japan versus more than 150 to 1 in the U.S. (Japan Death Penalty Information Center, www.jdpic.org). What is more, most people in Japan whose death sentences are finalized by the Supreme Court get executed, while that is not the case in much of America (Johnson 2006a:106).

such elaborate cruelty. In the Meiji period, the need to earn recognition and respect from the West produced one of the steepest death penalty declines in modern times. The U.S. occupation dictated the decision to retain capital punishment and established an environment of "censored democracy" that had lasting effects on the way Japan's death penalty is administered and discussed. After the Occupation, the decline of capital punishment was partly propelled by cross-national forces, including export-led economic growth, democratization (a main Occupation aim), and a homicide decline that was driven by larger economic and political changes. Even after the Tokyo subway attacks in 1995, the resurgence of capital punishment has been fueled by transnational developments, including anxiety about the rising number of foreigners resident in Japan and an increased emphasis on victims' rights. As historian Kenneth Pyle has summed it up, "few countries in modern history have been as subject—and as sensitive, responsive, and adaptive—to forces of the international environment as Japan. The international system has had a powerful effect on Japan's foreign policy, but it also exercised an extraordinary role in shaping Japan's domestic institutions. Repeatedly, Japan sweepingly reversed its domestic order to meet the needs of new configurations of the international order" (quoted in Zoellick 2006; see also Pyle 2007).

The domestic institution of capital punishment has frequently been "sensitive, responsive, and adaptive" to forces in Japan's international environment, and what stands out is how often Japan has looked to the West instead of Asia. Legal change in Japan has frequently occurred as a response to normative transformations in the West. In a variety of fields—tobacco control, equal employment opportunity, the treatment of persons with HIV or Hansen's disease, sexual harassment, domestic violence, prostitution, minority and children's rights, legal education, lay participation at trial, and others— domestic legal change was triggered by international frames and developments that activated a "norm of conformity with the West" (Feldman 2006; see also Chan-Tiberghien 2004). In the 21st century, transnational influences on Japanese capital punishment will continue to be refracted into a distinctly Japanese environment. If history is any guide, the most important outside influences may remain Western.

We caution, however, that there are also historical reasons to wonder whether Western appeals to the importance of "human rights" will push Japan away from capital punishment. As one of the world's leading social theorists put it in his synthesis of Japanese history, culture, and social organization, "all the characteristics of the Japanese program of modernity—*above all the negation of the universalistic claims of other civilizations*... distinguish it not only from the Western program but also from the response of other non-Western societies to the impingement of Western modernity" (Eisenstadt 1996:436; emphasis added). On this view, Japan has never been an "axial" civilization of the kind described by Karl Jaspers—a society (Jewish, Greek, Christian, Islamic, Buddhist, or Confucian) that deliberately tries to reconstruct the mundane world according to a transcendental vision (13). Indeed, despite centuries of continuous contact with axial civilizations, Japan has remained doggedly nonaxial.

The "denial of human rights norms covering capital punishment" has been a "major impediment" to abolition in many countries (Hood 2001:338), but the pattern of rejecting "universalistic claims" that one sees in Japanese history may mean this obstacle will be especially difficult to overcome in the Japanese context (Mishima 1958; Endo 1966; van Wolferen 1989:9; Murakami 2003:166).[51] The rapid rise in the number of abolitionist nations since 1980 has largely been driven by events in Europe, where a stand against capital punishment has become a "moral imperative believed necessary to the status of any civilized modern state" (Zimring 2003:17). This morality—and the "right to life" frame at its core—has been "exported to other nations with missionary vigor" and, at least in eastern Europe, with spectacular success (Zimring 2003:35).

But of course East Asia is not eastern Europe, and Japan is not Poland. Nor is Japan nearly as Christian as the Philippines or South Korea, where abolition of capital punishment is either a reality or a priority of national leaders, and where Christian individuals and organizations have played key roles in the abolition movements. By contrast, only about 1 percent of Japanese are Christian, and Nobuto Hosaka, one of the leaders of Japan's Parliamentary League for the Abolition of the Death Penalty, believes the weakness of Japan's Christian lobby not only distinguishes it from Europe and from Asian neighbors who have turned away from capital punishment, it also helps explain why religious groups in Japan tend to "cooperate in the death penalty" (quoted in McNeill and Mason 2007). At a deeper level, the lack of an organized Christian opposition to capital punishment may reflect the Japanese penchant for resisting "the universalistic claims of other civilizations" (Eisenstadt 1996:436).

Another history lesson from Japan is that large changes in the scale of capital punishment—and the Meiji decline especially—brought Japan to the symbolic end of the death penalty continuum well before many other nations reached a parallel point in their own histories.[52] The Meiji execution rate in 1900 (0.78 per million) was about one-half the rates in Virginia and Oklahoma a full century later (Hood 2002:92), and Japan's execution rate (0.29) in the 1930s was less than one-quarter of the American rate (1.31). In the postwar period, the continued decline of Japan's death penalty brought its execution rate lower than that in almost all other retentionist nations in Asia, though the resurgence of capital punishment since the Tokyo subway attacks is starting to change that standing.

51. As a senior prosecutor in Japan's Ministry of Justice stressed, "we believe that the decision whether to keep or abolish the death penalty should be the decision of each individual country, and should be based on the public sentiment of each country and the crime situation in each country" (quoted in Lane 2005b). There is no allowance for universalistic claims in this approach to capital punishment.

52. Many other nations, but not all. Between 1885 and 1894, the execution rate in Japan (1.8 per million) was about four times higher than the rates in Prussia (0.44) and England (0.44) (Evans 1996:918). But in modern Asia, we know of no other nation in which executions dropped as far and as early as they did in Meiji Japan.

To see that Japan has had a symbolic death penalty for more than a century is to recognize that executions stopped being needed for crime control there decades before the United States, South Korea, and Taiwan reached similar points in their own histories. For more than a century, Japan has retained capital punishment not so much because it needs it but because it wants it. The pursuit of at least one execution per year may keep the streak going and satisfy death penalty supporters in the procuracy and the Ministry of Justice, but it is hard to make a case that executions on such a small scale have anything to do with deterrence, incapacitation, or the other utilitarian purposes of punishment that provide the general justification for having criminal law in the first place. It is also ironic that in a nation where capital punishment has been symbolic for so long, its administration is surrounded by so much secrecy and silence (Johnson 2006c). The Japanese state is ambivalent not only toward using death as a criminal sanction but also toward talking about it.

The final lesson to stress from Japanese history is that from the standpoint of Western theories about when developed countries abolish capital punishment (Zimring 2003:16), the history of Japan since the U.S. occupation is an almost best case scenario for retention because the nation has been governed almost continuously by conservatives since 1955 (sometimes in coalition with other parties). In the absence of abolition during Japan's transition from authoritarianism to democracy following World War II, and in the absence of the election of a left-liberal party to power in the half century since the Occupation ended, Japan lacks both of the "precipitating circumstances" that stimulated abolition in postwar Europe (Zimring 2003:23). In this historical context, retention is neither a surprise nor does it need to be framed in terms of the nuances of Japanese culture.[53] Nevertheless, there is something

---

53. A related question concerns the efficacy of Japan's abolition movement, which was marginal until the late 1980s and then gained strength. In the United States, the retention of capital punishment can be partly explained by the ineffectiveness of the anti–death penalty movement, especially its failure to frame capital punishment in pragmatic terms that resonate with the American public (Haines 1996:5,22). The decline of American capital punishment since the late 1990s is partly the result of three factors: a marked decline in murder rates, the success abolitionists and their allies have had in exposing practical problems in the administration of capital punishment (wrongful conviction and botched executions especially), and the spread of LWOP alternatives to death. Japan's abolition movement would probably profit from a focus on frames more pragmatic than the "right to life," "human dignity," and "the rest of the world is abolishing" frames that now seem most salient in that country. Since "uncovering and clarifying the truth" is widely deemed to be the cardinal value in Japanese criminal justice (Johnson 2002a), a focus on wrongful convictions might be especially apt—if some could be exposed. The problem is that while some death row inmates do protest their innocence, none has been proved innocent since 1989 (Shikei Haishi Henshu Iinkai 2004). At the same time, Japan's abolition movement is handicapped by at least four other conditions: a shortage of resources, the structural disadvantage of being so organizationally centralized in Tokyo that it is difficult to address problems in outlying regions of the country, the absence of the option of life without parole

surprising, distinctive, and recurrent in postwar Japan's experience with capital punishment, and that is the conflict within the conservative ruling party, focused especially at the top of the Ministry of Justice and concentrated at the stage when prosecutors seek authorization for execution (Fukuda 2002; Schmidt 2002:62). This conflict, and the more intense conflict over capital punishment that exists in the very different American context (Zimring 2003:119), seem to reflect the problematic position the death penalty has acquired in developed democracies at this point in history.

■ Japanese Exceptionalism? On the Perseverance of Capital Punishment

Before considering the road ahead for the death penalty in Japan, important aspects of the current state of Japanese policy demand sustained attention. Japan is one of only two developed democracies with continuing executions. While there is an extensive death penalty literature on the United States, the other advanced democracy that uses execution, scholars have not explored what could be called Japan's death penalty exceptionalism. What differentiates Japan from the European and Commonwealth governments that ended executions between 1948 and 1981?

One possible answer is that Japan retains capital punishment because it is outside Europe's sphere of influence. Most developed countries that have abolished the death penalty have been close to the European experience and were influenced by it. Japan is not only geographically and culturally distant from Europe, it is situated in Asia, the only continent without a regional human rights enforcement agency (Bae 2007; Bae 2008b). But this is not a satisfactory explanation, for two reasons. First, the move away from the death penalty has been geographically broader than just Europe, with Canada, Australia, and New Zealand as the most obvious examples of developed nations that have abolished outside the European sphere (albeit with significant cultural connections to

---

(offenders sentenced to life are eligible for parole after 10 years, though on the average they serve more than 30 years before being released), and the general trend in Japanese society toward penal populism and harsher criminal sanctions (Shikei Haishi Henshu Iinkai 2000–2001; Hamai and Ellis 2008; Miyazawa 2008). Abolitionists in Japan are as passionate and committed as any in the world, but these are significant challenges.

The propriety of proposing a LWOP alternative to death—as a multiparty group of Japanese legislators did in 2008—is especially difficult to discern ("Shushinkei: Ze ka Hi ka" 2008; Vornic 2008). In some American jurisdictions, LWOP has helped reduce the number of death sentences. But American experience also suggests that the availability of LWOP often has little effect on executions and sometimes results in more people being sentenced to long terms of imprisonment than would have been the case without it ("Matter of Life" 2006; Johnson 2008c). More fundamentally, LWOP raises many of the same human rights issues that have been at the core of abolitionists' critique of capital punishment (Hood 2007; see also Appleton and Grover 2007; Hood and Hoyle 2008).

Europe). Second, Japan's ambivalence about execution and its reluctance to use state killing as a tool of government is evident in its history since it was opened to the West in the last half of the 19th century. The downturn in the use of execution as a criminal punishment not only started well over a century ago as a result of Japan's encounter with the West, it continued in the postwar period until the 40-month cessation of executions between 1989 and 1993.

Another possible explanation for Japanese exceptionalism is that Asian cultural and political values are different from Western ones and less hostile to execution as a tool of public policy. This "Asian values" theme certainly distinguishes Japan from Canada, Australia, and New Zealand, but it encounters difficulty explaining a number of Asian phenomena, such as the conflict over executions in Japan when ministers of justice make nonexecution a defining feature of their tenures. More generally, a broad theory of Asian affinity for capital punishment seems inconsistent with the recent histories of South Korea, Taiwan, and the Philippines.

Yet could a cultural difference that is distinctively "Japanese" explain Japan's death penalty exceptionalism? It seems not, for we see no discernable long-term trend in Japanese values or practice that suggests a cultural predisposition to continued use of the death penalty (Bae 2008c). Indeed, in the 150 years since Japan was opened to the West, there are few if any indicators that set Japan apart from other developed nations in death penalty sensibilities, and there are many good reasons—the large declines in death sentences and executions especially—to regard the historical trajectory of capital punishment in post-Meiji Japan as significantly similar to the trajectories that have been observed in other developed nations (Garland 2005:355).

If there is little about Japanese culture or values that seems distinctively pro–death penalty, there are features of Japanese politics and government that help explain the absence of abolition. The most striking political feature of postwar Japan is the sustained rule by a right-wing party. The LDP has been in power almost without interruption for the half century since 1955, albeit with several intervals of coalition government since the early 1990s (Kollner 2006). The hegemony of a conservative government is certainly part of the explanation for Japan's retention of capital punishment because the pattern in Europe involving nations such as Great Britain, Spain, and France is for complete abolition to occur only after a government left of political center comes to power. That explains why Great Britain abolished in the 1960s (under a Labour government) while Spain waited until the death of Franco and France maintained a capital statute until the socialists were elected in 1980.

Japan's continuous rule by the right seems a satisfactory explanation for the retention of the statutory power to execute, but it does not explain the increase in executions during the early 1990s, the rise in death sentences during the decade after the Tokyo subway attacks, or the surge in executions that started in 2007. What brought renewed attention to a penalty that was so long a symbolic but not practical tool of control? Even for a government of the right, an increased emphasis on capital punishment in the 1990s is something of a puzzle.

One feature of Japanese government that sets it apart from other industrial powers is its lack of authority to use military power or martial policies in the postwar period. The postwar occupation created a government that is pacifist by constitutional promise, pledged neither to threaten nor to use force of arms in international disputes. While Japan's Self Defense Forces (*jietai*) are among the most technologically advanced armed forces in the world, and while the nation's aggregate military expenditures were the seventh highest in the world in 2007, the constitutional commitment to pacifism removes one important means of governmental assertiveness when it feels threatened by hostile forces. If the symbolism of pacifism feels uncomfortably close to impotence for a government with conservative sentiments, then that discomfort could make the hangman an important symbol of governmental power. On this view, one reason the LDP put increased emphasis on the death penalty as an instrument of government in the 1990s may have been the absence of other martial options during a period in which many people inside Japan and out were calling on the country to develop a more assertive military posture in order to deal with new threats such as the rise of China, the miscreant North Korea, and conflict in the Middle East (Pyle 2007; Samuels 2007).[54]

■ Notes on the Future

Pondering the future of capital punishment in Japan is a high-risk venture but no less necessary for that reason. So much that will influence the character of Japanese society and government is unknown that it is anyone's guess where death penalty policy is going and how long it will take to get there. One could assume a conclusion from some normative frame—in our case the abolition of

---

54. This hunch about the perceived need to "make muscles" is based on the recognition that the death penalty performs important expressive functions (Masur 1989; Evans 1996; Sarat 1999; Sarat 2001; Sarat and Boulanger 2005). For most publics most of the time, politics is a parade of symbols and abstractions, and the political analysis of capital punishment must therefore consider not only tangible policies and practices but also what the death penalty means to people and how they are placated and aroused by it (Edelman 1964). As of this writing, there are at least 23 independent countries that do not maintain armies. According to Amnesty International, 17 have abolished the death penalty for all crimes (Andorra, Costa Rica, Haiti, Iceland, Kiribati, Liechtenstein, Marshall Islands, Mauritius, Micronesia, Monaco, Palau, Panama, Samoa, San Marino, Solomon Islands, Tuvalu, and Vatican City), 2 have abolished de facto (Grenada and Nauru), and 4 retain capital punishment in law but have not executed anyone in recent years (Dominica, Saint Kitts and Nevis, Saint Lucia, and Saint Vincent and the Grenadines). The overwhelmingly abolitionist policy of these pacifist nations may reflect three facts: all the nations are much smaller than Japan (the most populous is Haiti, with 8.3 million people), none has a history of militarism anything like Japan's effort to create a "Greater East Asia Co-Prosperity Sphere" in the first half of the 20th century, and (unlike Japan) most abolished the death penalty *before* they renounced the use of military force.

capital punishment—and then use information about Japan to explore how and why the nation might come to abolish. Much as we share the abolitionist preferences that would inform such a venture, we do not believe it is an appropriate approach because it seems more a branch of wishful thinking than Japanese studies.

The methodology we prefer is a more complicated and less comforting four-stage process. First, we outline a "government-centric" theory of how death penalty policies get made in Japan. Second, we describe the range of policies we believe to be the "field of choice" for Japan's death penalty policy. Third, we consider the motives Japanese governments could have for different policy choices, paying special attention to foreign influences. Fourth, we address how long it might take for Japanese policy to change and what factors may be leading indicators of governmental change.

A Government-centric Perspective

Whether or not there are major changes in death penalty policy in Japan is fundamentally a question of the desires of those who control the executive branch of the national government. In projecting this government-centric frame on the future, we assume a stable government without major crises. This is a Japan without war or major economic meltdown and with continuity in government structure.

Two features of Japanese government inform this perspective. First, once a finalized death sentence has been issued, the Ministry of Justice has discretionary authority over whether or not to execute, and without judicial interference. A condemned prisoner can be hanged one or two years after the final judicial decree, or he can die of old age three or four decades later. All power is in the national government, as is not the case with the federal system in the United States or the decentralized death penalty decision-making in China prior to 2007. But the most important assumption in this account concerns the relatively passive role of public opinion and social institutions on Japan's death penalty policy. Public opinion polls consistently show high levels of support for capital punishment, although these are temperatures taken in a climate of death penalty secrecy and "censored democracy" (Dower 1999; Johnson 2006a). There is no recent history of major public concern about capital punishment, and even during the death penalty resurgence that began in the 1990s, it was not a major concern in social or political institutions outside central government. Unless there are major changes in the way capital justice is administered and perceived, Japan's public and its social and legislative institutions will tolerate low levels of execution or even none at all.

To describe the structure of decision-making in Japanese capital punishment, one must distinguish the death sentencing process from the process that leads to execution. In both, it is prosecutors who seek death decisions, and in both there are other actors—judges and ministers of justice—who can prevent death penalty outcomes.

A death sentence can be issued in Japan only if prosecutors seek it and a court consisting of three judges agrees that death is deserved. Starting in May 2009, a panel of six lay assessors will sit with three professional judges to decide questions of guilt and sentence in capital and other serious cases, but even after that reform takes effect, a necessary condition for a death sentence to be imposed will be a prosecutor's decision to pursue it. In practice, however, the decision to seek death is not made by any individual prosecutor; it results from a collective and hierarchical process of case review and consultation (*kessai*). Thus, the rise of death sentences in Japan since the Tokyo subway attacks reflects an increased commitment to capital prosecution by the procuracy as an organization. Judges (and after 2009, mixed panels of judges and lay assessors) can disagree with the procuracy's decision to seek death, but in practice they do so only about one-third of the time, about half the disagreement level one finds in America's federal system.

For an execution to occur, a death sentence must be finalized, usually by the Supreme Court but occasionally by a lower court if the defendant waives the right to appeal. By law, the minister of justice is supposed to sign a death warrant within six months of the finalization of the sentence, and the execution must then occur within five days of the signing. In practice, death warrants are never issued as rapidly as the law requires, not because ministers try to slow the system down but because prosecutors in the Ministry of Justice who present cases to the minister for signing do so only after another long process of deliberation, consultation, and review. At least 10 and as many as 20 ministry prosecutors formally approve the decision to move toward execution before presenting a case to the minister for the signature that authorizes hanging, though in some cases prosecutors decide never to seek execution at all, even though all of the condemned's appeals have been exhausted.

It is the gatekeeping function prosecutors perform at the trial, sentencing, and execution stages that leads critics to conclude that they "play god" in Japan's capital process. Though the metaphor fits, it must be elaborated and qualified in at least three ways. First, a prosecutorial desire for execution can be frustrated by the acts of other officials. As noted at the outset of this chapter, some ministers of justice have refused to sign execution warrants, and judges always have the last word in capital trials and appeals. Similarly, the advent of Japan's new lay judge system in 2009 will give ordinary citizens some influence in sentencing at capital trials, though how they will use their authority remains to be seen (as we discuss later). Second, prosecutors in South Korea and Taiwan perform similar gatekeeping functions, and their politically influenced decisions to keep the gate closed have been one important proximate cause of these countries' moratoria on executions (see chapters 5 and 6). Third, depending on the case and the context, prosecutor policy in Japan runs in two directions: toward execution and toward nonexecution. This duality helps explain not only why Japan has averaged only about four executions a year since its own moratorium ended in 1993, but also why the age profile of inmates on Japan's death row is so much older than those in Taiwan

Table 3.2

Age of the condemned at time of execution in South Korea (1987–1997) and Japan
(1993–2006)

| Age | Executions in Korea | | Executions in Japan | |
	South Korea	Percent	Japan	Percent
20–29	44	44	0	0
30–39	41	41	1	2
40–49	11	11	14	28
50–59	4	4	16	32
60–69	1	1	17	34
70–79	0	0	3	6
Total	101	100	51	100

Sources: Shikei Haishi Henshu Iinkai 2006:269; B. Cho 2008.

and South Korea. In South Korea, for example, only 5 percent of the
most recent 101 executions were of people aged 50 or older, and nearly
85 percent of executions were of people in their twenties or thirties. In
Japan, by contrast, 70 percent of the most recent 51 executions were of people
aged 50 or older, while only 2 percent were under age 40. The estimated
average age at execution also differs markedly: 32 in South Korea versus 57 in
Japan. (See table 3.2.)

To understand this argument and its limits, it is necessary to distinguish
between the wide range of events and changes that might influence the path of
capital punishment in Japan and the way such influences can become changes
in policy. The powers to seek or not seek a death sentence, to make a judicially
completed death case eligible for execution, and to choose who will be
executed and when are all concentrated in the executive branch of the national
government. Influences on death penalty policy can and will come from all
over Japan and from other nations as well, but in order to influence policy, the
channel through which all these external stimuli must flow is that branch of
government. In the years to come, much will happen that could alter the
course of Japanese practice, but it must shape responses within government
before change can occur. In this sense, all roads for influence on Japanese
capital punishment must lead to Tokyo.

The Field of Choice for the Proximate Future

Four different policy clusters seem the most likely next steps in Japan's capital
punishment policy. The first three are non-legislative policies that emanate
from the executive branch of national government. One is a continuation of
the execution surge that started on Christmas 2006 and generated 23 executions

over an 18-month period–the biggest concentration of executions Japan has experienced in more than 30 years. The next possibility is a return to low-volume execution of the kind that prevailed until the recent surge. The third is administrative nonexecution—what could be called a ministerial moratorium—as a low-visibility probe into the propriety of ending executions altogether. And the final option for Japan is a formally acknowledged or announced cessation of execution that could come from either the executive or the legislative branch of government.

In the short run, executions may continue to occur at levels Japan has not seen since the mid-1970s. This is what we expect if future governments select proexecution hawks for the minister of justice position. In the years to come, there could also be considerable enthusiasm in the Ministry of Justice for executing the many members of Aum who are now on death row.

Regardless of who the future ministers are, it is also possible that the more general trend toward increased punitiveness in Japanese criminal justice (*genbatsuka*) could help generate annual execution totals that move Japan out of the "symbolic" and "nominal" execution policy categories which it inhabits in our tables 2.1 and 2.2 and into the "exceptional" category that in recent years has been represented by countries such as Vietnam and Pakistan. Japan's penal policy is becoming harsher in many respects, and if the wave of punitiveness continues, capital punishment could ride it for some years to come. What we do not know is how closely linked supportive public attitudes toward penal harshness in general are to historically more ambivalent feelings about executions.

There will not be any shortage of finalized death sentences to constrain the potential number of execution opportunities even if the Ministry of Justice works to sustain executions at 15 or 20 per year, and in this sense the power to determine the scale of executions is one government official wide. But even with the limited public dissemination of information on executions, the recent rise in executions has caught the attention of the media and elites and could destabilize attitudes and power relations within governmental circles. Unless there are political gains associated with the higher number of executions, the destabilizing influence may not generate political benefits worth the costs. In the near future, all of the power to decide how many persons get hanged in Japan resides in the Ministry of Justice and, of course, in the wider executive branch where decisions are made about who is appropriate to head it. The views of future justice ministers and of those who select them will thus be the key leading indicator of Japan's execution volume.

Assuming continued LDP dominance, an equally probable course for the future is a return to executions at the low volumes that occurred for most of the past half century. With few exceptions, the level of execution and the presence of a death penalty have not been important questions in Japanese politics, and the government is probably hoping that executions continue to maintain a low profile. There seems to be little to gain in pushing from three or four executions per year in a nation of 130 million to even 10 or 12, with no apparent public investment in particular hangings.

Before the current execution surge, one administrative concern was to make sure at least one execution happened in each calendar year. This policy was meant to demonstrate a commitment to the symbolic importance of execution as a continuing activity of government, but it also shows how close to zero and how far from an operational execution system Japan has come. However, there is a large difference between a government that strains to make sure at least one execution occurs each year and a state where operational inertia produces continued executions. The American state of Texas executed more persons in 1999 than Japan executed in the decade after 1996, and between 1977 and July 2004 one of Texas's 254 counties—Harris County (Houston)—had more executions (73) than did all of Japan (66) even though Japan's population was at least 35 times larger (Johnson 2006a:104). One push for more executions comes from a buildup of inmates on Japan's death row (persons with a finalized sentence of death), the population of which exceeded 100 in late 2006 and continued to expand thereafter, despite the execution surge. In fact, several of Japan's most recent executions were explained by government officials as necessary to keep the death row population below 100. Japan's death penalty resurgence will result in more opportunities for this jurisprudentially jejune justification to be used, but we do not expect the focus on a death row threshold of acceptability to last. If we are wrong, and if the number of finalized death sentences continues to climb, as most observers expect, then Japan will witness a sustained increase in executions for the first time since shoguns ruled the country. In comparative perspective, Thailand and the Philippines have maintained death row populations vastly larger than Japan's yet produced annual execution totals that were usually close to zero (see appendix D and chapter 4).

The third option for Japanese policy in the proximate future is cessation of executions as a low-visibility act of administrative government. What makes a ministerial moratorium on executions more likely than legislative or even high-visibility executive branch shifts in death penalty policy is the capacity of the current governmental system to end execution almost without friction. It is nearly as easy for the current Japanese system to produce consecutive periods of no execution as it is to produce executions. If both prosecutors in the Ministry of Justice and the minister of justice wanted executions to cease, they would. What makes this scenario less likely than continuing executions is not so much systemic inertia as the policy preferences within the Ministry of Justice. Career prosecutors in the ministry want executions to continue, and it takes as much affirmative action from them to schedule an execution as it does to halt progress toward one. In that context, the present level of executions indicates conscious choice more than bureaucratic momentum.

If the Ministry of Justice chose to stop executions, the easiest method would be quiet administrative action. Indeed, even if the executive branch of government wanted to abolish capital punishment (never yet an LDP position), the smoothest way to proceed would involve a long and low-visibility halt to executions with no announced policy change.[55] That would also be the least risky way to experiment with change from current policy without a commitment to eventual abolition. For those with personal or bureaucratic interests in maintaining executions, the major risk in a period of nonexecution is that the inertial forces that now make executions difficult could grow more substantial as soon as the expectation of execution no longer obtains. This is one reason why prosecutors have tried to make sure no calendar year goes by without a hanging. Perhaps Japan has not drifted into a moratorium because of governmental fear of exactly that trajectory. When and if this changes, a quiet moratorium is more likely than a major debate or widely discussed change in policy.

What might produce the fourth possible future, a sharper break with past practice and a more formal shift toward abolition? Such a shift is likely only if the stimulus for change comes from outside government and the question of capital punishment becomes more important than it is now or has been since 1945. As long as the death penalty is not a hot-button issue in Japanese politics, even a change in governing party might be more likely to produce quiet rather than loud initial steps toward the end of the death penalty. Only a capital punishment scandal—following a wrongful or botched execution, for example—or an international commitment that requires a formal shift in policy would push the death penalty into the legislative and public arena before a long informal moratorium. In Japan's Diet, there is neither the interest in the issue nor the legislative constituency for abolition that can be found in South Korea's National Assembly (see chapter 5). Hence, formal change in Japan's death penalty policy seems likely only if a political shift occurs in the legislature or if officials in the executive branch resist external pressure for change. And legislative pressure for abolition would not necessarily be strong even if the current LDP Diet majority were displaced by Japan's centrist opposition.

In sum, Japan's death penalty policy could sustain the surge in executions that started in 2006 or it could return to the steady but infrequent execution regime that prevailed for the previous several decades. In either event, the most probable beginning of the end of executions in Japan is their low-visibility cessation, which might be quietly maintained for many years before any explicit discourse about change follows the de facto moratorium. Less likely than any of these scenarios, and less likely in Japan than in other Asian settings such as South Korea and Taiwan, is an open and formal

---

55. This kind of quiet moratorium is what happened in Belgium, where the death penalty was finally abolished in 1996 after only one execution had occurred (in 1918) over the preceding 133 years (Council of Europe 1999:29).

discourse about abolition that starts before rather than after an administrative moratorium.

If these possibilities make up the field of choice for Japan's proximate death penalty future, what substantive factors could produce change?

Environments and Motivations for Change

Because we began with a "government-centric" theory about the power of the center in Japan's death penalty policy-making, the forces we consider here are those that could influence the priorities, values, and political judgments of the executive branch of national government. That does not reduce the number of influences to be explored, but it does provide a specific context for thinking about how various ones could produce policy change. There are three areas of possible influence: public opinion, government and politics, and foreign forces.

PUBLIC OPINION Public opinion in Japan can have important influence on official behavior even if it is several steps removed from the decisions made by governmental bureaucracies at the national level. But public attitudes toward capital punishment are unlikely to shift in such a way as to influence government decisions about levels of execution, or to reduce the number of annual executions to zero anytime soon. Public support for the death penalty in Japan has been high for a long time, and without a major scandal in the administration of capital punishment, there is no reason to suppose it will fall below a majority level. In many western European nations, publics continued to support the death penalty up to and even after abolition (Zimring and Hawkins 1986:15). Only when a despotic regime is overthrown is anti–death penalty public opinion a leading force for abolition, and even then—as in South Africa and the Philippines—public support for abolition is not guaranteed (Chiu 2006). Moreover, there is little indication that capital punishment is a pressing issue for most Japanese citizens. Majority support for the existing government policy seems to be as much an expression of support for government as of enthusiasm for executions (Zimring and Johnson 2006).[56]

---

56. Support for capital punishment is weaker among Japanese lawyers than in the public at large. A 1991 survey found the legal profession almost evenly divided: 47.6 percent wanted to retain the death penalty and 45.8 percent favored abolition (Kikuta 1999:15). A 1994 survey by the Tokyo Bar Association found even weaker support: only 32 percent of respondents (n = 1,329 attorneys) wanted to retain capital punishment while 61 percent wanted to abolish (and 81 percent of female lawyers wanted to abolish; see Tokyo Bengoshikai 1994:10). A survey by the Prime Minister's Office in the same year found that 73.8 percent of Japanese citizens supported the death penalty and only 13.6 percent opposed it (Schmidt 2002:166). Since then, public support for capital punishment in Japan has increased, reaching a high of 81 percent in 2005. For a summary of the problems with public opinion data about capital punishment in Japan, see Johnson (2006a:116).

So we regard public opinion about the death penalty as unlikely to change but also as an insignificant restriction on the government's freedom of action. A protracted moratorium on executions would not inflame public opinion even if, as seems probable, majority support for the death penalty persists. Until recently, questions of crime and punishment have not been centrally important in Japan's public discourse or political process, and even with the increasingly populist approach to policy-making that has developed in Japan's crime field over the past decade, the government retains substantial freedom of action with respect to capital punishment. This seems likely to continue.

That said, any changes in general political orientation that replaced the LDP with a left-of-center government could have substantial impact on death penalty policy if the experience in Europe, Canada, and Asian nations such as South Korea and Taiwan are repeated in Japan. This possibility is more appropriately considered a political and governmental change—the focus of the next section.

GOVERNMENT AND POLITICS   Two issues we identified in our earlier discussion of Japan's postwar history come into play here: the constitutional pacifism of Japan's postwar government, and the possibility of political change from right to left. The former is unique to Japan while the latter has played a role in most transitions away from capital punishment in other stable democracies.

Japan's constitutional rejection of military force has been associated with fears—within government as well as among a minority of the governed—that the state is weak and therefore ineffectual (Drifte 1998; Dower 1999:562; Pyle 2007:366). A government with circumscribed authority to use tanks and battleships may become more attached to executions and the executioner as symbols of its power. To the extent that executions have been of special importance because of the absence of other avenues to express state power, how might the recent and projected increases in Japanese military force and the willingness to use it influence the government's perceived need to execute criminal offenders?

Our hunch is that a broader array of instruments of state power may take pressure off the executioner as a symbol of government potency. The recent shift of concern in Japan from domestic threats (the Tokyo subway attacks in the mid-1990s) to foreign ones (North Korean bombs and missiles in 2007) seems to have brought with it a shift to a greater emphasis on the need to meet foreign threats with appropriate force. If this shift leads to constitutional revision and enhanced military potential, as some anticipate, then the next few years may witness a political transition in which an increased emphasis on bombs and rockets could diminish the significance of executions.

Just as the long supremacy of the right-wing LDP is one key cause of the government's continued commitment to capital punishment, the event in Japan's political future most likely to bring swift change to death penalty policy would be the election of a left-of-center party to effective control of national government. Since the early 1990s, a number of new challenges have arisen which threaten the LDP's dominance, including the creation of a centrist opposition party—the Democratic Party of Japan—that can seriously contend for power. One result is that government turnover appears to be more likely now than at almost any other time in postwar Japanese history (Kollner 2006:254). If and when a turnover occurs, there is reason to believe that a formal change rather than a quiet moratorium would signal the demise of the current death penalty policy.[57]

The historical instances of the ascendancy of a left-of-center party precipitating a shift away from the death penalty are numerous and are not limited to European or Western examples. Every time a stable democratic government in Europe has chosen to abolish the death penalty, the time for change arrived shortly after a shift from right-of-center to left-of-center control. This was the pattern in Austria (when the socialists joined the coalition government in 1950), Great Britain (under a Labour government in 1964 and again in 1997), Spain (after Franco in 1978), and France (when the socialists came to power in 1981). Outside Europe, the major reform in Canada was achieved by Lester Pearson, the Liberal leader in 1966; in Australia by the Labour government of Geoff Whitlam in 1973; and in New Zealand (twice) by a Labour government. A similar pattern of left-of-center national leadership generating change has also been evident among democratic governments of Asia. In both South Korea and Taiwan, the transition from right-of-center to left-of-center in the executive branch of government launched the campaigns to end capital punishment that are documented in chapters 5 and 6.

In contrast, a transition from right to left in the executive branch has never happened in Japan. This alone could be the sufficient explanation for Japan's persistence as a retentionist nation; no other aspect of the country's geography, culture, or social structure may be necessary to explain what we have called Japan's death penalty exceptionalism.

Does this mean that if or when the left comes to power the end of capital punishment is likely to be one by-product of the transition? The answer is yes,

---

57. Compared to South Korea's National Assembly, where more than half of legislators have supported abolition in recent years, Japan's Parliament has manifested little support for abolition. When Japan's de facto moratorium started late in 1989, 81 MPs said they opposed the death penalty, and by the time the moratorium ended in March 1993, 183 MPs, mainly from the Social Democratic Party, belonged to Forum 90, Japan's largest abolitionist organization (Schmidt 2002:79). A decade later, only 122 of the 762 MPs (16 percent) had joined the Diet Members League for the Abolition of Capital Punishment, an organization Forum 90 helped establish in 1994. In 2002, the chairman of this league, Shizuka Kamei, a faction chief in the LDP, predicted that membership would increase in the years to come, but it has not (Kamei 2002; Shimizu 2002c). As capital punishment accelerated after the Tokyo gas attacks in 1995, Japanese politicians became more reluctant to question or resist the institution (Shikei Haishi Henshu Iinkai 2005). Kamei himself never mentioned capital punishment during his campaign for prime minister in 2003 even though his three opponents staunchly supported the death penalty (Johnson 2005:270).

for at least two reasons. First, no developed nation with a left-of-center government has retained capital punishment after 1970—other than the United States, and even there, no executions were carried out by the federal government during the Democratic administrations of either Carter or Clinton, and neither president introduced any legislation authorizing a death penalty.[58] Second, two of the most rapidly developing nations in Asia that have experienced right-to-left transitions—South Korea and Taiwan—have traveled well down the road toward ending the death penalty. Thus, there are no suggestions yet that Asia is an exception to the general rule. Of course, the evidence of Asian conformity to this pattern in democratic politics could be stronger, for the transitions in South Korea and Taiwan are still unfinished. However, since both nations were much more prone to use execution in the generation before their transitions than was Japan during the same period of time, in any future transition, Japan has a much less dramatic shift to make than its two East Asian neighbors.

So if the left comes to power in Japan, one consequence could be a relatively swift change in death penalty policy, including an end to executions and perhaps a proposal for abolition. And if this does not happen, then for the first time in postwar history the empirical case will have been made that Japan's death penalty politics are exceptional.[59]

To say that a government of the left might end executions is not to say that Japan's retention of capital punishment has been a historical accident in the 1970s, 1980s, 1990s, and beyond, because the long dominance of the LDP is itself a product of other social and political features of contemporary Japan that may be linked to the persistence of capital punishment. Japan's recent history demonstrates an appetite and respect for authority reflected in the preservation and veneration of monarchy that is not necessarily Asian (see South Korea) but may be Japanese. As previously discussed, contemporary Japan also has limited governmental authority to deal with external enemies, not to mention xenophobia and a respect for hierarchy that find expression in the nation's political culture. All of these features suggest that the long

58. In 1998, President Clinton did sign a bill that was drafted and passed by a Republican-controlled House of Representatives.

59. For eight months in 1993–1994, a seven-party anti-LDP coalition did govern Japan, a temporary transition that was precipitated by a corruption scandal in the LDP (Curtis 1999:65). Some analysts believe the three executions in March 1993 that ended Japan's 40-month moratorium were calculated to divert attention from the shabby performance of the procuracy and the Ministry of Justice in that scandal (Schmidt 2002:61). In November 1993, a minister of justice in the anti-LDP government who personally opposed capital punishment authorized four more executions even though at least nine members of the cabinet also opposed the death penalty (Schmidt 2002:82). Those executions suggest that a brief transfer of power—even to a government with many members who oppose the death penalty—is an insufficient condition for abolition or even for a suspension of executions. A relatively durable change in Japan's ruling regime seems necessary.

hegemony of right-wing politics is anything but a historical accident. Indeed, the structural characteristics that underlie Japan's recent political history mean that a transition to left-of-center power is far from inevitable, and the same features that have limited the left would moderate the left-of-center orientation of an opposition party that displaces the LDP. Nonetheless, the major explanation for Japan's retention of capital punishment is the preferences of the current government, not extragovernmental social facts or values. If Japan's government changes, the policy may change, too.

A related issue is whether the retention of capital punishment and the continuation of executions might be reversed without the displacement of the LDP. There are few examples of abolition by the right in other developed nations, although in the late stages preceding abolition, long periods without execution have not been uncommon in Western governments of the right. Could the LDP end executions either de facto or de jure? If it happens, the key cause will be influence from other nations, to which we now turn.

FOREIGN INFLUENCES The most decisive influences on death penalty policy in the 19th century were Japanese leaders' responsiveness to an international system that impinged on their nation after more than two centuries of isolation and their sensitivity to foreign judgments about Japan's premodern penal system. The results of that responsiveness are striking: a 73 percent decline in death sentences and a 97 percent drop in executions in less than three decades. For students of history, a principal obligation and major challenge is to identify and explain the "profound forces" that impel a nation in one direction instead of another. In Japanese history, "the structure, governance, institutions, principles, and norms of the international system" have recurrently and decisively shaped modern Japan's international behavior and domestic politics and policy (Pyle 2006:393). When features of the international system have changed, Japan has consistently followed a strategy of "organizing the nation internally in order to succeed externally" (Pyle 2006:402). This is partly a matter of social facts "external to and coercive on" Japan (Durkheim 1982:50), but even when the influence of the external environment has been strong, considerable room for choice has remained (Samuels 2003). Moreover, while most of the preeminent statesmen in modern Japanese history have been conservative, their outlook has been, on the whole, "pragmatic," "non-doctrinaire," and strongly oriented toward "learning from others" (Rohlen 1992:326; Pyle 2006:408). The Meiji restoration proved to be a revolutionary event for Japan precisely because its leaders adapted and accommodated to the norms and institutions of a new international order. Closer to the present, the pervasive problems the nation experienced during the "lost decade" of the 1990s can be traced to radical changes in Japan's external environment—the end of the cold war, the rise of Asia, and the acceleration of globalization—and to the difficulties Japanese leaders encountered in trying to respond to them (Pyle 2006:415). In between these two periods, the effects of the international system on Japan were often powerful, and the strong and persistent disposition of Japanese elites was to give primacy to the demands of the international context. Many analysts regard that pattern as "an essential source of Japanese behavior" (Maruyama 1976; Dower 1999; Buruma 2003; Schaede and Grimes 2003; Pyle 2006:418; Pyle 2007).

If states have different "styles of being and behaving" that tend to persist through time (Aron 1966:279), then the core questions for the future of Japan's death penalty may be how Japan's leaders will respond to changes in the international environment and whether concerns about the nation's international reputation will stimulate changes in policy and practice. There are two reasons to believe that external forces will evoke adjustments in Japanese capital punishment: the recurrent concern in Japanese history and culture with the nation's reputation and international status, and the low costs of changing Japan's death penalty policy. Yet there is also one potentially critical difference between the foreign concerns that motivated change in the Meiji period and foreign influences on Japanese policy-making in the future. Western opinion was the predominant external force in Japanese policymaking in the 19th century, but influences on Japanese policy in the future will come from Asia as well as the West (Pempel 2005; Katzenstein 2006). Japan remains greatly concerned about its status compared to first-world nations of the West, but now it has become involved in status competitions with other Asian powers. In the not-too-distant future, this combination could affect issues as apparently peripheral as capital punishment.

Western nations. Japan is concerned about its status as a peer among the first-world nations of the West. With the creation of Europe as an almost-execution-free zone and Europe's aggressive advocacy for abolition throughout the world, the government of Japan is vulnerable to the rhetoric and reputational damage the Council of Europe tries to inflict on executing countries. Two factors have protected Japan from the brunt of European scorn. First, since Japan is not economically dependent on Europe, the economic coercion that put teeth into the crusade against the death penalty in central and eastern Europe is largely unavailable in its dealings with Japan (Bae 2007:24). Indeed, the extensive trade between western Europe and Japan is mutually beneficial, and disrupting it would inflict unthinkable harm on Europe. Pressure from Europe could even prove counterproductive if it provides Japanese officials with "a relatively cost-free way to savor a little old-fashioned national sovereignty" at a time when the nation is becoming increasingly nationalistic (Nathan 2004; Lane 2005b).

The second great protection Japan enjoys from the full force of European scorn comes from the United States. The example of America as a first-world power that executes can be used to counter Europe's moral example and to deflect a major portion of the European hostility to the death penalty away from Japan and toward the United States. The prominence of U.S. executions and the reality of American power make the United States a more attractive target than Japan. However, there is a sense in which Europe's concentration on American misdeeds may be counterproductive. The Japanese are quite sensitive to the judgment of other first-world cultures they admire, such as

Germany, France, and Italy. At the same time, Japan's insistence on whaling is an instance of elites remaining *insensitive* to first-world judgments, and the parallels to capital punishment suggest that Japan's death penalty exceptionalism could persevere for some time to come. In both whaling and capital punishment, the international movement to abolish is rooted in sensibilities about rights (animal and human). In both spheres, Japan remains an outlier, thumbing its nose at international society. In both spheres, there are American origins (in the postwar occupation) to Japan's persistent exceptionalism. In both spheres, Japan's government defends Japanese practice by invoking arguments about security and culture. In both spheres, cultural arguments emerged recently, apparently as one means of scratching a nationalist itch. And in both spheres, many Japanese resent pressure from the West to change (McNeill 2007; Onishi 2007c). One possibility, which we consider remote, is that Western pressure to abolish the death penalty will provoke stronger desires to preserve the institution (Onishi 2007c). That, anyway, is what has happened with whaling.[60]

Still, as long as the United States continues to execute, Japan will probably benefit from being a secondary target in Europe's anti–death penalty campaign. Even if Japan is only a secondary target, a larger number of negative judgments from individual European nations and from Europe's collective bureaucracies might not only disappoint Japanese elites, they could also influence them. More powerful would be a significant American move toward abolition, which would destabilize Japan's death penalty almost instantly by pushing it to the center of the bull's-eye for human rights assaults from the rest of the developed world. That said, in the first decade of the 21st century, there are few indications of any decisive movement away from capital punishment in the United States.

Asian nations. Absent any significant change in the United States, the most important foreign influences on Japan in the next decade will probably come from East Asia (Pempel 2005; Katzenstein 2006). But not all the nations of Asia are equally important to Japan's citizens and government. For starters, it is unlikely that abolition in the Philippines will have a major impact on Japanese sensibilities or policies because of the low regard in which most Japanese hold that nation. But South Korea is a challenge very much on the minds of many Japanese citizens and government officials.

Long regarded as a poor, primitive, and dependent relation to Japan, South Korea has made tremendous progress in economic sophistication and output, cultural achievement, and political development. Indeed, over the half generation since 1990, South Korea has made up much of the gap in wealth,

---

60. "Far from weakening in the face of worldwide condemnation, Japan's campaign to overturn the whale-hunting ban is gathering strength" (McNeill 2007). As of 2007, all of Japan's major political parties supported whaling, its Parliament boasted only one antiwhaling lawmaker (from Okinawa), and only 10 percent of the 98 members of Japan's Parliamentary Whaling League came from districts with a direct link to the whaling industry.

influence in Asia, and political status that separated the two nations for centuries. At the personal level, too, Japanese and Koreans have long felt the rivalries and hostilities of siblings. The rivalry is felt by citizens of both nations and regarded as important in both. If the Japanese are looking over their shoulders at any non-PRC competitors, it is the South Koreans, and the South Koreans seem at least as focused on the Japanese.

Although the focus of Korea's effort to abolish the death penalty is partly domestic (see chapter 5), it is likely that Korea's national pride in its human rights achievement will provoke invidious comparisons with the Japanese. Just as the Taiwanese are preoccupied with comparing themselves to the Chinese on the mainland, the first comparison a Korean tends to make is with the Japanese.

For Japan, falling behind the Koreans in any domain associated with "civilization and enlightenment" would be troublesome. As a Catholic priest in Seoul remarked, "if the Korean National Assembly votes to abolish the death penalty, Japan will follow because they hate for Korea to surpass them in anything" (quoted in Bae 2005:322). European accolades of Korean progress on human rights matters such as the death penalty could make matters worse, and being under pressure from two Asian neighbors abolishing the death penalty (if Taiwan joins in this) would be double trouble for the Japanese. Of course, Japan is not the most important point of reference for Taiwan, but Japanese might feel almost as bad about unfavorable judgments from foreigners in comparison to Taiwan as about Japan losing a human rights beauty contest to Korea. To fall behind both nations in European esteem could be too much to bear.

Thus, continued progress toward the end of capital punishment in South Korea and Taiwan could put pressure on Japan. If this happens, the most effective tactic for Europe will be to emphasize comparisons between East Asian nations, for this might not only invigorate the anti–death penalty movements in Korea and Taiwan (where status among developed nations is an important incentive for policy-making) but also generate significant status insecurity in Japan, which has long been concerned with taking its "proper station" in the world (Benedict 1946:44; Pyle 2007).

The other major rival of Japan early in the new millennium is the PRC, which does not pose the type of competition for human rights status that come from South Korea and Taiwan. Retrospective issues of war responsibility aside, it is hard to imagine China generating significant pressure on the Japanese to improve their human rights record. However, Japan's intense competition with the PRC for economic power and advantage, for regional influence, and for status on the world stage could subtly and indirectly pressure Japan to observe higher human rights standards as a means of enhancing its international standing. Competition between Japan and the PRC on dimensions like military might or brute economic strength is over before it begins. Japan's neighbor has ten times the population, many times the natural resources, and a developmental dynamic that has not been observed in any nation close to China's scale—including India (Luce 2007:18). This contrast in clout should create an incentive for Japan to focus its economic and status competition with the PRC in areas that promise a comparative advantage. In the economic sphere, Japan has emphasized property rights, intellectual property, and value added to the production of goods and services. In the competition for respect and status among major nations, Japan's comparative advantage is as a fully developed nation at the highest level. If human rights have become humanity's most "commonly shared bulwark" against brutality and cruelty (Hunt 2007), and if the push to frame capital punishment as a human rights issue takes root in Japan as it has in Europe and as seems to be happening in South Korea and Taiwan, then what Japan says through its capital punishment policy could become a low-cost way of expressing how it differs from China. At the same time, if the model to emulate is Sweden or Switzerland and Japan wants to draw the most favorable comparisons to China, then nostalgia for military might and affection for executions is not putting its best foot forward. One way to draw clear distinctions from China in future competitions would be to stop hanging people. In this sense, the ascendance of the PRC could serve as a negative role model that inspires Japan and other Asian nations to embrace human rights agendas and democratic values.

These scenarios of foreign influence are only a few of the many different forces that could affect Japanese policy in the future. But two points are primary. First, the opinions of other nations are important to the Japanese and will continue to be so for some time to come (Pyle 2007). We therefore expect that the international context and foreign developments and attitudes will substantially affect the future of capital punishment in Japan. Second, foreign influences are interactive, as is evident in some of the potential developments we have discussed. While there is an organizational logic to separating Western from Asian influences, the interactive dynamic of events crosses regional and national borders. If South Korea abolishes capital punishment, the most effective European assault on current Japanese practice might be a publicized comparison of Japan to South Korea. This kind of interaction contradicts tidy distinctions between Asian and Western influences in the smaller planet we all inhabit, and we expect this type of interactivity to be the norm in Japan's death penalty future.

Timing

Death penalty policy can change as quickly in Japan as in any nation with a civilized legal system. Without any change in formal law or judicial decision-making, Japan could carry out no hangings for the next ten years or it could carry out 40 in 2009! In this sense, the timing of change in Japan's execution policy is whatever the government wants it to be. But how long is that likely to last?

Some analysts believe that capital punishment is so "firmly established in Japan" that it "is likely to change glacially, if at all" (Schmidt 2002:83; Lane 2004). On this view—that the death penalty reflects "democracy at work"—Japan still has capital punishment because its "leaders are giving their people what they want," and what they want is unlikely to change anytime soon (Lane 2005b). Even those who predict the eventual end of the death penalty in Japan find it impossible to provide a timeline for that development (Johnson 2005:266).

Other analysts believe the introduction of the new trial system in Japan—the aforementioned inclusion of lay judges—"could well prove the necessary first step" of a gradual evolution toward abolition (Ambler 2006:23). But this view of lay judge impact is by no means a consensus. In our view, the question of the influence of this important reform is shrouded in uncertainty about the influence of citizen participation on death sentencing. Whatever the direct effects of the lay judge reform, the changes it will bring to the trial process and to the role of defense lawyers might produce shifts toward nontrial dispositions and other changes in the functioning of the criminal justice system that could powerfully influence the volume of death sentences.[61]

More generally, the gestation of political and social change in Japan is difficult to predict because the pace of change in that country differs from that of other East Asian nations. The conventional wisdom about reform in Japan is that it takes a long time, and social change does seem to occur more slowly there than in most of its neighbors (Upham 1987; Kerr 2001). The

61. When Japan had a jury system from 1923 to 1943, jury verdicts were substantially more lenient than decisions made by professional judges (Hayashi 1987; Johnson 2002a). In more recent years as well, mock jury trials in Japan have sometimes suggested that lay participation could make sentencing outcomes less severe. When South Korea introduced a jury-like system in 2008 (with jurors playing only an advisory role), lay participation seemed to make verdicts and sentencing outcomes less severe (S. Lee 2008). Some death penalty supporters in Japan fear that laypeople's attitudes will soften when they encounter concrete cases and individual defendants in the new trial system. This is one reason why the movement to introduce the harsh alternative of LWOP gained momentum just prior to 2009 ("Shushinkei: Ze ka Hi ka" 2008). Some observers even believe that the acceleration of executions in 2007–2008 was partly motivated by officials' anxiety that lay judges would be reluctant to impose sentences of death. On this view, the Ministry of Justice increased executions on the eve of the advent of the new system so that "the public will find it hard to oppose the death penalty when they are selected to take part" in it (Hongo, Fukada, and Nakamura 2008; Tanaka and Kinoshita 2008). But there are also reasons to wonder whether Japan's new trial system might lead to harsher outcomes. For one thing, the lay judge system could allow for the "death qualification" of lay assessors, in which case persons opposed to capital punishment would be dismissed from duty (Ambler 2006). In the United States, death-qualified jurors often tilt toward death (Sundby 2007). In addition, public opinion about punishment in contemporary Japan seems to be substantially more punitive than the opinion of the professional elites—prosecutors and judges especially—who now decide charge, guilt, and sentence (Hamilton and Sanders 1992:157; Johnson 2002a:30).

extraordinary pace of change in places like South Korea, Taiwan, and the PRC means that for the last two decades it is almost as if Japan and the rest of East Asia have been on two different clocks, with one operating two or three times faster than the other. When asked about the timing of political change in Japan, the first response should be about the relevant metric: Do you mean Asian time or Japanese time?

For the most part, governmental and social changes in Japan have been happening to the slower beat of "Japanese time" while economic and techno-logical changes have been somewhat swifter, in part because of international competitive pressure (Kingston 2004; Schoppa 2006; Vogel 2006). But there is reason to suppose that the fast pace of change in Asian nations will become more contagious. Indeed, there are "unmistakable signs" that Japan "is on the threshold of a new era in the way it relates to the international system" and "on the verge of a sea change" of the kind that has often surprised foreign observers in the past (Pyle 2006:417). A faster pace for Japan is especially probable if activity elsewhere in Asia helps motivate domestic reform. Thus, to the list of potential influences from other nations that we expect to see on Japanese policy-making, we can add some impact on the timing of death penalty reform. The contrast between Japanese and other East Asian patterns of change may prove too glaring for Japan to sustain. Here again, Japan may end up responding to features of its international context by following rather than leading other nations.

4

A Lesson Learned?
The Philippines

> The Philippines, a country that for me differed drastically from any other in the region—or, indeed, from any I had previously covered in Europe, Africa, or the Middle East.
>
> —Stanley Karnow, *In Our Image* (1989)

> Unfortunately, nations don't shed the past like snakes their skins.
>
> —Alan Berlow, *Dead Season* (1996)

In a study of the rise of Asia and its challenge to the Western world that was published in 1994, the journalist James Fallows located the Philippines "on the sidelines" because it was largely "left out" of the economic boom that many of its neighbors were experiencing at the time (Fallows 1994:326). Since that account was published, the Philippines has remained "on the sidelines" with respect to many measures of economic prosperity, democratic development, and social justice. During interviews David Johnson conducted in August 2006, some Filipino scholars and politicians even said their country had "retrograded" in the 20 years since dictator Ferdinand Marcos was overthrown by the People Power movement. Although that regime change has often been called a revolution, it was less revolutionary than it was the resurrection of institutions Marcos had dismantled and the reinstallation of old elites in their former positions of power and privilege (Karnow 1989:423). Democracy has been difficult to sow in the poisoned soil left behind by the Marcos dictatorship (Berlow 1996:xvi).

When it comes to capital punishment, however, the Philippines has hardly been a bystander, for it is difficult to find any other nation where death penalty policy has been so dynamic. Consider these developments during the last 20 years.

- After Marcos lost power, the Constitution of 1987 abolished capital punishment, "unless for compelling reasons involving heinous crimes, the Congress hereafter provides for it."
- In December 1993, the Philippines resurrected the death penalty by passing one of the most expansive capital statutes in Asia. The congressional votes were overwhelming: 123 to 6 in the House of Representatives (with two abstentions), and 17 to 4 in the Senate (with one abstention, by future president Gloria Macapagal Arroyo). Five

years after President Fidel Ramos signed the bill into law, the Philippines had one of the largest death rows in Asia (Gluckman 1999a).

- Of the 1,100 persons sent to death row in the first five years after the new capital statute was passed, seven were ultimately executed. All were men, and all were lethally injected between February 1999 and January 2000, during the administration of President Joseph Estrada. These were the Philippines' first judicial executions since 1976.

- In March 2000, Estrada announced a moratorium on executions, ostensibly out of respect for the Christian Jubilee Year. In December of the same year (on International Human Rights Day), while Estrada was under pressure for alleged acts of corruption that eventually led to his removal from office, he ordered all death sentences affirmed by the Supreme Court (more than 100) to be commuted to life imprisonment.

- Estrada's replacement, former vice president Gloria Macapagal Arroyo, vowed to lift the moratorium shortly after taking office in January 2001, and in subsequent years she made numerous public pronouncements that she would allow executions to occur. But no executions were carried out during her presidency, largely because she commuted and stayed hundreds of death sentences.

- On Easter 2006, Arroyo commuted more than 1,200 death sentences, including about 100 that had been finalized by the Supreme Court. This appears to be the largest commutation the world has ever seen. Two months later, Arroyo signed a bill into law that abolished capital punishment for the second time in 20 years. The bill easily passed both chambers of Congress: 120 to 20 in the House (with one abstention), and 16 to zero in the Senate (with one abstention).

In 1997, Amnesty International said the nations of Southeast Asia were riding "against the tide" of abolition (Tagayuna 2004:1). At present, however, 6 of the 11 nations of Southeast Asia are either abolitionist de facto (Brunei, Laos, and Myanmar) or completely abolitionist (Cambodia, East Timor, and the Philippines).[1] Of these six, the Philippines is the most populous and is the only nation to have abolished twice, and of the eleven nations in Southeast Asia, the Philippines has had by far the most vacillations in death penalty policy and practice.

After providing a brief history of capital punishment through the Marcos era, this chapter describes and explains the two Philippine abolitions and some of the other major death penalty developments that have occurred since Marcos was driven into Hawaiian exile and democratization began in this nation that now is home to 90 million people. Several themes are prominent, including volatility in death penalty policy and ambivalence about its usage, the high salience of capital punishment in the Philippine polity, the influence of the Catholic Church and of transnational flows of money and ideology, the Euro-

---

1. The retentionist nations of Southeast Asia are Indonesia, Malaysia, Singapore, Thailand, and Vietnam.

pean-like nature of the first abolition (in that it was precipitated by the removal of an authoritarian regime), the developmentally precocious nature and timing of the second abolition, and the high frequency of extrajudicial killing.

At the end of this story the question that remains is whether the second abolition has permanently ended the battle over capital punishment in the Philippines or whether it is just one milepost on a journey the Philippine death penalty will continue to travel. Although some observers believe capital punishment could be revived again, that seems unlikely, not least because the death penalty that was imagined at the time of restoration in 1994 turned out to be very different from the one that was delivered. What restorers wanted was an operational system of capital punishment that would deter crime and satisfy eye-for-an-eye urges in one of Asia's highest crime societies. What they got was a symbolic system that rarely resulted in execution and was so badly infected with bias, mistakes, and arbitrariness that it disappointed even many of its most ardent supporters. Some of those supporters turned into abolitionists only 12 years after they had worked to resurrect the death penalty. It appears a lesson was learned.

■ A Short History

There is little recorded history of the Philippines predating Ferdinand Magellan's arrival in 1521, and what little history there is speaks about capital punishment in at least two voices. On the one hand, "no death penalty is ever mentioned" in the indigenous law cases studied by scholars at the University of the Philippines (Barrameda 2005:64). On the other hand, pre-Spanish history in the Philippines does record the existence of the Code of Kalantiyaw, a common law used by indigenous people to impose punishments, including capital punishment, on persons deemed deviant (Zaide 1983; Tagayuna 2004:19). In either event, history becomes clearer after Magellan's arrival, and by the time General Emilio Aguinaldo declared independence in 1898, the Philippines had been a colony of Spain for over 300 years. That declaration coincided with Spain's defeat by the United States in the Spanish-American War and American military occupation of the Philippines.[2] Although Philippine guerrilla forces continued their struggle for independence against the Americans, in 1902, after incalculable casualties, the United States installed its own civilian administration (Karnow 1989:78–105).

---

2. In 1898, after the battleship *Maine* was blown up in Havana Harbor, the U.S. Congress authorized President William McKinley to use force to end Spanish rule in Cuba, and Assistant Secretary of the Navy Theodore Roosevelt ordered Commodore George Dewey to sail to Manila. On May 1, Dewey's ships sank the antiquated Spanish armada in Manila Bay, and on August 13 the United States and Spain signed the Treaty of Paris, granting U.S. sovereignty over the Philippines, which would last until the Japanese invaded the islands in December 1941 (Karnow 1989:436–437).

Table 4.1
Murder cases and death sentences in the Philippines, 1840–1885

Year	Murder cases	Death sentences	Percentage
1840	83	7	8.4
1856	246	21	8.5
1865	275	12	4.4
1871	270	4	1.5
1875	238	2	0.8
1880	291	0	0.0
1885	300	0	0.0
Total	1703	46	2.7

Source: Bankoff 1996:183.

Spanish colonizers brought with them medieval Europe's penal system, including the death penalty. During the early Spanish period, executions took a variety of forms, from decapitation, drowning, and hanging to garroting, stabbing, flaying, and burning. As in many other places, the death penalty in the Philippines was more than just one penal technique among many; "it was the base point from which other kinds of punishment deviated" as well as a "spectrum of penalties" that provided government officials with gradations of severity (dismemberment, burning, public display, and so on) above and below ordinary execution (see Banner 2002:54,86). With few exceptions, capital punishment "was only imposed on locals who challenged the established authority of the colonizers" (Mamamayang Tutol sa Bitay 2006:10).

Spanish rule during the 19th century, "while far from benevolent, was not entirely inhumane" (Karnow 1989:48), and some analysts suggest that "the Spanish Empire was one of the earliest colonial states with a moral conscience" (Bankoff 1996:95). The relative lenity of Spanish punishments can be seen in the infrequent use of capital punishment during this century.[3] From 1840 to 1885, for example, only 2.7 percent of murder cases resulted in a death sentence (and the percentage declined throughout that period). What is more, even murderers sentenced to death "were seldom executed," and "only in the case of rebellion was capital punishment frequently imposed" (Bankoff 1996:182). See table 4.1.

When executions did occur in the 19th century, they took one of three forms. Hanging was the usual means in ordinary capital cases until 1832, when the public spectacle of the gallows was abolished by royal decree because it was believed to reflect badly on Spain's international reputation. Garroting replaced hanging as the normal method in ordinary cases. And the firing squad was used mostly for military and political prisoners (after some habitual

3. Spain abolished capital punishment for ordinary crimes in 1978 and for all crimes in 1995. Its last execution occurred in 1975 (Hood 2002:250).

bandits were shot, their bodies were quartered and staked in places associated with their crimes). Traitors were shot in the back.[4] The executioner himself was often a condemned man spared from execution by agreeing to perform this function. He was well paid, receiving a salary of 20 pesos per month plus 16 pesos per head for each execution in 1895 (Bankoff 1996:183; see also Villamor 1909).

American colonizers adopted most provisions of the Spanish Penal Code of 1848, including the death penalty, and that code remained the main body of criminal law until the Revised Penal Code went into force in 1932. Execution data are unavailable for the early years of American rule (1898 to 1923), but from 1924 to 1933 18 persons were executed—an average of 1.8 per year (see table 4.2). In response to indigenous movements for independence, the Americans also passed several laws to sanction the use of the death penalty against nationalist Filipinos, including the Sedition Law of 1901, the Brigandage Act of 1902, the Reconcentration Act of 1903, and the Flag Law of 1907. On the whole, capital punishment during the American period "continued to be an integral part of the pacification process of the country, to suppress any resistance to American authority" (Mamamayang Tutol sa Bitay 2006:10). One of the most prominent targets of this "pacification" was Macario Sakay, president of the short-lived Republic of Katagalugan (1902–1907) in southern Luzon, who was executed by American authorities in 1907. In 1932, the Revised Penal Code came into force, providing for seven capital crimes: treason, piracy, parricide, murder, kidnapping, rape, and robbery with homicide (Amnesty International 1989a:2). But in January 1933, a year before the U.S. Congress passed the Tydings-McDuffie Act mandating a ten-year transition to Philippine independence, judicial executions ceased. There were no more until May 1950.

While there were no documented cases of judicial execution during the Japanese occupation of the Philippines (1941–1945), extrajudicial killings were numerous. Indeed, many analysts believe "the savagery vented by the Japanese" on American and Filipino prisoners "was unparalleled, at least in modern military annals" (Karnow 1989:302). Although the Japanese claimed they were "liberating" their fellow Asians from Western colonial exploitation, most Filipinos saw their new occupiers as "brutal conquerors" (Steinberg 2000:102). One enduring consequence of this bloody chapter in Philippine history is that "the war permitted violence to be institutionalized, and the use of weapons for whatever reason [to be] justified as patriotic." Even after

---

4. The most famous person to be executed in this way was Jose Rizal, a national hero of the Philippines. He was shot in the back by a Spanish firing squad on the morning of December 30, 1896 (Bankoff 1996:223). Rizal's execution for treason so enraged the indigenous intelligentsia (*ilustrado*) that "its members repudiated the last links to Spain and supported independence" (Steinberg 2000:50). Earlier, the execution of three Catholic clergymen in 1872 marked "the beginning of a nationalist consciousness" in the Philippines (Karnow 1989:67).

Table 4.2
Executions in the Philippines, 1898–2006

Years	Executions	Average executions per year
1898–1923 (American rule)	N/A	N/A
1924–1933 (American rule)	18	1.8
1934–1941 (transition to independence)	0	0.0
1941–1945 (Japanese rule)	0	0.0
1946–1965 (independence)	33	1.7
1965–1972 (President Marcos)	19	2.7
1973–1977 (President Marcos, martial law)	12	2.4
1977–1986 (President Marcos)	0	0.0
1987–1993 (death penalty abolished)	0	0.0
1994–1998 (death penalty restored)	0	0.0
1999–2000 (President Estrada)	7	3.5
2000–2006 (moratorium)	0	0.0
Total	89	1.1

Sources: Files of the Free Legal Assistance Group of the Philippines, University of the Philippines, Manila, consulted August 8, 2006; Amnesty International 1989a:24–25; Karnow 1989:437–442; Mamamayang Tutol sa Bitay 2006:10–11.

Note: The Philippines abolished capital punishment in February 1987, restored it in December 1993, and abolished it again in June 2006.

There were no executions in two-thirds of the years (54 out of 83 years) between 1924 and 2006. From 1924–2006, the five peak years for execution were as follows: 9 executions in 1928 (0.72 executions per million), 12 executions in 1967 (0.36), 6 executions in 1951 (0.29), 9 executions in 1974 (0.22), and 6 executions in 1999 (0.08). By comparison, in 1999 Japan had 5 executions (0.04 executions per million), South Korea zero, Singapore 43 (10.80), Taiwan 24 (1.09), and the United States 98 (0.35).

The 18 executions in 1924–1933 were carried out by electrocution at the Old Bilibid Prison in Manila. The 64 executions in 1946–1977 were carried out by electrocution at the New Bilibid Prison in Muntinlupa (the last on October 21, 1976). The seven executions in 1999–2000 were carried out by lethal injection at the New Bilibid Prison.

The moratorium of 2000–2006 occurred under presidents Joseph Estrada (March 2000–January 2001) and Gloria Macapagal Arroyo (January 2001–June 2006).

liberation was achieved in 1946, "the readiness to resort to force" has remained "a pervasive and disturbing feature of post-independence Philippine society" (Steinberg 2000:105).

No executions took place in the first four years of independence; they resumed in 1950, thus ending an unofficial moratorium of 17 years. One reason for the resumption was the Hukbalahap peasant rebellion in Central Luzon, which originated in the People's Anti-Japanese Army but developed into a formidable force challenging oligarchic control after the war, despite being outlawed in 1948 (Karnow 1989:341). By the mid-1950s, the Hukbalahap rebellion was effectively over, but the movement had led to the enactment of the first Anti-Subversion Law in the Philippines, Republic Act 1700. Though it carried the death penalty for leaders of the Philippine Communist Party, no executions ever occurred under this law (Amnesty International 1989a:3).

From 1950 to 1976, the Philippines carried out 64 executions—an average of 2.4 per year in a population that grew from 20 to 44 million during the same period. For much of that period, the Philippines had one of the highest homicide rates in the world. In 1964, for example, Manila recorded 800 murders, compared with fewer than 600 in New York City, whose population was eight times larger (Karnow 1989:364). At present, the Philippine homicide rate remains significantly higher than that of most other Asian nations. According to data from a recent report on violence by the World Health Organization, the homicide rate in the Philippines is almost 11 times higher than the rate in six industrialized nations of Asia, nearly eight times higher than the rate in China, and twice as high as the rate in Thailand. See table 4.3.

While President Ferdinand Marcos was in power (1965–1986), "deterrence" became the most salient justification for capital punishment, and it has remained so to the present. This was partly the result of political calculations, for Marcos's early frames and claims relied on the premise that crime was "out of control." Later on, the promulgation of numerous presidential decrees mandating the death penalty focused public attention on the "lawlessness"

Table 4.3
Homicide in the Philippines, Asia, and the United States (deaths per 100,000 population)

Nation	Homicide rate
Japan (2000)	0.6
Hong Kong (1996)	1.0
Singapore (1998)	1.3
New Zealand (1998)	1.5
Australia (1998)	1.6
China (1999)	1.8
South Korea (1997)	2.0
United States (2000)	6.0
Thailand (1994)	7.5
Philippines (1993)	14.2
Averages	
Industrialized Asia (n = 6)	1.3
Industrializing Asia (n = 3)	7.8
Total (n = 10)	3.8

Sources: World Health Organization 2002; Johnson 2006:77.
Note: Hong Kong is treated as a separate "nation."

that martial law was supposed to cure, thus justifying the emergency measures. This strategy also reinforced the impression that "a forceful executive was taking decisive measures to impose law and order" (Amnesty International 1989a:4). However, after the assassination in 1983 of Marcos's rival Benigno Aquino, which stimulated widespread resistance to Marcos's authoritarian rule, he employed a different "politics of law and order" and amended several presidential decrees so as to remove death as a sanction and demonstrate a desire to "liberalize" his government (Amnesty International 1989a:8). In these ways, Marcos adjusted capital punishment policy to display both severity and leniency, depending on the legitimation needs of the moment. This political strategy for manufacturing consent has a long pedigree (Hay 1975).

Although deterrence was also the main reason Marcos used to justify the declaration of martial law in 1972, judicial executions remained rare even during the martial law period, with only 12 executions from September 1972 to January 1981 and none at all during the last nine years of his presidency (1977–1986).[5] It appears that Marcos stopped judicial executions partly

---

5. One puzzle is why an authoritarian strongman like Marcos used the death penalty so sparingly. One answer, of course, is that he had other ways of exercising control, from incarceration without due process to extrajudicial execution—both of which were frequently employed. The Marcos regime jailed, tortured, and killed thousands— "in many cases using martial law as a pretext to liquidate local rivals or bilk innocent peasants" (Karnow 1989:396; Kessler 1989). Even compared to other authoritarian regimes of the time, the Marcos government was exceptionally lethal. By some accounts, Marcos's tally of 3,257 killed between 1972 and 1986 exceeds the 266 dead and missing during the Brazilian junta's most brutal period (1964–1979) and even the 2,115 extrajudicial deaths under General Augusto Pinochet in Chile (1973–1990). About three-quarters of the Filipinos killed were "salvaged"—that is, "tortured, murdered, and their remains dumped for display" (McCoy 2006:76). Yet some observers believe a more biographical reason also helps explain why this dictator seemed to be a reluctant user of judicial executions. In 1935, Marcos's father, Mariano, sought reelection to Congress but was defeated by Julio Nalundasan, whose supporters had ridiculed the senior Marcos during the campaign. Nalundasan was then murdered (by a single 22-caliber bullet in the back), and three years later Ferdinand was arrested for the crime. At the time of his arrest, Marcos was in his last year of law school (he would finish first in his class and would go on to achieve the nation's top score on the bar exam), and at the end of 1939 (at the age of 22) he was found guilty of murder and sentenced to 10 to 17 years in prison. Marcos argued his own appeal before the Supreme Court (in a white sharkskin suit and white shoes, to symbolize his purity), and his passionate defense moved one judge to tears. He was exonerated in an opinion written by Chief Justice Jose Laurel, who himself had been convicted of murder only to have it overturned as legitimate self-defense, and who in subsequent years would become one of Marcos's most reliable political allies (Steinberg 2000:116; see also Karnow 1989:368). In later years, Laurel's son became Corazon Aquino's running mate in the election that unseated the dictator (Berlow 1996:89). Aquilino Pimentel Jr., a veteran senator and a victim of multiple detentions under martial law, believes that Marcos's own murder conviction made him "squeamish" about using capital punishment in the years thereafter (interview by Johnson, August 8, 2006; see also Pimentel 2006).

because of "growing pressure and criticism from neighboring ASEAN countries and other Western allies" (Tagayuna 2004:19). If so, then even before the abolition of capital punishment became "an orthodoxy" in much of the developed world—a "moral imperative" believed necessary to the status of any civilized modern state—transnational forces were helping to shape death penalty practice in the Philippines (Zimring 2003:17).

The most publicized execution during Marcos's rule occurred four months before martial law was declared, when the president ordered television and radio stations to broadcast the electrocution (on May 17, 1972) of Jaime Jose, Basilio Pineda, and Edgardo Aquino as punishment for the gang rape of movie star Maggie dela Riva, even though the Revised Penal Code prohibited public executions. The same month, in a Senate hearing on a bill that would have abolished the death penalty, Supreme Court justice M. San Diego said the three executions had been "shamelessly played in television and the radio" and asked, "Who among us has not come out of this experience without a feeling of uncleanness, a feeling of lost self-respect?" (quoted in Amnesty International 1989a:7). None of the subsequent 12 executions under Marcos took place in public.

There were other significant death penalty developments under Marcos in addition to executions. The number of capital crimes increased to include the unlawful possession of firearms, embezzlement, drug-related crimes, illegal fishing, and cattle rustling. Military tribunals (agencies of the executive branch and not part of the judiciary) were used to try most capital crimes. The Supreme Court under President Corazon Aquino eventually exposed many of these tribunals' capital convictions as miscarriages of justice (Amnesty International 1989a:4,13; Tate and Haynie 1993). In October 1977, three months after Marcos declared that he was relaxing martial law, Senator Benigno Aquino Jr. was sentenced to death by a military tribunal for murder, subversion, and the illegal possession of firearms. A chief justice of the Supreme Court would later say that "the terrible consequence of subjecting civilians to trial by military process is best exemplified in the sham military trial" of Aquino (quoted in Amnesty International 1989a:5). Worldwide protests caused Marcos to reopen the trial, but his political rival remained confined and incarcerated for seven and a half years. Then, in May 1980, Imelda Marcos persuaded her husband to give Aquino permission to fly to the United States for heart treatment. It would look like "monkey business," she implored, if Aquino died during an operation in Manila (Karnow 1989:400).

"Ninoy" Aquino returned to the Philippines on August 21, 1983 (as Marcos was reported to be dying), only to be assassinated at the Manila airport moments after his arrival. The alleged assassin—a petty criminal named Rolando Galman—was immediately shot dead; he had been thrown from a waiting van. Although the Philippine government claimed that Ninoy was killed by this lone radical, few accepted the story. And while Ninoy's murder has never been solved, "his martyrdom altered the history of the Philippines," in large part because "the Marcos government never recovered its equilibrium"

NATIONAL PROFILES

112

(Steinberg 2000:xiv,142). Aquino "now ranks with Jose Rizal [who was executed in 1896] as the Philippine national messiah" (Karnow 1989:403). Two and a half years after his murder, Aquino's widow, Corazon, led the People Power movement that drove Marcos to Hawaii and her to the office of the presidency.[6]

■ The First Abolition

In 1987 the Philippines became "the first Asian nation to abolish capital punishment" (Hood 2002:44). But it was an ambivalent abolition and thus a continuation of the theme of mixed feelings that long characterized death penalty policy and practice in this country. During the 40 years before abolition, capital sentences had been imposed often but seldom carried out. Indeed, the 64 persons executed between independence in 1946 and abolition in 1987 "represent only a small fraction of the total sentenced to death in that period" (Amnesty International 1989a:6), and at the time of the first abolition over 500 of the inmates at the New Bilibid Prison in Muntinlupa had been condemned to die. The annual average number of executions was 2.3 in the 1950s, 2.3 in the 1960s, 1.8 in the 1970s, and zero in the 1980s. These two facts—many death sentences but few executions—make the Philippines before abolition resemble the state of California in the 1990s. A similar pattern reappeared after the Philippines restored the death penalty in December 1993.

In worldwide perspective, the most significant change in capital punishment during the postwar period has been the "remarkable increase" in the number of abolitionist countries (Hood 2001:331). For the most part, these abolitions have followed a "repetitive pattern" with four common elements: (1) a lag between de facto and de jure abolition; (2) public opposition to abolition; (3) political "leadership from the front"; and (4) a linkage between abolition and other civil liberties (Zimring and Hawkins 1986:21; Zimring

6. Apart from Jesus, Mary, and possibly Jose Rizal, it is impossible to find a more revered Filipino figure than Ninoy Aquino. Nonetheless, Aquino was realistic about his own capacity to improve the country. In the summer of 1983, on the eve of his fatal return to Manila, Aquino had this to say: "If you made me president of the Philippines today, my friend, in six months I would be smelling like horseshit. Because there's nothing I can do. I cannot provide employment. I cannot bring prices down. I cannot stop the criminality spawned by economic difficulties. I mean, let's face it. When people are hungry, you can bring Saint Peter down, and you won't get a stable government" (quoted in Karnow 1989:423). Cory Aquino soon discovered the limits of her own power during a presidency that raised expectations but disappointed many (Steinberg 2000:151). Some observers believe that the presidents who followed her (Ramos, Estrada, and Macapagal-Arroyo) ended up "smelling like horseshit," too (Berlow 1996; Hamilton-Paterson 1998; Hutchcroft 1998; Kang 2002; Pimentel-Simbulan 2005). For a view that the Ramos years (1992–1998) were actually "solid, stolid, and successful," see Steinberg (2000:193).

2003:22). The first abolition of capital punishment in the Philippines followed this repetitive pattern.[7]

First, when the death penalty was abolished by voter approval of the new constitution in February 1987, the Philippines had experienced no judicial executions for ten years and four months. By comparison, the lag between de facto and de jure abolition lasted 4 years in France, 11 years in Sweden, and 17 years in Australia (Hood 2002:249).

Second, while it appears that no surveys of death penalty attitudes were conducted in the Philippines during the 1980s, most knowledgeable observers believe that a majority of Filipino citizens opposed abolition, much as they did before the second abolition of June 2006 (Hands Off Cain 2002; interviews by Johnson, August 2006).

Third, abolition in 1987 was achieved through "leadership from the front" in the sense that public opinion was led, not followed. Despite little public pressure for abolition, the Constitutional Commission (CONCOM) created by President Corazon Aquino—48 delegates chosen almost exclusively from the political center, "educated, from the upper class, and predominantly lawyers"—decided to abolish as a sign of their commitment to democratization and as a way of distancing the Aquino government from Marcos's authoritarian regime (Steinberg 2000:154).[8]

7. There were several unsuccessful attempts to abolish capital punishment in the Philippines before 1987. In 1960, the Code Commission recommended abolition for all crimes except genocide, and the House Committee on Codification of Laws and Statutes supported the proposal. In 1968–1969, the Senate Committee on Justice conducted a comprehensive study of the Philippine penal system in order to propose legislation that would improve it. This committee recommended that "the death penalty must be abolished" because it is "the anti-thesis of reformation and rehabilitation," and committee chairman Salvador H. Laurel filed an abolition bill that did not make it out of Congress. Also in 1969, prisons director Alejo S. Santos publicly declared his opposition to capital punishment, stating that he did not believe "meting out the death sentence would correct the wrong done by a convict." In 1979, several assemblymen introduced a bill to commute a death sentence to *reclusion perpetua* after the condemned had served at least five years in prison (with good conduct) and if by that time the Supreme Court had not yet finalized the capital sentence. In the same year, another bill was introduced to eliminate the death penalty completely even though "at the time there was no sustained movement for abolition" (Lagman 2006:1–2).

8. The 48 members of the CONCOM were all "handpicked by Aquino from a list of about 2000 nominees" (Crisostomo 1997:186). They finished their draft of the constitution in 100 days, after holding public consultations across the country and a series of public hearings. Many people criticized the CONCOM for being an appointive rather than elective body, but when President Aquino issued Proclamation No. 3 (the interim "freedom constitution") in March 1986, she had established a "government under which she was vested with both executive and legislative powers and ruled as a dictator" (186). In addition to handpicking the members of the CONCOM, Aquino abolished the legislature, dismissed and replaced many members of the judiciary, replaced all elective officials and presidential appointees, and promulgated numerous laws.

The CONCOM debate about the death penalty took place mainly within the purview of the Committee on Citizenship, Bill of Rights, Political Rights and Obligations, and Human Rights (hereafter the Committee), a smaller body chaired by Father Joaquin Bernas of Ateneo University. At one key meeting, CONCOM member Bishop Teodor Bacani quoted from a 1979 statement submitted by the Catholic Bishops' Conference of the Philippines that endorsed abolition as "a step forward in the evangelical purification of consciences in favor of respect for life." Bishop Bacani also discussed his own experience as a parish priest in Subic Bay when one of his parishioners was wrongfully condemned to death (and later exonerated by the Supreme Court). In addition to the individual members of the Catholic clergy who supported abolition, the Catholic Church played an influential institutional role in the CONCOM debate, calling for "respect for life" and arguing that rehabilitative measures should be introduced into the penal code (Amnesty International 1997a:7). Similarly, CONCOM member Teodulo Natividad, who had written the 1972 Dangerous Drugs Act that provided for capital punishment for manufacturers and sellers of narcotics, explained why he changed his mind about the ultimate sanction. "Today we have more" narcotics addiction in the Philippines than before the 1972 law, Natividad said, and now he did not support the death penalty "because it is contrary to my concept of the Christian ethic" (Amnesty International 1989a:10). One of the most vigorous defenders of the death penalty on the Committee was Esteban Bautista, a professor at the University of the Philippines Law Center. He argued that eliminating the death penalty would "encourage the commission of barbaric acts," and he claimed that "some crimes are so outrageous that wrongdoers deserve the death penalty, regardless of whether or not it is a deterrent" (Amnesty International 1989a:9).[9]

9. On the whole, the Constitution of 1987 outlined "a moderate-progressive vision" of social justice and rights, though in some respects—especially land reform—it "reaffirmed the traditional elite verities that have been a hallmark of the Philippines since Rizal" (Steinberg 2000:154). There are moments in history when it is possible to reorganize hierarchies and redistribute power. After Marcos, President Aquino "had dramatic opportunity to address frontally the social contradictions and economic tensions of her nation," but she did not (or could not) do so (154–155). She focused instead on the goals of establishing good government, improving the economy, and restoring traditional political structures. Aquino's own secretary of agriculture, Carlos Dominguez, said that "more than anything we needed radical land reform, but Cory was too cautious. She had an opportunity and she blew it" (quoted in Karnow 1989:445). Early in 1986, Aquino proclaimed an interim "freedom constitution" that arrogated to herself "powers rivaling those exercised by Marcos under martial law" (Steinberg 2000:154). On the one hand, she was criticized for assuming "dictatorial" powers. On the other, she did not use that authority as aggressively as many wanted. Some analysts believe Aquino had "an astonishing capacity for obscuring, excusing, and romanticizing her country's afflictions" (Berlow 1996:268). Critics also contend that by the end of her presidency, "human rights were no longer a priority" of her government (254). For a more sympathetic view that also recognizes Aquino's shortcomings, see Steinberg (2000:181–192).

In the end, the Committee voted 8 to 3 to abolish the death penalty. After "acrimonious debate" in the CONCOM, abolition prevailed by a single vote, 19 to 18, on the condition that an amendment be added to allow for the possibility of reintroduction by Congress (Free Legal Assistance Group 1994:1).[10] Influenced by several liberal members of her cabinet, President Aquino supported abolition as one part of the new constitution (Steinberg 2000:153; Tagayuna 2004:5). Voters approved the constitution in a February 1987 referendum, but the very next year Aquino certified as "urgent" a bill to restore capital punishment, and in 1990, after she visited the parents of two young girls who had been raped, murdered, and mutilated, she vowed to "work hard for the reimposition of the death penalty for heinous crimes" (Amnesty International 1989b:9).

Fourth, the abolition of capital punishment in the Philippines was linked to other rights, in both the deliberations of the CONCOM and in the constitution's text itself, where the abolition clause is embedded in the bill of rights, which guarantees a wide variety of civil liberties (Tagayuna 2004:5). The abolition provision reads as follows: "Excessive fines shall not be imposed, nor cruel, degrading or inhuman punishment inflicted. Neither shall the death penalty be imposed, unless, for compelling reasons involving heinous crimes, the Congress hereafter provides for it. Any death penalty already imposed shall be reduced to *reclusion perpetua*" (Constitution of 1987, art. 3, sec. 19, para. 1).[11] In addition to the Philippines being the first Asian nation in modern times to abolish the death penalty, the most distinctive thing about this country's first abolition is the constitution's provision allowing Congress to reinstate capital punishment if it should ever desire to do so "for compelling reasons involving heinous crimes." Seven years later, that happened. In the interim, the constitution's double-footed approach invited a debate about whether the new charter had really abolished the death penalty. In *People v. Munoz* (1987), the Supreme Court addressed the issue when it ruled that the constitution had not abolished but "merely prohibits the imposition of the death penalty"—a distinction without a difference that the Court apparently felt compelled to make in order to avoid having to create a new penalty for murder (as required by a

10. The abolitionists on the CONCOM employed four main arguments: capital punishment is inhumane because it traumatizes both the condemned and his family; there is no solid evidence that the death penalty effectively deters serious crime; since life is a divine gift, it should not be put in the hands of human judges; and a modern penal system should favor rehabilitative treatments over retributive punishments (Amnesty International 1997a:7).

11. Until the second abolition occurred in 2006 (when a sentence of life without parole was established), *reclusion perpetua* was the Philippines' most severe sentence next to death. Often translated as "life imprisonment," this expression actually means incarceration for anywhere from 12 years and 1 day to 20 years (Free Legal Assistance Group 2004c:13), though in the past a sentence of *reclusion perpetua* meant a term of imprisonment from 20 years and one day to 40 years (Amnesty International 1997a:10).

separate Supreme Court ruling; see Free Legal Assistance Group 1994).[12] In the end, the first abolition in the Philippines did not just fail to achieve closure on the question of capital punishment, it did not even seek it. Most other nations that have abolished capital punishment as part of the process of regime change have been less ambivalent, with abolition for all crimes typically following (years and in some cases decades later) abolition for ordinary crimes (Hood 2001:249; Zimring 2003:16). What is more, new constitutions typically aspire to make bold, overarching normative assertions about rights. In the ambivalent Philippines, that is not the kind of language found in section 19.

■ Restoration

Six months after the death penalty was abolished, a bill to restore it was introduced in the House. That the restoration movement started so soon is a sign that the support for capital punishment that had prevailed prior to 1987 continued, as well as an indicator that the "kick me" clause in section 19 ("unless, for compelling reasons involving heinous crimes, the Congress hereafter provides for it") in fact had stimulated the reaction it seemed to invite. The prime mover behind the restoration movement was Fidel Ramos, general and chief of staff of the Armed Forces (Crisostomo 1997). A West Point graduate who "was often accused of tolerating human rights abuses" while he was head of the Philippine Constabulary during the Marcos years, Ramos was also—in a nation that is more than 80 percent Catholic—a Methodist, which seemed to liberate him from Catholic Church teachings on life-and-death subjects such as capital punishment and birth control (Steinberg 2000:194; Fidel Ramos, interview by Johnson, August 7, 2006).

In August 1987, Ramos called for capital punishment for the crimes of murder, drug trafficking, and rebellion. The next month, following a coup attempt against Aquino by a dissident group of soldiers, Ramos cited the

---

12. The *Munoz* decision was deeply divided (8–6) and widely regarded as dictum. Moreover, the deliberations of the CONCOM indicate that the framers of the constitution did intend abolition. For instance, committee chair Bernas said: "The effect [of section 19] is the abolition of the death penalty from these statutes—only the death penalty. The statute is not abolished, but the penalty is abolished" (Record of the Constitutional Commission). That abolition was intended can also be seen in the language of at least two clauses of the constitution. Article 3, section 19(1) says that any death sentence already imposed shall be *reduced* (not commuted) to *reclusion perpetua*. If the intent had been *not* to abolish, the CONCOM would have used the term "commuted" to describe all existing death sentences, thereby acknowledging that a penalty higher than *reclusion perpetua* existed. Similarly, article 3, section 13 states that the exception to the rule of bail as a matter of right exists when the accused is charged with an offense punishable by *reclusion perpetua*, not by a death sentence. There is no indication of any penalty higher than *reclusion perpetua* for purposes of denying bail (Free Legal Assistance Group 2006a).

abolition of capital punishment as one reason for the soldiers' low morale, thereby implying that it may have been "one factor in the restiveness that led to the coup" (Amnesty International 1989a:11). The same month, the Judge Advocate General's Office (the military's legal arm) drafted an internal security act that included capital punishment in order to strengthen the government's hand in the counterinsurgency campaign.

Military lobbying grew more intense when debate on the House bill started in October 1987. Ramos appeared before the legislators to urge them to facilitate the counterinsurgency fight by reintroducing the death penalty for serious crimes. The preamble to House Bill 295 acknowledged the military pressure: "In the light of the rising and mounting tide of criminality and lawlessness in the country, particularly the pestering insurgency and the alarming incidents of violent crimes, and considering further the observations and recommendations coming from the military and police establishment as well as from the courts of justice, it is hereby declared that for compelling reasons of public order and national security . . . the death penalty shall be imposed for certain heinous crimes." In May 1988, only 15 months after abolition, the House voted to restore capital punishment by a vote of 130 to 25. In addition to military and police influence, the key contexts of this act were an increase in killings of military and police personnel by the communist New People's Army, the first assassination of a cabinet member in the history of the Philippines, and repeated military coup attempts against President Aquino (Amnesty International 1989a:11; Steinberg 2000:151).

In 1989, three bills to restore capital punishment were put before the Senate, one of which Aquino certified as "urgent" after lobbying from Ramos following yet another coup attempt (Amnesty International 1997a:8). In 1990, the Senate suspended the vote for one year, and in 1991, "amidst vigorous public debate and intense lobbying by anti–death penalty groups," the Senate remained deadlocked (Amnesty International 1997a:8). Some of the strongest resistance to restoration came from Senator Rene Saguisag, who argued that Philippine history revealed that the administration of the death penalty is biased against the poor and disadvantaged. Outside the Senate, however, public opinion was "flowing in the direction of support for the death penalty" (Amnesty International 1997a:9). A survey of residents in Manila and ten other large cities (conducted by the Philippine News Agency) showed that in late 1992, one year before the restoration law was passed, 92 percent of Filipinos supported the death penalty while only 4 percent opposed it—a 23-to-1 ratio ("Poll" 1992).[13] Similarly, Jessica Soto, director of Amnesty International in the Philippines, estimates that "as many as 90 percent

13. A more informal survey of 23 respondents by the *Philippine Daily Inquirer* found that 16 persons (70 percent) favored the death penalty, six (26 percent) were opposed, and one was undecided (transcript of testimony submitted by Rep. Pablo Garcia to the House of Representatives Committee on Justice, November 12, 1992). Looking back at the anti–death penalty movement that helped produce the second abolition in 2006, Jose Manuel Diokno, the national chair of the Free Legal Assistance Group, said that "When we started the anti-death penalty campaign . . . public opinion was about 99 percent pro-death" (quoted in Burgonio 2008).

of the public supported the restoration of the death penalty" before it occurred. Five years later, during the wave of executions that occurred in 1999–2000, Soto said support had probably fallen to about two-thirds (Gluckman 1999a:3).

In June 1992, Ramos was elected president from among seven candidates with a modest 23.5 percent of the vote. He had been steadfastly loyal to President Aquino during the many coup attempts against her, and he became her successor largely because "he was clearly [her] choice and because he was a centrist in the middle of the political spectrum" (Steinberg 2000:194). In his first state of the nation address, Ramos cited "peace and security as the first urgent problem to overcome," and he singled out the restoration of the death penalty as a legislative priority (Crisostomo 1997:243). Citing the need to win the confidence of foreign investors and domestic entrepreneurs as well as the need to address public demands for improved "law and order," Ramos urged Congress to take speedy action. He was helped by the fact that a majority of those elected in Congress were from his own political party (Tagayuna 2004:6) and by the creation in 1993 of two law-and-order nongovernmental organizations (NGOs): the Citizens Action against Crime and the Movement for the Restoration of Peace and Order, both of which "were formed in response to the problem of rising criminality" and aimed "to pressure government to put more effort in its peace-and-order campaign" (Ang See 1997:128,138). Despite some diversity of opinion within these NGOs (their intellectual and organizational leader, Teresita Ang See, is herself opposed to capital punishment), they have consistently lobbied for greater use of capital punishment and other "tough on crime" measures.

When the congressional debate resumed in 1993, the list of crimes considered "heinous" was expanded to reflect the Ramos administration's emphasis on economic issues. In exchange, Ramos agreed to drop "political" offenses such as rebellion because of the effect such capital crimes might have on "national reconciliation" at a time when he was negotiating with (and offering amnesty to) members of the armed opposition groups (Amnesty International 1997a:9). Opponents of the bill argued that proponents had failed to prove "compelling reasons" for restoration, as required by the constitution, but a joint measure, Republic Act 7659, was approved by Congress and signed by Ramos in December 1993, to take effect on the first day of 1994. The vote in the House was 123 to 26, and the vote in the Senate was 17 to 4 (with one abstention, by future president Gloria Macapagal Arroyo).

"An Act to Restore the Death Penalty on Certain Heinous Crimes" identi-fied 13 capital offenses: treason, piracy, bribery, parricide, murder, infanticide, kidnapping and serious illegal detention, robbery with violence, arson, rape, plunder, certain drug offenses, and theft of a vehicle with rape or murder.[14]

---

14. In the next dozen years, the scope of the death penalty law expanded so much that it became one of the broadest capital codes in the world (Gluckman 1999b:4). By the time of the second abolition in 2006, there were 46 capital crimes: 25 mandatory, and 21 discretion-ary or "death eligible" (Free Legal Assistance Group 2004c:6).

For most of these crimes the death penalty was discretionary; the court was given a choice of punishments ranging from designated "short" and "medium" terms of imprisonment to *reclusion perpetua* and death. Under certain aggravating circumstances, however, such as using one's public position to extort bribes or committing murder during the course of rape or kidnapping for ransom, a death sentence was mandatory. The death penalty could not be imposed on persons aged under 18 or over 70 at the time of the crime, and death sentences were to be automatically reviewed by the Supreme Court sitting en banc. Supreme Court confirmation of a death sentence now only required a majority of justices to agree, in contrast to the rule of unanimity in the pre-1987 capital law.[15] The new death penalty law (article 81) also mandated death by electrocution, the same method that had been employed under the old capital law. Executions were to occur under the authority of the director of prisons, who was obligated to endeavor "so far as possible to mitigate the sufferings of the person under the sentence during electrocution as well as during the proceedings prior to the execution." If the condemned so desired, he could be "anaesthesized at the moment of execution." Unease about electrocution was also evident in a clause that mandated changing the method of execution to gas poisoning "as soon as facilities are provided by the Bureau of Prisons" (R.A. 7659, sec. 24). It was soon discovered, however, that the nation's one and only electric chair had been destroyed by fire in a prison riot years previously, and that installing a reliable gas chamber was both technologically difficult and prohibitively expensive (Wilkinson and Atkins 2000:62). In March 1996, Republic Act 8177 addressed this problem—a practical problem overlooked in the congressional deliberations, which had focused on matters of principle—by stipulating that the method of execution would be lethal injection "sufficient to cause the instantaneous death of the convict."

In comparative perspective, restorations of capital punishment such as the Philippines experienced are uncommon but not unheard of. In Europe, for example, Italy (1931) and Switzerland (1879) restored the death penalty after abolishing it late in the 19th century, and there were temporary death

---

15. Under the death penalty law in force until the first abolition, a single holdout on the Supreme Court could prevent the confirmation of a death sentence. A survey of capital cases from 1976 to 1986 found that one-third of the death sentences reviewed by the Supreme Court (154 out of 463 cases) were reduced because of a lack of votes. During the same period, only 18.6 percent of death sentences were affirmed by the Supreme Court; the remainder resulted in acquittal of the defendant or remand to another court for further proceedings (Free Legal Assistance Group 1994:7). The same study found that 9.56 years was the average length of time between the trial court's decision in a capital case and the Supreme Court verdict on review. Defendants acquitted on appeal (9.0 percent) and defendants sentenced by the Supreme Court to shorter terms of imprisonment than they had already suffered were thereby prejudiced.

penalty policy reversals after World War II in Belgium, Denmark, and the Netherlands, all of which had been occupied by Germany during the war (Zimring and Hawkins 1986:9,12,28). In Asia, New Zealand (1950), Nepal (1985), and Papua New Guinea (1991) restored the death penalty after abolition, though (as of this writing) in the latter two nations no executions have occurred since restoration (Hood 2002:43,45). In the United States, the number of jurisdictions that have abolished capital punishment only to restore it a few years later "is only slightly smaller than the number that have abolished it once and for all" (Bedau 2004:24). On the whole, however, the abolition of capital punishment tends to be a one-way street, and on the national level especially, countries that abolish the death penalty seldom restore it, and those that restore it rarely execute in large numbers. As we now shall see, the restoration of capital punishment in the Philippines led to hundreds of death sentences but only seven executions.

■ The Last Executions?

The restoration of capital punishment in the Philippines set off a "death rush" among trial court judges eager to appease the public's appetite for vengeance (Gluckman 1999b:4). Some condemned were even sent to death row in tee shirts printed with the words "Guillotine Club," gifts from judges who joined this club when they imposed a capital sentence (Gluckman 1999a:2). In child-rape cases especially, a "witch-hunt hysteria" ensued, as some judges seemed to compete with each other in handing down sentences calculated to gain publicity and popularity. At some trials, "jeering crowds of radical groups" urged the imposition of death (Wilkinson and Atkins 2000:63; see also Kandelia 2006).

In the first 11 months after capital punishment was restored (January to November 1994), 17 persons were sentenced to death: ten (59 percent) for killing one or more persons, and seven (41 percent) for crimes such as rape, robbery, and kidnapping that did not result in the loss of life (Free Legal Assistance Group 1994:7). By the time of the second abolition in June 2006, these percentages had traded places, with 40 percent of the persons on death row having been convicted of taking one or more lives, and the other 60 percent condemned for crimes that did not involve killing. Throughout the life of the law, nearly 40 percent of all condemned inmates were sentenced to death for the crime of rape without homicide. See table 4.4. One reason there were so many capital convictions for rape was that judges may have relaxed the "reasonable doubt" standard defined by the 1997 constitution, especially when the victim was a minor. Many judges quoted the same words in their decisions: "Greater weight must be given to the evidence of the victim than to the denials of the accused.... This Court cannot believe

Table 4.4
Crimes of death row inmates, the Philippines, 2004

Crime	Number	Percent
Murder	191	21.5%
Multiple murder	32	3.6%
Parricide	7	0.8%
Rape	405	45.5%
Rape with murder	55	6.2%
Kidnapping	129	14.5%
Kidnapping with murder	13	1.5%
Robbery	101	11.3%
Robbery with murder	83	9.3%
Carnapping	4	0.4%
Carnapping with murder	3	0.3%
Bribery	7	0.8%
Drugs	26	2.9%
Violation of Republic Act 7610	1	0.1%
Did not answer	19	2.1%
Total	890*	100.0%
Murder, all types	352	39.6%
Rape without murder	350	39.3%

Source: Survey of death row inmates by the Free Legal Assistance Group of the Philippines, May 2004 (Free Legal Assistance Group of the Philippines 2006b).

* At the time of the survey, there were 1,121 inmates on death row, of whom 890 (87 percent) responded to the survey.

that a Filipina of minor age would admit the loss of her chastity and possibly ruin her future marriage opportunities, unless it was true" (quoted in Wilkinson and Atkins 2000:63).[16]

16. For a detailed account of a British citizen named Albert Wilson who was wrongly condemned to death for the rape of his common-law stepdaughter, see Wilkinson and Atkins (2000). Because of international pressure, Wilson was acquitted by the Philippine Supreme Court in December 1999, only 14 months after the trial court condemned him to death. In less publicized capital cases, the appeals process took years. It is impossible to know how many miscarriages of justice occurred in capital rape cases in the Philippines. The country does have a pedophilia problem, in part because of strong demand for children from international sex tourists. Still, the available evidence suggests that the number of miscarriages in child rape cases has probably been substantial (legal professionals in Manila, interviews by Johnson, August 5–19, 2006; see also Kandelia 2006). For this reason, the first volume in the four-volume *Legal Reference on Capital Cases* (published by the Free Legal Assistance Group of the Philippines) is about rape, not homicide (Te 2006). For a critical study of the standard of proof in Philippine capital cases more generally, see Saifee (2005).

Of the first 17 capital convictions, 15 occurred on the island of Luzon—13 in Manila—and overall, the first to be condemned came from only three of the 14 regions in the country (Free Legal Assistance Group 1994:7). As in China, Japan, and the United States, capital sentences in the Philippines were geographically concentrated, and remained so until the second abolition.

Over the life of this new law (1994–2006), the Supreme Court reviewed more than 1,500 cases but affirmed only 270 (17.8 percent). See table 4.5.[17] Moreover, at the time of the second abolition in 2006, approximately 1,100 of the 1,205 persons on death row had not yet had their cases reviewed by the Supreme Court. Thus, during the 12-year life of R.A. 7659, trial courts in the Philippines produced approximately 2,600 death sentences, for an average of four new arrivals on death row each week.[18] Only seven of those sentences (1 in 371) resulted in execution. Compared to capital jurisdictions in the United States, where few death sentences result in execution, the conversion rate (of death sentences to executions) in the Philippines was low, even if one only takes into account the 270 persons sentenced to death whom the Supreme Court made eligible for execution when it finalized their sentences. In the Philippines, even when the condemned had exhausted all appeals, only about 1 in 40 actually met the executioner. On a per capita basis, the average number of death sentences under R.A. 7659—about 200 per year—exceeds the annual number of death sentences in most other Asian jurisdictions for which decent data exist. Trial courts in the Philippines produced about 20 times more death sentences per year in the 1990s than in Japan even though the Philippines' population was about one-third smaller than that of Japan and even though the number of death sentences in Japan increased markedly after the Tokyo subway attacks of 1995. (Japan, of course, has much lower rates of violent crime than the Philippines.) And compared to Taiwan, the Philippines produced more death sentences per capita every year that its restored capital law was in force.[19]

The ambivalence toward capital punishment reflected in the fact that so few death sentences resulted in execution can be seen by examining the presidential administrations—Ramos, Estrada, and Arroyo—in sequence. There were no executions under Ramos (1992–1998). This may seem like a puzzle, for as noted, Ramos was in many respects the prime mover behind the restoration of

17. Chief Justice Artemio V. Panganiban, a staunch opponent of capital punishment who spoke openly and often in favor of abolition, said that the Supreme Court's review of death penalty cases was "painstaking" and "meticulous" (Panganiban 2006:9; see also Panganiban 2003:54).

18. Another analyst has said that in the late 1990s, "thirty to forty" new persons were being added to the Philippine death row every month (Wilkinson and Atkins 2000:42). If so, then the Philippines was probably condemning to death about half as many people per capita as was the PRC.

19. The Philippine combination of many death sentences and few executions has one of its closest parallels in Thailand (see appendix D).

Table 4.5

Disposition of death penalty cases reviewed by the Supreme Court, the Philippines, 1994–2006

Disposition (as of January 2006)*	Number (percent)
Affirmed	270 (17.8%)
Acquitted	69 (4.6%)
Transferred (to the Court of Appeals)	456 (30.1%)
Modified	688 (45.5%)
Reduced (from death to *reclusion perpetua* or indeterminate sentence)	645 (43.0%)
Increased (from *reclusion perpetua* to death)	6 (4.0%)
Remanded for further proceedings	37 (2.4%)
Dismissed (due to death of the accused)	30 (2.0%)
Total cases	1,513 (100%)

Source: Mamamayang Tutol sa Bitay 2006:12.

* The death penalty was abolished in June 2006.

capital punishment. Ramos himself claims that the absence of executions on his watch was "because of the character of the President"—himself. He was not an "eager" advocate of executions, he insisted, but a supporter of executions only in "rare cases" that had been thoroughly reviewed by the courts and the executive (Fidel Ramos, interview by Johnson, August 7, 2006). But the truth seems more mundane. By law, a death sentence could only be administered after the Supreme Court finalized it, and this did not occur while Ramos was president because the time between the promulgation of the new capital statute (in January 1994) and the election of Joseph Estrada (in May 1998) was too short to enable the Court to finish its review.[20] Hence, public and presidential ambivalence does not explain why no executions occurred during the Ramos years. Unlike his successors, Ramos never had an opportunity to give the condemned clemency or a reprieve.

President Joseph Estrada is a strikingly different story. "Erap" ("friend" spelled backward in Tagalog), as he is known in the Philippines, has been called "an anomaly" because he was unconventional in many ways. In particular, Estrada was elected president "in happy defiance of a tradition of

20. After restoration, the first in line to be executed was Fernando Galera, who was sentenced to die for rape and robbery in April 1994. But "at the last minute" before execution, the Supreme Court unanimously declared his innocence and released him (Gluckman 1999b:4; *People v. Galera*, G.R. No. 115938, October 10, 1997). There appear to have been no other near executions during the Ramos presidency (attorney Frumencio A. Lagustan, interview by Johnson, August 7, 2006).

illustrado [indigenous intellectual] hegemony and technocratic dominance" (Steinberg 2000:210). Yet when it comes to capital punishment, Estrada's ambivalent actions were not anomalous; they resembled the actions of every post-Marcos president except Ramos.

A retired movie actor who played leading roles in more than 100 films over 32 years—often as a tough but kindhearted Robin Hood-like hero who helped the poor and dispossessed—Estrada was also one of the Philippines' most visible carousers (he boasted of having at least ten children; his wife was the mother of three). The action films helped mold Estrada's political image as a man of the masses and as the epitome of Filipino machismo. Using this reputation as a springboard into politics, Estrada also presented himself as "a beloved cartoonish character, full of faults but quintessentially Filipino" (Steinberg 2000:210).[21] In 1969 he became mayor of his hometown, San Juan, on the outskirts of Manila, where he served until 1986. He was elected to the Senate in 1987 and to the vice presidency in 1992.[22] In May 1998 he became president, winning the largest vote in Philippine election history with a strongly populist campaign. In his inaugural speech, Estrada declared that "the day is here" for "the common people who have waited long enough for their turn . . . . Now is the time for the masses to enjoy priority in the programs of the government" (quoted in Steinberg 2000:210). Thirty months later, the Senate opened an impeachment trial against Erap for a variety of corruption-related charges. In January 2001, the trial collapsed after some prosecution evidence was ruled inadmissible. Public anger spilled into the streets. Backed by the Catholic Church and the army, another People Power revolt drove Estrada from office, to be replaced by his vice president, Gloria Macapagal Arroyo. Ten months after that, Estrada found himself in the dock at his own criminal trial. One of the charges against him was plunder, a potentially capital offense. Estrada's trial lasted six years, and following his conviction in 2007 President Arroyo pardoned him, on condition that he return $80 million he had accumulated through gambling kickbacks and stolen excise taxes ("Ex-Philippine" 2008).

When Estrada became vice president in 1992, President Ramos assigned him the "thankless task of trying to curb the widespread criminality that had long plagued metropolitan Manila" (Steinberg 2000:202). Erap took to the task with a literal vengeance, and he used this position to promote his own political ambitions by leading many high-profile raids and theatrical shoot-outs. He also said that some criminals are "better dead than alive," and argued

21. Estrada's inelegant command of English also endeared him to Filipinos who speak a patois. On hearing one interviewer say that he heard Estrada had asthma as a youngster, the then–vice president said, "I beg your pardon, I have always been Catholic." When criticized for such malapropisms, Estrada once threatened, "I'll stop speaking in English. From now on, I'll just speak in the binocular" (quoted in Steinberg 2000:211).

22. In the Philippines, Senate races are national, and the race for vice president is separate from the presidential race.

that "it would be less expensive if they are dead" because taxpayers "would not have to pay for their meals in prison" (quoted in Steinberg 2000:218). Although Ramos was forced to dismiss Estrada from this position because too many criminal suspects were dying unexplained deaths in police custody, Erap continued to talk tough on crime after he was elected president. In his inaugural address, he focused extensively on crime and corruption, and in highly populist language:

> There is no excuse for the spread of crime in any society, unless government is an accomplice . . . . We know that the major crimes in this country are committed by hoodlums in uniform. We know that they are protected by hoodlums in *barong* [dress shirts] and acquitted by hoodlums in robes . . . . I promise to use all the powers of government to stamp out crime, big and small. There will be no excuses and no exceptions. No government is so helpless that it cannot prosecute criminals, especially when the criminals are officials operating in the open. (quoted in Steinberg 2000:7)[23]

In the two and a half years after this speech and before his own legal troubles began, Estrada carried out his "promise" and then some, using not only "all the powers of government" but some extralegal ones as well. In particular, he encouraged anticrime units to "shoot first and to talk later" (48 people were killed "resisting arrest"), and he spoke of his own desire to "arrest criminals and shoot them personally if the need arises" (quoted in Steinberg 2000:218; see also appendix G). Estrada further emphasized that he would not be an obstacle to executions under the new capital statute, repeatedly stressing the "need to be firm" in order to "send a message." He even urged judges who imposed noncapital sentences in capital cases to resign if they could not do their job (Wilkinson and Atkins 2000:108).

Despite this tough talk, Estrada repeatedly wavered when executions approached. The first execution that occurred on his watch—and the first in the Philippines since 1976—was of Leo Echegaray, on February 5, 1999. Echegaray had been convicted of repeatedly raping his 10-year-old stepdaughter. In 2006, just weeks before the Philippines abolished the death penalty for the second time, the chief justice of the Supreme Court delivered a speech stressing the "erroneous execution of Leo Echegaray" (Panganiban 2006:7). On this view, the indictment of Echegaray should not have alleged that the victim was his daughter because he was only the "confirmed lover" of the victim's mother (not her spouse), and thus by law should not have been subject to the

---

23. A popular joke in the Philippines illustrates what Estrada meant by "hoodlums in robes": a judge, before commencing trial, says, "I want you all to know that the plaintiff has given me 20,000 pesos ($400) to decide in his favor and the defendant has given me 30,000 pesos to decide his way. I am announcing that I am returning 10,000 pesos to the defendant in order for you all to know that this is going to be a fair trial" (quoted in Wilkinson and Atkins 2000:34).

mandatory death sentence he had received. The chief justice argued that "the outcome of this surreal case reinforces the strongest reason why the death penalty has no place in our statute books. After the execution of the appellant, errors in imposition become nightmarishly irreversible" (8).

But many Filipinos still believe that Echegaray deserved to die. By all accounts, he was not a nice man. Frequently drunk, this neighborhood bully was widely feared, and even after his rapes were exposed he remained unrepentant. His trial took place over the course of five hearings, each about one hour long, and he was represented by a series of different lawyers from the Public Attorney's Office (PAO), most of whom he barely remembered meeting. Only about 12–15 percent of capital defendants in the Philippines could afford private representation; The rest were served by the severely underfunded and undertrained PAO, "often with disastrous results" (Gluckman 1999b:3).[24] The judge who sentenced Echegaray to death in September 1994—Maximiano Asuncion—was the same man who gained notoriety for founding the Guillotine Club, whose members were judges who had imposed capital sentences and supported capital punishment.[25]

In June 1996, the Supreme Court finalized Echegaray's sentence—the first confirmed death sentence since the new capital law had come into force in 1994. But it would take almost three years for it to end in execution. In the meantime, a flurry of appeals occurred, evocative of American-style "appeals in the shadow of the gallows" (Zimring 2003:143). For instance, the Free Legal Assistance Group of the Philippines filed a supplementary appeal against Echegaray's capital sentence, alleging that the crime had not been proven beyond a reasonable doubt and that the defendant had not received a fair trial. In February 1997, the Supreme Court rejected that appeal and, in a decision upholding the constitutionality of the new death penalty law, confirmed Echegaray's death sentence "with finality" (see *People v. Echegaray*, 267 SCRA 682, February 7, 1997). In accordance with the new law, which stipulated

24. Private attorneys charged about $30 to attend each death sentence hearing—a lot of money for the majority of death row inmates, who earned less than $6 a day working as farmers, truckers, laborers, and the like before they were arrested. Until shortly before the second abolition, the 900 or so PAO attorneys received no special training for capital cases. And in addition to handling capital cases, these public attorneys were involved in more than 350,000 civil and criminal cases each year (about 400 cases per attorney per year), as well as millions of other filings and consultations. Many condemned persons complained that they were "railroaded into prison with limited or no representation" (Gluckman 1999b:3). In some cases, public defenders advised their clients to plead guilty in order to obtain a lighter sentence, unaware that the charges carried a mandatory death sentence (3).

25. Soon after imposing a death sentence on Echegaray, Judge Asuncion received a promotion to the Court of Appeals, but he died of a heart attack before Echegaray was executed. In general, "the more death penalties [a judge] meted out, the more one got one's name in the newspapers and the more likely one was to be considered for promotion" (Wilkinson and Atkins 2000:108).

that "the death sentence shall be carried out not later than one year after the judgment has become final," the Court subsequently ruled that Echegaray could be executed between February 28 and August 28, 1998. But another appeal, this time about the constitutionality of the new lethal injection law (R.A. 8177), delayed the execution again. This appeal was rejected by the Supreme Court on October 12, 1998 (*Echegaray v. Secretary of Justice*, 297 SCRA 754). On November 17 and in compliance with legal procedure, Quezon City judge Thelma Ponferrada set a new execution date for January 4, 1999, though the date was not made public. By law, a death sentence was to be executed under the authority of prison administrators, and their policy was to inform the condemned of the time of execution only after sunrise on the day of execution—about eight hours before the appointed time.

Echegaray's only hope seemed to lie with an appeal to Estrada for clemency or a stay, something the president had repeatedly vowed not to grant. But on January 4, 1999, just three hours before Echegaray's appointment with death, the Supreme Court granted a stay for up to six months. The cause was a last-minute appeal by Echegaray's lawyer, Theodore Te, who argued that several bills had been filed in Congress to repeal the new death penalty law, and that a treaty abolishing capital punishment was "headed for" ratification in the Senate (Panganiban 2006:3). Te's appeal was supported by a public call from a majority of Senators and 35 members of the House to review the new death penalty law. With the stay, the Supreme Court intended to give Congress time to conduct that review.

The result of the Supreme Court's last-minute intervention has been called "an unprecedented outpouring of what can only be described as blood-lust" (Wilkinson and Atkins 2000:109). Much of Philippine officialdom "reacted swiftly and furiously" (Panganiban 2006:3). Estrada reaffirmed his commitment to refuse clemency, saying, "No way. No way. I have to be firm to send a message to these future rapists that we mean business" (quoted in Wilkinson and Atkins 2000:112). Letters of protest flooded Philippine newspapers. Street rallies and demonstrations were organized, and angry citizens demanded the resignation of the eight justices who had voted for the stay. They were criticized as "incompetent, power-hungry, and insensitive to public opinion," and they and their families were insulted, booed, and threatened—sometimes with death.

This backlash peaked on January 11, when a rally was held in Makati, Manila's central business district. Vice President Arroyo marched arm-in-arm with the rape victim, "Baby" Echegaray (now aged 15), the latter with a towel over her head to hide her face. The rally cry was "Baby don't cry, Leo will die" (Wilkinson and Atkins 2000:111). "Baby" would go on to receive presents and offerings that included a new house and lot (from the Speaker of the House), two educational plans (one for her and one for her siblings), 150,000 pesos ($3,000) from members of the Chinese-Filipino community who had lobbied for victims' rights and for more severe punishments, and a film contract. It seems the victim had become "a locally famous and very rich person at the age of fifteen" (Wilkinson and Atkins 2000:111). The next year, Baby Echegaray would stand in front of a group of hundreds without a towel on her head and with TV cameras rolling, confidently delivering a five-minute speech on victims' rights.

As for the Supreme Court's stay, its last-minute timing prompted Congressman Roilo Golez—a tough-on-crime former military official who would support abolition in 2006—to sponsor a motion stating that the House of Representatives would not review the death penalty law anytime soon. When this motion passed, the Court lifted its stay, and a new execution date was set.

This date was kept. At 5:37 a.m. on February 5, 1999, Leo Echegaray was led from his cell on death row to a van that transported him to a holding cell near the lethal injection chamber at the New Bilibid Prison outside Manila. He wore an orange prison suit and a crucifix around his neck and carried a Bible in his hand. Although the date and time of execution were supposed to be secret, the information had been leaked, and Echegaray's final steps were covered by an unruly crowd of journalists and cameramen who "pushed, shoved, and howled" as they tried to cover the story (Wilkinson and Atkins 2000:112). Virtually all Philippine radios and televisions were tuned to catch the final few hours before this execution, the nation's first in 23 years.

In the end, Echegaray walked calmly to his death. He told his attorneys he had eaten well at breakfast, and he remained "upbeat" to the end (Te 1999). His last words were "I am hoping this will not push through. I am even smiling." But the execution did push through, in front of more than 30 witnesses, including the condemned man's wife (whom he had married five weeks earlier) and sister, both of whom sobbed incessantly.[26]

Despite appeals for clemency from the pope and the European Union, Estrada did nothing to stop or delay Echegaray's execution. But his actions after the fact betray an ambivalence that suggests (as one Supreme Court justice put it) "the seeming reluctance of the Executive Department to implement the death penalty lawfully" (Panganiban 2006:9).[27] In the immediate aftermath of Echegaray's execution, Estrada "toned down his elation of the previous days and meekly said he had done it only to protect women" (quoted in Wilkinson and Atkins 2000:113). In subsequent cases, the president wavered "each time a man was due to die" (Gluckman 1999b:2), granting more than

26. After the execution, senator and death penalty supporter Renato Cayetano extended his hand to Echegaray's lead attorney, Theodore Te. In notes recorded on execution day, Te said he "didn't want to take [Cayetano's] hand because he represented everything that I despised—a sleazy, despicable opportunist who would prance and preen at the slightest sight of a camera—but I was not myself then, I took his hand." Later, Te criticized Cayetano for saying that the execution had been "painless." In his view, the senator's comment was "a testimony to his monumental stupidity and craven and crass sleaziness that he would attempt to describe something that he has not even gone through" (Te 1999).

27. There were also mixed feelings within Estrada's family. His daughter Jackie secretly visited prisons to work for repeal of the new death penalty law (Gluckman 1999b:4).

100 clemencies and countless reprieves during his 30 months in office (Hands Off Cain 2000).[28] Before the execution of Eduardo Agbayani in June 1999—the first execution to occur after Echegaray—Estrada assented to an appeal from Manila bishop Teodoro Bacani only minutes after telling reporters that the execution of this convicted rapist would take place as planned later the same day. Using his home phone, Estrada then called the execution chamber, only to get a busy signal and a fax tone. By the time an aide reached the hotline in the presidential office, Agbayani had already been injected (Gluckman 1999a:1). He died two minutes after the mercy call arrived. Agbayani's victim (his daughter Eden) and her sisters had also appealed for clemency. Table 4.6 summarizes this and the other executions that occurred under President Estrada.

On August 18, 1999, there were three more executions (all on the same afternoon, and all for the robbery-homicide of an off-duty policeman who happened to be riding in the jeepney where the crimes occurred);[29] after that, Estrada suspended executions, pending review of each finalized capital case by a special group he called the Conscience Committee, which he established on the recommendation of Bishop Bacani and Estrada's own spiritual advisor, Brother Mike Velarde, who led the charismatic Roman Catholic group El Shaddai and who had been a strong advocate of executing Leo Echegaray six months earlier. Although the Conscience Committee was meant to be "purely a consultative and recommendatory body" that "shall not in any way limit or constrain the President's pardoning power" (Executive Order no. 147), Estrada always followed the committee's recommendations. At least one member of the committee believes the president established this organ as a "political buffer" to insulate himself from public pressure and criticism and to "distance himself" from the consequences of his decisions (former Conscience Committee member, interview by Johnson, August 19, 2006). If so, then Estrada's

28. Estrada granted some reprieves in order to allow DNA testing at a cost of $400 per test. That is a lot of money for a criminal justice system that spends only $240 dollars per inmate per year—66 cents per prisoner per day (Free Legal Assistance Group 2006a; see also Free Legal Assistance Group 2004d). In the United States and Japan, the cost of incarceration is about 100 times higher.

29. Two weeks after the executions of Dante Piandong, Jesus Morallos, and Archie Bulan for robbery-homicide in July 1999—three executions in three hours, more than had occurred in nearly a quarter century—the cover of *Asiaweek* featured a photo of a woman's hands holding a cross and a candle at a preexecution vigil. The accompanying headline said "Report from Death Row: Three More Down, a Thousand to Go." These three men all claimed to be innocent, alleging that the police had coerced their confessions through methods such as applying electric shocks to their genitals. Police abuse of force *is* widespread in the Philippines (Free Legal Assistance Group 2003b). Outside the prison before these executions, 100 or so death penalty opponents prayed for the executions to stop, while about 20 men and women "twirled rosaries, eyes shut, hands clasped to heaven" and beseeched God to "let the court-sanctioned killings continue" (Gluckman 1999b:1).

Table 4.6

Executions under Republic Act 7659, the Philippines, 1994–2006

Name	Crime	Date of execution
Leo Echegaray	Rape of 10-year-old stepdaughter	Feb. 5, 1999
Eduardo Agbayani	Rape of 14-year-old daughter	June 25, 1999
Dante Piandong	Robbery with homicide; victim was a policeman	July 8, 1999
Jesus Morallos	Robbery with homicide; victim was a policeman	July 8, 1999
Archie Bulan	Robbery with homicide; victim was a policeman	July 8, 1999
Pablito Andan	Rape with homicide; victim was a 20-year-old student of nursing	Oct. 26, 1999
Alex Bartolome	Rape of 14-year-old daughter who was pregnant by her boyfriend	Jan. 4, 2000

Source: Free Legal Assistance Group 2004b.

Note: Under R.A. 7659, the death penalty was mandatory for incestuous rape of a minor (of which Echegaray, Agbayani, and Bartolome were convicted).

conscience-by-committee approach to clemency review may be a Philippine manifestation of the "mechanisms of moral disengagement" that people frequently use in other countries and cultures to distance themselves from the moral implications of their death penalty actions (Haney 2005:143). Of all the cases this committee reviewed, it recommended "no clemency" in only one: the case of Alex Bartolome, who received a mandatory death sentence for raping his 14-year-old daughter.[30] Prior to that lethal injection, Bartolome himself urged Estrada to make his execution the last of the new millennium.

30. Three members of the five-member Conscience Committee interviewed Bartolome and his daughter Elena (the victim) after Bartolome's execution date was set. Under pressure from her aunt, Elena had written a letter to President Estrada asking that her father's life be spared, but when she was interviewed by members of the Conscience Committee, she said she believed that "he deserves to die" and that she "would be very frustrated if the President commutes the [death] sentence to life imprisonment" (internal memorandum of the Conscience Committee, 1999). In a separate interview, Bartolome suggested that Elena was "a loose girl," said he never hurt her, and claimed that their sex had been partly a response to his wife "having a relationship with a younger man." Based on these and other circumstances of the case, the committee "felt it more prudent and expedient to recommend that the decision of the courts be allowed to take its natural course." On the day Bartolome was executed, one committee member who favored the "no clemency" recommendation canceled the classes she was scheduled to teach and stayed in her room watching TV. The execution "bothered" her, she later explained. "You rationalize it by saying that the Supreme

So far, it has been. Two months after Bartolome died, Estrada announced a moratorium on executions, ostensibly in observance of the Christian Jubilee Year, although his reasoning was more complicated than that. As noted, Estrada showed signs of serious ambivalence after the first execution of his presidency and consistently thereafter. Some analysts believe his own participation in the execution process helped heighten his concerns about the practice. What is more, Estrada was in serious political trouble at the time he called the moratorium, and suspending executions may have been partly an effort to appeal to the powerful Catholic Church for support. Finally, Estrada's own secretary of justice (Sarafin Cuevas) reported that the president not only wanted "to be at peace with his conscience" (as the formation of his Conscience Committee suggests) but also worried that the Philippines might be branded as "the death penalty capital of the world" (quoted in Gluckman 1999b:4). Estrada's office received numerous appeals for clemency from foreign countries and citizens each time an execution approached, and this transnational pressure—and foreign media criticism as well—seems to have had an inhibiting effect on a man who—in a nation that strongly supported capital punishment—was famous for being a man of the masses.

■ The Second Abolition

Gloria Macapagal Arroyo became president when public demonstrations backed by the military and the Catholic Church drove Estrada from office for corruption in January 2001.[31] This was two years after she had marched arm-in-arm with Baby Echegaray to protest the Supreme Court's stay of Leo Echegaray's execution. Two months after becoming president, Arroyo announced that she was lifting the moratorium on executions Estrada had imposed in 2000. Although she would make similar statements on numerous occasions during the next five years, no judicial executions occurred during her presidency even though at least 100 persons were under finalized sentences of death and therefore eligible for execution at the time of the second abolition in 2006 (Amnesty International 2006c). As in the Aquino and

---

Court made the decision.... You try to assuage your own responsibility.... You recall the deliberations of the Conscience Committee.... And you remember the anger of the victim." In ways such as these, the presidential Conscience Committee clearly had effects on more than one conscience. The same person who shared these reflections said that she began working on the committee without strong feelings about capital punishment, but by the time she was done with it she harbored strong misgivings. "Where the administration of justice is extremely unjust, as in the Philippines," she explained, "you shouldn't even consider the death penalty" (interview by Johnson, August 19, 2006).

31. Arroyo is the daughter of Diosdado Macapagal, who was president of the Philippines from 1961 until Marcos defeated him in the 1965 election.

Estrada administrations, the theme of death penalty ambivalence characterized Arroyo's presidency too. See table 4.7.[32]

Arroyo signed R.A. 9346[33] on June 24, 2006, thereby abolishing the death
penalty for the second time in 20 years. A devout Catholic, she explained her
decision as a matter of yielding to "the high moral imperative dictated by God
to walk away from capital punishment" while at the same time assuring the
public that ending the death penalty did not mean she was "soft on crime"
(Toms 2006b).[34] Arroyo did not say when the "high moral imperative" of
abolition had been revealed to her, or explain how or why her position had
changed since marching with Baby Echegaray, or acknowledge her many
previous promises to permit execution of the "champions of darkness" who
committed capital crimes. She signed the abolition bill two months after the
Easter Sunday on which she had announced that she was commuting the
sentences of everyone on death row—the "largest ever commutation of death
sentences" (Amnesty International 2006b). Her commutation message was
not only delivered on the holiest of Christian days, it was framed in explicitly
Christian terms.

32. The contours of Arroyo's ambivalence are described in table 4.7; this note describes
two of the most striking manifestations in detail. First, following the 9/11 attacks on America
in 2001, Arroyo said she would order the immediate executions of up to 95 convicted
kidnappers after the Supreme Court had reviewed their cases. "Let us prepare the lethal
execution chamber for those champions of darkness for the sake of our society," she
declared. When Roman Catholic bishops chastised her, Arroyo called herself "a very good
Catholic" and explained, "You can interpret a Church law conservatively or liberally.
I've studied religion and theology long enough for me to know that there are ranges of
interpretation and I've taken this course because of my duties as President" ("Arroyo under
Fire" 2001). Similarly, in December 2003, Arroyo's office issued a news release that said:
"Persons convicted of kidnapping and high profile drug cases and meted the death penalty
will definitely get it.... No ifs or buts about it in these two cases.... The President is duty-
bound to serve the public interest, which lies in according the people the option of just
retribution for their own peace of mind.... Some may consider the death penalty too harsh
but it is what is prescribed by law, which in turn reflects the sentiments of the silent
majority... I shall no longer stand in the way of executions scheduled by the courts for
January 2004" (Free Legal Assistance Group 2003a). But Arroyo did stand in the way, and in
the next two and a half years before abolition she stayed and commuted hundreds of death
sentences. As of 2008, no judicial executions had occurred during her presidency.

33. The second abolition law does four main things: prohibits the imposition of
the death penalty; defines the punishments to be used instead of death (*reclusion perpetua*
for crimes involving the Revised Penal Code and life imprisonment for other crimes);
declares that persons convicted of offenses punished by *reclusion perpetua* or whose sentences will be reduced by this law to *reclusion perpetua* shall not be eligible for parole; and
mandates newspaper publication of the names of all persons whose sentences are reduced by
the law and who are being considered or recommended for commutation or pardon
(R.A. 9346).

34. Abolition day was the day after terrorists in Maguindanao killed six people with a car
bomb in the public square.

Table 4.7
Gloria Macapagal Arroyo's positions on capital punishment, 1993–2006

Date	Action reflecting position
December 1993	Abstains in Senate vote enacting new death penalty law; the vote is 17-4-1
June 1998	Elected vice president
January 1999	Marches arm-in-arm with rape victim "Baby" Echegaray to support the execution of Baby's father, Leo Echegaray, who is executed on February 5
January 2001	Becomes president when Joseph Estrada is ousted by public demonstrations over corruption
March 2001	Vows to lift Estrada's moratorium on executions
April 2001	Commutes at least 16 death sentences
October 2001	Says she will allow executions to proceed, especially for kidnappers
March 2002	Says the Senate's abolition bill is "urgent"
April 2002	Says that in order "to lick the kidnap menace, we have to use all our legal weapons"
July 2002	Says she "definitely" is not going to stay the execution of two kidnappers set for September and October; says she is going to adopt an "eye-for-an-eye" punishment policy; and says the death penalty is appropriate for some white-collar criminals
August 2002	Arroyo's press secretary says there will "definitely be some executions within the year"
July 2003	Says she wants drug traffickers to be executed
November 2003	Says she favors lifting the moratorium for kidnappers
December 2003	Lifts the moratorium and says executions will occur in January 2004; stresses that kidnapping and drug offenders "will definitely get it . . . no ifs or buts about it in these two cases"
January 2004	Says that after two executions this month, she may restore the moratorium
February 2004	Announces that 14 executions are scheduled for February; all are stayed or commuted
May 2004	Reelected president, defeating film actor Fernando Poe Jr.; scandal ensues over vote rigging
July 2004	Announces that ten executions are scheduled for September; all are stayed or commuted
February 2005	Says the moratorium will continue except for kidnapping and drug offenders
February 2005–December 2005	Stays at least 93 executions (an average of two per week)
February 2006	Commutes 280 death sentences and calls for abolition

(*Continued*)

Table 4.7 (*Continued*)

Date	Action reflecting position
April 2006	Commutes 1,200+ death sentences, including 100+ that have been finalized by the Supreme Court
June 2006	Signs the abolition bill into law, stressing that this is "God's will," and then visits Pope Benedict XVI at the Vatican, who commends her for abolishing

Easter Sunday completes the meaning of Christ's death on the Cross. From our great trials flow patience and experience that, in turn, elevate the hope of salvation. Christ suffered to show us how love can endure sacrifice and redeem souls. We must keep our hopes high as we carry our own crosses, rise from our failings, and fix our sights on a brighter horizon. Our beloved bishops spoke of the people's fear of more chaotic politics even as they struggle to make a decent living. We seek above all the nation's salvation from poverty and discord. *On the occasion of Easter, it is my honor to announce our policy to commute the death penalty to life imprisonment.* This nation will prevail in the loving hands of the Almighty. Happy Easter! (Arroyo 2006; emphasis added)

On the surface, these two steps toward abolition—Arroyo's mass commutation and her approval of the abolition law—seem to be motivated by religious objections to the death penalty. After the fact as well, a Christian frame was emphasized in the audience Arroyo had with Pope Benedict XVI two days after the bill became law. Some critics even accused the president of "rushing [the bill's] approval to please the pope" (Dalangin-Fernandez 2006). In the Philippines, where it usually takes months if not years to pass legislation, Congress had acted with unusual speed. It is therefore reasonable to ask: "What triggered the urgency to repeal a law that was rarely applied" (Toms 2006a) ?

To start with, Arroyo seemed to have complex and conflicted feelings about capital punishment—as many people do (Bohm 2003a; Haney 2005). Her ambivalence is evident in the fact that she expressed private and religious concerns about capital punishment at least as early as 1993 and yet took remarkably diverse public positions on the issue from that year forward. Although her changing public positions reflected different readings of the political landscape, a purely political interpretation cannot make sense of the frequency and timing of her many contradictory stands on the issue. Indeed, at times when permitting executions might have helped her political fortunes—as in the months leading up to her reelection by a narrow margin in May 2004—she stayed and commuted numerous executions despite broad public support for the death penalty. What is more, even afterward, when voters no longer could punish her at the ballot box, Arroyo's ambivalence continued. So we need to look at a wider array of situational factors in order to understand why she wavered on capital punishment and why that wavering eventually resulted in abolition.

Two such factors seem especially significant. First, Arroyo's narrow reelection victory in May 2004 was followed by widespread allegations that she had rigged the vote. The most damning evidence came from the former deputy director of the National Bureau of Investigation, who produced audiotapes of wiretapped conversations between Arroyo and a high-level official in the Commission on Elections in which the president made statements she later admitted were inappropriate. Evidence of this kind fueled a move to impeach her in 2005. It failed, but in 2006 similar impeachment charges were brought, and in the time between these two impeachment movements, Arroyo's popularity plummeted.[35] As a result, the mass commutation and the push to abolish both occurred during a period when the president sorely needed the support of the Catholic Church in order to weather a severe political storm. Although some analysts believe her desire to change the country's American-style presidential system into a parliamentary system also caused her to appeal for Church support through abolition (Toms 2006a), that motivation seems secondary to the imperative of political survival and the recognition that the Catholic Church had helped propel the People Power movements that drove presidents Marcos and Estrada from office (Steinberg 2000).[36]

Second, the transnational context of capital punishment also helps explain the second abolition. Spain's three centuries in the Philippines helped make it "the only Christian nation of Asia," and the Spanish and American occupations of the country have combined to make it "the most Westernized society in the region" (Karnow 1989:26). One result is that Philippine leaders frequently regard Western institutions as important points of reference and

35. Arroyo lost popularity for a variety of reasons. She instituted a "no permit, no rally" policy in order to discourage dissent. She forbade officials of the executive branch to appear in congressional inquiries without prior approval from her (a policy the Supreme Court later found unconstitutional). She declared a state of emergency (after an alleged coup attempt), thus giving herself power to make warrantless arrests and take over certain private institutions. She raided the office of the *Daily Tribune*, a newspaper that had criticized her. And she seemed to condone if not encourage the involvement of police and military officials in extrajudicial killings while fostering a "culture of impunity" that protected the killers from the law (Amnesty International 2006e; Alston 2007; see also appendix G). Arroyo's unpopularity persisted after the 2006 abolition (Ford 2008). In one national survey she was named "the most corrupt President in Philippine history" (Romero 2007).

36. Some observers have said that another reason Arroyo pushed for abolition was to weaken Church opposition to her efforts to revive mining in the Philippines (which some Catholic bishops opposed on environmental grounds). As one analyst saw it, "The abolition of the death penalty is one way of saying to the bishops 'I can't give you what you want over mining but I can give you something else, quid pro quo'" (quoted in Toms 2006a).

comparison (the Vatican being one conspicuous example). Moreover, chronic underdevelopment in the Philippines increased the economic leverage that developed countries had to export abolition to the Philippines. In fact, in the years between the restoration of capital punishment in 1994 and its abolition in 2006, numerous European countries and institutions pushed for the elimination of the death penalty in the Philippines, sometimes by directly lobbying institutions of the Philippine government and other times by supporting sympathetic NGOs.

The most important abolitionist NGO in the Philippines was the Free Legal Assistance Group (FLAG), which was founded by a small band of liberal lawyers in 1974, two years after Marcos declared martial law. For its first 20 years, FLAG was primarily committed to "developmental legal advocacy" (Free Legal Assistance Group 1994:6), but after capital punishment was restored in 1994 it increasingly focused on death penalty issues. Between restoration and abolition, FLAG received hundreds of thousands of dollars from the European Union and its members to support the organization's advocacy in capital cases and to underwrite a wide variety of death penalty workshops and publications. This support helped make FLAG the Philippines' foremost source of information on capital punishment, and that information had significant effects on many key decision-makers, including members of Congress who had supported restoration but later converted to an abolitionist position after exposure to better information (Orendain 2008). American Supreme Court justice Thurgood Marshall believed that if people were given reliable information about how capital punishment works in practice, "the great mass of citizens would conclude . . . that the death penalty is immoral and therefore unconstitutional" (*Furman v. Georgia,* 1972:361,363). In the Philippines, one encounters numerous stories about individuals who underwent Marshallian conversions. Maria "Cookie" Diokno, the executive director of FLAG, has said that when she spoke publicly about capital punishment, the number of people who supported the death penalty at the end of her talk was substantially smaller than the number at the beginning (interview by Johnson, August 18, 2006). When she spoke at De La Salle University in Manila, for example, 26 out of 28 students supported the death penalty at the beginning of her speech, but by the end "about half" had changed their minds (and several of those sent letters to her explaining their conversion experiences). In the Senate, Richard Gordon was a longtime supporter of capital punishment whose previous work as mayor of Olongapo (near Subic Bay) had helped "rid the town of the sleaze and scum associated with the American era" (Kirk 2005:90). (Gordon has been called the Filipino version of former New York City mayor Rudolph Giuliani, and he likes to point out that they have the same initials.) After the death penalty was restored in the Philippines, Gordon encountered so much information about its flawed administration—much of it from and through FLAG—that he voted to abolish in 2006, despite the fact that abolition was unpopular and even though he hopes to run for president in 2010 (90). He explained his change of mind as follows:

Although the death penalty is a political football in this country, in my case the decision to support abolition was a pragmatic thing. To start with, hardly anyone got executed anyway, and that probably made it easier to abolish because we were only legitimating present practice. . . . As for deterrence, it was never really put to the test because we executed in such small numbers. . . . If I became president, law and order would be my number one issue because crime and disorder are so bad in this country and because it [law and order] is a prerequisite to other major issues such as business growth, democratic development, neighborhood quality of life, and so on. . . . In order to be an effective leader you have to be macho and tough it out. . . . But law and order are especially bad for the poor and disadvantaged. My main concern with capital punishment is all of the problems and flaws in the criminal justice system. The evidence about the administration of the death penalty shows that it was not being applied fairly or reliably. In those circumstances, we should not be using it. You have to err on the side of justice. (Richard Gordon, interview by Johnson, August 14, 2006)

Other senators changed their minds for similar reasons. Franklin Drilon, who was secretary of justice under Ramos when capital punishment was restored, also voted for the second abolition. Although Ramos criticized Drilon for "flip-flopping" on the issue (Ramos, interview by Johnson, August 7, 2006), Drilon's reversal was largely data-driven, and much of the relevant data came to him through FLAG. He said:

Deterrence is the key issue in the Philippines because violence is so widespread. But there is no evidence that the death penalty has served as a deterrent.[37] In addition, there is much to be desired in our justice system, and for that reason I lack confidence in its ability to determine who is guilty and deserving [of death]. There are too many errors, and the capacity of police to enforce the law is spotty and biased against the lower classes . . . . Of course, the Europeans never missed an opportunity to remind this country that the death penalty is uncivilized, but because the United States has the death penalty too, a rhetorical deadlock usually ensued on this issue. I guess Europe and the United States cancelled each other out, so the weight of the European Union was not that great. Domestic considerations were primary. (Franklin Drilon, interview by Johnson, August 14, 2006)

37. There are no sound empirical studies of the death penalty and deterrence in the Philippines, but the statistics that are available suggest there was no deterrent effect. For example, from abolition in 1987 to restoration in 1994, the number of murders dropped steadily, from 12,305 to 6,446—a 48 percent decline in eight years (Free Legal Assistance Group 2004c:11). Similarly, the 1994 capital statute did not result in a decline in the rape rate (Wilkinson and Atkins 2000; Coalition against the Death Penalty 2005).

When asked whether he or other congresspersons feared that their support for abolition would generate a backlash among voters who support the death penalty, Drilon said not at all: "In my experience there is no relation between your legislative agenda and how many votes you get." In the Philippines, he averred, "you never get punished by voters for how you vote in Congress" (Franklin Drilon, interview by Johnson, August 14, 2006).

In the House of Representatives as well, many congresspersons rooted their support for abolition in concerns about the way the death penalty was administered, and those concerns were often based on information provided by European-funded organizations such as FLAG and the Philippine Coalition against the Death Penalty. After the second abolition, longtime abolitionist Representative Edcel Lagman explained that while people from the European Union seldom came directly to the House of Representatives to lobby against capital punishment, their indirect influence was "very significant." Indeed, for two years before President Arroyo pushed for abolition, "the House had abolition momentum, largely because my colleagues came to see that the death penalty is anti-poor and because they now know it is not an effective deterrent." In Lagman's view, "strong sentiment and pressure" from three sources helps explain the timing of the second abolition. First, NGOs like FLAG waged "incessant" educational campaigns and abolitionist advocacy. Second, House leaders who most seriously studied the available information on the death penalty were "trusted and believed" by their colleagues. And third, the worldwide trend toward abolition was a "key context" for the Philippines too (Edcel Lagman, interview by Johnson, August 16, 2006).

In explaining his vote for abolition, conservative representative Roilo Golez stressed similar reasons. Golez was the congressman who authored the resolution in 1999 responding to the Supreme Court's last-minute stay of Leo Echegaray's execution stating that the House had no intention of revising or repealing the death penalty law and whose immediate effects were to cause the Court to lift its stay and send Echegaray to his death. When Johnson interviewed Golez in August 2006, Golez said he had still supported capital punishment early in 2006, but when Arroyo certified abolition as urgent he had started to study the issue, and "as I studied I went through a conversion experience." Golez also displayed about 600 pages of photocopied materials in two volumes that he had collected during his crash course, and he said that the "key question" that motivated this study had been the puzzle of why all the European countries were against the death penalty even though many of them used to be vigorous users of it. The study materials that led him to conclude the death penalty "fails as a deterrent" and "discriminates against the poor" included information from the American Bar Association, the UN Economic and Social Council, the Death Penalty Information Center, Amnesty International, the Council of Europe, the University of Alaska Justice Center, the U.S. Bureau of Justice Statistics, news articles from around the world, and anti–death penalty studies and brochures produced and distributed by FLAG and other Philippine NGOs.

The reintroduction of capital punishment in the Philippines reflected a desire for an instrumental death penalty that would deter crime and achieve retribution while being administered fairly and reliably. But the resurrected death penalty was none of the above. The death penalty as it was actually administered involved bias against the poor and disadvantaged, frequent mistakes of law and fact, failure to satisfy the "burden of precision" that is a necessary condition of retribution (Turow 2003:63), and failure to generate a volume of executions that might have had a deterrent effect. This large gap between the vision and the reality helps explain why Gordon, Drilon, Golez, and others converted to abolition—and the conversion of Congress as an institution could hardly have been more extreme. When the death penalty was reintroduced in 1994, the new capital statute received 94 percent of the votes in the House and 77 percent of the votes in the Senate. In 2006, by contrast, only 14 percent of the members of the House voted against abolition, and nobody in the Senate did. Thus, there was an 80 percent change in opinion among the members of both chambers of Congress in only 12 years. It is difficult to think of a political issue in any other nation for which the shift in opinion has been so extreme. The Philippine Congress changed course largely because its members became educated about problems in the death penalty as it was actually administered. As Thurgood Marshall anticipated, when they became "informed as to the purposes of the penalty and its liabilities," they found it "shocking, unjust, and unacceptable" (*Furman v. Georgia*, 1972).

■ Ambivalence and State Killing

What we saw in the previous section was wholesale change in political opinion about one of the most salient issues in Philippine politics over a period of two decades. What remains to be seen is whether that change will endure. The dynamism of death penalty policy in the Philippines reflects the fact that capital punishment was frequently a "political football" that changed direction depending on what was happening in the larger political game (interviews by Johnson, August 2006). At the same time, the trajectory of the death penalty depended not only on domestic political considerations—such as the need to distance new regime from old (in 1987), the need to confront a perceived law-and-order crisis (in 1994), and the need to win support from the Catholic Church (in 2006)—but also on transnational developments, cash contributions, and information flows. At several stages in this story, the role of the Catholic Church was crucial—in driving Marcos from office, in creating the abolition clause in the new constitution, in enabling the Methodist Fidel Ramos to lead a restoration movement, in motivating President Estrada to stop all but seven scheduled executions, and in President Arroyo's decision to push for the second abolition. Indeed, there is no other Asian nation in which a religious organization has had such a strong influence on death penalty policy.

Another salient theme in this account of capital punishment is ambivalence, a notion which helps one understand and explain a range of behaviors and situations beyond the scope of rational-choice explanations. In the Philippines, ambivalence helps explain the instability of death penalty policy and practice, for ambivalence itself tends to be unstable, "expressing itself in different and sometimes contradictory ways as actors attempt to cope with it" (Smelser 1998:5). The simultaneous existence of attraction and repulsion toward capital punishment can be seen in at least four spheres of Philippine society.

First, *policy ambivalence* appeared initially in the proximate cause of abolition in 1987, the clause in the new constitution that invited the Philippine Congress to revisit the death penalty issue, which is exactly what started to happen only months after the new charter took effect. From that point on, policy ambivalence was a persistent theme in death penalty law and practice. A corollary of policy ambivalence is *political ambivalence,* both in Congress, where the Senate and House performed abrupt about-faces concerning the propriety of capital punishment, and in the executive branch of government, where presidents Aquino, Estrada, and Arroyo took markedly different stands on capital punishment, depending on the circumstances and exigencies of the moment. Even authoritarian Marcos, who casually used coercive force in so many other ways, proved surprisingly reluctant to employ judicial executions as a tool of his rule, and long before Marcos came to power in 1965, the Spanish and American colonial powers were also relatively sparing users of death as a criminal sanction.

Second, *public ambivalence* is evident in at least two aspects of this story. For one, there was little public backlash after either abolition, despite the fact that a large majority of Filipinos has consistently supported capital punishment. The contrast with American reactions to the U.S. Supreme Court's *Furman* decision in 1972 is stark, and it suggests that Filipinos are less passionately committed to the death penalty than are their U.S. counterparts, especially in the American South. Public ambivalence in the Philippines can also be seen in the contrast between citizens' steady support for the death penalty as an institution and their reluctance to execute individual offenders. Of course, this type of ambivalence is hardly a Filipino monopoly, for many people in the world are incapable of enthusiastically advocating a policy that is intended to take human life (Haney 2005:x).

Third, there has been significant *judicial ambivalence* about capital punishment in the Philippines. Putting aside the punitive trial court judges who belonged to the Guillotine Club, appellate judges often displayed mixed feelings about the death penalty. Most notably, the Supreme Court approved every major piece of death penalty legislation that Congress passed, yet when it came to particular issues in individual cases, the Court routinely slowed or stopped the machinery of death.[38]

---

38. There are also mixed feelings among the 1,200 persons who were on death row and were "saved" by the second abolition (interviews by Johnson, August 17, 2006). On the one

Fourth, there has been *ambivalence in the Philippine Catholic Church*. The church opposed capital punishment for the first five centuries of its existence, after which it took a retentionist position for the next 1600 years (Prejean 2005:115). In 1995, the year after the Philippines restored the death penalty, Pope John Paul II issued his *Evangelium Vitae* (Gospel of Life) encyclical stating that the practice of capital punishment in modern society should be "rare, if not nonexistent," and two years later the Vatican issued a new edition of the Catholic Church Catechism that said the death penalty is theoretically permissible when it is "the only possible way of effectively defending human lives against the unjust aggressor," though it went on to say that such circumstances are "practically nonexistent" in today's world. Since then, popes have consistently opposed the death penalty and asked Catholics to work toward its abolition. In the Philippines, however, Catholic leaders have remained divided about this issue (interviews by Johnson, August 2006). More fundamentally, there is far more support for capital punishment among the Catholic Filipino laity than there is in the clergy, a schism that helps explain why the Catholic Church seemed "helpless" to stop the seven executions that occurred in 1999 and 2000 (Wilkinson and Atkins 2000:114). Before the execution of Leo Echegaray, for example, Cardinal Jaime Sin publicly recognized that the Philippine nation "is divided by this raging issue" and that pro– and anti–death penalty Filipinos "both believe in God." He even stated that "it is time for us to pray and beg God to show us the right path" (quoted in Wilkinson and Atkins 2000:119). A man named Isidro Tan then appealed to Cardinal Sin to save Echegaray by promising to fast until his own death or until Echegaray's sentence was commuted. Although Tan was probably correct—Estrada would have commuted Echegaray's sentence rather than being made to look like the villain in this movie—the cardinal did not accept the challenge. For this execution and the six that followed it, the Church appeared more afraid of losing its flock than of upholding its official position (121). Yet subsequent events suggest that the Church's commitment to abolition may not have been at issue here. With the benefit of hindsight, it appears the cardinal may have been biding his time.[39]

_____

hand, they welcomed the 2006 abolition because it removed them from death row and afforded them a lifetime exemption from execution. On the other hand, many of them were resentenced to terms of imprisonment that were longer than those received by defendants who committed heinous crimes after abolition. The formerly condemned are also concerned that with the disappearance of capital punishment, legal aid, advocacy, and other forms of support will also disappear. For those inmates who have left death row but remain imprisoned and still have viable issues to appeal—including claims of actual innocence—abolition may have harmed their chances of prevailing or even of getting their cases heard.

39. Another form of ambivalence can be found among observers who applaud abolition whenever and wherever it occurs but who acknowledge that while judicial executions in the Philippines have ceased, extrajudicial killings have continued, with members of the military and police tolerating, condoning, and participating in them (Amnesty International 2006e; Alston 2007; Oliveros 2007; Ford 2008). Since 1977, the Philippines has experienced only

■ Is the Battle Over?

The first two decades in the Philippines after Marcos was driven from power demonstrate how ambivalent attitudes can generate volatility in capital punishment. As we have noted, one common pattern of change in national death penalty policy is for major transitions such as the formal end of capital punishment to take place in the wake of a shift in control of government. This happened in the United Kingdom after the replacement of a conservative government by the Labour Party in 1964, in Spain after the death of Franco, and in France after a Gaullist government was displaced by the socialists (Zimring 2003:23). In these instances, the change resulted when different people with differing beliefs from those in power took control of government.

This is not what happened in the Philippines. What changed in the Philippine Senate between 1994 and 2006 was not so much that an influx of new members had stronger anti–death penalty views as that the same senators who remained in office during the entire period changed their opinions and votes. Each Senate vote on capital punishment forced members of that body to transform profoundly mixed feelings about crime and capital punishment into a simple yes-or-no decision. The aggregate votes varied by a factor of 3 in the space of 20 years because the mixed feelings of so many senators produced contrasting individual outcomes when events pushed toward either fear or compassion.

---

seven judicial executions, which by some estimates is about how many extrajudicial killings occurred in an average week during the two years of the Arroyo administration before the second abolition. A local journalist in Davao City (population 1.36 million) said there have been, on the average, almost that many extrajudicial executions each week for the past 10 years—about 3,000 "Davao Death Squad" victims over the last decade—just in his city (the journalist "stopped counting when the local police began taking a keen interest in his arithmetic") (Miller 2008). But of course, the abolition of capital punishment not only ends judicial executions, it projects symbolic force as a legal and authoritative statement that the state will not intentionally kill its own citizens or residents, and the normative pressure of that position may discourage nonjudicial executions, too. Nonetheless, for people who care about state killing, whatever its incarnation, and for those who are inclined (as Noam Chomsky is) to assess a state's performance at least partly by "counting the bodies," the abolition of capital punishment in the Philippines could be deemed a limited achievement (MacFarquhar 2003). The relationships between judicial and extrajudicial state killing are explored in appendix G, and our argument there about "common causation" of judicial and extrajudicial executions may be receiving support from events in the Philippines since its second abolition. Since 2006, President Arroyo has taken several steps apparently aimed at controlling extrajudicial killing (Dalangin-Fernandez 2007; Salaverria 2007; "Philippine Rebels" 2008). According to separate reports from the Alliance for the Advance of People's Rights (Karapatan) and the Philippine National Police, there was "a huge drop in extrajudicial killings" in 2007 (Ager 2007; Dizon 2008).

For this reason, President Arroyo's frequent waffling between support for and opposition to capital punishment seems representative of the back-and-forth mood swings of Philippine political elites. The origin of that volatility is not so much changes in power as changes in sentiment among the elites, who have consistently participated in governance since Marcos's departure. If the emotional tugs that produce ambivalence—fear of violence, anger and disgust over sexual predation, fear of government error and excess—remain in place even after the second abolition, should we expect death penalty volatility to persist—perhaps in the form of a second reintroduction of capital punishment followed in a few years' time by a third abolition? We believe continued volatility is unlikely not because the political elite's mixed emotions have been resolved but because many of them have learned the lessons of the 1994–2006 period. On death penalty policy, they are less volatile because they are sadder and wiser.

As for the majority public opinion, which favors capital punishment, could it lead to restoration again in this still developing democracy? Or is the battle over? Since World War II, the usual pattern for the end of the death penalty in developed nations has been "leadership from the front": that is, governing elites have engineered abolition even though public opinion has favored retention (Zimring 2003:22). In the developed nations that have abolished capital punishment, it has rarely been resurrected. But should we expect the same pattern to appear in developing nations such as the Philippines, where pressure to demonstrate democratic legitimacy might make leaders more responsive to public opinion?

Some Filipino leaders believe the death penalty could come back, and there have even been some efforts toward that end. After the second abolition, for example, the abolitionist leader of the House of Representatives said: "restoration is always possible as a matter of law, and as a practical matter, advocates of restoration are already here, they just need to be motivated and mobilized" (Rep. Edcel Lagman, interview by Johnson, August 16, 2006). On this view, the enabling condition for another restoration would be some real or contrived crime crisis, as occurred before the restoration in 1994. As Lagman sees it, "such a crisis could easily come again." Several attempts to reinstate capital punishment have been made since the second abolition, and all occurred during major crime scares. In the first, in December 2006, the Chairman of the Committee on Human Rights in the House of Representatives—a former Baptist pastor named Bienvenido Abante, who was first elected to Congress in 2004—vowed to file a bill that would restore the death penalty. Abante made his promise during "a sudden rise in the commission of heinous crimes" around the country, but his pledge fell flat ("Bill to Restore Death Penalty Pushed" 2006). Seven months later, in July 2007, Representative Eduardo Nonato Joson, who was a member of the Congress that resurrected capital punishment in 1994, filed a bill to restore the death penalty for convicted killers-for-hire and for law enforcers found guilty of involvement in extrajudicial killing. Joson's bill was introduced "at a time when abductions and killings of politicians, journalists and political dissenters continue[d] to hog the head-lines," but it made little headway among the 600 other bills that were intro-duced at the same time ("Bill to Restore Death Penalty Filed" 2007).[40] In fact, later that month the Philippines signed the UN Second Optional Protocol to the International Covenant on Civil and Political Rights Aiming at the Aboli-tion of the Death Penalty, which committed the government to execute no one within its jurisdiction (Schabas 2002:397). The Philippines reinforced that commitment in January 2008 when it voted in favor of a UN resolution calling for a worldwide moratorium on executions with an eye toward abolition.[41]

These international commitments suggest that another resurrection of capital punishment will be difficult to achieve. And domestically, the conver-sion of many Filipino leaders to an abolitionist position was the result not of ephemeral political calculations but of exposure to information about how capital punishment was actually administered during the 12 years R.A. 7659 was in force.

One other feature of this nation's recent history also argues against another reversal in death penalty policy. Despite term limits and the great political volatility in the Philippines, a small political elite remains in the corridors of legislative and executive power. Many of the political figures who will influence Philippine penal policy in the next decade have lived through and witnessed not only the two abolitions of the death penalty but also the bluster, ambivalence, and ultimate impotence of the era of R.A. 7659—when all the disadvantages of capital punishment were in evidence and none of the consistency and firmness suppor-ters had hoped would return with the executioner. This firsthand experience gives this generation of leaders little nostalgia for a return to the penal realities of 1994–2006, and there are few fantasies that different laws or different judges will change things. The nation's modern history has meant the death of most hopes that capital punishment could provide either justice or security.

The end of executions in the Philippines is not a major landmark of either national development or the achievement of domestic security. This is a

40. Another effort to reinstate capital punishment occurred in May 2008 when Senator Juan Miguel Zubiri called for its restoration following a bank robbery in Laguna that led to the deaths of nine people. Police officials called the robbery-killings "the work of the devil," and the Catholic bishop of Laguna said the perpetrators were "worse than animals," but in the face of resistance from the president, the Catholic Church, and Zubiri's colleagues in the Senate, his efforts gained little traction ("Bishops Thumb" 2008; "Palace Not Keen" 2008).

41. The government's commitment to abolition is also evident in the efforts President Arroyo has made to prevent the execution of Filipinos in other countries. In July 2008, Philippine officials disclosed that through Arroyo's personal intervention with foreign kings and heads of state, she had "saved some 24 overseas Filipino workers from execution" since 2006. At the same time, Senate president Manuel Villar Jr. said there were still 35 overseas Filipino workers, or OFWs, facing capital punishment in other countries, including 10 in Malaysia, 9 in Saudi Arabia, 4 in Kuwait, 2 in China, 1 in Brunei, and 1 in the United States ("Palace: GMA" 2008).

country with major problems of crime and violence and weak control of the armed forces and the police. In the wake of the 2006 abolition, there was satisfaction but no euphoria, and abolition this time around has generated no high expectations.

If the lessons learned have been internalized—as interviews with Senators Drilon and Gordon seem to suggest—then the Philippines' death penalty battle is over for good.[42] European support for the Philippine abolition may also help it to endure. The European Union "hailed the Philippine government for 'turning its back' on capital punishment," and the European Union says it "looks forward to close cooperation with the Philippines...to encourage countries who have not yet done so"—especially in Asia (Contreras 2006).[43] The Philippines could even become part of the transnational movement to export abolition to nations that still retain the death penalty, though we think such a turn is unlikely. As chapter 9 explains, the Philippines enjoys little prestige or moral authority among other Asian nations, and has few incentives to offer its neighbors as an inducement to abolish. The continued occurrence of extrajudicial killings and the salience of Filipino ambivalence about capital punishment also seem to make this nation an unlikely member of the anti–death penalty missionary movement for some time to come.

42. Some abolitionists in the Philippines are not as sanguine as we are. Jose Manuel Diokno, national chair of the Free Legal Assistance Group, has said that "the death penalty is not totally foreclosed . . . It could be returned in the future," and Congressman Edcel Lagman has said that since efforts to reinstate capital punishment continue, "At no moment must we lower our guard" (Burgonio 2008).

43. King Juan Carlos I of Spain also praised President Arroyo for the 2006 abolition, though he did not mention that Spanish national Francisco Larranaga was one of those she had spared from capital punishment (Uy 2007).

5 ∎

The Vanguard
Change in South Korea

> Capital punishment goes against the foundation of democracy.
> Democracy regards the life of a human being as the most
> cherished thing in the world, and to end a person's life even in
> the name of law clearly runs counter to the basic principle of
> human rights.
>
> —Kim Dae Jung (February 2006)

> Taiwan and South Korea, of course, have much in common
> regarding the development of the rule of law.... There are
> obviously important differences between the [PRC] on the one
> hand and Taiwan and South Korea, on the other—especially the
> huge discrepancies in population and political systems.
> Nevertheless, some Chinese experts acknowledge that, as the
> PRC charts the course of its future law reform, there is much to
> be learned from the experience of both jurisdictions. Why this is
> so is easy to understand... I urge... our government's support
> for research on the development of the rule of law in Taiwan and
> South Korea and its relevance to law reform in the PRC.
>
> —Jerome A. Cohen, "Law in Political Transitions" (2005)

On December 30, 1997, South Korean officials hanged 19 men and 4 women at
five different prison facilities.[1] As of this writing—more than ten years later—
those executions are the last South Korea has experienced. In the 30 years
before executions ceased, South Korea's average execution rate (0.83 per
million per year) was more than seven times higher than Japan's (0.11).

---

1. Between 1987, when South Korea launched its democratic reforms, and December 29
1997, 78 people were hanged, of whom only one was a woman (B. Cho 2008). It is unclear
why South Korean officials selected four women for execution on December 30, 1997. In the
United States between 1976 and February 2007, 1 percent of all executed persons (11 out of
1,064) were women (see Death Penalty Information Center, www.deathpenaltyinfo.org),
while in Japan, the last execution of a woman occurred in August 1997, when Nobuko
Hidaka was hanged from the Sapporo gallows (with her husband) after being convicted of
arson-homicide (Johnson 2005:268). From 1998 through 2007, Japan executed 35 men.

In the 126 months since South Korean executions ended, Japan has hanged 45 men.

Executions stopped when Kim Dae Jung, who had been sentenced to death for sedition in 1980 and had spent six years in prison and 30 years under house arrest or in exile, started a moratorium after becoming president in February 1998. The moratorium lasted through Kim's five-year term and continued through the presidency of his successor, Roh Moo Hyun, a human rights lawyer and a leader of the "June Struggle" against dictator Chun Doo Hwan in 1987. At the end of 2007, the nation became (by Amnesty International's ten-year standard) de facto abolitionist. In 2005, South Korea's National Human Rights Commission (a state-affiliated human rights organization created by Kim Dae Jung in 2001) recommended that capital punishment be abolished, and in 2006 the Ministry of Justice followed with an announcement that it would "thoroughly examine the possibility of abolishing the death penalty as part of efforts to set up a human rights-oriented penal system" (K. Cho 2008; see also "South Korea Close" 2006). In 1999, 2001, and 2004, bills seeking the abolition of capital punishment were considered in the National Assembly, and legislator Yoo Ihn Tae has attempted to introduce legislation that would abolish the death penalty every year since. Yoo himself was sentenced to death in the 1970s for violating South Korea's National Security Law by sympathizing with North Korea, and more than 60 percent of the members of the Assembly say they support his bill. When Yoo initiated a bill in 2005 he said, "Although hatred of [killers] is understandable, it cannot match the feeling of desperation of those wrongly convicted and sentenced to death" (Bae 2007:63). Sentiments such as this are widespread among Korean political elites, not least because many of them have been personally touched by capital punishment or political repression.

What distinguishes South Korea's progress toward abolition from that of regimes elsewhere in Asia and the world is not so much the sharp declines in state killing (remarkable though they are) as the purposeful efforts of state officials to end executions altogether. In Korea, one finds not a slow drying up of executions over a prolonged period of time, as in Japan, or an aspiration to end executions at some distant but undefined point in the future, as in China. Rather, what one sees is the desire to do away with capital punishment now, through an aggressive program of policy change aimed at that end, and driven partly by painful lessons from the recent past and by personal experiences with human rights abuses and state killing. In this sense, death penalty policy in South Korea has distinctly domestic fingerprints. As we shall show in this chapter and the next one on Taiwan, efforts to end the death penalty have also been responsive to changes in the international context.

Capital punishment must be reckoned a peripheral institution in many societies. One prominent analyst argues that even in the United States,

> For all its symbolic significance and moral weight, capital punishment is hardly a major institution in contemporary society. It plays no structural

role in social organization, creates few vested interests and—with the important though numerically small exception of the people on death row, their families, lawyers and custodians—shapes none of the routines of everyday life. . . . Compared to imprisonment, probation and parole . . . it is a sanction with a miniscule impact. . . . Its importance is political and symbolic, not social or structural, and so it is liable to be more open to change than are other, more essential institutions (Garland 2005:361; see also Garland 2007a; Garland 2007b).

In South Korea and Taiwan, too, capital punishment has been highly "open to change" during the development and democratization processes, and its importance in those societies has frequently been "political and symbolic." But the death penalty in Korea cannot be called a minor institution with "minuscule impact," for democratic transitions in both places have pivoted on the imperative of distancing the present from a past in which capital punishment was a familiar feature of law and politics. Yoo Ihn Tae stressed the crucial importance of "distancing" when he explained that "the reason I support the abolition of capital punishment is to put an end to the shameful past of Korea" (quoted in Hands Off Cain, July 15, 2004).

This chapter addresses two central questions. First, what explains the rapid decline of capital punishment in South Korea during the last decade and the purposeful pursuit of abolition there? And second, to what extent will South Korea become an Asian vanguard, leading other jurisdictions in the region on the road to life without the death penalty?[2] We believe the extraordinary death penalty developments in this nation have important implications for its retentionist neighbors.

■ "My President Is Not a Communist!": A Cautionary Tale

On June 17, 2005, David Johnson interviewed South Korean minister of justice Kim Seung Kyu at his office in Seoul. Minister Kim said he believed Kim Dae Jung did not deserve the death sentence he received for allegedly

---

2. We focus on South Korea—population 49 million, and one of only three nations in the Organisation for Economic Co-operation and Development that retains capital punishment—instead of North Korea (population 23 million) for two main reasons. First, economic development and political democratization in the South (the Republic of Korea) make it a more instructive case for understanding the present and future of capital punishment in other Asian societies than would an analysis of the "horrible weirdness" in North Korea (the Democratic People's Republic of Korea). Second, reliable information about state killing in North Korea—a country that has been called a "hermit kingdom" and a "kingdom of lies"—is hard to come by (Cumings 1997:433; Gourevitch 2003:57,64). But the literature on North Korea does support several general assertions about capital punishment during the dynasty of Kim Il Sung and his son and successor Kim Jong Il. See appendix A.

leading the Kwangju uprising in 1980. "KDJ was merely an arch-rival of [President Chun Doo Hwan's] ruling party," Kim explained. "Bitter history such as that has made me and many South Koreans prudent about using the death penalty." Unlike most previous ministers—all of whom possessed the legal authority to authorize executions—Minister Kim was not an elected politician; he was a retired prosecutor (and an elder in the Presbyterian Church) who would go on to become head of the powerful Korean Central Intelligence Agency (KCIA), the same organization that kidnapped Kim Dae Jung from a Japanese hotel in 1973 and almost killed him on the return trip to Seoul.

When the subject of the interview turned toward death penalty trends in the contemporary world, Johnson could have been more prudent with the wording of a question that was prefaced with a description of the repetitive pattern of abolition in Europe. After noting that the death penalty in European nations had frequently disappeared when an authoritarian regime fell or a "left-liberal" party took power, Johnson observed: "It is interesting, and familiar too, that South Korea stopped executions when a left-liberal president [Kim Dae Jung] was elected, and it seems significant too, that the moratorium has continued under his left-liberal successor, President Roh Moo Hyun." Minister Kim fiddled with Johnson's name card while this statement was being translated and then gave a long and impassioned reply—perhaps ten sentences in all—which was reduced in translation to these six words: "My President is not a communist!"[3]

Johnson's encounter with Minister Kim Seung Kyu is telling in at least three respects. First, it reveals how much Korea's North-South division colors Korean politics and perceptions while at the same time illustrating how frames derived from other contexts (a "left-liberal" president) can get transformed ("he is not a communist!") when they are applied to this divided peninsula. Second, the interview of Kim shows that even some conservative officials have come to conclude that previous South Korean leaders frequently misused the death penalty in pursuit of political objectives. Minister Kim was no bleeding-heart liberal; he was a staunch death penalty supporter who spent most of his working life in one of the nation's most conservative organizations (the procuracy) and who would go on to pilot another (the KCIA) that was at least as ideologically mossback. Third, Kim's comments illustrate how much the politics of capital punishment in contemporary South Korea have been driven by "bitter" personal experiences with the ultimate sanction. The next section shows that the connection between the personal and the political is a pervasive contemporary reality.

3. Afterward, a senior prosecutor who attended the interview said that Minister Kim was "very troubled" by Johnson's "left-liberal" characterization of presidents Kim and Roh, while the translator said she was asked to omit the rest of the minister's response to that unfortunate formulation.

■ Politics and Punishment

The South Korean moratorium on executions initiated by President Kim Dae Jung in 1998 may have been motivated by personal experience. In the presidential election of 1971, Kim nearly defeated the incumbent, Park Chung Hee, despite massive vote buying by the incumbent. Though there were no elections in the 1970s after that, Kim continued to attract the attention of conservative Korean leaders. As Bruce Cumings summed it up, Kim

> was run over by a truck in 1971, kidnapped [by the KCIA] in 1973 [and nearly murdered], put under house arrest until 1979, indicted in 1980 [for treason] on trumped-up charges of having fomented the Kwangju Rebellion[4] and nearly executed until the Carter and Reagan administrations (one leaving, one incoming) jointly intervened in late 1980,[5] exiled to the United States in 1982, returned to house arrest again in 1985, and finally able to run in the 1987 direct presidential elections, only to lose when the opposition once again split and Kim Young Sam ran against him, thus electing Roh Tae Woo with a little over one-third of the vote. Kim's [charismatic power and] mass appeal sharply transformed Korea's pattern of authoritarianism and elite democracy, and he may yet become president of the Republic of Korea, assuming that elections remain direct and free. (Cumings 1997:361)

This prediction proved prescient: presidential elections did remain direct and free, and when Kim—a devout Catholic—entered the Blue House in 1998 he fulfilled his campaign promise to halt executions. This was less than two years after South Korea's strong and relatively independent Constitutional

---

4. By Kim Dae Jung's own account, he survived three "brushes with death" in addition to the Kwangju death sentence. The first was his imprisonment by the communists in the Korean War, during which 140 of 220 coprisoners were killed by the North Koreans (Kim 1987:186,321).

5. In 1980, President Chun Doo Hwan commuted Kim's death sentence to life imprisonment, largely because of international pressures on Chun. In a speech to the French Foreign Ministry in 2000, President Kim expressed his gratitude to late president François Mitterrand and Prime Minister Lionel Jospin for leading "an international movement" to save his life (Hands Off Cain, March 7, 2000). Similarly, while the United States failed to stop Chun's Kwangju massacre even though it probably could have, it did help stop Kim's execution. Chun had planned to execute Kim before Ronald Reagan's inauguration, but late in 1980, after Reagan's incoming national security advisor met with outgoing officials from Jimmy Carter's administration, the Americans agreed to offer Chun a state visit in exchange for commuting Kim's death sentence. The deal was never made public, but Chun was the first foreign head of state to visit President Reagan (Breen 2004:211).

Court had ruled that capital punishment was constitutional (Ginsburg 2003; K. Cho 2008).

As president, Kim reflected his extensive personal history with the death penalty not only by halting executions but also by reviewing individual death sentences, eventually commuting 13 (to life imprisonment, which in Korea usually means eligibility for parole after 25 years).[6] Kim Dae Jung was hardly the only South Korean president to be on the receiving end of the state's power to punish. Indeed, there may be no other nation in the modern world in which so many top leaders have been so directly touched by capital punishment. In addition to Kim Dae Jung and Chun Doo Hwan (who was sentenced to death after he left office), President Park Chung Hee, the most "towering figure" in South Korean history, received a death sentence in 1948 for his part in leading a revolt of junior army officers (Breen 2004:135). More generally, since Syngman Rhee took control of the southern part of a divided Korea in 1948, all of the major figures who held the Republic of Korea (ROK) presidency knew what it was like to be condemned to death (either before or after their presidencies) or to be arrested and imprisoned. Notably, all of their capital troubles stemmed from their real or alleged involvement in conflicts over national security issues. As the eighteenth-century English essayist Samuel Johnson said, "The realization that one is to be hanged in the morning concentrates the mind wonderfully." In South Korea, the realization that one had almost been hanged had a similarly concentrating effect on the views of capital punishment of several top leaders. See table 5.1.

More than half of the people executed between the founding of South Korea in 1948 and the election of President Roh Tae Woo in 1987 were condemned to death for violating the National Security Law, which "embraces every aspect of political, social, and artistic life" and under which any person who encourages or praises "antistate activities" can be criminally prosecuted (Cumings 1997:391). The law defines North Korea as an "antistate organization," and suspected sympathy or affiliation with it accounts for more than 400

---

6. Executive clemency is much more frequent in South Korea than in Japan or the United States (Sarat 2005; Johnson 2006c). In addition to commuting the capital sentences of 13 of the more than 50 inmates then on death row, President Kim Dae Jung pardoned more than 30,000 convicts and freed 3,586 prisoners in August 2000 (Hands Off Cain 2000). And at Kim's inauguration in 1998, "an amazing 5 million cases" received amnesty in a political gesture aimed at demonstrating the president's "leniency to 'victims' of the previous administration" of Kim Young Sam (Breen 2004:227). In February 2007, President Roh Moo Hyun pardoned 434 persons, including Kim's son and the son of former president Kim Young Sam (Kim Tong-hyung 2007). Although such acts of mercy are welcomed by many South Koreans, they also reflect what has long been a "main source of human rights abuse" in South Korea: "the domination of the legislature and judiciary by the executive branch" (Breen 2004:224).

Table 5.1
Presidents and punishment in South Korea, 1948–2008

President*	Personal experience with punishment
Syngman Rhee, 1948–1960	Arrested in 1897 for demonstrating against the monarchy and Japanese designs on Korea, tortured, and imprisoned from 1897 to 1904. Saved from a lynch mob in 1960 by the U.S. Central Intelligence Agency; died in exile in Honolulu in 1965.
Park Chung Hee, 1961–1979	Received death sentence in 1948 for leading a revolt of junior army officers. Murdered by the director of the Korean Central Intelligence Agency in 1979.
Chun Doo Hwan, 1980–1988	Received a death sentence in 1996 for treason, mutiny, murder, and corruption; reduced on appeal to life imprisonment; pardoned in 1997 by outgoing president Kim Young Sam and incoming president Kim Dae Jung.
Roh Tae Woo, 1988–1993	Received a life sentence in 1996 for treason, mutiny, and corruption; reduced on appeal to 17 years imprisonment; pardoned in 1997 by outgoing president Kim Young Sam and incoming president Kim Dae Jung.
Kim Young Sam, 1993–1998	Longtime opponent of authoritarian governments. Expelled from the National Assembly in 1979 and banned from politics 1980–1985.
Kim Dae Jung, 1998–2003	Kidnapped by the KCIA and almost murdered in 1973. Banned from politics and imprisoned in 1976, reduced to house arrest in 1978, reinstated in 1979. Sentenced to death for treason in 1980, commuted to 20 years in prison, then exiled to the United States; arrested again on return to Seoul in 1985.
Roh Moo Hyun, 2003–2008	Human rights lawyer who defended students. Prosecuted under the National Security Law. Helped lead the 1987 June Struggle against Chun Doo Hwan. Jailed for three weeks in September 1987 for abetting striking workers.

* Omitted: Yun Po Sun (1960–1962), who was controlled by Park Chung Hee, and Choe Kyu Ha (1979–1980), who was interim president for eight months after Park's murder.

of South Korea's hangings in the 30-year period after the nation was divided.[7]

"Antistate activities" have long ranked among Korea's most salient capital crimes. While data on rates of execution cannot be found for most of the period before 1945, the record does show that the death penalty was a fairly consistent feature of criminal justice and state control throughout (Yi 2001;

7. In the first full year after the enactment of the National Security Law in 1948, 188,621 people were arrested. The law has been revised several times since and has also been supplemented on numerous occasions with other national security laws and executive directives (Park 1993:10,15). In 1989, President Roh Tae Woo was still arresting dissidents under the law at the rate of 3.3 per day, for a total of about 1,200 for the year (Cumings

B. Cho 2008). The historical record also contains more evidence about conflict and executions among nobles than about punishment and control of the masses, and the narratives from history emphasize the extensive variation in leadership style between gentle and harsh rulers. The archetype of a gentle king in the early Choson period is Sejong (Cumings 1997:64), while Sejo and the aptly named Yonsan the Obscene represent the more violent cycles in early Korean administration (Breen 2004:92). The half century of Japanese rule after the *kabo* reforms of 1894 did not generate precise records of the incidence of or reasons for execution, but the general impression of harshness in Korea under Japanese rule contrasts with the relatively low level of execution in Japan during the late 19th and early 20th centuries (Duus 1998; Breen 2004:113; Dudden 2004; Botsman 2005:225; Lankov 2007a; see also chapter 3). In Taiwan, too, punishment of Japan's colonial subjects was much harsher than was punishment in domestic Japan (Roy 2003). From 1899 through 1901, for example, 2,616 Taiwanese were hanged, for an annual execution rate that was 367 times higher than the rate in the Japanese homeland (Botsman 2005:206).

The history of Korea prior to Japanese occupation suggests that the use of capital punishment was closely connected to elite interests and their concerns about national security. The use of capital punishment in the most recent authoritarian period—from the presidency of Syngman Rhee (1948–1961) and the prelude to the Korean War (1950–1953) until the democratic explosion of June 1987 led to direct presidential elections in December of that year—frequently reflected similar concerns about regime needs and national security.

1997:390). As of 1999, when "the world's longest-serving political prisoner" was released from jail after 40 years of confinement, South Korea still had more than 200 persons incarcerated for violations of the National Security Law. Woo Yong Gak, the Rip Van Winkle who was released in 1999, remained "a dedicated North Korean Communist" even after his release, perhaps because while in confinement he watched 12 of his friends die by torture (Kristof 1999). Similarly, Kim Song-myong, who was released in 1995 at the age of 73 after 44 years in prison, remained unrepentant. His jailers had tortured him and threatened him with execution and had executed his father and his sister in an effort to get him to confess (Cumings 1997:392). In January 2006, South Korea's National Human Rights Commission recommended abolishing the National Security Law (and capital punishment as well), something the U.S. State Department had urged 12 years earlier. But when the Ministry of Justice revealed its "roadmap for human rights protection" in 2007, it deferred action by saying "it is desirable to decide on the matter through national consensus after reviewing the related laws" ("Gov't Proposes" 2007). In 1997, historian Bruce Cumings called South Korea "a relatively industrialized, relatively democratic country" but also asked whether "we can dignify with the word 'democracy' a regime that continues to" incarcerate and attempt the conversion of political dissidents (Cumings 1997:16,393).

■ War and the Prelude to War: 1945–1953

The key context for the establishment of separate Korean governments in 1948 was "not in the realm of political parties" but in "the social and political conflict between left and right" that occurred throughout the peninsula after the Japanese occupation ended in 1945 (Cumings 1997:217). One prominent feature of that conflict was the use of "people's courts" to try and to execute landlords, policemen, and other government officials, especially those deemed to have collaborated with the Japanese. In places such as Cheju and Yosu, the left's revolutionary terror resulted in the lynching of hundreds. Similarly, after the incident at Ongjin sparked the Korean War (1950–1953), which resulted in a civilian death toll of two to three million, leftist guerrillas frequently assaulted the police. Police responses were brutal, too. Captured guerrillas were returned to their home villages and tortured for information, and then they were shot and tied to trees as object lessons. When North Korea's 1950 offensive pushed toward Pusan in the southeast, "people's committees" confiscated Japanese and ROK property and left the administration of justice to local people, many just released from Syngman Rhee's prisons. The result was a "reign of terror against their former antagonists, mostly in the police and youth groups" (269). North Korean soldiers also executed hundreds of American prisoners of war, usually through the "humane" method that was then customary: a single bullet behind the ear.

South Korea carried out many thousands of its own wartime executions. According to a "very conservative" estimate made by an historian on the country's Truth and Reconciliation Commission, over several weeks in a "summer of terror" in 1950, South Korean police and soldiers executed "at least 100,000 people" in a South Korean population of 20 million, and "the true toll may be twice that or more" (Hanley and Chang 2008). In three July days, for example, police killed 4,000–7,000 political prisoners in a village near the central city of Taejon. The victims were trucked in, decapitated by swords or shot in the head, and then stacked on top of each other "like sardines" (Cumings 1997:273; Cumings 2008). Twenty eye-witnesses said they saw two jeep-loads of American officers watch the killings. American and South Korean officials denied this atrocity, but later that month the head of the ROK national police acknowledged that those under him had executed 1,200 suspected communists during the first three weeks of the war. When the South occupied the North later in 1950, "newspapers all over the world reported eyewitness accounts of ROK executions of people under detention," including many women and children judged culpable because they were related to real and suspected "Reds" (Cumings 1997:282).

At the end of 1949, six months before the Korean War started, 80 percent of all South Korean court cases were against suspected communists, 30,000 political prisoners were locked up in President Syngman Rhee's jails, and 70,000 more were held in "guidance camps" because they could not be contained in the overcrowded prisons (Cumings 1997:223).[8] During "extermination weeks" in December 1949, up to 1,000 people a day were arrested and detained. The United States was tacitly supportive of and complicit in much of this repression, not least because American leaders, like the South Korean president himself (who relied on a kitchen cabinet of American advisors), thought harsh controls were necessary given the threat posed by the northern regime.[9] By the time the war ended in July 1953, at least 7 percent of the combined population of North and South had been killed, almost everything in northern and central Korea had been leveled, and many Koreans were living in caves and underground. Today, 10 million of the 70 million Koreans who live in the two countries are from families that were split by the war. One of the biggest tragedies of this "virtual holocaust" is that it solved little. The armistice merely marked the restoration of the status quo ante, and the tensions and problems that emerged after liberation from the Japanese continue to plague both halves of the divided nation today.

■ Syngman Rhee and Park Chung Hee: 1948–1979

South Korea's postwar industrialization resulted in one of the most highly touted economic success stories in the world—the "Korean model" of state-directed development without democratization that has been adopted and adapted in the PRC and in parts of Southeast Asia (Cumings 1997:325; Peerenboom 2007). But of course this model of development has several authoritarian dark sides. In particular, the first three decades after the South Korean state was founded were thick with violence, including considerable state killing, judicial and extrajudicial. At the same time, South Korea's

---

8. Comparison helps reveal how repressive Rhee's regime was. In 1949, the rate of incarceration of political prisoners (480 per 100,000) in South Korea was about the same as a mid-1990s estimate of North Korea's total incarceration rate (Cumings 1997:398), and about 50 percent higher than an estimate for North Korea that was made a few years later (Kang and Rigoulot 2001:xxiv). South Korea's rate of incarceration of political prisoners in 1949 was almost identical to the overall incarceration rate in 2000 for the United States, a country that imprisons people at four times the world average (Beck and Harrison 2001; Hartney 2006).

9. Although North Korea's regime has long been harshly repressive, it may not have killed its domestic enemies on a scale comparable to the slaughters undertaken by leftist regimes in China, Vietnam, and the former Soviet Union (Cumings 1997:232). In Bruce Cumings's comparison of political violence in both halves of the divided peninsula, "neither North nor South had qualms about using violence for political ends, but the North tended to be more discriminating, in part because its enemies were numerically small classes and groups, and also because of a political practice, perhaps growing out of the Korean leadership's experience with Chinese communism, of seeking to reeducate and reform political recalcitrants" (231).

democracy today has antecedents that long precede the democratic explosion of 1987. The long struggle in South Korea suggests that "democracy is not a gift or a political regime that one is born with but something that must be fought for every inch of the way, in every society" (Cumings 1997:339). If democracy and civil society now seem more vibrant in South Korea than in contemporary Japan, as some commentators contend (Diamond, Shin, and Sin 1999; Kim 2000), the difference partly reflects the fact that Koreans had to struggle for democratic change, whereas the democracy that emerged out of occupied Japan was in many respects the result of America's attempt to impose a "democratic revolution from above" (Dower 1999:65; Kim 2000). When Kim Dae Jung became ROK president in 1998, the struggle for Korean democracy and for controls on executive power culminated in a renunciation of capital punishment that has not occurred in Japan but has in Taiwan, the other Asian vanguard (see chapter 6). The next several pages discuss some of the actors and events that led to South Korea's about-face with the death penalty.

Syngman Rhee and Park Chung Hee were two of the most towering figures in South Korean history. Like succeeding presidents, both directly experienced the harshness of Korean criminal justice (see table 5.1). One of Rhee's biographers has said that "few heads in international politics have been battered longer or harder than his" (Oliver 1951:131). Rhee spent 41 years in exile with a price on his head and seven years in prison, beginning in 1897. For seven months of that incarceration, his feet were in stocks, his hands were cuffed, and his head was locked in place. He was beaten with rods, and his arms were wrapped with oily paper and set on fire. The same biographer said Rhee's fingers "were so horribly mashed that even today, in times of stress, he blows upon them" (133). Park, the son of a peasant rebel, took power in a bloodless coup in 1961, barely a year after Rhee was driven from office by student protests over brutality and ballot stuffing in a presidential election. As noted, Park was sentenced to death in 1948 (and later pardoned) for his role in a revolt of junior army officers. He went on to become the most popular leader in postwar South Korea (as 70 percent of Koreans said in a 1994 poll), a right-wing ruler almost brutally obsessed with economic growth who, early in his career, had decided to side with the political left after his brother had been killed by police during a communist-led uprising in Taegu (Breen 2004:135). Park hated the Rhee government, not only because of his own death sentence but also because of what he perceived to be its corruption and overdependence on the United States. Some Korean analysts have called Park an "emotional communist" because he so strongly desired to achieve Korean independence from both Japan and the United States. On this view, Park's long-term goal was *juche* (self-reliance), albeit by a different route from that taken by Kim Il Sung and Kim Jong Il in the North (136).

The North-South conflict colored the use of capital punishment in both the Rhee and Park regimes. According to the U.S. Central Intelligence Agency, Rhee possessed "an absolute and uncompromising" fear and hatred of communism (quoted in Cumings 1997:340), and Park acquired similarly reactionary reflexes. Their fear and hatred of the left translated into the frequent use of totalitarian tactics—police terrorism, strict censorship, brainwashing, and extrajudicial killing—in addition to a more aggressive policy of capital punishment than was employed by any of their successors.[10] Figure 5.1 and table 5.2 express South Korea's postwar execution patterns in two overlapping ways. Figure 5.1 shows judicial executions from 1911, the year after Japan annexed Korea, through 2007, the most recent year for which information is available. Executions declined during the 35 years of Japan's colonial rule, from an average of 52.7 per year in the 1910s to 26.8 per year in the 1920s, to 20.1 per year in the 1930s, to 15.0 per year in the first half of the 1940s. Despite this decline, the execution rate in occupied Korea remained three to four times higher than that in Japan.

After Japan's surrender in 1945, the highest peak for judicial executions occurred immediately before and during the start of the Korean War. Indeed, more executions occurred in the two years of 1949 and 1950 (578) than in the next 15 years combined. After that, executions declined, from an annual average of 88.6 per year in the 1950s to 19.6 per year in the 1960s and 18.9 per year in the 1970s.

After the 1950s, the next peak occurred in the early 1970s, when Park Chung Hee instituted martial law, declared himself president for life, ordered the KCIA to hunt suspected leftists throughout the country, and proclaimed his "Yushin system" of economic development, which was modeled on colonial Japan's "military-backed forced-pace industrialization" in Manchuria (Cumings 1997:311).[11] In 1972, 20 out of 34 executions (59 percent) were for violations of the National Security Law, as were 19 of 58 executions (33 percent) in 1974.[12] In 1974, the peak year for executions after 1956, George Ogle, an

10. In 1949, Rhee's government created a special body called the Union for the Guidance and Protection of the People (UGPP) in order to "reeducate" suspected communist sympathizers. By early 1950, the UGPP had more than 300,000 members. They were subjected to intense brainwashing, required to deliver regular penitence speeches, and obligated to report those who had not yet seen the greatness of the "free world" and the "crimes of communism." But "only a fraction" of UGPP members were actual communist sympathizers (Lankov 2007b). After North Korean troops began their southward march in June 1950, Rhee's regime decided to round up UGPP members and summarily execute them. The statistics are spotty, but best estimates suggest that at least 10,000 UGPP members were executed during the last half of 1950. Thus, many people who signed applications for the UGPP "unwittingly signed their own death sentence."

11. Park has been called an "economic warrior" and "a nation-builder with few peers in the modern world" (Clifford 1994:29).

12. Figure 5.1 and table 5.2 show no executions for 1975, but at least eight persons were executed that year following military court-martials (in the Inhyok-dang case). Although execution figures are missing for 1944–1946, a Ministry of Justice report issued in 2001 stated that Korea had 732 executions between liberation from Japan in August 1945 and the founding of the Republic of Korea in August 1948—an annual average of 244 executions for that three-year period (Hands Off Cain 2001).

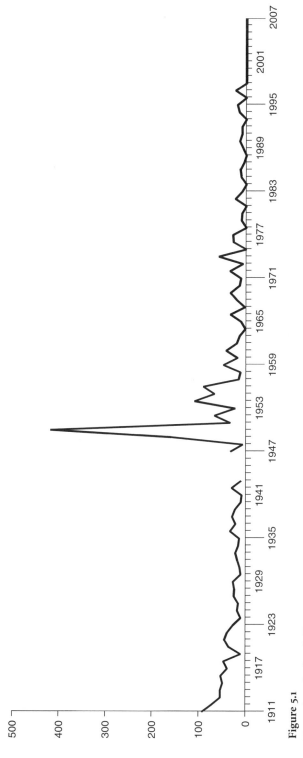

Figure 5.1
Executions in South Korea, 1911–2007
Source: B. Cho 2008.

Table 5.2
Executions in South Korea, 1945–2007

Years	Government[1]	Executions	Annual average Executions per year[2]	Execution rate	Percent NSL[3]
1945–1948	American military[4]	732	244.0	13.0	N/A
1948–1961	President Syngman Rhee	1,105	81.9	3.5	67.1
1962–1969	President Park Chung Hee	136	17.0	0.6	34.0
1970–1979	President Park Chung Hee	189	18.9	0.5	29.6
1980–1987	President Chun Doo Hwan	70	8.8	0.2	15.7
1988–1992	President Roh Tae Woo	39	7.8	0.2	0.0
1993–1997	President Kim Young Sam	57	11.4	0.3	0.0
1998–2002	President Kim Dae Jung	0	0.0	0.0	0.0
2003–2007	President Roh Moo Hyun	0	0.0	0.0	0.0

Sources: Han 2001; Hands Off Cain 2001; B. Cho 2008.

[1] Omitted: presidents Yun Po Sun (1960–1962) and Choe Kyu Ha (1979–1980) (see note for table 5.1). President Syngman Rhee left office April 26, 1960.
[2] The execution rate is expressed as the annual average number of executions per million population, based on the national population at the midpoint of the corresponding period of time. There were no executions in 1975, 1978, 1981, 1984, 1988, 1993, and 1996. Thus, since the presidency of Chun Doo Hwan, there have been no executions in the first year of every presidential term, a pattern Cho Byung Sun (2008) attributes to the perception that "execution could ruin the holy power" of a king or government.
[3] Percentage of all executions that were for violations of the National Security Law and related anticommunist laws.
[4] The American military government lasted from Korea's liberation from Japan until the founding of the Republic of Korea.

American Methodist missionary and labor rights activist, was taken to a place called South Mountain, where the KCIA conducted its most important interrogations and tortures.[13] Ogle was deemed an enemy of South Korean national

13. In 1974, in the midst of student protests that were critical of Park's authoritarian regime, Emergency Decree No. 4 also threatened students who cut classes with capital punishment. It is said that attendance improved considerably (Jerome Cohen, New York University professor of law, interview by Johnson and Zimring, January 25, 2008).

security because he had tried to defend eight men about to be executed for treason as socialists. The language used by the KCIA official who interrogated Ogle articulates some of the most salient assumptions held by members of the Park and Rhee regimes. After insisting that one of the eight condemned men must be a communist because he listened to North Korean radio and took notes on Kim Il Sung's speech, the interrogator screamed in Ogle's face: "These men are our enemies. We have got to kill them. This is war. In war even Christians pull the trigger and kill their enemies. If we don't kill them, they will kill us. We will kill them!"

George Ogle was deported in 1974. A year later, on April 9, 1975, the eight men he had attempted to help were hanged, 18 hours after the Supreme Court finalized the death sentences a military tribunal had imposed on them for forming a pro–North Korea political party that aimed to overthrow Park's government. In a 2007 retrial, the Seoul Central District Court acquitted all eight, holding that their confessions had been coerced through torture and finding that there was "no evidence to support the prosecution's claim" of guilt ("Court Clears" 2007). An earlier investigation by the National Intelligence Service concluded that its predecessor, the KCIA, had framed the members of this so-called Inhyok-dang (People's Revolutionary Party) on the orders of President Park, at a time when activists and college students were demonstrating against his dictatorship (B. Cho 2008; K. Cho 2008).

Table 5.2 gives execution summaries for the years from 1945 to 2007, broken down into nine political periods. It depicts three large execution drops during the authoritarian years, followed by another that led to the moratorium under presidents Kim Dae Jung and Roh Moo Hyun. The first was a 73 percent decline in the per capita execution rate from the period of American military government (1945–1948) to the period of Syngman Rhee's rule. Before Korea obtained independence on August 15, 1948, America's postwar military government used and condoned the use of capital punishment much more often in Korea than it did in occupied Japan.[14]

The second Korean drop was an 83 percent decline in the execution rate from the Rhee years (1948–1960) to the Park decades of the 1960s and 1970s. In significant part, this decline reflects the decreased use of the death penalty to punish violators of the National Security Law and related anticommunist statutes. As the last column in table 5.2 shows, about two-thirds of all executions in 1948–1961 were for "Red" violations, while the proportion dropped to less than one-third for the rest of the 1960s and the 1970s, and to 16 percent during the last dictatorship, that of Chun Doo Hwan (1980–1987). Since Chun,

---

14. It is unclear why American officials were keener on capital punishment in Korea than in Japan during the first few years after 1945, but the difference may reflect the fact that in Japan the military conflict had already ended, while in Korea there was considerable uncertainty and anxiety about how events on the peninsula would unfold.

the National Security Law has remained in force but there have been no executions for its violation.[15]

The third execution drop during the authoritarian years was the 64 percent decline in the execution rate from the 1960s and 1970s (the Park years) to the Chun years (1980–1987). Chun was removed by the democratic uprising of 1987. The next two presidents were Roh Tae Woo, Chun's high school class-mate and a military general who was elected to a five-year term in December 1987 when Kim Young Sam and Kim Dae Jung split the opposition vote, and Kim Young Sam, who served as president from 1993 to 1997. Both Roh and Kim Young Sam presided over administrations that continued to use executions at about the same rate as Chun's regime had, though there was a modest increase in the yearly rate of executions from the Chun and Roh regimes to Kim Young Sam, South Korea's first civilian president. As noted earlier, executions ceased when Kim Dae Jung became president in 1998, and that moratorium continued during President Roh Moo Hyun's administration. In these two administrations, there were ministers of justice who personally supported capital punishment but never signed death warrants because executions con-tradicted the president's policy.

Another striking feature of the distribution of executions in Korea is their lumpiness, as is clearly shown in figure 5.1, where years with many are interrupted by years with few or none at all. About one-quarter of the years between 1975 and the onset of the moratorium in 1998 had no executions, while in the years that executions did occur the average number was 14. This contrasts with Japan, where—except for the 40-month moratorium of 1989–1993—the Ministry of Justice has tried to ensure that at least one execution takes place each year.

Unlike the sharp peaks and valleys of executions, figure 5.2 shows a long and relatively smooth decline in death sentences from 1960 to 2005. Except for a small reversal from the Chun Doo Hwan years to the years of his successor Roh Tae Woo, South Korea's death sentence rate steadily decreased from the time of President Park, under whom district courts produced more than 0.80 death sentences per million, until the moratorium administrations of Kim Dae Jung (0.31) and Roh Moo Hyun (0.13). This decline is especially notable because South Korea's pool of potentially capital cases (which has consisted almost exclusively of homicide cases since the democratic revolution of 1987) rose rapidly during the same period, from an annual average of 287 homicide defendants for 1964–1969, to 417 for 1970–1979, to 489 for 1980–1987, to 648 for 1988–1997, and to 815 for 1998–2005. Thus, homicide trials and convictions nearly tripled during four decades in which the population did not even double, and yet the death sentence rate fell by nearly 85 percent (B. Cho 2008). The drop has been especially steep in the most recent years. In the 10 years from 1993–1996 to 2003–2006, the

15. The last year a death sentence was imposed for violating the National Security Law was 1990, the third year of Roh Tae Woo's presidency.

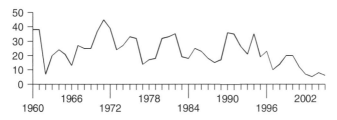

Figure 5.2
Death sentences in South Korea, 1960–2005
Source: B. Cho 2008.

total number of trial court death sentences fell from 108 to 25—a 77 percent decline (K. Cho 2008:14).

There has also been a significant change in the frequency of death sentences for violating the National Security Law. Between 1960 and 2005, 13.6 percent of all death sentences were imposed for such violations, approximately 85 percent of them during the reign of Park Chung Hee. During the nearly two decades of Park's presidency, almost a quarter of all death sentences were given to National Security Law offenders. The peak years were 1971 and 1972, when Park declared martial law and himself president for life (B. Cho 2008).

Since South Korea's democratic revolution in 1987, 90 percent of all first-instance death sentences have been imposed for the crimes of homicide or robbery-homicide.[16] This, too, reflects the movement away from using the death penalty as a tool of political repression. Most of the rest of the post-1987 death sentences were imposed under the Aggravated Punishment of Specified Crimes Act, which enhanced penalties for a variety of offenses (B. Cho 2008). Since Korea's democratic turn, the death penalty has become a sanction almost exclusively reserved for homicide offenders, and even for homicide, Korean courts have become increasingly reluctant to impose capital sentences. District courts became even more reluctant to impose death sentences after the moratorium on executions began in 1998. In the ten years before then (1988–1997), district courts issued an average of 23.7 death sentences per year, about

16. The 1995 revision to the 1950 Penal Code significantly reduced the scope of crimes subject to capital punishment. At present, however, 15 death penalty provisions remain in the Penal Code, in addition to 98 death penalty provisions in 20 other laws, for a total of 113 death penalty provisions in 21 laws. The total number of capital offenses in South Korea is about 160, of which 26 involve homicide, though in practice the vast majority of death sentences and executions are for homicide crimes (B. Cho 2008; K. Cho 2008). One recent exception to this general pattern is the death sentence the Cheongju District Court imposed on a 30-year-old man after he was convicted of committing 37 sexual assaults, including the rape of a mother in front of her daughter and the rape of a woman in front of her sister. "Since such crimes can be committed only by those who are a man in appearance but a brute in mind," the court said, "it is necessary to purge the accused permanently from society. " The court also stated that it needed to "dispel public fears" following "a series of high-profile sex crimes that rocked the nation" (quoted in Hands Off Cain, April 27, 2006).

Table 5.3

Death sentences in South Korea by president, 1960–2005 (courts of first instance)

Years	President[1]	Death sentences	Death sentences per year[2]	Death sentences rate[3]	Percent NSL[4]
1960–1969	Park Chung Hee	238	23.8	0.84	18.5
1970–1979	Park Chung Hee	286	28.6	0.81	27.0
1980–1987	Chun Doo Hwan	188	23.5	0.58	10.1
1988–1992	Roh Tae Woo	129	25.8	0.60	1.6
1993–1997	Kim Young Sam	108	21.6	0.48	0.0
1998–2002	Kim Dae Jung	73	14.6	0.31	0.0
2003–2005	Roh Moo Hyun	19	6.3	0.13	0.0
1960–2005	Total	1,041	22.6	N/A	13.6

Source: B. Cho 2008.

[1] Omitted (as from tables 5.1 and 5.2): President Yun Po Sun (1960–1962) and Choe Kyu Ha (1979–1980).

[2] Annual death sentence numbers are available only for the years since 1960.

[3] Death sentence rates are expressed as annual averages per million population, based on the national population at the midpoint of the corresponding period of time.

[4] Percentage of all death sentences that were imposed for violations of the National Security Law and related anticommunist laws. Between 1960 and 2005, approximately 90 percent of the death sentences imposed for violating the National Security Law occurred during the Park decades of the 1960s and 1970s.

one death sentence for every 27 homicide trials. Between 1998 and 2005, by contrast, district courts imposed 11.5 death sentences per year—only one death sentence for every 71 homicide trials. Per homicide trial, there were more than two and one half times more death sentences in the decade before the moratorium than in the decade afterward.

Table 5.4 summarizes death sentence reversal rates (the percentage of capital appeals in which a death sentence was reduced to some sentence less than death) for South Korea's Supreme Court and its five high courts. Two patterns stand out. First, the Supreme Court has rarely changed a death sentence to something less than death, doing so for only 17 of the 497 capital sentences (3.4 percent) it reviewed in 1970–2005, and with no increase in the likelihood of a sentence reduction over that period of time. As in the United States, capital prosecutors in South Korea try to prove the existence of one or more aggravating factors, while defense attorneys offer mitigating factors. Table 5.4 suggests that Korea's Supreme Court usually leaves it to the high courts to supervise how these factors are weighed at the trial level, though the Court has repeatedly emphasized that death "should be an extremely exceptional punishment" (decisions of June 13, 2003, and September 3, 2004). The Supreme Court's attitude "has made trial and appeal courts very cautious in imposing or affirming the death penalty," much as the Indian Supreme Court's "rarest of the rare" doctrine has in the Indian context (K. Cho 2008:16; see appendix F). Second, South Korean high courts have shown a remarkable increase in their propensity to reduce a death sentence to something less. From 1964 to 1969—a period of rapid economic growth and comparative political stability—high courts did not reduce a single

Table 5.4
Death sentence reversals in Supreme Court and high courts,
South Korea, 1964–2005

	Reviewed	*Reversed*	*Percent reversed*
Supreme Court (1970–2005)	497	17	3.4%
High courts (1964–2005)	770	402	52.2%
1964–1969	69 (11.5/year)	0	0.0%
1970–1979	268 (26.8/year)	129	48.1%
1980–1987	162 (20.3/year)	99	61.1%
1988–1997	209 (20.9/year)	131	62.7%
1998–2005	62 (7.8/year)	43	69.4%
High court reversals, by president			
Park Chung Hee (1964–1979)	337	129	38.3%
Chun Doo Hwan (1980–1987)	162	99	61.1%
Roh Tae Woo (1988–1992)	113	73	64.6%
Kim Young Sam (1993–1997)	96	58	60.4%
Kim Dae Jung (1998–2002)	46	32	69.6%
Roh Moo Hyun (2003–2005)	16	11	68.8%

Source: B. Cho 2008.

Note: In 1975–1980, high courts changed nine prison sentences to death sentences, and the Supreme Court did so once in 1982.

death sentence, but during the administration of Kim Dae Jung 20 years later (1998–2002), high courts reduced nearly 70 percent of death sentences, the vast majority to life in prison (and eligibility for parole after 25 years) or some lesser term.[17] The high reversal rates by appellate courts under presidents Kim Dae Jung and Roh Moo Hyun resemble the two-thirds of capital convictions in the United States that were overturned on appeal in 1973–1995 because of "serious errors" that "undermined the reliability of the outcome or otherwise 'harmed' the defendant" (Liebman, Fagan, and West 2000:1). In the United States, the high reversal rate is regarded as evidence of a "broken system" of capital justice. In South Korea it may reflect an analogous problem, but it is also a sign that appellate courts have achieved greater independence than they possessed in authoritarian times, and that they now scrutinize capital convictions much more carefully than they used to.[18]

Like South Korean society more generally, capital punishment has changed dramatically since dictators Syngman Rhee and Park Chung Hee held power. Courts have become much more careful about using death as a criminal sanction, both at the trial and appellate levels, and the last two presidential administrations have stopped executing entirely. As for the two dictators, Rhee resigned in disgrace in 1960 after students protesting violence and vote-rigging in that year's presidential election (in which Rhee received 89 percent of the vote) were shot and killed in the streets of Seoul. The previous year, Rhee's foremost political rival and former agriculture minister Cho Bong-am had been executed despite worldwide protests after an appellate court changed his prison sentence from five years to death (for allegedly contacting North Korea). Park Chung Hee's 20 years at the helm came to a violent end during a dinner in October 1979, when his own KCIA director, Kim Chae-gyu, shot and killed Park's bodyguard and then turned his pistol on the president. Military forces arrested Kim, who had graduated with Park in the 1946 class of the American occupation's military officers' school, and he was soon executed, despite his claim that the murder was an act of patriotism

17. During Park's rule in the 1970s, the High Court death sentence reversal rate was 48.1 percent, lower than the rate in any of the administrations that followed but a big change from the 1960s, when high courts never met a death sentence they disapproved. It is unclear how and why the high courts became more willing to reduce death sentences in the second decade of Park's administration, especially considering his turn toward "full-blown, formal authoritarianism" in the early 1970s (Cumings 1997:358). Park's control over all branches of government was also evident in the National Assembly, where not one of 306 administration-sponsored bills was rejected between 1967 and 1971 (356).

18. For an argument that South Korean courts were "subservient" to the executive branch in the authoritarian years, see Bae (2007:72). And for a fine collection of essays on the causes and consequences of judicial empowerment in authoritarian states (including Singapore and the PRC), see Ginsburg and Moustafa (2008).

because Park's dictatorship had undermined the development of Korean democracy.[19]

■ Chun Doo Hwan and Roh Tae Woo: 1980–1992

Forty-seven days after Park's murder, the man who headed the investigation into this crime—Major General Chun Doo Hwan—and his close friend and high school classmate General Roh Tae Woo led a junta that executed a coup that brought to power the 1955 graduating class of the Korean Military Academy. The *New York Times* believed this "shocking breach of Army discipline . . . would have been a hanging offense in any other military command structure" (quoted in Cumings 1997:375), but Chun and Roh, longtime acolytes and loyalists of Park, escaped punishment for the next 16 years. Their comeuppance came in 1996, during the presidency of Roh's successor, Kim Young Sam, when Chun was sentenced to death for murder (in the Kwangju massacre), treason and mutiny (in the coup that brought him to power), and corruption (he amassed a $900 million slush fund while president). Roh received a life sentence at the same 1996 trial, for mutiny, treason, and corruption (his slush fund was $650 million).[20] The laws by which they were convicted were enacted ex post facto under Roh's successor, Kim Young Sam, who then went on to pardon Chun and Roh in December 1997 as one of the last acts of his presidency, after consulting with incoming president Kim Dae Jung.[21]

Following the military coup that brought Chun to power, the signal event of the post-Park period was the Kwangju rebellion, which has been compared to China's Tiananmen massacre because "students and young people were slaughtered on a scale the same as or greater than that" in the PRC nine years later (Cumings 1997:338). This conflict in the southwestern city of Kwangju was sparked in May 1980 after Chun imposed martial law. In a display of "shocking brutality," ROK special forces beat, bayoneted, and used flame-throwers on protesters (Breen 2004:209). An estimated 1,000 people were killed. Chun claimed the rebellion was inspired by communist sympathizers led by Kim Dae Jung, who was behind bars at the time. Chun conducted additional purges in the same year. More than 8,000 officials were removed for corruption or other offenses, and almost 60,000 people were detained in his

19. Some analysts believe the United States had tired of Park's ways and wanted him out of the way, but the reality is that Park's murder has never been adequately explained (Cumings 1997:374).

20. South Korea remains corrupt, and there is considerable evidence that presidents Kim Young Sam, Kim Dae Jung, and Roh Moo Hyun amassed sizable political slush funds (Kristof 1996; Cumings 1997:364; D. Johnson 2004b).

21. Before those pardons, Chun's death sentence had been reduced on appeal to life in prison, while Roh's life sentence had been reduced to 17 years' imprisonment (West 1997; D. Johnson 2004b:53).

drive to "eliminate social evils." Two-thirds of the latter were sent to "purifi-cation camps," where at least 50 died. Since 1980, memorial rallies have been staged every May in Kwangju and on college campuses around the country. As one analyst has summarized, "the ghosts of murdered protesters haunted Chun Doo Hwan throughout his rule," and memories of the massacre paved the way for his own death sentence (216).[22]

Roh Tae Woo, who was president from 1988 through 1992, came to power on the heels of a popular uprising against Chun that was led, in part, by Roh Moo Hyun, a human rights attorney and Roman Catholic who would continue Kim Dae Jung's moratorium on executions after he became president in 2003. The event that sparked this uprising in June 1987 was the extrajudicial killing of a student by the Korean police and the subsequent cover-up, which led to a "mass movement embracing students, workers, and many in the middle class" that "finally brought a democratic breakthrough in Korea" (Cumings 1997:388). After four decades of Ameri-can support for Korean dictators, the Reagan administration pressured Chun and Roh to change their policies, and Roh responded by announcing amnesties for political prisoners (including Kim Dae Jung), guarantees of basic rights, and a direct presidential election for December 1987. Kim Dae Jung and Kim Young Sam split the opposition vote, and Roh won the election with only 36 percent of the vote. Though he went on to scapegoat Chun for the 1979 coup and for the 1980 massacre at Kwangju, he also protected his friend from prison and punishment. In many respects, Roh was a transitional figure in South Korean politics, more progressive than his predecessors but also the leader of a regime that continued to use military and police power to repress opposition and dissent. In 1989, for example, Roh's forces crushed numerous labor strikes and arrested an average of 3.3 dissidents per day—more than 1,200 for the year—under the National Security Law (390).

Chun and Roh not only took power in the same way Park did (by coup), they frequently employed Park-like tactics to repress popular demands for greater political openness and freedom. All the same, South Korea's execution rate dropped during Chun's presidency (despite a sharp rise in homicide), from an average of 18 executions per year in the Park years to an average of nine a year under Chun and eight a year under Roh. Executions for violations of the National Security Law fell as well, from more than 30 percent of all executions during the Park years to 16 percent under Chun, the last president under which such an execution occurred. Death sentences declined, too, though less sharply, as did the percentage of death sentences imposed on National Security Law offenders (B. Cho 2008).

---

22. Kwangju also paved the way for the KCIA to require Korean newspapers to "feature Chun's photo every single day," while the American media frequently praised the "new era" of political stability that this dictator allegedly achieved (Cumings 1997:380).

While the Chun and Roh regimes continued to use "Red scares" to quash political opposition, capital punishment became an increasingly insignificant weapon in their repressive arsenals. And while executions and death sentences decreased from Park to Chun and Roh, High Court reversal rates rose, reaching 61 percent under Chun and nearly 65 percent under Roh. Changes in these indicators—executions, death sentences, the use of the death penalty against violators of the National Security Law, and appellate reversal rates—reflect the decline of South Korean capital punishment *before* the democratic transition that began with the June Revolution of 1987. What explains this predemocratization decline?

The first thing to observe is that death penalty declines also occurred in the Philippines and Japan well before democratization. In the Philippines under Marcos, we could even call the decline "death penalty desuetude," for there were no executions for ten years before he was removed from power in 1987, and for ten years before that the annual average number of judicial executions was only 2.5.[23] In Meiji Japan as well, the execution rate at the turn of the 20th century was only one-40th the execution rate of the 1870s, while in Thailand there were no executions in 11 of the first 15 years after the Pacific war (1945–1956) and in 7 of the 10 years before the democratic election of 1992. The decline of capital punishment during authoritarian times is hardly unique to South Korea.[24]

In comparative perspective, what seems striking in Korea is that even when authoritarian regimes were threatened by popular demand for a more representative polity—and while violent crime rose simultaneously, from about 4,000 offenders handled by prosecutors in 1974 to almost 12,000 in 2003—the regimes usually responded *without* death penalty campaigns of the kind that became commonplace in the PRC after Deng Xiaoping gained control of the Chinese Communist Party (CCP) in the late 1970s.[25] If democratization was not a necessary condition for death penalty decline in Asian jurisdictions such as South Korea, Japan, the Philippines, and Thailand, exposure to international norms that are critical of capital punishment—an exposure that occurs in the context of a broader process of "socialization to the norms of

23. As in South Korea, Philippine appellate courts—and the Supreme Court especially—reversed a high percentage of death sentences during a relatively early period of political development (1994–2006). See chapter 4.

24. Table 5.2 shows that the decline of capital punishment under presidents Chun and Roh was actually the continuation of an ongoing pattern of death penalty decline that first became evident in the 1950s under President Syngman Rhee.

25. South and Central America have long been "in the vanguard" of the worldwide abolitionist movement, and in those decidedly non-Asian contexts capital punishment typically declined (and disappeared) in authoritarian times (Hood 2002:55). Today, democracy remains fragile and immature in many Latin American nations (Harrison 2006:105), but the hundred-year tradition of abolition still "holds sway over almost the entire region" (Hood 2002:58).

liberal-rational global culture"—does help explain the sometimes sparing use of capital punishment by authoritarian systems of government in these places (Lynch 2006). So does the availability of other repressive means of control such as extrajudicial killing (see appendix G).

Every Korean government before the one elected in 1992 began or ended in a popular uprising or a military coup. The longest, under Park Chung Hee, started with a coup and ended with murder, and the second longest, under Chun Doo Hwan, "began and ended with popular rebellions that shook the foundations of the system" (Cumings 1997:338). The next three sections continue the narrative of death penalty developments in postwar South Korea by summarizing the main events that occurred under the nation's first civilian presidents: Kim Young Sam, Kim Dae Jung, and Roh Moo Hyun.

■ Democratic South Korea: Kim Young Sam, 1993–1998

A one-time elder in his Presbyterian Church and a longtime opponent of authoritarian governments, Kim Young Sam did *not* attempt to abolish capital punishment or stop executions as many other left-liberal leaders have done after taking control of national government from their own authoritarian predecessors (Zimring 2003:22; K. Cho 2008:13).[26] But in some ways he did try to distance his regime from those that came before it. He retired the military to the barracks. He removed loyalists of Chun and Roh who had virtually monopolized key political positions. He appointed well-respected scholars and former dissidents to his cabinet. He pushed for the enactment of *ex post* laws that would enable prosecutors to indict ex-presidents Chun and Roh. He led South Korea's first major anticorruption drive and improved government and corporate transparency and accountability. And he even demolished the palatial presidential mansion that had been constructed by the Japanese for their governor-generals, replacing it with a building of more traditionally Korean design. In these ways and more, Kim Young Sam "effected drastic reform in many areas of Korean life" (Yoon 1996:511).

Kim's decision not to end capital punishment is all the more notable because of his long progressive record. In 1979 he was expelled from the National Assembly and then banned from politics until 1985. And in 1983 he started a hunger strike on the anniversary of the Kwangju massacre in an effort to push for more democracy. His fast lasted 26 days, at which point the authorities took him to a hospital and had him force-fed (Cumings 1987:380).[27]

26. In the 1992 presidential election, Kim Young Sam defeated Kim Dae Jung and Chong Chu-yong, one of the nation's most famous businessmen (Chong and his brother founded Hyundai in 1947) and the man who has been called "Korea's Ross Perot" (Cumings 1997:327).

27. In hindsight, Kim Young Sam has been regarded by some as a centrist or even a conservative politician, largely because of the prepresidential merger of his party with Roh Tae Woo's conservative party but also because his successor was more progressive

Thus, when Kim Young Sam took control of South Korea's national government in 1993, he seemed to be the kind of leader who possessed both the opportunity to push for abolition of capital punishment and also the appropriate background and motivation. Yet far from jettisoning the death penalty or ceasing executions, his government actually increased the hangman's workload. Under presidents Chun Doo Hwan and Roh Tae Woo, the annual average number of executions was 8.8 and 7.8, respectively, while under Kim Young Sam the number increased to 11.4 per year. Similarly, the High Court reversal rate of death sentences also dropped slightly during Kim's presidency, from 63 percent under Chun and 65 percent under Roh to 60 percent under Kim. That rate would rebound to nearly 70 percent under his two successors (B. Cho 2008).

Kim Young Sam's decision to retain capital punishment must be understood in terms of the larger political context of his presidency. His electoral victory based on 40 percent of the vote meant that his hold on power was shaky when tensions rose in March 1993, just one month into his presidency, after North Korea announced its withdrawal from the Nuclear Non-Proliferation Treaty. In the years that followed, there were persistent rumors that a restive "T-K group" (from the southeast provinces of Taegu and Kyongsang, the regional support bases of presidents Chun and Roh) "might once again intervene to destroy civilian electoral politics" (Cumings 1997:391). After North Korea's leader Kim Il Sung died the following year, Kim Young Sam spent much time and energy trying to placate South Korea's hard right wing "by issuing calumny after calumny over Kim's dead body—thus driving North-South relations into the deepest freeze in years" (391).[28] In the same year, a Gallup poll found that 70 percent of South Koreans wanted to retain the death penalty and only 20 percent favored abolition. Kim's capacity for action was further restrained by the heterogeneous mix of policy preferences in his own political party. Concerned that he would have a hard time getting elected president because of South Korea's highly skewed regional voting patterns, Kim merged his own party with Roh Tae Woo's ruling party and Kim Chong Pil's following in order to form a three-cornered, catchall party that was compared to Japan's LDP because it was intended to launch a similarly long run of stable one-party rule (390). The party itself did not last long (Kim renamed it after Chun and Roh were indicted in 1996), but it did help get Kim elected, and it complicated his choice set in several policy areas, including capital punishment.

Since Korean law restricts a president's stay in office to a single five-year term, reelection considerations could not have shaped Kim Young Sam's

---

than he was. But from the standpoint of what politics were like before Kim and what Kim himself did during his presidency, we believe he must be considered South Korea's first liberal reformist president (Yoon 1996).

28. Another key cause of the deepening freeze between North and South was the North's effort to develop nuclear weapons.

capital punishment decisions, but the need to appease those to his political right did seem to influence his policy. In deference to the traditional norm that "execution could ruin the holy power [of the government]" (B. Cho 2008), there were no executions in Kim's first year in office (1993), just as there had been none in the first full years (1981 and 1988) of his two predecessors. But on October 6, 1994, 15 persons were hanged: ten in Seoul, three in Taejon, and two in Pusan. Afterward, in a break from the no-announcement practice of previous regimes, a government spokesman proclaimed the fact of the executions, although not the names of the condemned. Thirteen months later, at 9:00 a.m. on November 2, 1995, 19 more executions occurred: 15 at the gallows in Seoul, 2 in Taegu, 1 in Pusan, and 1 in Kwangju. There were no executions in 1996, but on December 30, 1997, two months before the inauguration of Kim Dae Jung and once again at 9:00 in the morning, South Korea's most recent hangings occurred: 4 in Seoul, 6 in Taejon, 5 in Taegu, 6 in Pusan, and 2 in Kwangju. Kim Dae Jung had been elected 12 days earlier, and in the course of his election campaign he had stressed his intention to abolish the death penalty if he became president. Some Korean analysts believe Kim Young Sam "hurried up" the 23 executions so that they would occur before the calendar year in which his successor took office (B. Cho 2008). If so, then the hangings of 19 men and 4 women on the second-to-last day of 1997 might be considered a political expression of the year-end cleaning that has long been a custom in East Asian societies.[29] For the most part, however, Kim's motivations for these executions remain poorly understood, especially considering his generally progressive leanings.[30] If the all-on-one-day executions in 1994, 1995, and 1997 were aimed at deterrence—and Kim's unprecedented after-the-fact announcements suggest they may have been—they did not have the intended effect. An analysis of monthly homicide figures for January 1994 through December 1998 reveals that the concentrated execution policy failed to produce declines in homicide (B. Cho 2008).

But the main penal development under President Kim Young Sam was his decision to embark on what has been called South Korea's trial of the century,

29. As noted in chapter 3, Japan has carried out year-end executions in several recent years, apparently at least partly in an effort to prevent the occurrence of zero execution years.

30. As noted earlier, another puzzle is the decision to hang four women (along with 19 men) on December 30, 1997. We know of no parallels to the four-women-in-a-day event among similarly developed nations, nor do we know how or why these women were selected. One feature of Korean capital punishment that is not puzzling is that the condemned tend to come from disadvantaged backgrounds—as is the case in most executing states. Of the 101 people executed from 1987 to 1997, no one had graduated from college, 25 had graduated from high school, 30 from junior high school, 40 from elementary school, and six had no education at all (Bae 2007:70). And of the 64 persons who were on death row in 2007, only 18 had hired a private attorney at least once during their criminal proceedings. "The vast majority" of their legal counsel was provided by court-appointed attorneys, "whose quality has been criticized" (K. Cho 2008:15).

which ultimately led to the indictment and conviction of ex-presidents Chun and Roh and 23 of their associates, including nine business executives. The media and public opinion were important proximate causes of Chun's death sentence and the punishments imposed on the others. Late in 1995, daily revelations of the huge slush funds accumulated by Chun and Roh both reflected and reinforced public enthusiasm for indictment. At the same time, public frustration over the long-standing pattern of impunity for elites compelled the National Assembly to pass two special laws that enabled prosecutors to overcome legal obstacles—such as the principle of "no punishment without law"—that had stymied their investigations. Public anger over the prosecution's initial decision not to charge the ex-presidents also increased the pressure for indictment, as did public petitions asking the Constitutional Court to push for criminal charges (D. Johnson 2004:57).

Although many of these actions have been criticized for violating basic rule-of-law standards (Waters 1997; West 1997), Chun was sentenced to death in August 1996, and Roh was sentenced to life imprisonment. After their sentences were reduced on appeal, both were pardoned in December 1997. The persons who did the pardoning, outgoing president Kim Young Sam and incoming president Kim Dae Jung, said it was necessary in order to unite the country so that it could better face the severe economic challenges posed by the onset of the Asian financial crisis. While that no doubt figured into their calculus, it was also true that during the last year of his presidency, Kim Young Sam had descended into ignominy and near political impotence while his son was being investigated for bribery. As the Asian financial crisis caused the Korean economy to implode, a president who had entered office vowing to wipe out corruption became a paralyzed leader incapable of addressing the country's most pressing problems (D. Johnson 2004:66). Scandal had eroded his authority, as it would the authority of his successor, Kim Dae Jung. Thus, at the time of the pardons of Chun and Roh, the same president who had taken extraordinary measures to ensure that his predecessors would be prosecuted was eager to shift the focus away from questions about his own integrity. These pardon decisions were made at the intersection of the politics of corruption, the politics of finance, and the politics of capital punishment. Considering their timing, it is reasonable to wonder whether they were politically linked to the decision to execute 23 persons at the end of 1997. The answer appears to be no (Cho Byung Sun, personal communication, July 21, 2006).

There are two competing interpretations of the sentences imposed on former presidents Chun and Roh. According to one, "this was a fine moment for Korean democracy" because it held the powerful accountable and because it "vindicated the masses of Koreans who had fought for democratic rule over the past fifty years" (Cumings 1997:391). Despite the procedural shortcuts that were taken to achieve these convictions, there is an important element of truth in this view. The contrasting view is that Kim Young Sam's pursuit of Chun and Roh was merely another instance of a long-standing and vicious "cycle of revenge" in which the Korean incumbent turns on his predecessor ("Question of Revenge" 2001:40). This interpretation gained additional currency in 2001 when Kim Young Sam was himself accused (though not indicted) of amassing his own $80 million slush fund. This time the president who did the accusing was his successor, Kim Dae Jung.

■ Kim Dae Jung and the Moratorium on Executions, 1998–2003

When Kim Dae Jung campaigned for the presidency in 1997, he promised sweeping political changes. "Political reform must precede everything else," he stressed, and "the people must be treated as masters" (quoted in Gunness 2002). One prominent plank in his platform was the abolition of capital punishment, but that goal was not accomplished. In fact, Kim made few official statements about the death penalty during his presidency, though the man who has been called the Nelson Mandela of Asia and "the Gandhi of Korea" did initiate a moratorium on executions that has continued, as of this writing, for more than ten years (Bae 2007:73). One question is how consistent the moratorium is with Kim's claim that "the people must be treated as masters." During his presidency, at least four polls attempted to measure public opinion on the issue, and majorities favored retention in each: 66 percent and 50 percent in two 1999 surveys, and 55 percent and 64 percent in two surveys in 2001. But if Kim's death penalty policy was inconsistent with his assertion that the public should lead on reform issues, it had much in common with the pattern seen in other nations where abolitions and moratoria have frequently occurred despite majority public sentiment for retention. In this sense, Kim Dae Jung was very much engaged in political "leadership from the front" on the question of capital punishment (Zimring and Hawkins 1986:23).

Kim's policy was facilitated by a number of factors, individual, social, political, and geostrategic. As noted earlier, Kim himself was sentenced to death in 1980 and was subject to numerous other arrests and incarcerations. These trials and tribulations not only elicited widespread sympathy and support, they colored Kim's views about the propriety of capital punishment.[31] So did his Roman Catholic faith (Kim converted to Catholicism at age 31). By the time of his presidency, many religious leaders in South Korea had reached agreement about the desirability of abolition, and the Roman Catholic clergy, particularly those in the Korean Bishops Committee for Justice and Peace, played an especially important role in raising public awareness and pressuring politicians to pull away from capital punishment (Bae 2005:313; B. Cho 2008). In this respect, the Korean retreat from capital

31. Kim Dae Jung's experience also colored his views about the propriety of his opponents' political activities. In 2000, Kim and his Millennium Democratic Party demanded that opposition candidate Jung In-bong end his campaign for election to Parliament on the grounds that he had been one of the military prosecutors who had sought Kim's death sentence in 1980. Jung was also disciplined by the Korean Bar Association for delivering drugs to a prisoner (Hands Off Cain, April 8, 2000).

punishment had religious roots similar to those in the Philippines, the only country in Asia that is even more Christian than South Korea (Bae 2007:74).[32]

In the midst of the Asian financial crisis, with tensions about North Korea's nuclear ambitions relaxed and without any more former dictators to hold accountable, capital punishment in South Korea became a significantly less salient issue in Kim Dae Jung's presidency. Indeed, it is striking that Korea's moratorium started during the same period when Kim was pursuing his Sunshine Policy of opening to and engagement with North Korea, a diplomatic move that not only helped him win the Nobel Peace Prize in 2000 but also helped create an atmosphere in the South in which capital punishment could be more vigorously debated and critiqued than ever before.[33] In some political and cultural environments, the death penalty is perceived to be "abstractly desirable as part of society's permanent bulwark against crime" rather than in terms of the concrete actuality of executing real human beings (Zimring and Hawkins 1986:22). But in South Korea during Kim Dae Jung's Sunshine Policy, even the abstract desirability of the death penalty became a less pressing political issue, as can be seen in the support for abolition bills in the National Assembly. In 1999, 98 out of 273 (36 percent) legislators signed a bill calling for the abolition of capital punishment and its replacement with an LWOP alternative. Among national politicians, that is a much higher percentage of support for abolition than Japan has ever seen. In the same year, Kim Kichoon, the chairman of the conservative opposition's Grand National Party's Human Rights Committee and a former prosecutor general and minister of justice, said he believed abolition was "the ideal path to follow," though he added that such a move would be "premature" as long as the majority of Koreans still thought "the death penalty is needed to protect the innocent and deter crime" (Hands Off Cain 1999). By 2001, when another abolitionist bill was introduced and while a majority of Koreans still supported the death penalty, 155 members

32. Outside of religious organizations, which have led South Korea's anti–death penalty movement, there has been little anti–death penalty activism in this otherwise vigorous civil society, a passivity that Professor Sangmin Bae attributes to two main causes: the belief among Korean human rights activists that capital punishment is "very likely to be banned" in a few years anyway, making extra work toward that outcome unnecessary, and their concern that pushing for an end to the death penalty might alienate the many Koreans who still support capital punishment (Bae 2005:312). In Bae's view, the three main pillars of South Korea's anti–death penalty movement are the Catholic Church, Amnesty International, and legislators in the National Assembly (Bae 2007:82).

33. Although tensions about North Korea relaxed under Kim Dae Jung, they did not disappear, nor did the National Security Law. A South Korean student studying at the Australian National University was so confused to find himself in the same class with students from North Korea that he went to his local embassy to ask permission to speak to them. Permission was granted on the condition that he keep officials informed of what they discussed. South Korean law still forbids contact with North Koreans, and violators can be arrested and even sentenced to death for making unauthorized contact (Hands Off Cain, January 23, 2000).

(57 percent) of the National Assembly signed on, although the bill failed to make it out of the 15-member Law and Judicial Committee, primarily because of opposition from former prosecutors on the committee (B. Cho 2008).

Two other aspects of Kim Dae Jung's political environment shed light on his death penalty policy. First, Kim belonged to a liberal political party that was not beholden to conservatives (his Millennium Democratic Party had not merged with them), and this distinguishes his political situation from that of his progressive predecessor (Kim Young Sam). Second, Kim Dae Jung had considerable control over whether his minister of justice signed execution warrants. South Korean presidents have long dominated other branches and organs of government, and this control distinguishes South Korea from Japan, where prime ministers have historically had limited control over their formal agents in the bureaucracy, including those in the Ministry of Justice who must initiate the execution process (Johnson 2002a; Breen 2004:224). Thus, the power of the president in the South Korean context made "leadership from the front" on death penalty issues a more feasible aim than in the Japanese context when the LDP briefly fell out of power in the early 1990s. Of course, the same presidential power could be used to end the Korean moratorium after the presidency changes hands, as happened in February 2008 when conservative Lee Myung Bak took office. We examine this possibility later in this chapter.

The moratorium on executions was the biggest but hardly the only death penalty change that occurred while Kim Dae Jung was president. Despite a rise in homicide, District Court death sentences declined by a third, and the High Court death sentence reversal rate climbed from 60 percent under Kim Young Sam to nearly 70 percent under Kim Dae Jung. Kim also commuted the death sentences of 13 persons on death row—a far more vigorous use of capital clemency power than his predecessors exercised.

Nonetheless, at least two death penalty nonachievements during Kim Dae Jung's five-year presidency need to be noted. One is the failure to abolish or even restrict the legal scope of capital punishment, and the other is the decision not to commute the death sentences of everyone on death row. The failure of abolition was not for lack of effort. Twice during Kim's presidency an abolition bill was introduced in the National Assembly, first in 1999 and again in 2001. But despite majority support in 2001, the bill was blocked by members of the critical legislative committee. A number of factors help explain the blockage, including majority support in the electorate for retention; a belief among many in the major opposition party that death penalty policy should follow, not lead, public opinion; a similar belief among many members of the Korean Bar Association; and the relatively weak role played by secular human rights groups in the country's abolitionist movement (Hands Off Cain, November 22, 2001; Bae 2007:81). But most critical was the strong opposition to abolition from career prosecutors in the procuracy and the Ministry of Justice. In this context, it was not difficult for a handful of former prosecutors in the National Assembly to thwart Kim Dae Jung's abolitionist ambition.

Kim Dae Jung's decision not to commute all death sentences is more difficult to understand. Two months before he left office, Amnesty International petitioned him to do just that, and Korean lawmakers simultaneously launched a signature campaign with the same aim (Hands Off Cain, November 29, 2002). Kim was certainly familiar with his capital clemency power, having used it nine times before his final year in office, and he did commute the death sentences of 3 of the 54 inmates who were on death row when he was about to leave office. But he did not empty death row as Gloria Macapagal Arroyo did before the Philippines' second abolition, or as Illinois governor George Ryan did in 2003. In a speech given in 2007 "in appreciation of" the ten-year moratorium on executions that Kim had started, the former president said his efforts to commute the sentences of all death row inmates to life imprisonment failed "due to obstinate resistance of related authorities" (Kim 2007). Perhaps Kim also believed mass commutation was such a sweeping exercise of presidential power that it would have transgressed too severely the principle he stressed at his inauguration, that "the people must be treated as masters." The answer to this question—and a richer account of the contexts and conditions of Kim Dae Jung's moratorium—might be found in the archives of his presidential library at Yonsei University in Seoul.

■ Roh Moo Hyun Continues the Moratorium, 2003–2008

The moratorium on executions that began under Kim Dae Jung continued throughout the presidency of Roh Moo Hyun, who left office in February 2008. Roh, like the two presidents before him, was widely regarded as a progressive at the time he entered the Blue House, and like Kim Dae Jung he is a devout Roman Catholic who never attended college.[34] Before his narrow victory over former Supreme Court justice Lee Hoi-chong in the presidential race of December 2002, Roh was a prominent human rights lawyer. Although he entered office promising to overcome the entrenched regionalism that afflicts Korean politics and to resist American efforts to influence Korean affairs, this relative political outsider soon encountered major problems. A generational rift in the Millennium Democratic Party between older politicians who rose to power under Kim Dae Jung and younger legislators who identified with Roh meant that he could not always count on his own party's support in the National Assembly. His support became even more fragile when pro-Roh forces left the Millennium Democratic Party to form the new Uri Party in November 2003. Four months later, the opposition-controlled National Assembly voted to impeach Roh for illegal electioneering and incompetence, and he was replaced by an acting president (prime minister Goh Kun) while the charges were considered. In May 2004, the Constitutional Court overturned the

34. With a population of 49 million, South Korea has more than five million Catholic believers (Jin 2007).

impeachment decision and restored Roh as president, but a month earlier the Korean electorate had already issued its own verdict when it handed Roh's Uri Party a landslide victory in the April 2004 parliamentary election. Roh enjoyed renewed popularity for a short while after his return to office but then encountered more problems, including allegations of corruption, resistance to his plan to move the capital from Seoul to the Chungcheong region, and harsh criticism of his decision to deploy Korean troops in the United States–led war in Iraq. After the April 2004 parliamentary election, Roh's Uri Party lost in every by-election, including a zero-for-twenty-three showing in the April 2005 contest. To bolster support (which then languished at the 20 percent level), Roh proposed forming a grand coalition with the conservative opposition Grand National Party, arguing that the policy differences between the two parties were actually insignificant. But liberals in Roh's Uri Party were enraged, and the GNP repeatedly refused to negotiate with Roh. The merger plan was scrapped, having failed to gain support from either party, and throughout the last two years of his presidency Roh remained an unusually lame duck.

Through it all, the moratorium continued. Roh's decision to keep the hangmen unemployed despite his own persistent political problems reflects the fact that the death penalty became a relatively low-salience issue during the moratorium. More than 60 people were on death row, including several attractive candidates for hanging, such as serial killer Yoo Young-chul, who was convicted of murdering 20 women (and confessed to killing 11 more), and who said he objected to abolition and wanted to be executed because "isolating hideous criminals who cannot be reformed and making them die old is the cruelest punishment" of all (Hands Off Cain, March 22, 2006).[35] Yet Roh never authorized an execution.[36] For him, executions were wrong as a matter of

---

35. After the trial court ordered Yoo Young-chul to appear at the next trial session, he jumped on top of a court employee's desk in an effort to climb onto the judges' bench and express his displeasure personally, but he slipped and fell and was apprehended by about 20 court guards and prison officials. In his confession, Yoo said he "cut off faces, hips and genitals" of victims who had the same name as his ex-girlfriend (who had left him), and he also admitted eating six victims' internal organs "out of curiosity" and in order to treat his own bronchial disease ("Suspected" 2004).

36. In February 2007, following newspaper reports that Yoo Young-chul might be executed, minister of justice Kim Sung-ho told reporters, "There is an ongoing debate over whether or not to abolish the death penalty. How can I even consider executing anyone right now?" (quoted in B. Cho 2008). In interviews with Johnson in March 2004 and June 2005, numerous senior Korean prosecutors said that while there is resistance to the abolition of capital punishment in the Ministry of Justice and the procuracy, there is almost no resistance to the moratorium on executions. Kim Jong-bin, the minister of justice in June 2005, said the moratorium is "not a salient issue to prosecutors or the Prosecutors Office," and Cho Sung-wook, an executive prosecutor in Seoul, said capital punishment "does not rank among the 5 or 10 most important issues" for prosecutors. For him and for most other Korean prosecutors, issues such as corruption, justice system reform, and preserving prosecutor power in the criminal process matter more.

principle and, in more practical terms, were an unlikely route to renewed popularity. Opposition inaction on the moratorium issue suggests that conservative politicians also believed capital punishment was not a good way to build their own political capital.

Public opinion polls do not reveal a decline in postmoratorium support for capital punishment, but the most recent polls suggest there may have been a softening near the end of Roh's presidency. See table 5.5. In the five polls taken between 1994 and 2001—from Kim Young Sam through Kim Dae Jung—an average of 60 percent of Korean respondents said they wanted to retain the death penalty. By comparison, in seven polls taken during the Roh presidency, an average of 59 percent of respondents preferred retention to abolition. On the other hand, two polls in 2006 found that fewer than half of all respondents wanted to retain capital punishment—the lowest levels of support in all the surveys. The fact that at least seven death penalty polls were taken during the first four years of Roh's presidency suggests that if capital punishment was not an especially salient issue for politicians during the moratorium, it did have some currency in the media and public.

Table 5.6 disaggregates the results of a poll taken by Korea Daily Network between October and December 2003. The 2,200 respondents were not a random sample and were almost evenly divided between ordinary Korean citizens (n = 1,064), two-thirds of whom wanted to retain the death penalty, and persons working in nine specific occupational groups (n = 1136), six of which were in the law or penology fields (An 2004). Of the nine occupational categories, the strongest support for retention of capital punishment was found among medical personnel working in penal facilities (89 percent), prison guards (89 percent), and prosecutors (83 percent). On the death penalty issue, Korean prosecutors' closest equivalents were frontline prison employees. In contrast, the strongest support for abolition was found among citizens' group activists (86 percent), members of the corrections committee (81 percent), MPs (60 percent), lawyers (60 percent), journalists (60 percent), and judges (53 percent). In all six of these occupations, a majority of respondents said they wanted capital punishment to be abolished. The contrast in opinion among the three legal professions is also marked. Only one in six prosecutors supported abolition, compared with three in five lawyers and more than one in two judges.

It is difficult to discern whether judicial support for abolition in South Korea has increased in recent years, because (as far as we know) death penalty polls were not administered to them before or after the 2003 survey. By some accounts, "all major domestic judicial bodies" continue to oppose the abolition of capital punishment, including courts and lawyers' groups (Bae 2007:81). But we do have two sets of data that reveal temporal patterns in judicial outputs in capital cases, and in both the pattern is clear: South Korean judges have become increasingly cautious about imposing and affirming death sentences. As table 5.4 shows, High Court reversal rates rose from zero percent in the 1960s to nearly 70 percent in the late 1990s and 2000s. Similarly, despite a

Table 5.5
Death penalty polls in South Korea, 1994–2006

Date	Pollster	Retain	Abolish	Other
1994	Gallup Korea and *Chosun Ilbo*	70.0%	20.0%	10.0%
1999 (December)	World Research	65.7%	34.3%	0.0%
1999 (December)	Gallup Korea	50.0%	43.0%	7.0%
2001	Gallup Korea and *Chosun Ilbo*	54.6%	31.3%	14.1%
2001 (October)	Segye Ilbo	63.6%	36.4%	0.0%
2003	Gallup Korea and *Chosun Ilbo*	52.3%	40.1%	7.6%
2003 (October– December)	Korea Daily Network	66.0%	34.0%	0.0%
2004 (March)	National Human Rights Commission	65.9%	34.1%	0.0%
2004 (July)	Hankuk Sahoe Yeoron Chosaso and Sopress	66.3%	30.9%	2.8%
2005 (October)	Pollever	68.8%	31.2%	
2006 (February)	Realmeter andCBS	46.1%	37.9%	16.0%
2006 (September)	Realmeter and CBS	45.1%	33.8%	21.1%

Source: B. Cho 2008.

Table 5.6
Public opinion about capital punishment in South Korea: Ten groups

Group	% Abolish	% Retain
General citizens	34.0	66.0
Citizens' groups	85.8	14.2
National Assembly	60.0	40.0
Journalists	54.3	45.7
Judges	53.1	46.9
Prosecutors	16.7	83.3
Lawyers	60.0	40.0
Prison guards	11.3	88.7
Corrections officials	80.6	19.4
Medical personnel	11.0	89.0

Source: An 2004.

Question: "Do you support the abolition of capital punishment? N = 2,200 survey responses received: 1,064 from general citizens, and 1,136 from other persons in nine specific groups. Survey administered by Korea Data Network, October 22–December 10, 2003.

marked rise in homicides between 1995 and 2005, the average number of first-instance death sentences dropped from 21.6 per year under Kim Young Sam (1993–1997) to 14.6 per year under Kim Dae Jung (1998–2002) and to 6.3 per year in the first three years of Roh Moo Hyun's term (2003–2005). South

Korea's current death penalty policy is partly the aggregation of decisions by individual prosecutors and judges, and the decline in judicial use of the ultimate sanction seems to reflect the judiciary's institutional move away from capital punishment, even though the nation's two highest courts—the Supreme Court and the Constitutional Court—have reaffirmed the legality of capital punishment numerous times on the grounds that it remains a "necessary evil" (*pilyo-ak*). This linguistic formulation, which has been used in many of the judiciary's most significant capital decisions, reflects serious judicial ambivalence: the death penalty is bad, even evil, but is unfortunately necessary (B. Cho 2008; K. Cho 2008).

One sees signs of judicial ambivalence in other judicial acts as well. In 1996, the Constitutional Court struck down one part of the National Security Law that provided for capital punishment, and in 2003 it ruled that a sentence of death for selling drugs was "an excessive abuse of state power to punish" (K. Cho 2008:21–22). In August 2004, when the Supreme Court finalized the death sentence of a leader who had killed six people after they tried to leave his cult, it used language that denied the condemned his humanity, as if to say killing can only be justified when the victim is not human: "This ruling means those who committed brutal and inhumane crimes shall not be considered human beings. The death penalty in those cases will not go against the Constitution, which defines human dignity [because the condemned is not human]" (quoted in Hands Off Cain, September 8, 2004). In a separate decision one year later, South Korea's Supreme Court did not deny anyone's humanity but did feel compelled to explain that capital punishment is not inconsistent with being a "reasonable judiciary" in a "civilized country." "The death penalty," it said, "is a stern, extreme punishment to take away the life of one human being, and it is also an exceptional punishment which the reasonable judiciary of a civilized country can impose" (Hands Off Cain, August 25, 2005).

In November 2005, at confirmation hearings in the National Assembly for three persons who were appointed to the 13-member Supreme Court, all three expressed serious reservations about the death penalty. Kim Ji-hyung said, "abolishing the death penalty has to be considered more actively." Park Si-hwan said, "I think it would be better to review the law to abolish the death penalty." And Kim Hwang-si said, "I am personally an abolitionist of the death penalty but it is also true that as a Justice there are things to consider, including public opinion" (Hands Off Cain, November 16, 2005). The previous year, Supreme Court nominee Kim Young-ran said she believed capital punishment must be abolished in South Korea, emphasizing the emotional toll the death penalty takes on those who impose it: "Since judges are also humans, we try really hard to avoid sentencing the death penalty that deprives a human of his life. When we are forced to do so, we go through immense agony" (Hands Off Cain, August 11, 2004). And during a National Assembly confirmation hearing in July 2005 for Cho Dae-hyun, a former judge and lawyer who served as Roh Moo Hyun's legal counsel during his impeachment proceedings, the nominee said, "It seems right to give people another chance to become penitent by ruling out capital punishment and instead introducing life imprisonment" (Seo 2005).

We do not mean to exaggerate the Korean judiciary's support for abolition or its ambivalence about death penalty issues. Many Korean judges continue to support the death penalty and to impose and affirm death sentences, and in 2004 the judiciary as an institution formally opposed the National Human Rights Commission's recommendation that capital punishment be abolished. Nonetheless, the aforementioned signs do seem to suggest a significant lack of enthusiasm for capital punishment among Korean judges, especially compared to their counterparts in Japan, where judges have lowered the threshold for capital sentences and thereby helped fuel the recent resurgence of the death penalty.[37] There are similar signs of waning support for capital punishment among judges in Taiwan, which we will explore in the next chapter. In the next section of this chapter we summarize several special qualities and lessons that can be learned from the Korean case study.

■ The Extraordinary Present in South Korea

South Korean politics have been volatile for much of the past half century, but in the most recent two decades solid economic growth has been combined with maturing political institutions and public expectations of continuity and legality in democratic government (Sung 2006). Even the election in February 2008, which transferred the presidency to conservative Lee Myung Bak after a decade of left-liberal rule, does not signal a major policy shift because the institutional framework in which the shift took place will be significantly less likely to produce abrupt shifts in politics and priorities than the South Korea of 1985. Stable political institutions combined with dispersal of political power throughout the branches of national government are important features of the probable future of South Korean government, and they also form a key framework for future developments in death penalty policy.

The history of death penalty policy in South Korea suggests five features of the current situation that deserve special emphasis in predicting the road ahead. First, the death penalty has been a more important issue in political discourse—and was more important to political leaders in the 1990s—in Korea than anywhere else on the Asian mainland, and it continues to be so at this writing. The death penalty's high salience was evident on both sides of

37. Another sign of the judiciary's soft support for capital punishment is its treatment of Kim Dae Han, who in 2003 ignited a carton filled with gasoline on a subway car in Daegu, South Korea's third-largest city, killing 198 people and injuring 147 others. Prosecutors asked for the death penalty, but the Daegu District Court imposed a life sentence because Kim was deemed "repentant" and because he may have been "mentally unstable" when he committed the crime ("South Korea Man" 2003).

the transition of presidential power in 1998. The moratorium that started that year was one of the significant policies of new president Kim Dae Jung and an important expression of the political meaning of his coming to power. The moratorium was not only widely expected, it produced a single-day execution of 23 persons on the eve of the political transition. That is not the usual way stable democratic governments move toward ending capital punishment in peacetime; it was an emphatic statement that death penalty policy was considered important.

Second, the death penalty has been important in South Korean political life in large part because it has been more heavily used as a political tool there than anywhere else in Asia during the past generation. Indeed, capital punishment is imprinted on South Korean history in two distinct modes: for ordinary crimes of violence such as homicide and rape, and for political acts and actors that threaten regime interests. Although the second pattern has been all but absent for the last 20 years (at least in concrete death sentences and executions), the politics of capital punishment in contemporary South Korea continue to be conducted in the shadow of its relations with the North and in terms partly defined by personal experiences politicians have had with the death penalty and with other repressive state sanctions. In a system in which the president can almost single-handedly dictate how many executions there will be, some of South Korea's most important death penalty policies have been constructed at the intersection of individual biography and political history.

The political nature of South Korean capital punishment can be seen in the large number of death sentences and executions that have involved state security, treason, or collaboration with the North Korean enemy—all offenses more closely connected with political issues than common crime. But the most striking demonstration of the political salience of capital punishment is that three of the last six presidents of South Korea have been under a death sentence at some point in their careers: two prior to becoming president and one after. There can be no more straightforward indicator of the death penalty's relevance as a political tool, and this is one reason why leaders who have spent time on death row (or in prison) regard the practice as important. To quote Samuel Johnson again, the history of being under a capital sentence "concentrates the mind wonderfully."[38] The political history of capital punishment in South Korea brings human rights and limits of government concerns into death penalty debates early and often. In fact, there may be more emphasis on the broader governmental implications of state execution in

---

38. Of course, the lessons of experience with capital punishment are not inevitably abolitionist, as is demonstrated by the life course of Park Chung Hee, who survived his own death sentence only to go on to become an enthusiastic administrator of capital punishment and other forms of state killing. Notwithstanding this enthusiasm, we suspect President Park would agree that the death penalty's political history intensified the salience of the death penalty in South Korean politics.

South Korea than was evident in any of the western European nations that abolished it in recent decades. And in South Korea, much of the stress on the political dimensions of capital punishment is a homegrown phenomenon rather than the result of the influence of European rhetoric.

The third important feature of the current South Korean environment is the existence of a ten-year moratorium on state execution that has generated little controversy in either politics or public opinion. As one national newspaper editorialized on the occasion of the ten-year anniversary, "the time is ripe for abolition as the people have not shown any negative response to the fact that the nation has not carried out an execution over the past 10 years" ("Time Is Ripe" 2008). So while the death penalty is an important issue in Korean politics, the absence of execution has become an accomplished fact without continuing controversy or public concern. The fact of nonexecution has apparently become part of the South Korean status quo. If so, then this should alter how future policy shifts are perceived and should shape the political consequences of change in death penalty policy and practice.

To be sure, there are substantial differences between ten years of nonexecution and the complete absence of capital punishment—more than 60 finalized death sentences have been generated during the moratorium, and there are no legal or structural barriers to resuming executions.[39] Moreover, public opinion still supports the death penalty in South Korea, although public expectations (and those of governing elites) have been altered by the moratorium and by appellate court opinions during it (K. Cho 2008). Two signs of the changing environment are the attitudes of particular professional groups toward the death penalty and the shift in judicial willingness to reverse death penalty verdicts. The poll question in 2003 asked the general public and nine professional groups, "Do you support the abolition of capital punishment?" The result for the general public was based on a sample of more than a thousand people, while the results for the professional groups came from much smaller samples. (See fig. 5.3, which presents the information from table 5.6 in a different form.) The small samples of specialists and the absence of earlier or later polls that would enable comparison over time place substantial limits on the interpretation of these data. Still, one-third of the general public favored abolition—more than the percentage for prison guards and prosecutors, but much less than the majority support for abolition expressed by lawyers, judges, members of the National Assembly, and correctional officials. Of course, some of this support for abolition predated the moratorium and may have been one reason it happened, but at least some of the support has resulted from the environment generated by South Korea's nonexecution policy and by the lack of a public backlash to it.

39. As of January 2008, there were 64 persons with finalized sentences of death on South Korean death rows ("S. Korea Marks" 2007). All were males who had been convicted of murder, and their average age was 42 (K. Cho 2008:14–15).

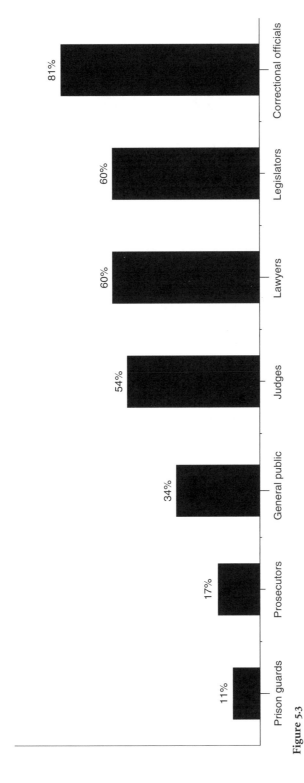

Figure 5.3
Support for the abolition of capital punishment in South Korea, 2003
Source: An 2004.

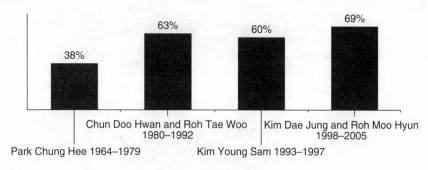

Figure 5.4
Reversal of death sentences by high courts in South Korea, 1964–2005
Source: B. Cho 2008.

Figure 5.4 (a chart showing the High Court death sentence reversal rates from table 5.4) shows that the changes over time are substantial. In only 40 years, the chance of a High Court reversal almost doubles and the chance of a death sentence being upheld is cut in half. One important part of this story is increasing judicial independence, a key feature of government where judges are more than three times as likely as prosecutors to favor abolition. But at the same time, signals from the moratorium—a period when nonexecution was imposed as the normative preference of the executive branch—also energized the judiciary. The last decade has been a period when elites in and out of government have expected no executions and when opposition to capital punishment has been the majority sentiment of legislators, lawyers, and judges.

One implication of the lack of friction over the moratorium is that in South Korea, unlike the United States, there do not seem to be many passionately ideological proponents of the death penalty. As abolitionist politician Yoo Ihn Tae has emphasized, the most important obstacle to abolition at present is prosecutors in the procuracy and the Ministry of Justice and former prosecutors in the National Assembly and elsewhere in government. Yet even in those circles (and in the Korean judiciary, too) there are signs of serious ambivalence. Few working prosecutors regard the death penalty as an especially important issue (interviews by Johnson, March 2004, June 2005, and June 2006), and in 2006 the Ministry of Justice—which is largely staffed and run by prosecutors—even announced that it would study the possibility of replacing capital punishment with life imprisonment without parole in order to respond to the rising number of calls to enhance the protection of human rights (Hands Off Cain, February 21, 2006). The draft the ministry released in February 2007 of its "roadmap for human rights protection" did not include recommendations made by the National Human Rights Commission to move toward abolishing the death penalty and the National Security Law ("Gov't Proposes" 2007), but prosecutors and officials elsewhere in government are clearly considering various death penalty futures.

While the moratorium on executions has for the most part encouraged greater opposition to capital punishment, the long absence of hangings and the strong public expectation that no executions are on the horizon has also relieved pressure on the legislature and the executive branch to push for immediate abolition. This may also be one reason why South Korea abstained in the UN vote on a resolution calling for a worldwide moratorium on executions with an eye toward abolishing the death penalty (which passed in December 2007 by a vote of 104 to 54, with 28 abstentions).[40] Draft legislation to abolish capital punishment has frequently been introduced in the National Assembly, only to be bottled up in committee. The government's commitment to nonexecution reduced the stakes involved in this kind of reform and thereby may have prolonged the status quo. Even if the 60 percent support for abolition reported in the 2003 poll (see fig. 5.3) is an accurate measure of current legislative sentiment, there has been no sense of urgency to generate any action that could carry political costs. If this helps explain the leisurely pace of legislation to make abolition a legal reality, then any shift in politics or policy that increases the likelihood of a resumption in executions might also increase the likelihood of efforts to achieve complete abolition. The relaxed legislative politics of death penalty reform may depend on expectations of nonexecution in the executive branch.

This interpretation of the impact of the moratorium on politics and elite attitudes leads us to two final conclusions about the South Korean present. First, the country is further down the road to full-scale abolition of capital punishment than any other major nation in Asia. There are a variety of indications of this: ten consecutive years without execution; the support for abolition of one-third of the public; high levels of support for abolition among legal elites and legislators; and the absence of political friction surrounding the nonexecution policy that has been a visible part of the last two presidents' terms (Han 2007). Indeed, the absence of executions caused no political trouble even during the term of President Roh Moo Hyun, who had little political capital with which to fend off sustained assaults on unpopular policies. Whenever there is public comment that South Korea might not be ready for abolition, the sentiment expressed seems to be much closer to "not yet" than to unqualified opposition. Even current president Lee Myung Bak, the Christian elder and a member of the conservative Grand National Party who replaced Roh in 2008, has qualified his desire to retain capital punishment

---

40. There are at least two other interpretations of South Korea's decision to abstain on the UN moratorium resolution. One is that South Korea is not the death penalty "vanguard" that this chapter has argued it is. The other concerns the timing of the moratorium vote, which occurred one day before conservative Lee Myung-bak defeated Chung Don-young—a candidate allied with lame duck liberal president Roh Moo Hyun—by 48.6 percent to 26.2 percent, the largest margin in a South Korean presidential election since 1987 (Onishi 2007b). The outgoing Roh government's decision to abstain on the resolution may have been motivated by the felt need to let a new administration make its own death penalty policy.

by stressing his intention to "use it with restraint" ("S. Korea Marks" 2007). In terms of public and elite sentiment, the operational aspects of criminal justice, and the organization and attitudes of legislators, South Korea has a short distance to travel from its current death penalty circumstance to formal abolition.

A final effect of the developments since 1998 has been a shift away from the pattern of abrupt changes in death penalty policy that accompanied transitions in executive power at many points in South Korea's modern history. The shift from 23 executions on one day at the end of 1997 to zero executions thereafter resembled the marked shifts that occurred at several previous moments. But the development of the institutions and traditions of democratic government in South Korea makes such abrupt changes in policy less likely during peacetime transitions of power, and the cumulative impact of ten years without executions makes sudden changes in execution policy both less likely to occur and a larger risk for the political actors who attempt them. The left-to-right presidential transition of 2008 will test how far Korea has evolved from abrupt shifts in death penalty policy, as will the general election in the same year that gave conservatives a majority of seats in the National Assembly ("Conservatives Win" 2008; Kim 2008). We believe the nation has come quite far indeed.

■ The Future

On the last day of 2007, one of South Korea's largest national newspapers, *Hankyoreh*, published a lead editorial titled "Doing Away with Death Penalty." As did many other articles published around the same time, this one stressed the international significance of a Korean abolition and the importance of continuing the cautious death penalty policy that had prevailed for the previous ten years:

> Starting yesterday, the international community recognizes Korea as a country that essentially no longer has capital punishment. Amnesty International classifies countries that do not execute anyone for a full decade as countries that have done away with capital punishment, and Saturday [December 29, 2007] marked ten years since Korea's last execution. This is very significant in that it means that Korea is a step closer to being seen by the international community as a country that respects human rights. What is important now is that we do not backtrack.... The value of life is absolute.... Japan and the United States remain countries not credited for their respect of human rights by the international community since both still have capital punishment. Korea has adopted much of its legal structure from those two countries, so it will be especially notable in the international community if we move to eliminate capital punishment before they do. During his

campaign, President-elect Lee Myung Bak took the position that the death penalty helps prevent crime. We hope he, too, can adopt a profoundly changed position and make the right decision. During the 17th National Assembly [April 2004–May 2008], some 175 legislators, more than half, signed a bill to abolish capital punishment, and no one in the country has really taken issue with the fact that executions have not been carried out for the last ten years, so the mood in society is ripe for doing away with it. Moving on the issue would also be meaningful as it could symbolize that [Lee] is a president who values civil rights.

There appear to be three alternative futures in the field of choice for capital punishment in South Korea: (1) a continuation of the current moratorium on execution with no formal abolition of the death penalty, (2) formal abolition of the death penalty for "ordinary crimes," and (3) efforts to resume executions, which could produce a renewal of anti–death penalty activism and either another moratorium or a legislative abolition. As the *Hankyoreh* editorial advocates, the most likely short-term outcome in South Korea is a continuation of the moratorium, while in the longer term abolition seems all but inevitable.

Two features of South Korea's recent history argue against a return to execution. The first is the institutional momentum of democratic development in the courts, the legislature, and the executive branch. The abrupt policy shifts and autocratic politics of 20 years ago are now ancient Korean history. And while passionate opposition to capital punishment is still a left-wing sentiment in the politics of the nation, the second major development of the last decade is the momentum generated by a decade of nonexecution. Because the moratorium has been a political success, its continuation seems likely under the new conservative president. On the other hand, formal abolition of capital punishment probably must await a presidency or strong legislative majority of the left (K. Cho 2008:26). Indeed, without a European-like regional mechanism for enforcing human rights in the Asia region, and with a more gradual transition to democracy than occurred in nations such as Ukraine and South Africa that abolished soon after they experienced "radical political transformations," South Korea may lack two of the elements that predict and explain compliance with the emerging international human rights norm of abolition (Bae 2007:123). But for the time being, anyway, it appears that no branch of South Korea's political mainstream is invested in restarting the execution of criminals. In fact, one development that could jumpstart a transition to formal abolition would be a political push to conduct executions. Legislative and judicial supporters of abolition have tolerated the procedural diversion of abolition proposals because of the security provided by the firm nonexecution policies of the two previous presidents. Any uncertainty about the executive branch's commitment to an execution-free South Korea might provoke a serious effort to hasten the formal abolition that many political actors believe is the eventual destiny of the nation.

The shift in emphasis by defenders of South Korea's current legal framework from a criminal justice to a national security justification for death penalty laws both illustrates how far down the path to abolition the nation has already come and suggests one possible compromise in abolition legislation. Many western European nations first abolished capital punishment for "ordinary" offenses, reserving the possibility of a death penalty for crimes during war (as in England's abolition for "ordinary" crimes in 1965 vs. its abolition for "all" crimes in 1998). Similarly, South Korea's focus on national security in an era of North-South division suggests a compromise in which abolition is enacted for ordinary crimes (which would cover all offenders currently under sentence of death) but is deferred for a prolonged period as a concession to the anxieties of those citizens and leaders who are concerned about acts of treason on the still divided peninsula.

In our view, the least likely short-run future of capital punishment in South Korea would be an attempt to reintroduce executions. There is no clear political advantage to advocating such a policy, and there appear to be real risks—particularly for a candidate of the right—in doing so. It might take some destabilizing emergency, such as an act of extreme North Korean terror, to overcome the caution of mainstream political actors in the South. If this prediction proves correct, it will demonstrate how far the South Korea of 2008 has moved from the circumstances in contemporary Japan, where executions have surged since Christmas 2006. An execution in South Korea now would be a radical change in policy, and that is a sign of how far the nation has traveled since 1997.

6

The Other China
Taiwan

Nothing spurs adoption of new ideas like other
actors doing the same.

—Lawrence W. Sherman, "Evidence-Based
Crime Prevention" (2004)

Ideas and products and messages and behaviors
spread just like viruses do.

—Malcolm Gladwell, *The Tipping Point* (2000)

■ Taiwan and South Korea

There are many similarities between Taiwan and South Korea in death penalty
policy and practice, both as a contemporary matter and in their recent
histories.[1] Most notably, both have been infected with the idea that capital
punishment is inconsistent with a commitment to human rights; both saw
executions decline dramatically after decades of authoritarian rule—in 2007,
Taiwan finished its second consecutive year with zero executions; and both
seem to be well on their way toward formal abolition. But there are also some
significant differences.

In general terms, the most important difference between Taiwan and South
Korea may concern what each regards as the defining countries of comparison
and contrast. For citizens and leaders in South Korea, how to relate to North
Korea and how to reunify the Korean peninsula remain the central questions
for the first decades of the 21st century (Cumings 1997:457). At the same time,
Japan continues to be a key reference point with respect to a wide variety of
economic, political, cultural, and legal issues. Indeed, it is in comparison to
and competition with Japan that South Koreans often define their success in
Asia and in the world.[2]

---

1. We accept the premise that Taiwan and the PRC are de facto separate countries.
Hence, we use the terms "Taiwan" and "Republic of China" (ROC) to refer to the island of 23
million people located 100 to 150 miles off the coast of Fujian Province, while "China" refers
strictly to mainland China (the PRC) (Roy 2003:ix).
2. With respect to recording criminal interrogations, Taiwan and South Korea have been
more progressive than Japan. Interrogation abuses have been one of the main causes of

In Taiwan, by contrast, the defining comparisons tend to be with the PRC, and the most pressing questions about the future concern Taiwan's relations with it. If the first theme of Taiwan's political history is democratization, the second is the persistence of political tensions with China (Roy 2003:239).

As for capital punishment in particular, the most salient comparative frame for Taiwan continues to be the PRC, although the United States has been important, too. The *Taiwan Human Rights Report 2000* illustrates the relevance of both references. Subtitled *The Taiwan Death Penalty in International Perspective*, the report begins by asserting that "almost no other country in the world is like Taiwan" because the death penalty there is so "taken for granted" and because citizens of Taiwan "refuse to face the issue" (Death Penalty Issue Research Group 2000). The report then states that if execution statistics were calculated relative to population, Taiwan would come out "on top" of cross-national comparisons, even standing "well ahead of China." The China frame reappears in the conclusion, where the reader is told that "in terms of the numbers of people executed, the Republic of China and the People's Republic of China are on the verge of 'unification'!" Although data difficulties for China make the veracity of these comparative assertions difficult to discern for the period summarized in this report (1989–2000), we will show that before democratization, Taiwan was one of the world's most aggressive executing states.

In the same report, one also finds numerous references to the United States, a nation that people in Taiwan "have relentlessly looked up to . . . as a model in almost all areas" (Death Penalty Issue Research Group 2000). If the United States "shares with [Taiwan] the 'distinction' of putting a lot of people to death," the situation in Taiwan is deemed much more problematic because death sentences there are imposed for a wide variety of crimes (not just homicide); executions occur soon after sentencing and in secrecy; the power of special appeal lies with prosecutors instead of defense lawyers; miscarriages of justice are common; and the system is biased against the young, the poor, and the uneducated. In the end, this report emphasizes, the United States has had the "courage and maturity" to face death penalty issues, and in this respect America is held up as a model for reform of capital punishment in Taiwan.

Setting aside the accuracy of these comparative assertions and the propriety of the suggestions for reform (the 2000 report appeared at about the same time that executions in the United States peaked), the contrast between Taiwan and South Korea consists chiefly in the fact that the special salience of the death penalty in South Korea centers on the history and practice of capital punishment in that nation itself, not on how that history and practice are perceived in comparison to other nations—whether North Korea, Japan, or the United

---

miscarriages of justice in all three nations, and there is much evidence from the United States and elsewhere that shows that tape or video recording helps prevent such problems. Recording also occurs in China, Mongolia, and Hong Kong (Johnson 2007b).

States.[3] By contrast, the death penalty in Taiwan is frequently framed and formulated in the context of an "irony of international isolation" that South Korea does not experience (Manthorpe 2005). To wit: Taiwan has been largely isolated from other nations and from the international human rights community as a result of its exclusion from the UN in 1971, yet its leaders and NGOs have struggled mightily to convince other nations and international organizations that it is a member in good standing of the democratic club, committed, above all, to respecting human rights. In this respect, "the quest for human rights invented modern Taiwan," and recent death penalty reforms reflect "Taiwan's ongoing invention of itself as a progressive nation" and its determination to demonstrate that identity to an international audience (Kennedy 2004:27).[4]

Though these contrasts are important, Taiwan and South Korea also share a great deal in common. Over the last four decades, the two nations have been similar in three large areas: history and culture, economic development, and political development. If history does not repeat itself, sometimes it does rhyme. The paragraphs that follow identify some of the most fundamental rhymes in order to lay the groundwork for our analysis of death penalty developments in Taiwan since the Republic of China regime fled mainland China in 1949 and made its new base an island that is one-third the size of the American state of Ohio.

History and Culture

This is not the place for an extended analysis of the historical and cultural similarities between Taiwan and South Korea, but a few prominent parallels do deserve mention. The Japanese occupations of Korea and Taiwan not only shaped execution regimes in both places but also originated some of the secrecy and silence that continue to surround capital punishment in each context. And while Japanese influence has been large, in certain respects China has been an even more important external influence. Some analysts regard Korea as "China's little brother" (Breen 2004:86). If Taiwan is an even smaller brother, it is also a closer one. China controlled much of Taiwan for more than two centuries—from 1684, when it incorporated Taiwan as a prefecture of Fujian Province (across the Taiwan Strait), until 1895, when Japan defeated

3. In some ways, the United States "looms larger than any other foreign country in the Korean national consciousness" (Choe and Onishi 2007), but with respect to capital punishment the most important Korean frames are not foreign.

4. Another irony concerns Taiwan's relationship with the United States. Some analysts believe that because the United States assisted Taiwan's economic and political liberalization while protecting it from seizure by the PRC, "Taiwan has been a shining example of successful American internationalism" (Roy 2003:243). If that is true, it is ironic that on the death penalty front Taiwan has moved much closer to abolition than has the United States—and at a surprisingly rapid rate.

China in the Sino-Japanese war. Taiwan reunited with China after Japan's defeat in the Pacific war, but it was such a "disastrous reunion"—bringing exploitation, discrimination, violence, and disappointed expectations—that Taiwanese perceptions of Japan's occupation are significantly more ambivalent than the more widespread South Korean view that their own colonization produced mostly suffering (Roy 2003:53,75).

The cultural similarities between Taiwan and South Korea are easy to exaggerate, but in the broader comparative contexts of Asia or the world the similarities do seem striking.[5] Among the most notable shared sensibilities are the primacy of family, the value of education, the salience of hierarchy, the importance of ritual performance, and the relationship between the individual and authority on the one hand and the individual and the group on the other (Fallows 1994; Reid 1999).

One final feature of the history and culture of Taiwan is the extent to which the modern nation was created in 1949 by the arrival and domination of the Kuomintang nationalist party (KMT) and its political infrastructure. The discontinuity between Taiwan's social structure and population prior to the nationalist retreat from mainland China and the almost six decades since 1949 are in some respects even more extreme than that of countries that have experienced political revolution. As many as two million soldiers and civilians were added to an existing population of six million, and the new arrivals and their descendants dominated Taiwan's government and economy for decades thereafter. Chiang Kai-shek did not merely occupy a country so much as attempt to construct a new nation much more discontinuously than even the nation-building adventure of South Korea after World War II. In a real sense, the society of modern Taiwan does not have the same kind of long history as do the more continuous societies of Korea, Japan, and many other Asian nations. In this respect, Taiwan is a modern invention.

Rapid Economic Development

In the first decade after its defeat in 1945, Japan resumed industrialization and progressed at a pace the world had never seen. Over the next four decades, Taiwan and South Korea (and Hong Kong and Singapore as well) modernized even more rapidly (Vogel 1991:1). Several circumstances helped make rapid growth possible, including massive aid from the United States, the destruction of old social orders by colonization and war, a sense of political and economic

---

5. Lionel Jensen, a historian of China, argues that there was no such thing as "Confucianism" until Jesuit missionaries "manufactured" it late in the 16th century, and he believes "the Confucian tradition" is perpetually reinvented in the context of present needs and concerns (1997). Though these claims may be true, they do not change the fact that several East Asian nations—including South Korea and Taiwan—share a similar core of values and beliefs that are rooted in their historical experiences in that region (Fingarette 1972; Reid 1999).

urgency that mobilized local support for all-out industrial development, eager and educated labor forces, and the availability of the Japanese model and Japanese technology and investment.

Yet situational factors alone cannot account for the Taiwanese and South Korean economic miracles; culture counted, too. In particular, several clusters of "industrial neo-Confucian" attitudes and institutions contributed to the capacity of these "little dragons" to industrialize (Vogel 1991:92). Those cultural qualities include a tradition of a meritocratic elite to guide economic development, a system of entrance exams that remained the crucial gateway to prestige and power, stress on the importance of groups over individuals, and traditions of "self-cultivation" that have been called "the closest analogue in Confucian culture" to the Protestant work ethic made famous by Max Weber (100).

Figure 6.1 shows the growth of GNP per capita in Taiwan and South Korea for the period 1960–2005. The exponential economic growth in Taiwan is similar in both magnitude and timing to the growth in South Korea. For each nation, a simple rule of thumb provides an accurate summary of a four-decade process: real GNP per capita doubles every 10 years until the mid-1990s, then slows a bit. By the logic of compound growth, the real economic output per person in both nations is 12 times greater in 2000 than it was in 1960.

Authoritarian Government and Political Rupture

Taiwan and South Korea both experienced long periods of authoritarian rule that started in the late 1940s and continued until the last half of the 1980s. And Taiwan was under martial law for almost 40 years, from 1949, when the KMT moved its government to Taiwan after it was defeated by Mao's forces on the Chinese mainland, until 1987, the year after opposition politicians defied a ban on new political parties and formed the Democratic Progressive Party (DPP). In its origins and early organizational development, the KMT displayed "striking similarities" to the Chinese Communist Party. The two parties have even been called "twins" because both acquired political hegemony in their territories, claimed an entitlement to govern, developed the organizational capacity to guard their political power, and frequently employed that power to repress opposition and dissent (Cheng and Lin 2006:1).

The break with authoritarianism also occurred at almost the same time in Taiwan and South Korea. In the latter, a mass movement for democracy that embraced students, workers, and people in the middle class finally produced "a democratic breakthrough" in 1987 (Cumings 1997:388). The same year, Taiwan's KMT-controlled government lifted martial law, and the next year the Chiang dynasty ended (after 40 years), and Lee Teng Hui of the KMT was elected president. In the years that followed, Taiwan and South Korea each developed lively and open civil societies—in some respects more open, vigorous, and contentious than those in Japan and the United States (Kim 2000; Madsen 2007).

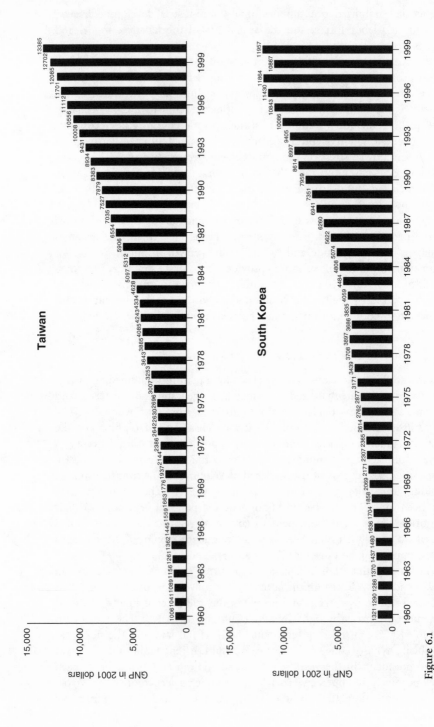

Figure 6.1
GNP per capita growth in Taiwan and South Korea

Note: Amounts are shown in constant U.S. dollars, normed to 2001 values to ensure that the growth shown does not reflect inflation.

Sources: See World Bank, http://genderstats.worldbank.org/genderstats/query/default.htm; government of Taiwan, http:eng.stat.gov.tw.

■ The Scale of Executions in Authoritarian Taiwan, 1947–1987

There was extensive state killing—judicial and extrajudicial—in Taiwan's recent past. Though the data are patchy, it appears there were even more executions under Chiang Kai-shek, who ruled from 1949 to 1975, and his son Chiang Ching-kuo (1975–1988) than there were in South Korea under presidents Rhee and Park. What is more, at some points in the last half century there apparently was as much state killing in Taiwan (per capita) under the Chiangs as there was in the PRC under Mao Zedong and Deng Xiaoping.

Chiang Kai-shek, the dominant figure in the KMT and in Taiwan's new political system, was "every bit as much a 'paramount leader' in his own (admittedly much smaller) sphere as was Mao on the [Chinese] mainland" (Roy 2003:82; Rubinstein 2006). If Chiang was not as enthusiastic about executions as Mao, the available evidence suggests that in some respects he was close. In the White Terror campaign he directed against intellectuals and others during the 1950s, estimates of the number of victims run as high as 90,000 arrested and "about half that number executed" (Roy 2003:90).[6] If 45,000 persons were executed during that decade, then Taiwan's rate of state killing in the 1950s was about 469 executions per million per year.[7]

Taiwan's execution rate in the 1950s was not only higher than South Korea's, it was not much lower than the levels of state killing that occurred in China during some years of Mao's rule.[8] Consider two comparisons. First, for the PRC to match Taiwan's per capita execution rate in the 1950s, it would need to have averaged 284,000 executions each year during that decade. From October 1950 to October 1951, Mao's nationwide campaign to suppress counterrevolutionaries resulted in an estimated 3 million deaths "by execution, mob violence or suicide"—a figure ten times higher than Chiang's annual rate for the 1950s (Chang and Halliday 2005:324). But not all of these deaths resulted from execution. Mao claimed the total number of people executed (not beaten or

6. Taiwan's Ministry of Justice regards the estimate of 45,000 executions as too high (Ministry of Justice officials Hui-Ming Chiang and Y. K. Huang, interview by Zimring, February 26, 2008).

7. Some sources indicate that following the "2-2-8 incident" of February 28, 1947, in which violence against a cigarette vendor by an agent of Taiwan's Monopoly Bureau sparked popular uprisings in the island's nine largest cities, Chiang Kai-shek sent a telegram from the Chinese mainland to Taiwan's governor-general Chen Yi with the order "Kill them all; keep it secret" (Roy 2003:71). During the recapture of the cities and the purges that followed, an estimated "several thousand to ten thousand" Taiwanese were killed, thousands more were imprisoned, and 3,000 dissidents fled the island (73).

8. In the six months after the June 1950 invasion of South Korea by North Korean forces, Syngman Rhee's regime summarily executed an estimated 10,000 suspected communist sympathizers (Lankov 2007b). Excluding deaths in combat, this may have been the peak year for state killing in South Korea. Even so, the South Korean rate of 481 executions per million in 1950 is about the same as estimates of Taiwan's annual average for the *entire decade* of the 1950s.

tortured to death or pressured to commit suicide) in this year was 700,000—a one-year rate about 2.5 times higher than Taiwan's rate for the entire decade of the 1950s (324). Yet even for Mao, this particular year involved an especially aggressive execution campaign.

The second comparison to the PRC involves the Great Purge that occurred during Mao's Cultural Revolution (1966–1976). The most well-known campaign of state killing in PRC history may have occurred during this decade: "at least 3 million people died violent deaths," for a per capita average of approximately 365 state killings per million people per year (Chang and Halliday 2005:547). Though the counts are imprecise, it appears that the per capita rate of state killing under Mao during the Cultural Revolution was not much higher, and may have been lower, than the rate of state killing during Chiang's White Terror campaign of the 1950s.[9] Moreover, from 1960 until Taiwan's democratic transition began in 1986, the number of arrests and executions "may have been lower, but a similar pattern continued" long after the official terror campaign ended (Roy 2003:90).

Chiang Ching-kuo followed as paramount ruler of Taiwan from the time of his father's death in 1975 until his own death in 1988. The younger Chiang was in some ways an "unexpected supporter of reform" who accommodated demands for liberalization with some frequency (Roy 2003:156). During the dozen years after he became chairman of the KMT Central Committee and before democratization, he allowed a proto-opposition movement to emerge, gave lower-level KMT cadres more input and responsibility, and presided over a shift in power from the KMT party to more formal institutions of government. But at the same time, Chiang continued to use capital punishment on a broad scale in order to repress deviance and dissent. Few records of executions in Taiwan are available for this period, and those that do exist do not include the majority of executions that were carried out as part of the national security crackdowns.[10]

In sum, the scale of execution in Taiwan before democratization seems to match or surpass that in almost all other nations, including South Korea. It is reasonable to wonder what the deterrent effects of all those executions were. The only known study of the issue was released (to limited circulation) by Taiwan's Research, Development, and Evaluation Commission in 1994. The research was based on data collected from official sources covering the 30-year period 1961–1990, and the results were unequivocal: the number of people

9. Mao also created a vast archipelago of prisons and labor camps. During his rule from 1949 to 1976, the number of inmates who died in such facilities "could well amount to 27 million"—or about one million deaths per year (Chang and Halliday 2005:325).

10. The challenges in obtaining decent death penalty data for Taiwan are even greater than for South Korea. Execution figures for the post–martial law period (1988 to the present) are reliable, but the only available figures for 1948–1987 do not list the large majority of executions that were carried out in secret (Ryden 2001:292).

executed "did not affect the incidence" of rape, violent crime, kidnapping, or other "general crimes." The study even found that "the greater the number of people executed, the higher the rate of homicide cases" (Death Penalty Issue Research Group 2000:4; Ryden 2001:293). If the threat of execution under the KMT cowed dissidents and potential political opponents (Roy 2003:93), it did little to control ordinary crime on the streets.

■ The Decline of Executions in Democratic Taiwan, 1987–2007

A decade after Taiwan's turn to democracy, its annual rate of executions per million people had declined markedly from the levels of the 1970s, yet in cross-national perspective the rate remained high. The most comprehensive available comparison (of 26 nations) for 1996 to 2000 shows that Taiwan's annual execution rate of 1.22 was surpassed in Asia only by that of Singapore (6.40) and the PRC (1.65, though this is a large underestimate), and elsewhere in the world was exceeded only by the war-torn nation of Sierra Leone (2.36) and the Muslim-majority nations of Saudi Arabia (4.46), Jordan (1.96), Iran (1.76), Kyrgyzstan (1.56), and (possibly) Kazakhstan (1.35 or 0.55). During the same five-year period, Taiwan's execution rate was approximately seven times higher than the rate for Vietnam, 12 times higher than the rate for South Korea, and 15 to 30 times higher than the rates for Thailand, Pakistan, and Japan (Hood 2002:92).

Figure 6.2 shows that between 1987 and 1997, the annual number of executions in Taiwan rose, fell, and then rose again before falling continuously after 1997. The first increase, from 6 in 1987 to 78 in 1990, reflects the fact that many executions before 1987 were carried out in secret (Ryden 2001:292). Some analysts believe this rise reflects not merely increased transparency but also a real and "dramatic" increase in state killing after the end of martial law (International Federation for Human Rights and Taiwan Alliance to End the Death Penalty 2006:7). On this view, democratization produced many social changes and much public anxiety (including widespread protests and demonstrations in 1987–1988), and Taiwanese courts responded by "getting tougher" on crime (Tsujimoto and Tsujimoto 1993:65). Indirect support for this view also can be found in the imprisonment rate for political offenders, which increased after martial law was lifted in July 1987 (Roy 2003:180). What is more, when Lee Teng-hui became president following Chiang Ching-kuo's death in 1988, there were deep divisions in the ruling KMT, and the new president had strong incentives to mollify the right wing of his party, which was concerned about the rapid pace of liberalization (185).

Until more records are released, it will be impossible to know for sure if the initial increase in executions after democratization was "real" or artifactual. Our view is that it probably was some of each. What *is* clear is that executions in Taiwan declined from a peak of 78 in 1990 to a low of 16 in 1995 before

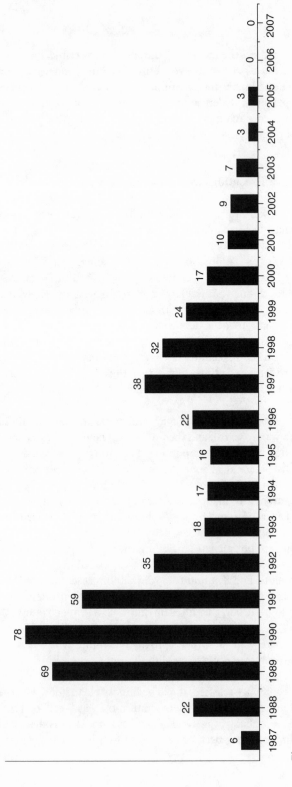

Figure 6.2

Executions in Taiwan, 1987–2006

Source: Liao 2008.

Table 6.1
Executions by crime, Taiwan, 1987–2006

Year	Homicide	Rape and homicide	Robbery	Kidnapping for ransom	Drugs	Banditry[1]	Total
1987[2]	4	1	0	0	0	1	6
1988	7	2	0	3	0	10	22
1989	15	2	0	1	0	51	69
1990	21	4	1	5	0	47	78
1991	16	2	0	2	0	39	59
1992	8	1	0	4	0	22	35
1993	4	1	0	2	1	10	18
1994	3	1	1	5	1	6	17
1995	5	0	1	2	2	6	16
1996	7	0	1	3	0	11	22
1997	12	3	1	6	2	14	38
1998	13	2	0	6	2	9	32
1999	6	0	0	2	3	13	24
2000	6	1	0	5	0	5	17
2001	7	1	0	0	1	1	10
2002	2	0	1	0	1	5	9
2003	1	1	4	1	0	0	7
2004	1	1	0	1	0	0	3
2005	3	0	0	0	0	0	3
2006	0	0	0	0	0	0	0
Total	141	23	10	48	13	250	485
Percent	29.1%	4.7%	2.1%	9.9%	2.7%	51.5%	100%

Sources: Ryden 2001; Liao 2008.

[1] The Act for the Control and Punishment of Banditry was abolished in January 2002. It mandated a death sentence for ten offenses. The act was imposed after the Nationalists regained Taiwan from the Japanese in 1945 and was imported from the Chinese mainland, where the ruling KMT used it to keep control while they fought with Japanese troops. The act proscribed not only murder, arson, and rape but also such activities as "organizing groups in the mountains or marshes in opposition to government authority." In theory, someone who merely trespassed on a military base could be charged and, if found guilty, sentenced to death. Between the 1940s and 1999, at least 257 people were executed for Banditry Act violations.

[2] The figures for 1987 and 1988 do not include executions carried out in secret under martial law, and this is the main reason for the sudden rise in executions from 1988 to 1989. For the number of annual executions that were *acknowledged* by the government in Taiwan between 1948 and 1986, see Edmund Ryden (2001:291). As he notes, it "seems as if there were more executions after the lifting of martial law than before, but in fact the reverse is the case." What increased after 1988 was not the actual number of executions but their transparency.

rebounding to 22 in 1996 and 38 in 1997. After that, executions decreased continuously until there were none at all in 2006 and 2007.[11] See table 6.1.[12]

The brief resurgence of executions in the mid-1990s corresponded to an increase in public and KMT concern about crime and corruption. In the years leading up to Taiwan's first direct presidential election in 1996, incumbent president Lee Teng-hui allowed executions to decline even while "military heavyweight" and "champion of law and order" Hau Pei-tsun served as premier (Roy 2003:187). But after Lee was reelected in March 1996 (with 54 percent of the vote), Taiwan experienced a series of high-profile crimes and a sharply increased demand for improved "law and order." In August 1996, a legislator in the National Assembly was kidnapped and incarcerated in a dog cage in Taiwan's mountains after he spoke out against organized crime. A month later, a county executive and eight of his associates were shot in the head after they announced their intention to tear down gangster-operated businesses in their district. It was called the worst mass murder in Taiwan's history. In December 1996, a prominent feminist, professor, and member of the DPP was raped and murdered. And in April 1997, gangsters kidnapped the 17-year-old daughter of a television variety show hostess and sent photos of the girl, along with her severed finger, to the mother. After the girl was killed, the ringleader, Chen Chin-hsing, remained at large and went on to kidnap and kill again. His crime spree ended in November 1997 after he held hostage the South African military attaché and his family. In an interview with television journalists while police had him surrounded, Chen demanded freedom for his detained relatives. Following a shootout in which the attaché and his daughter were wounded, Chen finally surrendered. The "most notorious criminal in Taiwan's modern history" was executed by firing squad 11 months later

11. Taiwan's last executions before the 2006 moratorium occurred on December 26, 2005, when two brothers were put to death for murdering one man and injuring another. The brothers expressed no remorse, said they wanted to be executed, and vowed to take revenge on the victims' families if they were ever released. According to Minister of Justice Morley Shih, these circumstances made it impossible for the government to pursue other avenues of extraordinary appeal that could have forestalled execution (Hands Off Cain, December 26, 2005).

12. There were some years after 2000 in which more Taiwanese were executed in the PRC than in Taiwan. In 2001 it was close: Taiwan had ten executions (at least two of PRC citizens), while at least seven Taiwanese were executed in the PRC. In 2004, three Taiwanese were executed in their home country and at least five were executed in the PRC, while in 2005 three Taiwanese were executed at home and at least eight were executed in the PRC (see Hands Off Cain reports for 2001, 2004, and 2005). Capital punishment sometimes stimulates a war of words between Taipei and Beijing, as when PRC authorities demanded severe punishments for the captain and crew of a Taiwanese smuggling boat who threw 20 Chinese women overboard when they were confronted by a coast guard patrol in August 2003 (Hands Off Cain, November 25, 2003). Six of the women died. The captain (Wang Chung-hsing) was sentenced to death in November 2003. He was executed in January 2005, just 17 months after the crimes occurred.

(207–208). In the years that followed, the mother of Chen's victim, famed entertainer Pai Ping-ping, became an outspoken opponent of the abolition of capital punishment.

President Lee's reaction to this crisis of law and order included a more aggressive execution policy, but only for a time. Executions peaked in 1997, then declined for the next decade. In the end, "the single most important reason" for the sharp drop in Lee's popularity during his final years in office was that many of Taiwan's people came to believe he was more interested in political and constitutional reform than he was in "tackling the public's greatest concern, crime and corruption" (Roy 2003:204). If Lee's decision to take his foot off the execution accelerator contributed to that perception, the public's disapproval did nothing to change his mind.[13]

Although some observers believe Taiwan's "progress toward abolition has been slow" since President Lee left office (International Federation for Human Rights and Taiwan Alliance to End the Death Penalty 2006), the execution decline that began in the 1990s continued after Chen Shui-bian was elected president in March 2000. Chen is, in many ways, Taiwan's counterpart to his South Korean contemporary, Roh Moo Hyun. Both were born poor, worked as left-leaning lawyers before entering politics, served time in prison for anti-regime activities, became president because other candidates split the conservative vote, and were plagued during their presidencies by scandal, political defections, and low approval ratings.[14] Yet both remained committed to

13. Three years after Lee left office, the *Washington Post* said he remained "the most controversial and most powerful politician in Taiwan—a kingmaker extraordinaire" (Pomfret 2003). A devout Marxist in his teens, Lee joined the Chinese Communist Party in 1946, ostensibly out of hatred for the KMT, but quit the party two years later. Lee's father was an aide to the Japanese police, his brother died in the Japanese imperial army, and Lee himself graduated with honors from Kyoto University. Since then, he has rarely tried to hide his pro-Japan sentiments. Lee is also a Presbyterian Christian who received a doctorate in agricultural economics from Cornell University. After Chen Shui-bian became president in 2000, Lee was expelled from the KMT for his inability to lead the party to victory. He then became (for a while) a confidant and ally of Chen and a more radical activist for Taiwan's independence. To achieve that end, Lee frequently called for Taiwan to reject a Chinese identity in favor of becoming a "New Taiwanese" nation, and frequently lambasted Chinese culture. "Chinese have a strange sense of history, with their obsession with 5000 years of their culture," he once averred. "When you meet an Italian, you don't see him dreaming about the greatness of Rome, do you? How can modern people have such ideas?" (Pomfret 2003).

14. In 2006, Chen's approval ratings dropped to Roh-like lows after his son-in-law was charged with insider trading, his wife was indicted for embezzling public funds, and the prosecutor of these cases announced he might indict Chen after his immunity as president expires (Yardley 2006b). (A few weeks later, Ma Ying-jeou, the mayor of Taipei and the rival KMT's presumptive presidential candidate for 2008, was indicted for involvement in a separate embezzlement scandal.) One scholar has called Chen "a pathetic failure" as president, not so much because he and his family were tainted by corruption as because he "used his office to divide the island's citizens, as if his domestic political opponents were Taiwan's

ending executions and, in rhetoric and reality, to abolishing the death penal-ty.[15] The execution rate in the first half of Chen's presidency (2000–2003) was little more than one-third what it was in Lee's final four years in office (1996–1999), while the rate fell by a further 80 percent in the first three years of Chen's second term. What is more, this decline was sustained despite a rash of high-profile gun crimes, including assassination attempts on Chen and his vice president (Ramzy 2004), some of the most aggressive, partisan, and sensationalistic media in Asia (Magnier 2005a), the creation of two and three strikes laws and the extension of what a "life" sentence meant from 20 to 30 or 40 years (Kennedy 2004:25), a prison population that nearly doubled between 1992 and 2003 (Hebenton 2007), and strong public support for capital punishment (Chiu 2006).[16]

Data on executions are available only for the second half of the period after Chiang Kai-shek took refuge in Taiwan, and reliable counts for the years when executions were at their highest do not exist. Nonetheless, the available evidence does show that during the 30 years after Chiang's death, Taiwan experienced a drop from over three executions per million in 1990 to none in 2006 and 2007. Its execution rate thus fell from a level that was perhaps half that of China to zero in only 16 years. This transition provides a setting in which we can search for historical evidence of the influence such a large change in executions has on the prison system, crime levels, and citizen attitudes. Those who wonder what sort of impacts a sharp decline in execution might have in the PRC should examine the historical record of Taiwan. The

---

mortal enemies"; he "balked" at Taiwan's further integration into the global economy; and he "pandered to the extreme wing" of his party and "mobilized his government to 'di-Sinicize' Taiwan culture" (Shaw 2006). Despite these pressing political problems, Chen did not push for more executions, exercising the same kind of restraint as Roh Moo Hyun did when he encountered similar problems as president in South Korea. In fact, prosecutors in Taiwan frequently filed extraordinary appeals in order to "keep prisoners sentenced to death alive" or at least "stall [their] executions as long as possible" ("Judiciary Disagrees" 2008; see also Kennedy and Guo 2006:5). That is what saved Chong Deshu from execution in December 2006, thus closing the first year in ROC history with no executions.

15. There are also significant similarities between Chen and Roh's predecessor as South Korean president, Kim Dae Jung. Both were targeted for assassination before entering office (Chen was targeted again while campaigning for reelection); both entered office aspiring to become their country's George Washington and ended up accused of being Boss Tweed; and both stressed the paramount importance of human rights—including the need to end capital punishment.

16. The "remarkable increase" in democratic Taiwan's imprisonment rate coincided with a sharp drop in eligibility for parole, a decreased use of suspended sentences, and a variety of "get tough" legislative changes (Hebenton 2007:4). In 2003, Taiwan's imprisonment rate of 224 per 100,000 was approximately 30 percent higher than the rate in the PRC, even when the PRC included nonprison forms of confinement such as camps for "reeducation through labor" (laojiao).

population and criminal justice system in the laboratory of Taiwan are much smaller than those in the PRC, but the scale of the decline in executions within one generation is the largest Asia has experienced since Japan's Meiji decline a century earlier.

■ A Profile of Capital Cases

A sociologist has summarized some of the legal, social, and economic aspects of capital cases that were tried by Taiwanese courts (all levels) from 1987 to 2000, the period from the end of martial law to the beginning of Chen Shui-bian's presidency. In this study, 324 capital cases—already decided and still in progress—were examined, and what was found (and what two earlier government surveys reinforce) resembles the death row profiles of Japan and South Korea, with a few important exceptions (Lee 2001).

First the similarities. Only 11 of 324 capital defendants in Taiwan were female, a proportion (3.4 percent) that differs little from the parallel female proportions in South Korea and Japan, and of the more than 130 executions that occurred in Taiwan between 1997 and November 2003, none was of a woman (Hands Off Cain, November 29, 2003). Taiwan had more than 150 capital offenses during the period under study, but two-thirds of capital cases involved homicide, either alone or in combination with other crimes such as robbery or rape. The next most frequent capital charges were for robbery and rape (9.6 percent), kidnapping for ransom (6.5 percent), and drug offenses (5.9 percent). Only one capital defendant was charged with a white-collar crime (corruption), and only 2.5 percent of capital defendants were foreigners (all eight of the foreigner defendants came from Asian countries). The defendant did not know the victim(s) in 75 percent of capital cases; 70 percent of defendants had no recorded arrests; and more than 80 percent had no prior convictions.[17] Nearly 50 percent of all capital crimes were committed in Taiwan's three largest cities: Taipei (25 percent), Taichung (14 percent), and Kaohsiung (10 percent). In all of these respects, the differences between Taiwan, Japan, and South Korea are insignificant.

But several dimensions of Taiwan's death row do stand out. The first is the age profile of the condemned. Of the 158 death row inmates who could be identified (not all with a finalized death sentence), almost 50 percent were 30 years old or younger, and 90 percent were 45 or less (Lee 2001:227). Data about age at execution could not be obtained, but it appears that the age profile of Taiwan's death row is much closer to the South Korean than to the geriatric Japanese distribution.

17. In November 2006, the Ministry of Justice released statistics that said 64 percent of the people executed since 1997 had prior criminal records (Hands Off Cain, November 29, 2003). There is thus a substantial discrepancy in accounts covering the same cases.

This comparative age difference is linked to a second striking fact concerning capital cases in Taiwan: they move rapidly. In the 130 cases for which information was available, the average length of time from the first report of an offense until the Supreme Court verdict was only 2.8 years, and 63 percent of cases took two years or less while 80 percent took less than three years (Lee 2001:235). Capital cases are processed much more slowly in Japan and somewhat more slowly in South Korea. In terms of time to completion of capital adjudication, the closest Asian counterparts to Taiwan, at least until the year 2000, seem to be Singapore, the PRC, North Korea, and perhaps Vietnam. If the quick is the enemy of the careful, then the speed of Taiwan's capital process may have generated a significant number of miscarriages of justice even after the nation's democratic turn. This possibility is also expressed by Taiwanese citizens, 88 percent of whom said (in a 2006 survey) "it is possible local courts have made mistakes in capital cases" (Chiu 2006:9). Miscarriage of justice has also been one of the concerns most frequently emphasized by abolitionists in Taiwan, though the issue apparently "has not aroused serious concerns" in Taiwanese society more generally (Anonymous 2006:33; see also Death Penalty Issue Research Group 2000; International Federation for Human Rights and Taiwan Alliance to End the Death Penalty 2006; Kennedy and Guo 2006).

When capital cases in Taiwan are adjudicated more slowly, the results are almost as troubling. After the Supreme Court rejects an appeal, a death judgment becomes final.[18] But if the appeal succeeds, the case is sent back to the relevant High Court, which must issue a new decision within one month. No matter what the High Court decides, the prosecutor and the defendant can appeal the result, and until final confirmation by the Supreme Court a conviction or sentence can be appealed by either side an unlimited number of times. One result is that some defendants who have been acquitted are subject to multiple retrials, remaining in a state of legal limbo for long periods of time while their case bounces back and forth between courts. In the case of the Hsih-chi trio—the most controversial capital case in ROC history—the three defendants underwent ten trials for the same murder charge in the first 15 years after they were arrested for allegedly stabbing to death a married couple in the town of Hsih-chi. At the time they were acquitted and released in 2003, more than 40 judges had upheld their death sentences, and as of 2006 the defendants were back on remand awaiting another retrial (International Federation for Human Rights and Taiwan Alliance to End the Death Penalty 2006:25). Even more dizzying was the ordeal of Hua Ding Guo, whose case

---

18. After a death sentence has been finalized, it is Taiwan's prosecutors and the attorney general, not defense lawyers, who have authority to file extraordinary appeals asking for additional appellate review. This has been criticized for being "in direct conflict with fundamental human rights principles" (Death Penalty Issue Research Group 2000:5), but during Chen's presidency, officials frequently used their authority to delay executions as long as possible (Kennedy and Guo 2006:5; "Judiciary Disagrees" 2008).

was sent back and forth between the High Court and the Supreme Court 18 times. Including his first-instance trial, Hua was acquitted seven times and sentenced to death 12 times before finally being sentenced to life imprisonment (International Federation for Human Rights and Taiwan Alliance to End the Death Penalty 2006:29). We know of no other jurisdiction in Asia or anyplace else where one nation combines such speedy processing in the large majority of capital cases with such instability and uncertainty at the appellate level in a small minority of cases (from offense to Supreme Court verdict, 3 percent of capital cases in Taiwan take 10 years or more; see Lee 2001:235). Here is one sign of death penalty ambivalence in Taiwan.[19] Ambivalence is also reflected in the reforms Taiwan performed in order to protect from execution some of the people the UN deems "vulnerable" (Hood 2002:114). As a result of legislation enacted during Chen's presidency, persons under age 18 and over age 80 are no longer subject to capital punishment, and the government claims that the execution of pregnant women and the mentally ill, though still permitted by law, does not occur as "a matter of practice" (International Federation for Human Rights and Taiwan Alliance to End the Death Penalty 2006:22).[20]

■ Executions and Ambivalence

Additional signs of ambivalence can be seen at the execution stage. Until recently—and in contrast to Japan and South Korea—the legally authorized means of execution in Taiwan was not hanging but the electric chair and the gas chamber. In cases where those facilities were not available (and it appears they never were), execution by firearm was permitted, and that has remained the standard method of execution since the ROC was founded (Tsujimoto and Tsujimoto 1993:64). In the early years, the condemned was required to stand facing a wall before being shot in the head, but in 1955 this procedure was changed to mandate death by bullets to the heart. At present, the condemned lies facedown on a mattress on the floor, a medical practitioner marks on the clothing where the heart is, and the

19. Prisons in Taiwan are overcrowded—some operate at more than 150 percent capacity—but prison conditions have "greatly improved in recent years" (International Federation for Human Rights and Taiwan Alliance to End the Death Penalty 2006:31). On death row, however, conditions remain problematic, at least as of September 2005, when 49 inmates had been condemned to death (no women or foreigners), of which six had finalized sentences of death. Death row inmates are usually detained in cells with one other long-term prisoner. Except for 30 minutes of daily exercise, they remain in their cells all day, shackled by a chain around both ankles, though the government contends such chains are only used to restrain real security risks (30,34).

20. In December 2005, two brothers asked to be executed after they were convicted of murder, despite claims by their defense lawyers that the younger brother was mentally ill (International Federation for Human Rights and Taiwan Alliance to End the Death Penalty 2006:22).

prisoner is shot three times from behind at close range—though not so close as to splatter the shooter with blood (65). The protocol changes when organs will be harvested. In this event, the inmate lies in a plastic bath so that the organs do not get contaminated, and the method of execution is a pistol shot to the back of the head, which causes less trauma to the organs that will be excised. The body of the condemned is also "put on a gurney and attached to a life support machine in order to preserve the organs" until they have been removed by a medical team on site (International Federation for Human Rights and Taiwan Alliance to End the Death Penalty 2006:35).[21] As in the United States, botched executions have stimulated reforms in Taiwan. In 1988, it took five shots to kill would-be organ-donor Wu Hsin-hua. His autopsy revealed that the bullets had missed the mark because his heart was located on the right side of his body (Tsujimoto and Tsujimoto 1993:73). In 1991, another condemned man had to be reexecuted after he was taken to the hospital—heart still beating—to have organs removed following an original execution effort that authorities thought had worked. Thirty-four hours later, the Ministry of Justice ordered the condemned taken from the hospital and returned to the execution chamber. Thirty days later, the execution law was reformed to create safeguards against a recurrence (65).[22]

Though the description so far reflects a straightforward, even practical, approach to execution in Taiwan, ambivalence is evident in at least three features of the execution process. First, Taiwan became the first government

21. In addition to the question of whether inmates on death row can freely consent to donate their organs, critics also contend that authorities do not allow enough time to determine whether the condemned is dead before his organs are removed. Accounts differ as to how often the practice occurs in Taiwan, but at least some reports suggest it is common. One recent report says "most death row prisoners sign an Organ Donation Agreement, authorizing organ donation, soon after they arrive in custody." On this view, organ donation is common because inmates regard it as a form of "redemption for their crimes" (International Federation for Human Rights and Taiwan Alliance to End the Death Penalty 2006:35). An earlier study found that more than 40 lives were saved by organs removed from the 137 death row inmates who were executed in 1990 and 1991 (Tsujimoto and Tsujimoto 1993:67). And in 2006, a Ministry of Justice official said 7 of the 13 persons executed in 2003–2005 "donated organs of their own free will" (Hands Off Cain, June 13, 2006). However, one study of capital cases from 1987 to 2000 found Taiwan's rate of organ donation to be "very low," occurring in only 5 out of 309 cases, or less than 2 percent (Lee 2001:236). There is little doubt that organ donations by death row inmates in the PRC are common. Between 2005 and 2007, the PRC's vice minister of health twice acknowledged publicly that "China routinely removes organs from executed prisoners for transplant—but only with prior consent" (Ang 2007). The claim about consent has been contradicted and criticized by a variety of foreign medical and human rights groups (Matas and Kilgour 2007). In Malaysia, the health director has said that his country will not consider calls to allow prisoners on death row to donate their organs after execution, and in Japan the practice is unheard of (Hands Off Cain, March 1, 1999).

22. Taiwan's safeguards include postexecution checks of the body by the attending prosecu-tor and medical personnel, and a provision that allows the condemned to withdraw consent for organ donation anytime prior to execution (Tsujimoto and Tsujimoto 1993:67–68).

outside of the United States to legislate lethal injection—even earlier than the Philippines, which legislated it in 1996. As of this writing, that method has not been used in Taiwan (Amnesty International 2007a).[23] Second, it is standard practice to give prisoners anesthesia so that they are unconscious at the time they are shot. This reform was implemented in 1975 because some among the condemned yelled or turned and stared at the executioner before the moment of truth, an interaction many executioners found unnerving (Tsujimoto and Tsujimoto 1993:65). Third, none of the 10–20 witnesses present at the execution is a member of the media or an independent observer who can report what transpired at the execution scene, and secrecy about the day of execution still remains the rule (Hands Off Cain, June 13, 2006). Of these three signs of ambivalence, only the last is also found in Japan and South Korea.

At the personal level, 68 percent of Taiwanese respondents said in a 2001 survey that they would be "willing to help carry out executions" (Shia 2001:70), but there is considerable ambivalence on the front lines of the execution chamber. A senior prosecutor in Kaohsiung who was in charge of executions for eight years said "I feel OK" if the condemned does not show any repentance, but acknowledged feeling "sympathetic when a prisoner expresses remorse to me before their execution" (Hands Off Cain, March 27, 2006). As the anesthesia reform of 1975 suggests, execution teams are not encouraged by last-minute displays of emotion from the condemned. According to another senior prosecutor who also had presided over executions, prisoners are offered alcohol and a last meal "a few hours before their executions," but "few of them are able to eat" and some "show huge fear when they know they are soon going to die." Many attempt to delay execution "by asking to smoke a cigarette or use the restroom." In order to drive away misfortune that might attend the officials who take life, it also is "customary" for Taiwanese executioners to place in their pockets a small amount of moxa (crushed leaves from the Chinese wormwood tree), a peach leaf, or a talisman (Tsujimoto and Tsujimoto 1993:64). Acts of magic such as these reveal that in Taiwan as in other death penalty environments, the system of capital punishment "asks normal people to participate in what, under normal circumstances, would be regarded as extraordinary, prohibited acts" (Haney 2005:x).

Thus, there is abundant evidence of ambivalence in Taiwanese capital punishment: in the coupling of speed with uncertainty in capital adjudication, the reforms to protect "vulnerable" populations from the death penalty, the changes in execution methods and protocols, the use of anesthesia before execution, the secrecy that surrounds death row, the personal feelings of

23. In law and in practice, Asia appears to be the world leader in capital punishment by lethal injection. In 1997, China became the second country (after the United States) to use it, and it has been enacted into law in Taiwan (1992), the Philippines (1996), and Thailand (2003). Similar reforms have been considered in Indonesia, India, Vietnam, and Papua New Guinea.

the prosecutors and judges who send people there, and the concern shown by Taiwan's legal profession (the Taipei Bar Association supports abolition; see International Federation for Human Rights and Taiwan Alliance to End the Death Penalty 2006:11). There are also signs of uneasiness with capital punishment in the KMT, which led the Pan-Blue Coalition that opposed the DPP during Chen Shui-bian's presidency. Ma Ying-Jeou, the successful KMT candidate for president in the 2008 election, said the party founded by Chiang Kai-shek hopes for abolition in the future, but only after alternative crime prevention policies are implemented and only if abolition "would not adversely effect the public's support of the criminal justice system" (International Federation for Human Rights and Taiwan Alliance to End the Death Penalty 2006:14). In this respect, the KMT position on capital punishment resembles what many PRC scholars, jurists, and government officials say about the future of capital punishment in their country. Ma's personal experience with the death penalty also reveals some apprehensions. When he was minister of justice under Lee Teng-hui, he refused to sign several execution orders because of concerns about innocence and flaws in the prosecution process.

■ Public Opinion and the Decline of the Death Penalty in Democratic Taiwan

On the other side of the ambivalence are Taiwan's consistently high levels of public support for capital punishment. In the end, public opinion cannot explain capital punishment's trajectory in democratic Taiwan, not least because Taiwanese citizens have been largely "secluded" from international death penalty developments (Death Penalty Issue Research Group 2000). Instead, the push toward a different international identity with respect to this issue has been led by elites and NGOs, as is typically the case when nations are socialized to global culture during the liberalization and democratization processes (Taiwan Alliance to End the Death Penalty 2004; Lynch 2006).

Tables 6.2 and 6.3 summarize the results of 15 death penalty surveys conducted in Taiwan between 1990 and 2006. The first 11 surveys reveal that as in Japan, the Philippines, South Korea, and societies such as Singapore, Hong Kong, and the PRC, public support for capital punishment in Taiwan is strong, ranging from 63 to 83 percent. That support seems largely rooted in "a cultural belief in retribution" and a strong "desire for vengeance" among ordinary Taiwanese (International Federation for Human Rights and Taiwan Alliance to End the Death Penalty 2006:9). Conversely, support for abolition has been consistently meager, ranging between 6 and 21 percent. Death penalty support does not come from only the general public. Two surveys of death row inmates found that most condemned men and women favor capital punishment, though these responses may partly reflect the "terrible situation of prisons in Taiwan" at the time the surveys were conducted (Chen 2001:285). And in Buddhism, the predominant religion in Taiwan, three of the four most influential figures "remain firmly opposed to the abolition of the death penalty" (International Federation for Human Rights and Taiwan Alliance to End the Death Penalty 2006:14). One, Hsin Yun, the founder of the Fo Guang Shan Buddhist Order, said: "The abolition of capital punishment does not conform to the notion of cause and effect (karma), for those that perform evil do not receive proper retribution. This is both unjust and not in accordance with the truth" (Lim 2006).[24] In contrast, Christian organizations have been active in the campaign to end capital punishment, with the Catholic Church playing "a leading moral role"—as it did in the Philippines and as it does in South Korea as well (Kennedy and Guo 2006:2). Especially notable have been the abolitionist efforts of scholars, students, priests, and laypeople affiliated with the John Paul II Peace Institute at Fujen Catholic University in Taipei (Ryden 2001).[25]

Tables 6.2 and 6.3 also show that death penalty opinion in Taiwan is considerably more complicated than the answers to simple retention-or-abolition questions seem to suggest (Chiu 2006:3). In fact, when Taiwanese are asked whether they would favor abolition if the alternative of life imprisonment without parole existed, more respondents say yes than no, with an average level of support for abolition of 49.8 percent and an average level of support for retention of 41.5 percent. Since all of the LWOP questions were asked after 2000, it is impossible to tell whether the public's qualified support for abolition increased as a result of the turn toward democracy, but that is certainly plausible.

When survey results from Taiwan are compared to public responses in other nations, the similarities are much more evident than any Taiwanese differences. Support for the death penalty is similar to the general population figures for South Korea discussed in chapter 6 and is not much different from totals for the United States. Indeed, the close to 50-50 finding when execution is explicitly compared to life without possibility of parole nearly duplicates the result observed in the United States. But because the question suggests the questioning agency seems to desire such a reform, the without-possibility-of-parole results may overestimate the degree to which support for abolition falls when this alternative is mentioned. Still, there is little evidence in East Asia that there are strong public objections to nonexecution. Notwithstanding the strong public support in South Korea for capital punishment, the country's decade-long moratorium has been uncontroversial. In Taiwan, too, there was little public concern when executions stopped in 2006 and 2007.

24. Many religious traditions have supported state violence (Juergensmeyer 2003; Harris 2005). In the Asian context, for a cautionary tale about Zen Buddhist support for Japanese militarism before and during the Pacific war, see Victoria (2006).

25. According to statistics released by the Ministry of the Interior in 2002, Taiwan's "total religious population" made up 55.5 percent of ROC residents, with the other 44.5 percent being "nonreligious." Of those who were religious, 23.8 percent were Buddhist, 19.7 percent were Taoist, and 3.9 percent were Christian, with Protestants outnumbering Catholics 2 to 1. About 8 percent of Taiwanese belonged to other religious organizations.

Table 6.2

Death penalty surveys in Taiwan, 1990–2006

Date	Released by	% Retain	% Abolish	% Other
1990	United Daily News Group	83%	6%	11%
1990	Public Opinion Survey Taiwan	75%	9%	16%
1991	Public Opinion Survey Taiwan	69%	13%	18%
1993	United Daily News Group	63%	13%	24%
1994	Ministry of Justice	72%	N/A	N/A
1994	Public Opinion Survey Taiwan	69%	16%	15%
2000	United Daily News Group	75%	13%	12%
2001	Taiwan government	71%	12%	17%
2002	Taiwan government	77%	10%	13%
2002	Basic Survey on Social Changes	79%	12%	9%
2006	Public Opinion Survey Taiwan	76%	21%	3%

Source: Chiu 2006.

Note: The wording of the question varied. First survey (1990): "Should a country have the death penalty?" Next eight surveys (1990–2002): "Are you for or against the death penalty?" Last two surveys (2002, 2006): "Are you in favor of abolishing the death penalty?"

In these 11 surveys, the average level of support for capital punishments is 73.5 percent; the average level of support for abolition is 12.5 percent; and the average ratio of support for retention to support for abolition is nearly 6 to 1.

Table 6.3

Death penalty surveys in Taiwan, 2000–2006

Date	Released by	% Retain if LWOP	% Abolish if LWOP	% Other
2000	United Daily News Group	41%	49%	10%
2001	Taiwan government	38%	52%	10%
2002	Taiwan government	43%	47%	10%
2006	Public Opinion Survey Taiwan	44%	51%	4%

Source: Chiu 2006.

Note: Question: "Are you in favor of abolishing the death penalty and replacing it with life imprisonment without parole?" With this question, the average level of support for retention is 41.5 percent, and the average level of support for abolition is 49.8 percent. Thus, when a LWOP alternative is offered, support for abolition increases fourfold, from 12.5 percent to nearly 50 percent, while support for retention decreases by 32 percentage points, from 73.5 percent to 41.5 percent.

Our case study of capital punishment in Taiwan reveals two intriguing ironies related to the role of public opinion in democratic policy-making. Both can be observed in other Asian environments such as South Korea and the Philippines. First, the steep decline of the death penalty in democratic Taiwan was enabled by a governmental commitment to human rights even while the general level of awareness of human rights in Taiwan remained "extremely low" (International Federation for Human Rights and Taiwan Alliance to End the Death Penalty 2006:15; see also Human Rights Policy White Paper of the Republic of China 2002). What is more, when governments such as Chen Shui-bian's "led from the front" on death penalty issues by framing capital punishment as a question of human rights, they did so despite the fact that the reforms they promoted restrained their own capacity to pursue ends such as "crime control" that their publics deemed important. The second irony is even more fundamental. At the heart of any coherent theory of democracy is some conception of majority rule, yet in nations such as Taiwan and South Korea where governments have pushed for abolition, large public majorities continued to support capital punishment even while their presidents said (as did Kim Dae Jung) that "the people must be treated as masters." Three things can be said about the second irony. First, the most fundamental death penalty changes in democratic Taiwan and South Korea were countermajoritarian and therefore undemocratic in this important sense. Second, "treating the people as masters" in penal policy-making tends to produce harsh penal policies and practices that undermine jurisprudential principles (desert, parsimony, proportionality) in addition to contradicting more general principles of decency (Tonry 2007). Third, the death penalty does not seem to rank very high on the average citizen's list of concerns in Taiwan or South Korea (or in Japan, China, or the Philippines). When people in these places are asked whether they support capital punishment, the large majority say yes, but that should not be construed as enthusiasm for the executions or as evidence of high salience. Rather, those replies tend to reflect how much people in Taiwan—and the other Asian places, too—take the death penalty for granted, precisely because they intensely dislike crime and the people who commit it (Death Penalty Issue Research Group 2000:1; Zimring and Johnson 2006).

■ Explaining Taiwan's Execution Drop

As in South Korea, there were major execution declines in Taiwan even in authoritarian times. Our explanation of this drop emphasizes two factors similar to the ones that seemed important in South Korea under presidents Rhee and Park: (1) exposure and socialization to international norms that were increasingly critical of capital punishment and other forms of domestic state killing (Lynch 2006), and (2) the availability of other repressive means of control in Taiwan's system of "submerged totalitarianism," where every potential dissident, activist, and opponent "knew what powers the state possessed to detect and punish its political enemies," and the authorities were often "ruthless in employing those powers," but some dissent was permitted to go unpunished so that the regime could claim, to audiences at home and abroad, that it tolerated criticism and therefore deserved support (Roy 2003:93). These circumstances combined to make capital punishment at the end of four decades of martial law a less central feature of Taiwan's political landscape than it had been at the beginning. Yet the forces were not all impersonal. Chiang Ching-kuo proved to be an unexpected supporter of changes that enabled opponents of his nationalist party's repressive practices to produce progressive reform. Once liberalization started, it had "a spiraling effect" that enabled Taiwan's political opposition to capitalize on domestic and international circumstances, culminating in a "breakthrough" that occurred at almost the same time as South Korea's turn to democracy (181). The decline of the death penalty in authoritarian Taiwan was one important aspect of this liberalizing process.

Similarly, as in South Korea after its democratic revolution of 1987, the execution decline in democratic Taiwan occurred in the context of a variety of factors that often support punitive policy and practice when they exist in other national and cultural environments. These factors include a steady supply of high-profile crimes, sensationalistic reporting by the mass media, frequent moral panics, public demand that the government "get tougher" on crime, an increasingly populist conception and system of democracy, and public support for capital punishment (Tonry 2007). But if these factors can fuel harsh penal practices, what explains the steady falloff of executions in democratic Taiwan even when they are present?

Proximate Causes

The proximate causes are not difficult to identify. The first and perhaps the most important is "leadership from the front." Chen Shui-bian made "human rights" the most prominent plank in his platform for the presidency, and one month after being elected he responded to the pope's call for abolition by advocating abolition himself—"the first time in Taiwan's history" that a political leader has done so (International Federation for Human Rights and Taiwan Alliance to End the Death Penalty 2006:8). In the years that followed, Chen's government repeatedly reasserted that position and tried to turn the death penalty into a public issue. In 2001, minister of justice Chen Ding-nan announced that he wanted capital punishment abolished within the three remaining years of Chen's first term, though he stressed that "only when the public accepts abolition" would the government push for the necessary legal changes (Ryden 2001:295). Abolition did not happen in that time frame, but in 2004 the Ministry of Justice reaffirmed its position by releasing a five-page statement entitled "The Policy of the Ministry of Justice of Taiwan with Regard to Abolition of the Death Penalty." In it, the ministry called human rights "the foundation of the nation" and encouraged "extensive discussion and research" in order to "form a popular consensus for abolition," after which legislation would be enacted to eliminate the death penalty altogether. This approach—to phase out the death penalty "in stages" and to abolish only after "consensus" has been forged—was criticized for being too "slow" (International Federation for Human Rights and Taiwan Alliance to End the Death Penalty 2006); it is also inconsistent with what is known about the circumstances in which abolition usually occurs. In most if not all cases of abolition, the death penalty disappears despite majority support for its continued use (Hood 2002:233). There are other critics who contend that "all the talk of abolition is mostly for foreign dignitaries, scholars, and media" (Taipei judge quoted in Kennedy and Guo 2006:3). But if the reluctance of Chen's government to push for a LWOP alternative to the death penalty seemed to make the Ministry of Justice's claim that it was seriously committed to ending the death penalty "ring a little hollow" (Kennedy and Guo 2006:4), especially when polls showed that about half of Taiwanese said they would support abolition if such an alternative existed (Chiu 2006), his government did display courage "in running counter to widely held and deeply rooted emotions in Taiwan over the death penalty" (Kennedy and Guo 2006:5). Chen also presided over the most sustained execution decline in ROC history.

Four other proximate causes help explain the sharp decline in executions during Taiwan's democratization.[26] First, between 1987 and 2006 there were several major revisions to Taiwan's capital statutes. As of 2002, the death penalty was still mandatory for about 60 offenses and was optional for another 96 (Hood 2002:46). By the end of 2006, all the mandatory laws had been eliminated or altered to make death sentences discretionary. The most important statutory reform was of the Bandit Law, which originated in China during the Pacific war and subsequently was applied to Taiwan. In the 1990s, this sweeping statute became increasingly unpopular because of its association with martial law, and eventually it was abolished in 2002. Prior to that, 10 to 73 percent of those executed in any given year had been people convicted of violating provisions of this legislation, which was a "strange mix" of ten different offenses whose original purpose was to provide a kind of "catchall" net that would allow the nationalists to execute a wide range of "criminal" offenders under color of law (Hands Off Cain 1999; see table 6.1). Reforms of the kidnapping and rape-with-homicide laws had similar but smaller effects on the volume of capital sentences and executions (Kennedy 2004; Liao 2008).[27]

Second, Taiwan's Criminal Procedure Law was amended 17 times between 1990 and 2006. Most notably, the presumption of innocence was confirmed

26. Two forces that do not *directly* explain democratic Taiwan's drop in executions are international law (Taiwan has ratified neither the International Covenant on Civil and Political Rights nor the International Bill of Rights), and constitutional provisions and interpretations (Taiwanese courts have long endorsed capital statutes and have never guaranteed the right to life). See Liao (2008).

27. Reforms to Taiwan's murder, robbery, and drug laws further narrowed the scope of capital statutes but had little effect on death penalty practice (Liao 2008).

and emphasized, the right to a defense lawyer was amplified, and the law of evidence was revised to require prosecutors to bear the burden of proof and to make judges tighten the rules on admissibility. These changes shifted the balance of power in Taiwan's criminal court communities. Suspects gained more legal protection, prosecutors assumed more responsibility, and judges took on a more neutral, umpire-like role. Table 6.4 shows that despite violent crime rates having remained "fairly flat" since the 1990s (Kennedy and Guo 2006:4), these changes in the balance of power have had two important effects on capital punishment: a two-thirds decline in the number of death sentences sought by prosecutors (from 268 in 1992 to 86 in 2005), and a sharp increase in the propensity of judges to impose noncapital sentences even when prosecutors have sought the ultimate sanction. From 1996 to 2000, the ratio of death sentences requested by prosecutors to death sentences imposed by judges fluctuated in a narrow range between 5 to 1 and 8 to 1, but by 2004 and 2005 the ratios had increased to 29 to 1 and 86 to 1, respectively.[28] Public opinion polls show that, at least in the abstract, judges in Taiwan are significantly less likely to oppose capital punishment than are their South Korean counterparts.[29] In practice, however, judges in jurisdictions from Taipei to Kaohsiung have become markedly more reluctant to impose the ultimate penalty.[30] The timing is striking, too, for most of the change occurred after the election of a left-liberal president (Liao 2008).[31]

28. The decline in Taiwanese prosecutors' capital case "win rate" is pronounced, but compared to Japan, where a death sentence is imposed more than half the time prosecutors seek it, the proportion of cases charged capital that result in a death sentence has long been low.

29. In a poll taken in 2000, 88 percent of Taiwanese criminal justice personnel (judges, prosecutors, police officers, and prison guards) said they supported capital punishment (unpublished manuscript available from the authors, 2007), and in other surveys fully 90 percent of judges and prosecutors favored it, making them "the strongest supporters" of the death penalty in Taiwan (International Federation for Human Rights and Taiwan Alliance to End the Death Penalty 2006:37). In South Korea, by contrast, 83 percent of prosecutors and 47 percent of judges said they supported capital punishment (see chapter 5).

30. In contrast to Japan and South Korea, polls show that 60 to 70 percent of citizens in Taiwan lack confidence in their judiciary and judicial system (Death Penalty Issue Research Group 2000:7). This lack of support is related to a more general pattern of distrust in officialdom, for "almost half of the people [in Taiwan] oppose whatever the government stands for" (unpublished manuscript available from the authors, 2007). The distrust may also reflect the history of immigration to Taiwan, for many of the people who came to be known as Taiwanese came to the island in order to get away from government repression in China (Roy 2003:31).

31. Judges on Taiwan's Supreme Court showed little reluctance in February 2006 when they imposed seven death sentences on former high school teacher Tseng Si-ru, who murdered a female colleague in 2002 after she caught him breaking into her apartment. Tseng hit the victim in the head with a dumbbell, slit her neck with a knife, and then turned on the gas before he left in order to make the death look like a suicide (Hands Off Cain, February 20, 2006).

Table 6.4

Death sentences sought by prosecutors and imposed by trial courts,
Taiwan, 1992–2006

Year	Death sentences sought (A)	Death sentences imposed (B)	Ratio of A to B
1992	268	37	7.2 to 1
1993	180	20	9.0 to 1
1994	147	16	9.2 to 1
1995	192	15	12.8 to 1
1996	157	20	7.9 to 1
1997	174	35	5.0 to 1
1998	158	31	5.1 to 1
1999	125	23	5.4 to 1
2000	94	18	5.2 to 1
2001	103	10	10.3 to 1
2002	103	9	11.4 to 1
2003	107	7	15.3 to 1
2004	116	4	29.0 to 1
2005	86	1	86.0 to 1
2006	N/A	0	N/A

Source: Liao 2008.

The third proximate cause of Taiwan's recent death penalty decline concerns the execution process, and this is not so much a legal change as a bureaucratic one that was stimulated by legal professionals' perception of unfairness in the capital process. As in South Korea and Japan, once a death sentence is finalized in Taiwan the minister of justice must issue a warrant in order for an execution to occur. After three persons were executed in October 1998, an attorney complained that he had not received the Supreme Court's final judgment until the day after his client had been killed. His complaint stimulated several Taiwanese NGOs to conduct a survey of defense lawyers, and the results revealed that similar problems (such as executions while appeals are still in progress) had occurred in at least 23 other cases. In turn, the survey elicited a critical opinion from the Control Yuan (a governmental watchdog) that prompted the Ministry of Justice to produce guidelines (in 1999) to improve its execution protocol by implementing more of the internal, bureaucratic review processes that long have been operative in Japan's Ministry of Justice. The effect has been a more cautious approach to execution in the Taiwanese organizations—the Ministry of Justice and the procuracy—that are finally responsible for turning inmates on death row into corpses. Since it is prosecutors in these organizations (not defense attorneys) who have authority to file extraordinary appeals after a death sentence has been finalized—an authority they often have used—the creation of "a better and more careful execution procedure" has also helped fuel Taiwan's execution decline (Kennedy and Guo 2006; Liao 2008).[32]

Finally, the personal backgrounds of several leaders of the Democratic Progressive Party have also influenced death penalty policy in Taiwan. Chapter 5 showed a pervasive overlap between political leadership in South Korea and personal experience with the death penalty and other criminal punishment. Many prominent politicians in Taiwan are also veterans of criminal prosecution, but only in the left-leaning party. Most notably, Annette Lu, Chen Shui-bian's vice president in the most recent DPP administration, was tried and convicted for treason after the Kaohsiung incident of 1979, and Chen himself and Frank Chang-ting Hsieh (the DPP presidential candidate in 2008) served as defense counsel in the case. No major figure in the right-leaning KMT party has had similar experience. Given this divergence, it is no mystery that it is the party of the left that is much more committed to the abolition of capital punishment (Kumamoto and Nishi 2008).

Fundamental Forces

In the background of the proximate causes that drove executions down in democratic Taiwan are two more fundamental motives that we call "push and pull factors." The first is the desire to *pull away* from the authoritarian excesses of Taiwan's recent past. Capital punishment and extrajudicial executions were prominent features of Taiwanese politics at least through the 1970s, and like other states—Italy, West Germany, Spain, and the Philippines—that moved away from state killing as part of the process of distancing themselves from the repressive practices of previous governments, Taiwan also pulled away from state killing when it turned toward democracy (Zimring 2003).

The second motive, which complements the first, is the desire to *push toward* a different identity in the world as a state committed to "a package of values that is associated not just with belonging to the same civilization" that most developed democracies belong to but also with "a substantial convergence in the norms, rules, institutions, and goals of the states concerned" (Buzan 2004:146; see also Lynch 2006:9). Under President Chen Shui-bian especially, Taiwan did much to push toward "convergence" with the human rights "norms, rules, institutions, and goals" that prevailed in devel-

---

32. In addition to the proximate causes discussed above, "general pardons" in 1988 (following the death of President Chiang Ching-kuo) and 1991 (to commemorate the 80th anniversary of the ROC's founding) reduced death sentences to life imprisonment for 26 and 38 death row inmates, respectively. These pardons had to go through the legislative process. As of this writing, presidents in democratic Taiwan, including Chen Shui-bian, have never used their constitutional power to grant amnesty to inmates on death row (Liao 2008). This contrasts with South Korea (see chapter 5).

oped democracies.[33] Taiwan's international isolation made this goal all the more imperative (Manthorpe 2005). In particular, the fear of being swallowed by China, that giant neighbor's shadow over much Taiwanese policy-making, and the perception that the high volume of executions in the PRC "perhaps shames the country internationally more than any other single question" (Bakken 2007:182) make capital punishment an especially attractive sphere for demonstrating that the ROC is a fundamentally different—and better— kind of regime than the PRC. Taiwan's symbolic power "has always been as a democratic counterpoint to China" (Yardley 2006b), and Taiwan's push toward ending the death penalty is one way that symbolic power has been amplified.[34] As President Chen said in his 2000 inaugural address:

> we are also willing to promise a more active contribution in
> safeguarding international human rights. The Republic of China cannot
> and will not remain outside global human rights trends. We will abide
> by the Universal Declaration of Human Rights, the International
> Covenant on Civil and Political Rights, and the Vienna Declaration
> and Program of Action. We will bring the Republic of China back
> into the international human rights system. (quoted in Ryden 2001:295)

33. One example of this push toward convergence occurred after the International Federation for Human Rights, an NGO that brings together 141 human rights organizations from 100 countries, and the Taiwan Alliance to End the Death Penalty released the results of their international fact-finding mission on the death penalty in Taiwan in June 2006. Their 50-page report was highly critical of many aspects of Taiwan's capital punishment system. The core claim was that because "momentum has been gathering in Taiwan for abolition," now is the time for its government "to take the final steps," a call that was later echoed by the *Taipei Times* newspaper ("Death to the Death Penalty" 2008). Taiwan did not abolish right away, but its Ministry of Justice did respond immediately to many of the report's criticisms (Hands Off Cain, June 13, 2006). By the end of 2006, the last three laws providing for mandatory death sentences had been amended.

34. There is also at least one way Taiwan might *emulate* China: by enacting a reform that would allow a death sentence to be suspended for two years while the behavior and attitude of the condemned is assessed. In the PRC, perhaps one-third of death sentences are suspended in this way, and the vast majority of those are ultimately reduced to some sentence less than death (see chapter 7). In Taiwan, there was considerable talk about this reform possibility in governmental and human rights circles during Chen's presidency (Hands Off Cain, December 31, 2005), and a survey in 2006 found that 62 percent of Taiwanese supported a policy that would allow the condemned to be resentenced to lifetime or long-term imprisonment if he or she was "well-behaved and/or expressed regret" during the period the death sentence was suspended; 35 percent of respondents were opposed (Chiu 2006:9). Japan considered a similar reform in the 1980s, but the proposal never made it to the Diet.

■ Taiwan Futures

The completion of a second consecutive year without executions was a major milestone for Taiwan in 2007 but probably far from the end of the era of state execution. At the time of this writing, the president most closely associated with opposition to capital punishment is four months out of office and in no position to leave any powerful political legacies, and there is nowhere near the legislative constituency for abolition in Taiwan that has existed in South Korea in recent years. The new president of Taiwan, Ma Ying-jeou, is from the KMT, and the landslide victory of the KMT in January 2008 also gave it control of more than 70 percent of the seats in the national legislature (Enav 2008). As of May 2008, therefore, the KMT has unified control of Taiwan's government for the first time in more than a decade and the potential to break the gridlock that slowed policy-making during President Chen's tenure (Lee et al. 2008).

Capital punishment was not an important issue in the 2008 presidential election campaign, but the results of that election did put some pressure on the new KMT executive to alter death penalty policy.[35] The issue of capital punishment came up only once in the campaign, when a question prepared by anti–death penalty activists put DPP candidate Frank Hsieh on record as supporting abolition as a human rights imperative, while Ma Ying-jeou argued that the death penalty should not be regarded as a human rights question.

The general climate in Taiwan supports the continuation of democratic reforms and political pluralism, and the rightward move in presidential politics is not a step back from either democracy or multiparty politics. In this respect, Taiwan will remain much closer to South Korea than to Singapore in the immediate future. Still, the large legislative majority of the right is a significant shift. What might it portend for executions? One possibility is an early end to the cessation of executions that started in 2006. As mentioned in chapter 2, Asian countries have experienced many multiyear moratoria that ended before reaching Amnesty International's ten-year threshold for de facto "abolition."

But perhaps executions in Taiwan will not resume under the new regime. During the 1990s, many crime and punishment issues were high-profile political matters in Taiwan (three strikes, mandatory prison terms, and so on), but the death penalty did not become a sharply contested political question ("Death to the Death Penalty" 2008). This is a strong contrast to the politics of criminal justice in the United States during the 1990s, and may

---

35. When eight NGO representatives were asked whether executions were likely to resume if Ma Ying-jeou won the March 2008 election, half of them said there would be at least one execution under Ma, and the reason most often given was pressure from conservative KMT legislators (Taiwan Alliance to End the Death Penalty, interview by Zimring, February 26, 2008).

suggest that in Taiwan capital punishment has already become an issue that transcends more ordinary crime and punishment concerns, at least for political leaders. Indeed, after Ma Ying-jeou was elected president in 2008, his appointment to the minister of justice position was Wang Ching-feng, a woman who previously held a number of high government posts and who personally disapproves of the death penalty. Upon being assigned to the position with responsibility for signing execution orders, Wang even told the media: "Life should not be taken away from a human being. I respect life. The removal of one life cannot restore a lost life" ("Taiwan Must Not" 2008). She also promised to consider abolishing the death penalty while at the same time warning that she did not know how to go about achieving that goal because it would run counter to public opinion. In response, one of Taiwan's largest newspapers published an editorial lamenting that "public opinion is a factor selectively ignored or drawn upon by policymakers presenting their case" and calling on "Taiwan's leaders to stop serving up excuses and set the [abolition] ball in motion" ("Death to the Death Penalty" 2008).[36] The other major influence in Taiwan during the spring of 2008 was the question of human rights that China's repression in Tibet pushed front and center for president-elect Ma. The violence in Tibet put pressure on Ma's government to emphasize respect for human rights, and while Ma has suggested that capital punishment in Taiwan is not a human rights issue, that assertion is contested. Whatever carryover human rights concerns might have for domestic capital punishment could result in a push toward a cautious continuation of nonexecution with no clear statement of policy intention. And whatever influence comes from the new KMT legislative majority could push toward a small number of executions, perhaps a few of the 29 execution-eligible persons in Ministry of Justice custody (Y. K. Huang, interview by Zimring, February 26, 2008). But it is easy to overestimate the political pressures on

36. A few days before Ma and Wang assumed their new posts, three seemingly progressive positions on the death penalty that had been taken by President Chen's Ministry of Justice were rejected by the Judicial Yuan, Taiwan's highest judicial organ. One would have required that a death sentence be imposed only when all judges agree on it (under current law a death sentence can be imposed by majority verdict). Another proposal would have required Supreme Court justices to meet and converse with attorneys representing the defendant when they review a death sentence on appeal (under current law the Supreme Court only reviews legal documents). The third proposal would have granted a stay of execution to death row defendants who file a petition for retrial or extraordinary appeal. In explaining its resistance to these reforms, the Judicial Yuan said that as the government agency in charge of administering capital punishment, the Ministry of Justice should decide the more fundamental question of the future of the death penalty rather than upholding death sentences and then placing restrictions on judges' authority to impose them ("Disagrees" 2008). If Chen's Ministry of Justice did not push as hard for abolition as it might have, it was considerably more progressive on death penalty issues than the Ministries of Justice in Japan and South Korea.

both sides of the capital punishment question, for the death penalty is simply not very important in the Taiwan of 2008.

In our view, there is much uncertainty about future death penalty policy in Taiwan, but the field of choice in likely policies is relatively narrow. The two most likely scenarios are a lengthening period of nonexecution—a low-visibility moratorium that receives little political fanfare—or a resumption of executions under a new president in small volume and with episodic regularity. Formal abolition in the next few years seems unlikely, but it would be equally surprising if the country were to use execution with anything near its vigor in 2000, when Taiwan ranked third among all 29 Asian jurisdictions.

Thus, the most likely future is either a quiet continuation of the 2006–2007 hiatus in executions or a more visible shift to five or fewer per year. The first scenario would involve little systemic change if it results from a continuation of the quiet executive branch inaction that began under President Chen, but any resumption of state killing would probably require shifts in the method of execution, a reduction in the number and definition of capital crimes, and reform in procedures for the review of death sentences. In this sense, a zero-execution future might involve less legal and political change than would a transition to symbolic rates of capital punishment, and uncertainty over procedural matters such as appeal and means of execution could provide the new government with reasons to delay the resumption of executions and perhaps even to create a study commission to advise the new executive. For the Ma presidency, the level of *uncertainty* about death penalty futures is high enough to merit a study commission strategy even though the level of public and political *salience* on this issue is low. In the middle-range future of an independent Taiwan, the prospects for formal abolition are closely tied to the fortunes of the left-wing DPP, which is now committed by its leadership to that goal. The KMT seems unlikely to second support for abolition.

Any analysis of future policy choices in Taiwan must also consider the looming presence of the PRC and the possibility of unification or confederation between the two governments. Penal policies are a minor part of the portfolio of concerns about future relations between the two Chinas, but the prospect of change in their relationship may be an important aspect of how senior leaders in Taiwan think about the future of capital punishment. What we have called a "human rights/limits of government" motivation for limiting or ending state executions takes on a special meaning when confederation or unification with the mainland is a possibility. Those who oppose the death penalty in Taiwan could employ the PRC example in discussions of appropriate domestic policy for their own country in two distinct ways: by using mainland policy as a basis for invidious comparisons with Taiwan (contrasting PRC brutality with Taiwanese legality and respect for human rights), or by arguing that clear policy limiting capital punishment must be created if Taiwanese views are to survive any future confederation with the mainland, as happened in Hong Kong and Macao (see appendix B).

So one can imagine a two-tiered dialogue on the death penalty in Taiwan, with proponents of execution stressing crime control concerns and abolitionists placing a stronger emphasis on human rights and the need to limit government than in other nations—stronger because in the future the governmental power under discussion may not be solely Taiwan's. Citizens' attention to the role of the PRC in Taiwan's future may stimulate a stronger receptiveness to arguments about the need to limit state power to use severe sanctions. It also seems likely that the more imminent confederation or collaboration with the PRC becomes, the more powerful becomes the argument for Taiwanese abolition as a useful element of a potential political effort to limit China's power to use execution as a repressive tool of government.

All of this could lead to an "only in Taiwan" variant of the left-versus-right political alignments that tend to prevail on capital punishment. Political actors interested in smoothing the path to cooperation with the PRC might be eager to keep the peace on potentially controversial punishment issues such as execution. A sustained moratorium on execution, or even abolition, could function as a gesture of Taiwan's independence and a reassurance to the Taiwanese electorate about the limits of PRC power that might help ease a transition to closer relations with Taiwan's enormous sibling state. Other developments in Asia could influence Taiwan's path, but none is as important as those in the PRC. A continuation of the South Korean moratorium might help Taiwan's abolition prospects, and a well-publicized abolition in South Korea that generated favorable comment on the Korean leadership could help even more, though it should be acknowledged that, so far anyway, neither Taiwan nor South Korea has paid much attention to the other when it comes to death penalty policy and practice.

Compared to South Korea, the issue of capital punishment in Taiwan is less important in the political sphere, and the future course of debate and legislation is far less clear. Taiwan's two major parties have contrasting positions typical of European governments late in the path toward abolition, with the left (now out of power) seeking to end the death penalty and the right deemphasizing the issue. But this political situation is a recent development and a by-product of Taiwan's swift march toward plural democracy. Compared to most other nations in Asia, the Taiwan story is one of striking change, from one of the highest rates of execution in the region to a multiyear moratorium and a national executive branch seeking a path to abolition. The magnitude of these changes is one of the most remarkable developments in Asian death penalty policy.

7

The Political Origins of China's Death Penalty Exceptionalism

> In trying to understand China today we need to know about China in the past; but how far back we carry that search remains, in a sense, the central question.
>
> —Jonathan D. Spence, *The Search for Modern China* (1990)

> Judicial exceptionalism in the practices of the death penalty existed in China before Mao.... But Mao radicalized this trend to an extreme degree.
>
> —Zhang Ning (2008)

A case study of death penalty policy in the PRC is, for this type of book, both indispensable and impossible. China is the most populous nation in Asia and the world and has probably carried out most of the executions on the planet for the last half century. How could we write a book on capital punishment in Asia without a chapter on the nation that by most estimates conducts more than 90 percent of the region's (and the world's) executions? Such a chapter is the sine qua non of case studies of Asian death penalties.

The problem is that by ordinary standards of empirical research, an acceptable profile of the death penalty in China is impossible. The number of persons executed in the PRC in 2007 is not merely unavailable, it is a state secret, disclosure of which triggers serious criminal liability. One result is that the number of executions for that year is unknown, with educated guesses ranging from 2,000 to 15,000. And since the number of executions has been a state secret for decades, there is no basis for constructing execution trends over time in either the short or the long term. Are executions in 2007 higher or lower than in 1990? Than in 2006? And by how much? We complained in chapter 6 about the absence of reliable execution estimates for Taiwan during the 1960s and 1970s, but the data available for Taiwan are vastly superior to the statistical black hole of Chinese capital punishment. These data constraints are fundamental, effectively limiting the range and reliability of any scholarship on the death penalty in the PRC. When we confronted similar data problems for Vietnam, the nation that may have the third highest execution rate in Asia, we excluded it as a candidate for detailed case study treatment (see appendix C). But since the PRC is too central to our subject to exclude, this chapter is constructed around limits that sound scholarship would ordinarily find unacceptable.

The statistical black hole is only the beginning of the empirical problems that bedevil efforts to comprehend China's criminal process. Jerome Cohen's pathbreaking book on the subject had to rely on information provided by Chinese expatriates (Cohen 1968:8). Although the situation has improved in some respects (Tanner 1999:ix; Trevaskes 2007), data on crime rates at any time, and therefore on crime trends as well, remain often unavailable and frequently unreliable (Bakken 2004; Bakken 2005). Similarly, information about critical stages and processes in the criminal justice system, including trials, appeals, and incarceration, is frequently difficult to obtain and evaluate. To study criminal justice in China is to operate in an environment where adjectives often must substitute for numbers and where many accounts of how the system works are highly provisional.

This chapter begins by providing a context for capital punishment in the PRC through descriptions of the scale of criminal justice there and the political organization of the criminal justice system. Next, we estimate execution incidence in the post-Mao reform period, 1976 to the present. We then contrast two explanations for the high rates of execution in recent years: Chinese history as an influence on contemporary penal culture, and the political legacy of the past half century. We argue that the proximate causes of China's death penalty exceptionalism are more rooted in the nation's recent history—and in the legacy of the PRC's founding fathers: Joseph Stalin, Mao Zedong, and Deng Xiaoping—than in the *Analects of Confucius*, the punishment philosophies of emperors or mandarins, or the social practices associated with these ideas.

We then move on to an analysis of the 2007 reinstitution of death sentence review by the Supreme People's Court (SPC), a reversal of a 1983 policy that decentralized appellate review in order to crack down on crime by encouraging and expediting executions. We examine the motives for the reform, the methods selected to implement the new system, and the reasons China has made this change a prominent part of its international profile. We also summarize some other recent death penalty reforms, including the issuance of guidelines for prosecuting and sentencing in capital cases, the advent of lethal injection as an execution method, and the effort to create a cash-for-clemency system. We then describe the likely impact of the 2007 reform and other recent changes on the number of executions, the administrative character and costs of the PRC's death penalty system, and the types of reform proposals that may emerge from China's renewed experience with SPC review.

The final section of this chapter focuses on the long-term future of capital punishment in China. The goal of many CCP leaders and most legal professionals in the PRC is criminal justice without executions, but this aspiration usually comes attached to qualifications that posit a long-term future in which the country is economically developed and its legal system is significantly more advanced than it is today. Is this vision a sincere ambition or a method of reassuring Western observers that the PRC will respect the principles of other developed nations? And if the aspiration is genuine, what major obstacles separate the status quo in China from a future in which the nation is capable of sustaining its criminal law without state executions? In an environment where change is a pervasive feature of national existence in every sphere from agriculture (O'Brien and Li 2006) to industry (Fallows 2007) and from sex (Druckerman 2007) to sects (Perry and Selden 2000), how far away is such a long-term future?

■ Government and Criminal Justice in the PRC

The natural starting point for any discussion of crime and punishment in modern China is the sheer size of the nation and the scale of institutions used to govern and sustain it. The national population of 1.3 billion is divided into a complicated, multilayered system of government with separations between the village, town, county, municipal, provincial, and central levels (Chen and Wu 2006:173). For most of China, one step below the central government are the provincial governments, analogous to state governments in the organizational chart of the U.S. federal system and the units of government with primary administrative responsibility for criminal justice functions such as courts and prisons. Several Chinese provinces are equal in population, size, and economic organization to modern Asian nations such as Vietnam and Thailand. If California, the most populous U.S. state, were part of the PRC, it would be only the 17th most populated province. As of 2007, three Chinese provinces—Henan, Shandong, and Sichuan—had larger populations than Germany, the most populous country in Europe, and China's total population was nearly three times greater than the aggregate population (454 million) of the 28 countries in the European Union. In the same year, 171 cities in China had populations of more than one million, compared to nine such cities in the United States (Schell 2008).

China's vast size and population have prevented it from supporting professional police forces that are as large, per capita, as those in neighboring countries, let alone in industrialized nations. This is one reason why it has frequently been attracted to "cheap deterrence" strategies such as the "Strike Hard" (*yanda*) campaigns, which rely heavily on public cooperation and activism in order to maintain social control (Tanner 2000:95).

The division of political authority for criminal justice matters between the different levels of Chinese government is different from that in federalist systems such as the United States (T. Lee 2000). In China, the exclusive authority to draft criminal laws (and thus authorize penalties) is in principle possessed by the national government, so for the most part variations between provinces in the definition of crimes or in the range of penalties authorized by law do not exist. This contrasts with the United States, where the federal criminal code is the authority for prosecution only in the federal courts, and each of the 50 states has its own penal code with different prohibitions and penalties.

But while the principles of crime and punishment are the monopoly of the national government in China, the institutions of punishment are almost exclusively the responsibility of local governments. The central Ministry of Justice maintains only one prison—Yancheng, outside Beijing. All other prisons are the administrative and financial responsibility of provincial and municipal governments (and of the five "autonomous regions" that have equivalent authority). Since jails and other short-term detention facilities are operated by provincial, county, or municipal governments (in practice most are run by the police), almost all of China's prisons and jails are provincial and local. Police are generally regulated by the national Ministry of Public Security but are employed, assigned, and usually controlled at the provincial, county, and municipal levels.[1]

Two practical points must supplement this formal description of the responsibilities of the levels of government in Chinese criminal justice. The first is true of all criminal justice systems: where local officials have discretionary power—and police, prosecutors, judges, and prison officials in China do—the exercise of it can make a huge difference in how the criminal law is enforced. In the campaigns against crime that have been a recurrent feature of Chinese society during the reform period, party leaders, police, prosecutors, and courts at the local level frequently stretch their new grants of authority to the limit, while the central institutions that might impose modest checks on their powers—such as the Supreme People's Procuratorate and the SPC—are either weakened by the campaign directives or voluntarily subordinate themselves to the local officials leading the crackdown (Tanner 1999; Tanner 2000:109; Trevaskes 2007). Thus, the large institutional role of local and provincial officials in China implies the power to shape and redefine the general principles announced by officials at the center.

The second practical point counterbalances the centrifugal force of local discretion and has special force in contemporary China. In the central government and the Communist Party, there are important loci of power and administrative attention that influence local decision-making and often control it. The government of the PRC is authoritarian, and the authority lies at the center of the system. Provincial and local police, prosecutors, courts, and prison administrators can ignore mandates from Beijing—and frequently do—but if the issue is crucial to the central government, they may pay a significant price (Chen and Wu 2006; Tanner and Green 2007).

Studies of criminal punishment too often divorce the death penalty from other penal sanctions (Gottschalk 2006). Figure 7.1 provides one measure of the scale and severity of Chinese criminal justice by comparing the estimated population of

---

1. In addition to the Ministry of Public Security, there is a separate Ministry of State Security that is administered by the central government and engages in policing and jailing operations.

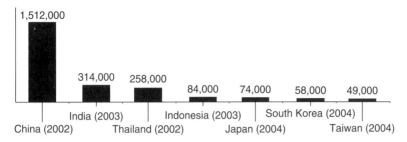

Figure 7.1
Scale of imprisonment in seven Asian nations
Note: Bars represent prisoners, including those in pretrial detention. *Source*: Walmsley
2004.

persons imprisoned in China and six other Asian jurisdictions. There are two
ways of illustrating the relative size of China's imprisonment system in its Asian
context: by comparing its prison population to those in other major Asian nations
individually, and by comparing the Chinese total to the collective size of the prisons
in the other six nations combined. China dominates the individual comparisons in
Asia, with five times as many persons in prison as India, the next largest prison
system. The only nation in the modern world with an aggregate prison population equal to that of the PRC is the United States. And even when the other six
Asian nations are considered in the aggregate, their combined total of 837,000
inmates is only a little more than half the number of prisoners in China alone.

The absolute size of China's prison system is important for many reasons
but it is not a good indicator of the relative impact of punishment and
criminal justice because there are no controls for the very different population
sizes of the nations reported in figure 7.1. Figure 7.2 shows the estimated rates
of imprisonment per 100,000 for the same seven nations after controls for
population have been applied.[2] When the focus shifts from the size of each

2. In figures 7.1 and 7.2, the imprisonment numbers for China do not reflect persons
kept in custody for "reeducation through labor" (*laojiao*), a system of administrative
detention in which the police detain persons for up to four years for minor crimes such as
petty theft or prostitution and for crimes against the state such as leading unregistered house
churches (Biddulph 2008; Yi 2008). *Laojiao* should be distinguished from *laogai* ("reform
through labor"), which denotes the Chinese prison system more generally. As of 2007, there
were an estimated 300,000 persons detained at *laojiao* centers, and the U.S. State Department
said about half of them were practitioners of the Falun Gong religion, which was banned in
1999. Scholar Fu Hualing has found that *laojiao* institutions are so strongly influenced by the
need to meet economic targets that the police intentionally increase arrests when they need
more labor to fulfill their quotas (Fu 2005:213). *Laojiao* sentences are imposed by the police
without judicial review, and *laojiao* detainees are held at facilities separate from the regular
prison system. Figures 7.1 and 7.2 also exclude detention for administrative violations for
periods of up to 15 days, which in recent years has numbered approximately five million
people per year (Jerome A. Cohen, New York University professor of law, interview by
Johnson and Zimring, January 25, 2008).

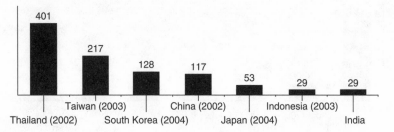

Figure 7.2
Rates of imprisonment in seven Asian nations per 100,000 population
Source: Walmsley 2004.

nation's prisons to the rate of imprisonment per unit of population, the PRC estimate puts China in the middle of the distribution of Asian nations. Two countries, Thailand and Taiwan, have rates of imprisonment that are clearly higher, while South Korea's imprisonment rate is approximately equal to China's. The reason China's prisons dwarf her neighbors' is that the other large nations in Asia—Japan, Indonesia, and India—have rates of imprisonment that vary from half (Japan) to one-quarter (India and Indonesia) of the Chinese rate. A similar pattern emerges when other populous nations of Asia are considered, such as Bangladesh (45 per 100,000) and Pakistan (59 per 100,000). Thus, China does not have the most severe imprisonment policy in Asia; it achieves its statistical prominence only because it is the most severe of the large Asian nations.

One careful analysis of confinement facilities and their populations in the PRC, by James Seymour, adds a series of prison- and jail-like institutions and arrives at a combined rate of around 160 inmates per 100,000, which is about one-third higher than the 117 per 100,000 in figure 7.2 (Seymour 2005). The higher number is probably closer to the true rate of Chinese incarceration, but we prefer to use the same source of data for China as for the other six nations in the comparison. We cannot tell what the results would be if Seymour's method were applied to the other nations, but even if the new rate of 160 per 100,000 were compared to the uncorrected estimates for the other six jurisdictions, the PRC's position would only move one slot to the left, from fourth to third. And if the 117 per 100,000 estimate for current imprisonment is correct, then the rate of imprisonment in contemporary China is not far removed from the nations of central and eastern Europe. Even at 160 per 100,000, the scale of imprisonment in China would be unexceptional by world and Asian standards, though it is substantially higher than the imprisonment rates in populous countries such as Indonesia and India.

But the size and aggregate cost of prisons in China is larger than in other big Asian nations. The total cost of Chinese jails and prisons and the unit cost per prisoner are not known, though one Chinese prosecutor has said that the annual operating budget of $210 million for San Quentin prison in California (with 5,222 inmates and 1,718 staff members as of March 2007) is "equal to that of 10 prisons of the same size in China" (Dan 2007a:5). We do know, however, that while imprisonment is a labor-intensive process, the level of skill required for most prison personnel is not high, and the security needs at most Chinese prisons are not especially stringent (prison officials, interview by Johnson, June 2007).

A related question about the political economy of Chinese imprisonment is the extent to which prison labor programs defray the costs of security and subsistence. Seymour's guess puts the figure at 40 percent (2005:157). With the right combination of jobs, employable prisoners, and well-governed institutions, Chinese provinces might come close to breaking even on their prisons, although we suspect there is substantial variation by region, province, and type of facility in the productivity and income of Chinese prison labor.

The final question about the political economy of Chinese prisons that we consider here is what level of government pays for their operating costs. Because the primary responsibility for prison administration is provincial, it is tempting to assume that fiscal responsibility is also a provincial matter, but this is not necessarily true. Seymour (2005:157) reports a series of national government commitments to subsidize prison construction and administration, but the ultimate nationwide total of central government support for operating prisons was planned to reach only 80 million yuan, which is less than 1 percent of the total estimated prison cost in the same study. It appears that the vast majority of prison costs in China are borne by governments at the provincial and local levels.

■ Estimating Executions in China

Profound data problems frustrate efforts to describe the trajectory of Chinese capital punishment in the last half of the 20th century (Hood 2002:90; Lu and Miethe 2007:x,73), as well as efforts to understand many other aspects of Chinese society.[3] "Intense secrecy and manipulation of information have

---

3. Two important problems of data reliability concern the size of China's economy and its rate of growth. In 2007, the Chinese economy seemed to shrink by about 40 percent overnight—losing a slice of the pie about the same size as Japan's national output—because the "purchasing power parity" measure that had been used to adjust for price differences between countries was determined to be based on an outdated survey of prices. Things in China have become significantly more expensive, and the result of the price rise is more than a technicality. Among other effects, the number of Chinese who live below the World Bank's poverty line of a dollar a day suddenly jumped from about 100 million to 300 million (Porter 2007). Similar data problems confound efforts to measure the growth rate of China's economy. The PRC currently claims that the national economy is growing at 10 to 11 percent per year, but the official statistic for the overall growth rate "is best regarded as an approximate growth rate of the economy of its cities" (Thurow 2007). The true overall growth rate may be somewhere between 4.5 percent and 6 percent a year.

long been regarded as an essential part of successful government and diplomacy" in the PRC (Becker 2000:2).[4] But at least two conclusions do emerge from the available evidence. First, the PRC has been a frequent user of execution for most of the six decades since the state was founded in 1949. Indeed, the number of annual executions in this nation must be counted with at least one more digit, and usually two or three, than executing states elsewhere. For the last two decades, the PRC has carried out thousands of executions each year, accounting for at least 90 percent (and probably more) of all the executions in the world. In absolute terms, this makes China the world's execution leader, and whatever country is in second place is not close. In per capita terms as well, China is, along with Singapore, one of only two jurisdictions in Asia with enough executions to warrant being called a nation with an "operational" system of capital punishment (see chapter 2). Our second conclusion is that China's huge national total probably obscures substantial variation across time and in the many different regions of the country. The evidence here is thinner, but it does seem clear that early in the 21st century, some parts of China use capital punishment markedly more than others.

This section summarizes the evidence supporting these conclusions about what can be called the vital statistics on capital punishment for the PRC.[5]

4. In 2007, the international NGO Human Rights in China released a 280-page report, "State Secrets: China's Legal Labyrinth," which examines how the PRC's "complex and opaque state secrets system sweeps a vast universe of information into the state secrets net," including the incidence of occupational illness, statistics on trafficking in women and children, information on unusual deaths in prisons and juvenile detention facilities, the frequency of strikes, and data on water and solid waste pollution. The report argues that China's state secrets system "is dangerous to the health of people not only in China but also worldwide, and undermines healthy governance and rule of law" (Human Rights in China 2007).

5. Because this book focuses on judicial executions, we do not discuss the incidence of extrajudicial killing in China or its trends over time (on extrajudicial killing generally, see appendix G). Note, however, that there are many accounts of gross and systemic human rights abuses in the PRC, including reports of organ seizures from practitioners of the Falun Gong religion. According to one source (the reliability of which is in dispute), many Falun Gong members have been murdered by military personnel so that their organs could be harvested and sold on China's lucrative organ transplantation market. See the report by Canadian attorneys David Matas and David Kilgour (2007). Ian Johnson's (2004:183–292) account of the repression of Falun Gong after the religion was designated an "evil cult" by the Chinese government in 1999 estimates that at least 30,000 faithful were jailed during the first two years after the crackdown started, while James D. Seymour says the number "is believed to have been in the tens of thousands" (2005:155). The government's repression of Falun Gong helped transform it into a transnational movement promoting human rights and the fall of communism in China (Hail 2008). On Chinese dissidents who have been imprisoned in mental hospitals and maltreated for being "political maniacs," see Robin Munro (2003). In 2006, Human Rights Watch said it had documented 3,000 cases of

After a brief exploration of two ways of thinking about whether China's current execution figures are large or small, we estimate the volume of executions in 1998–2006—a period that starts after a recent Strike Hard campaign and ends with the reintroduction of death sentence review by the SPC in 2007. Then, we identify the important and mostly unanswered questions that exist about execution trends over time for the past generation and about differences in rates of execution in different parts of this huge and diverse nation.

A Large or Small Number?

Mu Wang, president of the Chinese Society of Criminology, responded to a lecture Johnson gave in 2007 with the following comment: "I don't know what the exact number of executions in China is, but almost all Chinese students and scholars believe the figure is too large. Capital punishment has become a pain in the heart of many Chinese scholars and of many political leaders as well." The year before, Sun Huapu, a spokesman for the SPC, asserted that the PRC executes only "a very small number of criminals" each year ("Conditions" 2006). One similarity between these contrasting commentaries serves as a useful introduction to thinking about the scale of executions in contemporary China: the currency of discourse about executions in this country is adjectives rather than numbers. The volume of executions is never a number; it is "too large" or "very small." There is considerable ambiguity in these terms. "Too large" or "very small" compared to what? With 90 percent or more of the world's current executions, one obvious frame of reference for assessing China's execution volume is the scale of execution in other nations. But is there any standard (short of Alice in Wonderland–like stipulative definitions that allow words to mean whatever the user wants them to) by which China's annual execution total might be regarded as "very small"?

The answer is yes, for there are two types of comparison in which even a world-leading rate of execution might appear small. The first is when China's executions are compared to the much higher volume of criminal cases and sanctions. If one million people per year serve time in detention, labor camps, or prisons, even 10,000 executions is only a 1 percent share of substantive criminal punishments. The second standard is when the present rate is compared to the scale of state killing during the revolutionary and postrevolutionary periods. That scale of violence is discussed in detail later in this chapter.

---

psychiatric punishment of political dissidents since the early 1980s, and it reported that the use of penal mental asylums had increased in recent years. According to Munro, many of the diagnoses—delusions of grandeur, litigation mania, conspicuously enhanced pathological will—are "based on disreputable theories inherited from the Soviet Union that claim that certain types of dissident thinking and behavior can be attributed to severe mental pathology" (quoted in Kahn 2006b). On the treatment of dissidents in "greater China" more generally (Hong Kong, Tibet, Taiwan, Singapore, and the PRC), see Ian Buruma (2001a).

For now, we merely observe that if the annual total of political killing in the mid-20th century ranged from 100,000 to one million, then 10,000 executions a year in the 1990s would be only a 1 to 10 percent share of the previous rate of lethal violence. In short, both adjectival descriptions may be accurate, but only one of them carries substantial moral weight in the 21st century—even if the volume of executions is small compared with that of other eras or sanctions. The world-leading volume of executions in the PRC is uniquely problematic for a nation with ambitions for plenary development, and the most striking evidence of the problem is China's effort to keep death penalty statistics a state secret.[6] As sociologist Borge Bakken (2007:182) has observed, "The fact that China today executes many more people than the rest of the world combined is one that today perhaps shames the country internationally more than any other single question."[7]

From Adjectives to Numbers

Our effort to estimate the current volume of executions involves sifting through a variety of imperfect data sources and hoping that differently flawed data sets will point toward a consistent range. The fancy name for this methodology is triangulation of proof (Zeisel 1985:253). The sources we use all generate estimates for some part of the period 1998–2006, but since we do not have evidence of stability in execution volume, there may be variations within this period that we cannot recognize. The data we have sorted through are of four main types: Amnesty International execution reports; estimates from government sources and officials; informed estimates by nongovernmental experts; and projections of national execution volume from data that are available for local areas within the PRC. We use all of these sources other than the (unrealistically low) Amnesty numbers to generate our own execution estimates.

AMNESTY INTERNATIONAL As part of its worldwide data collection and advocacy efforts, Amnesty International has been collecting reports on executions from informants, media reports, and public records and compiling them into annual execution counts for all executing nations. For nations where executions are part of the public record, Amnesty's estimates are quite reliable, but when executions are both secret and unreported, the Amnesty totals underestimate actual execution volume. In China the undercount is very large. Table 7.1 reports the Amnesty estimates for the PRC by year from 1981 to 2006. By Amnesty's accounting, China executed at least 32,617 persons in 1981–2006—more than two-thirds of

6. Human Rights in China (www.hrichina.org) lists known executions by name, but the catalog is far from complete.

7. Similarly, Jerome Cohen believes "the Chinese government is so embarrassed by the number of executions it carries out that the precise figure is one of its most closely-guarded secrets" (2005:427).

all the executions in the world that Amnesty documented in that quarter century, and an average of 1,255 executions a year. By the same measure, China has averaged 2,030 executions a year since 1994, accounting for close to 85 percent of the world's executions as counted by Amnesty in that period. Since 2000, China has carried out 12,295 of the world's 13,256 known executions, which is nearly 93 percent of the total Amnesty tally.

The Amnesty method of recording and reporting executions has one large virtue and several limitations. The virtue is its reliability as a minimum estimate across a wide variety of regimes around the world. Amnesty bends over backward not to overestimate execution numbers. It is all the more credible, then, when Amnesty reports that the PRC sum since 2000 is more than 90 percent of the world total.

But bending over backward not to overcount what a closed and secretive government does actually guarantees a substantial undercount, and this produces several limits on the data. One is that the Amnesty total in a closed system is not a good way to estimate total volume. For any year in table 7.1, the Amnesty minimum is not a good estimate of total execution volume—not for the 135 in 1985 or the 3,400 in 2004.

But can changes over time in reported executions be considered a reliable index of changes in true volume? We know that 1,084 for 1991 and 6,100 for 1996 are undercounts, but might the variation be used to suggest that executions expanded nearly sixfold between these two years? The answer is no, because different levels of effort and different levels of information vary the ratio of known to actual executions over time, and there is no way to determine by how much. Amnesty reported 126 known executions in 1986 and 3,400 in 2004, but that is not good evidence that by 2004 the volume of executions increased to a level 26 times that of 1986. Nor is the decline in Amnesty's execution count from 1,010 in 2006 to 470 in 2007 compelling evidence that the true total dropped more than 50 percent in that one-year period. Indeed, in the same Amnesty report that estimated a total of "at least 470" executions in the PRC for 2007, Amnesty's U.K. director Kate Allen said that "[a]ccording to reliable estimates, on average China secretly executes around 22 prisoners every day," a figure which yields an annual total of 8,030 executions (Amnesty International 2008b).

Thus, Amnesty's minimum estimates are not a good foundation for projections of true execution rates at any particular time period or for trends over time. We are also skeptical of comparisons of partial Chinese numbers from Amnesty with better numbers from more open governments in other jurisdictions. Such comparisons provide a minimum measure of Chinese dominance but not an accurate one.

Roger Hood's execution estimates for China rely on figures from Amnesty International and on his own research as reported in the UN Secretary General's Quinquennial Reports and his own books (Hood 1989; Hood 1996; Hood 2002; Hood and Hoyle 2008). For the five years 1994–1998, Hood has estimated that China had a total of 12,338 executions, an average of 2,477

Table 7.1
Amnesty International execution estimates for China, 1981–2006

Year	Number of executions
1981	91
1982	65
1983	600
1984	292
1985	135
1986	195
1987	132
1988	126
1989	273
1990	730
1991	1,084
1992	1,079
1993	1,419
1994	1,791
1995	2,190
1996	6,100
1997	1,876
1998	1,067
1999	1,077
2000	>1,000
2001	2,468
2002	1,921
2003	726
2004	3,400
2005	1,770
2006	1,010

Sources: Amnesty International reports (various years); Hood 1989:49; Hood 1996:74; Lu and Miethe 2007:75.

Note: Total number of executions confirmed by Amnesty International during this 26-year period: 32,617; annual average: 1,255; ratio of high (6,100 executions in 1996) to low (65 in 1982): 94 to 1. Annual execution averages by decade: 212 for the 1980s (1981–1989); 1,841 for the 1990s; 1,756 for the 2000s (2000–2006).

executions a year and an annual execution rate per million of 2.01. By this count, China had the seventh highest execution rate out of 26 countries (Hood 2001:336). When the analysis was updated for 1996–2000, Hood found that China had a total of 10,275 known executions, for an average of 2,055 executions per year and an estimated annual rate per million of 1.65—again the seventh highest rate in a list of 26 countries with at least 20 executions over

Table 7.2

Execution estimates for China since 1998, from official sources and outside experts

Source	Period	Annual volume	Citation
Official sources			
CCP	1998–2001	15,000+ (including police killings)	Nathan and Gilley 2003
National People's Congress delegate	2004	"Nearly 10,000"in recent years	Bakken 2004; Qi 2005; Wang 2007; Yardley 2007
SPP prosecutor	2006	7,500	Interview by Johnson, 2007
Outside experts			
John Kamm, Dui Hua Foundation	1996	15,000	Hands Off Cain 2007; Yardley 2007
John Kamm, Dui Hua Foundation	2001	12,500	Yardley 2007
John Kamm, Dui Hua Foundation	2006	7,500	Yardley 2007
Liu Renwen, Chinese Academy of Social Sciences	2005	8,000	Interview by Johnson, 2006; Bezlova 2006b

that five-year period (Hood 2002:92).[8] Like Amnesty International, Hood makes it clear that the figures he uses for China are substantial underestimates, with the true number of executions perhaps "four- to fivefold greater than those publicly reported in the press" and in the Amnesty reports on which he relies (Hood 2002:90). We do not believe Hood's or Amnesty's numbers are a plausible estimate of total Chinese executions, so we do not use them even as a lower estimation bound.

ESTIMATING THE SCALE OF RECENT EXECUTIONS Three types of data can be used to construct more accurate estimates of the volume of executions in China: government sources, the opinions of expert observers, and projections of national totals from information about provinces and smaller governmental units. Table 7.2 summarizes what government sources and experts say about execution levels in the PRC since 1998.

The closest thing to a "smoking gun" that has been published in English is an account by Andrew Nathan and Bruce Gilley (2003) based on secret files of the CCP that reports more than 60,000 total executions and police killings in 1998–2001. That would be more than 15,000 killings a year over

8. Hood's execution estimates for China for 1994–1998 and 1996–2000 are slightly lower than the estimates in our table 7.1, probably because Amnesty International occasionally revises the estimates on which we both have relied.

this four-year period, with the nonjudicial killings probably accounting for no more than 10 percent of that total. This number is about ten times the Amnesty count for the same years, and it cannot be tested against either a statistical record or the testimony of government record keepers. The files used by Nathan and Gilley attribute leadership for this execution policy to Luo Gan, who was then the ninth-ranking member of the Politburo standing committee.

The 60,000 figure from the CCP personnel files has been relied on by several subsequent writers, including Nathan and Gilley themselves (2003) and Nicola Macbean and Li Qinglan, researchers on the death penalty in China at the European Initiative for Democracy and Human Rights, who have said that the figure of 15,000 is consistent with death penalty data they obtained from the Court Network of China on executions in the city of Yulin (Guangxi Province) for 2001 (Macbean and Li 2003:33). It is, of course, hearsay evidence, but it is not inconsistent with other data.

It is telling that the CCP files praise Luo Gan for "overseeing the killing of more criminals than any previous internal security leader" (Nathan and Gilley 2003:31). As of 2003, none of China's new leaders was known to "disagree with the view that the execution of thousands of criminals every year is necessary to maintain stability" (31,218). Although the CCP files do not make clear how many of the 60,000 state killings were judicial executions and how many were police killings of alleged criminals apprehended in the act, in flight, or during preconviction detention, we estimate the proportion to be at least 10 to 1.[9] If this is accurate, then China averaged more than 13,500 executions per year in 1998–2001. The CCP files do not indicate whether the distribution of executions across these years was more or less stable or whether there were significant fluctuations from year to year.

A second official source of information is Chen Zhonglin, who was a high-level delegate to the National People's Congress (China's national legislature) in 2004 and who revealed to journalists that his country had executed "nearly

9. In the United States in the late 1980s, police shot and killed 600 to 1,000 people per year. That number fell by about one-third during the 1990s to roughly 400 to 600 police killings per year, and since then the number has remained at approximately the same level (Klinger 2004:10). In 2005, 55 American police officers were murdered on the job and another 67 were accidentally killed. Thus, the proportion of American police killed on the job to people killed by the police is approximately 122 to 500, or about 1 to 4. If a similar proportion obtains in China, where citizens are vastly less armed but police behavior may be more brutal, and where the number of police killed on duty has averaged about 300 per year for the last 20 years—a tenfold increase over the period 1949 to 1981 (Bakken 2005:15)—then police in China may have killed about 1,200 people per year during the period covered in the CCP files (1998 to 2001). Although there is an obviously high margin of error in this manner of groping China's execution elephant, by this estimate the proportion of judicial executions to police killings is approximately 13,800 to 1200, or 11.5 to 1.

10,000" people per year in recent years (Bakken 2004:82; Qi 2005:9; Yardley 2005b).[10] Chen retracted this statement after it was published in the official newspaper *China Youth Daily*, but similar numbers have been reported by numerous other sources, including the Australian Broadcasting Corporation ("Purse-Snatching" 2006), which said China executes about 10,000 people a year, and the Dui Hua Foundation (2007b:1), a nonprofit organization dedicated to "advancing the protection of universally recognized human rights in China and the United States."[11]

The Dui Hua Foundation (2007b:2) has also posed one version of the puzzle we explore in the next section: "how China went from a country executing one or two thousand people per year in the early 1980s to, in less than a decade, one that was annually executing more than 10,000 people." This statement of the mystery was first formulated by Dui Hua director John Kamm, who has worked for many years on China matters and who says two "informed sources" told him their country executed about 7,500 people in 2006, a figure that matches the 2006 number given to the first author of this book by an official in China's Supreme People's Procuratorate in June 2007. Kamm believes the 7,500 executions in 2006 represents a 40 percent drop from 2001, the year China was chosen to be the host city for the 2008 Olympics (quoted in Yardley 2007), and a 50 percent drop since 1996 (quoted in Hands Off Cain 2007).[12] If so, then China executed approximately 15,000 people in

10. Chen's statement of "nearly 10,000" executions is ambiguous because the Chinese expression *yi wan* can mean either "ten thousand" or "a very large number" without being 10,000 exactly.

11. After Chen retracted his statement of 10,000 executions a year, Luo Gan said that the execution rate in China was "too high" (Bakken 2004:82; Lim 2004). As explained later in this chapter, this view, which is considerably more temperate than the positions expressed in the leaked CCP files, rapidly became China's official orthodoxy.

12. Part of this decrease probably can be attributed to the decline of the death penalty for theft, which is by far the largest crime category in contemporary China. The number of death sentences and executions for theft declined markedly in the 1990s, even before capital punishment for most types of theft was abolished by the new Criminal Law of 1997. According to statistics from one intermediate people's court, 41.4 percent of the people executed in that jurisdiction in 1991 had been sentenced to death on theft charges. That percentage fell to 22.73 percent for 1992 and to 10.71 percent for 1997. After the new Criminal Law took effect in 1997, "no one had been sentenced to death on theft charges" (Qi 2005:7; Wang 2008; Chinese judges, interviews by Johnson, June 2007). Similarly, in one of China's largest provinces, the number of unsuspended death sentences declined 48 percent between 1997 and 2006, and more than two-thirds of that decline occurred in the first year after the new Criminal Law took effect in 1997 (confidential report of a provincial High Court, in possession of anonymous source). In 2006, law professor Liu Renwen said that an estimate of about 8,000 executions annually was "realistic," and he estimated that China probably executed more than 10,000 people per year before capital punishment for theft was abolished in 1997 ("China Claims Big Fall" 2008).

1996 and 12,500 in 2001.[13] Both of these estimates are broadly consistent with the execution figures given in the leaked CCP files (Nathan and Gilley 2003).

Although the estimates in table 7.2 are surprisingly consistent with each other, one reason for this may be that outside experts have been exposed to data such as those that are found in the leaked CCP files. And of course the leaked documents have several weaknesses as data: the estimates are round numbers rather than precise counts; we are not told what original data the authors of the report had access to; and it is impossible to verify the claims. But if the personnel files are genuine, would there be any reason why the reporters would want to exaggerate reality? We do not know. A more likely problem with the leaked number is that the authors of the files in which it appears report as fact the rumors or hunches of others.

Table 7.3 introduces a new set of data, information on punishments from one province, one county, and one city that can be used as a separate basis for estimating execution volume at the national level. The largest jurisdiction in table 7.3 is southern China's Guangdong Province, with a population of about 70 million. Sentencing data for Guangdong are available for 1998 and 2001, but only for a category of serious sentences made up of death sentences, suspended death sentences, and life prison sentences.[14] The ratio of unsuspended death sentences to the total category is not available for Guangdong, but table 7.3 uses the ratio of unsuspended death sentences to the total of all death plus life for Maguan County—an estimate of one unsuspended death sentence to every two life or death sentences—to generate projected totals of unsuspended death sentences and executions in the province. Those projections—955 for 1998 and 798 for 2001—are then used to extrapolate national totals, on the assumption that the nation as a whole has the same rate as Guangdong. This is a double projection with two distinct margins of error, but the estimates generated,

13. Chen Xingliang, professor of law at Peking University, whose views on the death penalty have been "widely accepted" by Chinese officials, scholars, and citizens (Lu and Miethe 2007:125), has endorsed the execution estimates made by John Kamm (interview by Johnson, June 12, 2007). Liu Renwen, a scholar at the Chinese Academy of Social Sciences in Beijing, told us that China had approximately 8,000 executions in 2005 (interview by Johnson, April 15, 2006), a figure he has used in other interviews as well (Bezlova 2006b). In June 2007, a legal scholar at Peking University said that in his view, which was informed by dozens of conversations with Chinese judges and prosecutors on the subject of capital punishment, the PRC may have had 15,000 to 20,000 executions a year during the decade or so before the 2007 change that restored the authority of the SPC to review and approve death sentences (interview by Johnson, June 2007). And in July 2008, the Rome-based Hands Off Cain organization, which campaigns to end the death penalty, reported that China had conducted "at least 5,000 executions" in 2007. Its estimate was based on reports by the media and other human rights groups ("China Leads" 2008).

14. The suspended death sentence remains "one of the most unique features" of China's death penalty practice, and a variety of factors are considered in order to determine whether such sentences will be reduced to something less than death after the two-year period ends (Lu and Miethe 2007:66). The vast majority are.

Table 7.3
Estimating executions for China, 1990–2001: Extrapolations from local rates

Place and date	Data	Estimated number of local death sentences	Estimated national number
Guangdong Province, 1998 (pop. 70,000,000)	Class of sentences consisting of death sentences, death sentences with a two-year reprieve, and life sentences	955	17,000
Guangdong Province, 2001	Same as above	798	14,000
Yulin City, Guangxi Autonomous Region, 2001 (pop. 5,500,000)	Death sentences	61 for 8 months, 91 per year	21,000
Maguan County, Yunnan Province, 1990–1999 (pop. 300,000)	Death sentences	59 in 10 years	25,610

Sources: Macbean and Li 2003; Dui Hua Foundation 2007c.

17,000 and 14,000, are close to the estimates for the same periods that were generated by other means in table 7.2.

Our second projection comes from the city of Yulin in the Guangxi Autonomous Region of southwestern China, which has a population of 5.5 million and for which we have a figure of 61 unsuspended death sentences for an eight-month period of 2001 (Macbean and Li 2003). When that number is annualized by correcting for the number of months, we arrive at a total of 91 unsuspended death sentences, a rate to population that translates into 21,000 executions for all of China, an amount half again as much as the one generated from Guangdong. But here, too, there is a large margin for error, for Yulin is an urban area that may not reflect national patterns. It could have more death sentences than would a more representative jurisdiction, not least because Guangxi is generally believed to have more drug activity than many other parts of the country.

Our third and final projection comes from Maguan County in Yunnan Province, for which the Dui Hua Foundation has reported detailed death penalty data over a long period of time. There are two problems with the Maguan data set as a basis for national projections. The first is its small population—300,000—and small volume of death sentences. We correct for this by combining death sentences for ten years (1990–1999) to generate a total of 59 and a rate per population that is not highly sensitive to year-to-year variations. The second problem is that Yunnan Province may have a higher-than-average number of capital cases—particularly drug cases—because of its location and ethnic diversity. Thus, projecting the rate to population for

Maguan (19.7 per million per year for the 1990s) to the entire PRC produces an estimated volume of 25,600 executions, which may be substantially higher than the true national total.

Despite the various errors risked by these different projections, the pattern that emerges when the data are combined is one of clear support for a peak annual volume of 15,000 executions or more at the turn of the 21st century. That is as many executions in one year as the United States and its precursor colonies had in the four centuries since the first English settlers came to Jamestown in 1607 (Death Penalty Information Center, July 26, 2007). The triangulations of proof summarized in tables 7.2 and 7.3 support the conclusion that in recent years China has executed on a very large scale.

Patterns over Time and Cross-sectional Variation

The data thin out, however, and important questions go unanswered when addressing trends in executions in China over time and the nature of cross-sectional death penalty variation within the country. But some temporal themes do seem clear. The volume of executions increased substantially in the early 1980s, but this story must be told in adjectives rather than numbers (Trevaskes 2007). Was the Strike Hard expansion of executions twofold or tenfold? What crimes and geographical areas had the greatest changes and the least? We do not know.

The magnitude of the expansion in the 1980s may bear on the types of change to expect from current and anticipated reforms. If the 2006 execution total is 7,500—about half the late 1990s peak—then has the PRC returned to its prior level of execution, or are current rates five times greater than before the first Strike Hard initiative? Measuring the variability of executions after 1976 might also provide useful information about the independent effects of political and governmental forces rather than culture in explaining the extent of executions in the PRC. In any event, we hope that government permission and resources will soon be devoted to documenting the history of China's death penalty. While trends over time are currently described mostly by adjectives, those who are curious about the exact range of variation cannot even be sure what the right adjectives are!

So here are some of the more important unanswered questions about variation in the patterns of capital punishment in contemporary China. To start with, what is the extent of variation among China's 22 provinces, five autonomous regions, and four provincial-level municipalities? Some reports suggest that death penalty "verdicts vary wildly depending on region, party influence and a defendant's connections" (Glionna 2008). We believe the range of variation may be smaller than the 100-to-1 differences in execution rates that exist in U.S. states with death penalties, but how much smaller? Are execution rates higher in big cities where crime rates are higher or in rural areas where law enforcers and judges are less educated and more conservative (Chen and Wu 2006)? How much of the variation in execution rates is linked to drug crime? To ethnic and religious diversity? And how did the 1983 elimination of SPC review of most capital cases affect the variation across provinces and regions? Answers to these and related questions would provide important information about recent history and current policy. It would also help inform the evaluation of legal reforms that were implemented in the years leading up to the Beijing Olympic Games of 2008.

■ The Political Roots of China's Death Penalty Exceptionalism

How and when did the PRC come to use capital punishment as a standard criminal sanction in ways that distinguish it from every other major nation? China-watchers offer two principal explanations. The first emphasizes Chinese history and culture and considers the current use of capital punishment a continuation of earlier practices and priorities. On this view, "the death penalty has been widely used throughout Chinese history for purposes of social control, order maintenance, and regulation of individuals and private groups" (Lu and Miethe 2007:27), and China's contemporary system of capital punishment is firmly rooted in that tradition (Ho 2005:284). In contrast, the second theory stresses the impact of the communist revolution and the postrevolutionary political changes implemented by Mao Zedong and Deng Xiaoping. On this account, it is not excessive to speak of the current system of Chinese capital punishment as "specifically Maoist" (Zhang 2008). Our shorthand labels for these two theories are *cultural* and *political,* and we will argue here that the evidence favors the political one.[15] Chinese history does matter, of course—how could it not?—but the irony of our finding that politics is preeminent is that searches for the deep historical roots of China's current death penalty exceptionalism frequently fail to come to terms with the political cataclysms in the last century that have left the nation in an almost "constant state of self-repudiation and self-reinvention" (Schell 2006). Indeed, since Deng took the PRC down the reformist road in the late 1970s, the nation's intoxicating economic progress has made it possible for many Chinese elites to treat the socialist revolution as an irrelevant prelude to a new and invincible future. The reason for their amnesia is easy to see: the regime's legitimacy depends on protecting the record of the CCP and its founder, Chairman Mao, and it therefore suppresses discussion of the recent but painful past (Kahn 2006c; Shapiro 2006). But until that past is reckoned with, China's death penalty exceptionalism will remain in fuzzy focus.

15. For a similar argument about the primacy of politics over culture in shaping the PRC's mediation practices, see Lubman (1967).

State Killing in Imperial China

In a recorded legal history that goes back more than 2,500 years, killing as an instrument of governance was frequently employed on a grand scale and with extraordinary disrespect for the humanity of Chinese subjects (Bodde and Morris 1967; van der Sprenkel 1971; Schwartz 1985:321; MacCormack 1990; Head and Wang 2005; McKnight 2007). This is one source of age-old laments such as "The lives of Chinese have no worth" ("Zhongguoren de ming, buzhi qian"). It can be difficult to distinguish a clearly legal system of capital punishment from other varieties of state violence in some periods of imperial history, and the "inadequacies of existing records" sometimes make reliable counting impossible, but there is no doubt that state killing often occurred in huge numbers (Lu and Miethe 2007:204). One example is the Boxer Uprising at the turn of the 20th century, in which tens of thousands of Chinese Christians were killed in less than two years, mostly by frustrated peasants and the imperial forces who supported them (Spence 1990:234). Another is the Taiping Rebellion, which swept across China in 1845–1864, killing more than 20 million people, including "massive executions" after imperial forces defeated "the largest uprising in human history" (Spence 1996; Lu and Miethe 2007:199). As historian Frederic Wakeman put it, "the attrition exceeds the limits of historical imagination" (quoted in Schell 1996). The U.S. Civil War occurred about the same time (1861–1865) and took less than 700,000 lives[16]— about 4 percent of the Taiping total and just one-sixth its annual loss-of-life average—yet "on the Richter scale of barbarism in Chinese history the Taiping Rebellion is only a single blip" (Schell 1996). Other historical comparisons suggest that China may well be "the world leader in massacre" (Payne 2004:47). Civil wars have been numerous in Chinese history (one study counted 477 wars and revolts in just the 19th century), and in many of them it was common practice to slaughter people in the defeated region, leaving victims in the "scores of millions" (14). Sometimes the result was district depopulation "by 60, 70, or even 90 percent," and far from being ashamed of the carnage, many Chinese leaders "openly embraced it" (47).

Political murders were also common. Sociologist Daniel Tretiak, who studied patterns of political killing among high Chinese officials between 1600 and 1968, found three main types of political death: execution, forced suicide (usually to forestall execution), and assassination. Unlike the United States, where assassinations have often been the work of individuals acting alone, assassination in China was usually "part of the process of elite conflict" (Tretiak 1970:636). Overall, 13 to 28 percent of the deaths of Chinese high officials were by political murder of one of these three kinds (Payne 2004:98).[17] A key enabling condition

16. The death rate in the U.S. Civil War was more than five times higher than that in World War II (Payne 2004:10).

17. The prevalence of political violence and revenge during Mao's reign has led some analysts to describe his China as "a country of angry widows" (Apter and Saitch 1990; Mirsky

for this kind of political violence and for other forms of state killing was the fact that neither Confucianism nor Legalism—the sources for the two main schools of thought in China's legal tradition—regarded moral laws or individual rights as limits on state power (Nathan 1985:114).

In short, at the elite and popular levels of Chinese society, violence as a means of controlling and subduing others—political competitors, servants, tenants, and dependent family members—was "fully culturally approved, as were the most brutal of punishments against those construed as criminals, rebels, and other deviants" (Rowe 2007:5). In places such as Macheng County in Hubei Province, "persistently and systemically violent" local cultures were constructed over the course of many centuries, giving rise to "an absolute and uncompromising hatred of one's enemies that would sanction, across the spectrum of political ideology, the most grisly and inhuman actions against them" (326). But it is difficult to tell how much China differs in these aspects from other Asian nations. Korea, it will be remembered, once was ruled by the loathsome Yonsan the Obscene, yet the southern part of that divided peninsula currently maintains a ten-year moratorium on executions. Similarly, the decline of Choson Korea was accelerated by two wars with Japanese forces led by Tokugawa Hideyoshi, who ordered his men to cut off tens of thousands of Korean ears and noses, pickle them in salt, and bring them back to Japan to be buried (Cumings 1997:77). Japanese history was very bloody, too, and state killing was a major contributor, yet Japan's per capita execution rate during the last decade is only about 1/250th that of the PRC.

In the end, there seems to be nothing singular in China's long history that can be clearly or closely linked to the country's high current rate of execution and that distinguishes China from its neighbors. Moreover, periods of severity in punishment have alternated with cycles of leniency throughout Chinese history (Lu and Miethe 2007:37). In fact, the traditional Chinese judicial system "was often astonishingly benevolent," with the use of mercy to moderate severity probably most pronounced from the glory years of the Han dynasty (206 B.C.–220 A.D.) through the three centuries of the Sung (960–1279 A.D.; see McKnight 1981:112). During the Tang dynasty (618–907 A.D.), for example, "the vast majority" of criminal offenders had their sentences reduced by commutation or pardon (Lu and Miethe 2007:38). An anthropologist's attempt to summarize the meanings of violence in Chinese history even concludes that in comparison to others, Chinese culture abhors and condemns violence to an unusual degree (Harrell 1990). Similarly, a review of more than two millennia of Chinese history concludes that, "despite numerous violations, many, if not most, emperors were constrained by the rule of law that was valued in both theory and practice" (Fang 2008:40).

1994). After Mao's death, however, the suspended death sentence given to his wife Jiang Qing (in 1981) may have marked the passing of political murder in China. Since that time, there have been few high-level killings in the PRC (Payne 2004:98).

Capital punishment has been a prominent feature of government in many periods of Chinese history, much as it was in the premodern histories of Korea, Japan, Germany, England, and the United States. Like Korea and Japan, however, China experienced at least one period of death penalty abolition before the 20th century, for a little more than a decade (747 to 759) during the Tang dynasty (Benn 2002:209). Another abolition may have occurred for 70 to 80 years during the Yuan dynasty (1279 to 1368), though some historians believe that during this period executions declined markedly but still continued to occur (Chen 1979:45; Lu and Miethe 2007:196). In either event, the review of death sentences during the Yuan was apparently so lenient that "heavy criticisms" were frequently directed against it (Lu and Miethe 2007:38).

Dead Ends

Despite these and other periods of penal lenity, by the time of China's first clash with the West in the 19th century, the nation had acquired a reputation for barbarism in criminal punishment. China's penal system was harsh, but its standard of law and order "was probably comparable to that prevalent in Europe or the United States at the time" (Spence 1990:126), and in some respects may even have been less severe (Bourgon 2003; Bakken 2004:78).[18] Chinese law also held that "there was really no room within the system for special treatment of foreigners," and the execution of foreigners in the late 18th and early 19th centuries helped convince Western nations that "the Chinese must be compelled to yield up jurisdiction over cases involving foreign nationals" (Spence 1990:126–127). In this way, conflicts over capital punishment and extraterritoriality contributed significantly to a new force in Chinese history—antiforeign nationalism—and to major clashes between China and the West (Morse 1910), including the Opium War (1840–1842), which some scholars consider the most influential incident in the modern history of East Asia (Gordon 2007; Kitaoka 2007).

As the Qing dynasty (1644–1911) drew to a close, the main form of punishment was the "age-old death penalty," for the scope and scale of capital punishment had expanded significantly during this last imperial period (Chen 2006c:426).[19] The original Qing Code contained a total of 275 capital

18. As Ian Buruma observes, "there was a time when enlightened European thinkers saw the Chinese Empire as a model of sophisticated government. Voltaire, for example, liked the idea of a state led by scholarly mandarins, chosen on the basis of intellectual merit in a strict examination system. He saw them as high-minded, cultivated men (a bit like himself perhaps) whose moral and political philosophy was bound by reason, not religious superstition. China, to Voltaire and other Enlightenment philosophers, seemed far superior to France, where rational men were still persecuted by the clerics of a powerful and sometimes fanatical church" (Buruma 2001b).

19. As in 17th- and 18th-century America, the death penalty during the Qing period was more than just one punishment among many, it was the base point from which other kinds

offenses, but by the end of that era there were three times that number—more than 840. According to Chen Xingliang, one of the PRC's premier criminal law scholars, "China had seen nothing like these sheer numbers and this severity in punishment in thousands of years" (426). The perceived harshness of Chinese punishment provided one of the pretexts for Western powers to impose the same humiliating system of extraterritoriality on China that they imposed in other Asian places such as Japan and Korea. Partly as a response to this problem, Qing law was radically revised in 1910, reducing the 800-plus capital offenses to fewer than 30 (426). At the end of the Qing dynasty, China appeared to be embarking on the same kind of penal reform that had transformed punishment in Meiji Japan during the last decades of the 19th century, not only in the sphere of capital punishment but also in its efforts to construct a more "modern" prison system (Dikotter 2002:27; see also Dutton 1992:152).[20] In fact, some analysts argue that China's late imperial judiciary "was exceedingly chary about executing criminals, requiring a strict standard of evidence . . . and multiple levels of review for every capital case" (Sommer 2000:70; see also Bodde and Morris 1967:131; Conner 1979).[21]

Thus, when China became a republic after the Qing dynasty was overthrown in 1911 by a combination of military, parliamentary, and revolutionary forces, the nation seemed to be turning away from the heavy reliance on capital punishment that had characterized many parts of its history (Xu 2008). This

---

of punishment branched out. A variety of methods were used to create gradations of capital severity, with dismemberment through the excruciating "death by a thousand cuts" (*lingchi*) and public display of the corpse being two of the best known means of intensifying the death sanction. Note, however, that Chinese executions during the Qing dynasty were staged and understood very differently from the more visible, religious, ritualized, and legalized executions in the contemporaneous West (Ho 2000; Bourgon 2003). For a fascinating account of death by a thousand cuts, see Brook, Bourgon, and Blue (2008), who argue that while many Europeans recoiled from what appeared to be a gruesome, lingering death, regarding it as evidence of a uniquely Oriental ruthlessness, "it is hard to see much distinction in degrees of cruelty" between the Chinese practice and Western practices such as drawing and quartering.

20. "Democracy" is a contested concept, and some scholars believe China turned toward it at the end of the Qing dynasty. More precisely, the beginning of Chinese democracy has been dated to the year 1895, when China signed a disastrous peace treaty with Japan after it lost the Sino-Japanese war. The treaty created the conviction among many Chinese that "the nation's survival could no longer be left in the hands of officialdom" (Nathan 1985:x). Other scholars believe the Qing rulers "started to promote the adoption of European models of government after the disaster of the Boxer rebellion in 1900" (Dikotter 2002:1).

21. Western accounts of Chinese criminal justice tend to traffic in grim depictions of late Qing trials and to focus on the torture imperial officials used to coerce confessions from defendants (Spence 1990:124). But torture continues to be widespread in the PRC (Nowak 2006), and appeals against conviction are ordinarily fruitless. The result is a contemporary system of criminal justice "seemingly more arbitrary than that of the Qing—and less subject to the rule of law" (Conner 2000:155).

attempt to modernize capital punishment accelerated in the early Republican period (1911–1927) and under the leadership of the KMT (1927–1949). Indeed, there is substantial evidence that the same shift away from execution as a standard form of criminal punishment that has been documented in other parts of Asia and in Europe was well under way in China during the decades between the end of the Qing dynasty and the full-scale Japanese invasion of China in 1937. Though the historical record of criminal punishment in China's early Republican period is far from complete (not least because large parts of the country were controlled by local warlords who did as they pleased), the evidence of movement away from capital sanctions is striking. Figure 7.3, assembled from data reported by historian Frank Dikotter (2002), shows criminal cases and sentences for the Beijing district (including Tianjin) in 1918.

The district of Beijing included two large cities and a much more urban population than China generally had in that era. Detailed population estimates are not available,[22] but they also are not necessary to interpret the Beijing data because the ratios of criminal cases and of punishments to death sentences make the point well. In 1918, just over 9,000 cases were investigated, generating about 6,000 indictments. The vast majority of these produced convictions and sentences, and the right-hand side of figure 7.3 shows their distribution. The 6,000 indictments produced a total of six death sentences, a ratio of 1,000 to 1. The ratio of custodial sentences (mostly short) to death sentences is 686 to 1, and the ratio of prison sentences to death sentences is 359 to 1.

This analysis illustrates that by 1918 a death sentence had become an uncommon and extraordinary punishment in Beijing criminal courts. Most crimes in Beijing were not major, but "wounding and murder" were the next most common crimes in the Beijing caseload, accounting for "roughly a quarter" of the 6,000 indictments (Dikotter 2002:77). Only six death sentences out of 1,500 assaults and homicides seems a clear indication of the marginal importance of execution as a criminal sanction in China at the end of the second decade of the 20th century.[23] What is more, efforts to "civilize" execution methods also spread during the Republican period. In 1925, for example, the Ministry of Justice lamented the "waste of time and 'infinite suffering'" caused by traditional forms of capital punishment, and it proposed replacing human executioners with machines so as to achieve "an impartial and clinical death." Ten years later, the ministry even advocated the use of

22. The population of Beijing in 1916 was 801,136 (Chang 1965:318), and the population of Tianjin at that time was perhaps one-half to three-quarters that number, but we do not know the precise parameters of the combined district.

23. If the PRC under Deng Xiaoping had sentenced criminal offenders to death at the same rate at the start of the first Strike Hard campaign in 1983–1984 as the city of Beijing did in 1918, it would have had about 600 death sentences instead of more than 24,000 (Tanner 1999:98; Tanner 2005:174; Trevaskes 2007).

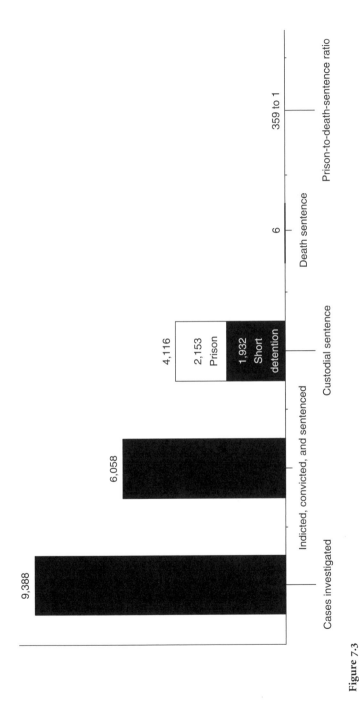

Figure 7.3

Criminal investigation and punishment in Beijing, 1918

Source: China Ministry of Justice, *Fifth Yearbook on Criminal Statistics 1921*, quoted in Dikotter 2002:77.

chloroform to lessen the pains of execution. Although these directives were not implemented, they do reflect a "profound concern" to minimize pain and an emerging conviction that the purpose of capital punishment "was no longer the infliction of pain in a retributive vision of revenge but the humane disposal of a life judged unworthy of continuation" (Dikotter 2002:137).

The marginal importance of executions in Beijing is also evident when that district is contrasted with Shanghai, China's largest city during the KMT era and one of the most cosmopolitan (it was called the Paris of the East) and corrupt cities in the world at the time (Clifford 1991; Wakeman 1995; Yatsko 2001). During the early 1920s, power in Shanghai was divided between foreigners and the Chinese (Spence 1990:298). In 1925, the foreigners numbered about 30,000 and ran the main concession areas, where their businesses and houses were congregated in what was called the International Settlement, under protection of extraterritoriality. This settlement was the largest and most important commercial and banking center in all of China, and some 810,000 Chinese lived there as well, under the jurisdiction of the Mixed Court, which dealt with people of Chinese nationality accused of crimes committed within the 8.7 square miles of the settlement (Stephens 1992:xi). The Mixed Court was established because foreigners—British, Portuguese, American, German, French—had no jurisdiction over Chinese nationals on Chinese soil. The Westerners therefore arranged for a Chinese magistrate to sit for this purpose within settlement limits, and they insisted that a representative from a Western consul sit with him in order "to monitor the proceedings and to ensure that western interests were protected and the proceedings were conducted as far as possible according to *western ideals* of criminal administration and judicial independence and probity" (Stephens 1992:xi; emphasis added). Outside the International Settlement and related concession areas, Chinese Shanghai and its population of almost two million were governed by a succession of Chinese warlords who competed among themselves for control (Spence 1990:298).

Though the Mixed Court of Shanghai owed no allegiance to any specific foreign power, the establishment of a court by foreigners for the trial and punishment of Chinese citizens on Chinese soil can hardly be seen as "anything other than an illegitimate arrogation" of China's sovereign powers (Stephens 1992:69).[24] At the same time, however, Westerners in Shanghai did believe that Chinese criminal justice was prone to excesses of cruelty and brutality, including the routine use of flogging and torture to obtain evidence from witnesses and confessions from suspects (Lee 1993; Lee 1995). The foreigners ultimately introduced several criminal justice reforms to address

---

24. The Mixed Court of Shanghai owed its existence and the definition of its powers to the consular body, which itself was "a mere ad hoc collective without any corporate existence, any sovereign power over Chinese, or any constitutional validity" (Stephens 1992:112).

those problems.[25] Counsel was allowed to represent the defendant, a procedure not permitted in traditional Chinese practice. Rules of evidence stressed the primacy of information given in court rather than hearsay, coerced confessions and testimony, or the magistrate's own investigations and intuitions. And torture and corporal punishment fell into disuse (Stephens 1992:47). If the main task of the Mixed Court was to maintain order among the Chinese, on the whole it did the job well (112).

For our purposes, however, what is most striking about the Shanghai Mixed Court is how aggressively it used death as a criminal sanction. In 1924, for example, "ninety-six executions took place at the instance of the Mixed Court," giving the International Settlement of Shanghai a rate of 118.5 executions per million, which is 22 times higher than the highest execution rate Hong Kong ever had under the British after World War II (Stephens 1992:57).[26] The contrast with Beijing is also stark: the volume of executions in the International Settlement—the most Westernized jurisdiction in Republican China—was 16 times greater in 1924 than the volume of judicial executions in the district that combined Beijing and Tianjin only six years earlier.

We also have national data on the distribution of punishments during the "Nanjing decade" between 1927, when the KMT took power, and 1937, when the Sino-Japanese war began. Figure 7.4 presents punishment data from three national judicial reports covering the years 1929, 1931, and 1933. Since the national government did not control all sectors of modern China and did not receive information from everywhere or from all of the same localities each year, the population covered in any year cannot be determined with precision. But we do know that these data describe a very large and diverse nation.

The three punishment profiles reflect a pattern quite consistent with the earlier data from Beijing: convictions range from 64,000 to 86,000, but the number of death sentences never exceeds 188. The ratio of convictions to death sentences starts at 358 to 1 in 1929 and rises to 705 to 1 in 1933, while the ratio of prison sentences to death sentences starts at 173 to 1 in 1929 and increases to 459 to 1 in 1933. Thus, both in absolute terms and relative to other criminal sanctions, the death penalty on the Chinese mainland under the KMT was an unusual sanction that was becoming more uncommon over time, even as extrajudicial killing continued at high levels.

Not only was capital punishment a tiny part of China's criminal process in the early Republican and KMT periods, the number of Chinese death sentences is comparable to that in other Asian nations of the same era. Japan had

25. For a description of the new *civil* courts that were established in Shanghai to protect foreigners in their commercial dealings with the Chinese, and for an explanation of how those new courts helped transform the economic and legal cultures of Shanghai, see Lee (1993).

26. If the same rate had prevailed in the PRC in 1998–2001, it would have had more than 600,000 executions instead of the 60,000 or so that actually occurred (Nathan and Gilley 2003:217).

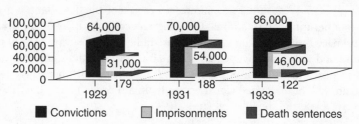

Figure 7.4
Criminal convictions, sentences of imprisonment, and death sentences in Nanjing-governed China, 1929, 1931, and 1933
Source: Dikotter 2002:230–231.

about one-tenth the population of China and reported death sentences of 21, 31, and 26 for the three years depicted in the China statistics of figure 7.4. The annual Japanese average was 26 death sentences, or one-sixth the Chinese average (163). Depending on the total population covered by the Chinese reports, Japan's death sentence rate was equal to or slightly higher than China's. For Korea, which was under Japanese control during this period, information on judicial sentences is not available, but execution rates are. The data presented in chapter 5 indicate that the execution rate in Korea was higher than in Japan: for a population of approximately 21 million, the Korean execution totals were 47 in 1918, 27 in 1929, 13 in 1931, and 22 in 1933. The 1929, 1931, and 1933 totals for Korea are well above the death sentence rate per million in nationalist China for the same years. If we assume nationalist authority over 60 percent of China's 490,000,000 people in 1933, then the 122 death sentences equal a rate of 0.42 death sentences per million. The average execution rates in Korea were much higher: 0.98 per million for 1929, 1931, and 1933, and over two per million for 1918. And if we assume that everyone condemned to die in Republican China was executed the same year they were sentenced, then China's execution rates for 1929, 1931, and 1933 were only about half Taiwan's execution rate for the year 2000, and only 2 to 4 percent of the execution rate that prevailed in the PRC in 1998–2001.

In sum, China between the Qing dynasty and Mao was not an aggressive user of death as a formal criminal sanction.[27] Outside the foreign settlements in Shanghai, where Western influence on China's criminal process was especially strong, there are no indications of higher-than-average levels of capital punishment in the Republican period. As Dikotter (2002:81) concludes, "judicial authorities, including those in provinces controlled by military governors, passed very few death sentences, in stark contrast to the many decades of political terror that would follow the communist victory in 1949." This stress on the relatively infrequent use of capital punishment in the Republican

27. The widespread extrajudicial killing by the nationalists is another story; see Spence (1990), Rummel (1994), Fenby (2003), Wakeman (2003), and Dutton (2005a).

period must be qualified by recognizing the persistent practice of extrajudicial killing, especially in the later years of the KMT era.

The Founding Fathers of Chinese Mass Execution

The point of departure in Jonathan Spence's unrivaled account of modern Chinese history is that "in trying to understand China today we need to know about China in the past; but how far back we carry that search remains, in a sense, the central question" (Spence 1990:xix). The previous section demonstrated that understanding the origins of China's current death penalty exceptionalism does not require returning to ancient emperors or mandarins. China's modest death penalty totals in the early 20th century do not merely differ from the political terror of the 1950s, they are a stark contrast to the death penalty rate for common crimes in the early years of the 21st century. How did the country go from 122 death sentences in 1933 to 100 times that many or more in 2000?

We will argue here that the origins of China's current death penalty policy can be found in the political carnage that occurred after the communists took power in 1949 and in the transitions in criminal justice and governance during the reform years of the 1980s that turned judicial execution into a common form of criminal punishment. This argument builds on our summary of state killing in China before the communist revolution by arguing that the founding fathers of execution policy in the PRC were Joseph Stalin, Mao Zedong, and Deng Xiaoping. This is not a "great man theory" of history; it merely recognizes that some outsized individuals can be both products and agents of large historical processes (Carr 1961:68). All three of these leaders were at once the representatives of and the creators of social forces that helped determine the shape of capital punishment in China's contemporary period.

STALIN'S INFLUENCE ON MAO Stalin was the 20th century's first great practitioner of mass killing as an instrument of communist governance. Although he never made Chinese policy, his design and administration of mass extermination in the Soviet Union from the time he took control of the party and government in 1929 until his death in 1953 was in some ways the model Mao adopted (Tanner 2007). The highest levels of violence under Stalin were far removed from the years of the Russian Revolution and were attached to a wide variety of agendas—from agrarian reorganization to the removal of threats from political rivals. While the killings were mostly governmental, they frequently failed to observe the forms or pretenses of judicial authorization of criminal sanctions (Bullock 1998; Mikhlin 1999).

The exact number of deaths by government under Stalin is not known, but the consensus estimates are all in the millions, and most are in the tens of millions. The most comprehensive effort to count the victims of the 20th century's "bloodiest megamurderers" ranks Stalin first in overall bloodletting (ahead of Mao, Hitler, and Chiang Kai-shek, in that order), with more than

42 million governmental killings in the quarter century he ruled the Soviet Union (Rummel 1994:8). Others put the number at closer to 20 million (Montefiore 2005). Whatever the exact count, state killing under Stalin was either "not far behind" the worldwide death rate from war during the 20th century—more than 100 people an hour—or it exceeded that rate by a significant margin (Rummel 1994:79; Glover 1999:237).

Many of Stalin's victims were arrested and executed after being denounced by jealous neighbors or targeted in order to fulfill a quota (Rayfield 2005). His chief of secret police once sent another official a telegram saying, "You are charged with the task of exterminating 10,000 enemies of the people. Report results by signal" (Glover 1999:239). The reply was a numbered list of those who had been shot. Mass executions usually were carried out at pits, with victims shot from behind so that they would fall or could be pushed inside. In the prison camps in Stalin's vast gulag, inmates were fed on the basis of how close they came to filling their work quotas.[28] Many inmates worked for years without meeting the quota once. Prisoners who collapsed while working or walking back to the barracks were shot, and the "guards had a way of testing if anyone was feigning by bashing their skulls in with a sledgehammer" (Glover 1999:240). Many suspected "counterrevolutionaries" in the camps were tortured to death (Conquest 2000).

In several central respects—the scale of state killing, the use of execution quotas, party involvement in decision-making, mass trials, methods of execution, the treatment of class as hereditary, and the mistreatment of prisoners in the camps—there are not only clear parallels between the Soviet Union under Stalin and the PRC under Mao Zedong, there is also significant evidence that Mao learned from Stalin (Spence 1995; Glover 1999:283; Becker 2000; Buruma 2000; Chang and Halliday 2005; Zhang 2008). Another key parallel concerns the ways state killings were justified. Stalin and Mao both stressed that they were carrying out the will of History, and both regarded executions as a necessary means to that utopian end (Glover 1999:252). But how could they kill on such a huge scale? Under Stalin, the answer had a lot to do with fear of the consequences of resistance and the power of human belief to numb the natural aversion to killing other people (Grossman 1996). Most Soviet citizens knew what was in store for those who stepped out of line, and the pressure on people to betray their own values was immense (Bullock 1998)—as it was in China under Mao (Chang 1991; Li 1994; Mirsky 1994; MacFarquhar and Schoenhals 2006). At the same time, beliefs about the righteousness of the communist cause "were central to what happened under Stalin" because they functioned to "deaden human responses" (Glover 1999:265).

---

28. The size of the Soviet gulag in Stalin's time has been estimated to range from 3 million prisoners early in his rule to a peak of 12 million at the time of his death in 1953. This translates into 2,000–8,000 inmates per 100,000 people in the general population (Seymour 2005:147).

Prohibitions against killing were rejected as "bourgeois morality," and this facilitated the process of hardening—of "turning into wood"—that made large-scale killing possible (Rayfield 2005). In the Soviet Union, this stress on hardness even extended to names.[29] The paramount leader had his surname changed from Dzhugashvili to Stalin, or "man of steel," and other Bolshevik leaders made similar name changes—to "man of stone," "the hammer," and so on (Glover 1999:260). In 1931, a visiting British lady asked Stalin a question no one else would: "How long will you keep killing people?" Stalin's interpreter froze, but the boss replied without pausing that "'the process would continue as long as was necessary' to establish communist society" (253).[30] On another occasion, when Stalin was signing lists of people to be executed, he asked two of his aides: "Who's going to remember all this riff-raff in ten or twenty years?" (256).

Like Stalin, Mao rejected traditional moral restraints and urged others to do the same. "We have so many people," he once said. "We can afford to lose a few. What difference does it make?" (quoted in Glover 1999:297). His personal physician, Li Zhisui (1994), described Mao as devoid of love, friendship, and warmth. In Mao's view, "mercy to the enemy" was deemed to be "cruelty to the people" (quoted in Glover 1999:291). Indeed, the quintessential political question for Mao, as for Stalin, was "Who are our enemies, who are friends?" (quoted in Dutton 2005a:3). This, above all, was the issue "germane to the revolution," and it would shape Chinese capital punishment long after Mao's death (Tanner 1999).

Our argument that Stalin was the first founding father of China's current death penalty exceptionalism must be qualified in three ways. First, Stalin himself is not an uncaused cause (though we have said little to indicate the major influences on him). From the earliest moments of the Russian Revolution, there was a hardened indifference to the individual victims who might be destroyed by the communists' new policies. Lenin stressed early and often the need to "exterminate one's enemies" (Glover 1999:255), he frequently expressed glee when ordering executions (Gellately 2007), and he mocked those philistine party members who complained about the mercilessness of his policies (Mirsky 1994). The causal chains leading to Stalin and Mao (as for all actors and acts) could be traced back indefinitely; there is no single origin.[31]

29. A commitment to "hardness" also made it possible for Stalin to introduce the death penalty for children as young as 12 (Glover 1999:26).

30. Belief in the ultimate value of the communist end and in the need to jettison "bourgeois values" in order to achieve it is further evident in Stalin's often-quoted adage "You can't make an omelet without breaking some eggs" (Glover 1999:255).

31. Some analysts argue that "the mold for all the great revolutionary butchers"—Stalin, Mao, Pol Pot, and so on—was set by Maximilien Robespierre, the chief architect of the French terror that resulted in the execution of at least 50,000 persons at the end of the 18th century (Hunt 2006). As in Russia and China, the motor of revolution in France was as much violence as ideology (Andress 2006; Scurr 2006).

Our second caveat is that while Mao was Stalin's truest heir, state killing differed under the two in several important ways. To start with, the cruelties perpetrated under Mao involved unparalleled mass participation, the origins of which can be traced back to communist campaigns before he came to power (Lieberthal 2003). Mao ruled by getting people to hate each other, especially in the period 1949–1955, when people's tribunals were widely employed, and again during the disastrous Cultural Revolution of 1966–1976. Mao's reliance on the masses for repression is one reason why some people believe China had no real equivalent of the KGB.[32] Instead, Mao "managed to turn the [Chinese] people into the ultimate weapon of dictatorship" (Chang 1991:659) by urging them to carry out the violence he required alongside police and prison officials (Wang 2007:178). In this way, "Mao's China was qualitatively different from Stalin's Soviet Union" (Glover 1999:292). The delegation of control to ordinary people and the decentralization of the power to review death sentences during Mao's reign has been called the "regionalization" of Chinese capital punishment, and this, too, distinguishes his approach from Stalin's more centralized one (Zhang 2008). So does Mao's use of "the death sentence with a two-year reprieve," which he invented in the 1950s "in an attempt to limit a situation that had become uncontrollable" (Zhang 2008).[33] Wang Youquin, who launched a Web site in 2000 recognizing the Chinese victims who died during the Cultural Revolution, notes that the Chinese have also produced "much less writing" on the violence under Mao than the Russians have generated about violence in their own Stalinist era. She believes one reason is that "the persecution in China was more serious than in Russia in some respects" (Wang 2007:177; see also McNett 2000).[34]

Mao seldom aspired to make the killings he conducted and orchestrated conform to preconceived notions of legality, and in this respect he diverged markedly from the legal pretense that frequently surrounded Stalinist killing in the Soviet Union (Zhang 2008). In this and related ways, Maoist institutions of capital punishment (and of criminal justice more generally) differed considerably from those in the Soviet Union, even when the CCP professed to be learning from its "elder brother" (Lubman 1969).

Our third qualification is that at the same time Mao drew on Soviet experience and on his own personal relationship with Stalin, he also looked

32. Mao did have the Central Case Examination Group, whose mandate was to investigate senior party personnel suspected of treachery, spying, or "collusion with the enemy," but some analysts say its scale of operation was significantly smaller than those of the Soviet KGB and the German Gestapo (Schoenhals 1996; Glover 1999).

33. The death sentence with two-year reprieve has many precursors in Chinese history, but the modern version was created by Mao (Zhang 2005a; Zhang 2008).

34. Wang's Web site is www.chinese-memorial.org. A year after it was launched, Chinese authorities blocked access from the mainland. As of 2007, Wang had only 1,000 names on this Web memorial, a small fraction of the 1.3 million victims' names that were published by a Russian human rights group in 2004 (Wang 2007:180).

to the Chinese past for instructive examples of how to rule. Mao was a voracious reader, and his "favorite rulers, whose biographies comprised much of his reading from the piles of books that littered his huge bed and lined his study, were China's most cruel emperors" (Mirsky 1994). Emperor Zhou of the 11th century B.C. mutilated his enemies and forced his servants to cavort in a wine-filled swimming pool, yet Mao believed those excesses were negligible because the emperor had expanded China's territory. And Mao not only thought Emperor Qin's myriad slaughters in the third century B.C. were justified because the victims had interfered with efforts to unify China and build an empire (Li 1994; Mirsky 1994), he even "spoke with contempt of the Qin emperor for killing fewer people than he himself had killed" (Zi 2007). Contemporaneous influences had the biggest effects on Mao, but it is neither necessary nor desirable to ignore the influences of the Chinese past on his death penalty policy (Tanner 1999:185).

MAO ZEDONG (1893–1976) The true heirs of Stalin were not the Soviet leaders who followed him, for they had no grand political scheme besides keeping the Soviet Union afloat. For huge Stalinist projects aimed at remaking society, one must turn to two Asian cases: Mao Zedong in China, and Pol Pot in Cambodia (Glover 1999:283).[35] Cambodia decided to abolish the death penalty after a holocaust that killed at least 15 to 20 percent of a total population of seven million (Kiernan 2002), and the main point of its abolition was to "mark with a powerful symbol" the end of Pol Pot's vicious regime (Hood 2002:43; Dunlop 2005). That abolition was confirmed in 1993 when Cambodia's new constitution mandated that "there shall be no capital punishment" (Cambodian League for the Promotion and Defence of Human Rights 2007). The death penalty in China, by contrast, outlived Mao with a vengeance not seen in the Soviet Union after Stalin.[36]

Mao has been called "the most destructive tyrant in recorded history," and intentional killing was one hallmark of his rule (Mirsky 1994; Chang

35. Though considerable, the Stalinist influences on Ho Chi Minh were not as strong as on Pol Pot and Mao. See appendix C.

36. Capital punishment in the former Soviet Union was abolished three times: in 1917–1918, 1920–1921, and (for peacetime offenses) 1947–1950. Each time, the death penalty was soon reinstated on the Leninist rationale that it was needed to "defend the revolution from its class enemies" (Mikhlin 1999; Hood 2002:30). From the 1960s until its dissolution in 1991, the Soviet Union executed an average of 730 people a year. In 1996, Russia imposed a moratorium on capital punishment, and in 1999 its Constitutional Court formally barred the practice until all of the country's courts had switched to jury trials. In December 2006, the State Duma effectively extended the ten-year moratorium for three more years by putting off the introduction of juries in Chechen courts (Murphy 2006). According to Victoria Sergeyeva, Penal Reform International's director for Russia, Ukraine, and Belarus, "it's possible that within the next two to three years, Russia will ratify Protocol No. 6 [to the European Convention for the Protection of Human Rights and Fundamental Freedoms] and strike out the death penalty from its national legislation" (quoted in Klomegah 2007).

and Halliday 2005). This view has been contested by some who believe Mao belongs in a different category from other 20th-century tyrants because, unlike Stalin and Hitler, he had a utopian dream to transform his country and because he never totally lost his belief in the efficacy of thought reform and the possibility of redemption (Short 2000). In the end, however, both Mao and Stalin had many people killed purely to expand their personal power, so it is difficult to see a categorical difference between them. Comparison to Hitler reveals significant similarities, too (Buruma 2000).

Of course, there were numerous actors and factors besides Mao that made the 20th century such a terrible one for so many Chinese. They include the depth and savagery of Japan's assault on China (Chang 1997), the reality of peasant deprivation in Republican China (Spence 1990), the collapse of local order and the spread of banditry in the early Republican period (Wakeman 1995), the strength of criminal gangs in many parts of the country (Wakeman 1995), the large-scale extrajudicial killing by Chiang Kai-shek and his nationalist party (Wakeman 2003), and the means-justify-the-ends mentality of many of Mao's comrades in the Communist Party (Chang and Halliday 2005).[37] This was the milieu in which Mao emerged, and accounts of his acts and influences must attend to these formative forces (Spence 2005). In the end, however, Mao had more control over more people than any leader in human history, and how he exercised that control was strongly shaped by his direct and indirect relationships with Joseph Stalin and by his decisions to adopt

---

37. Abolition of capital punishment and torture were popular aims of the early Chinese communists, and the CCP's charter of 1923 even included these among its goals (Chang and Halliday 2005:84). To this day, abolition remains a CCP objective, albeit only at some unspecified time in the future when the nation's "material and spiritual circumstances" have improved (Ho 2005:276; Chen 2006c; "China Defends Use" 2008). But there was also considerable enthusiasm for executions among Mao's comrades before the PRC was established. In 1928, for example, Peng Pai, the leader of one of the most famous communist bases in China, extolled the virtues of Lenin by saying that "His law has no detail. It just kills all opposition." Peng's communist base was known as Little Moscow (it had its own Red Square), and he called on his comrades to "disembowel and slice off heads . . . slaughter on the spot with no hesitation. Have absolutely not a shred of feeling. . . . Kill, kill freely. To kill is the topmost important work in an uprising" (quoted in Chang and Halliday 2005:61). In the 1930s, it was the communists who first introduced Soviet-style concentration camps into China (Spence 1995), but it was Chiang Kai-shek's government that first established the crime of "counterrevolution" when the KMT and the CCP split in 1927 (Becker 2000:322). The same year, Chiang's forces massacred many Communist Party members on the principle that "it was better to kill a thousand than let one go free" (250). While he was on the mainland, Chiang tried to adopt some of the elements of a modern liberal state, at least in his rhetoric, and some of his reform attempts actually were "astonishing in the context of Chinese history" in that they aimed to "lift the crushing hand of the Chinese state" (Becker 2000:14; see also Dikotter 2002; Xu 2008). But Chiang became increasingly dictatorial after splitting with the Communists (Fenby 2003).

many of the Soviet dictator's methods (Chang and Halliday 2005:337; Zhang 2008:118).[38]

Mao employed the Soviet model of death as an instrument of political action both during the long civil war of communist ascendancy and in its aftermath. When he and his comrades settled in Yan'an after their famous Long March, he established a domain that "was closely modeled on that of Stalin's Soviet Union" (Becker 2000:15). For nearly two decades before the founding of the People's Republic in 1949, the CCP borrowed from the Soviet Union, including capital punishment and numerous other institutions and practices of criminal justice (Cohen 1968:7; Lubman 1999:71). From the birth of the PRC until 1953, China's criminal process "served as a blunt instrument of terror," much as in the earliest days of the Soviet Union (Cohen 1968:9). Mao's main aims were to crush all sources of political opposition and to rid society of antisocial elements who threatened public order. Toward these ends, he developed a death penalty policy (and other policies as well) that relied on the fundamental distinction between "friends" and "enemies" and on the need to reform the former while ruthlessly punishing the latter (Dutton 2005a).

The next stage in the evolution of the PRC's criminal process lasted from 1954 to 1957, and it has been called, with some exaggeration, a "golden age of law" because during this period "Chinese communist leaders decided to develop further a Soviet-style legal system" (Cohen 1968:11). That effort was undertaken with the aid of many Soviet legal experts, and the party line on criminal justice "was the same as that for other aspects of the country's development—to adapt the advanced experiences of the Soviet Union to China's conditions" (Cohen 1968:11). This decision to learn from the Soviet Union was reversed by Mao's antirightist movement of 1957, after which the chairman and many Chinese writers increasingly emphasized the inappropriateness of the Soviet model for their country (Cohen 1968:15). By this time, however, several Stalinist death penalty tactics had already been institutionalized, including sustained campaigns of repression, mass trials and executions, and execution quotas (Lubman 1999:79). The de-Stalinization of Chinese criminal justice continued until the mid-1960s, when the PRC went back to the future by returning to a model of revolutionary justice that was administered through government agencies and

---

38. Writing in 1986, scholar Su Shaozhi argued that "the Stalin model and its traditions, alongside this [Chinese tradition of] feudal despotism is a potent combination which brings on sickness" (quoted in Dutton 1992:9). Similar views about the interaction of Stalinist influences with repressive currents of Chinese history are expressed in Xin (1997), Becker (2000), Buruma (2000), and Huchet (2002). More recently, some analysts have argued that China "inspired" the coercive interrogation techniques used by the United States in its war on terror (Shane 2008), but in fact many of those techniques were initiated and practiced in Stalin's Soviet Union long before China adopted them or the United States put them into practice. See, for example, Arthur Koestler's *Darkness at Noon* (1941) and Aleksandr Solzhenitsyn's *One Day in the Life of Ivan Denisovich* (1963).

the people themselves, as had been done during the first several years after the nation's founding (Tanner 1999:26). This approach continued until Mao died and the Cultural Revolution ended in 1976.

The last decade of Mao's life was characterized by "the utter breakdown of law and order" (Tanner 1999:13). Class struggle was elevated to a position of supremacy, law was denounced, ignored, and eliminated, and the core organs of criminal justice—public security, procuracy, and courts—were "rhetorically and literally attacked as the state lost its monopoly on coercive power" (Tanner 1999:13). This was, in many respects, an era of "law without lawyers" (Li 1977). A more juristic model of criminal justice (like the one advocated before the antirightist movement of 1957) began to appear after Deng Xiaoping became China's paramount leader in 1978, but those reforms were confined and deemphasized when Deng's call in 1983 for a Strike Hard campaign led to the return of Mao-like methods of repression (Tanner 2000:107; Trevaskes 2007).

Throughout much of the Maoist period, legal forms and judicial authority were not regarded as important or even necessary elements of state killing because the authority of the communist power structure was considered sufficient to provide whatever legitimacy the act required. As with Stalin, when terror was a weapon of state, legitimacy was not a pressing question. And as with Stalin, the death toll generated by Mao's policies is difficult to determine with precision but certainly numbers in the many millions.[39] In fact, if priority is placed on the sheer number of deaths (as opposed to the proportion of population killed, in which case Pol Pot comes out on top), then Mao's regime ranks among the most lethal governments of the 20th century (Rummel 1994:8). Mao wielded almost absolute power over the lives of one-quarter of the world's population from 1949 until his death in 1976, and during that period he was, according to his most recent biographers, "responsible for well over 70 million deaths in peacetime, more than any other twentieth-century leader" (Chang and Halliday 2005:3; Zhang 2008:132). That estimate has been disputed (Kristof 2005), and not all of the deaths for which he might be held "responsible" were state killings (perhaps 30 million Chinese died during the famine that followed the Great Leap Forward, and up to a million people a year died in Mao's vast labor camps), but the most comprehensive effort to determine the 20th century's most deadly killers concludes that Mao ranks second (after Stalin), with nearly 38 million victims between 1923 and

39. It is difficult to describe the trajectory of capital punishment after the revolution that brought Mao and the CCP to power not only because systematic data do not exist or have not been published but also because it is sometimes impossible to discern whether state killing was judicial or extrajudicial (MacFarquhar and Schoenhals 2006; Zhang 2008). Capital punishment is an inherently legal concept and practice. Under Mao, however, much law was eliminated, and even where it remained it was often disregarded if it happened not to suit party policies or purposes (Spence 1990:711; Lubman 1999:2). Appendix G briefly examines some of the connections between judicial and extrajudicial killing in China and other Asian jurisdictions.

1976 (this includes his guerrilla period; see Rummel 1994:8; Becker 1996; Chang and Halliday 2005:325).[40]

If Mao ranks with Stalin and Hitler on the government killing scale,[41] the leaders of the country he once ruled still perpetuate the benevolent myth of a man who in reality—and routinely—denied his people's desire and right to live.[42] His huge portrait still hangs in Tiananmen Square, his corpse (or something resembling it) continues to be viewed by throngs of visitors to that plaza, his face graces the country's currency, and, more generally, the leadership of the CCP continues to embrace and advocate fictions about a man whom many believe was "a hypocrite in his personal life and a terrorist from above in his politics" (Nathan 2006:4; see also Fairbank 1990; Li 1994; Mirsky 1994; Becker 1996; Buruma 2000; Chang and Halliday 2005). In this respect, too, Mao must be distinguished from Stalin (and Hitler), for his legacy lives on in a way theirs did not (Bullock 1998).[43]

40. Another estimate of the scale of Maoist violence during the Cultural Revolution can be found in MacFarquhar and Schoenhals (2006), who believe that in rural areas of China, 750,000–1,500,000 people were killed and roughly equal numbers were permanently injured in 1966–1971. By this conservative estimate, an average of at least 125,000 people were killed by the government each year, and the number would be "immensely greater" if killings in urban centers were added (Spence 2006). MacFarquhar and Schoenhals also note that Mao appears to have been in control of all key decisions concerning the Cultural Revolution's targets and direction, at least until he was weakened in the revolution's latter years by Lou Gehrig's disease and other ailments. On the whole, however, MacFarquhar and Schoenhals describe a Mao who was somewhat more reasonable than the person depicted by his former personal physician Li Zhisui (1994) and by analysts such as Jonathan Mirsky (1994), Ian Buruma (2000), Jung Chang and Jon Halliday (2005), and Andrew J. Nathan (2006).

41. As mentioned earlier, in one list of the 20th century's "bloodiest megamurderers," Stalin, Mao, and Hitler are followed by Chiang Kai-shek (Rummel 1994:8). On the terrible cruelties perpetrated by Chiang and Dai Li, his secret police and intelligence chief, see Fenby (2003) and Wakeman (2003).

42. After millions of people died of starvation and overwork in the Great Leap Forward and the resultant famine, Mao said: "Death is indeed to be rejoiced over. . . . We believe in dialectics, and so we can't not be in favor of death. . . . Deaths have benefits. They can fertilize the ground. . . . We are prepared to sacrifice 300 million Chinese for the victory of the world revolution. . . . Half the population wiped out—this happened quite a few times in Chinese history" (quoted in Chang and Halliday 2005:439). The famine of 1959–1962 actually killed about 30 million, and Mao and his adoption of policies that had already proved disastrous in the Soviet Union were largely responsible for it. The human desperation was so intense that it resulted in cannibalism, the selling of human flesh, and the swapping of children so that people could use them for food without committing the additional sin of eating their own (Becker 1996).

43. Since the CCP issued its "Resolution" on Mao in 1981, the official view has been that Mao's "merits are primary and his errors secondary" (for the quantitatively inclined, he was "70 percent good and 30 percent bad"). But outside the PRC, many analysts think it is impossible to regard him "with anything except horror and rage" (Mirsky 1994), even if he did help "lay the groundwork for the rebirth and rise of China after five centuries of slumber" (Kristof 2005). As for Stalin, his fan club has grown in recent years, at least inside Russia (Kramer 2007).

The peak period of Maoist killing occurred in the early 1950s. In October 1950, Mao launched a nationwide campaign to suppress counterrevolution-aries, and later he boasted that 712,000 persons had been executed in the year-long crackdown, which is more than 30 times more executions than there were death sentences in the first 12 months of China's famously harsh Strike Hard campaign in the early 1980s (Zhang 2008:123). The number for 1950–1951 does not include approximately three times that number who perished through mob violence or suicide (Chang and Halliday 2005:324). In 1956, after Nikita Khrushchev condemned Stalin's use of terror, Mao felt compelled to reduce the number of arrests and executions (416), but China remained an aggressive killing state, with state-sponsored executions "reaching their ex-treme in every province in 1968," a year early in the Cultural Revolution that was dominated by a campaign called Sort Out Class Ranks, the aim of which was to "inventory every single 'class enemy' in the entire population" (545). In the northern province of Inner Mongolia more than 16,000 persons died, while in the southern province of Yunnan some 17,000 people were executed, beaten to death, or driven to suicide (546). The new boss of Anhui Province made decisions about the appropriate scale of executions by defining his target as the average number of killings that occurred in two neighboring provinces (546). As noted earlier, Mao and his subordinates frequently used execution quotas. In 1951, for instance, the Ministry of Public Security promulgated his directive that, as a general rule, the number of counter-revolutionaries should be limited to one person in 1,000 in the countryside and half that amount in the cities, and one or two out of ten counter-revolutionaries were supposed to be executed. As we show in the next section, "a comparable logic" could still be perceived in the anticrime campaigns that were directed by Chinese capital punishment's final founding father, Deng Xiaoping (Zhang 2008).

DENG XIAOPING (1904–1997)   The title of the *New York Times* obituary for Deng Xiaoping was "A Political Wizard Who Put China on the Capitalist Road," and in it a former American ambassador to China (J. Stapleton Roy) observed that "if you look at the 150 years of modern China's history since the Opium Wars, then you can't avoid the conclusion that the last 15 years [under Deng] are the best 15 years in China's modern history" (Tyler 1997). In the nearly two decades that Deng was the PRC's top leader, his economic pragmatism helped nourish a boom that radically improved the lives of hundreds of millions of Chinese (Evans 1995; Yang 1997; Marti 2002). Real incomes in cities and in villages more than doubled during his rule (Tyler 1997).

Deng's economic pragmatism diverged from Mao's ideological extrem-ism, but there are significant continuities between the two leaders in the spheres of politics and criminal justice. Most broadly, both were stubbornly resistant to democratic stirrings, and both insisted on the preeminence of the Communist Party. As for capital punishment in particular, the policies of Mao and Deng did differ in some respects. Most notably, the blurry line between judicial and extrajudicial killing that existed under Mao became clearer under Deng as more law was created and used to administer the death penalty (Tanner 1999; Chen 2000; Bakken 2004:80), and the volume of extrajudicial executions decreased dramatically after Mao died and the Cultural Revolution ended (Payne 2004; Chang and Halliday 2005).[44]

Nonetheless, the similarities between Mao and Deng are striking and substantial, as are similarities in rhetoric and policy between the anticrime campaigns of the 1950s and the 1980s (Trevaskes 2007:138). Here is our list of 15 of the most salient death penalty resemblances, to which experts on China no doubt can add:

1. A strong reliance on harshness in punishment, including the frequent use of execution as a criminal sanction (Tanner 1999:136; Bakken 2004:80; Tanner 2005:174; Zhang 2008)

2. The use of execution targets and quotas, with different regions of the country sometimes competing against each other (Tanner 2005:177; Zhang 2008)

3. The decentralization of much death penalty decision-making (Tanner 2000; Zhang 2008)

4. The orchestration of mass campaigns to crack down on people and activities deemed threatening, the enlistment of mass involvement in these campaigns, the routinization of the campaigns, and faith in the general deterrent effects of public degradation rituals (Tanner 2000; Trevaskes 2002; Trevaskes 2004; Qi 2005; Qu 2005; Trevaskes 2007; Cody 2008; Zhang 2008)

5. The centrality of the distinction between "friends and enemies," with stress on reform for wayward members of the former category and severity for those in the latter (Tanner 2000; Dutton 2005a; Zhang 2008)

---

44. Deng diverged from Mao in other ways as well. For instance, the death penalty under Mao tended to target "counterrevolutionaries" instead of ordinary criminal offenders, and Mao stressed the need to appease public anger more often than Deng, who more consistently emphasized capital punishment's deterrent value. Borge Bakken (2004:80) uses two Chinese expressions to contrast the leaders' approaches to execution: Mao believed more in "justice in the public square" (*guangchanghua*), while Deng favored "justice in the [more legalized] theatre" (*juchanghua*). Bakken may have it wrong, however, when he claims that "from the mid-1950s until the mid-1960s, estimates of the number of executions are far lower than the estimates from the Deng era" (79). He provides no references for the Mao half of that assertion, and studies show that large-scale executions occurred during that decade of his rule as well (Chang and Halliday 2005; Zhang 2008; see also Pu 1994).

6. The leading role of the Communist Party in all capital punishment policy-making and the frequent intervention of party officials in individual cases (Tanner 1999:188; Maier 2005; Zhang 2008)

7. A view of law as a flexible instrument for achieving party and regime purposes (Tanner 1999:187; Tanner 2000; Trevaskes 2007:138; Zhang 2008)

8. Speedy decision-making in individual cases, with little allowance for defense lawyering, witness testimony, or meaningful appeal (Amnesty International 1997a; Tanner 2000; Trevaskes 2002; Qi 2005; Trevaskes 2007; Glionna 2008)

9. A heavy dependence on confessions for evidence and the routine use of torture to obtain them (Cohen 1968; Nowak 2006; Matas and Kilgour 2007)

10. A shortage of human and material resources to run the criminal justice system in a manner consistent with the law-on-the-books (Tanner 1999:187; Tanner 2000; Trevaskes 2007)

11. "A substantial degree of continuity" in substantive and procedural criminal law (Tanner 1999:6; Lubman 1999:71)

12. Reliance on public security officials and firearms as the primary execution method, with most condemned offenders shot in the back of the head ("Death Penalty in China" 2004; Ye 2006)

13. Extreme secrecy about execution totals, but with more caution about revealing the facts of specific executions to foreign than domestic audiences (Tanner 1999:103; Lu and Miethe 2007)

14. Almost no public criticism of death penalty policy or practice, and strong regime intolerance of the same (Bakken 2004; Ho 2005; Zhang 2005a)

15. An almost "constant recourse" in official rhetoric to "popular will" and to "public support" for harsh punishment policies (Dutton 1992:5; Ho 2005)

In short, Deng Xiaoping had a "golden opportunity" to change Chinese death penalty policy after he came to power in 1978, and he chose not to (Bakken 2004:79). The year 1978 marked "a turning point" for China in many ways, economically and socially, of course, but also in the crime field, as the belief that the nation was experiencing a huge upsurge in crime rapidly became orthodox (Dutton 1992:327). The belief may not have been well grounded (Bakken 2004), but things that are defined as real can be real in their consequences—and that is what happened in Deng's China. By the early 1980s, concerns about deteriorating public security prompted Deng and the Central Committee of the CCP to declare that they would "reverse the present abnormal situation" by showing "absolutely no mercy in striking determined blows against criminal elements" (quoted in Tanner 1999:83). Thus was born the first of China's Strike Hard (*yanda*) campaigns, which would become an almost perpetual feature of China's crime control policy for the next two decades (Trevaskes 2004; Qi 2005; Qu 2005; Tanner 2005; Trevaskes 2007).[45]

Reliable Strike Hard statistics are scarce, but many accounts suggest that these anticrime campaigns have been extraordinarily harsh (Trevaskes 2007). The Chinese editors of *Forty Years of Rule by the Chinese Communist*

45. For an account of the campaigns that were conducted by the communists long before they gained power in 1949 (and that shaped more recent Strike Hard policies and practices), see Lieberthal (2003). Several scholarly accounts have been given of the motives for the recent Strike Hard campaigns. Borge Bakken (2004:67) argues that the first campaign was "triggered by a moral panic about juvenile crime and to some extent economic crime in the early 1980s," while historian Harold Tanner (1999:86) cites an article in a Hong Kong magazine that said Deng took "a personal interest in the violent suppression of criminal activity" after robbers tried to hold him up as he rode in his limousine near the seaside resort of Beidaihe. One of the most comprehensive summaries comes from political scientist Murray Scot Tanner, who has identified a variety of motivations, including: (1) the leadership's desire to produce "a morally and ideologically civilized society to compliment [*sic*] the materially advanced society being forged by economic reform"; (2) the unconsciously felt need of public security officials to "redeploy" revered Maoist techniques of mass campaigning in order to deal with a major increase in crime; (3) the imperative felt by the political and public security leadership to adapt to China's "very low ratio" of professional police officers to citizens; (4) police concern that high-profile crimes could embolden citizen activists to think the state no longer controls the "balance of awe" in society; (5) the widespread belief that campaigns under Mao helped control crime, establish order, and encourage the masses to cooperate with the state against criminal offenders; and (6) a conviction among most security officials and political leaders that severe punishments deter crime (Tanner 2005:172–173). Tanner's earlier account makes a convincing case that what precipitated the first campaign was "the powerful cumulative impact of a series of high-profile crimes that shook the sensibilities of many Chinese in the early 1980s" (Tanner 2000:102). To Westerners, the best-known crime was the May 1983 hijacking to South Korea of a Chinese airplane—reportedly the first commercial hijacking in PRC history. More disturbing to Chinese citizens was "a spate of brutal gang rapes," some committed in broad daylight in front of large crowds of witnesses too frightened to complain or intervene. On this view, the original Strike Hard campaign reflected the leadership's "deep fear" that it was losing control over what Tanner terms the "balance of awe" between the party-state and criminals. "Without a decisive show of state force," Tanner says, "not only would criminals not be deterred from crime, but ordinary citizens would also be unwilling to give the state the popular assistance it needs to maintain social order" (94). For an analysis of Strike Hard campaigns that is based largely on a case study of the local court system in the city of Baotou in Inner Mongolia, see Susan Trevaskes (2007), who argues that in many respects, China's criminal justice practices in the 1980s paralleled those from the 1950s and "set the foundation for practices into the twenty-first century" (Trevaskes 2007:1,137–140). Trevaskes identifies four main strategies in the anticrime campaigns of the post-Mao period and today: announcing crime as a major national problem, making criminals the enemy of modernization, changing criminal procedure and sentencing practice (through speedy trials, party control over local criminal justice work, and the joint handling of cases by the police, prosecutors, and courts), and creating momentum for the campaign by mobilizing the masses and by acts of expressive punishment such as mass sentencing rallies (117–134).

Party believed the concentrated attack on crime in 1983 was "the largest since the campaign to Suppress Counter-Revolutionaries in 1950" (quoted in Tanner 1999:85). According to statistics provided by the Central Politico-Legal Affairs Commission in 1984, over 24,000 persons were sentenced to death in the four-month "high tide" of the campaign between August and December of 1983 (Tanner 1999:98; Tanner 2005:174). Of those, about 5,000 were sentenced to death with immediate execution, while the remaining 19,000 were sentenced to death with a two-year reprieve (most of the latter probably had their sentences commuted to something less than death). Professor Marina Svensson of Lund University in Sweden has offered a higher (and rougher) estimate, that "during the Strike Hard campaign of 1983 tens of thousands of people were sentenced to death and executed" (Svensson 2001:10). And Susan Trevaskes (2007:1) has observed that "some reports put the national figure of people sentenced to death over the three years [1983–1986] at over thirty thousand (including those sentenced to death with a two-year reprieve)." Whatever the exact numbers—and the data are scarce—it appears that judicial executions rapidly escalated in the first Strike Hard, perhaps tripling between 1978, when Deng took control and put the country on the capitalist road, and 1986, the year the first campaign ended (Scobell 1990).[46] Murray Tanner (2000:93) has called the first Strike Hard the "bloodiest chapter in post-Mao Chinese politics." In 1984, the year after it started, Deng attested to his own role in it when he told the Central Advisory Commission of the Communist Party "last year, I devoted myself to only one thing: a crackdown on criminal offenders" (quoted in Tanner 1999:86). He would go on to say on many other occasions that "only by being severe can we cure crime for good" (quoted in Bakken 2004:80), though the evidence suggests that China's death penalty "has not been an effective deterrent" in the reformist period (Tanner 1999:167; Tanner 2005:181). Some have even argued that the "brutalizing" effects of severe punishment might have contributed to increases in the incidence and seriousness of violent crime (Bakken 2000:394; Trevaskes 2007:183; but see also Zimring 2008).

Yet again, to say that Deng continued many of Mao's execution policies is not to say the two were twins. Crime was not the central concern of either Stalin or Mao, nor was execution as a specifically judicial sanction its central

---

46. In a subsequent article, Scobell said there were "at least 10,000 and perhaps as many as 20,000 executions" in 1978–1987, an estimate that is, even at the high end, almost certainly low (Scobell 1991:205). While doing research for his pathbreaking book on the birth and early development of China's Strike Hard strategy, Harold Tanner was told by two Chinese informants that their country executed about 8,000 people per year in the late 1980s and around 10,000 people in 1991 (Tanner 1999:141). Susan Trevaskes analyzed China's 2001 Strike Hard campaign and found that more than 3,000 people were executed in the first five months of that year (Trevaskes 2002:677). On Strike Hard campaigns since the 1990s, see also Amnesty International (1997a), Trevaskes (2004), Trevaskes (2007), Qi (2005), and Qu (2005).

form. It was Deng and his cadre who engineered the transformation of judicially ordered execution into a frequently used instrument of crime control (Bakken 2004:79). Little is known about the level of execution in China immediately before this change or about the peak rates that were reached after Strike Hard campaigns took effect. What we do know is that rising crime became an important public and governmental concern in the early 1980s, prompting the central government to mandate stern punishments and implement changes in the legal process that would reduce the costs and increase the rates of execution.

The most important of these Deng-era changes was the 1983 decision by the Standing Committee of the National People's Congress to relocate authority for reviewing death sentences away from the SPC, the nation's top judicial organ, to courts at the provincial level (Tanner 1999:73).[47] This decentralization helped fuel "a substantial increase in the use of capital punishment" (Scobell 1990; Bakken 2004:79), though the precise extent of the rise is difficult to gauge. Execution rates are not known for the 1980s or for the previous three decades, and the peak rates during Strike Hard remain state secrets. At the high end, however, informed guesses speak in terms of five-digit execution volumes in the early Strike Hard years, which is a huge number compared to modern rates of execution in other nations but a small fraction of the epic levels of state killing that occurred in China's revolutionary and postrevolution periods. If 15,000 executions were carried out in the first year of the initial Strike Hard campaign, that would be more than 90 percent of the world's judicial executions but less than 10 percent (and probably less than 5 percent) of the average annual volume of political killings that occurred during the decade-long Cultural Revolution that preceded Mao's death (Chang and Halliday 2005; MacFarquhar and Schoenhals 2006; Spence 2006).

The large difference between the scale of political killings in an era of terror and the much smaller number of state executions during Strike Hard suggests that political killings can provide precedent for broad campaigns of judicial execution. This difference may also help explain why Deng and his successors seem to have regarded their crackdowns as modest and moderate. Next to 100,000 or 500,000 political killings a year, 15,000 executions of convicted criminals may not feel extreme. Indeed, when contrasted with the scale of killings under Mao and their frequently dubious legality, even five-digit

47. A related directive issued at the same time by the National People's Congress gave county courts the authority to try first-instance capital cases, but because these courts were so swamped with cases and because they "made such a procedural mess of their casework," the SPC, the Supreme People's Procuratorate, and the Ministry of Public Security "issued a humiliating recision of the authority" only three months later (Tanner 2000:111,119). The decentralization of authority to review death sentences would last almost another quarter century.

execution figures probably seem like small beer.[48] And considering the strong levels of public support for capital punishment in contemporary China, the aggressive death penalty policies of Deng and his successors may well have bolstered their popularity (Bakken 2004:83; Ho 2005; Bakken 2007:181).[49]

But if state killing now is less common and more governed by law than it was under Mao, and if the majority of Chinese citizens hold a highly positive view of capital punishment, then what explains the state secrecy that surrounds the number of executions? One common explanation is the sensitivity of China's government to foreign opinion, and this is undoubtedly part of the story. But execution numbers are domestic secrets as well, even though a high level of execution presents no obvious political threat, given current public opinion, and even though publicizing a high execution rate would presumably increase deterrence. The connection between political killings and judicial executions provides an additional perspective on this issue. To the extent that political authorities like Deng regarded the two genres as linked, the tradition of treating state killing as an appropriate secret of the government in power may have carried over to the practice of judicial executions. Thus, core facts about the exercise of state power perhaps are being kept secret as much out of inertia as out of a traditional penchant for governmental secrecy or the fear of foreign criticisms that are framed in terms of human rights.

History and tradition are the "twin towers" usually used to legitimate capital punishment in contemporary China (Ho 2005:285), but we have argued here

48. In addition to serving as justifying precedent, political killings may have contributed some institutional and procedural precedent to the new generation of criminal justice execution. This criminal sanction is often called "judicial execution," but the term is seldom true in any literal sense because judges are not executioners in any modern system. Both the method of killing (shooting in the PRC of the mid-1980s) and the personnel doing it (the armed police) were the same for judicial executions under Deng as for many of the political killings that occurred under Mao.

49. Few surveys of public opinion on capital punishment have been conducted in the PRC, but those that have been done indicate high levels of support. When scholar Hu Yunteng (2002) surveyed 5,066 persons in 1995, only 0.78 percent said the death penalty should be abolished, and only 3.04 percent said it was used too much (Svensson 2001:2). Similarly, interviews that Virgil Ho, a professor at Hong Kong University of Science and Technology, conducted with ordinary Chinese citizens led him to conclude that public views about the death penalty are very similar to those held by government and party officials (Ho 2005:275). But the most rigorous survey of public opinion on capital punishment in the PRC also yields the most interesting findings. Based on face-to-face questionnaire interviews with 231 Chinese citizens in Beijing city and Hubei and Guangdong provinces, researchers at the Max Planck Institute in Freiburg found that 58 percent of respondents favored the death penalty, and only 25 percent said they are interested in the issue (Oberwittler and Qi 2008). If these findings are representative of Chinese public opinion on the death penalty more generally (and the minor differences between provinces suggest that they may be), then the level of support for capital punishment is lower in China than in most American states (Zimring 2003:11–12). More intriguingly, the low level of Chinese "interest" in the death penalty seems to suggest that "leadership from the front" to reform the nation's death penalty exceptionalism might not be hard to achieve.

that the current high rate of execution in the PRC has its proximate roots in the government that came to power in the mid-20th century rather than in ancient practices or enduring propunishment values. It is possible that long-standing patterns of Chinese culture contributed to the political appeal and public toleration of Mao's regime and its tactics. If so, then China's "legalist" tradition of reliance on harsh punishment for order could have played an indirect role in the exceptional policies of the present. But even if it did, the most important moving parts of China's current system of capital punishment are less than 60 years old and political at their core (Zi 2007; Bakken 2008).

To many China-watchers, foreign and domestic, the story of state killing under Mao now seems unreal, clouded over by the passage of time and irrelevant to the needs of a new China (Spence 2006). The CCP also continues to encourage and enforce forgetfulness about the most painful parts of that story (Kahn 2006c; Schell 2006). Still, all of China's leaders in 2007 were in their teens or early twenties when the brutalizing class warfare of the Cultural Revolution occurred, and they would not be human if the scars did not run deep. The culture of violence that Mao's party inhabited not only shaped the death penalty sensibilities of China's current leaders, it also dominated the thinking and feeling of the old men—Mao's comrades—who ordered the crackdowns in Beijing and elsewhere in 1989 (Apter and Saitch 1990; Mirsky 1994; Clark 2008) and the crackdown on Falun Gong ten years later (I. Johnson 2004; Matas and Kilgour 2007; Pan 2008). That is one reason to believe that Strike Hard campaigns may "continue to be used as the key political response to social change in China well into the first decades of the new century" (Trevaskes 2002:692; see also Tanner 2000:125). Another reason to anticipate more of the same is that crime is perceived to be the primary threat to China's economic development, widely considered the nation's top priority (Tanner 1999:190; Dutton 2005b; Trevaskes 2007). According to official statistics, the nation's crime rate in 2000 was almost 50 times higher than the rates observed in the 1950s and 1960s (Zhang, Messner, and Liu 2007:962). This increase may be greatly exaggerated by changes in crime reporting practices, and China's current crime rates are still low compared to many other nations (Bakken 2005), but the critical fact is that citizens and leaders alike *believe* the country's crime situation has worsened considerably. What Jiang Zemin stressed when he was in power remains the watchword today: "stability overrides everything" (quoted in Tanner 2000:94).[50]

50. There is also the problem of China's unbalanced sex ratio: "too many boys" are being born because girls are disproportionately aborted (Choe 2007d). Within 15 years, China may have 30 million men who cannot find wives, and "that could mean serious trouble" (Kurlantzick 2007), not least because single young men are much more likely to commit violence than their married peers (Hudson and den Boer 2005). In China today, "cities with the most unbalanced sex ratios have some of the highest crime rates" (Kurlantzick 2007a). When female infanticide generated skewed sex ratios in 19th-century China, a revolt, the Nien rebellion, spread across the countryside, and it took more than a decade for Beijing to repress it. Ultimately, the rebellion weakened the imperial court and hastened its downfall, and some analysts believe it is "a lesson China's current rulers surely have not forgotten." If the CCP cannot reverse China's sex ratio problem, and if it regards unattached young males

No matter how reasonable the expectation of more Maoist capital punishment may seem, it could be confounded. Indeed, China has already undertaken several important death penalty reforms, with apparently large effects on the volume of death sentences and executions. More declines may be on the way. Next we explore the motivations for the recent reforms and the meanings and consequences of the changes.

■ Recent Death Penalty Reforms

The peculiar governmental organization of punishment in China is one powerful reason why the national government must send clear signals in order to influence levels of punishment. As described in the first section of this chapter, all of China's major penal laws are national, but all the critical elements of law enforcement and punishment are provincial, municipal, or county. This means that one function of national policy on specific aspects of capital punishment is the signal it sends to those in provincial and local government about the desired scale of execution. To the limited extent that shifts in national regulation can be studied, they are important both for the specific rules they convey and for the general messages they transmit about whether to accelerate or moderate the use of the capital sanction (Trevaskes 2008).

Since the early 1980s, there appears to have been a cyclical pattern in death penalty signals from Beijing. During the periods when Strike Hard campaigns became a major focus of national government, as in 1983, 1996, and 2001, the signals from the center were unambiguous.[51] The clearest case of explicit encouragement for an aggressive execution policy in the provinces was the removal of the power to hear most death sentence appeals from the SPC in 1983. This preceded a large increase in executions throughout the PRC and probably led to greater variation in the different provinces' regimes of criminal procedure and rates of capital prosecution and execution. But since reliable data are unavailable for both the national rate of execution just prior to 1983 and the range of variation in execution rates among the provinces, the extent to which the 1983 change influenced death penalty rates and policy diversity cannot be established with any precision. What little we know, however, points in the predicted direction. Within months of the first Strike Hard campaign, local courts were so swamped with cases that the Chinese histories "report judges falling sick or even collapsing and dying from exhaustion," and the flood of new inmates into prisons combined with a new policy not to release those who had already served their sentences to create "massive overcrowding and sanitation problems" (Tanner 2000:119). One Chinese criminologist

as a serious threat to the social order, it may rely on capital punishment more than it otherwise would. Something similar can be said of other Asian governments with "surplus" male populations (Hudson and den Boer 2005).

51. Although three main Strike Hard campaigns have occurred since 1983 (Trevaskes 2007:1), it is also true that by the mid-1990s similar campaigns had become a more or less "permanent feature of Chinese life" (Lubman 1999:163; Trevaskes 2007:88).

estimated that the number of offenders undergoing reform through labor "increased dramatically from fewer than 600,000 to approximately 1,200,000" (quoted in Tanner 2000:120). And since the message from the center unleashed local party and political-legal officials to deliver "stern blows" as they saw fit, the first Strike Hard campaign also "became a textbook example of how local officials can reinterpret and stretch Beijing's directives to show their enthusiasm" for Politburo policy (Tanner 2000:115).

The first Strike Hard campaign gradually slowed in 1984 but did not really end until 1986. After that, two broad sets of changes influenced the jurisprudence of capital cases without any clear impact on execution rates. The first changes were part of the project to promote a "rule of law environment," particularly in the criminal justice system. While capital cases now do receive some special attention—scholar Wang Yunhai (2008) even speaks of China's own version of "super due process"—the ambition to create a rule of law within the justice system and to exercise control over the police is part of a larger developmental ambition. By some accounts, "virtually every element of contemporary Chinese law was either revived or newly created during the course of the last 25 years" (Lubman 2006). A number of recent procedural steps, such as creating opportunities for defense attorneys to present oral arguments in death penalty appeals and opening some appeals to public observers, are part of the effort to improve the appearance and the actuality of legality in capital cases. Two manifest aims of these reforms are to make the system more law-like and to reduce the inconsistency between "verdicts that vary widely depending on region, party influence and a defendant's connections" (Glionna 2008).[52] But an important effect may be to decrease executions by making it more difficult to generate capital convictions and sustain them through the appeals process. Indeed, it is precisely because it is so difficult to remove capital offenses from the Chinese statute books that many reformers focus on altering death penalty procedures as the most practical and immediate means of reducing the volume of executions.

Recent efforts to control police by restricting their power to interrogate and torture (by requiring, for example, that some interrogations be electronically recorded) and the recent discussions about cutting back police authority to impose detention without trial are important attempts to impose legal standards, but for the most part they have not been aimed at reducing the volume of death sentences or executions (Tanner and Green 2007; Biddulph 2008; Yi 2008). These proposed reforms began gathering momentum in the 1990s and have steadily gained support in Beijing (Clarke 2007). Though they have not been a central feature of the central government's attempt to influence execution policy in the anticrime crusades, one probable effect will be to influence the rate and cost of execution, as we will show.

---

52. For a critique of inconsistent sentencing in two capital cases that involved hired killers, see Zi (2007).

The addition and subtraction of offenses that can be punished by death is, by contrast, one fairly reliable indicator of political sentiment toward capital punishment in Beijing even though it is by no means clear that the death-eligible crimes that come and go in the penal code are a major source of capital prosecutions or executions. Wang Yunhai notes that the "Old Criminal Law" of 1979 had 28 capital offenses, while the "Current Criminal Law" of 1997 expanded the number to 68, but other analysts report that many of the capital offenses in the current law had already been added piecemeal by the National People's Congress in the years since the first Strike Hard, including some crimes for which death was mandatory (Qi 2005; Wang 2008). But whether or not the new capital crimes directly produced many executions, the proliferation of new death penalties since 1983 certainly signaled to prosecutors and judges in the provinces that capital punishment was a policy in favor in Beijing. The main exception to this pattern is the elimination of most types of capital theft in the 1997 law, which resulted in steep declines in executions for theft in at least some jurisdictions (Qi 2005).

The Central Importance of Supreme Court Review

The strongest signal that the national government is concerned about the accuracy of capital adjudication and the scale of execution was the decision to provide final appellate review by the SPC for all death sentences, a reform that became effective on January 1, 2007. Of all the legal reforms instituted in the last 25 years, this is the most important sign that the CCP and the national government are worried about the quantity and quality of death sentences. Although the procedures for review and the substantive standards for examining capital cases have not yet been settled, informed observers predict a substantial impact on executions.[53] As the Dui Hua Foundation observed shortly after the reform took effect, "There is no question that restoring the SPC's authority to review death sentences is intended to sharply reduce the rate of executions in China. . . . It should be possible to cut the rate of executions in half over the next two or three years, from 7,000 in 2006 to fewer than 3,500 in 2009" (Dui Hua Foundation 2007b; see also Yardley 2007). One reason for such predictions is that messages from the party-state that it desires fewer executions can lead to much lower prosecution and death sentence rates independently of the impact of how the capital appeals are conducted.

But how will the new program be run, and with what standards? The same SPC that now must review up to 10,000 death sentences per year reviewed only

---

53. The SPC often acts like a legislative body in issuing interpretations and opinions, and it is expected to do so for capital cases in the months and years to come, but it has not kept pace with the general reform trend in China toward increased transparency and public participation in the lawmaking and rule-making processes (post by Professor Randall Peerenboom to the Chinese Law Discussion List, 2008).

300 capital cases in 2003 (Dui Hua Foundation 2007b). The exponential increase in mandatory reviews has required the hiring and training of "several hundred" new SPC judges, mostly recruited from provincial courts and the ranks of qualified academics and lawyers, and some analysts predict that death penalty cases eventually "will make up more than 90 percent of the total number of cases heard by the court" (Ni 2007).[54] On this view, the SPC will be dominated by the large number of criminal court judges, and the sheer volume of capital cases on the docket could "overwhelm" the SPC by undermining its character, legitimacy, and functions (Ni 2007). In the provinces as well, teams of prosecutors will be necessary to defend death sentence appeals, and there is also the task of finding, training, and providing material support for defense attorneys to participate in capital review at the SPC, which will not be easy. China remained without a legal profession for 20 years before market reforms started in the late 1970s (Li 1977; Lubman 1999:156). In 2007, the nation had 2.5 times more lawyers than it did in 1997, but it still had only one attorney for every 10,650 people, compared with one for every 5200 in Japan and one for every 270 in the United States (Fowler, Canaves, and Ye 2008). Even when legal counsel is available, the Chinese state continues to impose serious institutional, procedural, and personal constraints on defense lawyers' activities (Macbean and Li 2003; Albrecht and Research Unit of the Death Penalty Cases Survey Institute of Law 2006; Gallagher 2006; Human Rights in China 2006; Michelson 2006b; Glionna 2008; Human Rights Watch 2008b; Halliday and Liu forthcoming).

Reform or Reinstatement?

All of this uncertainty about the scope of SPC review and the institutional arrangements needed to support it may seem overblown since the 2007 provision merely restores a power that the SPC had before 1983 (the power was originally legislated in 1954). What was the nature of review back then and what resources were necessary to support it? And why such a fuss over merely reinstating a process that was halted in the early 1980s?

There are two reasons to think of the new SPC system as a reform rather than a return to previous procedure. First, while SPC review was provided for in the 1979 legislation, a regime of SPC review never had a chance to become

---

54. Xuan Dong, a judge on the SPC for a ten-year period that ended in 2000, says he "had a hand in the executions of 1,000 people"—an average of about two per week every week for a decade (Glionna 2008). Dong left the bench to fight for human rights as a defense lawyer. On his worst days on the bench "he considered himself a Communist Party hanging judge," and he secretly "loathed rubber-stamping death sentences against people whom he thought rarely deserved such a fate." Dong's acknowledgement that there "were times when I didn't think a criminal deserved a capital punishment but I had to announce one simply because the judicial committee said so" also reflects our view that China's death penalty exceptionalism has political roots (Bakken 2008; L. Lee 2008).

institutionalized because the 1983 withdrawal of that authority for most capital cases swept aside four years of legislative efforts aimed at strengthening criminal justice procedures, thus nipping a new reform in the bud rather than eliminating a well-established practice. After nearly 25 years without SPC involvement in most final capital reviews, a new process had to be invented rather than restored. One major motivation for the invention was the revelation of serious miscarriages of justice in capital cases (Kahn 2005a; Kahn 2005b; Chen 2006b; Johnson 2007b; Lu and Miethe 2007:130; Yardley 2007).

Second, the evolving rule-of-law principles now being put in place are new. A death penalty appeal with an oral presentation by a defense advocate is an entirely different entity from a judicial read-through of briefs on paper—different in kind, not degree. Also important is the opening of most High Court appeals to public observation. Whatever the impact of oral argument or public access alone, the influence of the two together could generate a rather different setting for death penalty reviews in the years to come compared with what prevailed in the appellate practices of 1982.

Or not. The nature and intensity of High Court review has yet to be determined and implemented. What legal resources will the condemned receive? What facts found by trial courts can be challenged? Under what circumstances can issues such as the quality of defense counsel at trial be raised on appeal? What are the practical limits when poor defendants need trial lawyers, and what effect will this have on preserving grounds for appeal? If the SPC provides ambitious standards of procedure and legal representation for capital cases, what level of government will pay for the new services? And if capital trial practice is not reformed, how much change can come from High Court or SPC reversal of cases on appeal? It is too early to answer any of these questions, though some accounts do suggest that if present trends continue, the reforms could be "restricted" (Liebman and Wu 2007; Bezlova 2008b; McLaughlin 2008).

Guidelines

One other function of the SPC in capital cases differs from court functions in Anglo-American systems and may play an important role in the future of China's death penalty system: the practice of issuing guidelines to the provinces indicating when capital prosecutions and sentences are appropriate ("Chinese Judge" 2007). In American states, this function is often assigned to a separate sentencing commission, and U.S.-style guidelines are addressed to judges rather than prosecutors. It is not known which officials the SPC guidelines are addressing or what methods are planned to enforce them, but front-end controls such as guidelines are much less expensive than depending on appeals after the fact to enforce national standards for capital prosecution. This may be one reason the Supreme People's Procuratorate in August 2007 issued draft death penalty guidelines for its own prosecutors and, it appears, for judges on the SPC to consider in capital appeals (Li 2007). According to media reports, the new draft regulations are intended to plug the "sometimes-fatal hole" in criminal procedure by ordering prosecutors and judges to focus on the authenticity of evidence and the reliability of testimonies when conducting capital appeals ("Life and Death" 2007). On this view, most wrongful death sentences and executions—and there have been many—"have turned out to be based on questionable evidence or conflicting testimonies" ("Life and Death" 2007; see also Kahn 2005a; Yardley 2005a; Chen 2006b).

Lethal Injection

Two other recent changes in Chinese practice are more difficult to classify. The first is a series of legal and fiscal encouragements for lethal injection as a means of execution and for the use of mobile lethal injection vans to replace execution by shooting in some cities and provinces. This reform started in 1996 when the SPC "requested" that lower courts begin employing the new method, and it was first used in Kunming, the capital of southwestern China's Yunnan Province, which carried out four executions by lethal injection that year (Wang 2008; Yang 2008). By 2006, Liu Renwen, a scholar at the Chinese Academy of Social Sciences, estimated that the number of lethal injections may have reached 40 percent of the national execution total, with the new practice especially common in urban areas (MacLeod 2006). By 2008, about half of China's 404 intermediate people's courts were using lethal injection for some or all executions (Bezlova 2008). Chengdu (the capital of Sichuan Province) and Taiyuan (the capital of Shanxi Province) have abolished execution by shooting, and "many other cities" are planning to follow suit ("Final Shoot" 2008). In January 2008, the SPC "issued a circular requiring local courts to popularize the use of lethal injection according to their own conditions," and it promised to "help equip courts with all required facilities" and to "train more professionals, particularly in the central and western regions," though it gave no timetable for the change ("China to Expand" 2008; Yang 2008). The SPC also began to provide local courts with the chemicals for lethal injection free of charge. Previously, local court officials had to travel to Beijing to obtain the ingredients for the cocktail; one dose cost about $44 ("Final Shoot" 2008).

The official motivation for the lethal injection reform is said to be the desire to kill as painlessly and humanely as possible (the new process is said to "take no more than two minutes with some soft music"), and that is undoubtedly a message meant for audiences both domestic and foreign (Bezlova 2008; "China Favors" 2008; "Final Shoot" 2008). But other reasons seem relevant as well. Death by lethal injection is regarded by some as faster, easier, and cheaper than death by shooting; it can more easily be kept secret in some cases; it reduces family complaints about the condition of the corpse (heads and faces can be cabbaged by a bullet to the back of the skull); and it relieves concerns many Chinese have about bodily integrity after death (Bezlova 2006a; interviews by Johnson, June 2007). There is also mention of using the execution vans to remove and transport body organs for sale and use in China's lucrative organ transplantation business (Matas and Kilgour 2007). Yunnan province, with a total population of 44 million, reportedly has acquired 18 vans (Bezlova 2006a).[55] This seems to indicate that either Yunnan has the worst roads in China or well-connected persons stand to gain from high-volume involvement in organ transplantation.[56]

The introduction of lethal injection is probably not motivated by a desire to reduce the rate of execution. In practice, however, the public relations campaigns that come with the switch might function to encourage toleration of higher levels of execution, as happened in the United States in the 1980s (Zimring and Hawkins 1986:107). Oklahoma and Texas, two of the four states with the highest rates of execution, were the first to introduce lethal injection, and the new method may have facilitated their execution increases in subsequent years. In the PRC, large investments in new equipment for lethal injection may encourage higher rates of execution, especially if the practice is combined with lucrative commerce in human body parts.[57]

55. There are disagreements about the cost-effectiveness of lethal injection: some analysts say it is relatively cheap (Bezlova 2006a), and others claim it is expensive (Yang 2008). Whatever the reality, the stories that have surfaced about the economics of lethal injection are puzzling. Not only does the number of lethal injection vans for Yunnan Province seem high, but some experts estimate the cost of each van at 400,000 to 700,000 yuan ($57,000 to $100,000), which is 30 to 60 percent cheaper than the estimated expense of a fixed execution ground (1 million yuan or more) but still a substantial chunk of change for a country with a per capita income of $1,740 in 2006 and for a government with a chronic inability to collect tax revenue (I. Johnson 2004:295). If the experts' cost estimates are accurate, China's lethal injection reform is probably not being driven by cost savings, though its utility for lucrative organ transplantations is a separate issue.

56. At a conference in Boston in July 2006, a Chinese transplant doctor (Zhonghua Chen) said that Chinese doctors transplanted 8,102 kidneys, 3,741 livers, and 80 hearts in 2005. Some experts believe that "well over 90 percent of all organs transplanted in China come from executed prisoners" (Magnier and Zarembo 2006; Matas and Kilgour 2007). In recent years, the central government has publicly acknowledged several times that "China routinely removes organs from executed prisoners for transplants" while insisting that this occurs only with prior consent (Ang 2007). In April 2007, the State Council (China's cabinet) formalized rules issued the previous year that banned the sale of organs and required donors to provide written permission. But the new regulations do not mention prisoners. "Outside the prison population, voluntary organ donations are rare" because China's Confucian tradition holds that bodies must be kept intact out of respect for parents and ancestors and out of the belief that the body's condition at death may affect the person's condition in the afterlife (Ang 2007; Brook, Bourgon, and Blue 2008).

57. Lethal injection in the PRC has also generated considerable public criticism. Some citizens complain that the method is too lenient for heinous offenders and too out of touch with public sentiment about what the worst of the worst deserve, while others believe this method is mainly used to execute the rich and well connected, thus violating the principle of equality before the law (Bezlova 2008; "Final Shoot" 2008).

Cash for Clemency

A final policy innovation seems clearly aimed at reducing executions, at least for defendants from families with financial means. This is the effort to create a publicly regulated compensation or restitution system whereby payments from a defendant or his family to victims or their families will trigger the diversion of the defendant to some noncapital punishment. A similar practice is common in Islamic systems of justice (and was part of the Chinese past as well).[58] But in contemporary China, cases of cash for clemency have been reported in distinctly non-Islamic provinces such as Guangdong, Shandong, and Zhejiang. Although victims have often been marginalized in Chinese criminal justice (Peerenboom 1993), the practice of compensating victims in capital cases is proving contentious, not least because of the perception that the fate of defendants depends on the depth of their pockets and because many victims' families are so poor that they have little choice but to accept the money offered. In response to these concerns, some courts have imposed a limit on the compensation that can be offered or demanded. More generally, the restitution system conforms to the SPC's call to "hand out fewer death penalties and to do so prudently," and even some progressives support the innovation.[59] As a Shanghai lawyer recently wrote on an Internet forum, "If there is repentance and the criminal's behavior does not merit execution, why is it necessary to take a life?" (quoted in Bezlova 2007a).

The direct effect of cash for clemency will be to discourage execution in individual cases, but the emphasis on this kind of diversion could also reduce executions across the board by undermining the retributive credibility of the death penalty as a public punishment. If the rich can buy off victims' families, where is the retributive justice in shooting the poor?

■ Predicting the Impacts of Reform

The quixotic purpose of this section is to discuss how to evaluate the changes in death penalty policy that have started to arrive in clusters at the national level of government in the PRC. But since the data that would enable an

---

58. During the Qing dynasty, "a great many punishments could be commuted for cash," which "clearly benefited the wealthy" (Spence 1990:125).

59. Chen Xingliang, professor of law at Peking University, believes the establishment of an adequate victim compensation scheme is one of three preconditions for the abolition of capital punishment in the PRC. The other two requirements are a reformed punishment structure that reduces the gap that now exists between capital sentences and life sentences that result in practice in a maximum of 22 years served (most suspended death sentences result in a maximum of 24 years imprisonment), and improvements in society's capacity to exercise informal social control (interview by Johnson, June 12, 2007).

impact evaluation are still not available, the research method described below is hypothetical, almost wholly dependent on the availability of death penalty data in the Chinese future. This section might also serve as a memo to those in government who have access to the necessary information.

The previous section mentioned a variety of policy changes that might influence rates of capital prosecution and their outcomes. Two distinctions to help think about the effects of these different policies are the *direct* versus *indirect* effects of a policy shift, and the difference between policies that attempt *front-end* controls on capital cases versus those that focus on the *back end* of the process. The 1983 decision to decentralize final appellate review illustrates both distinctions. One direct effect of removing the SPC from the review process was to eliminate one stage from the back end of the appeal process. A second direct effect of the change was to increase the variation between death penalty policies in different provinces. We also suppose there may have been a decrease in the percentage of death cases reversed on appeal and a decrease in the delay between trial and execution. These are all direct effects.

But another major purpose of dropping SPC review was to send a signal to local police and prosecutors that the volume of capital cases should increase. This indirect effect takes place at the front end of the system, and it could have had much more impact on death sentences than any change in the rate of appellate success. Indeed, it would not surprise us if the indirect, front-end impact of Deng's 1983 signal was five or six times larger than the direct, back-end effect. The reestablishment of SPC jurisdiction in 2007 will probably also produce a mix of direct and indirect impacts. This time, the direct effects will be the addition of another stage at the back end of the process, some evening out of differences between the provinces, and a lengthening of the time between arrest and execution.[60] At the same time, the signal sent to prosecutors and judges to reduce death cases will have the indirect effect of reducing the supply of capital cases at the front end of the system. Table 7.4 illustrates how the effects of the SPC review reforms may be distributed between the front and back ends of the system.

By contrast, the direct effects of guidelines for instituting death penalty cases will be found at the front end of the system: the higher the standards for death cases, the smaller the number of cases filed, and the bigger the drop from

---

60. Of course, the possibility of swift execution remains even with the advent of SPC review. In July 2007, for example, Zheng Xiaoyu, the former head of China's food and drug administration, was executed by lethal injection for corruption and dereliction of duty, only four months after he was arrested. The value of the bribes Zheng confessed to taking—$850,000—was about 60 percent of the average monetary damage ($1.4 million) caused by other corruption defendants who were sentenced to death in China in 1994–2004 (Lu and Miethe 2007:86), but his misconduct attracted tremendous international and domestic criticism, which probably hastened his demise (Barboza 2007a; Barboza 2007b; Barboza 2007c; Barboza 2007d; Magnier 2007a).

Table 7.4
Potential impacts of the Supreme People's Court death sentence review,
effective January 1, 2007

	Front end	Back end
Direct	Few or none	Substantial increase in SPC appeals; increase in SPC reversals; new legal rules for trials
Indirect	Decrease in capital prosecutions, and an increase in guilty pleas to a death sentence with two-year reprieve	Increase in suspended death sentences at trial

pre-guideline policies. The indirect effects of guidelines might well include more scrutiny from appellate courts, particularly in borderline cases that "wobble" between a death sentence and something less than death, and a larger number of capital cases that result in suspended death sentences, especially in marginal cases that fall close to the lines in the new guidelines. Most of these indirect effects would probably come at the back end of the system. One further indirect effect of China's death penalty reforms may be the enhancement of legal standards for noncapital criminal cases. As some analysts see it, advances in China's capital process could "inevitably extend to all serious criminal cases" (Cohen 2007c:24). "Death is different," but it might not be different enough to prevent domestic diffusion in China's criminal process for very long.

Three points deserve emphasis in this general discussion of future impact evaluations. The first is that both direct and indirect effects must be examined in any evaluation exercise. To look only for direct effects of the 1983 change or the 2007 reversal would miss much of the impact these changes had on capital punishment in the PRC.

The second point is the danger of confusing impacts when two or more changes occur close together. One possible confusion concerns the 2007 appellate change and the new SPC capital case guidelines that are targeted for release in 2008 or 2009. If the only impact of national appellate review were on the back end of the capital process, and if the only influence of guidelines were on the front end, then the risk of confusing effects would be minimal. But since each type of change has potential impact in both the rates of beginning and the pattern of concluding capital cases, the potential for false attribution is much more substantial. Indeed, when two or more reforms take effect at the same time, the problem may be insolvable. On the other hand, if two or more changes are separated in time, disaggregation over time is the best hope for discerning their respective influences.

Our third point about the effects of change in Chinese death penalty policy is that front-end reforms will be much less costly and more efficient than back end reforms at making the system more selective. The material resources of the PRC's legal system are limited, and fully qualified lawyers are still a scarce national resource, especially for criminal cases in which the incentives to practice are small. With only about 122,000 lawyers available for all types of civil, administrative, and criminal cases, fully staffed trials, appeals, and reviews for thousands of capital cases may be an impossible undertaking (Fowler, Canaves, and Ye 2008). Indeed, 10,000 death cases a year could absorb the entire qualified bar if the procedures and standards of American states such as California or Illinois were used. And if our rough estimate of six to seven lawyer and judge work-years per capital case in Japan is close to correct, then Japanese style capital litigation would consume about half of all the lawyers in the PRC (assuming 10,000 cases per year). The point of these comparisons is not to predict a massive diversion of Chinese legal resources to capital cases. If present patterns hold, Chinese lawyers will remain more likely to serve the interests of financial capital than to serve the needs of capital defendants (Michelson 2006a). The point is rather that the necessary resources to vigorously defend and appeal capital cases are going to be very hard to locate, mobilize, and pay.

The scarcity of legal resources carries several implications for reform. The first is that many additions to the PRC's legal system may amount to less than the advertised intensity of service. Americans who live with a jury system that produces plea bargains in more than 90 percent of criminal cases know the gap between vision and reality well. The high cost of full procedure frequently encourages the exchange of lesser punishment for lower levels of legal procedure, even in systems like Japan's that formally forbid such bargaining (Johnson 2002b).[61] The second impact of scarce legal resources is that any real guarantees of special legal protection for capital defendants could create pressure to limit capital prosecutions. In these ways, the shortage of legal resources may weaken the substance of defendants' legal entitlements. Any real protections of defendants' rights that do appear could produce large front-end impacts on the rate of capital prosecution, and that is in fact a major motive for reform.[62]

■ Early Reports on the Impact of Reform

There are some signs that the death penalty was declining in China even before the 2007 reforms. In the 10 years before review power was returned to the SPC (1997–2006), the number of death sentences in one of China's largest and richest provinces dropped 48 percent. Similarly, between 2001, when China was chosen to be the host city for the 2008 Olympics, and the middle of

61. China has already started using summary procedure for some minor offenses, and some observers believe it could expand to cover more serious crimes (Margaret Lewis, New York University School of Law, letter to Zimring, January 16, 2008).

62. More broadly, some analysts believe China's death penalty reforms "cannot be confined to capital cases but will inevitably extend to all serious criminal cases" (Cohen 2007c:24).

2007, the volume of executions nationwide may have declined as much as 40 percent.[63] Some observers believe the need to look good for the world in the run-up to the Olympics was one major reason for the downturn (Bezlova 2007b; Cha 2008; Glionna 2008), while others contend that China cares little about what the rest of the world thinks (Buruma 2007a; Mann 2007; Rabkin 2008).

Although the early reports on the impact of the 2007 reforms are certainly incomplete and possibly unreliable, they all do point in the same general direction: down. In June 2007, less than six months after authority to review death sentences was restored to the SPC, judges in three Chinese jurisdictions said that death sentences had already "dropped dramatically" as a result of the change: by 10 percent or more in Beijing, by 20 to 30 percent in one large province, and (here comes another adjective) by a "large amount" in another. Two months later, government officials from a part of Yunnan Province well known for drug trafficking reported that before the authority to review death sentences was returned to the SPC, their jurisdiction, with a population of about one million, produced 200 to 300 death sentences each year. If the same per capita rate had obtained throughout the PRC—and it did not—the nation would have generated more than a quarter million death sentences per year. The Yunnan officials also said that in the first six months following the SPC reform of 2007, the number of first-instance death sentences in their jurisdiction dropped to one-third the average level for the corresponding periods of previous years (confidential correspondence, September 2007).[64] In a much larger and richer province than Yunnan, a high-level judge said the SPC had approved "about 100" death sentences from his province in 2007, which was a marked decline from the average of about 150 per year in the preceding period (confidential correspondence, February 2008). This is consistent with general reports from the state media that said "death sentences passed by Chinese courts fell by 30 percent" in 2007 ("China Claims" 2008). The decrease seems to be even larger in some jurisdictions. At a forum on the death penalty held in Liaoning Province in May 2008, a judge from a court in Liaocheng, Shandong Province, said that the number of death sentences "decreased by up to 40 percent" in that city in 2007 ("China Sees" 2008). According to a deputy chief justice of the intermediate court in a "large city in northwestern China" (perhaps Xian in Shaanxi Province), executions dropped from an average of "about 60" per year before the SPC reform to "only 10" in 2007—and with "no visible side effect on public order and security" ("Death Sentences" 2007). Finally, in November 2007, the chief justice of the SPC reported that "for the

---

63. The source for the provincial death sentence trend is a report to the SPC by judges in that province (and viewed by the first author in June 2007), while the source for the estimate of the nationwide decline in executions is Dui Hua director John Kamm (quoted in Yardley 2007).

64. It is impossible to verify the accuracy of this report, and it should be noted that the pre-reform figures given by these officials are much higher than the death sentence numbers presented earlier in this chapter for Yunnan's Maguan County.

first time in the history of the PRC, the number of death sentences with two years suspension exceeded the number of executions" ("Death Sentences" 2007; "Suspended" 2007).[65]

In short, China's recent death penalty decline appears to be so steep that some Chinese scholars and officials have even expressed concern that the drop may be too dramatic. As Wuhan University professor of law Ma Kechang put it, "I hope the speed of the decrease in the number of executions can be a little slower" ("Death Sentences" 2007). There have also been complaints from victims and their families, and some analysts worry that their discontent could cause the number of executions to rebound ("Death Sentences" 2007; Xie 2008). A similar worry has been voiced by Piers Bannister and Mark Allison, death penalty researchers at Amnesty International, who believe the slowdown in executions might be the result of a "logjam" that eventually could lead to "a rise in executions once a review by China's top court of all capital cases is concluded" (Chan 2008; "China Overturns" 2008). However long the current decline in death sentences and executions lasts, the return of review power to the SPC must be considered one of its most important causes. In June 2008, Gao Jinghong, the presiding judge of the SPC's Third Criminal Law Court, announced that the SPC had overturned about 15 percent of the death sentences handed down by high courts in the first half of that year (Xie 2008). The indirect effects of SPC review on the front end of the system also seem to be significant ("China Claims" 2008; Xie 2008).

■ Capital Punishment in the Middle and Long Runs

The proximate causes of high rates of execution in the PRC are for the most part political (Bakken 2008). The only sure relevance of cultural values in explaining current and recent execution levels is that they sometimes have encouraged and always have tolerated the high rates generated by the political system. The primacy of politics means that China's party-state has the capacity to change levels of execution quickly. But since executions remain a powerful symbol of governmental authority and a not unimportant method of controlling some

---

65. Another possible sign of China's recent death penalty decline concerns the aftermath of the riots in the Tibetan capital of Lhasa in March 2008. According to state media reports, the violence killed 18 civilians and one police officer, injured 382 civilians and 241 police, and resulted in a direct economic loss of about $47 million. But of the first 42 people who were tried and convicted of crimes, none received a death sentence (as of July 2008, another 116 defendants were still on trial or awaiting trial; see "No Death Penalty" 2008). In previous years, Chinese criminal justice in Tibet was frequently faster and harsher (Marshall et al. 2000; Shakya 2000; Seymour 2005:153; Magnier 2005b; Mishra 2006a:304). Equally striking are reports that even during the riots in Lhasa, Chinese security forces engaged in little if any extra-judicial killing, a "response that was highly unusual compared with their usual tactics for dealing with protests in Tibet and elsewhere in China" ("Illusion of Calm" 2008).

social problems, it is difficult to imagine executions dropping from 6,000 per year in the present to none at all in five or seven years. Even here, however, the issue is political will, not political capacity (Lubman 1999:299; Cohen 2007c:20).

A satisfactory analysis of the future of capital punishment in China would start with a comprehensive account of the economic, social, and political changes on the horizon for the country in the next 15 years. This we cannot do (the scenarios are numerous).[66] Our main assumption about political development is that evolutionary changes will continue to nibble away at the strong, single-party structure but will not produce major structural changes. Rapid growth in economic productivity and rising levels of education will put pressure on the party-state to become more accountable if not democratic. And economic centers of power outside government, including transnational corporations and foreign consumers, will influence China's domestic and international policies and actions. Even before there is major progress toward democracy, the increased availability of information about government and the economic and informational links with the outside world will increase as well (Ye and Fowler 2008). China will have to become a much less secret society before it becomes a much less authoritarian government.

A gradually moderating party-state will want to preserve a death penalty with strong central controls, a more extensive legal framework (though not an unfettered adversarial system), and far fewer executions than the 6,000 or so estimated for 2007 ("China's Chief Justice" 2008). The best alternative penal mechanism for a shift away from execution is the two-year suspended death sentence that already diverts to imprisonment the vast majority of its recipients (Scobell 1990; legal scholars and professionals, interviews by Johnson, April 2006 and June 2007). This Maoist invention provides what can be touted as the moral equivalent of a death penalty for local police and prosecutors and perhaps even for some victims and survivors—a symbolic sanction that expresses severity and stigma.[67]

66. Some of the best-informed speculations about China's future can be found in Turner, Feinerman, and Guy (2000), Gilley (2004), I. Johnson (2004), Cohen (2005), Shambaugh (2005), Lynch (2006), Rowen (2006), Zhao (2006), the roundtable "China in the Year 2020" (2007), Kang (2007), Mann (2007), Peerenboom (2007), and Bell (2008).

67. There are also at least two risks in using suspended death sentences. First, they are employed as an alternative to capital punishment with immediate execution in some cases where there is doubt about the evidence, which "runs counter to the principle of presumption of innocence" (Qi 2005). Second, the ultimate decision about whether to reduce a suspended death penalty to a term of imprisonment can involve subjective considerations about the offender—Is he repentant? Does she have overseas connections?—that may be shaped by the decision-maker's biases and prejudices (Zhao Xinghong 2006; Lu and Miethe 2007:66). In practice, a suspended death sentence in China usually results in a 24-year term of imprisonment, while a life sentence typically means 22 years. Some Chinese death penalty reformers believe the gap between a death sentence and other punishments is too large, and they advocate the introduction of a LWOP possibility as one necessary step toward the ultimate abolition of capital punishment (interviews by Johnson, June 2007; see also

This and related reforms, such as the restricted use of capital punishment for homicide offenders who kill a single victim (Ge 2006) or who plead guilty and are pardoned by the victim's family (Xie 2008), could reduce the number of executions per year to 1,000 or fewer, and could do so quickly and at modest cost. If 9,000 candidates for execution a year were diverted to prison for 22 to 24 years (the maximum time that can be served under a life sentence or commuted death sentence with a two-year reprieve), the result would be a cumulative increase of 13 to 14 percent in the prison population (ten years out, the increase is only 6 percent), creating an additional expenditure for the provinces that could be offset by reductions in the use of incarceration for noncapital offenders or by increased support from the central government for prison operations.

But if the exceptional level of executions in the PRC can be altered at the will of the central government, what stands in the way of total abolition? That is, after all, the avowed aim of the Communist Party (Li 2007). The obstacles to abolition are large, for possessing the power to take life remains an important element—perhaps a central element—in the self-concept of many top officials (Nathan and Gilley 2003:218). What Emperor Kang-Hsi said some 300 years ago still reflects much elite sentiment today: "Giving life to people and killing people—those are the powers that the [ruler] has" (quoted in Spence 1974:29). The political importance of capital punishment to an authoritarian government is no small matter, and this is as true in the PRC as in Singapore (see appendix E). Indeed, there are strong indications that even the low execution rate government of Japan attaches substantial symbolic importance to its death penalty and to the nearly totalitarian methods by which it selects, informs, and administers hangings.

In the short to middle term in the PRC, government stability and the absence of major political upheavals would be a more favorable environment for significant shrinkage of executions and increased central control over them than would political unrest and instability. Political reform of all kinds comes to China at the discretion of the party and the government, so a secure and stable party-state is apt to be a greater friend of moderation in execution than one that feels threatened by political competition. The problem, however, is that the more developed and prosperous China becomes, the more insecure and threatened the country's leaders feel and the more likely they may be to continue relying on executions as one way of keeping the lid on and themselves in power (Shirk 2007:5). Following the conflict in Tibet that occurred in March 2008, for example, Wang Shengjun, the new president of the SPC, "struck a markedly different tone than his predecessor" when he told judges that "where the law mandates the death sentence, the death sentence should be

note 59). In our view, they should be careful what they wish for because substituting LWOP for the death penalty raises many of the same human rights issues that lie at the core of concerns about the death penalty itself (Appleton and Grover 2007; Hood and Hoyle 2008:383).

given," especially for those offenders who "seriously threaten social order" ("China's Chief Justice" 2008).

In the longer term, a real diminishment of the strength of the authoritarian essence of Chinese government is probably necessary before the state voluntarily abolishes the death penalty. If so, then the political conditions that would foster moderation are quite different from those that would lead to abolition. No amount of economic development will shift capital punishment policy in the PRC the way it has shifted in South Korea and Taiwan. The political changes discussed in chapters 5 and 6 were necessary conditions for the "leadership from the front" that has occurred in those two nations. Progress in the PRC toward Korean or Taiwanese-style democratization would make abolition likely sooner rather than later, but no such political change is on the Chinese horizon (Mann 2007).

Could China abolish the death penalty without moving toward democracy? Some analysts think it is possible. In their view, the future of capital punishment depends much more on whether and when China becomes a "legal country" and on the extent to which the "rule of law" is institutionalized than it does on democratization (Wang 2008). For us, however, the key issue is the political will of the government rather than its capacity to effect change, and in present circumstances it is hard to imagine a set of external or internal pressures and inducements that would provide sufficient motivation for abolition by the PRC's authoritarian regime.[68] China is not Ukraine or South Africa (Bae 2007).

The closest analogy in recent history is the moratorium on executions the Europeans negotiated with Russia in 1996, yet even this parallel is not compelling, for three reasons. First, the Russian economy and government were in a weak position in 1996, badly in need of European trade and support. China, by contrast, is prospering and powerful. Second, under current conditions there are no inducements or penalties that could motivate the PRC leadership to walk away from capital punishment. China won the right to host the 2008 Olympics and obtained high-value international positions (like membership in the World Trade Organization) without making any major political concessions, and this reveals the strength of its current position. What is more, since two members of the G8 (Japan and the United States) still maintain their own death penalties, it would be difficult if not impossible to isolate the PRC and stigmatize its use of executions. Were the PRC to become the last great power with an active execution policy, the pressures and the inducements would change.

---

68. Externally, China has started to sign treaties that recognize the principle of no extradition of capital offenders. As of April 2008, the Standing Committee of the National People's Congress had ratified agreements with Spain, France, and Australia, and a treaty with Portugal had been signed but was not yet ratified. Even if these treaties multiply, they will probably do little to move China closer to abolition.

The third difference between Russia in 1996 and the PRC in the years to come is the seemingly secure position of the current Chinese government and the importance of the power to execute to it (Lynch 2006). It is possible to imagine China one day trading its death penalty for international status or benefits, but it is hard to imagine it selling this power cheaply. Still, the concession of autonomy to remain without a death penalty that helped induce the reabsorption of Hong Kong and Macao into the Chinese mainland suggests that negotiation on death penalty issues is possible (see appendix B). But neither the pressure to change nor the rewards that would motivate concession are anywhere in sight.

Thus, democratization and the growth of human rights seem the best hope for an execution-free PRC. How long this might take is not an issue this study can constructively address. However, there are two pieces of encouraging news for those alarmed by the scale and barbarity of executions in the PRC in recent decades. The first is the sharp declines in Chinese execution that have already appeared on the horizon. The days of 15,000 executions per year have probably passed into history. The institutional controls now being established could cut executions in China by 90 percent from their late 1990s peak if the current government so decreed, and that would cut *world* executions by as much as 80 percent. For the current regime, there is close to a zero marginal value of decentralized executions in the tens of thousands. Only if the party-state faced strong threats would it be tempted to return to the lethal politics of China's not-so-distant past. We believe that major declines in execution will come soon—they already have started—but executions will not cease.

The second piece of cheerful news for students of China's death penalty exceptionalism is the astonishing pace of change in that country. Two decades after the Soviet Union crumbled, the CCP is alive and reasonably well, and most observers only speak of liberalization and democracy as features of the long-term future. But the rate of change is rapid, not merely in the growth of cities and the economy but also in the social, cultural, and institutional spheres those developments shape. If we must wait for long-term developments, there is the consoling prospect that the long run in contemporary China sometimes feels like the day after tomorrow. The party-state has done a remarkable job of suppressing the growth of civil society, and the government's current stress on creating a "harmonious society" reflects its recognition that inequality must be reduced if stability is to be maintained. But material wealth, education, communication, and cross-cultural contact are social facts that authoritarian governments find it difficult to survive. The most modernized people in this rapidly evolving society are the children of the economic and governmental elites. In these circumstances, it might be prudent for China-watchers to turn to current conditions in Taiwan, South Korea, and Japan for a peek at the Chinese future.

Lessons and Prospects

The final two chapters draw lessons from our case studies of capital punishment and explore the future prospects of the death penalty in Asia. Chapter 8 presents the lessons to be learned from studying Asia that help one understand the death penalty as a modern political, legal, and human rights phenomenon, while chapter 9 considers future scenarios for capital punishment in the region. Because of chapter 9's forward-looking focus, the level of uncertainty that surrounds it is greater than for chapter 8. Comprehending the lessons from Asia is largely a process of looking backward at the historical materials in chapter 2 and in the case studies of part II and the appendixes. Chapter 9, however, has to assess Asian developments that have not yet occurred, and the margin of error for this kind of future-oriented policy analysis frequently bears a striking resemblance to fortune-telling. Valuable lessons about future trends can be gleaned from the recent histories in Asia, but there are many unknowns as well. In our view, a sustained look at the future of Asian death penalty policy is an adventure worth the risks.

8

Lessons

The comparative study of death penalty policy is a relatively new and un-practiced discipline, and few of the existing studies concentrate on regional rather than global comparisons. This chapter makes the case for a regional focus by reviewing the materials in the preceding chapters so as to gather insights from Asia about capital punishment in the world in the 21st century. The lessons are organized into three sections. First, we describe features of death penalty policy in Asia that are *consistent* with the experiences recorded in Europe and with the theories developed to explain Western changes. Next, we identify some of the most significant *variations* within the Asian region—in rates of execution, trends over time, and patterns of change—that contrast with the recent history of capital punishment in non-Asian locations and hence challenge conventional interpretations of death penalty policy and change. Finally, we discuss three ways the politics of capital punishment in Asia is *distinctive*: the limited role of international standards and transnational influences in many Asian jurisdictions; the presence of single-party domina-tion in several Asian political systems; and the persistence of communist versions of capital punishment in the Asia region.

Overall, the study of death penalty policy in Asia confirms many of the major themes that have emerged from studies of the postwar European and Commonwealth experiences. Most notably, there has been a decline in executions as a tool of crime control and in the political reputation of state execution throughout most of Asia. Economic development and political democracy are both correlated with declining executions and with the abolition of capital punishment, but neither prosperity nor democracy is a sufficient condition for ending the death penalty. Concerns about the concentration of state power and its misuse are as prominent a theme in anti–death penalty rhetoric in Asia as in the West, and the most important feature of Asian nations that predicts their level of execution is not culture, public opinion, or crime rate but rather the nature of the political regime. Only authoritarian governments use execution with any frequency in Asia (or elsewhere), and most of the hard-line authoritarian states in Asia where high rates of execution continue to occur are communist. Thus, while the political circumstances of Asia are different from those found in other parts of the world, the influence of political characteristics on death penalty policy are similar.

■ Consistencies

Scholarship about modern trends in capital punishment and the causes and contexts of death penalty decline is based almost exclusively on accounts of Western history. How many of the significant aspects of that story appear in Asian experiences? The number of parallels and the importance of each are to some extent a function of the judgment of the observer, but in our view the available evidence does reveal at least nine consistencies between the Asian histories we have studied and existing accounts of capital punishment in the West: (1) a long-term decline in the use of death as a criminal sanction; (2) a recent decline in executions in most countries; (3) a strong but not universal tendency for economically developed nations to curtail executions and consider abolition; (4) an even stronger relationship between the character of government (democratic vs. authoritarian) and the extent to which political elites accept and employ capital punishment; (5) the unimportance of "Asian values" as an explanation of death penalty policy; (6) the declining importance of capital punishment for crime control; (7) the common causation of judicial and extrajudicial killing; (8) reliance on "leadership from the front" rather than public opinion to change death penalty policy; and (9) the increased salience of "human rights" and "limits of government" perspectives in death penalty discourse.

Long-Term Decline

From Emile Durkheim's "two laws of penal evolution" to more empirically oriented histories of punishment, many studies have concluded that there has been a long-term shift away from executions and toward lesser punishments in Western countries. Durkheim (1983:114) believed that "deprivation of liberty and of liberty alone, varying in time according to the seriousness of the crime, tends to become more and more the normal means of social control." Pieter Spierenburg dates the beginning of Europe's long-term decline in executions to the 16th century (and somewhat later in England), concluding that "the scaffold eventually yielded its primacy to imprisonment and to transportation" (1995:52). By the late 18th century, "a long, slow, and uneven decline was in progress" in several Western nations, though "actual abolition of capital punishment did not begin until the 1860s" (Zimring 2003:17). By the turn of the 20th century, the death penalty had become an exceptional punishment in all Western democracies, reserved for only the most serious offenses, rarely imposed, and regarded as a particularly problematic governmental practice. This broad decline in Europe was interrupted after 1930 by a regressive torrent of state killing in Germany, Russia, and (to a lesser extent) Italy and Spain, but the long-term trend resumed at war's end in 1945.

Long-term data on patterns in Asia are not plentiful, but the general pattern found in most Asian nations does seem consistent with the European story. There were dramatic execution declines in Japan late in the 19th century—a 97 percent drop in less than 30 years (see chapter 3)—and Indonesia has had low rates of judicial execution since 1945 (Gelling 2008a), as has Thailand since 1940 (see appendix D). Execution levels have also declined in the abolitionist nations of Australia, New Zealand, Cambodia, East Timor, Nepal, Bhutan, and the Philippines and in the de facto abolitionist nations of Laos, Myanmar, Brunei, the Maldives, Papua New Guinea, and Sri Lanka. In Hong Kong, executions started to decline in the 1950s and stopped altogether in 1967, and in Macao there have been no executions for more than a century (see appendix B). In India, executions declined from an annual average of more than 160 in 1954–1963 to an average of less than 2 per year in 1995–2007 (Batra 2007).

The general trend down in Asia was interrupted by explosions of state killing at midcentury in China and Taiwan and by a smaller concentration in South Korea around the same period, and these surges may be slightly later parallels to the European eruptions that occurred between 1930 and 1945. By the 1980s, most Asian nations outside China had rates of execution well below the level necessary to play an important role in crime control. If the midcentury increases are treated as temporary interruptions of a long-term, downward trend, then the drops and stoppages in places such as Taiwan and South Korea can also be considered part of the broader pattern.

But what about China's half century of high execution rates? On the one hand, even the four- and five-digit execution volumes in recent years are a substantial decline from the levels of execution that prevailed under Chairman Mao. On the other hand, a streak this long has no parallel in Europe and must therefore be regarded as an exception to the more general pattern. Still, the long-term pattern elsewhere in Asia does conform to the most prominent pattern in Western history, and since most of the region lagged behind the West in rates of industrial growth until the last third of the 20th century, one might expect a similar lag in the decline of executions outside Asia's earliest developing countries, Japan and Singapore. The high rates of execution that persist in some Asian nations might then be considered temporary differences.

Unfortunately, the data are too thin and the time too early to test this theory of lag. The generality of the downward trend over time is easier to discern than its causes or ultimate course.[1]

Recent Declines and Recurrent Periods without Execution

The patterns in most Asian nations over the last generation are consistent with the longer-term declines in prevalence of executions, and many places in Asia now have execution rates close to zero. Chapter 2 reported that the decline in Asia in recent years is similar to that in Africa and distinct from the flat pattern over time in the Middle East. In 2006, 10 of 29 Asian jurisdictions had at least one execution, a 30 percent decline since 1995, and only five of the 29 executed every year in the period 1995–2006. In South Korea, a ten-year period without execution is widely viewed as a stage in the transition toward abolition, and Taiwan (in 2006–2007) recently joined South Korea as an Asian nation with no executions. The Philippines is the only large Asian nation to abolish in recent years, but several other nations have self-consciously moved closer to abolition, and in many other nations executions have become rare events. Even in China and Singapore, which continue to execute often, there is evidence that executions have declined in the most recent years (see chapter 7 and appendix E).

But if recent Asian trends are downward, there are exceptions, too. One exception is Japan, where death sentences tripled from 1996 to 2006 and where there were more executions in 2007 and the first half of 2008 than in the previous seven years combined (Shikei Haishi Henshu Iinkai 2007:7,267).[2] Another is Pakistan, where there were almost three times more executions in the one year of 2007 than in the five years between 1996 and 2000, and where executions increased from 18 in 2003, to 21 in 2004, to 52 in 2005, to 83 in 2006, to 135 in 2007 (Hood 2002:92; Ebrahim 2008).[3] The Asian nations that have participated

---

1. The declines of the death penalty in Europe and Asia are part of a broader movement away from violence and coercion that may be a "universal pattern" at work in "all human communities" (Payne 2004:vi; Pinker 2007).

2. In December 2007, shortly before the UN passed a nonbinding resolution calling for a worldwide moratorium on executions, Japan's justice minister Kunio Hatoyama said, "[E]ven if a UN resolution passes, it will have absolutely no limitation on our death penalty system." Despite this and other signs of enthusiasm for capital punishment, the Japanese ambivalence described in chapter 3 persists.

3. Although executions in Pakistan have increased sharply in recent years, there are also signs that the nation's death penalty system might be approaching a turning point. In February 2008, two months after opposition leader Benazir Bhutto was assassinated, Pakistan's two main opposition parties took control of government. In July of that year, the cabinet approved the proposal of Prime Minister Yousuf Raza Gilani to commute the sentences of all death row inmates to life imprisonment, except for terrorists and persons convicted of attempting to assassinate the president (Sarwar 2008b). At the time, Pakistan

in the death penalty downturn have moved away from execution at a pace that is slower than that of eastern Europe after 1990 and similar to that of the less-developed countries of Africa. But this Asian pattern is a rule with more exceptions than exist in the recent histories of some other regions. The higher variability in execution policy makes Asia a particularly interesting context in which to search for the features of politics, economy, and culture that explain the variation.

Economic Development and Death Penalty Decline

Two bodies of evidence suggest that economic development encourages decline in judicial execution and steps toward the cessation of capital punishment. The first is the cross-sectional pattern noted in figure 2.5. In 2006, Asia's least prosperous nations were twice as likely as its most prosperous ones to have carried out executions, and nations with middling levels of per capita GDP were in the middle position on execution prevalence. Yet this cross-sectional analysis also suggests that prosperity is neither a necessary nor a sufficient condition for the abolition of capital punishment. Cambodia, Nepal, Bhutan, and East Timor are some of Asia's poorest states, and the Philippines lags well behind the monumental success stories of East Asian economic development, but all of these nations have abolished the death penalty. Japan, on the other hand, has been rich for many decades yet still retains capital punishment, and Singapore is simultaneously one of Asia's most prosperous places and one of its most aggressive executing states.

The other evidence on the relationship between economic development and the end of executions concerns the economic status of the two "vanguard" nations profiled in chapters 5 and 6. As recently as 1995, South Korea and Taiwan (along with Japan and Singapore) could have been cited as clear

---

had more than 7,000 inmates on death row—about one-quarter of the world's condemned prisoners. Gilani, who spent nearly five years in prison after being convicted of corruption in 2001 by a special court formed by President Pervez Musharraf, said he made the recommendation in order to honor Bhutto's memory. In 1988, in one of her first acts as prime minister, Bhutto had commuted the death sentences of several hundred death row inmates. As of July 2008, the final approval of Gilani's commutation recommendation rested with the same President Musharraf who had imprisoned Gilani, and there were indications that he might approve the proposal (Sarwar 2008a; see also "Abolition" 2008; Nazar 2008). Some observers said that Gilani's commutation proposal emerged in a political context of "leaderless drift" in which no one was really in charge of Pakistan's new civilian government (Gall 2008), but the proposal might also have reflected the classic pattern of change in death penalty policy after a left party takes control of government (Zimring 2003:22). For an overview of the death penalty in Pakistan, see International Federation for Human Rights and Human Rights Commission of Pakistan (2007).

examples that economic development does not necessarily produce major death penalty declines, for three decades of rapid growth had not produced visible progress toward abolition of capital punishment or cessation of executions. But the events of the next decade pushed both nations into campaigns against execution. Why? One explanation is chance. Contingency is frequently a critical factor in the making of history (Kershaw 2007; Taleb 2007), and while the elections of presidents Kim Dae Jung and Chen Shui-bian can be explained retrospectively, they were not predictable ex ante. But a more satisfying and persuasive explanation for the Korean and Taiwanese death penalty dynamic during the last decade is that economic development fostered technological, educational, and moral improvements in both nations that ultimately produced pressures toward political reform and democratization (Friedman 2005).[4] On this account, economic development created the conditions in which political change was more likely to occur, and the latter was the precipitant for changes in death penalty policy. The causal sequence is two steps instead of one.[5]

If this is part of the story behind the decline of capital punishment in South Korea and Taiwan, then two more conclusions follow. First, the (eventual) role of economic development in altering death penalty policy is stronger than some cross-sectional comparisons suggest. Observers must wait for the intermediate changes in social and political structures to occur before they can see the full effects of economic growth. One interpretation of the atypical positions of China and Singapore in cross-national studies of the relationship between rights and economic development is that under some conditions, even 25 years of development may be "insufficient for the influence of eco-

4. Economic growth provides more than merely material benefits; it helps generate many of the hallmarks of a moral society, including fairness, democracy, tolerance, openness of opportunity, and economic and social mobility. As measured by Freedom House, rights and liberties are positively correlated with average per capita income and with income growth (the most striking exception is China), but the key to political and social liberalization seems to be growth, not merely a high standard of living. Even wealthy nations put their progressive values at risk when income levels stagnate (Friedman 2005:313,315). In these terms, the resurgence of capital punishment in Japan may partly reflect the economic stagnation it has experienced since its economy tanked in the early 1990s.

5. India, which has been called a "highly improbable" democracy because of its great diversity and widespread poverty, is another exception to this two-stage pattern because it democratized before it developed and because its per capita execution rate dropped by more than 99 percent in the half century between 1954–1963 and 1995–2007 (Dahl 1998:159; Batra 2008). To explain cases such as this, one probably needs to "abandon the methods of statistical social science—in which India will always be the exception to the rule—in favor of the more primitive techniques of the narrative historian" (Guha 2007:11). To our knowledge, a good narrative history of capital punishment in India does not exist, but for a brief overview of recent death penalty developments there, see appendix F.

nomic growth to manifest itself in a society's political institutions" (Friedman 2005:317; see also Pan 2008).

But the question persists: if the explanatory power of economic development is strong, why hasn't Japan (or the United States) abolished capital punishment? The second conclusion that flows from considering current reality in the two Asian vanguard countries is the importance of explaining why, among developed nations, Japan and Singapore differ so much from South Korea and Taiwan in their death penalty policies. For those interested in the Asian future, this question assumes special importance. The central issue seems to be the relationship between prosperity and plural democracy. Does economic development eventually produce liberal multiparty democracy, or can less responsive and more paternalistic regimes survive even long-term prosperity? The long-term dominance of the People's Action Party in Singapore and the LDP in Japan suggests that unprogressive regimes can thrive for long periods of time in wealthy nations, but the jury is still out on this important issue.

The Influence of Character of Government

Twentieth-century Europe demonstrated the importance of government orientation toward death penalty policy in three ways. First, fascist and totalitarian governments have obvious affection for high rates of execution. The Nazi and Soviet experiences were discussed in chapter 7, and the reversal of abolition by Mussolini in 1930 and state killing in Spain by Franco's regime would have achieved greater notoriety if their actions had not been overshadowed by those of Hitler and Stalin. Second, the rapid move toward abolition happened during two political transitions: the defeat of the Axis powers in 1945, and the end of Soviet hegemony in central and eastern Europe in 1989. Taking both transitions together, new regimes abolished the death penalty within five years of governmental change in a total of 13 nations. Third, shifts of governments from right-of-center to left-of-center have precipitated legal change. This happened in three European nations that retained the death penalty after 1950; abolition started in England in 1965, continued in Spain in the mid-1970s, and culminated with France in 1981. In two of the cases—England and France—the transitions were the result of scheduled elections, while for Spain the transition that triggered abolition was a shift away from the rightist, authoritarian government of Franco.

Because the range of political differences is much broader in contemporary Asia than in postwar Europe, the influence of character of government on death penalty policy should be more visible—and it is. The cross-sectional and historical experiences in Asia both indicate that the general political orientation of a government is a major shaper of death penalty policy, as some global studies have found (Anckar 2004; Miethe, Lu, and Deibert 2005; Greenberg and West 2008; Neumayer 2008). A cross-sectional tour of Asia in 2007 implicates governmental orientation at both ends of the execution spectrum. Depending on the true execution rates in North Korea and Vietnam (see appendixes A and C), there are between two and four high-execution-rate nations in Asia—China and Singapore are the surest members of this club—and all have highly authoritarian governments. Were it not for high-rate American states such as Texas, Virginia, and Oklahoma, we would be tempted to conclude that an authoritarian government is a necessary condition for persistently high rates of judicial execution as criminal punishment.[6]

One alternative explanation for high rates of execution is culture or public opinion, but the distribution of execution policy in Asia demonstrates that this account is incorrect. Singapore's strongman, Lee Kuan Yew, attributed his nation's high volume of executions to "Asian values" and a preference for collective over individual interests, but neither public opinion nor cultural features can explain patterns of execution in his society or in the rest of Asia.[7] As the preceding chapters show, public opinion supports capital punishment for serious crime all over the region, but executions occur frequently only in the PRC, Singapore, and (probably) Vietnam and North Korea. As we will show, most Asian nations that retain the death penalty use it with a rarity that contrasts sharply with operational users. The cultural differences between Hong Kong and Singapore, Singapore and Malaysia, and North and South Korea are not nearly large enough to explain the huge differences in execution policy. Political factors are the only explanation that fits with the variation in executions in Asia.

---

6. In 2006, Amnesty International reported that the states with the highest volume of executions after China were Iran (177), Pakistan (82), Iraq (65), Sudan (65), and the United States (53). Their per capita execution rates per million were as follows: Iran, 2.7; Pakistan, 0.5; Iraq, 2.4; Sudan, 1.6; and the United States, 0.2. All these nations except the United States score "not free" on Freedom House's measure of respect for political rights and civil liberties, as do China, Vietnam, and the high-execution-rate state of Saudi Arabia. Other high-rate states, including Singapore and Jordan, score "partly free" on the Freedom House index. It appears that among nations deemed "free" in Freedom House terms, the only jurisdictions that regularly have execution rates exceeding our 1.0 threshold for "operational" death penalty systems are American states such as Texas, Virginia, Oklahoma, Missouri, and South Carolina (Hood 2002:92). Similar patterns prevailed in 2007, when Amnesty reported that (after China) the states with the highest execution volumes were Iran (317), Saudia Arabia (143), Pakistan (135), and the United States (42). Their per capita execution rates were as follows: Iran, 4.8; Saudi Arabia, 5.3; Pakistan, 0.8; and the United States, 0.16.

7. As Lee's ambassador to the UN observed, if popular referendums were held, most Asian societies would "vote overwhelmingly in favor of the death penalty" (Mahbubani 2002:78). Some Singaporean elites also believe that "the aggressive promotion of democracy, human rights, and freedom of press to the Third World at the end of the Cold War was, and is, a colossal mistake" (60; see appendix E).

If cross-sectional comparisons in contemporary Asia suggest the importance of political influences on executions, the patterns over time documented in this book are decisive. It is one thing to posit intrinsic differences between Singapore and Malaysia that might help explain persistent differences in execution rates, but why did Singapore's rate stay high for a long time while the Malaysian rate dropped substantially? Has there been rapid cultural change in Kuala Lumpur but not across the straits? Our accounts of political change and seismic shifts in execution policy in South Korea and Taiwan are the strongest evidence we found of the powerful and primary role of democratization and changing structures of government in stimulating change in execution policy. The evidence that political change played a key causal role in these two jurisdictions is not a statistical inference from multivariate regression models but rather the conspicuous center of their recent histories. It is difficult to imagine a more compelling demonstration of the political influences on capital punishment than the tale of these two nations.

More subtle political processes also provide insight into some other puzzles of recent Asian history. Japan has one of Asia's most developed democracies and has been governed almost continuously by the LDP since 1955. This is the equivalent of the Gaullists remaining in power in France not until 1981 (when abolition occurred) but for at least two decades thereafter. The persistence of capital punishment in Japan may be explained by the failure of a left-of-center party to take control of government, although this reductionistic account requires some explanation of that failure—such as the LDP's responsiveness to public demands (Calder 1988; Curtis 1999). At the same time, some changes in Asian death penalty policy have not been the product of changes in political structure or of the end of control by a government of the right. The second abolition in the Philippines, for example, was a by-product of a minor shift in politics even though the first abolition was the result of a classic right-to-left "radical political transformation" (Bae 2007:122). Similarly, the downward trend of executions in Malaysia seems attributable to gradual changes in governance. Not all of the causal action in Asian capital punishment occurs in the political sphere, but much of it does.

The Myth of "Asian Values"

The previous section summarized the evidence that the political orientation of Asian governments is a much more powerful influence on variations in rates of execution in Asia than is any set of cultural values linked to executions or favoring collective interests over individual rights. Political factors—from right-wing dominance in Japan to authoritarian governments in the PRC, Vietnam, North Korea, and Singapore—provide a convincing explanation for the high incidence of execution in the Asian nations that use it most aggressively and for the persistence of executions in the region's most developed country. The other advantage of a political explanation is that it accounts for the sharp drops in executions that occurred after democratization in South

Korea and Taiwan. When the scope of inquiry is broadened to consider the full variety of death penalty policies in contemporary Asia and the recent history of Asian governments where policy has changed, there is little evidence that public attitudes influence the character or intensity of death penalty policy.

The first evidence against a strong cultural preference for capital punishment in Asia is the low incidence of executions among retentionist nations. Most Asian nations that retain the death penalty use it sparingly, and large nations such as India, Indonesia, and Thailand have gone for years between executions without producing public clamor for more.

The PRC's claim that Chinese culture requires high levels of execution is directly contradicted by recent history in two settings dominated by Chinese values. In Taiwan, a high rate of execution dropped sharply in the wake of democratization and the election of a left-of-center government—from over three executions per million per year in 1990 to none at all in 2006 and 2007—and this remarkable decline was a low-visibility event in national politics. As chapter 6 reported, the only pressure to discuss the death penalty in the presidential election of 2008 came from an NGO advocating abolition.

A second test of culture versus politics comes from Hong Kong, a setting that once combined a British colonial government and legal system with a thoroughly Chinese culture and local politics. As appendix B shows, British governance fully explains the absence of hangings in Hong Kong for the last third of the 20th century and the formal abolition of capital punishment in 1993. But why did the death penalty go so quietly in the 1990s, and why haven't the new political circumstances of Hong Kong since 1997 produced public demand for the restoration of capital punishment? The quiet demise of the death penalty in Hong Kong turns out to be a telling indicator of the lack of public reaction to reduction or elimination of executions that tends to occur in other Asian settings.

Is there any evidence of a distinctive cultural demand for executions in the region? Public opinion is no less punitive in Asia than elsewhere—and probably no more punitive either (see table 8.1). A Hong Kong newspaper reported that 60 percent of the public supported capital punishment for murder in the 1990s (see appendix B), a level of public support similar to those in South Korea and lower than those found in Germany and Great Britain at the points of their abolitions (Zimring and Hawkins 1986:13). Moreover, high public support for capital punishment in Japan and the PRC may represent support for official policy as much as evidence of potential opposition if governmental policy should change.

The "Asian values" argument is frequently a justification politicians and prosecutors advance in order to avoid taking responsibility for capital punishment as a governmental prerogative. Yet one searches the historical record in vain to find political backlashes—such as those that occurred in the United States in the 1970s—when Asian governments end or reduce executions. In Hong Kong, South Korea, Taiwan, and Japan, the pattern of public opinion and reaction is no more persistent or intense in its commitment to execution than it was in Europe or the Commonwealth nations, and even in the Philippines and Nepal—two Asian nations that have each abolished the death penalty twice—the reintroduction of capital punishment between their abolitions was mainly elite driven. Thus, the best available evidence suggests that the presence or absence of executions in Asia is usually a matter of little public importance and few intense feelings (Oberwittler and Qi 2008). Government officials use public sentiment as an excuse for executions all over the world, and the "Asian values" version of this argument differs little from the political justifications that are made in other places.[8]

The great diversity of execution policies in the region and the swift and quiet accommodations of the public to criminal justice without executions also help demonstrate the value of regional comparisons in the study of death penalty policy. The best and perhaps the only test of the "Asian values" hypothesis is comparison of policy over time and across jurisdictions in Asia. The evidence gathered in this study on this question is a testament to the value of a regional approach.

The Declining Importance of Capital Punishment for Crime Control

Most of Asia, like most of the rest of the world, manages to control crime and punish offenders without significantly relying on executions. The most important dividing line is not between the 13 Asian jurisdictions that continue to execute and the 16 that do not (see chapter 2) but between the 25 or 26 nations with zero or near-zero execution levels and the three or four nations in which execution remains an operational feature of criminal justice (Vietnam and North Korea can be considered "wobblers" because of data inadequacies). Thus, for 90 percent of Asian governments capital punishment is an absent or marginal feature of efforts to control crime, and the symbolic role of

---

8. Our stress on the political causes of capital punishment policy does not mean culture is irrelevant. Methodologically, the arbitrary separation of ideas from institutions can force researchers to confront insoluble questions (Douglas 1986; Thompson, Ellis, and Wildavsky 1990). And substantively, some cultures are more effective than others at promoting prosperity, democracy, and social justice (Harrison 2006; see also Harrison and Huntington 2000; Putnam 1993; Landes 1998; Stark 2005; Inglehart and Wenzel 2005). The British movement to abolish slavery had important cultural and religious roots (Loconte 2007), but when it comes to the abolition of capital punishment, the cultural antecedents are less clear (Alarid and Wang 2001; Anckar 2004; Miethe, Lu, and Deibert 2005; Sarat and Boulanger 2005; Bae 2007). Where culture does shape death penalty policy and practice, it tends to do so indirectly, by influencing things such as literacy, economic development, and political rights (Greenberg and West 2008:331). If the central conservative truth is that culture counts, the central liberal truth is what Daniel Patrick Moynihan observed: "politics can change a culture and save it from itself" (quoted in Harrison 2006:xvi). As this book has argued, politics—and "leadership from the front" especially—is usually critical in death penalty policy-making (Zimring 2003:22; Bae 2007:116,122).

executions in places such as Indonesia, Malaysia, India, Japan, and Thailand is close to the pattern that prevailed in western Europe during the 1950s. Execution policy in the PRC, Singapore, Vietnam, and North Korea is different and will be discussed in the next section of this chapter. Some large Asian nations—India, Indonesia, Japan—have had tiny execution levels for many years. In other places, such as Malaysia, Taiwan, and South Korea, the trajectory has turned downward recently as the result of conscious policy change.

Common Causation in State Killing

Execution as punishment for crime is only one form of killing that state agents commit. In addition to waging war, some officials of the state kill while making arrests or responding to attacks from insurgents, and in many circumstances governments use police, military, or other armed personnel to kill persons who have not even been tried for crimes, much less sentenced to death (see appendix G). Such proactive government killing violates values of personal dignity and individual liberty and contradicts principles of due process and "power control" (Dan Cohen 1984). One important but neglected issue is the relationship between death as a criminal penalty and the rates of death from other forms of proactive state killing. There appear to be three possibilities: independence, complementarity, and common causation.

The independence hypothesis posits that rates of capital punishment and rates of other forms of proactive state killing are unrelated. On this view, knowing that a state does not conduct judicial executions tells little about whether its rate of proactive extrajudicial killing is high or low. The complementarity theory is that capital punishment may reduce the pressure for extrajudicial killing by providing a legal means of causing state enemies to "disappear." If this theory holds true, there is an inverse relationship between judicial and extrajudicial executions because the two behaviors are complementary.

The third and most probable relationship between the two forms of state killing is a positive correlation: the higher the one rate, the higher the other. Most of the conditions that explain high rates of capital punishment—low regard for citizen rights, a low level of economic development, belief in lethal violence as a legitimate expression of state power, fear of disorder—seem also to encourage higher than average rates of extrajudicial killing. This notion can be called a theory of common causation because the two forms of state killing are shaped by similar forces, though it should be stressed that what tends to generate high rates of extrajudicial execution are values and views about the propriety of state killing rather than the judicial executions themselves.

For the most part, the history of Europe supports the common causation claim that judicial and extrajudicial executions are linked. The most aggressive users of execution in 20th-century Europe were the same regimes that killed promiscuously without judicial sanction, Hitler's Germany and Stalin's Soviet Union being the most notable cases. What is more, the period after the abolition of capital punishment in Europe has evinced no upward pressure on extrajudicial killing, which contradicts the expectation of the complementarity theory.

The experience in Asia is also broadly consistent with a theory of common causation. Chapters 5, 6, and 7 described three jurisdictions in which judicial and extrajudicial executions rose to epidemic levels together before falling concurrently. In two of these cases, South Korea and Taiwan, executions fell to zero without any increase in extrajudicial killing. The mere fact of abolishing capital punishment is not a sufficient condition for ending extrajudicial executions (as appendix G notes), but when the death penalty ends there appears to be no hydraulic transfer of pressure to increase extrajudicial violence by the state.

Reliance on "Leadership from the Front" for Reform

Whatever separates major Asian nations that are pulling away from the death penalty from their less mobile neighbors, it is not public opinion about the appropriate punishment for murder. At the point of abolition in Hong Kong, public opinion on the death penalty was at 68 percent support, a percentage close to the levels of public support that exist in Japan, South Korea, and Taiwan. This 2-to-1 pattern of support is consistent with public opinion just prior to abolition in Western nations such as Great Britain, Canada, and the Federal Republic of Germany (Zimring and Hawkins 1986:22). In all of these democratic settings, the political momentum for reform was achieved through what has been called "leadership from the front" (Zimring 2003:22). And in both of the vanguard nations examined in this book, critical leadership came from the very top of the political power structure—elected presidents (see chapters 5 and 6). In South Korea—scene of the longest of these adventures—public support for capital punishment has not generated a substantial backlash since the current moratorium started in 1998. The Korean story also displays a large gap between public support for abolition (34 percent) and support among legal and political elites (60 percent; see fig. 6.1). A similar pattern can be observed in Malaysia, where the public supports the death penalty and 80 percent of lawyers want to eliminate it. A less heroic story of presidential initiative in response to interest group pressure and corruption allegations was documented for the Philippines in chapter 4. More generally, a large gap between public opinion and leadership from the front seems to be a recurrent theme in several Asian settings where disengagement from the death penalty has already occurred or is in progress. See table 8.1.

Political leadership from the front is a two-way street in contemporary Asia because government elites also provide the major impetus to maintain high rates of execution or even increase them. The difference that fuels the gap in execution rates between Singapore and Malaysia is not between the opinions of the average "man on the street," unless that man in Singapore happens to be Lee Kuan Yew. In Singapore, the PRC, North Korea, and Vietnam, the key

Table 8.1
Public support for the death penalty in Asia

Nation	Year	Percent supporting	Source
Japan	2005	81%	Cabinet Office 2005[1]
Philippines	1999	80%	*Philippine Daily Inquirer* (in Tagayuna 2004)[2]
South Korea	1999	66%	World Research (in B. Cho 2008)[3]
Taiwan	2001	80%	Ben Chang Shiah (in Ryden 2001)[4]
China	1995	99%	Hu Yunteng, Chinese Academy of Social Sciences[5]
Hong Kong	1986	68%	Gaylord and Galliher 1994[6]
Singapore	2006	96%	*Straits Times* (in Hands Off Cain 2006)[7]
Thailand	2005	84%	Dhurakij Pundit University (in International Federation for Human Rights 2005)[8]

Note: In southern India, a (nonrepresentative) survey of 434 undergraduate students at a large university in the state of Andhra Pradesh found opinion split, with 43 percent supporting the death penalty, 44 percent opposing it, and 13 percent uncertain (Lambert et al. 2008).

[1] Highest level of support for capital punishment in the nation's postwar history (Schmidt 2002:165).

[2] Poll conducted during the controversy surrounding the execution of Leo Echegaray, the first person to be executed in that nation after the death penalty was reinstated in 1993.

[3] Poll conducted one year after President Kim Dae Jung declared a moratorium on executions; support for capital punishment has softened in subsequent years (B. Cho 2008).

[4] Poll (n = 1,381) conducted by Ben Chang Shiah, professor of statistics, Fujen University (Ryden 2001:70).

[5] Poll (n = 5,006) conducted by Hu Yunteng, a scholar at the Chinese Academy of Social Sciences, who found that only 0.78 percent said the death penalty should be abolished while another 3.04 percent said it was used too much (Svensson 2001). A second death penalty poll was conducted in 2002 and 2003 by Virgil Ho (2005), who received 86 responses to a survey he administered to a group of mostly middle-class professionals in South China; 85 percent said they supported capital punishment. But a more recent poll conducted in 2007–2008 found only 58 percent of Chinese in favor of capital punishment (Oberwittler and Qi 2008; see note 49 in chapter 7).

[6] Poll conducted in 1986, two decades after the moratorium began (Gaylord and Galliher 1994:29). A similar poll conducted after the Tiananmen massacre in 1989 found that 50 percent of Hong Kong residents supported capital punishment (Vagg 1997:398).

[7] Poll surveyed 425 citizens and permanent residents aged 20 and older. Most said they wanted the death penalty to remain mandatory, and almost three-quarters believed Singapore should stand its ground on capital punishment even if more countries abolish (Hands Off Cain 2006).

[8] Poll conducted by researchers at Dhurakij Pundit University; 1,154 persons surveyed nationwide (International Federation for Human Rights and Union for Civil Liberty 2005). In 2001, in a narrower survey administered to 1,357 residents of Bangkok, 89 percent said they supported capital punishment, and 59 percent said they wanted executions to be more publicized (International Federation for Human Rights and Union for Civil Liberty 2005).

determinant of high execution levels is the preference of strong governments with pervasive authority over executive and judicial actions. This kind of leadership from the front is of course less remarkable than the kind that pulls away from capital punishment, because there is no pattern of democratic control in any of the four authoritarian political structures. In these settings, leadership comes from the front on all matters and it frequently contradicts public opinion. Still, if the PRC is now launching a campaign to curtail executions, in some respects it will resemble the liberal death penalty reforms undertaken in Asian and European democracies. Whatever the governmental system, the most likely proximate cause of substantive change in death penalty policy is the leadership of political elites.

"Human Rights" and "Limits of Government" Influences

Emphasis on the need to limit government power and respect the human rights of criminal offenders was not evident in the domestic debates that produced abolition in western Europe. "Neither the friends nor the foes of capital punishment made any serious effort to build a position on the death penalty into a larger framework of human rights in either law or moral argument" (Zimring 2003:25). The human-rights/limits-of-government perspective took hold in Europe only in the 1980s and 1990s, after western Europe had already become an execution-free zone. In chapter 1 we asked whether this broadly political view of state execution influences death penalty discourse in Asia now, and the answer is a resounding yes. But the Asian nations where the impact of these concerns has been greatest—South Korea and Taiwan especially—have been influenced by their own domestic histories more than the global abstractions of European human rights rhetoric. Still, to the extent that execution policy is discussed in contemporary Asia, questions about limits on government are highly salient and usually close to the center of debate.

The clearest cases of concern for human rights and limits on government are South Korea and Taiwan. At the other extreme is the limited range of domestic discourse on capital punishment in the PRC and Singapore, though in these two places the failure to employ political frames may mainly result from self-censorship in constrained circumstances (Lydgate 2003; Zhang 2005a).[9] What the Asian situation seems to reveal is not that the political aspects of capital punishment are more important in present-day Asia than they were in Europe before the 1980s, but rather that the passage of time has produced a substantial increase in human rights concerns about capital punishment around the world (Schabas 2000; Schabas 2002; Schabas 2004). In the 21st century,

---

9. It also needs to be acknowledged that the quantity and quality of death penalty discourse in Singapore and the PRC have increased in recent years (Zhang 2005a; Hood and Hoyle 2008:101; see also chapter 7 and appendix E).

rights-related issues will be prominent in any serious discussion of capital punishment, for it is time rather than geography that is the critical variable.[10]

While human rights have become highly salient and transnational NGOs now lobby on death penalty policy and collect information on how it is practiced around the world, the main arena for death penalty debates and decisions remains the nation-state. There is no transnational body in Asia seeking to play a role in death penalty policy parallel to that played by the Council of Europe after 1982 (see chapter 9). Despite this "every nation on its own" orientation, the region is replicating the pattern that characterized Europe during the 36 years between the end of World War II and France's abolition in 1981. For abolitionists in Asia, this time lag, and the heightened regard for human rights it has produced, may be the most important "advantage of followership" (Pyle 1974).

■ Variations

In regional terms, the outstanding difference between western Europe of the postwar period and the current circumstances of Asia is the much wider variation in political, social, and economic environments in Asia. By the 1960s, many of the forces believed necessary for the abolition of capital punishment in Europe were either completed or (as in the case of Spain, then in the hands of an aging dictator) all but inevitable. From the standpoint of observing the preconditions for the death penalty's demise, arriving in western Europe at midcentury was like arriving at a theater at the start of act 3. After a brief flurry of executions for wartime offenses, conditions in western Europe varied little from country to country, and in their practice of capital punishment most nations combined low rates with an end-of-an-era mood. There was poverty in the immediate wake of World War II, and there were gaps in wealth between north and south in western Europe, but there was considerably less variation in circumstances than there is now in Asia. Today the range of economic conditions in Asia is as great as the range worldwide, from Japan, Singapore, and Hong Kong on the high end to Nepal, East Timor, and Laos on the low. The political systems of Asia also vary greatly, from the totalitarianism of North Korea and the military authoritarianism of Myanmar to a wide variety of functioning democracies, and these sharp political differences distinguish more than merely a few extreme cases. The PRC and Vietnam are both functioning governments dominated by authoritarian

---

10. The belief that "human rights" should trump other claims and values is of relatively recent origin but is rapidly becoming conventional. The very concept of "human right" implies three interlocking qualities that seem to entail universality: "rights must be natural (inherent in human beings); equal (the same for everyone); and universal (applicable everywhere)" (Hunt 2007:20).

communist parties, while Singapore is administered with an authoritarian intolerance for dissent that would arouse the envy of Spain's Generalissimo Franco (Buruma 2001a:125; Lydgate 2003). Changes in forms of government in Asia are frequent over time as well.

All of this variation, over time and between nations, makes Asia an essential laboratory for examining how political, economic, and social forces shape death penalty policy. Rather than listing a wide range of environmental factors and calling them Asian variations, we will focus here on three main dimensions of Asia's diversity: execution rates, the pace of change in death penalty policy, and the policy content of low-rate retentionist nations. One purpose of describing these Asian variations is to establish the contexts that inform our discussion of Asian differences in the final section of this chapter.

Death Penalty Policy and Rates of Execution

In recent years, Singapore and the PRC have used execution at rates above five per million per year, which is more than a thousand times the best estimate of the execution rate in the "improbable democracy" of India (Dahl 1998:159; Hood 2002:92; Batra 2007:2). As striking as this illustration is of the range of variation in Asia, an equally instructive contrast concerns Singapore and Malaysia, two contiguous nations with a common colonial history and legal heritages that were only separated after a postcolonial attempt at national unity. Figure 8.1 shows the execution rates for Singapore (population four million in 2000) and Malaysia (population 23 million in 2000) for a recent period in which executions can be documented.

Singapore and Malaysia both have a British colonial past, common law foundations for their legal systems, and government structures that are authoritarian and dominated by a single "strongman" who now wields authority

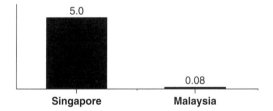

Figure 8.1

Execution rates per million population, Singapore and Malaysia, 2000–2005
Note: Singapore had 89 executions between 2000 and October 2003 and 27 executions in 2004–2005. The nine-month total of 13 executions for 2003 has been extrapolated to a one-year estimate of 17 for the year, yielding a total of 111 executions (89 + 4 + 27) for the entire six-year period 2000–2005 (Amnesty International 2004b). The figure is based on 111 estimated Singapore executions and 11 in Malaysia. *Sources*: Amnesty International 2004b; see also Singapore Ministry of Home Affairs 2004; Hands Off Cain (various years).

informally. These two nations also have a variety of mandatory capital statutes, substantial numbers of death sentences (Malaysia had 159 people on death row in May 2006), and differing proportions of Muslims in their populations (15 percent in Singapore vs. 53 percent in Malaysia). Nonetheless, the annual rate of executions in Singapore is 62 times higher than that in Malaysia, and the gap has grown wider over time. A difference of this magnitude cannot be attributed to differences in culture, government, or political structure. It seems to reflect a taste for execution in Singapore's government—and in Lee Kuan Yew especially—that is no longer found among Malaysian political elites. In 2006, Malaysia's minister of justice even said he supported the abolition of capital punishment because "no one has the right to take someone else's life, even if that person is a murderer" (quoted in Malaysians against Death Penalty and Torture [MADPET], March 21, 2006). Preferences as strikingly different as these appear in few policy areas outside capital punishment. According to Freedom House, Singapore and Malaysia received identical scores for "political rights" and "civil liberties" until 2005, when Malaysia's score for the former was raised by one point on a seven-point scale (see www.freedom-house.org, as well as Friedman 2005:313).[11]

It is difficult to tell how long the Malaysia-Singapore contrast in executions will endure. As of this writing, Lee Kuan Yew, the 83-year-old British-educated lawyer and creator of modern Singapore who led the nation for 31 years before stepping down as prime minister in 1990 to become "minister mentor," continues to respond to critics who condemn the city-state for being too tightly controlled by stressing Singapore's "vulnerability" in a world and a region full of perils. "To survive," he says, "we have to do these things" (quoted in Mydans and Arnold 2007).[12] But Lee also emphasizes that his is a country of

---

11. Malaysia used to use execution much more aggressively. In 1970–1996, there were 349 executions by hanging—an average of 13 per year—and 150 of them (43 percent) were for drug offenses (Hood 2002:48). In February 2005, opposition leader Lim Kit Siang received statistics from prime minister Abdullah Ahmad Badawi revealing that there had been 358 executions in the previous 24 years—an average of 15 per year (Hands Off Cain 2005). In 2000–2006, by contrast, Malaysia carried out only 11 executions—an average of 1.6 per year for a country that was 80 percent more populous in 2006 than in 1980. In recent years, about 14 percent of the persons executed in Malaysia have been foreign nationals, which is about one-fourth to one-third the corresponding percentage for Singapore (Amnesty International 2004b; Singapore Ministry of Home Affairs 2004). In 1999–2003, almost three-quarters of Singapore's executions were for drug offenses, a substantially larger share than that in Malaysia (43 percent) in the period 1970–1996 (Hood 2002:48; Hands Off Cain 2004).

12. When the octogenarian Lee was asked if he had ever gone too far with repressing political opponents, he said: "No. I don't think so. I never killed them. I never destroyed them. Politically, they destroyed themselves" (Lee 2007). It is true that Lee did not execute political rivals as his authoritarian counterparts in China and Vietnam did, but he did destroy many of his enemies (Seow 1994; Harding and Chu Harding 2002; Lydgate 2003). The chief instrument of destruction was often an emasculated judiciary that Lee and his successors employed for purposes of political persecution and revenge (Seow 2007; see also appendixes E and G).

"pragmatists" who will "have to go in whatever direction world conditions dictate if we are to survive and be part of the modern world." Some observers believe there is "an unquestionable trend towards universal abolition of capital punishment" (Schabas 2000:280). If that prognosis is correct, and if Lee Kuan Yew is right about Singapore's need to adjust to changes in its environment, then when the execution contrast between Singapore and Malaysia does diminish or disappear, it will be because Singapore converges toward Malaysia—and toward most of the rest of the region and the world. The true test will begin when the minister mentor leaves the political scene. In the meantime, it is worth noting that executions in the nation Lee built may have already started to merge toward a more Malaysian level (see appendix E).[13]

WHO GETS EXECUTED IN HIGH-EXECUTION NATIONS? In describing Asian variations, one important question concerns the types of offenses and offenders who get executed in high-execution jurisdictions and periods. Though the data are patchy in many respects, Asia has had several high-execution eras: China and Singapore throughout the past generation, Taiwan until 2000 or so, Vietnam, North Korea, and South Korea in the 1950s and 1960s, and probably Vietnam and North Korea more recently. What kinds of offenders and offenses receive the death penalty when its reach expands? Although many crimes are death-eligible in Asia, and the particular subjects of capital punishment vary from nation to nation, only a few common crimes—murder and drug offenses especially—account for the large majority of executions in the region. For the most part, the persons most likely to get executed in contemporary Asia's high-execution environments are members of what is generally known as the "criminal class"—especially the poor and poorly connected.

The first common characteristic in high-volume environments is the large number of different crimes for which death is a possible punishment. China has had 68 such offenses since its criminal code was reformed in 1997 (Lu and Miethe 2007:54); Taiwan retains 50 capital crimes even since its capital laws have been narrowed (Liao 2008); Vietnam had 44 capital offenses until the number was cut back to 29 in 2000 (B. Cho 2003); and the death penalty in Singapore continues to be prescribed for "a wide range of offenses" (Amnesty International 2004b).

The particular subjects of capital punishment vary from country to country. South Korea aggressively enforced national security offenses well into the 1980s, as did Taiwan before democratization. Political offenses are often capital too, though the reform of China's Criminal Code in 1997 did shift the government's focal concern away from the kinds of political crimes that had frequently led to execution in the past and toward economic and social issues in the present (Wang 2008). Forcible rape and other sexual offenses have carried the possibility

13. Following an average of 22.4 executions per year during the five-year period 2000–2004, Singapore carried out only 13 executions in 2005–2007. Over a three-year period ten years earlier (1995–1997), Singapore conducted 138 executions.

of capital punishment in several Asian jurisdictions—most notably the Philippines between its two abolitions (Wilkinson 2000; Kandelia 2006). In the PRC and Vietnam, death remains a sanction for public corruption and aggravated crimes of theft, but in both locations there have been attempts to restrict capital punishment for white-collar and property offenses.

Drug offending is capital in many high and low execution nations, especially in Southeast Asia. As of 2007, at least 34 of the world's 64 retentionist countries that had carried out executions in the preceding decade had legislation authorizing the death penalty for drug-related crimes (the comparable count in 1985 was 22). Almost half of those 34 nations are located in Asia.[14] Despite the international trend toward abolition during the last two decades, "the number of countries expanding the application of the death penalty to include drug offenses" has increased, especially in Asia (Lines 2007:6). Concern about drug trafficking is also prominently featured in pro–death penalty rhetoric throughout the region, with many Asian governments insisting that capital punishment deters drug crime. But a 1991 report on Malaysia's mandatory death penalty for drugs concluded that the capital solution to the drug problem "is not effective" (Harring 1991). In fact, Malaysia had "one of the world's highest per capita populations of drug addicts and users," a fact "vehemently denied by the government but supported by its own official statistics" (Lines 2007:14). More recently, a member of Malaysia's ruling party acknowledged that "the mandatory death sentence . . . has not been effective in curtailing drug trafficking" ("229 Executed" 2005). Similarly, a recent report from the U.S. State Department found that "drug laws remain very tough in Vietnam," including provisions for mandatory death sentences, yet "drug trafficking continues to rise" (U.S. State Department 2003). And in Singapore, where "the vast majority" of executions are for drug offenses, the government ceased publishing crime statistics in the 1980s, "making its claims of the death penalty's effectiveness impossible to test" (Lines 2007:15). One might expect a government that frequently stresses the deterrence effect of capital punishment on drug crime—and publishes high-quality statistics in many other policy spheres—to collect and release data on this important question. But one would be wrong. "Statistical data [on the death penalty and drug deterrence] are not provided in any consistent or meaningful way by [Singapore's] government," and one "can

14. According to the Anti–Death Penalty Asia Network (ADPAN), 16 Asian nations retain death penalty laws on the books for drug offenders: Bangladesh, Brunei, China, India, Indonesia, Laos, Malaysia, Myanmar, North Korea, Pakistan, Singapore, South Korea, Sri Lanka, Taiwan, Thailand, and Vietnam (see also Hood and Hoyle 2008:137). Outside the abolitionist nations of Asia, therefore, only four countries in the region do not retain the death penalty for drug offenders: Japan, the Maldives, Mongolia, and Papua New Guinea. The death penalty remains a prominent feature of punishment systems in many Asian nations even though the "Golden Triangle" of Southeast Asia (an opium-growing region 350,000 square kilometers in an area that includes parts of Myanmar, Laos, Thailand, Vietnam, and China's Yunnan Province) produced only about 5 percent of the world's supply of opium in 2007, compared with more than 70 percent three decades earlier (Fuller 2007).

only speculate why" (Hor 2004:105). One possibility is that the evidence does not support the government's policy preference.

The list of potentially capital crimes is a misleading guide to actual patterns of execution in most Asian nations because a handful of offenses at the top of the priority list usually accounts for the majority of executions. Murder without mitigation and major drug crimes are the two offenses most commonly considered most serious. Police and prosecutorial discretion sometimes reduces the punishment for such offenses to something less than death, but the mandatory death label indicates that these are crimes where execution outcomes are expected and normal. Murder and banditry have been especially high-volume execution crimes in the PRC and Taiwan, while the available evidence suggests that in Indonesia, Malaysia, Singapore, Thailand, and Vietnam, "the majority of death penalty cases are for drug crimes" (Anti–Death Penalty Asia Network 2007).[15] In the Philippines, three of the seven persons executed between February 1999 and January 2000 had been convicted of capital rape without homicide.

As for offender characteristics, in most recent high-execution environments, the "criminal class" accounts for the vast majority of executions, and it most frequently consists of the poor and ethnic minorities. Executed offenders do not all come from the bottom rungs of the social ladder, but there is substantial overrepresentation of the least well off. In Pakistan, for example, there is some economic diversity among the 7,000 persons on death row, but the Islamic practice of cash for clemency (*diyat*) means that the large majority of executions are of persons from poor families. In the Muslim-majority nation of Malaysia, an estimated 90 percent of the 300 or so persons on death row are poor. In Japan, the richest nation in Asia and one in which more than 90 percent of the population self-identifies as "middle class," most of the more than 100 inmates on death row "have no choice but to have . . . court-appointed defense counsels," says Akiko Takada, a leading member of Forum 90, Japan's largest abolitionist organization (quoted in Hadji-Ristic 2007). And in China, Huan Jinting's interviews on death row in a Chongqing prison paint a troubling portrait of the harsh life circumstances of 22 petty offenders who were condemned to die (Huan 2006). Another China study examined 1,010 serious criminal cases and found that 81 percent of the 544 persons who received unsuspended death sentences had killed at least one

15. In Southeast Asia, the percentage of drug offenses of any kind that end in execution is not known, and since the volume of drug prosecutions is also unknown, the odds of a death sentence for drug offending cannot be estimated. In contrast to the Southeast Asian nations where the majority of executions are for drug offending, in the one Chinese province for which we were able to acquire detailed information on the distribution of capital convictions by crime, more than 60 percent of death sentences in 2006 were for intentional homicide, about 25 percent were for robbery, 3 percent were for assault, and 1 percent were for rape. In this province, where drug use and sale are probably not as common as in provinces such as Yunnan and Guangxi, drug offenses accounted for less than 10 percent of all death sentences. In contrast, government officials in two parts of Yunnan Province inside the Golden Triangle report that approximately 90 percent of their death sentences are for drug trafficking.

victim, and 62 percent of all capital offenders were either unemployed or lived in rural areas, while 42 percent were "transients." In the same study, 70 percent of all capital offenders who were employed held low-status jobs (Lu and Miethe 2007:80). In many Asian nations, including Singapore, Malaysia, and Indonesia, foreigners are more prominent in death penalty totals than in the broader population of criminal defendants (Amnesty International 2004b; Hands Off Cain 2007). As for white-collar offenders, the corrupt government officials who occasionally get executed in China (as did Zheng Xiaoyu in 2007) get tremendous publicity but represent a fraction of 1 percent of the death toll from Strike Hard campaigns. At peak rates of execution in the PRC, 1 percent of the *annual* total of executions would be 150 persons, and our sources indicate that 150 government officials have not been executed in any *decade* in China since the 1980s.

The good news about the concentration of executions among the "criminal classes" and poor and minority populations is the apparent scarcity of political offenders and social dissidents who get executed. If such cases are not a prominent feature of the current landscape of Asian executions (except perhaps in North Korea), then this marks a major departure from death penalty practice in the PRC and Taiwan in the first few decades after midcentury, in South Korea under presidents Syngman Rhee and Park Chung Hee, and in Vietnam under Ho Chi Minh. But the problem with declarations that dissidents are seldom executed is that political executions are likely to be among the most secretive government actions, so they may be underrepresented in the tightly controlled death penalty statistics that characterize some Asian regimes. In Taiwan, for example, an entire class of executions was excluded from official records until 1977, and what separates that system's method of accounting from those used in several other Asian governments is Taiwan's candor in acknowledging the omission. Similarly, in China, dissidents are precisely the kinds of offenders the government would most like to keep off its own death penalty rolls and those of the NGOs that monitor the country (Matas and Kilgour 2007). It is impossible to tell to what extent such an execution pattern can be kept secret, but even if places remain in the PRC where overtly political executions can occur without notice to the outside world, the capacity to hide them is shrinking every day (Ye and Fowler 2008).[16] In South Korea and Taiwan, we can be confident that executions of political opponents have not happened on any significant scale since their democratic turns, while in the more secretive

16. In North Korea's closed system, it appears that political dissidents continue to be executed on a regular basis "under the loving care of dear leader" Kim Jong Il (Martin 2006; see appendix A). In October 2007, for example, a factory manager was executed by firing squad in front of a crowd of 150,000. He was condemned to death for making international phone calls. The Associated Press reported that public executions in the hermit kingdom had declined since 2000 because of international criticism, but late in 2007 the South Korean aid agency Good Friends reported that the North Korean government had orchestrated at least five public executions in recent months, some involving persons deemed insufficiently deferent to the country's dictator (see Tim Goodwin's Asia Death Penalty Blog, December 6, 2007).

environments of Singapore and Vietnam the evidence suggests that large numbers of political dissidents and enemies are not executed.

In sum, the wide variation in Asian rates of execution is not reflected in a diversity of types of offenders subject to execution. The bulk of executed persons are common offenders convicted of homicide, robbery, or drug crimes. This is a shift away from the explicitly political executions that were commonplace in previous generations in South Korea, Taiwan, Vietnam, Cambodia, and China. Moreover, the huge variation in execution rates for homicide, drug, and robbery offenders across the jurisdictions of Asia does *not* reflect differences in crime rates between nations with high and low execution rates—with one exception. Crime problems do not distinguish high-rate Singapore from low-rate Malaysia and Thailand, and the same can be said of Vietnam and Indonesia. Similarly, China does not seem to have significantly higher crime rates than Taiwan or South Korea (Bakken 2005; Johnson 2006b:86; Hebenton 2007). Only in Japan might a low crime rate be an important contributing cause of a low rate of execution, and even there the surge in death sentences that has occurred in recent years—and the acceleration in executions—have been accompanied by a homicide rate that has remained flat (Johnson 2008b).

The Pace of Change in Execution Rates

The prevailing pattern in western European nations that dropped the death penalty without changing the form of government was a long decline that produced substantial periods with few executions preceding the onset of non-execution. The paths to abolition in other regions of the world have been more varied (Hood 2007), but as a matter of common sense if not formal theory, one expects those nations with the lowest rates of execution in the 1980s and 1990s to be prime candidates for intentional stoppages in execution in the 2000s. In Europe, the main exceptions to this pattern were the abolitions that occurred in Italy and Germany in the mid-1940s after their repressive regimes had been decisively rejected, and the abolitions that took place in the Soviet client states of eastern Europe after their regimes were overthrown following the fall of the Berlin wall (Zimring 2003).

But of the three governments that moved dramatically toward ending executions in the most recent history of East Asia—the Philippines, South Korea, and Taiwan—only the Philippines was at the low end of the execution scale long prior to the move, while nations such as Japan, Thailand, Indonesia, and India all had much lower execution rates than South Korea and Taiwan did before they began to dismantle capital punishment. Indeed, the execution rate in Taiwan was many times higher than in Japan or Thailand, and South Korea's execution rate was also substantially higher. Figure 8.2 illustrates the "leapfrog" status of Taiwan and South Korea by comparing execution rates in seven Asian nations for 1990, 1995, and 2006.

The main cause of South Korea's and Taiwan's decisive move to limit executions was political change in a democratic direction. Thus, explaining

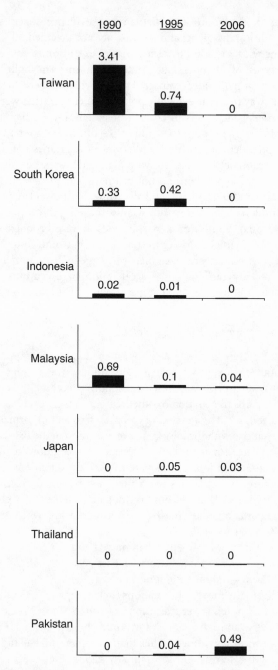

Figure 8.2
Execution rates in seven Asian nations, 1990, 1995, and 2006
Sources: Amnesty International (various years).

the rapid pace of change in these two nations is not difficult: the most important moving parts are shifts in power, political sentiment, and leadership. In some circumstances, the absence of political change also helps explain stasis in execution policy. The persistence of executions in Japan is at least partly a by-product of a half century of (almost) continuous conservative control of government. Later we will present the persistence of hard-line authoritarian regimes as an important element distinctive of Asia. Here we merely observe that the great leaps forward toward ending executions in South Korea and Taiwan during the last decade are inextricably linked to the decline of right-wing autocratic regimes in the preceding years.

The Policy Content of Low-Rate Retentionist Nations

While the rate of executions is one important dimension of death penalty policy in those Asian nations that retain and use the death penalty, there are significant differences between nations with similar execution records. In some low-execution settings, the central government seems to make little effort to attend to or control capital punishment. India may be the best example of this decentralized orientation, though even there the "rarest of the rare" doctrine that restricts the scope of cases qualifying as capital emerged from the Supreme Court in Delhi (Batra 2007). In other low-rate settings, long periods pass without any executions even though no formal reshaping of policy seems to occur. In both Indonesia and Thailand, substantial periods without execution have been punctuated by occasional executions despite no alteration in substantive policy. In Japan, by contrast, a low rate of execution has been consciously maintained and carefully administered by a central government that regards regular executions as a necessity. Some nations that use execution—China, Thailand, and (before its second abolition) the Philippines—have tried to soften their image by using lethal injection,[17] but in Japan there is

---

17. In China, the revised Criminal Procedure Law of 1997 added the possibility of lethal injection, and some experts have estimated that by 2007 more than half of executions in some jurisdictions were being performed by this method (see chapter 7). Thailand's lethal injection reform of 2003 replaced execution by firing squad; as of 2007 it had been used four times. In the Philippines, all seven of the executions (in 1999–2000) that occurred between the two abolitions were by lethal injection. In 1992, Taiwan's Legislative Assembly passed a law permitting execution by lethal injection as an alternative to shooting, but as of 2007 it had never been used, perhaps because the necessary facilities have not been prepared. In India, Vietnam, and Papua New Guinea, the introduction of lethal injection has been proposed, but no legislation has been passed. Outside of Asia, the only jurisdictions to have passed lethal injection laws are in the United States (beginning with Oklahoma in 1977) and Guatemala (in 1996). Guatemala's reform was stimulated by a botched double execution by firing squad that was televised; the first lethal injection—also televised—was also botched (Amnesty International 2007a).

little momentum toward this reform or toward a softening of the secretive and arbitrary executions described in chapter 3.[18]

All of this suggests that the importance of a handful of hangings in Japan is out of all proportion to the value of that enterprise for criminal justice or crime control. One way of distinguishing Japan's policy from India's is to call India's death penalty a low-salience system and Japan's a high-salience system of significant importance to the ruling party and the national government. A complementary way to describe the difference between Indian or Indonesian policy and that of Japan is to distinguish a hit-or-miss pattern of "inertial retention," by which the former governments respond without enthusiasm to their long-standing death penalty systems, from the pattern of "intentional retention" that prevails in Japan, where the government gives significant time and attention to capital punishment and regards it as a positive part of its criminal justice system without (until 2007) pushing for more executions.

Japan's intentional, high-salience model of execution policy generates its own puzzles. Most important, if the value of executions is so substantial, why carry out so few? There are two answers that help explain this Japanese pattern. First, only a few executions are needed to serve the symbolic purpose of validating the government's authority. Why execute 30 inmates a year if fewer serve the purpose just as well? In this sense, there seems to be a real difference between what the death penalty *says* and what it *does* to accomplish utilitarian purposes such as deterrence, the marginal benefits of which are easy to imagine but difficult to demonstrate. The second reason Japan executes rarely, despite the high symbolic value it places on continuing to put criminals to death, is its substantial ambivalence about the propriety of state killing, both in government circles and among the general public (Johnson 2006a; Johnson 2006c). Reservations about the propriety of execution almost certainly play a role in this low-rate but committed execution regime, for the perception that a larger number of executions will be politically costly or risky seems to be the only discernible motive for maintaining execution totals in the single digits for a generation. The Japanese pattern of low volume with high salience reflects a conflict in which both the interests served by executions and the costs of execution are deemed to be substantial. Although this conflict is not reflected in the blunt instrument of public opinion polls or in political

18. In October 2007, Japanese minister of justice Kunio Hatoyama did say: "[F]rankly I feel there must be some more peaceful method" (of killing death row inmates than hanging), after which a study group in his ministry began researching the issue, but for the preceding four decades there had been almost no discussion of execution methods in the media or in policy-making circles ("Japan Minister" 2007). Similarly, after Japan hanged three men in December 2007, the government announced for the first time the names of the persons who had been executed, the crimes for which they had been condemned, and their execution locales, but there was no prior notification to the inmates or to anyone else, leading some analysts to criticize this "opening" as only a "small step forward" (Hogg 2007).

debates in the Diet, it is evident in the sharply different policies that various ministers of justice have adopted. In India and Indonesia, by contrast, the issue of the death penalty simply appears to be less important, perhaps because the governments of these still developing nations believe they have more pressing concerns.

It is unclear which type of low-rate environment, intentional or inertial, is the better harbinger of policy shifts toward abolition among the diverse range of retentionist nations in the Asia region. In low-salience inertial contexts such as India, Indonesia, and perhaps Mongolia, abolition might require less political energy, but at the same time there may also be less interest in mobilizing opposition to capital punishment. Though the death penalty appears to be a more important question in rich Japan than in those developing nations, this difference cannot be translated into a confident prediction of which countries will abolish first.

■ Distinctions

Three features of contemporary Asia distinguish capital punishment policies there from those in the West and other parts of the world. First, national control over death penalty policy persists, with weakness of international involvement. Second, long-term single-party rule is prevalent. Third, hard-line authoritarian regimes endure, especially in three of the world's last remaining communist nations—China, Vietnam, and North Korea.

The Persistence of National Autonomy

In Europe, transnational organizations assumed leadership on death penalty issues in 1983 when the Council of Europe promoted Protocol No. 6 of the European Convention on Human Rights. Since then, transnational standards have become important substantive principles in negotiations with the new national governments of eastern and central Europe and with the governments of Russia, Turkey, and the Ukraine, ultimately leading to the "fastest and most complete regional abolition in history" (Zimring 2003:35).

The situation in Asia is distinct in several respects. First, there are no international Asian organizations with substantial pan-Asian authority or influence, for many reasons (Studwell 2007:193). The major political variations on the continent make common standards harder to find, and on most questions there is little enthusiasm for regional authority that might constrain national autonomy. For example, when the heads of state of the Association of Southeast Asian Nations (ASEAN) signed a new charter in November 2007, the result was a lowest-common-denominator content in which the denominator was very low indeed. Under the new charter, the principle of "noninterference" in the affairs of member states continues to take precedence over adherence to democracy, the rule of law, and constitutional governance, leaving ASEAN largely powerless to respond to the acts of repressive regimes such as Myanmar's ruling junta. This failure to call members to account undermines ASEAN's legitimacy and raises the specter of its irrelevance ("ASEAN's Broken Heart" 2007). More generally, since there is no "Asian community" or "East Asian community" of nations to parallel the expanding European Community, the lack of powerful international organizations and top-down moral and political regulation follows as a matter of course.

The weakness of international involvement is one piece of a larger pattern of national autonomy on death penalty issues in Asia, for there are few efforts by individual nations in the region to influence death penalty policy in other countries. With so much variation in Asia's political systems, and with almost all of the region's large nations still retentionist, the absence of an orthodox set of values on capital punishment is unsurprising, as is the absence of missionary zeal to export whatever abolitionist enthusiasm exists.[19] What is harder to understand is the near absence of discourse on death penalty matters between Asian nations and the weakness of efforts by Asia's more developed countries to try to influence death penalty policy in neighboring jurisdictions. Even in Australia, which last used execution in 1967 and abolished capital punishment in 1985, opposition to the death penalty is "the formal policy of both the Labor and the Liberal parties," but under prime minister John Howard, who led the country for almost 12 years between 1996 and 2007, the government's "covert position" was to endorse the death penalty in certain cases, as it did for the six Bali bombers who were sentenced to death in Indonesia for killing 88 Australians (and 114 other persons) in October 2002 (Lindsey 2007). Australia also says little against the death penalty in international forums, directs "no criticism" at capital punishment in China or the United States (two of its largest trading partners), and has "long been quietly content" to let Indonesia execute Indonesians (Lindsey 2007). Only when the life at stake was Australian did Howard's government protest with any vigor against capital punishment.[20]

Japan, the most developed nation in East Asia, has not attempted to influence death penalty policy in other Asian countries either, for two main reasons. The first is a matter of style: Japan has neither the desire to be a pan-Asian political leader nor the reservoir of goodwill to bring this type of leadership off, for many neighboring nations are only a half century removed

19. ADPAN (see note 14), an informal network of Asian individuals and organizations coordinated by Amnesty International and committed to abolition, was only launched in October 2006 (see http://asiapacific.amnesty.org/apro/aproweb.nsf/pages/adpan).

20. During the election campaign in October 2007, when Robert McLelland, the foreign affairs spokesman for opposition leader Kevin Rudd, promised to campaign against capital punishment in Southeast Asia if Rudd became prime minister (as he did two months later), Prime Minister Howard strongly rebuked his rival, arguing that pleading for mercy for the condemned Bali bombers "would be seen as 'distasteful' by all Australians" (Harrison 2007).

from Japanese colonialism.[21] The second obstacle to Japan taking a leadership position in Asia is that its government does not have a deeply felt and confident position on capital punishment. In this sphere as in other political realms, ambivalence is hardly a selling point. Nations that recently abolished the death penalty are poor candidates for pan-Asian leadership too, because they lack the economic clout and cultural influence to command respectful attention. Whatever their virtues may be, Cambodia, Nepal, Bhutan, and the Philippines are seldom considered models for economic or political development.

The weakness of challenges to national autonomy on capital punishment does not mean that issues pursued by international bodies are unimportant in Asian death penalty debates. Rather, international opinion becomes impor-tant in places like South Korea and Taiwan when it is injected into domestic discourse by domestic political actors. Human rights are important in Taiwan because Taiwanese politicians and civil society have tried to make them so, and similar agents have been at work in South Korea. But one consequence of this practice of domestic adoption and adaptation of human rights frames is that achievements that occur in one Asian nation are not contagious in any direct sense. Human rights NGOs operating in Asia have had only modest success across borders (Keck and Sikkink 1998:89).

Might this change? For reasons we will discuss, some Asian nations would regard better coordinated regional human rights campaigns as unwelcome violations of national sovereignty; Japan, China, and Singapore are the three most prominent examples.[22] But some governments that are presiding over what we have called the inertial retention of low-salience death penalties—such as India and Indonesia—might listen to credible leadership efforts from a high-status Asian nation. The most likely source of this style of leadership is South Korea, especially if it crosses the boundary from de facto to de jure abolition.[23] South Korea is small for a regional power, but its cultural influence

---

21. Some Japan-watchers believe Asia's richest nation is developing more confidence in foreign affairs (Pyle 2007; Samuels 2007). If that trend continues, and if official ambivalence about capital punishment declines, as some observers expect (Shikei Haishi Henshu Iinkai 2006), then Japan could become more assertive on death penalty issues in the region. But we believe a Japanese shift to a more missionary position is unlikely.

22. The effort to pass a nonbinding resolution in the UN calling for a worldwide moratorium on executions met especially strong resistance from Singapore's UN envoy, Vanu Menon, who criticized the European-led effort for "trying to impose a particular set of beliefs on everyone else" (quoted in Kuppusamy 2007b). But the resolution passed, with 104 nations voting in favor, 54 against, and 29 abstaining. Of the jurisdictions described as "Asian" in chapter 2 (minus Hong Kong, Macao, and Taiwan, which are not represented in the UN), Asian nations were 2.5 times more likely to oppose the resolution than were the nations in the rest of the world (Hands Off Cain 2007).

23. In December 2007, on the verge of the ten-year anniversary of its own moratorium, South Korea let pass a high-profile opportunity to exercise such leadership when it abstained

is substantial in many Asian nations, and it does have incentives to assert its influence in competitive contrast to Japan.

For the foreseeable future, the lack of challenges to national autonomy on death penalty questions will probably remain an important fact of life in Asia, though even modest efforts by developed nations such as South Korea to start discussions with other countries in the region could make a meaningful difference. In recent years, the main attempts at regional influence have involved complaints about nationals from one Asian nation under sentence of death in another. One typical circumstance is a death sentence in Singapore, Vietnam, or Indonesia for an Australian national, often in a drug case. National governments in abolitionist jurisdictions are understandably concerned when their citizens are sentenced to death elsewhere. It is "inconsistent" and "even hypocritical," however, when only these circumstances provoke protests by non–death penalty governments (Lindsey 2007). When concern is limited to the welfare of citizens from the complaining nations, the objection cannot be credibly framed in terms of broad principles of human rights or of limited government power. More practically, "that sort of unprincipled policy differentiation sure won't fly" in most Asian nations (Lindsey 2007).

Single-Party Dominance

In most developed political systems of the West, frequent shifts in power are accepted and expected. Indeed, transfers of power are not only the norm in western Europe and the former nations of the Commonwealth, they are considered a hallmark of democratic government (Dahl 1998). Where nondemocratic governments have persisted, as in Spain and Portugal until the 1970s and in the Soviet-dominated satellite states during the decades of the cold war, regimes endured because they were unwilling to share or relinquish power and because they possessed the means to realize their will.

Governments in Asia are more likely to maintain power for long periods of time, and a substantial number of them have been nondemocratic. China, North Korea, and Vietnam are communist, authoritarian, single-party states, while Taiwan and South Korea (until the 1980s) and Singapore (to the present) have had authoritarian regimes of the right. Other nations such as the Philippines, Indonesia, Pakistan, and Malaysia are more difficult to classify on a left-right continuum but must be considered undemocratic for most of their modern histories. Even Japan, with a fully functioning democratic system, has experienced more than 50 years of almost uninterrupted one-party dominance (Curtis 1999; Vogel 2006).

---

from the vote on the death penalty moratorium resolution in the UN. The resolution passed anyway; the seven Asian nations that voted in its favor were Australia, Cambodia, Nepal, New Zealand, the Philippines, and East Timor (all abolitionist), and abolitionist de facto Sri Lanka (Hands Off Cain 2007).

Regimes in power for long periods of time tend to retard the capacity for developing political liberties and establishing limits on state power—and this is especially the case for long-lasting authoritarian regimes (Ginsburg and Moustafa 2008a). In this respect, there are no clear differences between governments of the hard left and the hard right. (For some regimes such as the PRC since Deng Xiaoping, it is difficult to classify the government's policies on a left-right continuum.) But simply adding the populations of the countries listed in the previous paragraph produces a present total of more than two billion people living in one-party governments or in nations that have only recently pushed toward plural democracy.

The pace of economic change has been rapid in much of East and Southeast Asia, and shifts from agriculture to manufacturing have produced powerful demographic shifts as well. Where high rates of economic development have been sustained for decades, as in Taiwan, South Korea, and Singapore, changes in levels of education, training, and social mobility are frequent too. The contrast between fast-moving economic and social shifts and slow-moving governmental and political processes produces lags between socioeconomic developments and legal and political accommodations, largely because governments are often oriented to their own interests more than those of the governed. A persistent gap between economic change and political reform creates pressure for political change. If that pressure builds up and is not suppressed, long periods of economic development without significant political change will be followed by structural change in government. This has already happened in South Korea and Taiwan but not (yet) in China, Vietnam, or Singapore.

Again, one consequence of the difference in pace between economic and political change is a time lag between economic and social changes and the political adjustments they promote. But even if causation is direct, it may not be swift. Long delays between economic development and political liberalization are not decisive evidence against economic causation. But does economic development mean the inevitable end of right-wing authoritarian government? The jury is still out on this question in East Asia—but not very far out. Authoritarian governments of the right have been reformed in Korea, Taiwan, Indonesia, and the Philippines, and they have been significantly softened in Malaysia and (between coups anyway) Thailand. On the continent, only Singapore, Myanmar, Pakistan, and (since 2007) Bangladesh remain substantially intact as authoritarian, right-wing regimes. The actuarial prospects for right-wing governments to generate sustained economic growth and enhanced educational and social opportunity do not look promising.

The prospects for left-wing authoritarianism in Asia have been less dismal. China, Vietnam, and North Korea remain politically unreconstructed despite substantial economic development in the first two. This cluster of communist states—and their strong commitments to capital punishment—is the third major distinction between Asia and other regions of the world.

Communism and Capital Punishment

The implosion of the Soviet Union as a regime and superpower helped produce a striking contrast between Europe and Asia regarding the presence of hard-line communist governments. Communism has almost disappeared in Europe and Central Asia, replaced by various gradations of democracy and other types of authoritarian government. Nearly all of the Soviet Union's satellite states had formal death penalties on their statute books before the fall of the Berlin wall (though East Germany abolished in 1987), and most of those states abolished capital punishment under European pressure early in their post-Soviet careers (Zimring 2003:16). There were multiple routes to abolition in this region, with 11 cases of abolition through legislative action and 5 involving the prominent role of a constitutional court, but in many respects—especially the influence of the Council of Europe and Amnesty International—"similarities prevailed" (Puhar 2003:55,107).

There are few hard-line (authoritarian) communist states on the world map in 2008, but almost all of them are in Asia. Cuba has a communist government with some aspects of authoritarianism, but it is a softer regime than classic Stalinist governments were, and none of Latin America's other new left governments seem close to communist.[24] In contrast, three Asian nations fit the hard-line communist classification: China, Vietnam, and North Korea.[25]

---

24. As explained in our analysis of Vietnam's death penalty in appendix C, Cuba is believed to have executed 5,000 to 6,000 people in 1959–2003, an average of 111 to 133 executions per year in a nation with a current population of about 11 million. On this estimate, Cuba's average execution rate since the revolution that brought Castro to power is higher than Chinese execution rates after Mao died in 1976. Between 1999 and 2007, however, Cuba only executed three people (Grogg 2006), though the regime remains repressive in many other ways. Cuba has imprisoned dozens of journalists who published criticisms of the regime, and many Cubans are so afraid of being labeled critics that they are reluctant to utter Castro's name in public. Instead, "they silently pantomime stroking a beard when referring to their leader" ("Cuban Revolution" 2007).

25. Laos is also communist, and has been since the communist victory in Vietnam in 1975, but it has not had any judicial executions since 1989 and has not issued a death sentence since 1993 (Hood 2002:45,248; Hood and Hoyle 2008:88). There were purges of state and party leaders in Laos in 1979 and 1990, but they were not as bloody as those undertaken by other communist regimes in the region (Margolin 1999:576). The literature on Laos is too thin to permit confident conclusions about why Laotian communism seems less committed to capital punishment than the other communist regimes in the region, but the explanation may involve the strong influence of Theravada Buddhism in Lao society. In noncommunist Myanmar as well, the dominant role of Theravada Buddhism may help explain why this military regime of the right has not carried out any judicial executions since 1989 (Myint-U 2006; Hood and Hoyle 2008:88). For a general account of history, politics, and society in Laos, a nation of nearly six million people, see Brett Dakin's *Another Quiet American*, in which the author says he ultimately left the country because he "couldn't live in a place that people were always trying to escape from" (Dakin 2003:273).

All are long-standing, self-perpetuating governments that have been in power for at least half a century (Vietnam united in 1975, but the communists came to power in the north in 1954), and all make regular use of death as a criminal sanction. While North Korea is dependent and dysfunctional in many ways, and may even be well on the way to collapsing (Kaplan 2006; Lankov 2006), the PRC and Vietnam are developing rapidly and show few signs of governmental weakness or instability (SarDesai 2005; Pan 2008).

Hard-line communist states, like all authoritarian governments, are unfriendly to notions of limiting government power or extending personal liberty. This enthusiasm for state power is reflected in periods of high-rate state killing in both China (chapter 7) and Vietnam (appendix C). The affinity of communist governments for capital punishment is more a matter of practice than principle. Communist theory (which hopes for the withering away of the state) typically endorses the ultimate abolition of execution, and a rhetoric of eventual abolition is manifest in the PRC and Vietnam now as it was in the Soviet Union under Lenin and Stalin.[26] In practice, however, hard-line communist governments tend to use capital punishment aggressively, in many instances more aggressively than other authoritarian systems (Courtois et al. 1999).

But while all types of hard-line government tend to endorse capital punishment and resist limits on its application, the prospects for deeper change in Asian death penalty policy are closely tied to the behavior of communists in power because hard-line regimes of the right were reformed or significantly softened in the late 20th century. South Korea and Taiwan are the most notable examples, but significant steps toward democracy also have been taken in Thailand, Indonesia, Malaysia, and the Philippines. A similar softening of the communist regime in Laos may have occurred, but external pressures to effect regime change were necessary for the more dramatic shifts in Cambodia since the Khmer Rouge.

One critical question is what the impact would be of sustained economic growth for multiple decades, in the pattern of Taiwan and South Korea, on the authoritarian proclivities of a hard-line nation like China (Cohen 2005). We do not yet know but may find out in the not-too-distant future. China and Vietnam are both experiencing rapid economic development, and while both are still relatively early in the process, they may cross important developmental boundaries soon. The PRC already helps administer the wealthy regions of Hong Kong and Macao—without relying on capital punishment—and the CCP hopes and expects that the PRC's

26. Lenin considered capital punishment "an efficient weapon in the class struggle" but believed "the need for the death penalty would lapse" under genuine communism (Puhar 2003:57). In a widely read essay published in 1853, Karl Marx said that "the world has never allowed itself to be either reformed or deterred by the death penalty," though he also thought killing was a necessary part of the revolution (57).

"middle class" will expand to more than half of its total population by 2020, which would be an exponential increase from the 4–5 percent of the total population that could be called "middle class" in 2006 ("China Aims" 2007). It is possible that the same kinds of economic and social forces that broke down regimes of the authoritarian right might have similar effects in China and Vietnam. This seems more plausible as a description of the PRC's potential accommodation of citizen pressure—an adaptive softening of the regime—rather than as a forecast of a "people power" overthrow of the current government. A second possibility is that the democratization process in China will take longer and generate more costs and conflicts than similar processes have in other countries. Yet in some situations, the party-state's accommodation of citizens' challenges even reinforces its hold on power (Pan 2008). And a third possibility is that regime reaction to the push for democratization will stunt the social and economic changes now taking place, in which case the government might crack down (Gilley 2004). On this reading, China's rulers would prefer hard-line control to prosperity, a choice they did not have to make in the aftermath of Tiananmen Square.

Whatever the outcomes of the interactions between developmental pressures and communist governments, this aspect of Asia's present and future has no direct precedent in recent European history. If hard-line communist regimes such as China and Vietnam are as prone to democratic change through the steady pressure of development as the autocracies of the right were, this lesson will have to be learned in the years to come. Communist regimes may compromise on capital punishment without more general democratization—and by 2007 the PRC may already have initiated such a two-track approach—but such compromise seems likely to occur only if international concern about the death penalty in Asia intensifies, as it seemed to do in the period leading up to the 2008 Olympics in Beijing. Unless the major communist nations of Asia implode in the Soviet pattern, the future will test how hard-line communist states respond to the same dynamics that have already reshaped many other authoritarian governments in the region. This is a topic of defining importance to the future of the death penalty in the region, and we will revisit it in the last section of the next chapter.

■ Conclusion

First, a reminder of the empirical limits of this study. A comprehensive account of how the recent history of capital punishment in Asia compares to the records in other regions would require two kinds of data that are unavailable to us. The first is a more complete picture of Asia than could be assembled in this volume. The biggest missing pieces in the materials presented here are the nations of South Asia: India (see appendix F), Pakistan (see footnote 3 of this chapter), Bangladesh (Mash 2007), and Sri Lanka (Hood and Hoyle 2008:88).[27] Similarly, Indonesia (in Southeast Asia) deserves the same kind of case study attention we have given to the nations profiled in chapters 3 through 7.[28] We hope

27. Sri Lanka ceased judicial executions in 1976, but in 2004 President Chandrika Kumaratunga's government threatened to reactivate the nation's dormant death penalty for murder, rape, and drug trafficking. The precipitating event for this pronouncement was the murder of Judge Sarath Ambepitiya by a suspected drug gang in the capital city of Colombo (Wickramasinghe 2004). As of 2008, no executions had been carried out but death sentences continued to be imposed. Two of the most recent condemned men were sentenced to death for "grabbing a gold chain from a woman caught in the 2004 tsunami before letting her be swept to her death" (Hood and Hoyle 2008:88).

28. When Indonesia became independent from the Netherlands in 1950, there was no legal provision for capital punishment. The death penalty was introduced in subsequent years, but few judicial executions occurred before Suharto came to power in 1965. According to Amnesty International, 33 persons were executed in the 11 years between 1985 and 1995. Then there was a pause until 2001, when executions resumed (Hood and Hoyle 2008:95). When Indonesia executed Ayub Bulubili in April 2007 for murdering a family of six persons eight years earlier, it was the country's 14th reported execution since 1995 (Asia Death Penalty Blog, April 29, 2007). Over this 12-year period, Indonesia had an average annual execution rate of 0.005 executions per million. In the same period, Japan's execution rate (0.03) was six times higher. As Amnesty International's Kathryn Duff put it, Indonesia is "not typically an enthusiastic executioner" (quoted in Gelling 2008a).

But in 2008 there were several signs suggesting that Indonesia was beginning a Japan-like execution surge (see chapter 3), perhaps because President Susilo Bambang Yudhoyono was "under mounting pressure" to prove his "tough on crime" credentials with general elections less than a year away ("Indonesia Bucks" 2008), and perhaps because he wanted to deflect attention away from corruption scandals in his government (there were even proposals to impose capital punishment for some forms of corruption; see Khalik 2008; Michelmore 2008). Whatever the causes, in June 2008, on the International Day against Drug Abuse and Illicit Trafficking, Indonesia executed two Nigerian men for trafficking in heroin, and over the next three weeks there were four more executions—all of convicted murderers—in addition to a promise from the attorney general to execute three of the Bali bombers "as soon as possible" (Michelmore 2008). Following the June executions—Indonesia's first drug executions in four years—the attorney general also said that other executions might be accelerated. As of July 2008, 58 of Indonesia's 112 inmates on death row had been condemned for drug-related crimes, and seven of the 112 had exhausted all their appeals and were "expected to be executed soon" (Gelling 2008b). Four years before there had been 54 persons on death row—30 for drug trafficking—and 20 of the 22 foreigners on death row at that time had been sentenced to death for drug charges (Lynch 2008:41).

Executions in Indonesia are carried out by a firing squad of 12 people: six with live ammunition and six with blanks (Hands Off Cain 2006). "A single shot is fired from each rifle, carefully aimed at the chest. If that does not kill the prisoner, the commander will fire a point-blank shot to the head" ("Execution Plans" 2008; Gelling 2008b).

In 2007, Indonesia's Constitutional Court rejected an appeal by three Australian men and two Indonesian women, all condemned to death for drug trafficking, by a vote of 6 to 3. The court ruled that foreigners do not have legal standing to challenge the constitution, and it

our effort will inspire others to uncover more country-level detail about capital punishment in these and other neglected nations. We also hope that vital information now shrouded in government secrecy in places such as China, Vietnam, North Korea, and Singapore will be revealed in the near future. There is still much to be learned about the history and current practice of capital punishment in Asia that could enrich and modify the themes of this chapter. If some of our interpretations are proved wrong or nearsighted, we will still consider this project a success so long as it helps stimulate additional studies of the subject. They are sorely needed.

But Asia is hardly the only place where large gaps exist in our understanding of death penalty developments over time. A comprehensive history of the death penalty in Germany (Evans 1996), Radzinowicz's *History of English Criminal Law* (1948 and 1986), and a magnificent study of public executions in England (Gattrell 1994) seem to be the only 20th-century studies of capital punishment in Europe that examine more than recent decades, while Forst's (1999) account of the campaign for abolition in France covers the postwar story there (see also Badinter 2000). But little is known about the politics and administration of capital punishment in central and eastern Europe (Puhar 2003), the Baltic states, and Scandinavia, and studies are scant about the history of capital punishment and its abolition in Latin America, a region where the death penalty disappeared before economic development and political democratization were very far along (Hood 2002:55; Timmons 2005). A richer understanding of the 19th- and 20th-century histories in a wider variety of nations could reveal a great deal about how closely abolition is tied to political change and economic growth. More study also might illuminate other cases of transition away from capital punishment and generate comparative data on rates of execution in Latin America and central Europe before

---

rejected the Indonesians' appeal on the grounds that the right to life is not absolute but has to be balanced against the rights of persons victimized by drugs. According to the Ministry of Health, Indonesia's population of 238 million includes an estimated 18 million drug addicts—one person in every 13—and according to the National Narcotics Agency, there are 41 deaths in Indonesia every day due to drug overdose or drug-related HIV/AIDS (Lynch 2008:39). The Constitutional Court further averred that all existing death sentences should be carried out while also proposing a ten-year moratorium on executions (Lynch 2008:61). According to Professor Tim Lindsey of Melbourne University, this decision is "good news" for human rights in Indonesia because it is "a tentative step towards abolishing the death penalty" (quoted in Asia Death Penalty Blog, October 30, 2007). But President Yudhoyono, a "staunch supporter of the death penalty" since taking office in 2004, has said publicly that he "would not pardon drug offenders" (Gelling 2008b). As Lindsey (2008) has observed, "in most of South-East Asia drugs offences are, rightly or wrongly, often seen by authorities as being as bad as murder." For an analysis of Indonesia's use of the death penalty for drug-trafficking crimes, see Lynch (2008).

For an analysis of efforts to spread "international human rights" to Indonesia and the other nations of Southeast Asia, see Eldridge (2001). And for a book that sees parallels between law reform in Southeast Asia and the rest of the developing world, see Lindsey (2006).

abolition. One reason it is difficult to arrive at confident conclusions about the distinctiveness of Asia is the striking ignorance about capital punishment in so many other places. The more we learn about other regions, the clearer our vision will be of the aspects that make Asia similar and distinctive.

At this point in the comparative study of capital punishment, what sets Asia apart from western Europe of the 1950s is first and foremost the much greater variety of political and economic circumstances. Only one Asian nation (Japan) maintains a death penalty in circumstances where European experience would predict abolition, and that seeming anomaly is at least partly a function of the LDP's right-of-center hegemony for the past half century. In all of the other large or most developed Asian societies, the direction of political change and of death penalty policy seems consistent with Western patterns, though it is moving more slowly and is less closely linked to transnational organizations and influences. In the years to come, the great variety of Asian political situations and Asia's rapidly developing but still authoritarian governments will provide clearer clues about the circumstances in which development pushes toward plural democracy, human rights, limits on government, and abolition of capital punishment. To paraphrase a proverb, the citizens of Asia's rapidly developing nations are living in interesting times.

9

The Pace of Change

By some measures, Asia is as far removed from the goal of abolishing capital punishment as any region on earth. While the number of executing nations has dropped, the number of executions in the region is far larger than anywhere else, and this is not solely the product of Strike Hard campaigns in the PRC. At present, three or four of the world's top seven or eight execution rates are in Asia—China, Singapore, Vietnam, and probably North Korea— and Japan, the region's most developed nation, is one of the world's two wealthy democracies that still executes consistently. An impartial observer might be justified in concluding that contemporary Asia is separated from the abolition of capital punishment by several major changes in policy throughout the continent and by a substantial period of time. Much needs to happen before Asia becomes what the Europeans call "an execution-free zone," and many of the necessary changes will require substantial gestation periods. Nonetheless, our outlook for the future is like that of Robert Badinter, the former justice minister of France, who believes the most formidable obstacle to abolition in the world is "the Islamic countries, especially the regimes run by fundamentalists," not the nations of Asia ("Death Penalty: Dialogue" 2007).

There are three indications that the abolition of death as a criminal punishment is a possible feature of Asia's future. The first is the substantial downward trend in both the number of executions and the social reputation of capital punishment in the region. Executions have been declining in most of Asia for a long time, and current events strongly suggest that China is joining this downturn in a significant way. With the possible exception of Singapore, the reputation of state executions in Asia is not good, and even in Singapore the execution total for 2005–2007 (13) was less than one-tenth the total for 1995–1997 (138). Any government with aspirations to exert human rights leadership recognizes that it must try to avoid executions. More generally, most governments now recognize that high rates of execution are an obstacle to being regarded as "decent" by the rest of the world (Bae 2007). This recognition is one of the main reasons Asia's most aggressive executing states—China, Singapore, Vietnam, and North Korea—release so little information about the reality of capital punishment in their jurisdictions. In December 2007, when the UN General Assembly adopted a resolution calling for a worldwide moratorium on the death penalty with a view toward abolishing it, one of those four nations—Vietnam—even abstained rather than opposed the resolution.

The second sign that state execution faces long-term difficulties is the widespread ambition in Asia for economic development and democratic politics. With few exceptions, what citizens in Asia seem to want is the prosperity and freedom they see in rich democracies, and many governments in the region, including authoritarian ones, endorse such sentiments. Even China's long-term goals include aspects of participatory democracy, although the long term turns out to be very long indeed in some scenarios. The economic and political ambitions in Asia cast a shadow over executions because of the authoritarian ethos that pervades state killing, notwithstanding high levels of popular support for some form of capital punishment. With the important exception of the United States, the kind of government most Asian citizens desire has not been well disposed toward executions for half a century.

The third reason to expect a continued decline of capital punishment in Asia is the widespread agreement on the ultimate demise of the death penalty as a goal of political development in many nations. Chinese prosecutors reassure Western advocates of abolition by contrasting the long-term desirability of an execution-free criminal law with the short-term needs they say make execution a necessary but temporary evil. The distinction between the needs of the present and a nonspecified future without executions can function as a rhetoric of permanent deferral, but even when it does, this way of framing the issue makes important concessions of principle to the abolitionist agenda. Almost everywhere in Asia, the moral high ground has been ceded to those who want to end the death penalty, and this fact will have long-run implications.

On current evidence, the abolition of capital punishment in Asia is not a question of whether but of when, and the critical issues seem to concern the pace and processes of change rather than the direction changes will take or their eventual end point. That said, a large margin of error accompanies efforts to guess how quickly Asian capital punishment will change. Should we think in terms of a few years, a few decades, or a few centuries? What are the leading indicators of the cessation of executions? And what contingencies could slow the process? These are the central concerns of this concluding chapter.

■ Organizing the Future

Several options are available for organizing a presentation on the future developments of Asian death penalty policy, and when choosing between them one must make substantive judgments about future trends. One example of this linkage between the substantive and the organizational serves as an introduction to the path we selected.

The most obvious way to organize the future is by subdividing the endless hereafter into more manageable temporal components, beginning with a discussion of likely developments in the short run, then peering more deeply into a crystal ball in order to make predictions about more distant possibilities. Since some trends are cyclical, it is often necessary to distinguish predictions for the short and long range. In a book about capital punishment in the United States, Zimring and Hawkins (1986:149) felt compelled to distinguish between short-term futures in which executions would probably increase and a longer term in which executions would decline. This up-then-down forecast was confirmed by an increase in executions that culminated in a 1999 peak, followed by an eight-year decline that has continued to the present. When different eras seem likely to produce contrasting policies, separate accounts of the short and long terms are necessary.

In this chapter, we decided *not* to divide the future into periods, for two main reasons. First, there is no discontinuity in trends on Asia's death penalty horizon for as far as we can see. An immediate increase was easy to predict for the United States of 1986, and its subsequent reversal was plausible if not foregone conclusion. The Asian trend of the last 15 years is a decline in the prevalence of execution and in the incidence of execution after the PRC reached its peak rate during this recent period. We believe the future of Asian death penalty policy will be a continuous but uneven process of decline. How long the road will be until abolition is achieved is not known, but at present there is no reason to suppose future events will produce major reversals in policy direction. We also acknowledge that "Black Swans"—events that lie outside the realm of regular expectations and have extreme impact but are prospectively unpredictable—often shape human history in profound ways, and could do so in the future of capital punishment too (Taleb 2007).

The second argument against dividing this discussion of Asia into short- and long-term futures is the uncertainty and margin of error in defining the boundary between near and far when facing forward. Is 2018 the long term or the short term in societies as dynamic as Taiwan and South Korea? And if China's middle class expands tenfold in the next 12 years (as the CCP predicts), should that be considered a long-term development ("China Aims" 2007)? These questions require a more specific context and content: are we asking about population, politics, or women's status? Yet even then, dividing the future into the short and long terms invites arbitrary and erroneous judgments. Population patterns change so gradually that the demographic "long term" can last a generation or more, while politics can evolve much more quickly. For death penalty policy, where is the line between sooner and later?

When reversals of direction can be anticipated, the guessing game about the timing of turning points becomes a necessary part of thinking about the future. In the United States of the 1980s, one had to decide whether the execution peak was one or three decades away. But if we are correct to assume continuity in Asian trends, then predicting turning points is unnecessary because the turnaround has already occurred. There may be differences from country to country in the pace of change, and there will be periods when change accelerates or slows down, but the future trajectory for Asia has been established. In this important sense, the long term has already started for Asia's death penalty policy.

Our belief that the long term has already begun contradicts the assumption of those Chinese officials who reassure visitors that in the long term their government will abolish capital punishment. The utopian future they imagine is as far removed from the Chinese present as an active imagination can make it, for it is a future without crime, poverty, or discord. The rhetorical point of situating abolition in this long-term perspective is to protect present practices from criticism. From this perspective, the notion that Asia has already embarked on its long-term future may be frightening to those who prosper in the present.

This chapter organizes the potential influences on Asian death penalty policy into three categories. First, we examine some of the forces that are likely to come from outside Asia. Second, we discuss the types of influence that could come from within the region, both from regional organizations and from the example and influence of specific Asian nations. Third, we explore national-level influences: the political, social, economic, and legal changes within individual Asian nations that will shape the pace of change. The power to determine death penalty policy seems likely to remain a national prerogative for some time to come, and the most powerful influences on national policy will probably remain within national boundaries for as long as the present distribution of decision-making authority lasts. Thus, the national-level influences are likely to be especially important even though the range of potentially significant factors is great and the processes of influence on death penalty policy are frequently subtle.

■ External Influences

The influences least directly connected to capital punishment in Asia are those that come from outside the region. Four factors in the broader community of nations will affect the pace of change of Asian death penalty policy: (1) the intensity of international concern with human rights and criminal justice issues; (2) the changing status of capital punishment in non-Asian nations that have influence in Asia; (3) the importance of Asian capital punishment to non-Asian nations and international organizations; and (4) the degree to which death penalty issues influence international security and law enforcement coordination in matters of concern to Asian nations.

Human rights issues have become a high-priority concern for developed nations and international organizations only in the past quarter century. One question is whether this increased concern will continue and intensify in the years to come. The prospects seem good for stable or increased levels of interest in human rights and criminal justice, for a variety of reasons (Hunt 2007:213). First, the amount of information about foreign practices has increased dramatically over the past decade, and the interest of citizens in developed nations in the politics and living conditions of other nations has kept pace with the information boom. The earth is a smaller planet in 2008 than it was in 1993, and this shrinkage has produced much higher interest in foreign conditions than there was in earlier eras (Nelson and Dorsey 2008). In addition, there is now an institutional structure of NGOs that focus on human rights issues and depend on public and governmental attention to help define them as problematic. These groups all but guarantee sustained attention on human rights in the years to come. Indeed, some such groups show signs of permanent prominence in the public life of developed nations (Keck and Sikkink 1998; Nelson and Dorsey 2008). In these circumstances, our conservative expectation is for continued activity in western European nations, together with increased emphasis on human rights in developing nations such as Mexico and Brazil.

If levels of national concern stay high in developed and developing nations, then international organizations' level of involvement in human rights and criminal justice issues is likely to increase. Transnational organizations such as the UN sometimes lag behind developed nations and NGOs in their attention to human rights, in part because UN-like organizations serve the interests of member nations. But since the staying power of human rights interest groups generates pressure on international organizations to create credible human rights programs, greater concern in these transnational organizations seems all but inevitable. The clash of human rights interest groups with national claims to sovereignty will likely inhibit the emergence of powerful regulatory structures in the UN and in regional organizations outside Asia, but informal standards and transnational publicity about problematic practices in individual Asian nations have already emerged as influential tools for some international organizations. Moral principles alone seldom determine political behavior in Asia or anyplace else, but most of the governments in Asia care about both the material consequences of their behavior and what has been called the "logic of appropriateness" of their activities (Bae 2007:126).

Since any increase in concern for general human rights will almost certainly translate into increased attention to death penalty practices, one important indicator of the status of capital punishment in Asia will be the level of human rights consciousness in international organizations and in Western and third-world nations outside the region. At the same time, many other factors will influence the status of capital punishment and the importance of death penalty concerns in the international community. If the number of abolitionist jurisdictions increases in Africa, the Americas, and the Middle East, there will be added pressure on executing nations in Asia to join the trend. It is less certain whether the international anti–death penalty movement will accelerate even more than it has since the 1980s (Hood 2001:339). In assessing the future pressure that could come from further expansion in the number of nonexecuting nations, much depends on the intensity of support for abolition and on the priority that recently converted nations attach to the international campaign against capital punishment.

The example of the United States "paves the way for the use of capital punishment in many parts of the world" (Anckar 2004:58), and the changing status of the death penalty in the United States could significantly influence Asia. If U.S. executions continue to decline, and if individual states continue their hold on executions or even withdraw death penalty legislation in the future—as New Jersey did in 2007 and as other states have indicated they might—then the diminished enthusiasm in the U.S. setting will provide less support for Asian governments of the right (such as Japan and Singapore) that respect the United States.[1] On the other hand, a sharp increase in U.S. executions would provide a defense for Asian nations against European-inspired criticism and stigma. In either event, the expansion of conflict over capital punishment in the United States seems easier to foresee than the impact of that conflict on executions in America and abroad. Whoever takes office as president in 2009 seems unlikely to provide the same support for executions as the second Bush presidency has, but the right-wing appointments made to the Supreme Court by recent Republican presidents have made it more difficult for court-based arguments to restrict capital punishment (Toobin 2007). In this respect, the future of death penalty policy in the world depends on not only the future of capital punishment in the United States but also the views of "a few hand-picked jurists" in that nation (Anckar 2004:178).

The United States and the European Union are the usual suspects in Asian discussions of foreign influence, but another factor that could heighten the importance of executions on the international agenda would be greater attention to death penalty issues in third-world nations such as South Africa, Brazil, and Mexico. In these three countries, the death penalty has been retired for some time. South Africa became the new kid on the block when it abolished in

---

1. The United States conducted 42 executions in 2007, compared with a post-1951 peak of 98 executions in 1999. Twenty-six of the executions (62 percent) occurred in Texas, and no other state executed more than three people. Some analysts believe "the day is not far off when essentially all executions in the United States will take place in Texas" (Liptak 2007), but we think that is an unlikely prospect. Death sentences in the United States also have dropped, from almost 300 in 1998 to about 110 in 2007.

1995 (Bae 2007:41), Mexico has not conducted judicial executions since 1930 (Timmons 2005), and Brazil has had none since 1855 (Hood and Hoyle 2008:409)—yet their governments have not been significant players in international anti–death penalty activism.[2] If the core constituency of anti–death penalty nations diversifies to include third-world countries without substantial colonial histories, then the breadth of the campaign will change in ways that could affect Asian nations such as India and Thailand. And if Turkey, a more recent and less voluntary convert to abolition, gets involved in the international campaign against capital punishment, the Islamic credentials of its new government might carry special weight in Muslim-majority nations such as Indonesia, Malaysia, Pakistan, and Bangladesh. In these ways, one innovation of the near future could be a broadening of the base and a diversifying of the constituency for abolition in the international community.

A third significant influence of non-Asian policy on Asian death penalty matters could be the extent to which Asian practices become a higher priority in Western and third-world death penalty campaigns. In the 1990s, a main priority of the Council of Europe and the European Union was the elimination of capital punishment from European soil, and their secondary target was executions in the United States. The Europeans' success on their home turf has left death penalty activists with energy and resources for other geographic zones. If death penalty issues continue to command the interest that was evident at the turn of the 21st century, then more of the missionary vigor of European activists will get directed at countries in Asia. Two Asian death penalty stories have already generated considerable attention in Europe and the Commonwealth: Japan became the first Asian target for the Council of Europe because of its status as Asia's most developed democracy, and then China became a target of the European Union because of its huge volume of executions and its increasing economic and geopolitical clout. And in 2007, Amnesty International conducted a special campaign to eliminate capital punishment in South Korea.

There may also be some spillover of interest in Asian capital punishment from European concerns about political repression in Myanmar, instability in Thailand, and authoritarian development in Vietnam (Zin 2008; appendixes C and D). To the extent that European concern for capital punishment is produced by distrust of state power, interest in Asian death penalty issues will remain a natural extension of the interest in placing limits on autocratic governments and on encouraging democratic discourse. Increased interest in Asia can be expected from Europe and Scandinavia, but whether third-world nations will focus more attention on Asia is less certain, though their actions may help determine whether international organizations become more active in monitoring and evaluating the death penalty policy of Asian nations.

---

2. Mexican officials have lobbied and lectured American governments about the need to end the death penalty. In 2002, for example, President Vicente Fox canceled a visit to President George W. Bush's ranch because Texas had executed a Mexican national, Javier Suarez Medina (Timmons 2005).

There are two different ways that "spillover" effects could generate greater outside attention to Asian capital punishment: the case-specific, and the general. A case-specific suspicion of capital punishment focuses attention on the issue when there is evidence that political dissidents, repressed minorities, or foreigners have been subject to capital sanctions in a particular country. Concerns about the political and repressive uses of capital punishment have been directed at North Korea, Vietnam, and China, but since these forms of state killing frequently do not involve criminal adjudication or judicial sentencing (as may be the case with executions of members of Falun Gong in the PRC), critiques are customarily framed in terms of human rights rather than capital punishment (Matas and Kilgour 2007). Case-specific criticisms of capital punishment most commonly occur when citizens of an abolitionist country are subject to the capital process in a state that uses execution. Vietnam responded with leniency to several appeals for clemency from foreign governments, but the execution of Canadian citizen Nguyen Thi Hiep by firing squad in 1999, despite persistent protests from Canadian officials, sparked a major diplomatic rift between the two nations. In comparison, Singapore takes a firmer position against foreign appeals for mercy, as it did when the Philippines unsuccessfully tried to save condemned domestic worker Flor Contemplacion in 1995, and again in 2005 when it rejected Australia's pleas for clemency in the case of convicted heroin trafficker Nguyen Tuong Van. (Singapore did extend the condemned Australian several special privileges before he was hanged, including access to family members and reporters, that other persons on death row are denied).

A more general "spillover" occurs when outside observers are suspicious of a repressive regime's death penalty process even when there are no indications that dissidents, minorities, or foreigners are being executed. In this pattern, problems in the PRC (such as the attacks at Tiananmen Square or the suppression of Falun Gong faithful) create distrust of execution even though the objects of execution are different types of people. Having determined that a government abuses power, there is no appetite for capital punishment because it is believed to produce—inevitably—its own forms of abuse.

This broader incubator of death penalty opposition seems a more likely basis for generating concern about capital punishment in Asia. Once attention and distrust are directed at other problems in the region, state execution can become an important target even if it is somewhat removed from the arena of governmental activity that originally produced the concern. Particularly in places where the death penalty itself has been stigmatized as an abuse of human rights, evidence of regime abuse that stops well short of political execution can still excite the interest of outside observers. And where secrecy about capital punishment is the rule (as in China and Vietnam), there is ample justification for skepticism and distrust. In this way, one by-product of external concern with capital punishment in Asia may be greater pressure toward disclosure and accountability in its administration.

International Practicalities

In 2007, when Rwanda became the 100th nation to abolish capital punishment, the announced reason for abandoning state killing illustrated another way the security and cooperation imperatives that emerge from living on a smaller planet could involve non-Asian nations in Asian death penalty policy. The existence of the death penalty in Rwanda conflicted with the rules of the International Criminal Court and the European Union that forbid turning over persons in their custody to a criminal process in which execution is a possibility. Abolition of a domestic death penalty was therefore deemed necessary in order for Rwanda to obtain the return of a large group of defendants in one of the 20th century's worst genocides. A series of low-tech slaughters—performed mainly with machetes—had been carried out with frightening speed in the spring and early summer of 1994. Of an original population of 7.5 million, at least 800,000 people were killed in just 100 days, meaning "the dead of Rwanda accumulated at nearly three times the rate of Jewish dead during the Holocaust" (Gourevitch 1998:3). A massacre of this magnitude would seem to be a powerful motive for retaining capital punishment, but in the context of the movement toward international prohibition, the death penalty actually became an impediment to closing the books on Rwanda's national nightmare.

Several problems involving security and law enforcement cross national and regional boundaries. Depending on how other nations regard state execution, the presence of the death penalty in a nation requesting criminal justice assistance may produce a number of disabilities. The narrowest restriction a domestic death penalty generates is the requirement that a nation requesting extradition of a criminal suspect provide credible assurance to the rendering organization or nation that capital punishment will not result from the custodial transfer. This requirement is increasingly common in country-to-country extradition negotiations and protocols, and it has prevented the return of numerous offenders to their countries of origin, including China's "most wanted man," the "outlaw entrepreneur" Lai Changxing, who fled to Canada in 1999 after Chinese officials decided they could no longer turn a blind eye to his smuggling operations or the bribes he paid to facilitate a multitude of "nearly legal" enterprises (August 2007). A related requirement is that the transfer of a suspect can only take place if the legal charges involved will not result in capital punishment. Further, some nations refuse to provide evidence or investigative information to other countries if the requesting nation might use it to seek a death sentence. This happened in the case of Zacarias Moussaoui, the French national of Moroccan descent who was charged with being an active conspirator in the attacks of September 11, 2001. The French government refused to grant a request for investigative files and information on the defendant unless the U.S. government agreed not to seek a death penalty (Zimring 2003:43).

In addition to country-to-country relationships in which the death penalty is an obstacle to cooperation, international organizations that only share information with associated members or that impose minimum standards on nations that qualify for assistance may disapprove of the death penalty and thus restrict the access of those nations who retain it. To date, the restrictions imposed by nations and international organizations have been linked to extradition or cooperation in capital prosecution rather than to more general refusals to cooperate with nations that use execution. But there also are indications that international cooperation is becoming more important to the security needs of some nations at the same time that the pressures to impose human rights standards (which may forbid capital punishment) are increasing.

Crime prevention and control have more prominent multinational dimensions in an era of accelerating globalization. Terrorism, transnational drug trafficking, counterfeiting, and fraud are all increasingly international phenomena in the 21st century, and transnational cooperation is increasingly required to identify criminal suspects and make them available to the nations where their victims reside. Police authorities in numerous countries may have information on multinational fraud, terror, or drug enterprises, and offenders with passports or computers or both can be part of the crime problem in several places simultaneously. These aspects of globalization will increase the number and scale of law enforcement problems that cross national borders and will heighten the importance of international cooperation.

But in some developed nations, concern about governmental abuse of human rights has been growing almost as quickly as the need for transnational law enforcement and cooperation in extradition. We live in the era not only of the "war on terror" but also of Human Rights Watch, Amnesty International, and Doctors without Borders. As long as a large number of powerful nations retained capital punishment, international agencies and organizations were reluctant to offend those important constituents. But the growing number of abolitionist nations and of nations nearing abolition seems to be bringing international bodies closer to a tipping point. In sheer numbers, something close to that might be on the horizon were it not for the extraordinary influence of the United States. Yet if 25 more nations can be added to the abolitionist category in the next 15 years, organizational pressures to exclude death penalty states from credentialed participation will become substantial.[3]

In sum, two trends may converge sometime soon: the increasing need for cooperation in international law enforcement, and the increasing stigma associated with capital punishment in many regions of the world. The impact of this convergence on death penalty policies in Asian nations would be

---

3. Even taking into account the shrinking pool of retentionist nations that could still convert, this scenario is plausible. Compared with a global total of 20 "completely abolitionist" nations in 1980, there were 91 in 2008—an increase of 71 nations in 28 years (Zimring 2003:35; Amnesty International reports for various years). By Amnesty's count, only 63 of the world's 197 countries retained capital punishment in 2007, and only 24 of them—one nation in eight—carried out executions in that year.

indirect, but it would also be important, even if the precise effects are difficult to discern. In 2007, Rwanda was an exceptional situation in one respect but also typical of nations willing to respond to sanctions and incentives (Bae 2007:23). What set Rwanda apart was the huge stake it had in obtaining help from the International Criminal Court, which had jurisdiction in this case over a bumper crop of 57 criminal defendants. What was typical was the nation's soft commitment to capital punishment. Domestic genocide prosecutions had produced 22 death sentences and executions in 1998, yet this was not an experience Rwanda's government was eager to repeat. Instead, the need to obtain suspects from the International Criminal Court functioned as the justification to do what the government was willing to do anyway, as is indicated by its decision to formally end the death penalty rather than just guarantee no capital sentences for the 57 defendants.

It is reasonable to suppose that the practical problems international organizations might impose on death penalty nations would have greatest influence on Asian states without a strong commitment to capital punishment and on those where domestic policies generate substantial ambivalence. As discussed in chapter 8, India, Indonesia, and Thailand seem to be cases of inertial retention of capital punishment, and in places such as these the practical consequences of retention might be perceived as sufficiently negative to warrant reconsideration of some death penalty policies. But where the national commitment to use execution is stronger, the practical problems that arise from international sanctions can create a boomerang effect if the sanctioned nation resents the threat to autonomy implied by the pressure. Singapore and China sometimes seem to recoil in this way, and even a low-execution-rate nation such as Japan, with its strong symbolic attachment to execution as an expression of state power, could forcefully oppose execution-based sanctions, especially if they are perceived to be a manifestation of inappropriate meddling in the nation's domestic affairs.

One final irony about the politics of capital punishment in what has been called the "age of terrorism" concerns the way changing international standards can influence law enforcement needs. In domestic politics, the fear of transnational terrorism frequently generates a powerful appeal for greater state power over individual life and for fewer limits on governmental action (Zimring 2008). "Antiterrorism" is thus a context in which government power tends to expand. But when there is a shift from national to international enforcement activities, the need for minimum human rights guarantees can restrict the range of control activities by individual states. In this way, international standards can become a sign of the stigma now associated with capital punishment.

■ Regional Influences

Of the three framing categories employed in this chapter, that of the regional influences within Asia has the weakest historical justification. Many parts of

Asia have had social and cultural interactions that go back centuries, and not long ago large parts of the region were under the military and political control of Japan (Kang 2007). But most of the contemporary determinants of death penalty policy turn out to be national in origin, and the variations among nations in institutions such as courts, prosecution, and justice ministries now seem more important than their overlapping ancestries. At the same time, there are few regional organizations in contemporary Asia to parallel the institutions that have existed for decades in Europe (Bae 2007:113).

Nonetheless, there are economic and political interactions in various parts of Asia that create not only regional similarities in situation and orientation but also self-conscious comparisons to other nations in the region. Most of the nations of Asia feel closer to each other than to nations elsewhere, and these identity and reference group phenomena extend to political matters as well as economic ones. There is also a growing awareness of shared interests in the region as the result of transnational events such as the financial crisis of 1997 (Studwell 2007:125) and the tsunami of 2004 (Kalis and Brooke 2005). For many nations in Asia, common identities and interests often seem to outweigh historical animosities (Kang 2007). Whether the comparisons each nation makes to its neighbors are primarily cooperative or competitive may not be as important as the importance Asian nations attach to the policies of their peers. But it would be easy to overstate the foundations for common action in contemporary Asia. There are big political differences between systems of government among the region's major powers—contrast Japan, China, and India—and there are ongoing conflicts (as between India and Pakistan) that inhibit the willingness to cede some autonomy to transnational entities (Emmott 2008). Still, the nations of Asia do measure their policies and achievements against each other, and in many areas they are more concerned with the policies and status of their Asian neighbors than with nations in other regions.

The two major influences discussed in this section are the impact of domestic death penalty changes on the perceptions and ambitions of other Asian nations, and the potential for loose associations of governments in the region to direct soft power at downsizing death as a criminal punishment and at raising expectations for procedural protections in capital cases.

The first major development that could alter the dynamics of capital punishment in Asia is the formal abolition of the death penalty by a government with leadership status in the region. Only a small number of Asian nations are credible candidates for this status, and none of them has yet abolished completely.

Formal abolition by a nation with first-echelon leadership status in Asia could create substantial shifts in the regional ecology of capital punishment. We count three to five such nations in East Asia—Japan, South Korea, and the PRC for sure, and perhaps Thailand and Vietnam as well—and two more possibilities in South Asia: India and Indonesia. After briefly describing our criteria for this classification, we will discuss how formal abolition among the leadership nations might change the dynamics of death penalty policy in other Asian places.

Japan is an obvious candidate for leadership status in Asia in every way: population, economic and political development, education, status (including respectful enmity), and a history of exercising power in the region. After several decades of "economy first" politics following its surrender in the Pacific war, Japan is also experiencing a significant resurgence of power and purpose (Pyle 2007; Samuels 2007) while at the same time starting to shed its "traditional indifference" to other nations in the region (Fackler 2008). The PRC is another noncontroversial candidate for leadership because of its huge aggregate economic, military, and political power and its rapid recent development (Shambaugh 2005). After millennia of influence in a wide variety of cultural, institutional, and linguistic spheres, China's status in Asia is also high (Kang 2007). South Korea has less than half the population of the Philippines but substantial cultural, media, and symbolic influence in the region in addition to democratic political institutions, a vibrant civil society, and the ambition to be a major player in international relations (Borland and Kanellos 2004; Choe 2007b).[4]

Thailand has 50 percent more people than South Korea, but it has been chronically unstable, with frequent coups and no fewer than 17 constitutions in the last 75 years (ten of them since 1972). Although its status in Asia is generally positive, it is well below that of South Korea. Vietnam is twice the size of South Korea and possesses substantial military power, yet despite its PRC-like pace of economic development in recent years, it remains a nation run by an authoritarian regime that lags well behind the first tier of Asian governments in external esteem. To the south, India and Indonesia are both large nations with substantial but uneven rates of development. They are regarded as powerful but are not accorded the same status the Japanese enjoy or the Koreans covet and are close to achieving. Even China's status in the region is considerably higher than India's, despite the latter's superior democratic and technological credentials (Meredith 2007).

Finally, we do not consider Taiwan a credible candidate for leadership in Asia for two main reasons: it is small, and it has failed to attain recognition as an independent entity by most Asian governments. Although Taiwan is a striking example of the movement away from authoritarian politics and frequent execution, it does not possess sufficient status in Asia to inspire emulation, and it seems unlikely to acquire that standing anytime soon.

---

4. South Korea, once one of Asia's most rigidly patriarchal societies, recently became the first country in the region with a large sex imbalance to reverse the trend toward "too many boys." In 1990, 116.5 boys were born for every 100 girls, but by 2006 the ratio had declined to 107.4 to 100. China and India also have large sex imbalances (largely from the selective abortion of female fetuses), and both are "closely studying South Korea as a trendsetter" in order to learn how a similar turnaround can be accomplished in their own societies (Choe 2007d; see also Hudson and den Boer 2005).

This focus on leadership potential in Asia is necessary because the paucity of death penalty discourse among governments in the region results in part from the absence of an Asian nation that combines leadership status with a commitment to ending capital punishment. While none of the five to seven leadership nations has abolished the death penalty so far, only China and Vietnam remain far removed from that end. Our case studies and appendixes discuss the prospects of policy change in all of these nations except Indonesia. An exemplary abolition would be a prod to other Asian nations that regard it as a peer even if the leading nation made no deliberate attempt to direct capital punishment claims at other countries. This is frequently "how claims spread" cross-nationally (Best 2001). By abolishing the death penalty, for example, South Korea could have immediate influence on Taiwan (which harbors similar ambitions), while at the same time putting pressure on Japan and providing talking points for inertial retentionist nations such as Thailand, India, and Indonesia.[5] A South Korean or Japanese abolition would also be considered an inconvenience or even an embarrassment to the "Asian values" rhetoric that is used to justify high levels of execution in Singapore. Exemplary abolition in Asia also would put greater pressure on China to reduce executions, develop the rule of law, and make the processes that govern capital cases more transparent. All of these changes could occur simply as the result of the emergence of a national leader and without the generation of European-like death penalty discussions at the regional level in Asia's own transnational organizations. If a national leader does emerge, changes in capital punishment policy elsewhere in the region could happen in a hurry, for "nothing spurs adoption of new ideas like other actors doing the same" (Sherman 2004:91; see also Gladwell 2000).

Organizations

There are a great variety of regional and subregional organizations in Asia that have interests in economic, political, and social conditions in member countries, including ASEAN, which is composed of Brunei, Cambodia, Indonesia, Laos, Malaysia, Myanmar, the Philippines, Singapore, Thailand, and Vietnam; ASEAN Plus Three, which adds the East Asian nations of China, Japan, and South Korea to the ASEAN club; East Asia Summit, which includes

5. South Korea has leadership aspirations in Asia, and its leaders frequently use comparison with Japan to measure how it is doing. In a New Year's speech in 2008, for example, president-elect Lee Myung Bak announced the goal to "overtake Japan within ten years" (Kim 2008), an objective that may be realistic in some respects. According to International Monetary Fund data, GDP per capita (at current prices) grew 51.3 percent in South Korea in 1996–2006 while shrinking in Japan by 1.47 percent (Arudou 2007). On the other hand, Japan's population is more than 2.5 times larger than South Korea's (127 million vs. 49 million), its per capita income is still about one-third higher ($33,100 vs. $24,500), and its sense of "power and purpose" in foreign affairs seems to be rising (Pyle 2007; Samuels 2007).

the previous 13 nations in addition to India, Australia, and New Zealand; and Asia-Pacific Economic Cooperation (APEC), the oldest such forum and generally recognized as the highest-level multilateral process in the region (Chu 2007). But APEC is "fundamentally an economic dialogue body," and though it has focused more on security issues such as counterterrorism in recent years, "its potential for becoming a workable economic, political, or security mechanism which can create tangible results is slight" (Chu 2007). More generally, there is no tradition of centralization in Asia or in any of its subregions that can generate collective authority on issues regarded as important to sovereign nations. Even when regional organizations in Asia act, it is the collective opinion of the nations behind their actions rather than the authority of the organization that carries the potential for influence. When ASEAN communicated concern about Myanmar's repression of demonstrations in the fall of 2007, the protest was deemed significant only to the extent that individual members of the organization expressed disapproval. There was little evidence that the organizational whole was greater than the sum of its parts, and the collective expression of concern sent only a weak signal to a repressive government that was operating in the region with near impunity ("ASEAN's Broken Heart" 2007). Might a more powerful organized response play a larger role in Asian death penalty policy in the future?

At present, the prospects for a more active role in death penalty matters are as limited by the lack of consensus on capital punishment as by the lack of strong transnational organizations. The nations of ASEAN include five that are abolitionist in law or practice (Cambodia, the Philippines, Brunei Darussalam, Laos, and Myanmar), five with active death penalties (Indonesia, Malaysia, Thailand, Singapore, and Vietnam), and two (Singapore and Vietnam) with high rates of execution. Under such circumstances, generating a substantive stance against capital punishment seems highly unlikely.[6] What is more, ASEAN has a tradition of "much talk and little action" on a wide variety of issues (Studwell 2007:193). When the organization created a new charter on its 40th anniversary in 2007, it was intended to push the region toward more complete integration and coherence, but the final product actually "falls considerably short of that ambitious design," especially on human rights issues ("ASEAN's Broken Heart" 2007).[7]

6. The organization ASEAN Plus Three is even more diverse than ASEAN, and "its future direction is not very clear" (Chu 2007). The East Asia Summit adds the democracies of India, Australia, and New Zealand to the 13 countries of ASEAN Plus Three, and so may be more motivated to engage political issues such as capital punishment, but currently it serves "merely as a 'forum' for 'dialogue'" (Chu 2007). If it maintains that function in the years to come, "it will not develop into anything more than just a 'talk shop'" and "will be neither as productive as ASEAN Plus Three nor as prestigious as APEC" (Chu 2007).

7. The new charter of ASEAN does call for the promotion and protection of human rights, but that admonition is qualified by the need to do so "with due regard to the rights

There are, however, some aspects of death penalty policy that could produce consensus in Asian transnational organizations. In the capital punishment portfolio, the closest issue to the political repression that provoked ASEAN comment about Myanmar is the execution of dissidents or political prisoners, a practice strongly disapproved of by most governments in the region. Should an outlier nation like North Korea be suspected of political killings, the nations with an interest in human rights might raise the matter as a potential consensus issue. For similar reasons, procedural guarantees such as the right to trial counsel and to appeal in a capital case could create enough agreement between death penalty and non–death penalty jurisdictions to produce meaningful action.

The special protection of political activity from capital punishment does have precedent. The American Convention on Human Rights, for example, contains this prohibition: "In no case shall capital punishment be inflicted for political offenses or related common crimes" (1144 U.N.T.S. 123 O.A.St. no. 36). This proscription could serve as a model for protection against political executions in Asia as well.

Organizations with worldwide memberships that include Asian nations may have stronger incentives to involve themselves in Asian death penalty issues and to provoke action from Asian members. When Western observers stress the importance of China fully committing itself to the UN Covenant on Civil and Political Rights, it is partly to assert that China, as a ratifying nation, has a symbolic commitment to compliance, but it also helps produce a standard against which outside observers can judge China's performance (Cohen 2007c). Asian branches of the UN and UNESCO might then be drawn into concern about the procedural commitments made to the covenant. In this way, some global organizations could get involved in death penalty matters before indigenous Asian organizations do, and before the emergence of the substantive consensus that would be necessary to substantially limit capital punishment in the region.

After 15 years of anti–death penalty campaigning at the UN and repeated failures to pass similar resolutions, this is what happened in 2007, when the UN General Assembly adopted a nonbinding resolution calling for a worldwide moratorium on capital punishment with a view toward abolishing it. The final vote was 104 nations in favor with 54 opposed and 29 abstentions, thus confirming how the arithmetic of international sentiment on capital punishment has changed since the 1980s. Massimo D-Alema, deputy prime minister and minister of foreign affairs of Italy—the nation that led the moratorium

and responsibilities of the member states" of the organization. "Noninterference" in the affairs of member states is also mentioned before other principles such as democracy, the rule of law, and constitutional governance (Lynch 2008). On the whole, the new charter is not a bold step forward in the European fashion; it is merely "the codification of existing norms" ("ASEAN's Broken Heart" 2007).

movement—called the resolution "a major milestone," while other leaders of the transnational anti–death penalty movement hailed it as "glorious news" (World Coalition against the Death Penalty), a "historic step" (Amnesty International), "a historical achievement and . . . the beginning of the end for the 'state killer'" (Hands Off Cain), and "a significant step toward the definitive abolition of capital punishment" (UN High Commissioner for Human Rights) (quoted in D-Alema 2008; Arbour 2007; Rouwenhorst 2007; Marcel 2008). But among the jurisdictions considered "Asian" in chapter 2 (excluding Hong Kong, Macao, and Taiwan, which do not have representation in the UN), the vote on the resolution was 7 in favor with 15 opposed and 4 abstentions.[8] There was, therefore, less than half the level of support for the moratorium resolution among our "Asian" nations (7/26 = 27 percent) as among the other countries of the world (97/161 = 60 percent).[9]

The more quickly abolition takes hold in Asia, the more likely it is that regional organizations will get involved in death penalty matters. This may mean that those organizations have little distinctive value because they are only active in situations where they are not really needed. But when the aspiration to eliminate capital punishment has a broad Asian constituency, transgovernmental organizations could become a meeting place for NGOs and for low- to midlevel officials from nations in the region, thus becoming a setting that is less politically risky for discussing death penalty issues than a

---

8. Asian nations voted on the UN resolution as follows. *In favor*: Australia, Cambodia, East Timor, Nepal, New Zealand, the Philippines, and Sri Lanka. *Opposed*: Bangladesh, Brunei Darussalam, China, India, Indonesia, Japan, Malaysia, Maldives, Mongolia, Myanmar, North Korea, Pakistan, Papua New Guinea, Singapore, and Thailand. *Abstained*: Bhutan, Laos, South Korea, and Vietnam. Thus, all of the retentionist Asian nations except Vietnam opposed the resolution, and all of the completely abolitionist nations of Asia except Bhutan supported it. The seven de facto abolitionist Asian jurisdictions were split: Sri Lanka supported the resolution; Brunei, the Maldives, Myanmar, and Papua New Guinea opposed it; Laos and South Korea abstained. For abolitionists, South Korea's abstention was especially disappointing, though at the time of the vote (December 18, 2007) that nation was still 12 days away from marking its ten-year moratorium.

9. Outside of Asia, the distribution of votes by region on the UN moratorium resolution was as follows. Middle East: 1 in favor (Israel), 10 opposed, 2 abstentions (Lebanon, United Arab Emirates); Arab countries: 1 in favor (Algeria), 15 opposed, 4 abstentions, 1 absent (Tunisia); Caribbean: 2 in favor (Dominican Republic, Haiti), 10 opposed, 1 abstention (Cuba); Africa: 17 in favor, 11 opposed, 20 abstentions, 4 absent; North America: 2 in favor (Canada, Mexico), 1 opposed (United States); Central America: 6 in favor, 1 opposed (Belize); South America: 9 in favor, 2 opposed (Guyana, Suriname), 1 absent (Peru); Oceania: 8 in favor, 2 opposed (Solomon Islands, Tonga), 1 abstention (Fiji); Europe: all nations in favor except Belarus, which abstained (Boumedra 2008). As a region, therefore, Asia was substantially more supportive of the moratorium than were the Middle East and Caribbean regions, but it was less abolitionist than Africa (where 61 percent of the countries that took a position favored the moratorium, compared with 32 percent in Asia), the Americas, Oceania, and Europe.

national capital would be. The larger the number of leadership nations that suspend or abolish the death penalty, the greater the motivation for the regional organizations that see themselves as forums for discussion and agents of change. The moral high ground abolition occupies in Asia, even as the region executes thousands each year, magnifies the impact of national-level steps toward abolition on the attitudes and conduct of organizations in the region. The combination of national-level movement away from execution and pressure on regional institutions from sister organizations outside Asia may well provoke more discourse in the future. Regional organizations will not soon become independent powers in Asia, but discourse on the death penalty in some of these settings can make them important even if they are weak.

■ The Pace of National Change

The most important aspects of death penalty policy in Asia are the policies adopted by individual nations. Changes in the world or in the region do influence attitudes about executions and inspire or restrain changes at the national level, but the centers of control for capital punishment in Asia remain the nation-states. This section begins with an analysis of the political economy of executions in modern states. After that we discuss the pace of change in Asian democracies and the prospects for change in the death penalty policies of hard-line communist regimes.

The Political Economy of Executions

What benefits and costs do governments consider when making death penalty policy? Before answering this question for contemporary Asia, we will use the rapid abolition of capital punishment in central and eastern Europe during the 1990s as a tutorial in the political economics of executions.

EUROPE AS A TUTORIAL Why, in retrospect, was the transition of central and eastern Europe from low execution rates to abolition (and binding promises from Russia not to use execution) so quick and painless? One way to frame this transition is in cost-benefit terms, and one important element of such an account has already been discussed: the material incentives for abolition were the opportunity to join Europe and thereby gain substantial economic benefits. In this sense, the European rush to abolition was a one-time opportunity to see how quickly death penalty policies will change when large economic incentives are presented to a group of countries that are undergoing rapid political changes and inertial retention of the death penalty. The absence of any protracted struggle to retain capital punishment in these circumstances suggests that the death penalty was a policy of low pecuniary value to governments that long retained it (Puhar 2003; Bae 2007:23–40).

The unusual financial incentives that precipitated rapid changes in Europe aside, are the modest benefits that led central and eastern European countries to retain death penalties 25 years ago true as well for Asian nations that retain capital punishment in 2008? If the material benefits that accrue to countries that use execution tend to be modest, this might help predict the (generally low) degree of resistance to abolition that governments display on pecuniary grounds, and could also arbitrate between symbolic and material explanations for continued resistance to the end of capital punishment.

THE IMPORTANCE OF EXECUTIONS IN ASIA   If we are correct in our assessment that almost all of the active execution systems of Asia concentrate on common criminals and not on political dissidents or rivals, then the practical value of that style of capital punishment is insubstantial to the regimes that employ it for crime control. However, since this low value is (ironically) the result of the cessation of state killing as a tool of political conflict, the lack of death penalty utility must be a recent phenomenon in the nations where authoritarian governments formerly used execution as an instrument of political control. As we will show, the comparative advantage of executing political rivals instead of imprisoning them is much greater than execution for the control of common criminals. Hence, for authoritarian regimes, the value of a death penalty for political cases may be higher than that of a death penalty restricted to common crimes, even if the capital sanction is currently used only for common criminals in noncrisis periods.

What makes killing more effective than confinement for political threats is the permanent removal of potential rivals, whereas imprisonment is especially inefficient if the rivals have followers. Myanmar joins South Africa and Poland and Czechoslovakia during the Soviet era in illustrating these points. When a regime's political future is uncertain, locking up political opponents can seem a risky solution, while killing them represents a more plausible path to incapacitation. By contrast, imprisonment is as effective as execution for the control of common criminals in stable regimes. Nobody is going to storm the Bastille to release incarcerated drug dealers and street robbers.

But isn't execution at least less expensive than imprisonment? While the economic costs of imprisonment are substantial, it turns out that only a death penalty system without special legal protections for the condemned is less costly than prison. In legal and economic systems at the lowest end of the development scale, capital punishment might have some economies to offer if it carried no special legal protections, but even a small dose of due process costs much more than prison guards (Bohm 2003c). In the system now evolving in China, SPC review with legal representation and sentencing guideline enforcement will probably raise the cost per execution well above the marginal cost of protracted imprisonment.

But if the capital sanction has no significant economic advantage for crime control, why do governments insist on retaining and using it? Partly because it is a symbol of state power that reassures both the state and its citizens that the government is more powerful than its enemies. For authoritarian governments, however, an operational death penalty may also function as an insurance policy against political instability and future threats to the regime. Under normal circumstances, it is much easier to expand the scope of an operational death penalty system to include political or national security cases than to attempt to reintroduce the death penalty from scratch when the political weather turns stormy. To governments that are dedicated to political control, the possibility of political usages, which gives political dissidents reason to fear the expansion of operating death penalties, may be more important than the utility or cost-effectiveness of "strike hard" campaigns against street crime.

If this analysis helps explain hard-line authoritarian states' affection for capital punishment, it also suggests a potentially effective method of under-mining the commitment to capital punishment on the part of authoritarian governments that have stopped executing political offenders. A substantial majority of Asian governments share the sentiment that execution for political offenses should be prohibited. Generating commitments to a ban on political executions might therefore remove or reduce the relevance of one of the most significant unacknowledged rationales for death penalty retention in authori-tarian states. The more difficult it is to obtain such a political commitment, the greater the chance that it represents a step toward ending executions.

THE GEOGRAPHY OF INCENTIVES   The contrast between the pecuniary politics of central and eastern Europe in the 1990s and the practical concerns in contemporary Asia is a function of the benefits of abolition much more than its costs. The swift end to capital punishment in the new European regimes of the 1990s resulted from large incentives that overwhelmed the modest pecuniary value of retaining the death penalty (Puhar 2003; Zimring 2003; Bae 2008b). The major contrast with Asia is the lack of strong incentives to abolish. For most Asian nations that retain capital punishment, the practi-cal value of retention is small, as are the pecuniary incentives to abolish, so the issue can be decided in purely symbolic terms. In Indonesia and India, for instance, the death penalty issue is not very important, but there is also no significant incentive to eliminate it.

In authoritarian nations that have recently used execution as a political tool, the potential to use it again may be a shadow benefit that inhibits movement away from using death as a punishment for any offender. In these contexts, the low value of other uses raises the relative importance of political motives. For this and related reasons, the two sections that follow discuss separately the prospects for reforming death penalty policy in both authoritarian and nonauthoritarian governments.

Nonauthoritarian Nations

There is abundant evidence that in all of Asia's nonauthoritarian nations that retain a capital sanction, the death penalty has little utility. The rates of execution in India, Indonesia, Thailand, and Japan are a small fraction of the rate per million in the United States (Hood 2002:92; Batra 2007), and Taiwan and South Korea have not used execution for the last two years and ten years, respectively. Similarly, executions in Malaysia have declined markedly, from an average of 15 per year during 1980–2000 to an average of less than two per year during 2000–2007 (Kuppusamy 2007). In Bangladesh, the execution rate per million in 1997–2005 was only 1/20th the American rate over the same period of time and less than 1/100th the rate in Texas (Mash 2007). Execution rates are higher in Pakistan, but even there, after executions increased to 135 in 2007, the per capita rate of 0.8 did not reach what we regard as the threshold for an operational system of capital punishment (see chapter 2), and it was almost 30 percent lower than the execution rate in the American state of Texas. In none of these nations is there evidence that executions play an important role in crime control and public safety.[10] But while the material benefits of execution are modest, there is little pressure in either domestic politics or international relations to end capital punishment in these nonauthoritarian countries. The death penalty is simply not a central question in the politics of these low-use nations, nor are there powerful institutions in domestic political life that make capital punishment a high-priority concern.

The low profile of capital punishment in the political life of most Asian nations is best illustrated by contrast with the higher salience the issue has had in two other nations. In the Philippines, the death penalty was a more important question during the first two post-Marcos decades as it was abolished, reintroduced, and then abolished again. What distinguished the Philippines from places like India, Thailand, and Indonesia was not the rate of actual executions, for that had been low for a long time. Even though crime rates in the Philippines were very high by Asian standards, executions had not been a key aspect of crime control for more than a century. What made capital punishment a salient issue from 1986 onward was its connection to progressive politics and its importance to the powerful Catholic Church and Cardinal Jaime Sin, the Church's Filipino leader. There is no parallel to this high priority in the domestic politics of Japan, India, Indonesia, and Thailand. The Philippine Catholic Church attached to capital punishment a much higher profile in the national agenda and in political horse-trading even though the issue was probably no more salient to the ordinary people in Manila than those in Tokyo, Delhi, Jakarta, or Bangkok. But the high priority of capital punishment to the nation's Catholic hierarchy combined with the educational and lobbying activities of the Free Legal Assistance Group were enough to overcome the usual combination of public hostility to criminals and legislative inertia. In this respect, the recent story of abolition in the Philippines is another demonstration of the low practical importance of capital punishment.

---

10. In Texas, too, the death penalty's deterrent effect is invisible (Fagan, Zimring, and Geller 2006).

The second instructive contrast is with the United States, where the death penalty carries higher priority in many jurisdictions than it does in nonauthoritarian nations of Asia such as Indonesia and Thailand. This is not a claim about the proportion of the public that supports a death penalty for persons who commit murder, for that is as high or higher in most Asian countries as in the United States. But the question of capital punishment seems substantially more important to the ordinary person in Houston or Los Angeles than in Bandung or Chiang Mai. Data to support this assertion would have to come from a survey that asked samples in a variety of nations to rank capital punishment among other economic and political issues, enabling one to compare across jurisdictions the proportion of citizens who say executions or their absence are more important than unemployment, inflation, education, traffic, corruption, or health care. If such a survey were conducted, we expect that the salience of capital punishment would be significantly higher in the United States than in the nonauthoritarian Asian nations that seldom use death as a criminal sanction (Zimring and Johnson 2006).

LOW SALIENCE AND THE PACE OF CHANGE   What does the low importance of the death penalty portend for whether and when the nonauthoritarian nations of Asia that retain capital punishment might give it up? One consequence of the low intensity of the issue is reduced predictability about how quickly change will come. For India, Indonesia, and other nonauthoritarian nations, the reasons for retaining capital punishment are not especially important—but neither are the reasons to abolish it. Much depends on the attitudes of high public officials, though the low priority of the topic in domestic politics also makes foreign attitudes and incentives important. The lack of intense feeling among citizens in most nations where there is inertial retention could create some tendency for them to change policies in clusters, with abolition in one place sparking heightened concern in other low-usage countries. That did not occur after Cambodia, Nepal, East Timor, and Bhutan abolished, but if more visible nations—say, India or South Korea—abolished, more dominoes might fall. Another implication of the modest domestic importance of the death penalty in nations with inertial retention is the larger relative importance of foreign influences, including the stigma associated with execution that now exists in most countries of the world. The fact that capital punishment is a low-stakes political game in many of the world's nations magnifies the influence of weak political actors. In this respect, the European groups that have had little success lobbying against the death penalty in the United States could find more encouraging prospects in Asian nations where capital punishment is less important.

One story of significant external influence on death penalty policy in Asia comes from the role of FLAG in the campaign that culminated in the second abolition in the Philippines. A full-time, fact-rich NGO lobby such as this one is by no means a sufficient condition for policy reform in any nation, but the FLAG example does show that the impact of relatively small investments (in this case from Europe) on a low-priority issue can still be impressive.

Of course, not all low-rate, nonauthoritarian nations regard the death penalty as unimportant in national politics. In Japan, executions are controlled by the central executive and carried out at least once a year. As long as the conservative party continues in power, sustaining this policy seems likely to remain a matter of importance to the government, partly as a means of demonstrating state power in a nation with a pacifist constitution that restricts the use of military force (see chapter 3). To the extent that there is a greater attachment to executions in Japan than in other low-rate nations, more importance must be given to abolition by actors who wish to achieve it than in low-rate inertial retention nations such as India or Indonesia. In any event, we do not expect Japan to be the earliest of Asia's currently executing nations to abolish, though the generality of Japan's commitment to capital punishment can only be known after a non-LDP government rules for a while.

Of the more developed nonauthoritarian nations in Asia, only Malaysia and Taiwan used execution in nontoken amounts in the years before 2000, and both have experienced steep drops. As of this writing, Taiwan has gone two years without using execution (2006–2007), a huge decline from the most recent peaks of 78 executions in 1990 and 38 in 1997. Malaysia, which averaged 13 executions a year in 1970–1996, had no executions for the four years before November 2000 or in 2003–2005 (Hood 2002:48; Hands Off Cain 2007). Pakistan and Bangladesh are far less developed, but Bangladesh carried out no executions in four out of the ten years from 1997 to 2006 (Hands Off Cain 2007; Mash 2007), while executions in Pakistan have fluctuated markedly from year to year during the last decade (International Federation for Human Rights and Human Rights Commission of Pakistan 2007). In 1996–2000, Pakistan's execution rate—0.07 per million (Hood 2002:92)—was lower than the rates in South Korea (0.10) and Thailand (0.08) and only about one-quarter of that in the United States (0.27). Even when Pakistan's execution volume surged to 135 in 2007, its execution rate of 0.8 per million remained "exceptional" (according to the typology we introduced in table 2.1).

As noted in the second section of this chapter, the most likely first abolition in the group of currently retaining nations is South Korea.[11] But which nations

---

11. In December 2007, Lee Myung Bak—a former Hyundai executive and mayor of Seoul—of the conservative opposition Grand National Party was elected president of South Korea by the largest margin since democratic elections began 20 years earlier. Lee, a Christian elder in the Presbyterian Church, is known as a probusiness, pragmatic politician, and his campaign made several central promises: to put the economy first; heal the South's divided society and achieve national harmony; get tougher on North Korea; and mend ties with the United States (Onishi 2007b). But on questions of capital punishment, Lee has been careful and discreet. His clearest statements suggest that he plans to "maintain the death penalty but use it with restraint" (AFP 2007; "Time Is Ripe" 2008). Like many of his

might follow South Korea's lead? Two related predictors are the existence of an intentional moratorium and politicians sympathetic to nonexecution. Taiwan has had both of these features, and Ma Ying-jeou, the new president elected in 2008—replacing the one who has been most sympathetic to abolition (Chen Shui-bian)—has expressed no hostility to the moratorium or to the rapid decline in capital sentences that has occurred in recent years (Liao 2008).

By most accounts, the commitment to execution seems relatively weak in Thailand, Indonesia, and India. But in India, because of complicated level-of-government issues, national abolition depends on an exercise of uncharacteristic federal power by either the Supreme Court or the prime minister. The Supreme Court has shown limited ability to restrain government's power to punish (Epp 1998:71), and the prime minister, who leads a sprawling multi-party coalition, lacks the necessary political capital to pursue that end (Luce 2007:180). Since the limited importance of capital punishment in Indian politics makes the issue a poor candidate for initiative by the prime minister, only an emboldened Supreme Court and a significantly strengthened "support structure" for implementing rights (Epp 1998) seem likely to push the nation onto the early track of abolition (see appendix F).[12] Indonesia's stronger executive might find national abolition easier to accomplish than India's would, but what has been missing in both the internal politics of Indonesia and its external relations is a strong motive to do so (see chapter 8, footnote 28). As for Thailand, it could quickly and completely end executions and death sentences if the king made a commitment to abolish, but that political will has not been evident despite frequent years with few or no executions.

All else equal, nations with strong incentives to appear as champions of human rights will be more motivated to reform their death penalty policies, and this tendency is likely to intensify after the formal abolition of capital punishment occurs in a first-echelon state like South Korea. Whether this would create a chain reaction in other retentionist nations is difficult to predict because the central question is whether abolition in a leading country

---

predecessors in office, Lee has spent time in prison. In 1964, he served six months for his role in student demonstrations against the normalization of Korea-Japan relations. Following his release, Lee found himself on a government blacklist and unable to find work. Instead of studying overseas like others in his predicament, he wrote a letter of complaint to President Park Chung Hee, which led to a meeting with one of Park's presidential aides. Shortly thereafter, Lee joined Hyundai Construction (Onishi 2007a). It is difficult to tell what effect Lee's personal encounters with state repression will have on his attitudes toward execution. His public approval ratings plummeted soon after he took office, in part because he was perceived to be "kowtowing to the United States" and "reversing democratic achievements" ("Lee Administration" 2008).

12. The Indian state of Maharashtra—home to Mumbai, the most populous city in the world—has the most populous death row in the nation, with 42 condemned convicts at the end of 2007. But Maharashtra, with a population twice that of South Korea, has not had a hanging since July 1995 ("Mumbai" 2007; see appendix F).

would help transform capital punishment from a mostly national issue into a question with regional significance. As long as the death penalty agenda was set mainly within a nation's borders, the issues to be discussed were, for the most part, a function of domestic considerations and understandings. In Japan, for example, it has been mainly a matter of Japanese sensibilities whether capital punishment should be considered an issue of human rights or of the appropriate limits on government. But once the death penalty becomes an important regional topic, the definition of key terms and frames will be determined outside Japan's national boundaries. If capital punishment issues generate competition for status among governments in the region, one result could be pressure on Japan, especially if there is South Korean leadership in death penalty discourse that is perceived as an attempt to undermine Japan's preeminence in the region. How this would affect the domestic politics of execution in Japan is an open question; refusal to change is as plausible a scenario as a rush to maintain Japan's status by ending executions or significantly softening its execution policy.

Politics and Capital Punishment in Authoritarian Regimes

Capital punishment is an important policy in many authoritarian governments, and one reason for the affinity between authoritarian regimes and the death penalty is ideological: state interests are accorded high value by authoritarian regimes, and personal interests and rights are discounted. In contests between government goals and individual claims, the former are invariably favored. Beyond ideology, killing permanently removes political rivals who would remain threatening with less drastic controls. Authoritarian regimes have frequently used state killing on a grand scale in political conflict, and even when hard-line governments have not used capital punishment on political rivals in periods of stability, they have often regarded the death penalty as insurance for political conflict that could threaten them later.

Whatever its causes, the tendency for authoritarian governments of the left and right to use capital punishment for a wide variety of crimes and to carry out high volumes of executions is as clear in the Asia of the 21st century as it was in Europe during the Nazi and Stalinist periods. In the middle third of the 20th century in Asia, right-wing hard-line regimes were as numerous as left-wing ones, and the right-wing regimes in Taiwan and South Korea were among the most repressive (see chapters 5 and 6). But political reforms have left only one small right-wing regime in the region (Singapore), three hard-line communist governments (China, Vietnam, and North Korea), and a military junta in Myanmar that has not carried out judicial executions since 1989 (Hood and Hoyle 2008:88). Singapore and the three communist countries all retain capital punishment and generate levels of execution at the top of the distributions for Asia and the world. Indeed, these four regimes account for more than 98 percent of the region's executions, and even without China, the three others probably carry out more executions than the other nine Asian nations that retain the death penalty. The prospects for reform in these authoritarian nations are obviously a key part of Asia's death penalty future.

We review the prospects for change in Asia's authoritarian regimes in three stages. First, we consider the likelihood of political reform—liberalization or overthrow of the current structure of government—that could precipitate the end of capital punishment in these regimes. We then acknowledge some "retrograde possibilities" before discussing the prospects for change in death penalty policy even if there are no fundamental shifts in the form of government in Asia's authoritarian nations.

PROSPECTS FOR POLITICAL CHANGE   One of the most important causes of the declining prevalence of executions in Asia over the past two decades has been political reform in previously authoritarian governments that has resulted in high-execution-rate nations such as Taiwan and South Korea first reducing their executions and then stopping the practice altogether. What are the prospects for this kind of change in Asia's remaining authoritarian nations?

Singapore seems a likely candidate for liberalization in the near future because it has high levels of the usual precursors to democratization, especially prosperity and education. The relative lack of hard-line restrictions in Singapore also predicts reform. Of the countries we consider "authoritarian," Singapore's government has by far the softest central structure; it could even be called "authoritarian lite" in comparison to North Korea or Vietnam (see www.freedomhouse. org). All of these features suggest that the current government could become more open and democratic with little friction. Singapore's softer controls also expose its citizens to more of the signals and symbols of liberal governance that come from other nations. The experiences of Taiwan and South Korea also indicate that Singapore could be close to change. Unless Singapore's situation is singular—and it is a small city–state—the softening of other right-wing governments in the region suggests that a similar fate awaits what critics have called "Disneyland with the death penalty" (Gibson 1993). What is more, the recent histories of Taiwan and South Korea indicate that an end to executions may not be far removed from decisive steps toward democratization. The key question, then, is whether a "culture of developmentalism" that has subordinated individual rights to the larger "needs" of the nation will continue to promote a society of fear and paranoia and an extensive and repressive apparatus of control (as it has for the past 40 years), or whether development will lead to more liberal democracy and less reliance on capital punishment, as it did in South Korea and Taiwan. Although the answer is unclear, right-wing authoritarianism is something of an endangered species in the prosperous neighborhoods of contemporary Asia. The smart money should bet against the continued singularity of Singapore's government (see appendix E).

By contrast, Vietnam is less vulnerable to political reform because it is less prosperous, its citizenry is less educated, and it is more tightly controlled. As a result, the entrenched controls of the current system—including capital punishment—may be difficult to displace. But while the inertial properties of the current government seem substantial, the pace of economic change has been remarkably rapid. Vietnam also seems more susceptible to foreign influence than China, a vulnerability that may have been evident in 2007 when it was the only Asian retentionist nation that did not oppose the UN resolution for a worldwide moratorium on executions (it abstained). With fewer public protests to address, those who govern Vietnam may also prove more flexible than Chinese leaders have been since Tiananmen Square. Still, how Vietnam's political leaders will respond to the challenges of rapid development remains as much a matter of fortune-telling as academic analysis (see appendix C).

What makes North Korea vulnerable to change is not any flexibility of its leadership but the current regime's epic failure to sustain a functioning economy or feed its people. There is little chance the government will liberalize voluntarily but a substantial chance that it will be replaced after some catastrophic failure or foreign incursion. There are also signs that the world's last Stalinist system is "dying a natural death" as information flows in, the centrally planned economy collapses, and political controls diminish (Lankov 2006). However the hermit kingdom falls, one possible successor would be a government dependent on the PRC. This would not foreclose the possibility of a successor government honoring the current regime's pretense of no executions, but the probability of this scenario is difficult to assess. A second possibility for postfailure North Korea is a confederation with South Korea, which would probably produce a far more liberal government but may be unlikely because of the substantial financial costs such a merger would entail and because China could oppose it on sphere-of-influence grounds. The analogy with German reunification after 1989 seems inapt because China has now and will continue to enjoy a much stronger position in East Asia than the stumbling skeleton of the Soviet Union that existed in the late 1980s. Only if the North Korean government pushes toward a confederation with the South might Korean reunification survive Chinese resistance (see appendix A).

Finally, what are the possibilities for democratization in China itself during the next 15 to 20 years? Despite rapid growth in the number and scale of public protests, the current government still has a strong grip on state and society. The challenges that confront the PRC are huge, but the best hope for liberalization seems to be the incremental reform of the current government rather than its failure and replacement. Compared to other countries at its income level, China has already made progress in several significant respects (Peerenboom 2007:viii). Greater opening of government and more respect for civil and political rights will undoubtedly come in the high-growth Chinese future, but how much and when? These are critical questions—and open ones (Gilley 2004; Pan 2008). What does seem clear is that the more China reforms, the better the prospects will be for political reform elsewhere in the region. Some scholars even believe China is becoming "a model for the rest" of the nations in Asia and the world that aspire to modernization (Peerenboom 2007).

RETROGRADE POSSIBILITIES   There is no law of history that says all political changes will be in the direction of more democratic government and increased respect for human rights (Dahl 1998; Friedman 2005). Because authoritarian regimes tend to retain and use capital punishment, a political survey of future prospects in Asia should consider political and policy changes that might shift away from liberalization and regard for rights. One such possibility is that the only authoritarian state in Asia that does not use execution—Myanmar—might start using it. There is also the possibility of authoritarian takeovers in places such as Pakistan and Bangladesh. Less likely but by no means impossible would be long-term, hard-line takeovers in countries like Indonesia and Thailand. Just as democratic reform tends to foster decline of the death penalty and eventual abolition, authoritarian regimes are often good news for the execution industry. We expect that the forces of development and globalization will continue to push Asia toward political democracy, but there are likely to be significant failures and regressions along the way.

HOW LIKELY IS AUTHORITARIAN ABOLITION?   How closely linked are the political characteristics of national governments and the instruments a state uses to control its enemies and achieve state purposes? Pain and death are important weapons of power in the modern state unless a government denies itself recourse to such tools. That has been the paradoxical ambition of governments in many liberal states. Could the liberal sense of limits on authority take root in authoritarian governments that until recently have been averse to self-restraint? And from what sources might such a sense of limits be found for an authoritarian government such as China that is only 30 years removed from Mao Zedong?

The voluntary abolition of capital punishment by authoritarian regimes has not been a common occurrence in Asia (Cambodia and Bhutan seem to be the two closest cases), and a large part of the explanation for this pattern is the absence of substantial incentives of the kind that helped end executions in Russia and produced abolition in the Ukraine (Bae 2007:23). For the authoritarian nations of Asia, the material benefits of capital punishment are small, but so are the costs. Several small steps could increase the costs of execution and reduce the incentives for retention. Pressure for procedural reforms in capital cases and appeals will increase system costs. Such changes have already started in China but not in Vietnam. Greater international attention to the number of executions and minimum standards for legal representation and appeals also might generate public relations problems for capital punishment. If executions were to end in Japan or in other first-tier nations of Asia, an increase in the stigma attached to state killing would put additional pressure on high-execution-rate states. International treaties protecting political crimes and prisoners might also make the retention of the death penalty less attractive to hard-line regimes. What distinguishes the impact of these sorts of pressure from the program that succeeded in central and eastern Europe is the lack of real incentives to reform. The stigma associated with execution is limited as long as first-world nations like the United States and Japan dilute the moral force of abolitionist appeals by continuing to conduct executions, and large economic incentives simply do not exist in Asia.

But stigma and pressure can achieve two meaningful, if preliminary, steps toward reform in the Asian environment. The first is a reduction in executions and at least modest reforms in the legal procedures for capital cases. The second step is capital punishment reform becoming a higher priority in the hard-line authoritarian nations which will at some point embark on liberalization. Singapore may not stop executing as long as its government remains committed to its current priorities, but moving the high rate of executions closer to the top of the list of reforms to be considered when liberalization does begin will probably push the hangman's retirement many years forward. Every authoritarian regime in Asia is at risk of reform in the near future, and even if authoritarian regimes are poor candidates for abolition, the prospects for significant death penalty change are brighter than they have ever been because of a reform dynamic that we expect will remain a broad and important feature of the Asian future.

The rate of executions and the prevalence of executing nations in Asia are declining and probably will continue to decline. Some of these decreases are a function of economic development and democratic reform, but the status of execution has also dropped. Increased attention from abroad and efforts to generate interest in the death penalty within regional organizations should help focus attention on capital punishment and generate further change in death penalty policy. A number of nations retain capital punishment without strong commitments to it, and these "inertial retention" countries appear to be prime candidates for early change. At the same time, Asia's hard-line authoritarian states are not strong candidates for swift abolition, but considering the extraordinary pace of change in the region, efforts to make their death penalty policies a higher priority could pay off sooner rather than later.

Appendixes

Appendix A: North Korea

Chapter 5 focuses on South Korea (population 49 million) instead of North Korea (population 23 million) for two main reasons: because economic and political development in the South make it a more instructive case for understanding the present and future of capital punishment in other Asian societies than would an analysis of the "horrible weirdness" in North Korea, and because reliable information about state killing in North Korea—a country that has been called a "hermit kingdom" and a "kingdom of lies"—is hard to come by (Cumings 1997:433; Gourevitch 2003:57,64). Our accounts of capital punishment in China (chapter 7) and Vietnam (appendix C) describe some of the death penalty data problems in those countries, but "in North Korea perhaps more than anywhere else, the effects of Communism are difficult to translate into numbers," making it impossible to provide a precise picture of the country or the realities of capital punishment there (Rigoulot 1999:546,563). Nonetheless, the available evidence does support at least nine general statements about the death penalty during the dynasty of Kim Il Sung, the "Great Leader" who ruled the Democratic People's Republic of Korea (DPRK) from the time it declared independence in 1948 until his death in 1994, and of his son and successor Kim Jong Il, the "Dear Leader" and "Lodestar of the 21st Century" who has wielded power since.

First, North Korean authorities "maintain that the last execution took place in 1992" (Hood and Hoyle 2008:96), but there is considerable evidence that executions continue to occur on a regular basis and at high but unknown rates (Kang and Rigoulot 2001:137; Gourevitch 2003:60; Becker 2005:37; Martin

2006:290). Executions were suspended for one month after Kim Il Sung died in July 1994, but it seems his son soon wanted to "hear the sound of gunshots again," and in January 1995 he reportedly issued orders demanding the execution of all criminals within three months (Becker 2005:98). For a time there were "executions every day by stoning or hanging 'criminals' who had stolen two pounds of maize or a couple of eggs," and a refugee interviewed in Bangkok said he saw 28 "criminals" executed in one day (98). During the food shortages and famines of the 1990s, resistance to the regime increased, with protests, strikes, local uprisings, and even the killing of some officials and their families. Kim Jong Il responded with more terror, including "waves of purges and a countrywide pattern of summary public trials and executions" (36). Some refugees told of watching prisoners who were "garroted or hung or tied to a stake and their relatives forced to light the fire" (37), and one inmate who escaped from a labor camp told Doctors Without Borders that he personally witnessed more than 1,000 executions (37).

Similar execution patterns have characterized North Korea for the last 60 years. Kang Koo Chin, a specialist on North Korea's legal system, has estimated that in 1958–1960 at least 9,000 people were ejected from the Communist Party, tried, and sentenced to death. In the late 1990s, a French scholar extrapolated from this estimate "to include the other nine purges of a similar scale," arriving at a figure of 90,000 to 100,000 executions over a 40-year period, a Mao-like rate of more than 100 executions per million per year (Rigoulot 1999:552,564; Becker 2005:62). This is only the number of people executed in party purges (not ordinary criminal cases) and does not include the estimated 1.5 million deaths in concentration camps, many of which resulted from an excruciating process of "slow capital punishment" whereby inmates deemed no longer productive or useful were worked and starved to death (Rigoulot 1999:564; Becker 2005:36,94).

The second North Korean death penalty reality is the regime's claim (in its 2001 report to the UN Human Rights Committee) that it had reduced the number of capital offenses from 33 to 5. The remaining offenses were said to be conspiracy against state power, treason, terrorism, antinational treachery, and intentional murder. According to the UN, four of these capital crimes are "essentially political" and are "couched in terms so broad that the imposition of the death penalty may be subject to essentially subjective criteria, and not confined to the 'most high crimes' only" (Hands Off Cain, May 31, 2006). The crimes on this short list are highly elastic. Since all property in the DPRK belongs to the state, anyone found "stealing" corn from a field, chopping down a tree, or killing a cow without authorization is guilty of a crime against the state (Becker 2005:37). At the same time, there is substantial evidence that North Korea continues to execute people for crimes not on this short list, including theft, smuggling, and other nonviolent offenses (Amnesty International 2005b).

What is striking about these first two facts is not only the high execution volume for a wide variety of offenses but also the fact that a "rogue regime" that frequently defies international norms in other areas—diplomacy, trade, terrorism, nuclear weapons, narcotics, and human rights—apparently feels the need to tell the world that it is a decent state when it comes to capital punishment. This is a window onto the symbolic importance of death penalty policy even in "the most closed state in the world" and even though its claims about capital punishment reform have been thoroughly discredited (Rigoulot 1999:547). It is also a testament to the power of international human rights norms and the "logic of appropriateness" to shape the death penalty sensibilities of political leaders in repressive regimes (Bae 2007:126).

Third, "uncounted critics" of the North Korean regime have been executed since Kim Il Sung became paramount leader in the 1940s (Cumings 1997:407; Martin 2006:290). Some observers believe North Korea's purge of politically disloyal subjects is even "more brutal than the Chinese Cultural Revolution" (Martin 2006:293), while others contend that North Korea has been "more discriminating" in its use of violence for political ends than were the dictators in South Korea (Cumings 1997:231). Whatever the historical reality—and the most comprehensive account of "death by government" concludes that Kim Il Sung's regime killed twice the percentage of his country's population than Mao did of his (Rummel 1994:4)—the present reality is that Kim Jong Il continues to execute political and personal enemies. Dozens if not hundreds of military officers have been executed, including at least ten who were shot for opposing Kim's succession (Becker 2005:197). Kim also had one of his mistresses—an actress born in Japan—executed for being unfaithful; she was shot before a crowd of 5,000 shouting "kill, kill" (135). One of Kim's former bodyguards claims the dictator had his barber shot for botching his bouffant hairdo (142). These political, personal, and capricious motivations for killing resemble no one so much as Mao Zedong. They also distinguish state killing in North Korea from state killing in present-day China and Vietnam—Asia's other large communist countries—where capital punishment is no longer directed at explicitly political targets except in isolated cases.

Fourth, North Korean authorities often use torture to extract confessions, and many persons have been executed without receiving the benefit of a criminal trial, much less due process (Ichikawa 2006; Martin 2006:302). North Korea's justice system exists mainly to promote the interests of the regime. "All judges and almost all lawyers act on the orders of the Party and are explicitly instructed to work along strict Marxist-Leninist lines" (Rigoulot 1999:553). Some victims of "interrogation" are beaten with iron chains, rubber belts, and wooden sticks. Others are tied with ropes and then hanged upside down and electrocuted. One detainee was ordered to clean the toilet hole in his cell with his tongue for 30 minutes, and the same degradation ritual was inflicted on a fellow prisoner for five consecutive days as punishment for sleeping on his side instead of his back. Suspects and inmates who try to escape these barbarisms are sometimes executed. One would-be escapee was killed by being dragged behind a car, and other prisoners were forced to "file past and place their hands on his bloodied corpse" (Becker 2005:94). Some of

North Korea's penal techniques—such as its underground torture chambers—were adopted and adapted from its Japanese occupiers, a form of learning that also occurred in the South. But unlike the present-day South, little attention is paid to legal processes or protections. From the purges of party officials that followed the signing of the armistice in 1953 to the executions under Kim Jong Il, real trials—where evidence counts and guilt can be contested—have been a rarity. All too often, victims simply disappear and law is simply dispensed with—"no charges, no formal sentencing, no documents, and no appeals" (62).

Fifth, underpinning the North Korean state's elaborate apparatus of social control is "a principle of collective family responsibility that makes every member of a household accountable for the conduct of his immediate kin, so that the deviations of one are the calamity of all" (Gourevitch 2003:60). What matters in North Korea is not merely what you do but also what your family once was (Delisle 2005; Hoare and Pares 2005), and the belief that political deviance is hereditary extends to capital punishment (Kang and Rigoulot 2001). Pregnant women who have given birth in Korea after being repatriated from China have even had their babies killed because they were "tainted with foreign blood" (Becker 2005:95). Conversely, some criminal suspects escape punishment altogether because of their family backgrounds. According to a report by the South Korean Bar Association, the children of former activists who protested Japan's colonization of Korea often receive "automatic rulings of innocence" (Ichikawa 2006).

Sixth, executions have frequently been staged in public during the Kim dynasty and continue to be so staged in North Korea today even though the regime claims that public spectacles were ended in 2003 (Kang and Rigoulot 2001:137–144; Amnesty International 2005b; Martin 2006:290–304; Hood and Hoyle 2008:96). In March 2005, for example, a 104-minute videotape of two public executions in the city of Hoeryang was smuggled out of North Korea (via China) into Seoul. It shows about 1,500 persons scattered around a rocky ravine watching two men (described as "prostitute traffickers") get tied to white posts and shot from the rear by three soldiers, each of whom fires three times. Before the executions, a North Korean official with a megaphone reads the charges aloud, and afterward he can be heard saying "how pathetic is the end of these traitors of the fatherland" (quoted in Marquand 2005). Other public executions have been documented through interviews with North Korean defectors (Ichikawa 2006) and through Good Friend, a support organization for North Korea that has documented the public execution of offenders charged with selling videotapes or electric cables (Hands Off Cain, June 27, 2006). In October 2007, a factory boss in South Pyongon Province was reportedly executed by firing squad in front of a stadium crowd of 150,000; he was condemned for making international phone calls on 13 phones he had installed in a factory basement (Kwang-Tae Kim 2007; "N. Korea Resumes" 2007). Kang Chol-hwan, who was purged as a nine-year-old boy with the rest of his family and who spent ten years in North Korea's largest prison camp

(Yodok), says in his memoirs that he attended some 15 executions between 1977 and 1987. After one, "the two or three thousand prisoners in attendance were instructed to each pick up a stone and hurl it at the corpses while yelling, 'Down with the traitors of the people!'" Kang says they "did as [they] were told" (Kang and Rigoulot 2001:14). An inmate released from another prison camp said authorities at his facility "would stage public executions fifteen or twenty times" each year (Martin 2006:299). Since there are approximately 20 prison camps in the North Korean gulag, there may be a public execution somewhere in the country almost every day. In some cases, people are not only summoned to watch, they are urged to participate through shouts of hatred, insults, and (as Kang's experiences suggest) kicking, beating, and stone-throwing (Becker 2005:190).

Seventh, in addition to the execution of political prisoners and more run-of-the-mill criminal offenders by shooting and hanging, between 100,000 and 300,000 persons are incarcerated in North Korea's gulag (Cumings 1997:398; Kang and Rigoulot 2001:xxiv). This gives a state whose crimes stand out as the most striking contemporary expression of "savage Communism" an estimated per capita imprisonment rate about equal to that in the United States (Rigoulot 1999). For those North Koreans who are placed in "hard-labor zones," the work is "conceived solely for the purpose of driving prisoners to their graves" (Kang and Rigoulot 2001:xi, 144), an agonizing species of slow execution (Becker 2005:36). According to the South Korean Bar Association, in North Korean prisons that accommodate political prisoners, "inmates are forced to work for between 12 and 15 hours a day, 361 days of the year" (Ichikawa 2006). Some analysts believe a million or more North Koreans may have died in these prisons under the two Kims, which would be an average of more than 15,000 deaths per year (Rigoulot 1999; Becker 2005).

Eighth, since the summit meeting in 2000 between Kim Jong Il, the "central brain" of North Korea, and South Korean president Kim Dae Jung, officials in Seoul have largely avoided drawing attention to human rights abuses in the North, seemingly out of fear of harming North-South relations (Marquand 2005). Among South Korean citizens too, many people "have turned a blind eye" to the truth about North Korean concentration camps and capital punishment (Kang and Rigoulot 2001:viii). It is hard to tell if more international attention would have changed the North's death penalty policy, for the regime remains isolated, insulated, and incorrigible in many respects. But since international opinion has sometimes been an agent of positive death penalty change in Asia's other communist regimes—China and Vietnam especially—it is reasonable to wonder if more external attention to North Korea's state killing would have made a difference there too.

Finally, there seem to be many significant similarities between the death penalty practices of North Korea and those of China and Vietnam. In all three of these communist states one sees the use of execution targets and quotas, the orchestration of campaigns and crackdowns and the enlistment of mass participation in them, the centrality of the distinction between "friends" and "enemies," the treatment of law as a flexible instrument for achieving regime aims, a heavy reliance on confessions for evidence and the frequent use of "the third degree" for obtaining them, little in the way of legal protection or rights for criminal suspects and offenders, extreme secrecy about the death penalty (especially vis-à-vis foreign audiences), and the routine recourse in official rhetoric to "popular will" and "public support" for harsh punishment practices. There are differences too, of course. In North Korea, capital punishment continues to target political enemies to an extent no longer seen in China and Vietnam. But East Asia is almost the only place on earth where communists still rule, and if there is a specifically "Asian" brand of communism in this region, as some analysts argue (Margolin and Rigoulot 1999:636), there appears to be an identifiably Asian version of communist capital punishment as well.

As for the future of North Korea—the most militarized country in the world—and its possible effects elsewhere, some observers believe the real threat from Kim Jong Il's regime is not nuclear missiles but the prospect of its catastrophic collapse, which "could determine the balance of power in Asia for decades" to come (Kaplan 2006:64). If the North Korean regime does collapse—and experts have wrongly predicted it would for at least 35 years (Cumings 1997:433)—the case of German unification following the fall of the Berlin wall in 1990 suggests that criminal justice in the North would likely converge to the prevailing patterns in the South (Markovits 1995). Some analysts believe Kim Jong Il's regime is already dying "a natural death," as "the last fifteen years have witnessed the gradual wearing away of North Korean Stalinism" (Lankov 2006). On the other hand, Bruce Cumings, one of the most astute students of Korean history, believes North Korea has always been "closer to a Neo-Confucian kingdom than to Stalin's Russia," and he argues that the Kim regime's skill at drawing deeply from "the well of Korean tradition and anticolonial nationalism" may well give it "staying power" for some time to come (1997:407,433). If that prediction proves prescient, the Korean peninsula will remain home to two of the most radically different death penalty systems in all of Asia. We do not think "culture" can explain that difference.

Appendix B: Hong Kong and Macao

In 2007, ten years after Hong Kong returned to the Chinese mainland under the PRC's "one country, two systems" policy, it remained the richest, freest, and most Westernized part of China (with a higher income per capita than Britain's) even while its politics were less democratic than India's before independence (Morris 1997; Buruma 2001a:234). If Hong Kong were an independent country, its population of seven million would place it about 100th out of 238 nations, below Switzerland and above Israel (and about the same as the American states of Washington or Indiana). But of course Hong Kong is not an independent country; it is (under the terms of the 1984 Sino-British Joint Declaration) a Special Administrative Region (SAR) of the PRC that has been allowed to retain its capitalist system and some degree of autonomy until 2047. Under this scheme, the central government of the PRC is responsible for the territory's defense and foreign affairs, while Hong Kong maintains its own legal system, police force, customs policy, monetary system, and delegates to international organizations and events.

The first four sections of this appendix describe and explain the major turning points in Hong Kong's death penalty policy since the British took control of the islands in 1842, and the fifth section explores the significance of abolition in Hong Kong for other parts of the region. The final section examines capital punishment in Macao, a separate SAR of the PRC that was ruled by Portugal for more than 400 years before its return to the Chinese mainland in 1999. Under the terms of their return, both Hong Kong and Macao have retained their status as death-penalty-free zones, although occasionally they have had to negotiate jurisdictional issues with China's central and provincial governments. There were also significant similarities between the two cities before their returns, for as colonies both Hong Kong and Macao administered capital punishment policies that reflected, for the most part, the policies that prevailed in the home jurisdictions of their respective colonizers.[1]

■ The Death Penalty in Hong Kong before Britain's Abolition

In 1838, China's Emperor Daoguang tried to stop his country's importation of opium, which had been a critical part of Britain's international balance-of-payments strategy and a central feature of its foreign policy. The British responded with military force, and three years later were able to impose a treaty that "fundamentally altered the structure of Qing relations with foreign powers" by ending a long pattern of history in which China's rulers had imposed effective controls over foreigners on their soil (Spence 1990:139). Among other benefits for Britain, the 1842 Treaty of Nanjing—"the most important treaty settlement in China's modern history" (158)—declared that Hong Kong (Victoria Island) was to be "possessed in perpetuity" by Queen Victoria and her successors and ruled as they "shall see fit." In the century and a half between that treaty and Hong Kong's decision to abolish the death penalty in 1993, capital punishment in the colony reflected death penalty policy in Britain, albeit with a substantially more aggressive approach to execution in Hong Kong than in the home country during the period that both were still executing.[2]

Table B.1 shows executions and death sentence commutations in Hong Kong for the first half century after World War II (1946–1992). The "last colony's" last executions occurred in 1966, the year after Britain abolished the death penalty for ordinary crimes (Buruma 2001a:209; Hood 2002:251). In the two decades (1946–1966) before Hong Kong's hangmen went on permanent

---

1. A majority of countries that are now independent used to be colonies in one empire or another, and it seems "very likely indeed" that death penalty policy in former colonies has been shaped by the former mother country (Anckar 2004:75). A recent analysis of colonialism and capital punishment found that "countries without a colonial past tend to be markedly more restrictive toward the use of capital punishment than countries with a British or French colonial past," but that was only at the global level (87). At the regional level there was no association, perhaps because almost all of the colonial powers were European (Anckar 2004:167).

2. From 1946 to 1955, the per capita execution rate in Hong Kong (3.6 per million) was about 12 times higher than that in England and Wales (0.3), while the Hong Kong rate in 1956–1964 (1.1) was about 18 times higher than the rate in England and Wales (0.06). Annual execution figures for England and Wales can be found at the Web site of Richard Clark (www.richard.clark32.btinternet.co.uk/hanged2.html).

Table B.1
Executions and commutations in Hong Kong, 1946–1992

Year	Executions	Commutations
1946–1947	10	5
1947–1948	11	2
1948–1949	6	0
1949–1950	3	3
1950–1951	12	1
1951–1952	8	0
1952–1953	8	2
1953–1954	5	2
1954–1955	4	0
1955–1956	6	0
1956–1957	4	1
1957–1958	4	1
1958–1959	5	0
1959–1960	9	2
1960–1961	2	1
1961–1962	3	2
1962–1963	4	2
1963–1964	0	2
1964–1965	0	1
1965–1966	0	4
1966–1967	2	2
1967	0	4
1968	0	5
1969	0	3
1970	0	0
1971	0	5
1972	0	6
1973	0	12
1974	0	13
1975	0	15
1976	0	19
1977	0	10
1978	0	7
1979	0	16
1980	0	3
1981	0	12
1982	0	16
1983	0	13
1984	0	9
1985	0	22

(*Continued*)

Table B.1 (*Continued*)

Year	Executions	Commutations
1986	0	5
1987	0	20
1988	0	16
1989	0	6
1990	0	6
1991	0	5
1992	0	13
Total	106	294

Source: Gaylord and Galliher 1994:24.

vacation, they executed a total of 106 persons—an average of five per year. The peak year for execution was 1950, with 12, making Hong Kong's per capita rate that year (5.4 executions per million) and in several other years rise to a level resembling those that prevailed in the PRC and Singapore some 50 years later. For the last 20 years that Hong Kong was executing, its average annual rate of 1.84 executions per million was well above the 1.0 threshold that we used in chapter 2 to define operational death penalty systems. As long as Britain retained capital punishment, Hong Kong remained a vigorous executing colony. Executions in the territory only started to wither away in the early 1960s, after double-digit executions in England and Wales had ceased (in 1956) and just before Britain formally abolished.[3]

■ Hong Kong's Moratorium

Between the British abolition of 1965 and Hong Kong's abolition of 1993, the territory retained the death penalty in its statute books for a number of offenses, and death was the mandatory sentence on conviction for several (Vagg 1997:393). After Britain abolished, however, Hong Kong's colonial governors were forced by edict of the home government to commute death sentences to life imprisonment (Gaylord and Galliher 1994:19).[4] In the two

3. England and Wales averaged 3.2 executions per year in the nine years before they abolished (1956–1964), compared with 14.6 executions per year in the nine years before that (1947–1955).

4. The sole exception seems to be Hong Kong governor Murray MacLehose's refusal to commute the death sentence of Tsoi Kwok-cheung, a convicted murderer, in 1973. The governor's reluctance probably was influenced by the "steady build-up of public pressure"

decades before 1965, those governors commuted an average of 1.6 death sentences per year, a figure that increased sixfold (to 9.7) for the period 1966–1992. (See table B.1.)

For at least the first decade after Britain's abolition, the externally imposed moratorium on execution proved to be an unpopular policy among many Hong Kong citizens. In the early 1970s, traditional neighborhood leaders (Kaifong chiefs), the president of the Chinese Manufacturers Association, and the leader of the Buddhist Sangha Association all expressed frustration over the nonexecution policy (Gaylord and Galliher 1994:28), and Hong Kong newspaper editorials joined in the chorus by denouncing the nonenforcement policy. As the *China Mail* put it in 1973, "To pay lip service to a law that cannot be enforced is to make a mockery of all law. And once the rule of law is mocked, all society is threatened" (quoted in Gaylord and Galliher 1994:28). Some writers even looked forward to Hong Kong's return to a Chinese government that would not be squeamish about execution. In 1986, two decades into Hong Kong's moratorium, a survey of 1,312 residents found that 68 percent supported the death penalty for convicted murderers while only 12 percent opposed it (Gaylord and Galliher 1994:29).

Another death penalty poll was conducted in Hong Kong after the June 1989 massacres at Tiananmen Square in Beijing and in many other cities around China. An exact body count is impossible to come by, but estimates range from 300 to 2,700 people killed—most shot in the neck by single bullets (Buruma 2001a:5). In this context, Hong Kong's enthusiasm for capital punishment softened. Fifty percent of respondents still said Hong Kong should retain the death penalty (vs. 30 percent who said it should not), but on the question of whether condemned persons should actually be executed, less than 30 percent thought they should while nearly 50 percent said death sentences should be commuted to imprisonment for life or a shorter period (Vagg 1997:398).[5] After Tiananmen,

on the local government to carry out an execution, based on the prevalent view that Chinese rather than Western sensibilities about punishment should be observed when dealing with convicted offenders (Gaylord and Galliher 1994:23). Governor MacLehose dispatched his chief justice and attorney general to London in order to stress Hong Kong's desire to see Tsoi executed, but in the end British policy prevailed. Tsoi was saved by a reprieve from the Queen and then, more decisively, by a grant of mercy from the British secretary of state (Gaylord and Galliher 1994:25).

5. The persistence of public support for capital punishment in Hong Kong long after executions ceased is consistent with the experiences of many nations, but not all (Zimring and Hawkins 1986:21). According to poll results released by the Uzbek Public Opinion Study Center in July 2008, just six months after a presidential ordinance had abolished the death penalty in Uzbekistan, 92.8 percent of citizens in that Central Asian nation said they supported the abolition. "Citizens are increasingly aware of the need to humanize the criminal justice system," said one Uzbek analyst. "This [abolition] is a major precondition for the democratization of Uzbekistan" ("Over 90%" 2008). Similarly, in Turkey, where a moratorium on executions lasted from 1984 until the death penalty was formally abolished in 2002, "public opinion supported the abolition" (Lynch 2008:43; see also Hood and Hoyle 2008:48).

public opinion generally seemed comfortable with de facto abolition, and for a few years thereafter "the death penalty was effectively a non-issue" (394). A law that was neither enforced nor abolished seemed to appease two key audiences: the pro–capital punishment Chinese population in Hong Kong, and a majority of anti–death penalty legislators in the British Parliament (Gaylord and Galliher 1994:33).

■ Hong Kong's Abolition

It is possible to tell the story of Hong Kong's abolition in at least two different ways. One approach focuses narrowly on how Hong Kong legislators responded to an armed robbery wave that started in the late 1980s, and on the unexpected outcome—abolition—of a few politicians' attempts to score points with the electorate by posturing as "tough on crime." On this view, Hong Kong's abolition is ironic, for the death penalty's demise was the result of the punitive reactions of local legislators to a rise in serious, violent, and firearms-related crime in a city that traditionally had enjoyed levels of violence as low as those in Nordic countries (Vagg 1997).

But a broader and better approach to explaining Hong Kong's abolition frames the issue by situating death penalty policy-making in the context of two key events involving the PRC. The first is the Tiananmen massacre of 1989 and the Chinese government's suppression of the prodemocracy movement, a one-two punch that motivated a variety of protective responses in Hong Kong aimed at alleviating the local crisis of confidence that ensued in the soon-to-be-swallowed city. One of the most important reactions was the enactment in 1991 of a bill of rights that reproduced the strongly prorights language of the International Covenant on Civil and Political Rights. The new bill of rights enabled Hong Kong courts to strike down laws, including the death penalty, that violated human rights standards. After its enactment, "it became even more unlikely that Hong Kong would bring back the rope for as long as the colony remained under British control" (Gaylord and Galliher 1994:34).

The second major fact that stimulated abolition in Hong Kong was its approaching return to the Chinese mainland in 1997. The fear of what future governments might do in Beijing and in a SAR that would be at least partly controlled from the center "left no room for complacency on the part of the colonial government" (Gaylord and Galliher 1994:34). Thus, anxiety about China's future conduct combined with concern about its behavior in the recent past to impel Hong Kong's legislature to pass a Crimes Amendment Ordinance that abolished the death penalty after it received royal assent in April 1993 (Vagg 1997:402).

The framework of law and government built up by the British over the previous 150 years—and especially a legal system that, however imperfect in practice, was based on rule-of-law principles—provided the critical domestic context for the enactment of Hong Kong's abolition law. A similar legal system was handed down to Singapore when it gained independence in 1965, but it was undermined by Singaporean politicians—and by Lee Kuan Yew especially—almost as soon as the British left (Buruma 2001a:215). One of the clearest expressions of Singapore's authoritarian turn is the PRC-like rates of execution that have prevailed there since independence (see appendix E). In the first three years after Hong Kong abolished, for example, Singapore, with 3.5 million people—a little more than half the population of Hong Kong at the time—performed at least 199 executions, for an average annual execution rate of 19 per million population (Amnesty International 2004b). This three-year total is nearly twice as many executions as Hong Kong had (106) in the 47 years before it abolished.[6]

■ Hong Kong after Abolition

Two death penalty issues persist in Hong Kong after abolition. The first are jurisdictional: can a resident of Hong Kong be executed if he or she commits a capital offense on the Chinese mainland and is tried there? And what about offenders who flee to Hong Kong from mainland provinces? These issues have not been clearly resolved, but capital punishment is sometimes employed in both situations.

Some offenders who have fled to Hong Kong from elsewhere in China have been returned to the mainland and executed there through the process of "rendition" (Hood 2002:95). Questions have been raised about the validity of this practice, but it seems less controversial than the "rendition" of suspects and offenders who committed the bulk of their criminal acts in Hong Kong territory. In 2002, the *South China Morning Post* reported that "a total of 23 Hong Kong residents were either executed or sentenced to death in mainland China" in 2001 (quoted in Hands Off Cain 2002).[7] Although Chinese authorities justify these death penalties on the grounds that the crimes were cross-border or were planned on the mainland, their view has been vigorously contested by civic groups in Hong Kong. Whatever the propriety of using capital punishment against Hong Kong citizens and residents—and even if the 23 death penalties for 2001 are triple the true total—the SAR's per capita rate of 1.13 executions and death sentences per million would be higher than the United States' combined execution and death sentence rate (0.81) in the same year (and Chinese death sentences are more likely to end in execution

6. Despite the radically different execution policies in Hong Kong and Singapore, their homicide rates have tracked each other closely since at least the late 1970s. In a comparison of two cities that are similar in many social, cultural, and economic respects, the deterrent effects of Singapore's aggressive execution policy are invisible (Zimring, Johnson, and Fagan 2008).

7. The original source of the figure for 2001 is Hong Kong's Joint Committee for the Abolition of the Death Penalty (Hands Off Cain 2002).

than are U.S. ones). What is more, human rights activists in Hong Kong contend that "the number of known SAR residents executed [in China] is just the tip of the iceberg" (quoted in Hands Off Cain 2002). Despite the formal abolition that occurred in 1993, the death penalty remains a reality in Hong Kong because of its close proximity to the PRC and because of the PRC's willingness to use the death penalty against a wide variety of offenders.

The other persistent death penalty issue for Hong Kong is whether China's central government will try to formally reintroduce capital punishment in Hong Kong in the years to come. There is little question that the PRC could do so if it really wanted to (its relationship with Hong Kong is hardly egalitarian), but it appears to have little to gain by making such an attempt (Hood and Hoyle 2008:84). Hong Kong has one of the world's highest population densities but one of its lowest homicide rates (Gaylord and Galliher 1994:22; Johnson 2006b:77), and its other crime problems do not seem especially significant by PRC standards. In addition, the process of rendition already enables the PRC to use the death penalty against offenders from Hong Kong. But perhaps the biggest obstacle to reintroducing the death penalty in Hong Kong is public relations. China's ruling regime would likely encounter "highly negative public feelings" in Hong Kong if it took a high-handed approach to this issue (Vagg 1997:403), and the demonstration effect in Taiwan could be even worse. For the Communist Party to pursue a policy that would restart capital trials and judicial executions on Hong Kong turf would be to violate the letter and the spirit of the "one country, two systems" agreement and to alienate the prodigal sibling—Taiwan—that it wants to return to the fold. For these reasons, we do not expect to see any change in Hong Kong's abolitionist status before the current PRC–Hong Kong agreement expires in 2047. By then, China itself may no longer be communist or retentionist.

■ The Regional Importance of Hong Kong

Hong Kong is an important precedent for the impact of death penalty abolition in Asia but is not a significant participant in discourse about death as a punishment in the region. The value of Hong Kong as precedent is not in the mechanism of its abolition, for that was tied to its colonial status, but rather in the political and cultural response that occurred in an East Asian setting where there were few and then no executions. The political backlash to abolition in Hong Kong was very mild, almost nonexistent. Cultural ties to capital punishment had little visibility in the municipal life of Hong Kong in the quarter century after 1980, and the impact of the change on crime rates and perceptions of public safety was negligible. Thus, abolition in Hong Kong can be called a success story in these criminological and social senses. This is good news for those seeking to abolish the death penalty in Taiwan, and highly relevant news for those who claim the roots of the mainland's prodigious rates of execution are Chinese cultural values.

Two Newspapers

In order to study the importance of the death penalty and attitudes about it in Hong Kong, we analyzed the coverage of capital punishment in two Hong Kong newspapers over the 12-year period beginning January 1995—two years after the death penalty was formally abolished, and two years before the transfer of power from Britain to the PRC. The first newspaper surveyed was the *South China Morning Post*, the largest English-language daily newspaper in Hong Kong, with an average daily circulation in 2007 of 106,054. Both "death penalty" and "capital punishment" were searched.

Table B.2 shows the total number of death penalty mentions in the *Post* and breaks down the stories into those concerned with Hong Kong, those concerned with the rest of the PRC, and those related to other jurisdictions in the world. The annual total of death penalty mentions varies between 39 (in 2001) and 110 (in 1995) with no clear pattern over time; the highest year was 1995, but the second highest total was for 2005.

This relatively stable death penalty coverage was almost always concentrated on death penalty stories outside of Hong Kong. In every year except 1998, there were more stories and comments on the death penalty in the PRC than about Hong Kong, and there is a clear temporal pattern away from local concerns with the death penalty in Hong Kong. Over the period 1995–1998, 62

Table B.2

Death penalty–related articles and commentaries in the *South China Morning Post*, 1995–2006, by geographic area that is the subject of comment

	Mainland China	Hong Kong	Others	Total
1995	30	16	64	110
1996	22	13	24	59
1997	12	7	23	42
1998	24	26	13	63
1999	31	7	14	52
2000	44	4	22	70
2001	26	3	10	39
2002	46	2	15	63
2003	18	4	18	40
2004	16	8	35	59
2005	36	0	40	76
2006	35	3	30	68

Source: Analysis of *South China Morning Post* by Jiang Su, visiting scholar, Boalt Hall School of Law, University of California at Berkeley, March 2008.

of the 274 newspaper items concerning the death penalty were about Hong Kong—23 percent of all death penalty stories. In the seven years after 1998, only 31 of 467 death penalty stories concerned Hong Kong—just 7 percent. By the turn of the 21st century in Hong Kong, capital punishment was PRC and foreign news. The major concern in Hong Kong is of course policy in the PRC, so that China stories accounted for 46 percent of all death penalty coverage in the 12-year period. In the seven years after 1998, the *Post* ran 252 mentions of capital punishment in the PRC, which is 53 percent of all death penalty coverage and more than eight times as many stories as there were about the death penalty in Hong Kong.

For the most part, the death penalty stories concerning Hong Kong were neither long nor about legislation. Individual crimes and defendants were the focus of many, and short letters to the editor from private citizens proposing or opposing a death penalty also appeared from time to time.

One long substantive analysis appeared in the *Post* on January 15, 1995, outlining the way a post-1997 SAR might reintroduce capital punishment. In the words of Nihal Jayawickrama, a professor at Hong Kong University, "the constraints of British policy will not be in place after 1997 and if the Legislative Council wants [a death penalty] the SAR won't stop it. It will depend on the nature of public opinion at the time and the intentions of the SAR" (quoted in *South China Morning Post*, January 15, 1995). Putting aside whether Jayawickrama accurately described the SAR's intentions, the notion that reviving a death penalty was politically possible once the British left would seem like an open invitation to a campaign to bring back the executioner after this Chinese region is liberated from its British yoke. If ever there was to be a clean test of the influence of "Asian values" on capital punishment, the transition of Hong Kong from British to PRC control would seem a prime candidate. But a review of the *Post* from 1995 through 2006 provides no evidence of any sustained or organized effort to bring back capital punishment in Chinese Hong Kong.

The published record of pro–death penalty sentiment in the *Post* is strikingly sparse: one letter to the editor said that "criminals who commit atrocious crimes . . . should be executed" (January 18, 1995), and the father of an arson-murder victim complained that the offender's "sentence is too light . . . We should bring back the death penalty" (January 22, 1995). But no political candidates or public figures responded to the *Post*'s story of January 15, 1995, on the political possibility of resurrecting capital punishment. Indeed, 12 years of newspaper coverage produced only two persons of any public prominence in the governance of Hong Kong who went on record as supporting the death penalty.

The first was an official in Hong Kong's equivalent of a police union, the Hong Kong Police Inspectors' Association. In January 1995, the *Post* reported that "in August, Mr. Robert Chan Chuen-Kung, the outspoken chairman of the Local Inspector's Association, was strongly rebuked by force management after he spoke up in favor of the death penalty being reintroduced after 1997"

(January 2, 1995). A second story reports the same "controversy" over his championing the possible reintroduction of the death penalty (February 27, 1995). Five months later, the *Post* reports, "The outspoken chairman of the local Inspector's Association . . . Senior Inspector Robert Chan Chuen-Kung stepped down today. . . . Last year he angered officers by calling for revival of capital punishment" (July 19, 1995).

The second pro–death penalty voice was the only political figure in Hong Kong who is on record in the *Post* as a proponent of capital punishment: "David Chu Yu-Lin, a member of the pro-China Preliminary Working Committee," who said, "[T]he local judiciary appears nowadays to have gone soft. . . . I am one of the chorus calling out for the return of the death penalty, at least on the statute books" (January 15, 1995). Yet the next time this death penalty "chorus" made the *Post* was more than two and a half years later, when Chu, now a legislator, suggested a "package of proposed police reforms that include the restoration of the death penalty for those who kill police officers" (October 6, 1997). In the same story, unnamed human rights activists branded the proposed reform as "crazy." The idea then disappeared from view for the next nine years in the *Post* while the world's most active executioners took over the administration of the SAR. The few death penalty stories that do appear in Hong Kong in this period describe the vigilance and concern of human rights lawyers and the pledges of political candidates "not to restore" capital punishment (November 12 and December 2, 1996). There is, in short, no visible campaign to reintroduce the death penalty in Hong Kong's leading English-language newspaper.

Table B.3 provides parallel information for the *Singtao Daily*, a Chinese-language newspaper in Hong Kong that claims a daily circulation of approximately 180,000. The 12 years covered in this analysis (1996–2007) start one year later than that of the *South China Morning Post* (the later start was made necessary because the first year with computerized records is 1996). The pattern of coverage in the *Singtao Daily* is almost identical to that in the *Post*. The annual number of stories varies from a low of 87 to a high of 144, with no clear temporal trend, and most of the coverage concerns the PRC, with more stories focusing on it than on Hong Kong in every year. As with the *Post*, the peak year for Hong Kong–related stories is 1998, and the drop-off after that is pronounced, with 41 stories in 1998 and fewer than eight stories in every subsequent year. For the nine years after 1998, there are a total of 21 Hong Kong death penalty stories, an average of about two per year and less than 5 percent of the 462 stories with a PRC focus. Hong Kong itself all but disappears from the death penalty news in the *Singtao Daily*, while about two death penalty stories each week are published focusing on the PRC or other countries.

Capital punishment has also disappeared as a local political question in Hong Kong newspapers, a vanishing act that is easy to explain. Human rights priorities in Hong Kong are self-centered. What is important to Hong Kong is what is at issue or at risk between the city and the PRC government, and the death penalty is neither at issue nor at risk. Because Hong Kong has neither

Table B.3

Death penalty–related articles and commentaries in *Singtao Daily*, 1996–2007, by geographic area that is the subject of comment

	Mainland China	*Hong Kong*	*Others*	*Total*
1996	47	4	53	104
1997	45	7	51	103
1998	59	41	44	144
1999	52	3	42	97
2000	53	2	43	98
2001	55	2	45	102
2002	52	3	38	93
2003	40	3	54	97
2004	39	7	41	87
2005	56	0	57	113
2006	57	1	46	104
2007	58	0	42	100

Source: Analysis of *Singtao Daily* by Jiang Su, visiting scholar, Boalt Hall School of Law, University of California at Berkeley, March 2008.

the desire nor the power to become a force in regional human rights matters, current concern about capital punishment is low. But this does not mean Hong Kong would quietly comply with efforts of its mainland masters to restore executions. The resignation of Robert Chan Chuen-Kung from the Local Police Inspectors' Association in 1995 suggests quite the opposite. The penal autonomy of Hong Kong is a bellwether of the long-term ability of the city to survive in the PRC's embrace. Reintroduction of capital punishment by mainland fiat would risk a firestorm, and Beijing knows it.

The Dog That Didn't Bark

What of locally generated demand for capital punishment? The Beijing government would likely be pleased with a demonstration of the cultural demand for capital punishment that it says pervades its nation, yet there has been no grassroots movement to restore the death penalty in Hong Kong. Perhaps one reason a grassroots or indigenous movement to bring back execution has not been launched is that local political elites in Hong Kong would distrust the authenticity of the "grassroots" origins of any call for more capital punishment. Recall that the *South China Morning Post* was quick to identify the connection of Chu to "the pro-China Preliminary Working Committee" when he became a one-man "chorus" in favor of the death penalty. Distrust of PRC power is mixed with heavy suspicion that "local" pressure on issues like capital punishment is not really local.

That Hong Kong has experienced no significant push back toward execution contradicts what any explanation that roots PRC executions in Chinese "cultural values" would expect. Hong Kong's reputation for public safety and effective law enforcement might be one reason why there has been little "law-and-order" outcry in the populace (Broadhurst 2005). Even so, the 15 years since the formal abolition of capital punishment in Hong Kong can be regarded as a controlled experiment testing the relative validity of the competing explanations of the high levels of execution in the PRC: "Asian values" versus the Chinese government as prime mover. Hong Kong represents a Chinese population and cultural setting that differs mainly in political structure and political tradition from mainland China. That the executioner is not needed in this environment is eloquent testimony to the power of a political explanation of death penalty policy, and is also an important demonstration of the value of regional comparisons as a method of research on capital punishment.

■ The Death Penalty in Macao

Macao can be distinguished from Hong Kong in numerous ways. For starters, its population of 430,000 at the time of its return to the Chinese mainland in 1999 was less than 7 percent of the population of Hong Kong at the time of its return two years earlier. The economy of this "Las Vegas of Asia" is also heavily dependent on a single industry—gambling—from which the local government obtains more than half its operating revenues (Godinho 2007). Gambling has also produced a more pronounced problem with organized crime and violence than Hong Kong has had to deal with (Broadhurst 2005). Indeed, on the eve of Macao's return to China in 1999, the city's "biggest complaint" concerned crime (McGivering 1999), and Edmund Ho, the SAR's first chief executive, promised that controlling it would be his government's top priority because residents were so concerned about law and order (Chinoy 1999). By many accounts, the people of Macao are also more patriotic toward the Chinese mainland than their Hong Kong counterparts are.[8] At the turn of the 21st century, almost half of Macao's population had settled in the city only in the previous 15 years, which may help explain why most Macanese seem to lack the sense of separateness and superiority that many residents of Hong Kong seem to express toward the mainland. Unlike Hong Kong, Macao also has lacked an influential middle class and a vocal political opposition (McGivering 1999),

8. Another contrast concerns Christianity. In Macao, the birthplace of Catholicism in China and East Asia, "the number of Roman Catholics and their proportion of Macao's population have been in steep decline," which is a stark contrast to the flourishing of Catholic and other churches on the Chinese mainland and in Hong Kong (Aikman 2003; Greenlees 2007).

not to mention respect for the country—Portugal—that colonized the territory for 450 years. By the end of that occupation, many locals believed the Portuguese administration was corrupt and inefficient and blamed it for failing to prevent crime and being remote and irrelevant in a wide variety of policy arenas.[9]

But if Macao is not merely a smaller, more espresso-loving version of Hong Kong, the death penalties in the two SARs have traversed broadly similar trajectories. Most notably, Macao's capital punishment policy has long been determined by outside forces. Portugal was the first European country to abolish the death penalty for murder (in 1867), and with the exception of executions for military crimes that occurred between 1916 and 1918, its last execution took place in 1849 (Hood 2002:23). Abolition for all crimes happened in 1976 as part of the political transition from Antonio Salazar's authoritarian regime (Hood 2002:250; Zimring 2003:23). A study of the relationship between colonial heritage and capital punishment has found that as of the year 2000, Portugal was the only former empire *all* of whose former colonies—five out of five—had completely abolished the death penalty. The prevalence of capital punishment in the former colonies of the Japanese, British, French, Spanish, Dutch, Belgian, Soviet, and American empires was considerably greater (Anckar 2004:87).

It is not clear exactly when Portuguese officials carried out their last execution in Macao, but in 1997 Amnesty International reported that none had taken place "for over a century." In 1995, this long-standing practice was enshrined into law when Macao's new Penal Code banned the death penalty and life imprisonment. The official press in the PRC reported that during the consultations on the Penal Code held earlier that year, "the Chinese side did not challenge the provision for abolishing the death penalty" and assured Macao representatives that they could retain an abolitionist policy as long as Macao deemed it necessary (quoted in Hands Off Cain 1999). In subsequent negotiations related to the handover, Portuguese officials requested and received assurances from the PRC that human rights would be respected and the death penalty would not be reintroduced. To drive the point home, Portugal's president issued a series of decrees in July 1999 that extended to Macao several international human rights standards. The decrees were suspended when Macao's legislative assembly complained that it had not been consulted, but they were reinstated a month later. In November 1999,

9. In 1974, Portugal's government even tried to return Macao to China, only to be rebuffed because "the time wasn't ripe." Some observers believe Lisbon effectively surrendered control of Macao affairs after riots and a general strike gripped the enclave in 1966, at the beginning of China's Cultural Revolution. Thereafter, local politics were dominated by leftist labor unions and pro-Beijing neighborhood associations, and the local media acquired "a pronounced pro-Beijing bias" (Crowell and Law 1998a; Crowell and Law 1998b). To some, these developments made Macao a "semiliberated" part of China, despite the Portuguese presence.

just one month before Macao's Portuguese period ended, Beijing informed the government of Portugal that it planned to pass 20 new laws as soon as Macao was handed back to China—and the death penalty was not among them. Since then, the death penalty has not been used in Macao territory, though jurisdictional ambiguities remain, much as they do in Hong Kong (Hood and Hoyle 2008:84).

Macao has experienced less controversy and debate about human rights issues than Hong Kong, both before and after their returns to the mainland. Britain and China rowed bitterly after Hong Kong's last British governor, Chris Patten, tried to increase the level of democracy at the 11th hour, and many Hong Kongers regarded him as their champion (McGivering 1999). Near the end of the British period, all the major government posts in Hong Kong were filled by ethnic Chinese except for those of attorney general and governor. In Macao, by contrast, all of the top administrative positions were held by Portuguese expatriates right up until the moment of transfer in 1999. The weaker localization of government and policy-making seemed to foster passivity in the local population in Macao and probably stunted civil society there as well (Crowell and Law 1998a; Crowell and Law 1998b). These differences, and the differences in levels of crime and in Chinese patriotism mentioned earlier, might mean the PRC would have an easier time installing a death penalty in Macao than in Hong Kong, but we think both outcomes are unlikely. Through the process of rendition, China already uses capital punishment against some Macao offenders, much as it does for criminals from Hong Kong. More important, a PRC move to reintroduce the death penalty in Macao would almost certainly generate blowback reactions in Hong Kong and Taiwan that the CCP would be loath to see. For these reasons, Macao seems likely to remain Casino City without capital punishment for a long time to come.

Appendix C: Vietnam

The real heirs of Stalin were not the Soviet leaders who followed him but two Asian dictators—Mao Zedong and Pol Pot—who aimed to remake their nations in an image consistent with their own Marxist-Leninist visions of a good society (Glover 1999:283). Cambodia abolished the death penalty in 1989 as part of the process of distancing a new government from the brutality of Pol Pot's regime,[1] while in the PRC a Maoist system of capital punishment outlived the chairman by 30 years (see chapter 7).

---

1. Pol Pot's vision of a better Cambodia produced "a revolution of unparalleled ferocity" in which "hundreds of thousands" were executed and one-fifth to one-third of the nation's seven million people died of starvation, overwork, and other unnatural causes (Kiernan 2002; Dunlop 2005:3; Kiernan 2005). Communist regimes everywhere have sought to level income disparities, monopolize the press, limit migration to cities, control communications with the outside world, and make law an instrument of policy, but Pol Pot's regime pursued even more radical reforms. "Money, law, courts, newspapers, the postal system and foreign telecommunications—even the concept of the city—were all simply abolished. Individual rights were not curtailed in favour of the collective, but extinguished altogether. Individual creativity, initiative, originality were condemned *per se*. Individual consciousness was systematically demolished" (Short 2004:11). Some analysts regard Cambodia as the "exception that proves the rule" because unlike other communist countries in Asia such as China, Vietnam, and North Korea, it was "never affected by Confucianism." On this view, the absence of a Confucian tradition "may be one of the main reasons that violence [in Cambodia] was so widespread and bloody. It is possible that what happened there was the effect of applying Sino-Vietnamese ideas to a

If Vietnam's Ho Chi Minh was not as enthusiastic a proponent of Stalinist death penalty methods as his counterparts in Cambodia and China, he and his successors were strongly influenced by the Russian dictator's approach to governing and state killing—and by Maoist methods as well. Indeed, "the line of inheritance from Stalin, to Mao, to Ho, to Kim Il Sung, to Pol Pot was quite clear, with each new leader receiving both material aid and ideological inspiration from his predecessor" (Malia 1999:xiv). In Vietnam, the result is a contemporary death penalty system that in several central respects looks a lot like China's, with high levels of execution, a wide range of capital offenses, heavy reliance on confessions, few due process protections, strict control of death penalty information, little public criticism of the party-state's policy, and a leading role for the Communist Party in capital punishment policy-making.

■ Contexts

The Socialist Republic of Vietnam (SRV) shares many features in common with the PRC even though its population of 85 million—about the same size as China's Sichuan Province—is only one-fifteenth that of its large neighbor to the north. To start with, Vietnam is a one-party communist state (one of five remaining communist governments in the world)[2] that uses violence and threats of violence to maintain its monopoly on power (Abuza 2006), and the Vietnamese Communist Party (VCP) presents most of its decisions as if they were the unanimous word of all parts of government. The SRV also tends to present its history—to itself and to outsiders—as a simple and heroic tale of resistance to foreign imperialists—Japanese, French, American, Chinese—and of reunification, revolution, and victory. Its constitution even makes it a criminal offense to "doubt the fruits of the revolution" that brought Ho Chi Minh's party to power after the military defeat of Japan in 1945.

In addition to regime type and orientation, there are numerous other similarities between Asia's two largest communist countries. Most fundamentally, Vietnam and China have both created hybrid economic systems that combine

---

population that was fundamentally opposed to them" (Margolin and Rigoulot 1999a:641). More research is needed about the reasons for Cambodia's crimes against humanity and the events that led to its abolition of capital punishment in 1989 (Cambodian League for the Promotion and Defence of Human Rights 2007).

2. As of September 2007, communist governments exist in four Asian countries— Vietnam, China, North Korea, and Laos—and in Cuba. Two main features distinguish the contemporary Asian versions of communism from communism as it operated in Europe. First, the communist governments of Asia (with the partial exception of Cambodia) are still in power. Second, communist regimes in Asia such as Vietnam and China "established themselves through their own efforts and built independent political systems with a strongly nationalist character" (Courtois et al. 1999:459).

elements of Leninism with capitalism (Jamieson 1995). In Vietnam the result is, in recent years, Asia's second-fastest-growing economy (after China), with 8 to 9 percent growth since 2005 (Bradsher 2006; Collins 2008), and Saigon had the fastest-growing economy of any major city in Asia during the mid-1990s (Templer 1998:15). Vietnam's economic "renovation" (*doi moi*) started in 1986 at the Sixth Communist Party Congress following a disastrous famine that plagued almost the entire country and was caused by the failures of the command economy that was put in place after the country was reunified in 1975. The reforms accelerated around 1991, opening new doors of opportunity and shortening the reach of some state powers. In the past ten years, Vietnam has halved its poverty rate, doubled its per capita income, and become the second-largest exporter of rice in the world (Finlay and Clark 2006:xvii). As in China, the vast bureaucracy that once tried to monitor the lives of millions of Vietnamese people now cares less what they do—so long as they stay out of politics. Vietnam also remains overwhelmingly rural, with about three-quarters of its people still working the land. As in the PRC, the inequality between urban and rural residents in Vietnam is large and growing, and corruption has become a serious problem since the economic reforms started (Collins 2008).

Some analysts inaccurately depict Vietnam's complex, hybrid culture as the dullard offspring of a far more sophisticated Chinese culture (Fitzgerald 1972), but much of what is described as Vietnamese culture does have its origins in China (Templer 1998:17,35). More generally, China has not only been a "perennial problem" for Vietnam for centuries, it has had a profound influence on attitudes, institutions, and policy in the nation that sometimes is called "China lite" (Templer 1998:283; Collins 2008). Whether Vietnam likes it or not, its economic fate and the durability of its party-state may be inextricably linked to those of its powerful neighbor.

Besides the differences in territorial size and population,[3] there are many other ways the most heavily bombed country in history is not merely a smaller version of the PRC.[4] Two of the most salient are as follows. First, the

---

3. Like China, Vietnam also has a "complex ethnic diversity," with six to eight million of its people belonging to 54 distinct ethnic minorities (Finlay and Clark 2006:xix). Despite some government attempts at proactive legislation, these minorities remain, for the most part, "socially, politically, and economically marginalized" (xx). So do many of the people who practice their religions outside the handful of state-approved faiths, although Vietnam's six to eight million Christians (mostly Catholic) do exercise a "disproportionate" influence on Vietnamese society (42).

4. A foreign diplomat in Hanoi who previously served in Beijing has said with some hyperbole that "everything" in Vietnam "is more moderate than in China" (quoted in Collins 2008:5). Vietnam is "a bit less harsh with dissidents than China"; its capitalism is "less red in tooth and claw"; Vietnam's version of "the Great Firewall of China" seems to be less forbidding of communication on the Internet; Vietnam has a two-child policy "pursued half-heartedly" instead of a one-child policy enforced harshly; Vietnam has a more consensual style of leadership in which power is shared by the president, the party boss,

experiment in social engineering that was agricultural reform in Vietnam was carried out simultaneously with reform of the Communist Party, whereas in the PRC agrarian reform preceded party reform by several years. Because the privileged class in Vietnam was much smaller than that in China, the period of large-scale state killing was less protracted (Margolin 1999:569). Second, ac-knowledging the damage caused by communism in Vietnam is "still anathema to many Westerners" who took a stand against French colonialism and Amer-ican imperialism in the 20th century (Margolin 1999:565). In this respect, recognizing the historical precursors of capital punishment in contemporary Vietnam may be as difficult for some Western progressives as it is hard for Chinese citizens and officials to appreciate the Maoist roots of their own government's current death penalty policy (see chapter 7).

■ Communist Foundations

Ho Chi Minh has been called a "missionary of revolution"—an evangelist of radical change through force—and the "father" of the modern nation of Vietnam (Brocheux 2007:23,95). Discussions of his legacy tend to describe him in one of three ways. To some, he was a saint who liberated the oppressed Vietnamese people from the yoke of Western imperialism. To others, he was a tyrant committed to the spread of communist totalitarianism throughout the world. To yet others, he was an unprincipled opportunist who, like Mao, exploited his reputation for integrity and simplicity in order to amass power and glorify himself (Duiker 2000:569). All of these descriptions capture part of the truth about a complex man who consciously cultivated an air of mystery regarding his own biography and achievements (Ho adopted more than 50 assumed names during his lifetime).[5]

But Ho was nobody's carbon copy. He relied more on a strategy of collective leadership than did Stalin and Mao, who consistently asserted their personal dominance in political and policy matters, and he also seemed more "a man of situations" than were his more ideologically driven counter-parts in Russia and China (Macdonald 1993:340; Brocheux 2007:187). In the last analysis, however, Ho's role in Vietnam was often paramount, and the influences on him from outside the country were just as often profound (SarDesai 2005:141).[6] Most important, Ho "fully adopted the Soviet Socialist

and the prime minister; and the decision-making process in Vietnam tends to be slower—and more equitable—than the one in China (Collins 2008:6).

5. Though Ho never adopted their names, one of his biographers concluded that he "was half Lenin and half Gandhi" (Duiker 2000:576).

6. Ho not only founded the VCP (at a conference in Hong Kong in 1930) and served as president from 1946 to 1969, he was the nation's top strategist for much of his adult life and, four decades after his death, remains its "most inspiring symbol" (Duiker 2000:576). The communist victories in the wars against France and the United States and the

model and never repudiated it," thereby establishing and reinforcing severe limits on individual freedoms and human rights (Brocheux 2007:187). If he sometimes seemed more Vietnamese than communist, his revolutionary doctrine—and the violence it bred—ultimately triumphed over his more unifying and temporizing patriotism (187). At the end of his life, Ho himself was "crushed" by the weight of the implacable communist system he had helped put in place through his "indisputable charisma" (187).

The communist influences on Vietnamese capital punishment have been similarly significant. From 1911, when Ho took a job working in the kitchen of a French ship, until 1941, when he returned to Vietnam to found the League for the Independence of Vietnam, he traveled abroad, frequently moving between Russia and China. He was a fervent follower of Lenin, writing on the occasion of Lenin's funeral in 1924 that the Soviet leader "was our father, teacher, comrade, and adviser. Now he is our guiding star that leads to social revolution. Lenin lives on in our deeds." Ho also appropriated many elements of Mao's model for revolution (Kamm 1997; SarDesai 2005). When he was asked why he did not write much himself he simply replied, "Mao had said it all" (quoted in Templer 1998:294). It would be absurd to question the sincerity of the nationalist aspirations of Ho or his Communist Party, for they fought against the imperialist Japanese, French, and Americans with remarkable determination. For them, accusations of "collaboration" with "the enemy" carried the same force as the "counterrevolutionary" label did in China—and stimulated similarly severe responses. In capital punishment as in other policy spheres, there worked beneath the surface of Vietnamese nationalism "a Stalinist form of Maoism that followed its prototypes extremely closely" (Margolin 1999:566).

Consider a few examples of China-like death penalty policy in Vietnam. In the revolution of August 1945 through which the communists took control, Ho consolidated his power by executing some 10,000 "enemies" and imprisoning tens of thousands more (Vo 2004:24). The aim was to "liquidate all competition" (Margolin 1999:566). In the Northern Land Reform of 1953–1956, the party's main goal was the total control of a population that had not been sufficiently receptive to the communist takeover, and state killing was one of the main means of achieving it. Approximately 50,000 people were executed during this campaign—a per capita scale of state killing not far removed from that in some years of Mao's China—and another 300,000 to 500,000 either died of starvation or committed suicide to escape execution (Vo 2004:26). The VCP's methods during this land reform "were identical" to those used

---

dominance of the Communist Party in subsequent decades are above all "a legacy of the vision, the will, and the leadership" of this man (2). But for many people in Vietnam as for many people in the other communist countries of Asia, "life under right-wing Asian strongmen was, on the whole, to be preferred to life under Mao, Pol Pot, Kim Il Sung or even Ho Chi Minh" (Buruma 2007b).

by the CCP in China's agrarian reforms of 1946–1952 (Margolin 1999:568). And in Vietnam as in China, communist activists sometimes incited the poorer peasants to protest and urged them to put their enemies on public trial. Many victims were chosen arbitrarily, their show trials were frequently farcical, and quotas (up to 4 or 5 percent of the population in some circumstances) were used to generate the desired scale of convictions and executions. In these respects and more, revolutionary justice in Vietnam closely resembled its Chinese uncle (568). The result was an "extraordinary" scale of violence, with hatred of the "enemy" its most prominent ideological theme. Even Vietnam's motto resembled those used in Mao's China: "Better ten innocent deaths than one enemy survivor" (quoted in Margolin 1999:569).

Large-scale executions continued in the years after land reform ended, though it can be (as in China) difficult to discern which ones were judicial and which were not. What is not hard to see are the high rates of state killing. In 1966–1969, at least 18,000 persons were assassinated by the party-state, a per capita rate of explicitly political killing that rivals what happened in the PRC during the same period. In 1968, in the city of Hue (which lies near the South China Sea coast about halfway between Hanoi and Saigon) "between 3,000 and 5,000 South Vietnamese citizens were executed in cold blood" (Vo 2004:30). The Vietnamese communists' most aggressive campaign of violence followed the fall of Saigon in 1975. In the subsequent 18 months, an estimated 100,000 to 250,000 persons were executed and more than two million suspected "dissidents" were imprisoned, making up almost 7 percent of the 30 million residents in the southern part of the nation where this campaign was concentrated. For Mao's China to match this execution rate—1,400 to 3,400 executions per million—it would have had to execute one to three million people per year. The Cultural Revolution was extremely bloody, but even it was not that bad (MacFarquhar and Schoenhals 2006).[7]

The scale of execution, the use of quotas, and the reliance on distinctions between "friends" and "enemies" are hardly the only aspects of state killing in Vietnam that had parallels in the PRC. Trials in the "people's courts" involved little in the way of legal process, and persons sentenced to death were often executed immediately and in public (Vo 2004:139). At some prison camps, loudspeakers announced the names of the condemned twice each week, followed by an account of the crimes they were found to have committed and the offenders' public degradation. Thousands were convicted of "counterrevolutionary crimes," which frequently amounted to nothing more than being insufficiently enthusiastic about the party's purposes and policies. Torture was hidden but ever-present (Margolin 1999:573), and many people were pressured or forced

---

7. See Truong (1986) for an account by a former Vietcong minister of justice who defected to the West after becoming convinced that the Communist Party was an obstacle to democratic revolution, and see Kamm (1997) for interviews with other Vietnamese defectors who experienced the VCP's repression.

to falsely accuse others in order to protect themselves. Reeducation through "thought reform" (*cai tao*) was widely practiced, and its main aims were to eliminate individual and capitalist thoughts, instill Marxist-Leninist beliefs, and create "new socialist men" through such mechanisms as self-criticism (Vo 2004:143). In the bamboo gulags, tens of thousands died from starvation (rations were so small that death often came in weeks), even larger numbers were beaten and abused, and when it was difficult or costly to transfer inmates from one facility to another, many were "simply liquidated rather than moved" (Margolin 1999:571). In the mid-1970s, the official Saigon prison (Chi Hoa) held more than 40,000 inmates, about five times the number incarcerated under the previous regime in conditions that already were "universally condemned" (574). The concentration camps outside the official system (usually far out in the jungle) were in some ways even worse, with many inmates sentenced to a lifetime of forced labor without any legal means of presenting a defense or appeal (Doan 1986).[8] One testament about prison conditions that was "signed" orally by 48 inmates pleaded with the Red Cross and "humanitarian organizations throughout the world" to "send us cyanide capsules as soon as possible so that we can put an end to our suffering ourselves. We want to die now! Help us to carry out this act, and help us kill ourselves as soon as possible. We would be eternally in your debt" (Doan 1986; Margolin 1999:574).

■ Contemporary Realities

Although the "renovation" that began in 1986 has altered many aspects of life in Vietnam, continuities are conspicuous in several spheres of capital punishment. The SRV remains, like the PRC, highly secretive about its death penalty policy and practice, so it is difficult to discern the scale of capital punishment. And since NGOs and international media focus significantly less attention on Vietnam than on China, it is even more difficult to estimate death sentences and executions there than in the PRC. What we do know suggests that Vietnam ranks among the most aggressive death penalty states in Asia and the world. In table C.1, which summarizes what has been reported about Vietnamese death sentences and executions over the course of the last decade, all the plus signs indicate that the true figures are probably higher—sometimes substantially so (Amnesty International 2003a; Amnesty International 2003b). The death penalty numbers from both Amnesty International and Hands Off Cain are based mainly on information provided by Vietnam's tightly controlled state media. "No independent

---

8. One of the hallmarks of government repression in Vietnam, China, Cambodia, and North Korea was "the absence of even cursory references to the mechanisms of law and justice: everything was political" (Margolin and Rigoulot 1999:640). In China (in 1979) and Vietnam (in 1986), the introduction of a penal code marked the end of the period of terror.

Table C.1
Death sentences and executions in Vietnam, 1995–2007

Years	Death sentences	Executions	Source
1995	104+[1]	11+	Amnesty International
1996– 2000	N/A	64+ (average: 13/year)	Hood 2002:92
1997– 2002	931+ (average: 155/year)	N/A	Supreme People's Court and Amnesty International
2000	112+	12+	Hood 2002:51; Amnesty International
2001	N/A	N/A	
2002	48+	27+	Amnesty International
2002	N/A	34+	Hands Off Cain
2003	103+	64+	Amnesty International
2003	N/A	69+	Hands Off Cain
2004	88+	64+	Amnesty International
2004	N/A	82+	Hands Off Cain
2005	65+	21+[2]	Amnesty International
2005	N/A	27+	Hands Off Cain
2005	N/A	100+/yr	Forum Asia Democracy
2006	116+	N/A	Vietnam News
2007	95+ (as of November 30)	25+	Vietnam News; Hands Off Cain

Sources: Hood 2002; Supreme People's Court of Vietnam; Amnesty International (various years); Hands Off Cain (various years); Foreign Asia Democracy 2005; West Australian 2007; "Vietnam Considers" 2008.

Note: National population: 67.2 million in 1990; 79.0 million in 2000; 85.3 million in 2007.

[1] Plus sign indicates true figure is probably higher.

[2] In January 2004, the prime minister issued a decree declaring death penalty statistics a state secret, and reporting and disseminating them became criminal acts. The apparent decline in executions from 2004 to 2005 may reflect changes in reporting practices.

media organs have been allowed" in Vietnam, and the few attempts by dissidents to publish outside approved channels "have met with harsh and immediate crackdowns by the state" (Abuza 2006:3).[9]

Between 1995 and 2005, Vietnam's annual execution estimates range from a low of 13 per year during the first half of that period (an annual rate of

9. The VCP is particularly "concerned about the power of the internet and the ability of dissidents both to post their views and to form relationships with people overseas, especially ethnic Vietnamese" (Abuza 2006:3). Secrecy and censorship are found in numerous policy areas besides capital punishment. As in China, "many budgets, policies, and issues are still categorized as 'state secrets,' and hence any investigation into them is a punishable offense" (12).

0.16 executions per million population) to (according to a Forum Asia Democracy report released in 2005) more than 100 executions per year in the early 2000s (1.2 executions or more per million population). By the former measure, Vietnam carried out executions in the last half of the 1990s about 40 percent less often than the United States and 40 times less often than Singapore, but by the latter count—over 100 executions annually—Vietnam ranks well above the threshold of 1.0 executions per million that we have used to define operational death penalty systems (see chapter 2). Even by the conservative counts of Amnesty International and Hands Off Cain, Vietnam's execution rate has approached that threshold in several recent years—despite the problem of under reporting. The apparent drop in executions after 2004 may largely reflect the government's decision in that year to treat death penalty statistics as a top state secret, thereby ratcheting up the degree of concealment above an already high level. The change in reporting was at least partly motivated by the party-state's desire to defuse criticism from European governments and international human rights organizations (Hands Off Cain 2007).

The most striking figure in table C.1 comes from the "incomplete statistics" provided by the SPC for the period 1997–2002 (Amnesty International 2003b). By the government's own accounting, there was an annual average of 155 death sentences during this six-year interval: 57 percent for murder and other violence resulting in death, 33 percent for drug crimes, 3 percent for corruption, 0.5 percent for other property offenses, and 6 percent for all other offenses. Amnesty International has reported that "most people sentenced to death [in Vietnam] are executed once their cases have gone through the appeals procedure" and that commutations from the president "are rare" (2003b). If so, then Vietnam's execution rate may have approached 2 executions per million in the years covered by the SPC's report, a level matched or exceeded only by China, Singapore, Saudi Arabia, Sierra Leone, and Belarus during the same period (Hood 2002:92). According to the *Vietnam News,* the number of death sentences remains high in the most recent years for which information is available, with 116 in 2006 and 95 in 2007 ("Vietnam Considers" 2008).

In addition to the sizable scale of capital punishment and the secrecy that surrounds it, there are several similarities between the SRV and the PRC in how death as a criminal sanction is administered. Most fundamentally, the VCP maintains a monopoly on power and therefore dictates almost all aspects of death penalty policy in addition to intervening in individual cases, when necessary, to achieve the outcomes it wants. In 2000, the VCP's general secretary declared that it would transform Vietnam into a "law-governed society," and toward that end legal codification has "increased dramatically." But article 2 of the constitution still places the party—and some of its members—above the law, while indicted persons are presumed guilty under the same charter (Abuza 2006). Taking a page out of Lee Kuan Yew's book for stifling criticism and crushing dissent (Lydgate 2003), the VCP issued a new libel law in 2004 that requires journalists to pay monetary damages to individuals or organizations who have been harmed by their reports—even if they were accurate (Abuza 2006). In other ways as well, including efforts to recruit the best and the brightest to its inner circle at an early stage, the VCP often looks to Singapore, "a one-party state whose government still controls the commanding heights of the economy" (Collins 2008:6).

Vietnam's death penalty process provides suspects and defendants with few meaningful protections against the party-state's power. Police torture is common, and many confessions are coerced. Defense lawyers are not allowed to call or question their own witnesses, have limited freedom to meet with the suspects and defendants they represent, and in many cases can do little more than plead for clemency on a capital defendant's behalf. On the whole, the capital process "falls far short" of international standards (Amnesty International 2003b; B. Cho 2003). Some trials are so scripted that judges announce the dates for verdict and sentencing at the very first hearing.[10]

Although capital trials and executions in Vietnam are not publicized as much as they were in the war years and the first decade or so thereafter, executions continue to be carried out in public, and people with no direct links to the parties are frequently "encouraged to attend" (Amnesty International 2003b). In 2003, for example, ten persons were publicly executed in Nam Dinh Province in front of nearly 1,000 spectators. Five years earlier, six men and one woman were executed outside Hanoi in front of a crowd of similar size (Amnesty International 2003a). The woman was so distressed that she fainted three times before being shot.

Executions are carried out by a firing squad of five people, often ending with a "make-sure" shot to the head, and usually after a longer wait on death row than is customary in China.[11] Relatives of the condemned are not informed beforehand, but two or three days after the fact they are asked to

10. For descriptions of the biggest criminal proceeding in Vietnam's history, which culminated in the execution of a gangster known as "Vietnam's godfather" and four of his captains, see "Vietnam Officials" (2002), "Nam Cam" (2004), and Finlay and Clark (2006). Altogether, more than 150 people went on trial with the mob boss known as Nam Cam, including several high-level police and prosecutors who had protected his criminal enterprises, and at least two members of the VCP's Central Committee were expelled from the party. The Nam Cam case came to symbolize the seriousness of corruption in Vietnam, growing public anger about it, and the VCP's perception that this problem poses a serious threat to its continued rule, as is also the case in China.

11. In the PRC, executions usually occur within seven days of the finalization of a death sentence, whereas most condemned prisoners in Vietnam wait on death row—often in leg irons and shackles that severely restrict mobility—for at least one year after the appeals process has been exhausted. The reasons for the longer lag in Vietnam are unclear. According to Amnesty International (2003b), as of 2003, the minimum time for a defendant to go through the capital appeals process in Vietnam was five months and the maximum was four years. In China, the maximum appeal period is about the same as in Vietnam but the minimum period is substantially shorter—sometimes as brief as a week or two (Lu and Miethe 2007:109).

collect the deceased's belongings. The family has no right to receive the corpse of the condemned; in fact, handing over the body is banned (though family members with means may be able to acquire it by paying a bribe). Some accounts say that condemned prisoners are taken to the execution grounds blindfolded and gagged (as also occurs in China), presumably to prevent last-minute protests (Amnesty International 2003b). The party-state has proposed several reforms to this execution process. In 2005, the Ministry of Justice proposed legislation that would introduce the alternative of lethal injection and authorize the family of the executed to obtain the body for proper burial, which in Vietnam's religious tradition is deemed a necessary step to peaceful passage to the next stage of existence. One year earlier, officials proposed replacing firing squads with some form of mechanized gun in order to "overcome the problem of 'trembling hands' of nervous firing squad members" (Amnesty International 2005b) and to shield the execution team from "trauma" (Hands Off Cain, April 8, 2006). Proposals such as these may also have been prompted by the regime's perceived need to be seen as a civilized member of the international community (Lynch 2006; Bae 2007).

Foreign considerations also seem evident in three other realms of Vietnamese capital punishment. First, in 1999 the SRV reduced the number of capital offenses from 44 to 29 (though Amnesty International reported a substantial rise in the use of capital punishment after this reform, especially for drug-related crime and economic offenses).[12] In subsequent years Vietnam announced several times that it was considering reducing the scope of its death penalty laws even further, especially for economic offenses such as fraud and bribery, but as of this writing the second wave of reform has not occurred (Tran 2006; "Vietnam Considers" 2008). Second, legislation in 2000 allowed death sentences for pregnant women and mothers of children up to 36 months old to be reduced to life imprisonment (Hood 2002:51; "Pregnancy" 2006). This reform is consistent with internationally recognized safeguards to protect "vulnerable groups" from capital punishment (Hood 2002:114). Third, Vietnam has executed only one Westerner for drug trafficking since 1975: a Canadian of Vietnamese origin named Nguyen Thi Hiep, who was executed by firing squad in April 2000. During the same period, Vietnam spared the lives of at least four Australian nationals who had been sentenced to death on drug charges, in addition to an unknown number of drug-offending foreigners with other national origins who had been condemned to die (Bunce 2006). This relative lenity toward foreign drug offenders contrasts sharply with death penalty policy in Singapore, where 73 percent of known executions in 1991–2000 were for drug trafficking and 53 percent of the executions recorded by

12. Since the death penalty for drugs was introduced in 1992, Vietnam has practiced some of the toughest drug enforcement in the world. A death sentence is mandatory for anyone caught with more than 600 grams of heroin (1.3 pounds) or more than 20 kilograms of opium (44 pounds). See "Death Penalty for 15" (2007).

Amnesty International in 1993–2003 were of foreign nationals (Amnesty International 2004b).[13] Here, too, Vietnam's relatively cautious approach to capital punishment for foreigners may reflect the regime's need—economically and politically—to avoid censure by abolitionist nations to which its own future is linked. Indeed, fear of possible censure may have been one reason why Vietnam was the only retentionist nation in Asia that did not oppose the UN resolution in December 2007 calling for a worldwide moratorium on executions with an eye toward abolition (it abstained).

■ Conclusion

Death penalty policy in contemporary Vietnam was created in a communist context. In turn, Vietnam's version of communism has been, like most national communisms are and were, "linked by an umbilical cord to the Soviet womb" and to "the genius" Joseph Stalin, who was "the hero of world Communism" for 30 years (Courtois 1999a:23,28). This linkage to Moscow lends a surprising amount of similarity to the various communist histories, which for our purposes can be reduced to three family resemblances. First, communist regimes did not just commit criminal acts, as all states do on occasion, they frequently "ruled lawlessly, by violence, and without regard for human life" (Malia 1999 : xvii). The widespread use of capital punishment and of more lawless forms of state killing are two leading indicators that this communist pattern was incarnated in the Vietnamese context too. Second, there never was a benign, initial phase of communism before it took a wrong turn off track. In the SRV as in the Soviet Union and the PRC, the need to crush "class enemies" animated Communist Party policy from the start and frequently fueled the machinery of death thereafter. Third, the terror and violence that are the defining characteristics of communist regimes in the 20th century "cannot be explained as the prolongation of pre-revolutionary political cultures," for they originated in neither traditional autocracies "from above" nor in traditional folk practices "from below" (xviii). Rather, in Vietnam as in Russia, China, Cambodia, and North Korea, state violence against the population was "a deliberate policy of the new revolutionary order," and its scope and inhumanity "far exceeded anything in the national past" (xviii).

With the exception of Cuba, Asia is the only place on the planet where communists still rule, and it is therefore reasonable to wonder whether it

---

13. Two weeks after Amnesty International published the Singapore figures, Singapore's Ministry of Foreign Affairs published a lengthy response claiming that between 1993 and 2003, 64 percent of the persons who had been executed were Singaporeans (Singapore Ministry of Home Affairs 2004). Even if the official figure is accurate, Singapore still executes many more foreigners than Vietnam does (see appendix E).

makes sense to speak of a specifically Asian brand of communism that has shaped capital punishment and other criminal justice policies.[14] We think it might, for at least three reasons. First, the key link among communist Asian countries and the way they practice capital punishment is "more often Beijing than Moscow" (Courtois 1999a:638). Comparative chronologies of the various Asian communisms show that policy initiatives not only came from China on a regular basis, they were frequently followed so closely that "the similarity sometimes seems to border on cloning" (639). In death penalty policy more particularly, Vietnamese practices bear a striking resemblance to the patterns that have prevailed in China. Second, communism in Asia sought to transform the whole of society by trusting that the mind of every individual can be completely filled with new, better ideas and that those individuals' future actions will reflect their new knowledge. In Vietnam as in the other Asian communisms, an aggressive policy of capital punishment frequently coexisted with a more thoroughgoing regime of thought control than existed in communisms elsewhere in the world (Margolin and Rigoulot 1999:639). Third, communism in East and Southeast Asia aimed to spread this ideology of political correctness and belief in the individual's willpower from the

---

14. Cuba does not publish statistics on its prisoners, death sentences, or executions, but according to Elizardo Sanchez, the president of a Havana-based human rights organization without legal status that Fidel Castro's government has tolerated, Cuba executed between 5,000 and 6,000 people in 1959–2003, an average of 111 to 133 executions per year for a nation with a current population of 11.2 million (Grogg 2006). All were men (Hood 2002:121). If this estimate is accurate, then Cuba's average execution rate since the revolution that brought Castro to power is higher than this book's estimates of Chinese execution rates after Mao died. The scope of capital punishment in Cuba is also broad: a death sentence can be imposed for 79 violations of state security and for 33 common crimes (Hood 2002:51). Capital punishment in Cuba was banned by the 1940 constitution that was in effect when Castro took power, but in 1959 his regime passed a law to reestablish its use, and that provision was subsequently incorporated into the 1976 constitution. In recent years, however, Cuba has seldom executed. The only executions between 1999 and 2007 seem to be the ones that occurred in April 2003, after three Cubans were convicted of hijacking a ferry carrying dozens of passengers in an attempt to reach the United States. Those executions and the summary trial that preceded them drew widespread condemnation, even from Castro's staunch supporters, and the Comandante himself expressed ambivalence about them after the fact. At a 1992 Earth Summit meeting in Brazil, Castro said his government was willing to sign a multilateral treaty to abolish the death penalty but would not get rid of the punishment on its own because "it is a tool in the struggle against those intent on destroying our country." In 2004, Castro's foreign ministry told the UN high commissioner for human rights that abolition in Cuba would be linked to "a cease in the hostility, terrorism, and economic, commercial, and financial warfare to which its people have been subjected for over 40 years by the United States" (Grogg 2006). And in 2008, new Cuban president Raul Castro (Fidel's brother) commuted all death sentences to prison terms of 30 years to life (about 30 inmates benefited), except for three people who had been condemned to death for terrorism (Frank 2008).

Communist Party to society as a whole—and with some success. This generalization of belief happened in a more attenuated way in the Soviet Union and eastern Europe, perhaps because they lacked a preexisting culture of Confucianism that, in a variety of Asian contexts, defined a way of life for *all* classes (640). Future research may discover that Confucianism mitigated some of the harms of Asian communisms (641).[15] If it had that effect in Vietnam, the result was still a state that frequently used violence, coercion, and capital punishment as tools of governance.[16]

The future of death penalty policy in Vietnam depends on the fate of the SRV and, perhaps more fundamentally, on the fortunes of the CCP (Puhar 2003). As we argued in chapter 7, it is difficult to imagine external pressures or inducements that could motivate abolition by authoritarian regimes of the kind that still exist in the PRC and the SRV. China is not Lithuania, nor is Vietnam. As in China, therefore, so, too, in Vietnam: democratization and a deeper commitment to human rights seem to be the best hope for an execution-free society. How long this will take is hard to tell. Since the *doi moi* reforms started in 1986, Vietnam "has had to endure the difficult and protracted process of scraping off the sticky tar of communism," and that task has been easier in economic matters than in political areas such as capital punishment (Templer 1998:46; Collins 2008:14). The reader should also recall our two pieces of encouraging news for people alarmed by the scale and barbarity of executions in contemporary China: the recent appearance of sharp declines in death sentences and executions, and the astonishing pace of change in that country (see chapter 7). Decent death penalty data for Vietnam are so sparse that we cannot

15. When Lee Kuan Yew visited Vietnam in 1995, he said the country "had a certain something" (Confucianism) that would ensure its future success (quoted in Templer 1998:289). What the sage of "Asian values" meant was that in cultural terms, Vietnam resembles the Asian nations that have experienced rapid economic growth. But this analysis is at best incomplete (Mahbubani 2008:51). No Southeast Asian nation is predominantly Confucian, and three success stories in the region—Malaysia, Indonesia, and Thailand— have no Confucian background at all. What is more, Lee's own Singapore was hostile to the philosophy during much of its high-growth period (Templer 1998:290).

16. One puzzle is why communist-controlled Laos has not had an execution since 1989 and has not issued a death sentence since 1993 (Hood 2002:45,248; Hood and Hoyle 2008:88). There were purges of state and party leaders in 1979 and 1990, but they were not bloody (Margolin 1999:576). Laos became communist in the aftermath of the communist victory in Vietnam in 1975. Thereafter, about 10 percent of the population fled the country, including more than 30 percent of the Hmong minority in the mountains and 90 percent of all intellectuals, technicians, and officials. In communist Asia, only North Korea during the Korean War of 1950–1953 saw a larger share of its population leave the country, causing some commentators to call the Lao People's Democratic Republic "a population in flight" (Margolin 1999:575). If the fate of Laos's 5.8 million people depends on that of Vietnam, as many analysts believe, then the divergent death penalty policies in the two countries are all the more puzzling (Kremmer 1998; Dakin 2003; Evans and Osborne 2003; "Country Profile: Laos" 2007).

tell if the first piece of good news has any echoes there. We do know, however, that Vietnam is changing at a remarkably rapid rate (Jamieson 1995; Mai Elliott 1999; SarDesai 2005; Collins 2008). As a former revolutionary peasant told a delegation of Westerners, "my country has developed more in the last ten years than in the previous thousand" (quoted in Finlay and Clark 2006:xvii).

So a great deal has changed in Vietnam, and much of it is for the better, but in the process of change Vietnam also has acquired many of the problems that afflict the former communist countries of eastern Europe: corruption, organized crime, drug abuse, prostitution, declining educational standards, increasing inequality, pollution, and a sagging infrastructure. In the name of "stability," the VCP has put off many of the changes it eventually will be forced to make, such as the creation of independent courts and media, the establishment of mechanisms of governmental accountability, and the encouragement of respect for civil liberties (Abuza 2006). Unable to regain the control or esteem that it once commanded, the VCP's response in recent years has been to "clench and release its grip on the economy and society in an increasingly desperate manner as its power slips slowly away" (Templer 1998:355; Collins 2008:14–16). Sooner or later it will have to let go. When it does, we expect to see major declines in execution and perhaps even outright abolition of the kind that occurred when communist regimes collapsed in Cambodia and in central European nations such as Hungary, Romania, and Czechoslovakia.

Appendix D: Thailand

■ Contexts

The large and rapidly developing nation of Thailand is culturally and politically distinct from most of the rest of Southeast Asia. With an area somewhat larger than California and about the same size as France, Thailand was home to nearly 63 million people in 2007, making it the ninth most populous country in Asia and the 20th most populous country in the world. About 95 percent of Thai people are adherents of Theravada Buddhism, a religion that is in many ways central to Thai identity and culture (Jackson 2003). The country has close to 300,000 Buddhist monks (one for every 210 people), and two key Buddhist values are the commitment to abstain from taking life (the first of five precepts in the *pancasila* code) and the principle of nonviolence (*ahimsa*). Nonetheless, Buddhist authorities have taken little action against the death penalty, and many leading monks support the institution (Alarid and Wang 2001; interview with Amnesty International chairperson Somsri Hananuntasuk in Death Penalty Thailand Blog, January 31, 2006).

There are at least three reasons for the tolerant attitudes toward capital punishment among Thailand's Buddhist monks. First, most monks come from rural regions of the country where support for the death penalty is especially strong. Second, many monks lack information about the reality of capital punishment in their country. Since the death penalty is "not considered a pressing issue in Thailand," the media, the government, and NGOs direct little attention toward it, and public ignorance is one result (International

Federation for Human Rights and Union for Civil Liberty 2005:11).[1] Third and perhaps most important, "political authorities strictly control the Buddhist administration" in Thailand (14). The supreme patriarch of the nation's Buddhist *sangha* (congregation) is appointed by the king; the state (through the king) has sole power to bestow ecclesiastical titles on monks; and the law forbids monks from making political statements (15).

Thailand had one of the world's highest rates of economic growth between 1985 and 1996, averaging almost 9 percent annually until the Asian financial crisis occurred in 1997. The Thai economy floundered for some time thereafter, but by 2002, annual growth was back above 5 percent. The financial crisis hit the middle class hard, but the most intense pain was felt by tens of millions of Thais whose incomes fell under, or close to, the poverty line as real wages dropped and prices and unemployment rose. Many have still not recovered. According to the World Bank's 2006 *World Development Report*, 32 percent of Thais live on $1 to $2 a day. The comparable figures for Indonesia, Brazil, and Argentina are 52 percent, 22 percent, and 14 percent, respectively (Studwell 2007:179).

The singular feature of Thailand's government is the influence and importance of the king in politics. The octogenarian monarch, Bhumibol Adulyadej, is not a figurehead in the tradition of Japan's postwar emperor but a real ruling force and a critical center of power during the frequent constitutional crises that have visited Thailand since he ascended to the throne in 1946 (Handley 2006). In other respects, the Thai government "has long echoed the polity of the Philippines," with the similarities today "more apparent than ever" (Studwell 2007:181). Most notably, the Thai economic elite has increased its control of the country's political process by winning a growing share of seats in the nation's parliament. This development reached its peak with the rise of Thaksin Shinawatra, a billionaire businessman and politician who is often compared to Silvio Berlusconi, the "tycoon populist" who combined vast wealth, a virtual media monopoly, and "rank criminality" during a multi-chapter career in Italian politics (Stille 2006; see also Pongsudhirak 2006; Rafferty 2006).[2] Thaksin became Thailand's prime minister in 2001 and was

---

1. The Thailand surveys that have been done indicate high levels of public support for capital punishment (International Federation for Human Rights and Union for Civil Liberty 2005:11). Our table 8.1 also cites a poll that revealed 84 percent public support for the death penalty in 2005.

2. Thaksin's first career was in the police force, where he served from 1973 to 1987, and he is the only Asian leader we know to have earned an advanced degree in criminology. In 1978, he received a doctorate in criminal justice at Sam Houston State University in Texas, where he wrote a dissertation titled "An Analysis of the Relationship between the Criminal Justice Educational Process and the Attitude of the Student toward the Rule of Law." Many Thais wondered about Thaksin's own attitude toward the rule of law during the widespread extrajudicial killing that occurred while he was prime minister in 2001–2006 (Macan-Markar 2007).

reelected to that post by a landslide in 2005 before resigning in 2006 following street protests against his rule and the party he led (Wehrfritz and Cochrane 2006).[3] After a snap election marked by controversy, a military coup took over the government in September 2006, sending Thaksin into self-imposed exile in Europe. It was the country's 18th coup since Thailand became a constitutional monarchy in 1932.[4]

Thailand carried out 26 judicial executions during Thaksin's period as prime minister, and police, military, and other government officials summarily killed at least 4,000 persons extrajudicially ("Silent Night" 2004; Munsgool 2007; "A Law" 2008).[5] That is 12.5 times more extrajudicial executions than there were judicial executions in the entire country during the 65 years before Thaksin took power. Thaksin himself seemed to authorize the lethal violence when he declared that "because drug traders are ruthless to our children, being ruthless to them is not a bad thing. It may be necessary to have casualties. . . . If there are deaths among [drug] traders, it's normal" (quoted in Macan-Markar 2007). Thaksin also blocked several attempts to investigate the extrajudicial killings that occurred under his leadership. In August 2007, while he was in exile in Britain, Thailand's Supreme Court approved a warrant to arrest him for crimes of corruption, and Thai human rights advocates were lobbying to have him booked for murder as well (Macan-Markar 2007; see also appendix G).

3. In May 2007, Thaksin and 111 members of his party were banned from engaging in politics for five years by Thailand's Constitutional Court (Paddock 2006; "Party" 2007). In March 2008, Thaksin pleaded not guilty in the first of several criminal corruption cases brought against him. Three months later, three of his lawyers were found guilty and sentenced to six months in prison for attempting to bribe Supreme Court judges who were hearing a high-profile case against Thaksin and his wife. Their $60,000 bribe was brought to the court hidden in a cake box, leading the Thai media to call the case "pastrygate" (Head 2008).

4. On the eve of an election in December 2007 that was supposed to return power to a civilian government, Thitinan Pongsudhirak, a professor at Chulalongkorn University in Bangkok, said, "Thailand is stuck in an anachronism. We have a neo-feudal hierarchy that is untenable. It's just incompatible with the 21st century. This contest between the older established order and the newly emerging order is being played out in the twilight of the king's glorious reign" (quoted in Mydans 2007b). Except for the absence of royalty, similar conflicts between old and new have characterized politics in the Philippines (see chapter 4; see also Karnow 1989; Berlow 1996; Steinberg 2000; Studwell 2007).

5. Thaksin's government drew up lists of suspected drug dealers and other undesirables, and some of them were summarily executed after leaving police stations where they had gone to turn themselves in (Hands Off Cain 2004). Other extrajudicial killings have occurred in the country's southernmost provinces where Islamic insurgents are active. From 2004 to 2008, an estimated 3,000 people in those provinces died as the result of police and military abuses ("A Law" 2008; "Thailand Fears" 2008). Here, too, there are parallels with the Philippines.

■ Capital Crimes, Death Sentences, and the War on Drugs

Thailand has 51 capital offenses on its statute books and a large volume of death sentences issued by its trial courts (International Federation for Human Rights and Union for Civil Liberty 2005). The number of persons on death row tripled during the first three years of Thaksin's rule (2001–2003), and by the end of 2004 there were 971 persons in the country who had been condemned to death: 855 men and 116 women (Hands Off Cain 2004; International Federation for Human Rights and Union for Civil Liberty 2005:9,32). As of September 2006, 757 condemned prisoners were appealing their death sentences at an appeals court or the Supreme Court, and 58 percent of their cases were for drug offenses. Of the 87 women appealing death sentences, 84 percent had drug convictions (Death Penalty Thailand Blog, September 16, 2006). According to Amnesty International (2007b), Thailand is one of five Southeast Asian nations in which "the majority of death penalty cases are for drug crimes." A death sentence is mandatory for many offenses in Thailand, including the manufacture and distribution of drugs, of which methamphetamine is deemed the most worrisome. The government's "war on drugs" is in many ways a crucial context for understanding recent death penalty developments, for its popularity has made it "very difficult to dissociate the question of the death penalty from drug issues in the Thai context" (International Federation for Human Rights and Union for Civil Liberty 2005:11).[6]

More broadly, the war on drugs and related "get-tough" policies have resulted in a huge rise in Thailand's prison population, from 73,309 inmates in 1992 to 257,196 in 2002—a 250 percent increase in only 11 years (International Federation for Human Rights and Union for Civil Liberty 2005:29).[7] By 2002, Thailand not only had the highest incarceration rate (401 prisoners per 100,000 population) of all the countries in East, South, and Southeast Asia (except for the tiny jurisdiction of the Maldives), its incarceration rate was almost triple the average rate of the 22 other jurisdictions in these subregions for which data are available (see International Centre for Prison Studies, www.kcl.ac.uk.depsta/law/research/icps). Prison conditions in Thailand are frequently wretched, although "money talks" for the few who have it—as is also the case in the Philippines (Fellows 1998; International Federation for

---

6. As in most death penalty systems, "the poor and uneducated are over represented" on Thailand's death row (International Federation for Human Rights and Union for Civil Liberty 2005:22; Hadji-Ristic 2007). Of the 49 death row inmates who indicated their level of education in a 2004 survey, 19 said they had only attended primary school.

7. By the end of 2004, Thailand's prison population had declined to 195,000, apparently because of a general pardon issued by King Bhumibol on the occasion of the queen's 72nd birthday in August of that year. About 40,000 of the prisoners were women (20.5 percent) and 9,000 were foreigners (4.6 percent), including 5,000 Burmese, 2,000 Cambodians, and 1,000 Laotians (International Federation for Human Rights and Union for Civil Liberty 2005:29).

Human Rights and Union for Civil Liberty 2005:30). Inmates on death row are required to wear leg chains 24 hours a day, and prisoners believe "the size of the chains [for condemned drug offenders] relates to the quantity of the drugs" involved in their crimes (International Federation for Human Rights and Union for Civil Liberty 2005:32).

Figure D.1 depicts the distribution of death sentences by year for the 11 years beginning in 1996, the only period for which data could be obtained. The annual number of first-instance death sentences remained level at around 100 per year for the four years 1996–1999 before quadrupling during the next three years. From a peak of 447 death sentences in 2002, the number fell back by about one-quarter in 2003 and then remained fairly steady at around 300 death sentences per year for the next three years. The most likely cause of the spike in death sentences in 1999–2002 is Thailand's campaign against drug trafficking. An official "war on drugs" was not declared until February 2003, but antidrug offensives were launched before that. The stepwise increase in death sentences at the turn of the century also seems consistent with a causal account that stresses changes in punishment policy rather than shifts in rates of violence or other criminal offenses.

■ Executions

Although death sentences in the most recent years are three to four times more numerous than they were in the years before the new millennium, executions have remained rare events as they have been for decades, largely because the king commutes most death sentences. The gap between death sentences and executions is striking. The 447 death sentences generated in 2002 was 124 more than the 323 executions that the government recorded in the 72 years 1935–2006.[8] In its peak death sentence year of 2002, Thailand had more than twice as many death sentences as the United States (447 vs. 169) but a lower rate of execution per million (0.18 vs. 0.25). Table D.1 presents the yearly count of executions since 1935.

Table D.1 shows that executions in Thailand were unevenly distributed over the past seven decades, with one of the years (1939) accounting for fully 15 percent of all the executions that have occurred since Thailand changed from death by beheading to death by gunshot in 1934. Conversely, 27 of the 72 years had zero executions, and these years cluster together, with one six-year streak (1945–1950), one eight-year streak (1988–1995), and two three-year moratoria (1952–1954 and 2004–2006). As in South Korea, where executions were bunched in the period before 1998, the uneven distribution of executions in Thailand suggests that its execution patterns are the result of policy choices made by the central government. One aspect of that policy has been to execute mainly murderers and persons

---

8. Three of the 323 executions were of women, the most recent in 1999 (International Federation for Human Rights and Union for Civil Liberty 2005:33).

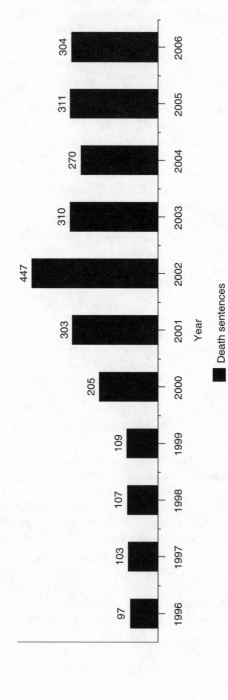

Figure D.1

First-instance death sentences in Thailand, 1996–2006

Source: Data from the Thailand Court of Justice, translated and interpreted by Parichart Munsgool.

Table D.1
Executions in Thailand, 1935–2007

Year	Executions	Year	Executions	Year	Executions	Year	Executions
1935	1	1953	—	1971	2	1989	—
1936	0	1954	—	1972	14	1990	—
1937	1	1955	4	1973	4	1991	—
1938	4	1956	2	1974	12	1992	—
1939	48	1957	—	1975	—	1993	—
1940	0	1958	—	1976	—	1994	—
1941	9	1959	3	1977	14	1995	—
1942	8	1960	8	1978	7	1996	1
1943	12	1961	4	1979	7	1997	2
1944	4	1962	11	1980	4	1998	2
1945	—	1963	15	1981	4	1999	16
1946	—	1964	3	1982	5	2000	1
1947	—	1965	5	1983	—	2001	11
1948	—	1966	3	1984	15	2002	11
1949	—	1967	7	1985	2	2003	4
1950	—	1968	2	1986	6	2004	—
1951	3	1969	4	1987	16	2005	—
1952	—	1970	1	1988	—	2006	—
Total							323

Source: Data from Thailand Department of Corrections 2007; see www.correct.go.th/commit.html (last accessed November 6, 2007).

who have committed offenses against the king or the security of the kingdom. Of the 323 executions that occurred between 1935 and 2006, 81 percent were for some kind of homicide offense, while 10 percent were for offenses against the king or the kingdom, and less than 9 percent were for drug offenses (data from the Thailand Department of Corrections, obtained by Parichart Munsgool, November 2007).

In addition to the uneven clustering of executions in Thailand, there has been some downward drift in executions over time. After only 12 executions in the decade of the 1950s, the average number of executions in the 1960s, 1970s, and 1980s—nearly six per year—was more than twice the annual average (2.8) for the period since 1990. And strikingly, there have been no executions in 12 of the 20 most recent years (1988–1995 and 2004–2007).[9]

9. Thailand changed its method of execution to lethal injection in 2003, and officials said the change was made to make the process more humane and to bring the country into

■ The King and Clemency

The decision about whether and when to execute is controlled by Thailand's central government, with the king playing two key roles. First, any condemned offender may file a pardon petition, and no execution is permitted until the king has rejected it. Although the data from Thailand's Department of Corrections cover many fewer cases of pardon petitions than of death sentences (315 petitions submitted vs. 1,641 death sentences issued in 2001–2005), the probability that a petitioner will succeed in obtaining a punishment reduction is quite good. In 2004, 78 of 82 petitions received a commutation (95 percent), and 98 of 110 did in 2005 (89 percent).[10] In developed countries such as Japan and the United States, executive clemency in capital cases has declined substantially in recent decades as political leaders have responded to forces in their political cultures that have discouraged acts of mercy that would

---

compliance with article 7 of the International Covenant on Civil and Political Rights (International Federation for Human Rights and Union for Civil Liberty 2005:35). In October 2003, a ceremony was held to mark the transition: monks prayed in the execution room; outgoing executioner Chavoret Jaruboon handed his duties over to a prison staff that would perform four lethal injections later that year; the German-made HKMP-5 submachine gun that had been used in many of the previous 319 executions was locked up in a crate; 319 balloons were released into the sky to represent the souls of the executed convicts; and the old execution area was turned into a museum (Hands Off Cain 2003). Before 2003, executions were carried out by gunshot in the back. The condemned stood behind a screen, tied to a pole and blindfolded, and the executioner would ask for forgiveness from the prisoner. "A target was painted on the screen which was placed between the prisoner and the submachine gun stand, thus allowing the executioner to pull the trigger and fire the hail of bullets through the bulls-eye marking, without seeing his real target" (International Federation for Human Rights and Union for Civil Liberty 2005:10). For a photograph of this execution scene, see Richard Clark's Web site (www.richard.clark32.btinternet.co.uk/bangkwan.jpg), and for a critical review of "a distasteful book" written by Thailand's last gunshot executioner (Chavoret Jaruboon), see the Death Penalty Thailand Blog entry for November 22, 2006 (http://deathpenaltythailand.blogspot.com).

In 1934, death by gunshot replaced death by beheading because the new method was considered cheaper, less complicated (no ritual dance or ceremonial music was needed), and more humane (International Federation for Human Rights and Union for Civil Liberty 2005:10). Three hundred years earlier, Gijsbert Heeck, a medical specialist working for the Dutch East India Company in what was then called Siam, observed several memorable execution methods. In interactions at the king's court, "The least sign of disobedience caused the guilty to be thrown alive in front of elephants to be torn to pieces, or beaten almost to a mash," and even a glance at the ruler's face could result in immediate decapitation (Terwiel 2008). For lesser offenses, a favorite response was to smear the dishes and drinking bowls of the accused with buffalo dung, "forcing them to eat and drink from these until they were either killed or acquitted" (Richie 2008).

10. In 2001–2003, the king received a total of 123 petitions for individual pardon and rejected only 26. We thank Parichart Munsgool for her help in locating these and other data presented in this appendix.

mitigate penal severity (Sarat 2005; Shikei Haishi Henshu Iinkai 2005). In Thailand, by contrast, "the vast majority of persons who are sentenced to death benefit from the royal pardon" (International Federation for Human Rights and Union for Civil Liberty 2005:27). In this respect, Thailand resembles the Philippines before it abolished in 2006, though of course clemency in the Philippines was a presidential prerogative, not a royal one (see chapter 4).

The second critical power the Thai king possesses in the administration of capital punishment is the discretion *not* to act on a pardon petition, which prevents the possibility of execution. Thus, the king can stay executions by refusing to act in addition to proactively conferring mercy through grants of clemency. He routinely does both.[11]

In the mid-1990s, when executions resumed after an eight-year moratorium, it became clear that King Bhumibol had grown more willing to reject appeals for clemency. Thai observers offered two interpretations of a change in policy that was unaccompanied by official announcement or explanation: some thought the king "had just become impatient with society as his reign neared its end," while others supposed that in the context of the government's law-and-order crackdown the king had come to conclude the death penalty was "a utilitarian means of keeping order" (Handley 2006:375). Whatever the causes of the executioner's comeback, two consequences seem clear: it altered the king's image from compassionate and forgiving to one of tougher justice—"making him someone to fear as much as to love," and it "set an example for justice generally"—and perhaps for the extrajudicial executions that took place in subsequent years (Handley 2006:375; see also appendix G).

The gap between death sentences and executions in Thailand is among the largest to be found in jurisdictions that retain capital punishment, perhaps matched only by California, Pakistan, and the Philippines before its second abolition. The Thai government reported 27 executions and 2,150 death sentences in the seven years after January 2000, a ratio of one execution for every 80 death sentences. There is no evidence that the execution risk is rising in the new millennium, for 85 percent of the country's executions since 2000 had already occurred by the end of 2002. At the time of this writing, Thailand has just entered the fifth year of a moratorium (2004–2008) that receives little recognition inside the country or out.

King Bhumibol may be the most important proximate cause of the postwar stops and starts in execution displayed in table D.1 (Handley 2006:374), but if he is, we do not know what moves this devoutly Buddhist leader to change his mind so frequently (there have been 12 stops or starts since 1945). And if the king is not the main moving part, then it would seem either officials in the Ministry of Justice are able to influence the flow of pardon petitions that make their way to

---

11. In recent years, some drug offenders have apparently been considered "unqualified" for royal pardon, though we do not have disaggregated data that would enable us to determine what effect, if any, this change has had on execution outcomes (International Federation for Human Rights and Union for Civil Liberty 2005:27).

the throne, or (as some Thai insiders believe) the prime minister is able to pressure Ministry of Justice officials to carry out the execution of some death row inmates whose clemency decisions the king has delayed.

■ Leadership from the Throne

The mechanisms used to administer capital punishment in Thailand differ from those used in other Southeast Asian nations, but the low rate and episodic pattern of executions is similar to other countries in the region. The republican government of Indonesia has even lower execution rates than Thailand, and the temporal trends in recent Malaysian executions seem roughly parallel to those in Thailand. Similarly, the infrequent and sporadic pattern of executions in the Philippines between its two abolitions resembles the pattern that has prevailed in Thailand for more than 60 years. It is therefore unclear how much of the substance of Thailand's death penalty policy can be attributed to the distinctive government structure that regulates death sentences and executions.

But one element of Thailand's death penalty policy does clearly differ from most other nations in the modern world, and that is the strong influence of a reigning monarch. "Leadership from the front" is a common feature of the reduction and abolition of capital punishment in many parts of the world (Zimring 2003:22), but Thailand is one of only a few Asian nations in which there is potential for what could be called "leadership from the throne." Royal influence was one element of Nepal's abolition in the late 1990s (Hood 2002:43), and in tiny Bhutan a Buddhist king was the principal force responsible for ending capital punishment in 2004. In Thailand, King Bhumibol may have possessed this potential power for decades but not used it (International Federation for Human Rights and Union for Civil Liberty 2005), and he may well be the last monarch in that country to possess such significant authority (Handley 2006:427). There is both irony and poetic justice when hereditary royal authority—one of the oldest forms of concentrated power—becomes a principal means for limiting a government's power to punish.

Appendix E: Singapore

The basic difference in our approach [to capital punishment] springs from our traditional Asian value system which places the interests of the community over and above that of the individual.

—Lee Kuan Yew (2002)

The Singapore Government makes no apology for its tough law and order system. Singapore is widely acknowledged to have a transparent and fair justice system and is one of the safest places in the world to live and work in.

—Singapore Ministry of Home Affairs (2004)

During the deliberations that preceded the UN General Assembly vote in December 2007 on the resolution calling for a worldwide moratorium on executions—a resolution that passed by a 104 to 54 margin—Singapore's strong pro–death penalty stand left many people wondering why the city-state of 4.5 million was "willing to risk international condemnation to pursue the death penalty so publicly as a solution to crime" (Kuppusamy 2007b). Singapore's UN envoy, Vanu Menon, who led the resistance to the resolution, insisted that capital punishment is not a human rights issue but rather "first and foremost" a criminal justice and law-and-order activity that is not prohibited under international law. "Every state," he said, "has the sovereign right to choose its own political, economic, social and legal systems based on what is in their own best interests" (quoted in Deen 2007).

Singapore's leaders have long chosen to administer one of the most aggressive death penalty systems in the world, one in which judges must impose a sentence of death on every defendant convicted of murder or drug trafficking (Vijayan 2007). Compare the city of Houston, the most aggressive executing jurisdiction in the most aggressive executing state in the most aggressive executing democracy in the world. Houston's homicide rate of 12.0 per 100,000 population in 2000 was 58 percent lower than its average homicide rate in the 1980s (28.7) but was still nine times higher than the homicide rate in Singapore (1.3) in 1998 (Johnson 2006b:77; Zimring 2007:238). From 1976, when the U.S. Supreme Court reinstated capital punishment, until July 2004, Harris County in Texas—the Houston metropolitan area—had 73 executions, seven more than the entire nation of Japan had over the same period of time (Johnson 2006a:104). Singapore, by comparison, with a population only a little larger than Harris County, had at least 76 executions in 1994, 73 more in 1995, and at least 76 in 2000–2002. By many accounts, Singapore has been considered the "world execution capital" ("Singapore" 1999:25; see also Hood 2002:91; Amnesty International 2004b; Hood and Hoyle 2008:96).

Sngapore officials say that their "general policy" is "not to give any information on the death penalty" (Hands Off Cain 2002), and their secrecy policy helps explain why capital punishment tends to be a "nonissue" that "evokes little discussion or debate" (Oehlers and Tarulevicz 2005:292). But concern about the country's death penalty policy is sometimes voiced by Singapore's own citizens. During the UN deliberations on the moratorium resolution, one senior Singapore attorney (who declined to be named for fear that government officials would retaliate against his legal business) asked: "Why is Singapore so ham-fisted in wanting the death penalty when the majority of nations are against it? We should go with the trend in the world which is to abolish—or at least place a moratorium on—state-sanctioned killing. If we can be the first one to commercially fly the Airbus 380, why are we among the last in the world to defend and insist on carrying out state killings? After all we pride ourselves as world trend-setters" (quoted in Kuppusamy 2007b).

In this appendix we explore why the nation with the third highest per capita income in Asia (after Japan and Australia) has been so strongly committed to capital punishment.[1] First we describe the social, political, and economic contexts that have shaped Singapore's death penalty. Next we sketch the main contours of the country's death penalty policy and practice, focusing especially on two puzzles: why executions surged in the 1990s, and why they have declined in recent years. In the final section we discuss how Singapore's system of capital punishment could change in the years to come.

■ Contexts

The story of modern Singapore is inextricably linked to the personality, power, and vision of Harry Lee Kuan Yew, a fourth-generation Singaporean who was born in 1923 and educated in law at Cambridge University before becoming a translator for Japanese forces during World War II. After working as a legal advisor to student and trade unions, Lee and his friends established the People's

---

1. In 2003, prime minister Goh Chok Tong told the BBC that Singapore had executed "about 70 to 80" people in the first nine months of the year, and when pressed about why he did not know the exact number said, "I have got more important things to worry about" (quoted in Hands Off Cain 2003). Amnesty International's execution count for the first nine months of 2003 was only 13, which Goh's pronouncement exceeded by a factor of five. Whatever the true number (see table E.1 and accompanying text), Goh's unambivalent approach to capital punishment characterizes many Singapore elites (Mahbubani 2002:78,112).

Action Party (PAP) in 1954. It was "a marriage of convenience with pro-communist trades unions, " and it has controlled Parliament continuously since Singapore established self-government as part of the British Empire in 1959 (Studwell 2007:287).[2] That was the same year Lee became Singapore's top executive, and he has remained its paramount leader for almost half a century since, first as prime minister (1959–1990), and then as "senior minister" and "minister mentor" (1990 to the present). What Mahathir was to Malaysia, Marcos to the Philippines, Suharto to Indonesia, Mao to China, and Chiang Kai-shek to Taiwan, Lee has been to little Singapore—only more so.[3] This brilliant, outspoken, controversial leader has been called "one of the seminal figures of Asia" and "a man who, almost single-handedly, built a great nation from a small island."[4] He may have shaped his country more than any other leader in Asia.

Lee's core values—and his commitment to economic development especially—were well expressed in January 2008, when he visited the bedside of Indonesia's ailing former president Suharto, who stole an estimated 15 to 35 billion dollars in state assets during his 32 years in power and who directed and condoned the killing of at least 500,000 Indonesian citizens before an economic collapse and widespread rioting drove him from office in 1998. Lee described his dying friend as "a quiet man, courteous and punctilious on form and protocol," who may have given "favors to his family and friends" but who presided over "real growth, real progress" while in power. "He educated the population. He built roads and infrastructure," Lee stressed before noting that Suharto had seized power (in a coup) in 1965, just a few years after Ne Win took control in what is now called Myanmar. "Compare," Lee urged. "Who's better off? Who deserves to be honored? What's a few billion dollars lost in bad excesses? [Suharto] built hundreds of billions of dollars worth of assets" (quoted in Mydans 2008b).[5]

2. In the general election of 2006, the PAP won 67 percent of the vote and 98 percent of the seats in Parliament (82 of 84 seats). That was much the same outcome as in the previous two elections (1996 and 2001), when opposition candidates won only two seats.

3. According to some analysts, Southeast Asia's four major postwar autocrats of the right—Lee, Suharto, Mahathir, and Marcos—"all had a fundamentally racist view of life," which was good news for the "godfathers" who dominated their national economies and who were, for the most part, ethnically Chinese (Studwell 2007:46).

4. Henry Kissinger, former U.S. secretary of state, and Kiichi Miyazawa, former minister of finance of Japan (quoted in Lee Kuan Yew 2000).

5. This is not to say Lee and Suharto behaved identically. For one thing, Lee was not extravagantly corrupt as Suharto was, though he and his family have been accused of various financial improprieties. For another, Lee did not order many (if any) extrajudicial killings (see appendix G). In the years after Suharto left office, Indonesia became "the standard bearer of democracy in Southeast Asia," in part because coups and coup attempts largely discredited two other exemplars of democracy in the region—Thailand and the Philippines (Mydans 2008b). Singapore, by contrast, has continued to be ruled by the "vast political machinery" of Lee's PAP even after Lee stepped down from a formal position of leadership, and significant political change seems unlikely to happen before he passes from the scene

Table E.1

Executions in Singapore, 1981–2007

Year	Executions	Execution rate per million
1981	3	1.3
1982	0	—
1983	2	0.7
1984	2	0.7
1985	1	0.4
1986	1	0.4
1987	0	—
1988	4	1.4
1989	5	1.7
1990	3	1
1991	6	1.94
1992	21	6.56
1993	7	2.12
1994	76	22.35
1995	73	20.86
1996	50	13.89
1997	15	4.05
1998	28	7.37
1999	43	11.03
2000	21	5.20
2001	27	6.55
2002	28	6.67
2003	19	4.44
2004	8	1.84
2005	8	1.81
2006	5	1.11
2007	2	0.5

Sources: Amnesty International 2004b; see also Hood 2001; Hood 2002; Lim and Yong 2006; Hood and Hoyle 2008.

Lee's emphasis on national development and his taste for capital punishment as a means of maintaining "law and order" were forged during the political turmoil of the 1960s (Lee Kuan Yew 2000). In 1963, Singapore declared independence from Britain (which had governed the island since 1858) and

altogether (Studwell 2007:185). Despite these differences, Lee and Suharto were alike in their pragmatic approaches to policy-making and in their commitments to economic development as the first priority of nation-building.

Table E.2
Thresholds for mandatory capital punishment in drug cases in Singapore, 2007

Drug	Quantity
Diamorphine*(heroin)	15 grams (0.5 ounces)
Cocaine	30 grams (1.1 ounces)
Methamphetamine	250 grams (8.8 ounces)
Cannabis	500 grams (17.6 ounces)

Sources: Hands Off Cain (various years); Lines 2007.
* The pharmaceutical name for prescription-grade heroin. Singapore's government contends that 15 grams of pure diamorphine is equivalent to "a slab of approximately 750g of street heroin"(quoted in Lines 2007:22).

merged with Malaya, Sabah, and Sarawak to form the nation of Malaysia. Two years later, in August 1965, Singapore was expelled from Malaysia following a bloody period of terrorism and rioting.[6] When Malaysia's prime minister, Tunku Abdul Rahman, told Lee that Singapore had to leave the Malaysian federation, the former British colony became "a geopolitical freak—a tiny, overpopulated, predominantly Chinese island, surrounded by hostile giants, an amputated capital dangling from the Malay peninsula like the head of a guillotined noble" (Lydgate 2003:48).[7] Lee believed separation would be a disaster, calling it "a political, economic, and geographical absurdity" (quoted in Lydgate 2003:48). But in subsequent decades, he and his lieutenants largely solved some of Singapore's most pressing problems—including survival and economic development—while consistently treating human rights as luxuries the nation could ill afford to protect or respect. The trauma of this separation engendered "a siege mentality" among Lee and his closest confidants "that would persist into the next millennium" and would motivate Singapore's aggressive death penalty policy (Lydgate 2003:49).

Today there is little room for critics, dissidents, or criminals in Singapore. They are, at best, "misguided losers, too stupid to understand the necessity for 'strong leadership,' or, at worst, dangerous 'Communists' who would plunge the land into chaos and darkness" (Buruma 2001a:128). The nomenclature may be different, but the fact that many deviants "are called Communists in Singapore and counterrevolutionaries in China is incidental; the underlying sentiments of the rulers are the same," including the desire for "complete control over the public and, where possible, even the private lives"

6. In an effort to destabilize the new Malaysian nation, Indonesian strongman Sukarno pursued a policy of terrorist confrontation in which saboteurs set off more than 40 bombs in Singapore between September 1963 and May 1965. Ethnic and religious riots in July 1964 killed 22 people and injured hundreds more (Lydgate 2003:48).

7. As of 2007, Singapore was 75 percent Chinese, 14 percent Malay, 9 percent Indian, and about 2 percent "Eurasian."

of their subjects (128,144; see also Trocki 2006). In policy-making more generally, "Singapore is blessed, or some might say cursed, with an overwhelming commitment to pragmatism. Nothing has value in itself; everything is valued in terms of functionality. It is perhaps as pure a utilitarianism as is humanly possible" (Hor 2002:512).

In the year 2000, Singapore's population of four million people would have made it the 10th most populous city in China, and its 2008 population of 4.6 million was about three times larger than the number of persons who lived in the city in 1959 when Lee first became prime minister. But Singapore's development has been more than demographic. Real economic growth averaged 8 percent between 1960 and 1990, one of the most rapid rates in the world, and between 1990 and 2007 the nation's GDP more than tripled. As of 2005, Singapore's GDP of $111 billion was nearly double the combined GDP of five other nations in Southeast Asia—Vietnam, Cambodia, Laos, Myanmar, and Brunei—even though those five countries had 37 times more people. In recent years Singapore has regularly been rated the most "business friendly" economy in the world, and it is now the world's fourth largest foreign exchange trading center (after London, New York City, and Tokyo) and the 17th wealthiest country in the world in GDP per capita. Singapore also has one of the lowest infant mortality rates and one of the highest life expectancies in the world, and in 2002 it ranked 28th in the world in the World Bank's Quality of Governance ratings, with a ranking right at the top on the dimensions of "government effectiveness," "regulatory quality," and "control of corruption" (Peerenboom 2007:47). In 1996 and 2002, Singapore ranked first among all Asian nations in the World Bank's Rule of Law ratings, well ahead of Japan, Hong Kong, South Korea, and Taiwan—and also ahead of the United States (Chan 1996; Peerenboom 2007:59).

Despite these remarkable achievements, justice in Singapore is Janus-faced. When adjudicating commercial cases, Singapore courts can be relied on to administer law fairly, and judges have a high reputation for integrity in this sphere. But in "politically-freighted cases," the same judges have "repeatedly demonstrated a singular facility at bending over backwards to render decisions favorable to the Singapore government and its leaders," and "their judicial contortions have acquired an international notoriety" that has long concerned human rights observers (Seow 2006:xv; see also Safire 1997; Safire 1999; "Democracy" 2008; Mydans 2008a). As one prominent critic of Singapore's compliant judiciary asks, even "with the best will in the world, is it really conceivable for any judge in Singapore to decide a case against Harry Lee Kuan Yew and his PAP cohorts?" (Seow 2006:xviii). Singapore does not use capital punishment to repress political opponents, but many observers believe that in ordinary capital cases, too, courts often tilt toward the government (Gibson 1993; Tan 2002; Amnesty International 2004b; Lines 2007).[8]

8. In Malaysia as well, there is considerable evidence that the judiciary under former prime minister Mahathir Mohamad "was deeply corrupt and under the thumbs of well-

The "Singapore model" of economic development has focused on promoting export-oriented industries, much as Japan, South Korea, and Taiwan did during their high-growth years. The PAP has constructed a "culture of developmentalism," with three key elements designed to foster the ultimate ends of national strength, status, and security: the subordination of individuals to the larger nation; the submission of individuals to the imperative of economic productivity; and the cultivation of a distinct sense of nationalism (Oehlers and Tarulevicz 2005:295). Singapore's system of capital punishment may be the logical culmination of the government's penchant for "crushing dissent" (Lydgate 2003) and micromanaging the social affairs and experiences of the residents of this nation's 63 islands (Buruma 2001a; Trocki 2006). On this view, Singapore is more than merely "the world's leading nanny state" (Studwell 2007:46), it is "Disneyland with the death penalty" in that judicial executions are employed to ensure "a relentlessly G-rated experience" (Gibson 1993) and to obtain high levels of compliance with the dictates of the "developmental" state (Oehlers and Tarulevicz 2005:293).

■ Two Death Penalty Puzzles

Chapter 8 shows that the annual per capita rate of executions in Singapore from 2000 to 2005 was 62 times higher than in neighboring Malaysia, and attributes this huge gap to a taste for executions in Singapore's government—and in Lee Kuan Yew especially—that is no longer found among Malaysian political elites. Chapter 8 also notes that this gap has grown wider over time. There may be serious and asymmetric problems of undercounting, but Malaysia had at least 69 executions in 1983–1987, while Singapore recorded only six. By these measures, Malaysia's per capita execution rate was more than twice as high as Singapore's. A decade later, Singapore's annual rate over a similar five-year period (1993–1997) had risen to 12.6 executions per million, while Malaysia went four consecutive years in the late 1990s without a single execution (Hood 2002:92).

Table E.1 presents Amnesty's execution estimates for Singapore from 1981 to 2007. It shows modest numbers for the first decade or so, followed by a huge jump in the 1990s and then a sustained drop after 1999, leading to rates for the most recent years that are more than 90 percent lower than the peaks in 1994 and 1995. The years 2003–2007 reflect an average annual execution rate (1.9) that is less than one-sixth the corresponding rate (12.7) for 1993–1997, and the

---

connected businessmen and politicians" (Kuppusamy 2008b). A video clip of a conversation between Mahathir's top lawyer and the chief justice of Malaysia that was shot in 2002 and surfaced five years later revealed that the principals focused on the promotion of judges "friendly" to Mahathir's government and on "how to end the careers of judges considered to be 'unfriendly and difficult' to the interest of their cabal" (Ibrahim and Anbalagan 2008; Kuppusamy 2008b).

most recent two years of 2006–2007 have an average annual rate (0.8) that is less than 4 percent of the peak two-year average (21.6 in 1994–1995) and less than 9 percent of the two-year average ten years earlier (9.0 in 1996–1997).

The numbers in table E.1 generate two puzzles: Why did executions in Singapore increase so substantially in the 1990s? And why have they declined in the most recent years?

The War on Drugs and the Rise in Executions

The apparent rise in Singapore's execution rate after the 1980s could be an artifact of reporting changes by the government. As Singapore prison officials have said on numerous occasions, the state's general policy is "not to give any information on the death penalty" (Tan 2002), which might mean there was "a hidden toll of executions" before the 1990s that studies could not capture (Hood 1989; Amnesty International 2004b). Here as in many other parts of Asia, it is impossible to know for sure whether there are undisclosed death penalty figures or how large they are.

But if the apparent surge in executions is not merely a statistical artifact— and we believe it is not—it is at least partly the result of Singapore's intensified attempts to deter drug offending through state killing. The homicide rate in Singapore is only slightly higher than in other industrialized Asian nations or in the countries of the European Union, and it is much lower than in the industrializing countries around the world (Johnson 2006b:77). Singapore's homicide rate also declined during the 1990s, from 1.8 deaths per 100,000 residents in 1991 to 1.3 in 1998 (LaFree 1999:130; Johnson 2006b:77). Thus, it is not the level of lethal violence or its trend over time that distinguishes Singapore's crime-and-punishment profile from those of its Asian neighbors, it is its response to drug and other offenses. Similarly, there was no surge in lethal violence that might explain the apparent rise in executions from the 1980s to the 1990s. The main proximate cause of that increase appears to be Singapore's drug policy.[9] Another contributing cause could be the new chief justice of the Supreme Court who "set upon speeding up capital trials" in the 1990s in order to reduce a backlog of cases that had grown in previous years (Michael Hor, professor of law at National University of Singapore, e-mail to Johnson, May 29, 2008).

Singapore introduced the death penalty for drug offenses in 1975 (Hands Off Cain 2002), and as its "culture of developmentalism" deepened in subsequent years, so did the salience of drug trafficking and possession in

---

9. Aggressive drug enforcement also helps explain the rapid rise in Singapore's incarceration rate, which doubled in 12 years, from 196 inmates per 100,000 population in 1992 to 392 in 2004. By mid-2006, the rate had declined about 20 percent, to 309 inmates per 100,000, but this still left Singapore with one of the highest imprisonment rates in the region (see http://www.kcl.ac.uk/schools/law/research/icps). As we explain later, Singapore's execution rate may have fallen even more rapidly than its incarceration rate in recent years.

the government's "construction of criminality" (Oehlers and Tarulevicz 2005:297). Punishment in independent Singapore has always been punitive and retributive.[10] But as crime came to be construed as rebellion against the nation, as a perverse attempt to escape the effort and responsibility of work, and as characteristically committed by "outsiders" who have little stake in the system, drug offenders came to be regarded as more and more deserving of death as "saboteurs" of the Singapore system (303). As the Central Narcotics Bureau reported in 2003: "[D]rug abuse inflicts a high cost on society as a whole. The government has to expend much effort and money to treat and rehabilitate addicts. *The number of productive man-hours lost and the opportunity cost involved are enormous*" (quoted in Oehlers and Tarulevicz 2005:302; emphasis added).

One centerpiece of Singapore's system of capital punishment is a statutory scheme that attaches a mandatory death penalty to convictions for possession of drugs with intent to traffic in extremely low quantities: 15 grams of heroin, 30 grams of cocaine, 250 grams of methamphetamines, or 500 grams of cannabis (Hands Off Cain 2007). And in Singapore as in Malaysia and some other nations, the usual burden of proof is reversed in capital cases, so an individual arrested in possession of a quantity of drugs greater than those just mentioned is presumed to be trafficking unless he or she can prove otherwise.[11] Singapore is not alone in threatening execution for low quantities of drugs, but available data suggest it is singular in its willingness to carry out the threat. In Malaysia, for example, the threshold for a capital heroin offense is only 1/50th the quantity of drugs required to make a similar case capital in Singapore, but in recent years Singapore's per capita execution rate has been more than 50 times higher than Malaysia's. See table E.2.

10. Singapore not only has one of the world's highest rates of execution and one of the highest incarceration rates in Asia, it also practices judicial caning (up to 24 strokes), as do the neighboring nations (and former British colonies) of Malaysia and Brunei. Introduced to Singapore by the British, caning is mandatory for more than 40 offenses, including rape, robbery, drug trafficking, and vandalism (it is discretionary for many other crimes). Offenders are not caned if they have been sentenced to death. In 1993, a year in which there were seven recorded executions, 3,244 persons were caned, or about one resident in 1,000, while in 2004 there were 11,790 arrests for immigration violations, which in Singapore carry a mandatory sentence of at least three strokes. Lee Kuan Yew's statements about caning indicate that he intends it to be both painful and humiliating; Lee himself was caned as a schoolboy at Raffles College in the 1930s (Farrell 2006). For a video of an actual caning that probably took place in Malaysia's Seremban Prison around 2004, see www.corpun.com/vidju.htm. And for a commercially successful film that dramatizes some of the challenges ex-offenders face reintegrating into Singapore society, see director Jack Neo's critically acclaimed *One More Chance* (2005).

11. This presumption has been criticized by many human rights monitors, including the UN Commission on Human Rights (Lines 2007:10).

In January 2004, Amnesty International released a report on the death penalty in Singapore that said 72.6 percent of the executions that had occurred between 1991 and 2000 had been for drug trafficking (Amnesty International 2004b). Two weeks later, Singapore's Ministry of Home Affairs released an angry response claiming that "AI has deliberately misrepresented or distorted the facts concerning the death penalty in Singapore," yet the government acknowledged that 110 of the 138 persons executed in 1999–2003–80 percent of all executions—had been condemned for "drug-related offenses" (Singapore Ministry of Home Affairs 2004).[12] Over the same five-year period there were 28 executions for murder and other non-drug-related offenses. If those had been Singapore's only executions—if the 110 drug executions had not occurred—then Singapore's execution rate of 1.4 per million per year would have been a little higher than that of Texas and a little lower than those of Virginia and Oklahoma at about the same period of time instead of being among the highest rates in the world, surpassed, perhaps, by only the PRC (Hood 2002:92; see chapter 7).

Singapore's strongly antidrug, pro–death penalty stand has long been visible in airport advertisements and other public places, and it also was evident in a book, *David's Diary*, that the government made part of the curriculum in 169 secondary schools in 2002. Commissioned by the National Council against Drug Abuse and supported by the Central Narcotics Bureau and the Prisons Department, the book tells the story of a 21-year-old drug addict whose encounter with heroin turns him into a trafficker and ultimately gets him sent to the gallows. The text focuses on the thoughts and fears of the condemned as he lives out his days on death row: his girlfriend's family returns all his letters; the prison chaplain is little help as the terror of execution approaches; and a hood is placed over his head, the reader learns, in order to prevent him from moving when the lever is pulled and in order to reduce rope marks and burns around his neck. If one message of the book is that drugs can ruin and end lives, another is that (as the little girl Wednesday says in the film *Addams Family Values*) drug users in Singapore should "be afraid, be very afraid."

Singapore's enthusiasm for executing drug offenders may also help explain why foreigners make up a high proportion of those executed. About one-quarter of the residents of Singapore are not Singapore citizens, but of the 174 executions recorded by Amnesty International (2004b) from press reports in 1993–2003, 53 percent (93) were of foreigners, primarily migrant workers. The Singapore government says the true figure for the same period is actually 36

---

12. In 2002, Hands Off Cain reported that 82 percent of the executions in Singapore in 1991–2000 (247 out of 300) were for drug trafficking, and in 2001 Singapore's Ministry of Home Affairs told the UN that 76 percent of all executions in 1994–1999 were for drug-related offenses (Hands Off Cain 2002; Lines 2007:9).

percent, and it claims the percentage dropped to 27 percent for the five years 1999–2003 (Singapore Ministry of Home Affairs 2004).[13] Whatever the true figure, it was (until recently) significantly higher than the percentage of foreigners in the population, and it is substantially higher than the proportion of all prisoners in Singapore who are foreign—about 20 percent as of July 2005 (see www.kcl.ac.uk/schools/law/research/icps).[14]

Lee Kuan Yew and other Singapore officials have long argued that the country's aggressive death penalty policy has deterred drug and other crime and helped make Singapore one of the safest places in the world (Mahbubani 2002). As Professor Michael Hor has observed, "there is widespread belief amongst lawmakers and the public in Singapore that the death penalty has worked" (Michael Hor, quoted in Hands Off Cain 2002).[15] But the evidence

13. Singapore has not been reluctant to execute foreigners, even in the face of strong protests from abroad. Consider five high-profile examples. (1) In 1994, Singapore's government stirred up a diplomatic storm when it hanged a Dutch engineer named Johannes van Damme for heroin trafficking. He was the first European executed in Singapore since its independence. (2) In 1999, the execution of a Filipina domestic worker named Flor Contemplacion (for murder) prompted Philippines president Fidel Ramos to recall his ambassador to Singapore and to cancel many bilateral exchanges between the two countries. (3) In 2005, the impending execution of Australian citizen Van Tuon Nguyen for trafficking in heroin prompted numerous vigils in Australia (and a few in Singapore too) in addition to several high-level appeals for clemency. After Nguyen was hanged, there were widespread displays of protest and sympathy, including an official minute of silence in the Queensland Legislative Assembly. (4) In 2006, Took Leng How, a Chinese Malaysian, was hanged for murder after Singapore's government rejected a petition from Took's lawyers that had 34,000 signatures. (5) In 2007, Iwuchukwu Amara Tochi, a Nigerian national, was hanged for heroin trafficking despite an appeal from the Nigerian president and pressure from several European nations and organizations.

14. The 20 percent of prisoners who are foreign gives Singapore one of the highest foreigner prisoner percentages in Asia, exceeded only by Malaysia (30 percent), Brunei Darussalam (28 percent), and the Chinese SARs of Macao (40 percent) and Hong Kong (34 percent). In Luxembourg, Liechtenstein, and Switzerland about 70 percent of prisoners are foreign, while in Saudi Arabia the proportion is almost one-half (see http://www.kcl.ac.uk/schools/law/research/icps).

15. Singapore's government also claims that its system of capital punishment is fairly administered (Singapore Ministry of Foreign Affairs 2004). Although the death penalty does fall disproportionately on "the poorest, least educated and most vulnerable members of society" in Singapore as in most other nations (Amnesty International 2004b), the state has not been reluctant to execute the well-to-do. The most prominent person executed in recent years was Shanmugam Murugesu, a former jet ski champion, military veteran, and civil servant who was arrested in 2003 after six packets containing just over a kilogram of cannabis were found in his bags when he was returning from a trip to Malaysia. Murugesu's hanging in May 2005 sparked a rare show of public dissent and an even rarer display of anti–death penalty sentiment, through pamphlets, prayer vigils, petitions, and public rallies.

supporting that verdict is neither clear nor convincing. For one thing, Singapore ceased regular publication of crime statistics in the 1980s, thereby making it impossible to test government claims about the death penalty's effectiveness. When the government did release totals for "drug abusers arrested" between 1993 and 2003 (in response to Amnesty International's critical 2004 report), the data showed a decline from a high of 6,165 arrests in 1994 to a low of 1,785 in 2003 even though reported executions over the same period fluctuated between a low of 7 in 1993 and a high of 76 in 1994, and with six reversals of slope in only 11 years. In the American context, where crime and execution data are plentiful, the bulk of the evidence suggests that executions are no more effective as a deterrent than long terms of imprisonment (Peterson and Bailey 2003; Fagan, Zimring, and Geller 2006). In Singapore, too, the available evidence strongly suggests that the deterrent effect of the death penalty on homicide is invisible (Zimring, Johnson, and Fagan 2008). More evidence would be welcome, of course, especially about drug crime, but the paucity of data provided by Singapore's government is itself interesting. As Professor Hor wondered on a separate occasion, "one might have expected that if the death penalty is being imposed on drug offences in order to deter or incapacitate, the government would be keenly interested in statistical and other studies to find out if, in fact, the increased penalties are working. But such studies, if they exist, are seldom revealed. Statistical data are not provided in any consistent or meaningful way by the government. One can only speculate why" (quoted in Lines 2007:14).

(Why) Are Executions Declining?

The execution decline in table E.1 is striking. The number of executions has fallen markedly since 2002, with the annual average of 5 executions for the most recent three years (2005–2007) just one-seventh the annual average for the 1990s (35.4) and only one-fourth the annual average for the first five years of the 21st century (20.6). How can this drop be explained?

There appear to be four possibilities. First, the execution decline could be just a temporary series of blips on the radar. Executions in the single digits were also recorded in 1991 and 1993, after which they jumped elevenfold in 1994. It is possible that executions in Singapore will rebound similarly in the

---

Murugesu's twin sons (age 14) even handed out flyers in the busy Orchard Road shopping district saying that the execution of their father would make them orphans (Murugesu was divorced). One week before Murugesu was executed, a three-hour vigil for him was held at the Furama Hotel. It was the first public gathering in Singapore organized solely by citizens demanding a change in the nation's death penalty policy. The mainstream local media ignored the event (they are required to report in the "public interest"), and the police shut down an open microphone session just as the first speaker was hitting stride, leading Sinapan Samydorai, president of the NGO Think Centre, to say, "we'll be lucky to get anywhere in 10 or even 20 years. But at least Singaporeans are finally speaking out" (quoted in Hands Off Cain 2005; see also Mydans 2006).

years to come. Second, Singapore's government and its compliant local press could be cooking the books by withholding execution information that it sometimes disclosed in the past. This explanation is plausible because Singapore is far from transparent about its death penalty policy and practice and because the highly critical death penalty report released by Amnesty International in 2004 focused considerable attention on Singapore's system of capital punishment and stimulated vehement defenses and denials from the Singapore government (Singapore Ministry of Home Affairs 2004). For all of their bluster in the international community—"We are Asian! We are sovereign! We will do what we want!"—Singapore's political elites are highly sensitive to foreign criticism. If either or both of these explanations are true, then Singapore's recent execution decline is more apparent than real.

But there are at least two reasons to believe Singapore's execution decline might not be a mirage. The first is that Lee Kuan Yew has been in some ways receding from the center of political power. His PAP still controls the vast majority of seats in the national parliament and continues to crush dissent (Lydgate 2003) and control the judiciary (Seow 2006), but Lee himself seems to be less involved in day-to-day governance and decision-making than in previous years. One theme of this book and of many other works on capital punishment is the importance of "leadership from the front." There is no other leader in recent Asian history who has led so long and so completely as Lee Kuan Yew, and as his power wanes it stands to reason that some policies will change. Capital punishment could be one of them.

The other reason to believe Singapore's death penalty decline is real has been suggested by Lee himself. The "minister mentor" continues to respond to critics who condemn Singapore for being too tightly controlled by stressing its "vulnerability" in a world and a region full of dangers (Mydans and Arnold 2007). Yet Lee increasingly stresses that Singapore is a country of "pragmatists" who must "go in whatever direction world conditions dictate if we are to survive and be part of the modern world" (Lee 2007). The death penalty is on the decline in many parts of the world, including Asia, and this "world condition" may be softening Singapore's enthusiasm for the death penalty even while its leaders continue to insist—loudly, publicly, and often—that executions are an integral part of "the Singapore model" and an important cause of its remarkable postwar achievements.

■ Regional Perspectives on the Future of Singapore's Death Penalty

The history of capital punishment in other Asian nations suggests one conclusion about Singapore's current death penalty policy and two possibilities for its future. The obvious but important finding about the origin of Singapore's high rates of execution is that they are not the result of historical or cultural features of the society that preceded the current regime but rather are an outgrowth of contemporary political choices. The great variability in Singapore's execution rate is just one more sign that variations in Asian rates of execution reflect political choices, and nowhere is this truer than in this city-state.

There also are signs in the politics of Asia that suggest Singapore will not remain a high-rate outlier for long. One threat to its aggressive execution policy is the pronounced tendency for developed nations to democratize. Countries like South Korea and Taiwan remained authoritarian in governance through much of their rapid economic development, only to shift from one-party control to highly competitive democratic systems in the late 1980s and early 1990s. These transitions to plural democracy have been associated with declining rates of execution and substantial steps toward ending executions in both of those nations, leaving only Japan as a model of democratic government in Asia with a continuing commitment to capital punishment. It is reasonable to wonder whether political evolutions in the manner of South Korea and Taiwan could have a similar influence on executions in Singapore (Mydans 2006).

But even if Singapore's authoritarian government survives the passing of Lee Kuan Yew, its high rates of execution could drop for two other reasons. First, one strategy for maintaining political power in authoritarian systems is the selective softening of controls and restraints. This is what happened in South Korea and Taiwan before they turned more fully toward democracy, and similar softenings can be seen in liberalizing Malaysia, Thailand, and Indonesia (Mydans 2008b). In recent years, Singapore's government has introduced casino gambling and allowed more gum chewing, gay rights activism, and bookstore selections than were permitted in earlier times. As controls weaken further—and we expect they will—it will become increasingly difficult to administer such a harsh and rigid death penalty system. Indeed, for the first time in memory there are signs of domestic ambivalence toward Singapore's severe system. In 2007, the Law Society, long cowed and co-opted by the PAP (Buruma 2001a:148), issued a report to the Ministry of Home Affairs calling for the scrapping of mandatory death sentences and a switch to a system in which judges have discretion to decide between capital and lesser sentences. We do not know the details of the report (our request for a copy was denied), but news articles did hint at the recommendation's justifications: "This flexibility in sentencing humanizes the law and reflects the evolving standards of decency in Singapore society" (quoted in sgforums.com, April 5, 2007).[16] We also do not know how seriously Singapore's government is considering this reform. It is worth noting, however, that executions in Taiwan declined dramatically after mandatory capital statutes were made discretionary (Liao 2008).

16. The Law Society simultaneously made several other reform proposals, including one that would decriminalize homosexual acts among consenting men (Vijayan 2007). As for government control of heterosexual activity, prostitution is legal in Singapore, and brothels are licensed and regulated by the state. Most sex workers are foreigners, and the minimum age for prostitution is 16, though there has been debate about whether the age should be raised to 18 (Bell 2008:59,205,208).

Another sign of domestic discomfort with the death penalty in Singapore was evident in the government's difficulty finding a successor for 73-year-old chief executioner Darshan Singh, who as of 2005 had hanged 850 people in the preceding 46 years—an average of 18 hangings per year.[17] By law, Singapore's executioners are forbidden to speak publicly about their job, but one of Singh's colleagues did tell a Reuters reporter that Singh tried to train two replacements. When it came time to pull the lever, "they both froze and could not do it." One of the trainees "became so distraught he walked out immediately and resigned from the prison service altogether" (Hands Off Cain 2005). Concern about capital punishment may also be evident in Singapore's decision to conduct a death penalty survey early in 2006 following two executions that attracted extraordinary criticism and publicity in the previous year (of Shanmugam Murugesu, a former sports star, and of Van Tuong Nguyen, an Australian national). Although the poll of 425 residents showed that 96 percent supported capital punishment and that most wanted it to remain mandatory (Lim and Yong 2006), the most extraordinary aspect of the exercise may be that a government policy long "shrouded in silence" was subject to survey at all (Tan 2002). In our view, it is possible that governmental elites felt the need to buttress their own death penalty preferences with a social fact they could construct through a public opinion poll and could repress if the results turned out to be inconvenient.[18]

The second regional reason a PAP government might use execution less promiscuously in future years is the growing association of high rates of execution with communist political culture. As Asian studies expert Ian Buruma observes, "nothing is more Chinese about Singapore than its punishments" (2001a:127). A generation ago, Singapore's aggressive system of capital punishment was not isolated on Asia's political right wing, for Taiwan, Malaysia, and South Korea were not far removed. Now, the only Asian company Singapore keeps is China, Vietnam, and perhaps North Korea. From the PAP's point of view, this exclusively communist company might be considered a

17. By comparison, Albert Pierrepoint, whose career as Britain's "most prolific executioner" was dramatized in the (2005) film *The Last Hangman*, executed some 608 persons between 1933 and the end of his career in 1955 (47 of them were Nazis executed at Nuremberg). Although Singh's execution total is 40 percent higher than Pierrepoint's, Pierrepoint averaged 26.4 executions per year, which is 43 percent higher than the Singapore septuagenarian's (Casciani 2006; Coslett 2006; Milmo 2006a; Milmo 2006b). In the state of New York, Edwin F. Davis, the electrician at Auburn Prison who built America's original electric chair in 1890, executed 240 people before he retired in 1914—an average of about ten per year (Banner 2002:195).

18. The death penalty poll was published by the local *Straits Times* newspaper but was permitted and perhaps even ordered by the PAP. In the words of Lee Kuan Yew, the news media must be subordinated to "the overriding needs of Singapore, and to the primacy of purpose of government," an imperative that has long been realized in practice (quoted in Seow 2006:xix; see also Safire 1997; Safire 1999; Buruma 2001a; Lydgate 2003).

form of guilt by association that is best avoided.[19] Since Singapore's crime control problems are quite ordinary, and since the utilitarian benefits of hanging are hardly obvious, substantial drops in execution could occur quickly and cheaply.[20] The information we have presented here suggests that the nation Lee Kuan Yew built may already be in the midst of such a drop.

19. A similar "guilt by association" dynamic is already occurring in Malaysia. In 2007, after China imposed a death sentence for drug trafficking on a young Malaysian woman, "much national outrage" was focused on the possibility of the Chinese government taking Umi Azlim Mohamad Lazim's life, and some observers said Malaysia's stand on the death penalty was "wavering" as the country united in "sympathy and outrage" over her plight. The ruling United Malays National Organization and its rival, the Islamic fundamentalist Pan Malaysian Islamic Party, were even "vying in their efforts" to save Lazim from execution. More generally, the fate of young Malaysians caught ferrying drugs in foreign countries is a "major embarrassment" to the [Malaysian] government (Kuppusamy 2008a).

20. For a brief statement on the death penalty's limited deterrent value for drug crime in Singapore, see Amnesty International (2004b), and for similar statements about the death penalty's weak deterrent effect on drug offenses in Singapore, Malaysia, Vietnam, and Indonesia, see Lines (2007), Fagan (2007), and Lynch (2008). On the death penalty's invisible influence on homicide rates in Singapore, see Zimring, Johnson, and Fagan (2008).

Appendix F: India

I cannot in all conscience agree to anyone being sent to the gallows. God alone can take life because He alone gives it.

—Mahatma Gandhi

Nowadays who remembers Gandhi?

—Satish, a hit man in Mumbai (2004)

Among nations that retain death as a criminal punishment, India is as extraordinary in its policies and practices as the PRC or any place else. In the ten years 1998–2007, India executed only one person (in 2004), giving it a rate of less than one execution per ten billion people per year. Over the same ten-year period, China's execution rate was at least 50,000 times higher, and in per capita terms even low-execution-rate Japan hanged criminal offenders about 300 times more often than India did. If the rest of the world shared India's execution rate over the course of the most recent decade, there would have been—worldwide—just over one execution every other year.

We first describe the social, political, and economic contexts in which India's death penalty policy has been shaped. Next, we describe and explain several key features of India's death penalty policy and practice, including the decline in executions that occurred after India gained independence from Britain in 1947 and the expansion of capital crimes and death sentences in the most recent years even while executions dropped to nearly zero. In the final section we speculate briefly about the future.

■ Contexts

With more than 1.1 billion people, India is the second most populous country in the world, home to three of the world's eight largest cities (Mumbai, Delhi, and Kolkata) even though nearly 70 percent of its residents live in rural areas.

Ten of India's 28 states have more people than South Korea. As of 2005, the world's largest democracy also had the tenth biggest GDP in the world and the world's fourth largest economy in terms of purchasing power (after the United States, China, and Japan). *Foreign Affairs* recently called India "a roaring capital success story," and many other analysts believe it is well along the road to "economic superstardom" (Mishra 2006a; Tharoor 2007b; Mahbubani 2008; Panagariva 2008). Since 1991, when India started to liberalize, its economy has expanded at 6 percent per year, a rate that rose to 7 to 9 percent average annual growth after 2004—not far behind China's recent record-setting rates of development. On this trajectory, if India is not on autopilot to economic greatness, "it would take an incompetent pilot to crash the plane" (Luce 2007:353).

By some measures the Indian economy has come a long way. In the first three decades after India gained independence from Britain in 1947, its average aggregate rate of economic growth was just 3.2 percent, leading many commentators to call it "the Hindu rate of growth" because it was barely higher than the rate of population growth and did little to raise per capita living standards.[1] In subsequent years, India has grown at almost double that rate, and since there has also been a steady decline in the rate of population growth, the relative growth in individual incomes has improved considerably, from an annual average of 1.2 percent increase in personal income before 1995 to 4 percent annual growth after. For the last two decades, India's economy has also consistently outperformed Pakistan's, with a growth rate of 6 percent almost doubling that of its neighbor. If India maintains its current rate of growth, the size of its economy will double every 12 years, and the nation will overtake Japan sometime in the 2020s to become the third largest economy in the world in GDP terms (Luce 2007:258).

While there is reason to welcome India's economic improvements, there also remain many causes for concern about its current state of development. As chapter 7 describes, China experienced widespread terror during the first 30 years of its communist period, yet its current per capita income is now more than double that of India even though Asia's two giants started at the same level in the late 1940s (Luce 2007:27). China also exports six times more products and services than India. Unlike China, independent India has managed to avoid famine, chiefly because it is a democracy (Sen 1992), but Indian democracy also has a much worse record than authoritarian China at protecting its poor from other afflictions such as malnutrition, tuberculosis, and illiteracy (Luce 2007:80). In many parts of rural India, crushing debt and

---

1. Although the "Hindu rate of growth" between 1947 and 1980 did little to improve the fortunes of ordinary Indians, it was a big improvement over the 1 percent average growth that occurred under British rule in the first half of the 20th century (Luce 2007:25). It is possible to credit the British with leaving some positive legacies in its former colony, but when they left India they also left behind literacy levels in the single digits and life expectancy of less than 30 years (Chakravorty 2008).

crashing markets have caused an epidemic of suicides by farmers, and in south India—the country's information technology center—young men and women have some of the highest suicide rates in the world (Sainath 1996; Aaron et al. 2004; Guha 2004; Iype 2004; Nanjappa 2008). India also has significantly lower rates of life expectancy and adult literacy than Indonesia and the Philippines and a per capita GDP that is only about three-fifths of those in the two most populous nations of Southeast Asia. Within Asia, it is mainly in comparison to the other nations of South Asia—Pakistan, Bangladesh, Nepal, Sri Lanka, Bhutan, and the Maldives—that India ranks average or above on measures of national and individual development.

India is a country of so much diversity and so many contrasts and contradictions that it has been called an "unnatural nation" and an "improbable democracy" (Dahl 1998:151; Guha 2007:7; Oldenburg 2007:7). The puzzles abound. For one, the country is emerging as a major economic and political force in the world even though it remains, on the whole, intensely religious, spiritual, and superstitious, leading some analysts to conclude that its recent economic achievements have occurred "in spite of the gods" (Luce 2007). Alone among large nations, India embraced democracy long before it had a sizable middle class or majority literacy among its voters, and the rapid expansion of the Indian economy in recent years has occurred without the country going through a broad-based industrial revolution of the kind that is under way in China. For this reason, India has been criticized for trying to "pole-vault over the basics" (Mehta 2004:24). India's rise is also striking because of the volatile and harsh character of its politics. For the foreseeable future, "deeply fragmented and often incoherent government is likely to be the norm" (Luce 2007:19).

In addition to the challenges India poses to conventional understandings about the conditions and sequence of development, it is a land where severe social conflicts frequently occur across the intersecting axes of caste, class, religion, language, and gender (Oldenburg 2007:7). By comparison, China is far less divided and much less poor (Guha 2007:737). Although India's caste system was legally eliminated in 1950, it persists in practice—especially in matters of political identity—even if it has been severed from its economic and religious roots in some circumstances (Sengupta 2008). Today, one-sixth of Indians—nearly 200 million people—belong to the "untouchable" (*dalit*) undercaste, a nation within a nation that is branded as impure from the moment of birth and subject to extreme exploitation and violence (O'Neill 2003). Arguably, "caste violence—the daily humiliation and killing of *dalits*— is the central faultline of contemporary Indian society" (Menon 2006:viii).

Caste overlaps with class, and India is a nation of huge class disparities too (Galanter 1984; Sen 2005:204). Some Indian entrepreneurs have become fabulously wealthy in recent years, but an estimated 380 million individuals— more people than reside in Pakistan, Bangladesh, and Sri Lanka put together—still live on income below a poverty line defined as $1 a day. About two-thirds of Indians live in rural villages, and many of the poorest of the poor are landless agricultural laborers and small farmers (Sainath 1996). Celebrations of India's economic rise also tend to obscure the fact that in 2006, the country's per capita GDP of $730 was only slightly higher than that of sub-Saharan Africa, and its rank of 127 on the Human Development Index placed it just two rungs above Myanmar and more than 70 below Cuba and Mexico (Mishra 2006a; Mishra 2006b). Half of all Indian children are malnourished, and the official literacy rate of 61 percent (which includes many people who can barely write their names) is 30 percentage points lower than that in China. In West Bengal, the heart of Indian trade unionism and communism, the school dropout rate is 88 percent, and the dropout rate in chronically backward Bihar state is even higher ("Lowest" 2008). India has become a world leader in information technology and business outsourcing, but that growth has largely been jobless. Only 1.3 million people out of a working population of 480 million are employed in the industries of the "new economy," and only 35 million workers—1 in 14—pay any kind of income tax, a low proportion even by the standards of other developing countries. Just 7 percent of Indian men and women between the ages of 18 and 24 go to college, half the proportion for the rest of Asia.

India is also divided by religion, and much of the communal violence that plagues the nation is organized around fractures of faith—Hindu, Islamic, Christian, and Sikh (Nussbaum 2007). Around 80 percent of Indians are Hindu, but the 11 percent who are Muslim give this country the world's third largest Muslim population (after Indonesia and Pakistan). Along with the untouchables, Muslims are one of the nation's most disadvantaged groups: 52 percent of Muslim men and 91 percent of Muslim women are unemployed, and 40 percent of India's prison population is Muslim, making them almost as overrepresented in Indian prisons as are blacks in American prisons (Shankardass 2000; Nomani 2007). Many Indian police "see Muslims as criminals, much as some American police view African Americans" (Mehta 2004:49).

Other social divisions occur across language. India's constitution recognizes 22 "official" languages, the most important of which is Hindi, spoken by more than 400 million people. Many of the other languages boast millions of speakers, and each is written in a distinct script, making linguistic diversity and national unity sometimes difficult to reconcile. The most important political split in India—the partitioning of Pakistan from India in 1947—was "created on the basis of religion, but divided on the basis of language" (Guha 2007:743).

Finally, the social axis of gender frequently cuts across the other dimensions of conflict. Here, too, the contrasts and contradictions are stark. Indira Gandhi served as prime minister of India for 15 years, and her daughter-in-law Sonia Gandhi has been president of the powerful Congress Party for the past decade (1998–2008), yet female infanticide and foeticide (sex-selective abortions) are still common, as are dowries, wage disparities, and the tendency for holy men to assign women an inferior status in this world and the next (Aravamudan 2007; Epp 1998; Sengupta 2008).

In these ways and more, the nation of India really consists of a multitude of different countries (Guha 2007). It is far more diverse than the continent of Europe ever was, and remains a laboratory of social variety and cultural conflict at least as interesting as the Europe of the 19th century. Because India is also a democracy with a free press and a largely independent judiciary, conflicts and contradictions are much more visible than they were in Europe a century or two ago. It may well be that "at no other time or place in human history have social conflicts been so richly diverse, so vigorously articulated, so eloquently manifest in art and literature, or addressed with such directness by the political system and the media" (10).

While India's recent economic achievements are real and impressive, it still faces many major challenges, including the problems of poverty, overpopulation, religious tensions, communal violence, and some of the world's worst levels of environmental degradation and HIV infection (Luce 2007). But if India's economic development is still a work-in-progress, "the real success story" of the country "lies not in the domain of economics but in that of politics" (Guha 2007:10). As political scientist Robert Dahl has observed, India has long had many conditions unfavorable for democracy, including low levels of income and literacy and high levels of social conflict, yet it has remained a vibrant democracy with regular elections, a free and vigorous press, and a relatively independent judiciary (Dahl 1998:159). What is more, India became a democratic nation without an armed conflict or even the threat of one.

To say that India's biggest success is its democracy is not to say that its democracy has been a complete success. For starters, Indian officials are among the most corrupt and lawless in Asia.[2] As of 2005, almost 100 of India's 545 MPs had been indicted for one or more crimes. For many of them, the main incentive for getting elected is the protection Parliament affords against criminal conviction, for once they are in office it becomes "virtually impossible to convict them" (Luce 2007:117; Wonacott 2007). "The quality of Indian parliamentarians has declined markedly over the last generation," and "this has taken its toll on the quality of public reasoning" in the nation (Luce 2007:349). Many of India's political parties have also become family firms, with internal democracy all but absent in party decision-making and with leadership positions dominated by one family or clique (as in the Congress Party since Jawaharlal Nehru became India's first prime minister in 1947). For

2. According to a former chief justice of India's Supreme Court, 20 percent of the Indian judiciary is corrupt, a figure some observers believe is too low (legal professionals in Delhi, interviews by Johnson, March 2008). One brazen act of judicial corruption involved a magistrate in Ahmedabad who in return for 40,000 rupees ($1,000) issued arrest warrants against the president of India, the chief justice of India, a sitting judge of the Supreme Court, and the former president of the Supreme Court Bar Association. "It was not that the not-so-learned magistrate had anything against these individuals; it was simply that, for the right price, he was prepared to issue a warrant against anyone" (Tharoor 2007a:305; see also Oldenburg 2007:7).

these reasons, some commentators regard India as a "50-50 democracy," possessing the requisite hardware of democracy—elections, parties, laws, courts, and rights—but lacking the software that would make the hardware run effectively (Guha 2007:738).

Even by this "half a democracy" assessment, India remains an impressive political achievement, surviving for more than half a century despite frequent predictions of its decline or dissolution (Oldenburg 2007). In our view, it is this political context—and especially the aspirations of India's improbable democracy—that best accounts for several striking features of Indian capital punishment.

■ Capital Punishment

Like most Asian nations, India has a long history of using death as a criminal punishment, and the execution of offenders was common throughout much of it (Upadhyaya 1982; Gupta 1986; Raghavan 2004). The main exception concerns Emperor Ashoka, who is still widely revered as one of India's greatest rulers. A key aspect of Ashoka's emphasis on *ahimsa* (nonviolence) in the "golden age of Buddhism" he fostered in the 2nd century B.C.E. was a policy that greatly restricted the use of capital punishment, making his kingdom one of the first jurisdictions in the world to significantly curtail the use of death as a criminal sanction (Horigan 2001). But capital punishment rapidly recovered after Ashoka died and his empire decomposed. Indeed, before the Mughal dynasty swept down from central Asia into north India in the early 16th century, the story of the many states of the Indian subcontinent was one of almost continual fragmentation and warfare in which capital punishment and other forms of official killing were ordinary occurrences (Dasgupta 1973; Lahiri 1986). After the Mughal invasion, the death penalty remained a normal punishment in the period of Indian unity that prevailed during two centuries of Muslim control and two centuries of rule by the British (Yang 1985; Sangara 1998).

Capital punishment was not only common throughout much of Indian history, it was closely connected to caste and class. When a Chinese visitor recorded his observations about a trip to India in the 5th century, he concentrated on caste, noting that India's sacred texts prescribed different punishments for the same crime depending on the offender's position in the prevailing hierarchy. Among other distinctions, a Sudra (farmer, servant, or foot soldier) who insulted a Brahmin (priest) faced death, whereas a Brahmin who murdered a Sudra was given the same light penalty (usually a fine) as he would have received for killing a dog or a cat (Luce 2007:107). For centuries after this observation was made, the death penalty in India remained a caste-and-class-inflected punishment. By most accounts, it still is today (Muralidhar 1998; Clifford 2004; Gangania 2006; Batra 2007; interviews by Johnson, Delhi, March 2008).

Executions in Independent India

Counting executions is almost as difficult in independent India as in China, Vietnam, and other authoritarian states, though the obstacles to reliable counting seem to have less to do with a governmental penchant for secrecy (and a fear of criticism that secrecy is meant to prevent) as with the logistical complexity of collecting decent data in the nation's highly fragmented political system, and with the low priority India's central government attaches to counting of this kind.[3] Nonetheless, several execution estimates have been published in recent years, and we summarize them in table F.1.

Despite many data inadequacies, four main patterns are evident in these execution estimates. First is the reality of decline over time. From an average of 140 judicial executions per year in 1954–1963—a figure that may well be low because the source for these years did not canvass all Indian states—the annual average drops to one execution per year for the period 1996–2000 (Hood 2001:5), and to only one execution in the ten-year period 1998–2007. The single execution that did occur during the most recent decade took place in Kolkata (formerly Calcutta) in the state of West Bengal, a jurisdiction with more people than Thailand and one that has been ruled by a communist party for three decades, making it the longest-serving democratically elected communist government in the world. The execution also occurred at a time when the left-of-center Congress Party was the ruling power in Delhi (Kaplan 2008). The man who was hanged, 39-year-old Dhananjoy Chatterjee, had been convicted in 1991 for the 1990 rape and murder of a 14-year-old girl who lived in the building where he worked as a security guard. It was a heinous crime, but there was little about the offender or the offense to distinguish this case from the 500 or so other persons who were then on India's death row and who have escaped execution to this day.[4]

---

3. Indian governments have difficulty finding and facing the facts in a wide variety of policy spheres. Among other problems, statements made by ministers in the highest forum of Indian democracy—Parliament—are frequently "misleading, if not entirely made up" ("Face the Facts" 2008). It is unclear how many of the execution numbers reported in table F.1 are misleading or made up, but at least the ones since the 1990s do seem reliable (legal professionals in Delhi, interviews by Johnson, March 2008; Hood and Hoyle 2008:92). Before the People's Union for Democratic Rights discovered the execution figures for 1953–1963, Indian officials frequently said the country had executed only 55 persons since gaining independence in 1947—a lie, a mistake, or a fabrication that was off by at least a factor of 25 and probably by a factor of 60 or more (Batra 2005c). As do several other Asian jurisdictions, India badly needs baseline research on the empirical contours of capital punishment (Muralidhar 1998; Clifford 2004; Batra 2008). To make that happen, Indian officials will have to be more cooperative with researchers and NGOs than they have been so far.

4. Chatterjee's executioner was 83-year-old hangman Nata Mullick, assisted by his 21-year-old grandson. Five years earlier, Mullick had joined a citizens' group fighting for the abolition of capital punishment, explaining: "I performed an inhuman job for four decades. But I have realized that hanging is no answer for crime. The death penalty has been abolished in 104 countries and India too must stop hanging criminals. We must find an

Table F.1

Estimating judicial executions in independent India, 1953–2007

Years	Executions	Source
1953	21	Batra 2005b
1954	108	Batra 2005b
1955	150	Batra 2005b
1956	151	Batra 2005b
1957	153	Batra 2005b
1958	144	Batra 2005b
1959	181	Batra 2005b
1960	174	Batra 2005b
1961	150	Batra 2005b
1962	107	Batra 2005b
1963	73	Batra 2005b
Total, 1953–1963	1,422[1]	Batra 2005b
1974–1978	68[2]	Hood 1989
1979–1983	45	Hood 1989
1982–1985	35[3]	Clifford 2004
1995–1998	24[4]	National Crime Records Bureau
1996–2000	5[5]	Hood 2001
1998	0	Batra 2007
1999	0	Batra 2007
2000	0	Batra 2007
2001	0	Batra 2007
2002	0	Batra 2007
2003	0	Batra 2007
2004	1	Batra 2007
2005	0	Batra 2007
2006	0	Batra 2007
2007	0	Batra 2007

Note: Batra estimates a total of 3,500 executions for the first 60 years of Indian independence, 1947–2007 (interview by Johnson, March 11, 2008).

[1] The annual execution totals for 1953–1963 and the summary total for the same 11-year period come from an appendix to a 1967 report by the Law Commission of India that was unearthed by the People's Union for Democratic Rights in 2005 following government claims that post independence India had executed only 55 persons. The true total for this period is probably higher because the report covers only 16 of 28 states; and the total of 21 executions for 1953 is probably much too low because it only reflects execution figures for 4 of the 16 states covered in the 1967 appendix. In addition, 86 percent of the 1,422 executions recorded for this period occurred in the five states of Madras (485), Uttar Pradesh (397), Punjab (140), Andhra Pradesh (119), and Kerala (84).

[2] The attorney general gave this figure in a statement he made to the Supreme Court during arguments in *Kehar Singh v. Union of India*, as reported in Muralidhar (1998:25).

[3] From a report released in Parliament as summarized by Tom Clifford (2004:20), who said the count for this "three-year period"represented "the most complete and reliable execution numbers" that were available at the time of his writing.

[4] According to lawyer and researcher Bikram Jeet Batra, this figure, as recorded by the National Crime Records Bureau of India's Home Affairs Ministry, may not be exact, but "there are unlikely to have been far more executions"during this period (Batra 2007:2).

[5] According to Hood (2001), India had 49 death sentences during this period.

The second execution pattern is regional, although here the best evidence is dated. Of the 1,422 judicial executions that were recorded in 16 Indian states in 1953–1963, 86 percent—6 out of every 7—occurred in five states that collectively made up one-third of the national population, and 62 percent took place in two states—Madras in the south and Uttar Pradesh in the north—that together accounted for less than one-quarter of the nation's population (Batra 2005b). By these measures, executions were more geographically clustered in India than they were in the United States, where executions have long been concentrated in a handful of southern states (Zimring 2003:94). It is unclear whether or how long this Indian pattern persisted, and in any event it makes no sense to speak of executions "clustering" in a contemporary India that has carried out only one in the last ten years. Still, at least some informed observers believe death sentencing and execution rates in India's southern states (which tend to be more developed) have long been lower than in other parts of the country (Clifford 2004:41).[5]

---

alternative to killing the killers" (quoted in Hands Off Cain, November 24, 1999). But Mullick's conversion (which occurred after he had tied the noose and pulled the lever at least 22 times) was impermanent. He became something of a celebrity prior to Chatterjee's hanging, and before waxing the rope with soap and ripe bananas in 2004, Mullick told the Associated Press that "criminals like Chatterjee ought to be hanged so that others don't commit such crimes. I'm only making society safer" (quoted in Hands Off Cain, August 14, 2004). After that execution, Mullick fell ill and had to be carried home on a stretcher. Prison officials said he had been drinking heavily during the previous three days. For a documentary account of this execution, see Joshy Joseph's film *One Day from a Hangman's Life*, which was released in 2005 but withdrawn by the chief minister of West Bengal (Budddhadev Bhattacharjee), apparently because he objected to the content (Hands Off Cain, June 21, 2005). And for a work of fiction that explores the emotional and practical dilemmas of an Indian executioner and is based on the life of Janardhanan Pillai, who became the hangman for the king of Travancore (present-day Kerala in southern India) in the early 1940s and performed 117 executions over the subsequent three decades, see Warrier (2000).

5. On June 13, 2001, the *Times of India* summarized death sentencing patterns for India's four largest states: two in the north (Uttar Pradesh and Bihar), one in the east (West Bengal), and one in the west (Maharashtra). Of these, Uttar Pradesh and Bihar—the two most illiterate and impoverished states in India and also the two with the most recorded murders—issued the largest number of first-instance death sentences (Clifford 2004). The annual death sentence totals ranged from 4 to 38 in Uttar Pradesh (population 166 million), from 4 to 37 in Bihar (83 million), from 1 to 9 in West Bengal (80 million), and from 2 to 11 in Maharashtra (97 million). As one article on the death penalty in India has observed, "the correlation between 'higher frequency' death penalty states and poverty has not gone unnoticed in Indian politics" (Clifford 2004:42). In a 1961 floor debate on the abolition of capital punishment in the upper house of Parliament, one MP said that of the 145 condemned prisoners he had interviewed, 93 (64 percent) came from the scheduled castes and tribes—population groupings that are explicitly recognized by India's constitution as previously "depressed" (Gupta 2000:342). In a dissenting opinion in 1980, Supreme Court justice Bhagwati wrote: "There can be no doubt that the death penalty in its actual operation is discriminatory for it strikes mostly against the poor and deprived sections of the

The third fact that stands out in table F.1 is the low aggregate total of judicial executions in independent India. The estimated total of 3,500 executions over a 60-year period is about the same number of executions as in a typical three-to-six month period in recent years in the PRC (see chapter 7), and on an annual per capita basis, the same rate of execution as Japan over the same six decades.[6] If we consider only the 30 years since 1977, when executions resumed in the United States after a ten-year moratorium, then India has executed (in absolute terms) only one-fourth or one-fifth as many persons as the United States. In per capita terms, that means the world's second most populous democracy—America—has for the past three decades been executing at a rate that is 10 to 15 times higher than the world's largest democracy.

The final striking feature of independent India's execution record is the present rate that hovers barely above zero. No retentionist nation in the world executes at a lower rate than India, and the only way India's own rate could go any lower is if it falls out of the retentionist category altogether.[7] The rest of this appendix explains how the execution rate reached this low level and why India's exit from the retentionist league of nations seems an unlikely prospect for the immediate future even though the current execution gridlock has all but retired the country's hangmen.

---

community and the rich and affluent usually escape from its clutches" (*Bachan Singh v. State of Punjab*, 1980). More recently, Bikram Jeet Batra has noted that there is "no research which can prove such caste-class discrimination, but given that competent legal representation is rarely available to the poor, it will be no surprise if they form the large chunk of those on death row" (Batra 2007:24; see also Clifford 2004; Gangania 2006; Batra 2008:117,203).

6. Between 1947 and 2007, Japan executed 614 persons, an average of 10.1 executions per year. With a population of 112 million at the midpoint of this period (1977), Japan's annual execution rate per million is 10.1/112 = 0.09. If India executed 3,500 people in 1947–2007, then it averaged 57.4 executions per year, and with a population of 640 million at the midpoint of this period (1977), its annual execution rate per million would be 57.4/640 = 0.09.

7. On the whole, South Asia uses capital punishment less aggressively than either East or Southeast Asia. Two out of seven South Asian nations have formally abolished the death penalty: Nepal in 1997, and Bhutan in 2004. Two more have abolished de facto: Sri Lanka has not conducted a judicial execution since 1976, and the Maldives—the most developed country in South Asia—has not had one since 1952. And two of the three South Asian nations that retain capital punishment—India and Bangladesh—have for the past decade or more performed judicial executions much less frequently than have the developed democracies of the United States and Japan (Mash 2007). The only nation that executes with any frequency in South Asia is Pakistan, where executions increased from 18 in 2003 to 134 in 2007 (Ebrahim 2008; see also International Federation for Human Rights and Human Rights Commission of Pakistan 2007). But even in Pakistan there are signs (such as the prime minister's proposal in 2008 to commute all death sentences to life imprisonment except for terrorists and persons convicted of attempting to assassinate the president) that executions might fall in the near future (Sarwar 2008b; see chapter 8).

Explaining Executions

India's low execution rate is something of a puzzle for at least three reasons. First, the country has serious problems with lethal violence and a large supply of potentially capital cases. Its homicide rate at the turn of the 21st century— 3.6 per 100,000 population—was six times higher than Japan's, nearly three times higher than Singapore's, and twice as high as China's (Clifford 2004:14; Johnson 2006b:77). What is more, India has long had serious problems with insurgencies, insurrections, political conflicts, terrorism, and communal violence.[8] These irruptions produce a steady supply of potential poster boys for execution, such as Mohammad Afzal Guru, who has been condemned to die for attacking the Indian Parliament in December 2001 and, some observers believe, who will be the next person India hangs (Mehta 2004; Mishra 2006b; Champa 2007; Guha 2007; Luce 2007; Chakravarti 2008).[9] Beginning in the mid-1980s, Parliament also expanded the scope of capital punishment to cover a number of new capital offenses, from acts of terrorism and organized crime to drug offending and kidnapping for ransom (Batra 2007). One result has been the expansion of death row, which grew from 110 in 2001 to 563 in 2004 (Batra 2007).

Second, the large supply of heinous offenses combines with an independent and frequently sensationalistic media to make "law-and-order" concerns highly salient in the court of public opinion. Although systematic surveys of

---

8. During the riots that rocked Mumbai in 1992–1993, killing 1,400 people, printing presses ran overtime producing two sets of name cards for some worried residents, one with a Muslim name and one with a Hindu name. "When you were out in the city, if you got stopped your life depended on whether you answered to Ram or Rahim" (Mehta 2004:45). Hardly anyone was punished for this orgy of communal violence. As of March 1998, the criminal justice system had produced only eight convictions—one for every 175 murders (109).

9. In March 2008, two advocates working in the Patiala House Courts in New Delhi told Johnson that in that jurisdiction alone approximately 10,000 out of the 500,000 cases then "pending" (on trial, waiting to be tried, or on appeal) were "potentially capital" in the sense that they involved defendants who were eligible to receive a death sentence. Nationwide, about 13.2 million criminal cases are pending in India's subordinate courts, to be tried or otherwise disposed of by 12,200 judges—a backlog of more than 1,000 cases per judge. On the average, India's lower courts can dispose of about 19 percent of pending criminal cases each year—around 2.5 million cases—but in recent years about 5 million new crimes have been registered each year. The net effect is long and growing delay in processing cases and very low conviction rates. By one report, fewer than 45 percent of persons charged with serious Penal Code offenses are ultimately convicted (Nariman 2006:85), and an even lower percentage of criminal offenses are registered in the first place. According to Kiran Bedi, a former high-level police official in Delhi, only about 5 percent of crimes in India are ever registered with the police, and for murders the registration rate is less than 20 percent (interviews by Johnson, March 2008). Two former chief justices of India's Supreme Court have lamented that the nation's criminal justice system has "already collapsed" or is close to "collapsing" (Nariman 2006:83).

public attitudes toward capital punishment have apparently not been done, the evidence that does exist generally suggests public support for the death penalty at levels comparable to the other Asian jurisdictions covered in this book and summarized in chapter 8. As one analyst has observed, "human rights activists [in India] stand largely alone in their opposition to capital punishment" (Eckert 2005:196). Before Dhananjoy Chatterjee was executed in Kolkata in 2004, there was widespread enthusiasm for his hanging, both in the state of West Bengal, where the execution occurred and where the local government pressured the central government not to provide clemency, and in much of the rest of the country, where the issue attracted enormous public and media attention. Similarly, a small-scale survey conducted in India in the mid-1980s found "strong support [for capital punishment] among university and college teachers, doctors, and, to a lesser extent, lawyers" (Hood 2001:244). Unless support for the death penalty in India is much weaker than the levels of support found everywhere else in Asia where this issue has been systematically studied, the interaction of heinous crime, lurid reporting, and public opinion would seem to constitute a recipe of support for the death penalty that elected leaders in India's highly populist form of democracy would be eager to satisfy (Guha 2007:681).[10] Yet even when India's major party of the right—the strongly nationalist Bharatiya Janata Party, or BJP—controlled the reins of central government for more than six years between March 1998 and May 2004, not a single judicial execution occurred even though there were more than 500 people on death row at the end of that period (Batra 2007). The infrequency of execution cannot be attributed to India's anti–death penalty movement, which is as weak, unorganized, and underfunded as many other progressive movements in the country (Epp 1998:90). One fact that does help explain the absence of executions under the BJP is the fact that a Congress Party politician—the liberal Kocheril Raman Narayanan—was president from 1997 to 2002. Many clemency decisions are made by the president in India's system of government, but since presidents are required to consult with members of the cabinet before making such decisions, Narayanan's presidency does not fully explain why there were no executions during this period (Batra 2008:229; legal professionals in Delhi, interviews by Johnson, March 2008).

Third, the Indian state has shown little reluctance to kill extrajudicially, and for the most part there has been "no reaction from the public, no outrage" that police have become executioners outside the law (Mehta 2004:173; Mitta and

---

10. A recent study of death penalty views in India found that opinion was evenly divided among undergraduates (n = 434) at a large metropolitan public university in the southern state of Andhra Pradesh, with 44 percent opposing capital punishment and 43 percent supporting it (Lambert et al. 2008). As the authors of this study acknowledge, the sample is far from representative, and it is uncertain how the level of death penalty support among college students at this one university compares to opinion in the general public. Most informed observers seem to believe that the majority of Indians support capital punishment for murder and for offenses such as "terrorism" (Batra 2007:1). There is little evidence of "demand."

Phoolka 2007). Few governments can match the enthusiasm for state killing that is found among some Indian officials (Baxi 1982; Subramanian 2007). Between 1999 and 2000, the Indian National Human Rights Commission reported that at least 1,143 persons had died in police custody. The numbers are similar for other years and the true total may well be higher (Rothman and Neier 1991; Batra 2007). Many if not most of these people died from police torture.[11] Hundreds of other Indian citizens "disappear" each year, abducted by police or military officials and detained in secret and without due process. Many are feared dead. In addition, hundreds of Indian civilians die each year in what are euphemistically called "encounters" between the police and citizens (Mehta 2004:169; Eckert 2005:198). Some police forces even maintain "encounter specialists" whose kill totals number in the dozens or hundreds and whose murders are authorized by high-ranking officers (Mehta 2004:174; Eckert 2005:205; Luce 2007:96). Between 1998 and 2001, police in Mumbai killed at least 305 purported "gangsters," giving the "thin khaki line" of this city of 14 million an annual extrajudicial execution rate of 5.4 per million population—a figure that does not include killings in police custody. The Wikipedia entry for "Mumbai Encounter Squad" even has a heading ("Active Inspectors in Encounter Squad and Encounter Killings Count") under which the names of six high-profile officers are listed along with their "encounter killing" totals—104, 82, 77, 51, 48, and 80—counts that are very much in line with those reported by other sources (Perry 2003; Ahmed 2004; Mehta 2004; Luce 2007:96). And the Mumbai police are "still fairly considered the best in India" (Mehta 2004:160). In the year 2000, more than 100 civilians were killed in "encounters" with the police in Mumbai, and not a single policeman was killed (Eckert 2005:214). These state-paid assassins do little to hide the nature or scope of their work, perhaps because the police, the courts, and the media help to maintain the fiction that the bad guys always fired first while the police shot only in self-defense (Mehta 2004:172).

One explanation favored by police—and by some outside observers as well—is that "encounter" killings and other forms of extrajudicial execution are common in India because the criminal justice system does such an

11. It is believed that at least 200 people were tortured to death in 1997 in the state of Maharashtra (whose capital is Mumbai), a record for police brutality "that outstrips that of many military dictatorships around the world" (Mehta 2004:163; Subramanian 2007). Thirty years earlier, the Bhagalpur police in the state of Bihar blinded at least 31 suspects in their custody by using needles and acid. When Upendra Baxi documented these abuses in his classic *Crisis of the Indian Legal System*, he concluded that chroniclers of governmental lawlessness in India are "condemned to labours as arduous and fruitless as those of Sisyphus" (Baxi 1982:348). Baxi was even more pessimistic in 2008. "The more things change the more they stay the same," he said. "Almost everything I said about government lawlessness [in my 1982 book] remains true today, and many problems are significantly aggravated. . . . The basic structures of exploitation and lawlessness have not changed" (Upendra Baxi, interview by Johnson, Delhi, March 19, 2008).

ineffective job of convicting and punishing offenders. In Mumbai in 2000, for example, the conviction rate fell to an all-time low of 4 percent (Mehta 2004:175), and conviction rates elsewhere in the country are notoriously low as well (Nariman 2006:85). So, too, is the proportion of crime that gets reported to the police in the first place (former police executive Kiran Bedi, interview by Johnson, March 20, 2008). As sociologist Donald Black has noted, crimes tend to proliferate as a form of "social control" in locations where formal state controls are weak or absent (Black 1983).

In sum, there are good reasons to wonder why India is not a significantly more aggressive death penalty state. What explains the gap between expectation and reality and the significant decline in executions shown in table F.1?

Capital Gridlock and Indian Politics

Two institutional actors play a major role in producing India's near-zero rate of judicial execution: courts, which are required by law to impose capital punishment only in the "rarest of rare" circumstances, and executive clemency, which is routinely used at the state and federal levels to delay executions indefinitely and to reduce death sentences to something less than death. These two obstacles to execution have created a kind of capital gridlock over the last 15 years—a profoundly inertial death penalty system that generates remarkably few executions.

Consider courts first. The Constitution of 1950 did not abolish capital punishment, and several attempts by Parliament to eliminate the death penalty failed in subsequent years, but until a new Code of Criminal Procedure took effect in 1973, the death penalty remained so much "the natural and preferred punishment for murder" that sentencing judges had to record special reasons when they chose to impose noncapital sentences, much as was done under the British before independence (Batra 2007:5). The new Code reversed this presumption by turning death into an exceptional punishment and requiring judges to record "special reasons" only when they awarded a capital sentence. The new Code also introduced a special sentencing hearing to be held after conviction at trial. Today, capital cases in India begin in trial courts at the state level and unfold in two stages, first determining guilt and then deciding sentence (Batra 2008:50).

The Indian legal system is federal, and under a constitutionally defined system of three "lists" that delineate the lawmaking powers of the state and central governments, the power to legislate criminal law rests in the hands of both. This means there is no such thing as an abolitionist Indian state because state-specific legislation is not required for a state to employ capital punishment, so long as the central government retains death penalty statutes. In fact, if an Indian state tried to abolish capital punishment by passing a law to prohibit it, the law would have no legal effect (Clifford 2004:11).

In practice, the vast majority of capital cases in India begin at the local level, but prosecutors do little of the screening that their counterparts do in places such as Japan, South Korea, China, Taiwan, and the United States. In murder cases, for example, Indian prosecutors "routinely" and "mechanically" seek a death sentence after the defendant has been convicted at trial (legal professionals in Delhi, interviews by Johnson, March 2008). In contrast to criminal justice systems in which prosecutors play a more primary role in deciding what cases are capital, in Indian criminal justice the onus is on courts to determine who deserves death, and they use the ultimate sanction sparingly. In the four-year period from 1999 to 2002, Indian trial courts issued a total of 94 death sentences—just 16 to 30 death sentences per year during a period in which India had more than 30,000 murders each year. Over the same period of time, trial courts in the United States produced 19 to 35 times more death sentences per murder (Clifford 2004:17). In 2007, the most recent year for which data are available, Indian trial courts imposed only 25 death sentences, 12 of them in one bombing case in Mumbai ("Mumbai Courts" 2007).[12] On a single day in October of that year, trial courts in Uttar Pradesh, Tamil Nadu, and Delhi awarded more than 60 sentences of life imprisonment but not a single sentence of death ("Abolishing" 2007).

More filtering is done by India's appellate courts. One study found that in 1980–1990, high courts upheld 65 percent of death sentences, while the Supreme Court upheld 40 percent of the capital sentences it reviewed during the same decade (Clifford 2004:29).[13] If Indian appellate courts confirm death sentences at similar rates today—and some observers believe they do—then only about one-quarter ($0.65 \times 0.40 = 0.26$) of first-instance death sentences survive the appeals process, a degree of selectivity that may be matched only by appellate courts in South Korea and the United States (legal professionals in Delhi, interviews by Johnson, March 2008).

The jurisprudential roots of the judicial reluctance to impose and uphold death sentences can be found in appellate decisions, especially the 1980 landmark case of *Bachan Singh v. State of Punjab*, which held that "a real and abiding concern for the dignity of human life postulates resistance to taking a life through law's instrumentality. That ought not to be done save in the *rarest of rare* cases when the alternative opinion is unquestionably foreclosed" (emphasis added). In this decision and subsequent ones, the Indian Supreme Court tried to define the "aggravating circumstances" and "mitigating circumstances" that would distinguish the "rarest of the rare" cases from more run-of-the-mill crimes. The 1983 case of *Macchi Singh and Others v. State of Punjab* held that the "rarest of the rare" requirement is satisfied when the "collective conscience" of the community has

---

12. In 2005, Indian courts sentenced 77 defendants to death (Hood and Hoyle 2008:92).

13. Another study found that almost 100 of 700 death penalty appeals heard by India's Supreme Court ended in acquittal (Batra 2007:27; Batra 2008).

been "shocked" and when the balance sheet of aggravating and mitigating circumstances indicates that a sentence of life imprisonment would be "inadequate" because it would denigrate the seriousness of the crime (Batra 2007:10).[14]

India's framework for discerning what crimes are the "worst of the worst" is largely borrowed from the United States, where the "aggravating" and "mitigating" categories were elaborated in the aftermath of the U.S. Supreme Court's *Furman* and *Gregg* decisions of the 1970s. In fact, the creation of the "rarest of rare" formula in 1980 was partly a reaction by India's Supreme Court against the state-level backlashes that occurred in the United States when the U.S. Supreme Court held (in 1972) that the death penalty as then administered was unconstitutionally "cruel and unusual" because it was applied so haphazardly. Having observed the controversy this decision sparked in America, and having watched the U.S. Supreme Court reverse course four years later, India's Supreme Court at the time (which was quite progressive) deemed it imprudent to attempt the judicial abolition of capital punishment, electing instead to curtail the circumstances in which death could be imposed. In this respect, many analysts regard the Indian Supreme Court's "rarest of the rare" doctrine as a "pragmatic compromise" (legal professionals in Delhi, interviews by Johnson, March 2008).

The attempts by Indian courts to impose substantive standards on death penalty decision-making have had mixed results. Death sentences are now imposed infrequently, and at least some of that judicial caution can be attributed to the Supreme Court's leadership. As one account concludes, "India is choosy with the death penalty and truly executes only the 'rarest of the rare'" (Clifford 2004:44). But India pays a high price for this achievement, for a system with capital statutes as broad as India's that carries out only a handful of executions in response to more than 30,000 murders per year is lawless in the sense that nothing about the nation's capital jurisprudence can explain who gets sentenced to death or hanged when hundreds of equally or more culpable offenders escape the death penalty altogether. In this sense, the first feature of India's capital gridlock—the judiciary—not only helps prevent many executions, it does so in a manner that undermines the doctrinal predictability that the "rarest of the rare" formula is supposed to serve. For this reason, Indian capital punishment has been called a "lethal lottery" (Batra 2008).[15]

14. India does not have LWOP. Offenders who receive a sentence of life are frequently released after 14 years in prison (legal professionals in Delhi, interviews by Johnson, March 2008).

15. Indian courts have also been criticized for being too quick to challenge decisions made by the other branches of government, but Chief Justice K. G. Balakrishnan has defended the judiciary by saying that "if its interventions annoyed other organs of the state, so be it." In his view, "the only function of the court is to protect the rights of the people, and all its actions are directed to further this function" (quoted in Mahapatra 2008; see also Epp 1998:71).

The second component of India's capital gridlock is executive clemency. If India's legislature speaks broadly in favor of capital punishment and Indian courts have upheld the constitutionality of the practice while restricting the volume of death sentences, the executive branch of government has spoken, through its silence and its mercy, in a rather different voice. All convicted criminals have the right to submit petitions for clemency to the governor of the state in which they were convicted and to the president of India. By law, neither executive can exercise clemency powers on his or her own initiative; each must act on the aid and advice of the ministers in their respective governments, and in some circumstances their clemency decisions are even subject to judicial review. Still, the scope of executive clemency power is broad, and it is often used to prevent executions in the same two ways that the king of Thailand prevents many executions there: by proactively granting sentence reductions to death row petitioners, and by passively withholding decisions on how the petitioner's request will be processed, often for many years (Batra 2007:27). Since there is no limit to the number of mercy petitions that can be filed, and since the law forbids executions while such petitions are pending, some condemned inmates are able to postpone an appointment with the hangman indefinitely by submitting repeated requests for mercy (Batra 2007:5; Batra 2008:227).

The institutional arrangements of recent years do not themselves reveal the deeper reasons why the rate of execution has dropped more than 99 percent since the 1960s. Even considering the generally low rates of execution that prevail among retentionist nations in Asia, the zero execution consistency and the byzantine complexity of India's current system are a substantial puzzle. In part, India's death penalty gridlock may be caused by the same large gap between ideology and material achievement that has produced a vibrant democracy and a free press in this economically underdeveloped nation. India is committed to democratic aspirations and institutions that are usually found in nations far more developed. The visions of Gandhi and Nehru remain a "precious inheritance" and an important part of Indian political consciousness even though there are huge inconsistencies between vision and reality in politics, social welfare, civil liberties, and the rule of law (Mehta 2003; Oldenburg 2007:11). India knows better than it does. The informal but powerful death penalty gridlock of the present is evidence that Indian governments realize that judicial executions are inconsistent with the nation's own political ideals. What the principal author of India's constitution concluded in 1949 still holds true today:

This country by and large believes in the principle of non-violence. It has been its ancient tradition, and although people may not be following it in actual practice, they certainly adhere to the principle of non-violence as a moral mandate which they ought to observe as far as they possibly can and I think that having regard to this fact, the proper thing to do is to abolish the death sentence altogether. (Bhimrao Ambedkar, quoted in Batra 2008:19)

■ **Policy Futures**

The most probable future of the death penalty in India is a long but informal continuation of few or zero executions without formal abolition. As of 2008, 27 of the 28 Indian states were already in Amnesty International's de facto abolitionist category because they had conducted no executions for a decade or more. Since this lack of executions has rarely become a visible political issue and has created few evident costs or conflicts, a continuation of the current low- and no-execution practice would seem to carry little political risk.

But if India's execution-free environment generates so little conflict about capital punishment, why not formal abolition? Two reasons that in-country activists do not think abolition is probable are the lack of political support for it and the possibility that public concern about insurgencies, crime, and disorder could create a backlash against an abolitionist push. There is no significant institution in India with a commitment to abolition that can parallel the Catholic Church in the Philippines, and there is no legislative constituency for abolition in India to parallel the situation in South Korea. A transition from the near moratorium of the present to formal abolition would require a species of "leadership from the front" on capital punishment with no precedent in Indian politics. Since another paradox of modern India is that its impressive democracy is peopled, for the most part, by "unimpressive" and "complacent" politicians, the final steps toward formal abolition may be all the more unlikely (Luce 2007:349).

Without strong political support for abolition, could an aggressive nationalist party like the BJP produce a resurgence in executions of the kind that is under way in Japan? The first reason this is unlikely is the lack of pressure in that direction in the current political environment. Even when the BJP held power, there was little effort to translate capital punishment into political capital, perhaps because any strong push toward execution would have transformed India's extraordinary ambivalence about execution into the conspicuous political force it has never been. A hard push for more executions creates the risk of a backlash. As one Indian scholar put it, "no regime can go very far on capital punishment and still survive" (interview by Johnson, Delhi, March 14, 2008). So Indian leaders have little to gain and much to lose by trying to break through the gridlock that prevents almost all executions, especially in a political context in which multiparty coalitions have become the norm and a fragmented political culture makes it difficult for governments to take decisive action (Luce 2007). In any event, a nation the size of India would need to average 44 executions a year in order to exit the "symbolic" category of retentionist countries that we introduced in chapter 2. That is as improbable an execution total for India as it is for the PRC.

Just as the ideologies of Gandhi and Nehru inspired and supported India's precocious democratic institutions, the opposition of India's founding fathers to state execution is an important element of its current death penalty policy—a spiritual "leadership from the front" that is embedded in Indian history and absent in other Asian nations. Now that nonexecution has become an orthodox part of the ideology of most progressive nations, India seems likely—sooner or later—to realize its founders' ideals. In this sense, the cynical query that opened this appendix—"Who remembers Gandhi?"—misreads an essential feature of Indian national identity.

Appendix G: Judicial and Extrajudicial Killing

Labels such as "state killing" and "the killing state" are frequently used to describe the legally permitted and regulated "judicial killing" that occurs in systems of capital punishment (Amnesty International 1989b; Sarat 1999; Sarat 2001; Zimring 2003; Kassymbekova 2005; Sarat and Boulanger 2005; Johnson 2006c; Amnesty International 2007b). But states kill extrajudicially too, and sometimes the scale so far exceeds the volume of judicial executions that it seems reasonable to wonder whether death penalty reductions or even outright abolitions are comparatively small potatoes (Rummel 1994; Horowitz 2001; Kiernan 2007; Vieira 2007; Hagan and Rymond-Richmond 2008).[1]

1. William Schabas has noted that "few more dramatic examples of the spread and success of human rights law can be found" than the widespread reductions in capital punishment that have occurred in recent decades (Schabas 2004:419). But as Roger Hood observes, "alarming reports" of extrajudicial killing continue to surface in the work of the special rapporteur on extrajudicial, summary, or arbitrary executions to the UN Commission on Human Rights (Hood 2002:155; see www.ohchr.org/english/issues/executions; see also www.extrajudicialexecutions.org, the Web site for the Project on Extrajudicial Executions in the Center for Human Rights and Global Justice at the New York University School of Law). Hood believes the findings from projects such as these constitute "a dreadful catalogue of nonjudicially sanctioned killings in far too many countries of the world, certainly on a scale out of all proportion to executions carried out under the due process of law and sometimes amounting to genocide" (Hood 2002:155; Hood and Hoyle 2008:6).

In this appendix we explore the relationship between judicial and extrajudicial killing in Asia. Our analysis depends on a fundamental distinction between two types of extrajudicial killing: (1) the use of lethal force in reactive, unpremeditated, and legally legitimate ways (as when the police shoot an armed felon in response to an attack), and (2) killing as an instrument of a government policy designed to eliminate perceived enemies of the state in a proactive, premeditated, and illegal manner (as the PRC is alleged to do with practitioners of the Falun Gong religion, and as Taiwan did in the years of the White Terror under Chiang Kai-shek). Our focus is on the connections between extrajudicial killing that is "proactive" in the type 2 sense and the judicially authorized executions that occur in systems of capital punishment. This approach to state killing largely ignores "reactive" killings of the type 1 kind because history and common sense suggest that police and soldiers tend to shoot back when insurgents or fleeing felons shoot at them first. If the Tamil Tigers (the world's leading suicide terrorist organization) were operating in Switzerland instead of Sri Lanka, the rate of Swiss state killing would rise substantially (Pape 2005:139).

Although the distinction between reactive and proactive extrajudicial killing seems theoretically sound, in practice it can be difficult to discern which has occurred. When states respond to insurgencies such as those that are ongoing in Sri Lanka, Nepal, and the Philippines, they often respond with both reactive lethal force and with proactive, preemptive strikes—and it is sometimes impossible to tell the two apart. Even at Tiananmen Square in 1989—when "the whole world was watching"—it can be difficult to tell whether Chinese forces were responding to a riot or engaging in deliberate massacre (Calhoun 1997; Gitlin 2003; Clark 2008). Moreover, many jurisdictions lack reliable counts of extrajudicial killings over time. Data difficulties such as these inhibit confident conclusions, but the available evidence does seem to suggest that the trajectories of capital punishment and proactive extrajudicial killing tend to track each other. This finding is important because it indicates that Asia's death penalty declines may reflect improvement in other spheres of state activity and because it means Asian governments tend not to compensate for reductions in their use of capital punishment by conducting more extrajudicial executions.

■ The Appearance of Independence

Table G.1 depicts some of the variation in state killing that exists in contemporary Asia by reducing the complexity of that phenomenon to two dimensions: judicial executions (low vs. high), and proactive extrajudicial executions (low vs. high). In this simplified scheme, it may be reasonable to resist our placement of some individual nations, but minor-to-modest adjustments do not alter the fact that at least one Asian nation can be found for each of the four cells in the table.

Table G.1
Judicial and extrajudicial killings in 21 Asian nations

	Extrajudicial killings		
	Low	*High*	
Low	Japan	Philippines	India
	South Korea	Nepal	Indonesia
	Taiwan	Cambodia	Myanmar
	Bhutan	East Timor	Papua New Guinea
	Malaysia	Bangladesh	Sri Lanka
Judicial killings			Thailand
High	Singapore	China	
		North Korea	
		Pakistan	
		Vietnam	

The distribution of Asian nations across all four cells of table G.1 could be taken as evidence that judicial and extrajudicial killing are unrelated in the Asian context. If so, then the Asian pattern might surprise those students of state killing in the United States who believe the history of lynching and capital punishment in the southern part of the country suggests that "a culture that carried out so much unofficial capital punishment [as some southern states did] could hardly be squeamish about the official variety" (Banner 2002:229). On this view, the aggressive use of death as a criminal sanction follows directly or indirectly from a cultural commitment to violence and from the race relations and attitudes that were a central feature of that culture. In the U.S. context, there is some evidence that the two forms of state killing are positively correlated, both during the post–Civil War period and after lynchings peaked early in the 20th century (Zimring 2003; Jacobs, Carmichael, and Kent 2005; Garland 2006; Garland 2007a; Garland 2007b).[2] If there is a positive linkage between lynchings in the past and judicial executions in the present, it may involve the persistence of "vigilante values" (Zimring 2003:89; see also Garland 2005). But there is also American evidence for an inverse relationship between legal executions and extralegal lynchings (Bowers 1984), and there is theoretical reason to wonder whether a formal control such as capital punishment tends to vary inversely with informal controls such as extrajudicial execution (Black 1976:107; Miethe, Lu, and Deibert 2005:120). In contrast to this ambiguous American evidence, some of which suggests a positive

2. Miethe, Lu, and Deibert (2005:127) reach a similar conclusion in their cross-sectional analysis of judicial and extrajudicial killing in 185 nations ("a significant positive bivariate relationship between the availability of legal and extrajudicial executions").

correlation between judicial and extrajudicial executions and some of which suggests an inverse relationship, the cross-sectional evidence summarized in table G.1 suggests that the two forms of state killing may be independent in the Asian context.

But there are at least two problems with using a cross-sectional approach to study state killing in Asia. First, the evidence on judicial and extrajudicial killing for many Asian jurisdictions is hardly high quality, not least because it is impossible to control for the incidence of crimes and rebellions that provoke lethal responses from the state. Second, since table G.1 does not take into account trends over time, the cross-sectional snapshots it presents may obscure longitudinal patterns.

■ State Killing in Temporal Perspective

The appearance of independence between the two types of state killing largely disappears when one considers the temporal dimension which is missing in table G.1. Indeed, when judicial and extrajudicial executions in Asia are examined over time, the initial impression of independence turns out to be misleading because as judicial executions have declined in many Asian countries, so have extrajudicial killings.

Before illustrating this temporal correspondence with several examples, we need to make two observations about the distribution of Asian nations across the two categories of state killing. First, there are at most five nations that conduct judicial executions at a "high" level of frequency (two of those—Pakistan and Vietnam—could be considered borderline in some recent years), and four of the five also rank "high" on the index of extrajudicial killing. The only exception is Singapore, where judicial executions are common but extrajudicial killings are all but unknown. Were it not for this city-state, we would be tempted to conclude that governments that kill a lot "legally" have little compunction about killing illegally as well. Second, despite the strikingly bottom-heavy distribution of judicial executions in Asia we described in chapter 2, extrajudicial killing remains common in many parts of the region, including nations that have formally abolished the death penalty, such as the Philippines (Berlow 1996; Amnesty International 2006d; Alston 2007), Nepal (Mishra 2006b:288), and Cambodia (Miethe, Lu, and Deibert 2005:128), and nations that seldom conduct judicial executions, such as Bangladesh (Islam 2008), India (Mehta 2004; Eckert 2005), Indonesia (Friend 2003; Nevins 2005), Myanmar (Myint-U 2006), Papua New Guinea (Human Rights Watch 2007), Sri Lanka (Human Rights Watch 2008a), and Thailand (see appendix D).

Consider first the Philippines and Nepal, the two largest abolitionist nations in Asia, with populations of 91 million and 29 million, respectively. Both countries have abolished the death penalty twice. Both conducted few judicial executions during the years before their first abolition. Both rarely carried out judicial executions after the death penalty was reintroduced (there were seven executions in the Philippines and none at all in Nepal). Both reabolished the death penalty shortly after its reintroduction (the interval was 12 years in the Philippines and 14 years in Nepal). Both have continued to conduct extrajudicial killing on a large scale since the second abolition. And in both nations, the state's extrajudicial killing mainly seems to target "communist" insurgents and their sympathizers and supporters.

In the Philippines, hundreds of people have been killed extrajudicially by police or by members of the armed forces, but as of March 2007 there had not been a single criminal conviction of these killers. The number of attacks on leftist activists and community workers also rose sharply during the years immediately preceding the second abolition that occurred in 2006 (Amnesty International 2007b). Similarly, there have been no judicial executions in Nepal since 1979, but observers describe "the routine torture and extrajudicial killing of suspected Maoists," which "had risen to a startling average of eight a day" by 2005 (Mishra 2006b:288). Nepal also may have "the highest number of unexplained disappearances in the world," and the institution believed responsible for most of them—the army—enjoys "massive impunity" (288).

The cases of the Philippines and Nepal illustrate how state killing can survive and even thrive after capital punishment ends. In temporal perspective, however, the volume of extrajudicial executions in both of these nations seems to have declined over the course of the last several decades (though there have been occasional resurgences). The evidence for a reduction in extrajudicial killing is clearest for the Philippines, where even the most conservative counts indicate that at least 3,000 victims were killed in the Marcos years, from 1965 to 1986—an average of 150 per year (McCoy 1999a; McCoy 1999b; McCoy 2006:76). By comparison, Amnesty International reported 66 extrajudicial "political killings" for all of 2005 (and this was after a significant surge in summary executions), while between 2001 and June 2006 the Philippines government recorded 114 political killings of leftists—an average of about 20 per year (Amnesty International 2006e). If these counts are close to accurate (and the latter is undoubtedly low), then they reflect a substantial decline in extrajudicial killing since the demise of Marcos's dictatorship (see also Berlow 1996).

Figures are harder to come by for Nepal, but there, too, one temporal trend seems to be a decline in unprovoked extrajudicial killing even though the democratic movement of 1989 and 1990 has "let the country down" so comprehensively that some analysts believe "today's Nepal has regressed, politically, by nearly half a century" (Crossette 2005–2006:69; International Nepal Solidarity Network 2007; Lawoti 2007). Much of the state killing that has continued to occur in Nepal since its second abolition of capital punishment (for ordinary crimes in 1990 and for all crimes in 1997) is committed by the army in response to "an extreme armed Maoist movement" that engages in "almost unimaginable brutality and terror" and aims to overthrow the present government (Crossette 2005–2006:70). As Louise Arbour, UN high commissioner for human rights, observed when she opened a branch office in Kathmandu, Nepal's "grave human rights crisis" involves abuses by both the Nepali state and the Maoist insurgents (quoted in Crossette 2005–2006:73). It is impossible to tell what share of Nepal's extrajudicial killings is provoked by illegal violence, but whatever the exact proportion it appears to be substantial (Mishra 2006b:285). State killings that are proactive in the sense that they are unprovoked by violence are problematic as a matter of law and morality, but they may be no more numerous now than they were in earlier periods of Nepal's modern history.

The decline of judicial executions in several other Asian nations also seems to correlate with a general decrease in the practice of extrajudicial killing. In Indonesia, for example, hundreds of thousands of persons were killed in the political purges of the 1960s and in the massacres on East Timor after Portugal withdrew from its colony in 1975 (Nevins 2005). But extrajudicial killing in the world's most populous Muslim-majority nation is much less common today than it was during those bloody and tumultuous periods (Friend 2003), while judicial executions have been infrequent events for more than 20 years, with only 33 in 1985–1995 (Hood 2002:48) and no executions at all in seven of the next eight years (1996–2000 and 2002–2003). Similarly, the rate of judicial execution in Bangladesh is only 1/20th what it is in the United States (and less than 1/100th the rate in Texas), and though extrajudicial killing remains a problem, the volume has declined significantly since Bangladesh declared independence in 1971 (Baxter 1997). In Myanmar, which with China, North Korea, and Vietnam has one of the most repressive regimes in Asia, the onset of a de facto moratorium on judicial executions in 1989 corresponded with an apparent decline in the military junta's willingness to kill its own civilians (Myint-U 2006). Military generals have ruled Myanmar for the past 45 years, ever since Ne Win, a tyrant, numerologist, playboy, and ex-postal clerk, took control of the government in 1962. When a new junta seized power in 1988, some 3,000 people died in the massacres that followed (Mydans 2007a). That junta took control at a moment much like the one that occurred in 2007, when masses rose up in a peaceful nationwide protest that was fueled by economic and political grievances. But in 2007, extrajudicial killing occurred on a much smaller scale, with death toll estimates ranging between 15 and 31—less than 1 percent of the body count 20 years earlier (Mydans 2007d). Thus, even among Burmese despots who "rule by fear" and who "really believe the country would fall apart without them," the willingness to kill people who demonstrate against them and their policies seems significantly weaker now than it was before the nation's death penalty moratorium began (Mydans 2007c). Of course, this parallelism does not mean that Myanmar's death penalty policy has dictated its orientation to extrajudicial killing, but it does suggest that there has been little or no effort to compensate for the decline in legal executions by bolstering extrajudicial killings.

If the temporal evidence on judicial and extrajudicial executions seems patchy for some of the countries just discussed—the Philippines, Nepal, Indonesia, Bangladesh, and Myanmar—the evidence of the case studies in part II of this book points more unambiguously in the same direction: the two forms of state killing frequently fall together. The huge decline in judicial executions that accompanied Meiji Japan's opening to the West in the last half of the 19th century occurred during the same period in which other forms of domestic state violence were tamed (Beasley 1990; Botsman 2005). In South Korea and Taiwan, the most marked declines in execution are more recent, and they reflect a much increased and more generalized reluctance to use killing as a tool of governance in the years since democratization began than in the preceding decades (Roy 2003; Choe 2007b; Choe 2007c; Han 2007). In China, where judicial executions have dropped in recent years, there is evidence that extrajudicial killing has remained an important tool of the communist party-state during the current reform period (Buruma 2001; Matas and Kilgour 2007), but there is vastly less state killing now than there was under Chairman Mao, who was responsible for millions of violent deaths during his nearly three decades as the "Great Helmsman" (see chapter 7).

Our final illustration of the apparently positive correlation between judicial and extrajudicial executions concerns Cambodia, where from 1975 to 1978 Pol Pot's vicious regime probably killed a larger percentage of the national population than any modern regime ever has (Rummel 1994). Cambodia abolished capital punishment in 1989, one decade after the end of a genocide that killed at least 15 percent of a total population of seven million people (Kiernan 2002; Cambodian League for the Promotion and Defence of Human Rights 2007). The main point of the abolition was to "mark with a powerful symbol" the end of the killing fields (Hood 2002:43; Dunlop 2005). As of 2008, Cambodia has not conducted any judicial executions for at least 20 years, and though extrajudicial killing still occurs, it is far less commonplace now than when the Khmer Rouge's lethal logic was aimed at "manufacturing difference" and achieving "disproportionate revenge" (Hinton 2005:45,211; Broadhurst and Bouhors 2008).

■ Common Causation?

Extrajudicial killing persists in several Asian nations that have abolished capital punishment or nearly abandoned the practice of judicial execution. One result is that there appears to be little correlation between a state's level of extrajudicial killing and its death penalty policy, at least when the two types of killing are examined at a single point in time. But a different pattern emerges in temporal perspective, for judicial and extrajudicial executions seem to have declined over time in several Asian jurisdictions, including Japan, South Korea, Taiwan, China, Cambodia, Indonesia, Burma, Bangladesh, the Philippines, and probably Nepal. The evidence is too thin and the relationship between judicial and extrajudicial killings too fuzzy to tell whether a similar historical pattern obtains in countries such as India and Thailand. Over the past several years, there has been considerable proactive state killing in both of these nations. In Thailand, for example, the police and other authorities summarily killed more than 2,000 people during the first three months of a "war on drugs" that started in February 2003 (Macan-Markar 2007; Munsgool 2007). That is seven times more extrajudicial killings than there were judicial executions in all of Thailand in the previous seven decades (see appendix D). The antidrug campaign continued until at least the end of 2003, killing many more persons (Fritsch 2004), and according to a Thai researcher for Human Rights Watch, "the majority was innocent people, not drug traffickers" (Macan-Markar 2007). In India as well, extrajudicial killings (also known as "fake encounters") appear to be widespread (see appendix F). An Indian policeman in Mumbai who confessed to participating in "about fifty" extrajudicial killings claimed this number is "not very many" compared to some of his colleagues; he also said that "freelance" encounter killings are "very rare" (Luce 2007:96). "I have never been involved in a killing that hasn't either been approved or requested by the senior commissioner of police," this encounter specialist explained. And he stressed: "We do not break the chain of command" (quoted in Luce 2007 : 96; see also Baxi 1982; Roberts 2003; Mehta 2004; Eckert 2005; Chandra 2007; Mitta and Phoolka 2007; Subramanian 2007; Human Rights Watch 2008c). But if agents of the Indian state continue to kill on a large scale even though the nation's level of judicial execution has remained close to zero for the last decade, it is also true that fake encounter killings date back at least to the violent repression of the Telengana peasant movement (1945–1951) in the postwar and early postindependence period, while in the 1960s and 1970s, when judicial executions in India were much more numerous than they are today, the extrajudicial execution of Naxalites— members of the radical, revolutionary communist groups that were born out of the Sino-Soviet split—"became standard police practice" (Pratirodh 2007; Chakravarti 2008). What is more, technology and media have advanced so rapidly during the last few decades that there is today vastly more information available about the previously hidden and isolated parts of countries such as India and Thailand, making it difficult to discern how much of the salience of proactive extrajudicial killing in the present is a function of better information and reporting (Gitlin 2003).

The relationship between judicial and extra-judicial killing is one of the most important but understudied areas of criminology (Hood 2002:155). We close, therefore, with a call for other researchers to explore more systematically than we have here the relationships between different forms of state killing, both in the Asian contexts that are the focus of this book and in other regions and societies. For now, anyway, the evidence from Asia seems to suggest that at least in this part of the world, the relationship between judicial and extrajudicial killing tends to be one of neither independence (as the distribution of countries in table G.1 might seem to suggest) nor of substitution effects (as may be the case in some Latin American contexts; see Godoy 2006). Instead, these two forms of state killing appear to be connected mainly through a process of common causation, with the same forces that predict and explain the decline of judicial executions also accounting for the fall of proactive extrajudicial killing in a variety of Asian environments.

Bibliography

Aaron, R., A. Joseph, S. Abraham, J. Muliyil, K. George, J. Prasad, S. Minz, V. Abraham, and A. Bose. 2004. "Suicides in Young People in Rural Southern India." *The Lancet* 363:1117–1118.

Abdymen, Kuban. 2007a. "Central Asia: Abolition Close, but Spectre of Death Remains." Inter Press Service. September 24.

Abdymen, Kuban. 2007b. "Central Asia Nearing Abolition." Inter Press Service. March 29.

Abdymen, Kuban. 2008. "Uzbek Abolition Draws Line under Past." Inter Press Service. January 17.

"Abolishing Death Penalty Possible." 2007. Yahoo! India. November 12.

"Abolition of Death Penalty." 2008. Editorial. *Pakistan Times.* July 4.

Abramsky, Sasha. 2007. *American Furies: Crime, Punishment, and Vengeance in the Age of Mass Imprisonment.* Boston: Beacon Press.

Abuza, Zachary. 2006. "Country Report—Vietnam." In *Freedom House, Countries at the Crossroads 2006*, 1–13. www.freedomhouse.org.

Ager, Maila. 2007. "Int'l Pressure Leads to Decline in Killings—Karapatan: 'Stop Military Aid, Oust Arroyo.'" *Philippine Inquirer.* December 3.

Ahmed, Zubair. 2004. "Bombay's Crack 'Encounter' Police." BBC News. June 9.

Aikman, David. 2003. *Jesus in Beijing: How Christianity Is Transforming China and Changing the Global Balance of Power.* Washington, DC: Regnery.

Akiyama, Kenzo. 2002. *Saibankan wa Naze Ayamaru no ka.* Tokyo: Iwanami Shoten.

Alarid, Leanne Fiftal, and Hsiao-Ming Wang. 2001. "Mercy and Punishment: Buddhism and the Death Penalty." *Social Justice* 28(1):231–247.

Albrecht, Hans-Jorg, and Research Unit of the Death Penalty Cases Survey Institute of Law. 2006. *Strengthening the Defence in Death Penalty Cases in the People's Republic of China: Empirical Research into the Role of Defense Councils in Criminal Cases*

Eligible for the Death Penalty. Munich: Max Planck Institute for Foreign and International Criminal Law. October.

Alston, Philip. 2007. *Report of the Special Rapporteur on Extrajudicial, Summary, or Arbitrary Executions, Philip Alston, on His Mission to the Philippines (February 12–21, 2007).* www.extrajudicialexecutions.org/reports/A_HRC_8_Philippines_Advance_Edited.pdf.

Ambler, Leah. 2006. "The People Decide: The Effect of the Introduction of the Quasi-jury System (Saiban-in Seido) on the Death Penalty in Japan." Honors thesis, College of Law, Australian National University.

Amnesty International. 1989a. "Philippines: Case Studies in the Use of the Death Penalty." ASA 35/08/89. April.

Amnesty International. 1989b. *When the State Kills: The Death Penalty vs. Human Rights.* London: Amnesty International.

Amnesty International. 1996. "The Death Penalty in the Socialist Republic of Vietnam." ASA 41/02/96. February.

Amnesty International. 1997a. "People's Republic of China: The Death Penalty in China: Breaking Records, Breaking Rules." ASA 17/38/97. August.

Amnesty International. 1997b. "Philippines: The Death Penalty: Criminality, Justice, and Human Rights." ASA 35/09/97. October 21.

Amnesty International. 1997c. "Philippines: The Death Penalty: Some Questions and Answers and Appeal Cases." ASA 35/10/97. October.

Amnesty International. 1997d. "Macao."

Amnesty International. 2002a. "Republic of Korea: Commute Death Sentences." December 2.

Amnesty International. 2002b. "State Killing in the English Speaking Caribbean: A Legacy of Colonial Times." AMR 05/006/2002. April 23.

Amnesty International. 2003a. "Sharp Increase in Vietnamese Executions." Amnesty International. September 4.

Amnesty International. 2003b. "Socialist Republic of Viet Nam: The Death Penalty—Inhumane and Ineffective." ASA 41/023/2003. August.

Amnesty International. 2004a. "People's Republic of China: Executed 'According to Law'?—The Death Penalty in China." Amnesty International.

Amnesty International. 2004b. "Singapore—The Death Penalty: A Hidden Toll of Executions." ASA 36/001/2004. January 15.

Amnesty International. 2005a. "Mechanizing the Death Penalty in Viet Nam—Progress or Barbarism?"

Amnesty International. 2005b. "North Korea: Briefing on Present Situation." ASA 24/002/2005. July 28.

Amnesty International. 2005c. "South Korea: Death Penalty Abolition: Historic Opportunity." ASA 25/003/2005.

Amnesty International. 2005d. "Viet Nam."

Amnesty International. 2006a. "The Death Penalty." www.amnesty.org/deathpenalty.

Amnesty International. 2006b. "People's Republic of China: The Olympic Countdown—Failing to Keep Human Rights Promises."

Amnesty International. 2006c. "Philippines: Largest Ever Commutation of Death Sentences." ASA 35/003/2006. April 19.

Amnesty International. 2006d. "Philippines: Political Killings, Human Rights and the Peace Process." ASA 35/006/2006. August 15.

Amnesty International. 2006e. "Viet Nam."

Amnesty International. 2006f. "Will This Day Be My Last? The Death Penalty in Japan." ASA 22/006/2006. July.

Amnesty International. 2007a. "Execution by Lethal Injection: A Quarter Century of State Poisoning." POL 30/021/2007. October 4. www.amnesty.org/en/report/info/ACT50/007/2007.

Amnesty International. 2007b. "Stop the State Killing." ACT 50/11/2007. http://web.amnesty.org/library/pdf/ACT500112007ENGLISH/$File/ACT5001107.pdf.

Amnesty International. 2008a. "Abolitionist and Retentionist Countries."

Amnesty International. 2008b. "Death Penalty: World Trend Down but Secrecy Surrounds China Execution Figures—New Report." April 14.

An, Byung Ho. 2004. "Kankoku ni okeru Shikei Seido ni kan suru Ishiki Chosa." *Forum 90 Newsletter* 77:8–9.

Anckar, Carsten. 2004. *Determinants of the Death Penalty: A Comparative Study of the World*. London: Routledge.

Anderson, Kent, and Mark Nolan. 2004. "Lay Participation in the Japanese Justice System: A Few Preliminary Thoughts Regarding the Lay Assessor System (*saiban-in seido*) from Domestic, Historical, and International Psychological Perspectives." *Vanderbilt Journal of Transnational Law* 37(4):935–992.

Anderson, Mary Jo. 2008. "Using the United Nations against Itself." *Catholic Online.* February 7.

Andress, David. 2006. *The Terror: The Merciless War for Freedom in Revolutionary France*. New York: Farrar, Straus, and Giroux.

Ang, Audra. 2007. "Executions Fill Transplant Needs: Death-Row Harvest: Inmates Supply Organs." *Honolulu Star Bulletin.* April 22.

Ang See, Teresita. 1997. "People of the Philippines vs. Crimes: CAAC-MRPO, the Criminal Justice System, and the Fight against Crime." In Marlon A. Wui and Glenda S. Lopez, eds., *State–Civil Society Relations in Policy-Making*. Quezon City: Third World Studies Center, University of the Philippines, 125–146.

Anonymous. 2006. "Execution for Preserving Humanity and Morality: Capital Punishment in Contemporary Taiwan." Manuscript submitted to *Punishment and Society.*

Appleton, Catherine, and Bent Grover. 2007. "The Pros and Cons of Life without Parole." *British Journal of Criminology* 47:597–615.

Apter, David, and Tony Saitch. 1990. *Revolutionary Discourse in Mao's Republic*. New York: Columbia University Press.

Aravamudan, Gita. 2007. *Disappearing Daughters: The Tragedy of Female Foeticide*. New Delhi: Penguin.

Arbour, Louise. 2007. "The U.N.'s Death Blow." *Los Angeles Times.* December 19.

"Armed Policemen Explain How the Death Penalty Is Carried Out." 2004. Boxun. www.zonaeuropa.com/20041202_1.htm. [Originally published in Chinese at www.boxun.com, November 26.]

Armstrong, David K., ed. 2002. *Korean Society: Civil Society, Democracy and the State*. New York: Routledge.

Aron, Raymond. 1966. *Peace and War: A Theory of International Relations*. Garden City, NY: Doubleday.

Arrighi, Giovanni, Takeshi Hamashita, and Mark Selden. 2003. *The Resurgence of East Asia: 500, 150 and 50 Year Perspectives*. London: Routledge.

Arroyo, Gloria Macapagal. 2006. "President Gloria Macapagal-Arroyo's 2006 Easter Message." April 15. www.ops.gov.ph/speeches2006/speech-2006_apr15.htm.

"Arroyo under Fire from Catholic Bishops." 2001. BBC News. October 19. http://news.bbc.co.uk/2/hi/asia-pacific/1608317.stm.

Arudou, Debito. 2007. "The Myopic State We're In." *Japan Times.* December 18.

"ASEAN's Broken Heart." 2007. *Japan Times.* November 22.

August, Oliver. 2002. "Emperor Who? China's New Ruler Keeps His Secrets." *The Times.* November 15. www.oliveraugust.com/journalism_emperor-who.htm.

August, Oliver. 2007. *Inside the Red Mansion: On the Trail of China's Most Wanted Man.* New York: Houghton Mifflin.

Austin, W. Timothy. 1999. *Banana Justice: Field Notes on Philippine Crime and Custom.* Westport, CT: Greenwood.

Aya, Philip, Theodora Christou, and Juan-Pablo Raymond. 2005. "B.I.I.C.L. Report: The Application of the Death Penalty in Africa." *Amicus Journal* 13:17–21.

Badinter, Robert. 2000. *L'Abolition.* Paris: Fayard.

Bae, Sangmin. 2005. "Ending State Killing in South Korea: Challenging the Asian Capital Punishment Status Quo." In Austin Sarat and Christian Boulanger, eds., *The Cultural Lives of Capital Punishment: Comparative Perspectives.* Stanford, CA: Stanford University Press, 308–327.

Bae, Sangmin. 2007. *When the State No Longer Kills: International Human Rights Norms and Abolition of Capital Punishment.* Albany: State University of New York Press.

Bae, Sangmin. 2008a. "The Death Penalty and the Peculiarity of American Political Institutions." *Human Rights Review* 9(2).

Bae, Sangmin. 2008b. "Friends Do Not Let Friends Execute: The Council of Europe and the Anti-Death Penalty Movement." *International Politics* 45(2):129–145.

Bae, Sangmin. 2008c. "Is the Death Penalty an Asian Value?" *Asian Affairs* 39(1):47–56.

Bakken, Borge. 2000. *The Exemplary Society: Human Improvement, Social Control and the Dangers of Modernity in China.* New York: Oxford University Press.

Bakken, Borge. 2004. "Moral Panics, Crime Rates and Harsh Punishment in China." *Australian and New Zealand Journal of Criminology* 37(supp.):67–89.

Bakken, Borge, ed. 2005. *Crime, Punishment, and Policing in China.* Lanham, MD: Rowman and Littlefield.

Bakken, Borge. 2007. Review of *Die Todesstrafe in der VR China* [The Death Penalty in the People's Republic of China], by Astrid Maier. *China Journal* 57:180–182.

Bakken, Borge. 2008. "The Culture of Revenge and the Power of Politics: A Comparative Attempt to Explain the Punitive." *Journal of Power* 1(2):169–187.

Bankoff, Greg. 1996. *Crime, Society, and the State in the Nineteenth Century Philippines.* Manila: Ateneo de Manila University Press.

Banner, Stuart. 2002. *The Death Penalty: An American History.* Cambridge, MA: Harvard University Press.

Barboza, David. 2007a. "China Sentences Former Drug Regulator to Death." *New York Times.* May 29.

Barboza, David. 2007b. "China Sentences Official to Death for Corruption." *New York Times.* July 7.

Barboza, David. 2007c. "A Chinese Reformer Betrays His Cause, and Pays." *New York Times.* July 13.

Barboza, David. 2007d. "For Two Children, Ban of a Drug Came Too Late." *New York Times.* July 13.

Barrameda, Mary Constancy. 2005. "Death Penalty and Indigenous Law." In *Stop the Execution! A Source Book on the Death Penalty*. Manila: Coalition against the Death Penalty, 58–67.

Batra, Bikram Jeet. 2004. "Sentenced to Die, Non-Unanimously." *India Together*. July.

Batra, Bikram Jeet. 2005a. "Life Imprisonment and Powers of Remission." *Hindu*. September 10.

Batra, Bikram Jeet. 2005b. "1422 Executions in 10 Years, Many More?" *India Together*. April 2.

Batra, Bikram Jeet. 2005c. "Public Prosecution—In Need of Reform." *India Together*. July 5. www.indiatogether.org/2005/apr/hrt-pudr1422.htm.

Batra, Bikram Jeet. 2007. "The Death Penalty in India—Issues and Aspects." Background paper for launch seminar, Sino-EU project "Moving the Debate Forward on the Death Penalty in China," Beijing, June 20–21.

Batra, Bikram Jeet. 2008. *Lethal Lottery: The Death Penalty in India: A Study of Supreme Court Judgments in Death Penalty Cases, 1950–2006*. Tamil Nadu and Puducherry: Amnesty International India and People's Union for Civil Liberties.

Baxi, Upendra. 1982. *The Crisis of the Indian Legal System*. New Delhi: Vikas.

Baxter, Craig. 1997. *Bangladesh: From a Nation to a State*. Boulder, CO: Westview Press.

Bayley, David H. 1991. *Forces of Order: Policing Modern Japan*. Berkeley: University of California Press.

Beasley, W. G. 1990. *The Rise of Modern Japan*. New York: St. Martin's Press.

Beck, Allen J., and Paige M. Harrison. 2001. "Prisoners in 2000." In *Bureau of Justice Statistics Bulletin*. NCJ 188207. Washington, DC: U.S. Department of Justice. August.

Becker, Jasper. 1996. *Hungry Ghosts: Mao's Secret Famine*. New York: Free Press.

Becker, Jasper. 2000. *The Chinese: An Insider's Look at the Issues Which Affect and Shape China Today*. New York: Oxford University Press.

Becker, Jasper. 2005. *Rogue Regime: Kim Jong Il and the Looming Threat of North Korea*. New York: Oxford University Press.

Bedau, Hugo Adam. 2004. "An Abolitionist's Survey of the Death Penalty in America Today." In Hugo Adam Bedau and Paul G. Cassell, eds., *Debating the Death Penalty: Should America Have Capital Punishment? The Experts on Both Sides Make Their Best Case*. New York: Oxford University Press, 15–50.

Beer, Lawrence W., and John M. Maki. 2002. *From Imperial Myth to Democracy: Japan's Two Constitutions*. Boulder: University Press of Colorado.

Bell, Daniel A. 2000. *East Meets West: Human Rights and Democracy in East Asia*. Princeton, NJ: Princeton University Press.

Bell, Daniel A. 2008. *China's New Confucianism: Politics and Everyday Life in a Changing Society*. Princeton, NJ: Princeton University Press.

Benac, Nancy. 2006. "Death Penalty Trials a Painstaking Process." Associated Press. February 27.

Benedict, Ruth. 1946. *The Chrysanthemum and the Sword: Patterns of Japanese Culture*. Cleveland, OH: Meridian Books.

Benn, Charles. 2002. *Daily Life in Traditional China: The Tang Dynasty*. Westport, CT: Greenwood.

Berger, Peter. 1963. *Invitation to Sociology: A Humanistic Perspective*. Garden City, NY: Anchor Books.

Berlow, Alan. 1996. *Dead Season: A Story of Murder and Revenge*. New York: Vintage Books.

Best, Antony. 2007. *International History of East Asia, 1900–1968: Trade, Ideology and the Quest for Order*. London: Routledge.

Best, Joel, ed. 2001. *How Claims Spread: Cross-national Diffusion of Social Problems*. New York: de Gruyter.

Bezlova, Antoaneta. 2006a. "China's Mobile Death Fleet." *Asia Times Online*. July 21.

Bezlova, Antoaneta. 2006b. "China to 'Kill Fewer, Kill Carefully.'" *Asia Times Online*. March 31.

Bezlova, Antoaneta. 2007a. "China Considers Cash for Clemency." Inter Press Service. June 17.

Bezlova, Antoaneta. 2007b. "Death Penalty—China: Going Easy on Executions ahead of Olympics." Inter Press Service. November 23.

Bezlova, Antoaneta. 2007c. "Letters from Death Row." Inter Press Service. March 24.

Bezlova, Antoaneta. 2008a. "China: Will the People Choose the Death Penalty?" Inter Press Service. June 14.

Bezlova, Antoaneta. 2008b. "China: War on Drugs Prompts More Executions." Inter Press Service. July 16.

Biddulph, Sarah. 2008. *Legal Reform and Administrative Detention Powers in China*. Cambridge: Cambridge University Press.

"Bill to Restore Death Penalty Filed at House." 2007. *Manila Bulletin Online*. July 3.

"Bill to Restore Death Penalty Pushed by Abante." 2006. *Manila Bulletin Online*. December 23.

"Bishops Thumb Down Death Penalty Revival." 2008. GMA News. May 18.

Bix, Herbert P. 2000. *Hirohito and the Making of Modern Japan*. New York: HarperCollins.

Bix, Herbert P. 2005. "The Emperor, Modern Japan, and the U.S.-Japan Relationship: An Interview with Herbert P. Bix." *Japan Focus*. August 26. Article ID 368. http://japanfocus.org.

Black, Donald. 1976. *The Behavior of Law*. New York: Academic Press.

Black, Donald. 1983. "Crime as Social Control." *American Sociological Review* 48:34–45.

Blume, John, Theodore Eisenberg, and Martin T. Wells. 2004. "Explaining Death Row's Population and Racial Composition." *Journal of Empirical Legal Studies* 1(1):165–207.

Blumenthal, Ralph. 2007. "A Twelfth Dallas Convict Is Exonerated by DNA." *New York Times*. January 18.

Bodde, Derk, and Clarence Morris. 1967. *Law in Imperial China, Exemplified by 190 Ch'ing Dynasty Cases*. Cambridge, MA: Harvard University Press.

Bohm, Robert M. 2003a. "American Death Penalty Opinion: Past, Present, and Future." In James R. Acker, Robert M. Bohm, and Charles S. Lanier, eds., *America's Experiment with Capital Punishment: Reflections on the Past, Present, and Future of the Ultimate Penal Sanction*. Durham, NC: Carolina Academic Press, 27–54.

Bohm, Robert M. 2003b. *Deathquest II: An Introduction to the Theory and Practice of Capital Punishment in the United States*. Cincinnati, OH: Anderson.

Bohm, Robert M. 2003c. "The Economic Costs of Capital Punishment: Past, Present, and Future." In James R. Acker, Robert M. Bohm, and Charles S. Lanier, eds., *America's Experiment with Capital Punishment: Reflections on the Past, Present, and Future of the Ultimate Penal Sanction*. Durham, NC: Carolina Academic Press, 573–594.

Borland, John, and Michael Kanellos. 2004. "South Korea Leads the Way." CNET News. July 28. www.news.com/South-Korea-leads-the-way/2009-1034_3-5261393.html.

Borthwick, Mark. 2007. *Pacific Century: The Emergence of Modern Pacific Asia.* 3rd ed. Boulder, CO: Westview Press.

Bos, J. N. W. 2002. "Crown Prince Sado of Korea." www.xs4all.nl/~kvenjb/madmonarchs/sado/sado_tekst.htm.

"Botched Manila Coup a Warning to Would-Be Plotters." 2007. Reuters. November 30.

Botsman, Daniel. 2005. *Punishment and Power in the Making of Modern Japan.* Princeton, NJ: Princeton University Press.

Boumedra, Tahar. 2008. "Arab Legislations Go Far beyond Islamic Law." Interview. *Inter Press Service.* May 29.

Bourgon, Jerome. 2003. "Chinese Executions: Visualizing Their Differences with European Supplices." *European Journal of East Asian Studies* 2(1):153–184.

Bowers, William J. 1984. *Legal Homicide: Death as Punishment in America, 1864–1982.* Boston: Northeastern University Press.

"Boxer Sentenced in '68 to Hang Innocent: Judge." 2007. *Japan Times.* March 10.

Brackman, Arnold C. 1988. *The Other Nuremberg.* New York: HarperCollins.

Bradsher, Keith. 2006. "Vietnam's Roaring Economy Is Set for World Stage." *New York Times.* October 25.

Breen, Michael. 2004. *The Koreans: Who They Are, What They Want, Where Their Future Lies.* New York: Thomas Dunne Books.

Brinton, Mary. 2003. "Fact-Rich, Data-Poor: Japan as Sociologists' Heaven and Hell." In Theodore C. Bestor, Patricia G. Steinhoff, and Victoria Lyon Bestor, eds., *Doing Field Work in Japan.* Honolulu: University of Hawaii Press, 195–213.

Broadhurst, Rod. 2005. "Crime Trends in Hong Kong." In Richard J. Estes, ed., *Social Development in Hong Kong: The Unfinished Agenda.* New York: Oxford University Press, 185–192.

Broadhurst, Rod, and Thierry Bouhours. 2008. "Policing in Cambodia: Legitimacy in the Making?" *Policing and Society* 18.

Brocheux, Pierre. 2007. *Ho Chi Minh: A Biography.* Trans. Claire Duiker. Cambridge: Cambridge University Press.

Brook, Timothy, Jerome Bourgon, and Gregory Blue. 2008. *Death by a Thousand Cuts.* Cambridge, MA: Harvard University Press.

Bullock, Alan. 1998. *Hitler and Stalin: Parallel Lives.* London: Fontana Press.

Bunce, Jane. 2006. "Australian Spared Death Penalty." *Australian.* November 17.

Burgonio, T. J. 2008. "'Not in Our Name': Book Shows Folly of Death Penalty." *Philippine Inquirer.* June 25.

Burnham, Margaret A. 2005. "Indigenous Constitutionalism and the Death Penalty: The Case of the Commonwealth Caribbean." *International Journal of Constitutional Law* 3(4):582–616.

Buruma, Ian. 2000. "Divine Killer." *New York Review of Books* 47(3).

Buruma, Ian. 2001a. *Bad Elements: Chinese Rebels from Los Angeles to Beijing.* New York: Vintage Books.

Buruma, Ian. 2001b. "The Mandate of Heaven." *New York Times.* March 18.

Buruma, Ian 2003. *Inventing Japan, 1853–1964.* New York: Modern Library.

Buruma, Ian. 2007a. "Political Games." *New York Times.* September 23.

Buruma, Ian. 2007b. "Who Freed Asia?" *Los Angeles Times.* August 31.

Buzan, Barry. 2004. *From International to World Society? English School Theory and the Social Structure of Globalisation.* Cambridge: Cambridge University Press.

Cabana, Donald A. 1996. *Death at Midnight: The Confession of an Executioner.* Boston: Northeastern University Press.

Calder, Kent E. 1988. *Crisis and Compensation: Public Policy and Political Stability in Japan, 1949–1986.* Princeton, NJ: Princeton University Press.

Calhoun, Craig. 1997. *Neither Gods nor Emperors: Students and the Struggle for Democracy in China.* Berkeley: University of California Press.

Cambodian League for the Promotion and Defence of Human Rights. 2007. "Abolition of Death Penalty: Ratification of Second Optional Protocol to the ICCPR and Cambodia." Phnom Penh. January. www.licadho.org/reports/files/ 102LICADHOPaper2ndOptionalProtocolCCPR07.pdf.

Camus, Albert. 1960. "Reflections on the Guillotine." In *Resistance, Rebellion, and Death.* New York: Vintage Books, 173–234.

Carr, Edward Hallett. 1961. *What Is History?* New York: Vintage Books.

Casciani, Dominic. 2006. "How Britain Made Its Executioners." BBC News. June 1.

Cha, Victor D. 2008. "In China, the Game Has Changed." *Los Angeles Times.* June 15.

Chakravati, Sudeep. 2008. *Red Sun: Travels in Naxalite Country.* New Delhi: Penguin.

Chakravorty, Sanjoy. 2008. "Post-colonial Studies." *Atlantic Monthly* (April):13.

Champa. 2007. *The Afzal Petition: A Quest for Justice.* New Delhi: Promilla.

Chan, Heng Hee. 1996. "Singapore Doesn't Claim to Be Model for Anyone." *New York Times.* October 24.

Chan, Kelvin. 2008. "Report: China Still Tops in Executions." *Honolulu Advertiser.* April 15:A8.

Chandra, Vikram. 2007. *Sacred Games: A Novel.* New York: Harper.

Chang, David Wen-Wei, and Richard Y. Chuang. 1997. *Politics of Hong Kong's Reversion to China.* UK: Palgrave Macmillan.

Chang, Iris. 1997. *The Rape of Nanking: The Forgotten Holocaust of World War II.* New York: Penguin.

Chang, Jung. 1991. *Wild Swans: Three Daughters of China.* New York: Simon and Schuster.

Chang, Jung, and Jon Halliday. 2005. *The Unknown Story of Mao.* New York: Knopf.

Chang, Ling-yin. 2005. "Cannibals Handed Death Penalty." *Taiwan News.* November 24.

Chang, Rich. 2006. "Nation Keeps Death Penalty, but Reduces Executions." *Taipei Times.* January 2.

Chang, Rich, Ko Shu-ling, and Shih Hsiu-chuan. 2007. "Cabinet Mulls Amnesty for Criminals." *Taipei Times.* April 25.

Chang, Sen-dou. 1965. "Peking: The Growing Metropolis of Communist China." *Geographical Review* 55(3): 313–327.

Chan-Tiberghien, Jennifer. 2004. *Gender and Human Rights Politics in Japan: Global Norms and Domestic Networks.* Stanford, CA: Stanford University Press.

Chen, Guidi, and Wu Chuntao. 2006. *Will the Boat Sink the Water? The Life of China's Peasants.* New York: PublicAffairs.

Chen, Hannah. 2001. "Christianity and Abolition." In Edmund Ryden, ed., *Taiwan Opposes the Death Penalty.* Taipei: John Paul II Peace Institute of Fujen Catholic University, 285.

Chen, Jianfu. 2000. *Chinese Law: Toward an Understanding of Chinese Law, Its Nature and Development.* The Hague: Kluwer.

Chen, Paul H. 1979. *Chinese Legal Tradition under the Mongols: The Code of 1291 as Reconstructed.* Princeton, NJ: Princeton University Press.

Chen, Xingliang. 2005. "History, Status Quo and Future of the Death Penalty in China." Special issue: The Death Penalty. *Peking University Law Journal* 17(5): 513–533. [In Chinese.]

Chen, Xingliang. 2006a. "Destiny of the Death Penalty in China in the Contemporary Era." *Frontiers of Law in China* 1:53–71.

Chen, Xingliang. 2006b. "An Examination of the Death Penalty in China." In *The Death Penalty in China*. Wuhan: Wuhan University Press, 428–447.

Chen, Xingliang. 2006c. "Opinions on Retention versus Abolition of the Death Penalty." In *The Death Penalty in China*. Wuhan: Wuhan University Press, 418–427.

Cheng, Tun-jen, and Gang Lin. 2006. "Competitive Elections and the Transformation of the Hegemonic Party: Experience in Taiwan and Recent Development in China." Paper presented at the conference "Democratization in Greater China: What Can We Learn from Taiwan's Past for China's Future?" Stanford University, October 20–21.

Chenwi, Lilian. 2007. *Towards the Abolition of the Death Penalty in Africa: A Human Rights Perspective*. Pretoria: Pretoria University Law Press.

Chin, Ko-lin. 2003. *Heijin: Organized Crime, Business, and Politics in Taiwan*. Armonk, NY: M. E. Sharpe.

"China Aims to Foster Bigger Middle Class." 2007. *Wall Street Journal*. December 26.

"China Claims Big Fall in Death Sentences, Keeps Figures Secret." 2008. *Monsters and Critics*. May 10.

"China Defends Use of Death Penalty, Says Conditions Not Right to Abolish It." 2008. *International Herald Tribune*. April 15.

"China Favors Execution by Lethal Injection." 2008. Reuters. January 2.

"China in the Year 2020." 2007. *Asia Policy*. July.

"China Leads the World in Executions, Rights Group Says." 2008. *Honolulu Advertiser*. July 25.

"China Overturns Fifteen Percent of Death Sentences." *Pravda*. June 27.

"China's Arbitrary State." 1996. *Economist*. March 23:31–32.

"China's Chief Justice Calls for Death, Harsh Punishments for Violent Crimes." 2008. *International Herald Tribune*. April 12.

"China Sees Thirty Percent Drop in Death Penalty." 2008. *Xinhua*. May 9.

"China to Expand Lethal Injections." 2008. BBC News. January 3.

"China Vice President Warns Corruption Could Lead to End of Ruling Party." 2006. *Forbes*. September 20.

Chinese Human Rights Defenders. 2008. "Human Rights Activists under House Arrest during U.S. Congress Visit." June 30.

"Chinese Judge Says Death Penalty Applied Unevenly across Nation, Seeks to Unify Standards." 2007. *International Herald Tribune*. July 5.

Ching, Frank. 2007. "When Beijing Games End, Will Buzzer Sound on Human Rights?" *Honolulu Star-Bulletin*. March 4.

Chinoy, Mike. 1999. "Will China Clean up Macau's Crime Problem?" *ASIANOW*. December 20.

Chiu, Hey-yuan. 2006. "Deterrence, Dignity, and the Death Penalty: Analyzing Taiwanese Attitudes toward the Abolition of the Death Penalty." *Taiwanese Journal of Sociology*.

Cho, Byung Sun. 2003. "The International Covenant on Civil and Political Rights (ICCPR) and the Second Optional Protocol to the ICCPR on the Death Penalty in Vietnam." Unpublished paper presented at conference sponsored by the government of Vietnam and the Danish Institute for Human Rights.

Cho, Byung Sun. 2004. "The Death Penalty in South Korea and Japan: 'Asian Values" and the Debate about Capital Punishment?" In Peter Hodgkinson and William

A. Schabas, eds., *Capital Punishment: Strategies for Abolition*. Cambridge: Cambridge University Press, 253–272.

Cho, Byung Sun. 2008. "South Korea's Changing Capital Punishment Policy: The Road from De Facto to Formal Abolition." *Punishment and Society* 10:171–205.

Cho, Kuk. 2002. "Unfinished 'Criminal Procedure Revolution' of Post-Democratization Korea." *Denver Journal of International Law and Policy* 30(3):377–394.

Cho, Kuk. 2008. "Death Penalty in Korea: From Unofficial Moratorium to Abolition?" *Asian Journal of Comparative Law* 3(1):1–28.

Choe, Sang-Hun. 2007a. "Lee Wins Election for Presidency in South Korea." *New York Times*. December 20.

Choe, Sang-Hun. 2007b. "South Korea Reviews Its Dark Past, but the Pace Is Slow." *New York Times*. March 11.

Choe, Sang-Hun. 2007c. "Unearthing War's Horrors Years Later in South Korea." *New York Times*. December 3.

Choe, Sang-Hun. 2007d. "Where Boys Were Kings, a Shift toward Baby Girls." *New York Times*. December 23.

Choe, Sang-Hun, and Norimitsu Onishi. 2007. "South Koreans React to Shooting in Virginia." *New York Times*. April 18.

Christie, Kenneth, and Denny Roy. 2001. *The Politics of Human Rights in East Asia*. London: Pluto Press.

Chu, Henry. 2000. "China Keeping Its Executioners Busy: Tacit Consent of U.S. over Death Penalty." *San Francisco Chronicle*. August 1.

Chu, Shulong. 2007. "The East Asia Summit: Looking for an Identity." Brookings Institution. February 1. www.brookings.edu/opinions/2007/02northeastasia_chu.aspx?p=1.

Chyung, Dai-Chul. 2001. "Shikei Haishi ni kan suru Tokubetsu Hoan Teian Setsumei" [A Proposed Explanation for the Special Bill Regarding Abolition of the Death Penalty]. November 15.

Clammer, John. 1997. "Framing the Other: Criminality, Social Exclusion and Social Engineering in Developing Singapore." *Social Policy and Administration* 31 (December):136–153.

Clark, Gregory. 2008. "Birth of a Massacre Myth." *Japan Times*. July 21.

"Clark Doesn't Support 'Death' for Bali Bombers." 2008. *New Zealand Herald*. July 22.

Clarke, Donald C. 2007. "Introduction: The Chinese Legal System since 1995: Steady Development and Striking Continuities." *The China Quarterly* 191 (September):555–566.

Clifford, Mark L. 1994. *Troubled Tiger: Businessmen, Bureaucrats and Generals in South Korea*. Armonk, NY: M. E. Sharpe.

Clifford, Nicholas R. 1991. *Spoilt Children of Empire: Westerners in Shanghai and the Chinese Revolution of the 1920s*. Hanover, NH: Middlebury College Press.

Clifford, Tom. 2004. "Death Penalty in India: A Comparative View." Unpublished paper. Boalt Hall School of Law, University of California at Berkeley.

Coalition against the Death Penalty. 2005. *Stop the Execution! A Source Book on the Death Penalty*. Manila: CADP.

Cody, Edward. 2008. "Across China, Security instead of Celebration." *Washington Post*. July 19.

Cohen, Jerome A. 1966. "Chinese Mediation on the Eve of Modernization." *California Law Review* 54(3):1201–1226.

Cohen, Jerome A. 1968. *The Criminal Process in the People's Republic of China: An Introduction*. Cambridge, MA: Harvard University Press.

Cohen, Jerome A. 2005. "Law in Political Transitions: Lessons from East Asia and the Road Ahead for China." *New York University Journal of International Law and Politics* 37:423–439.

Cohen, Jerome A. 2006a. "China's Legal Reform at the Crossroads." *Far Eastern Economic Review* 169(March):23–28.

Cohen, Jerome A. 2006b. "The Great Stonewall of China." *Wall Street Journal*. April 15:A6.

Cohen, Jerome A. 2006c. "Human Rights and the Rule of Law in China." Written statement prepared for the Congressional-Executive Commission on China. Washington, DC, September 20.

Cohen, Jerome A. 2007a. "Can, and Should, the Rule of Law Be Transplanted outside the West? The Case of China." *AmCham* (January):14–16. www.amcham.org.hk/images/pressCenter/Speeches/cohen.doc.

Cohen, Jerome A. 2007b. "A Just Legal System." *International Herald Tribune*. December 11.

Cohen, Jerome A. 2007c. "A Slow March to Legal Reform." *Far Eastern Economic Review* (October):20–24.

Cohen, Jerome A., Merle Goldman, Perry Link, Robin Munro, Andrew J. Nathan, and Sophie Richardson. 2006. Letter to President Hu Jintao. September 14.

Collins, Peter. 2008. "Half-Way from Rags to Riches: A Special Report on Vietnam." *The Economist*. April 26:1–16.

"Communism and Nazism: Compare and Contrast." 2007. *Economist*. August 11:75.

"Conditions Not Ripe for China to Abolish Death Penalty: Spokesman." 2006. *China View*. March 11.

Conner, Alison W. 1979. "The Law of Evidence during the Qing Dynasty." Ph.D. diss., Cornell University.

Conner, Alison W. 2000. "True Confessions? Chinese Confessions Then and Now." In Karen G. Turner, James V. Feinerman, and R. Kent Guy, eds., *The Limits of the Rule of Law in China*. Seattle: University of Washington Press, 132–162.

Conquest, Robert. 2000. *Stalin*. London: Weidenfeld and Nicholson.

"Conservatives Win Again in South Korea." *Japan Times*. April 12.

Contreras, Volt. 2006. "Europe Hails RP for 'Turning Its Back' on Death Penalty." *Philippine Daily Inquirer*. http://services.inq7.net/print/printphp?article_id=25030.

Coonan, Clifford, and David McNeill. 2006. "Japan's Rich Buy Organs from Executed Chinese Prisoners." *The Independent*. March 21.

Cortazzi, Hugh. 2007. "British Crime and Punishment: Blair's Failed Crackdown." *Japan Times*. March 19.

Coslett, Paul. 2006. "Albert Pierrepoint." BBC News. April 27.

Council of Europe. 1999. *The Death Penalty: Abolition in Europe*. Strasbourg: Council of Europe.

"Country Profile: Laos." 2007. BBC News. June 4.

"Country Profile: Vietnam." 2007. BBC News. August 11.

"Court Clears Victims Executed for Treason in 1975." 2007. Yonhap News. January 23.

Courtois, Stephane. 1999a. "Conclusion: Why?" In Stephane Courtois, Nicolas Werth, Jean-Louis Panne, Andrzej Paczkowski, Karel Bartosek, and Jean-Louis Margolin, *The Black Book of Communism: Crime, Terror, Repression*. Cambridge, MA: Harvard University Press, 727–757.

Courtois, Stephane. 1999b. "Introduction: The Crimes of Communism." In Stephane Courtois, Nicolas Werth, Jean-Louis Panne, Andrzej Paczkowski, Karel Bartosek, and Jean-Louis Margolin, *The Black Book of Communism: Crime, Terror, Repression*. Cambridge, MA: Harvard University Press, 1–31.

Courtois, Stephane, Nicolas Werth, Jean-Louis Panne, Andrzej Paczkowski, Karel Bartosek, and Jean-Louis Margolin. 1999. *The Black Book of Communism: Crime, Terror, Repression*. Cambridge, MA: Harvard University Press.

Crisostomo, Isabelo T. 1997. *Fidel Valdez Ramos: Builder, Reformer, Peacemaker*. Quezon City: J. Kriz.

Crossette, Barbara. 2005–2006. "Nepal: The Politics of Failure." *World Policy Journal* (Winter):69–76.

Crowell, Todd, and Law Siu-lan. 1998a. "Rumbles in Gangland." *Asiaweek*. April 24.

Crowell, Todd, and Law Siu-lan. 1998b. "Troubled Transition." *Asiaweek*. April 24.

"Cuban Revolution." 2007. *Wall Street Journal*. December 22.

Cumings, Bruce. 1997. *Korea's Place in the Sun: A Modern History*. New York: Norton.

Cumings, Bruce. 2008. "The South Korean Massacre at Taejon: New Evidence on US Responsibility and Coverup." *Japan Focus*. July 23.

Curtis, Gerald. 1999. *The Logic of Japanese Politics: Leaders, Institutions, and the Limits of Change*. New York: Columbia University Press.

DaCapo. 2003. "Shikeishu: Sono 'Kyokugen' no Sekai o Mita." 527(December 3): 10–39.

Dahl, Robert A. 1998. *On Democracy*. New Haven, CT: Yale University Press.

Dakin, Brett. 2003. *Another Quiet American: Stories of Life in Laos*. Bangkok: Asia Books.

Dalangin-Fernandez, Lira. 2006. "Arroyo Signs Law Abolishing the Death Penalty." *Philippine Daily Inquirer*. June 24. http://newsinfo.inq7.net/breakingnews/nation/view_article.php?article_id=6417.

Dalangin-Fernandez, Lira. 2007. "Palace Orders Wider Probe of Military in Political Slays: Melo Panel to Continue Work." *Philippine Daily Inquirer*. January 30.

D'Alema, Massimo. 2008. "Global Shift against Death Penalty." *Baltimore Sun*. January 1.

Dan, Wei. 2007a. "An Old Tree in Need of Trimming: Reflections on San Quentin." *Dialogue* [Dui Hua Foundation] 27(Spring):4–5.

Dan, Wei. 2007b. "The Role of The Supreme People's Procuratorate in Promoting Respect for Human Rights and Rule of Law in China." Paper presented at the Boalt Hall School of Law, University of California at Berkeley. March 12.

Dan Cohen, Meier. 1984. "Decision Rules and Conduct Rules: On Acoustic Separation in Criminal Law." *Harvard Law Review* 97(3):625–677.

Dando, Shigemitsu. 1996. "Toward the Abolition of the Death Penalty." *Indiana Law Journal* 72:7–43.

Dando, Shigemitsu. 2000. *Shikei Haishiron*. 6th ed. Tokyo: Yuihaku.

Dasgupta, Ramaprasad. 1973. *Crime and Punishment in Ancient India*. New Delhi: Varanasi Bhartiya.

"Death Penalty: Abolition Is Desirable, but Don't Hurry." 2006. *Korea Times*. February 22.

"Death Penalty: Dialogue with Islamic Countries Difficult, Says Former French Justice Minister." 2007. *Italy Global Nation*. December 17.

"Death Penalty for Fifteen Drug Traffickers." 2007. *West Australian*. November 30. www.thewest.com.au/default.aspx?MenuID=29andContentID=49022.

"The Death Penalty in China." 2004. EastSouthWestNorth Web site. www.zonaeuropa. com.

Death Penalty Information Center. 2005. "Taiwan President Promises to Abolish the Death Penalty." Washington, DC. September 14.

Death Penalty Information Center. 2007. "Updated Historical Execution Database Provides Unique Look at History of the Death Penalty in the U.S." Washington, DC. July 26.

Death Penalty Issue Research Group. 2000. *Taiwan Human Rights Report 2000: The Taiwan Death Penalty Issue in International Perspective.* Trans. Jessie Yeh. www.tahr.org.tw/site/data/report00/eng00/death.htm.

"Death Penalty: Medieval Relic." 2008. *Charleston Gazette.* July 24.

"Death Penalty Sentences in Japan Hit Record Level in 2007." 2007. *Mainichi Daily News.* December 29.

Death Penalty Thailand Blog. 2007. http://deathpenaltythailand.blogspot.com.

"Death Sentences Review: A Turbulent Year." 2007. *Nanfang Daily.* December 20. [Trans. Jiang Su. Original Chinese version: http://news.xinhuanet.com/legal/2007-12/20/content_7284509.htm.]

"Death to the Death Penalty." 2008. *Taipei Times.* May 28.

Deen, Thalif. 2007. "Death Penalty Threatens to Split World Body." *Inter Press Service.* October 31.

Delisle, Guy. 2005. *Pyongyang: A Journey in North Korea.* Trans. Helge Dascher. Montreal: Drawn and Quarterly.

"Democracy in Singapore." 2008. *Wall Street Journal.* June 26.

Denno, Deborah W. 2003. "Lethally Humane? The Evolution of Execution Methods in the United States." In James R. Acker, Robert M. Bohm, and Charles S. Lanier, eds., *America's Experiment with Capital Punishment: Reflections on the Past, Present, and Future of the Ultimate Penal Sanction.* Durham, NC: Carolina Academic Press, 693–762.

Dent, Christopher M. 2008. *East Asian Regionalism.* London: Routledge.

Diamant, Neil J., Stanley B. Lubman, and Kevin J. O'Brien, eds. 2005. *Engaging the Law in China: State, Society, and Possibilities for Justice.* Stanford, CA: Stanford University Press.

Diamante, Rodolfo S., and Jovenal D. Velasco, eds. 2005. *Stop the Execution! A Source Book on the Death Penalty.* Manila: Coalition against the Death Penalty (with funding assistance from the Royal Netherlands Embassy in Manila).

Diamond, Larry, and Marc F. Plattner, eds. 1998. *Democracy in East Asia.* Baltimore: Johns Hopkins University Press.

Diamond, Larry, Doh C. Shin, and To-Chol Sin, eds. 1999. *Institutional Reform and Democratic Consolidation in Korea.* Stanford, CA: Hoover Institution Press.

Dikotter, Frank. 2002. *Crime, Punishment, and the Prison in Modern China: 1895–1949.* New York: Columbia University Press.

Dizon, Nikko. 2008. "PNP: Extrajudicial Killings Fell by 83% in 2007." *Philippine Inquirer.* January 14.

Doan, Van Toai. 1986. *The Vietnamese Gulag.* Trans. Sylvie Romanowski and Francois Simon-Miller. New York: Simon and Schuster.

"Doing Away with Death Penalty." 2007. Editorial. *Hankyoreh.* December 31.

Domikova-Hashimoto, Dana. 1996. "Japan and Capital Punishment." *Human Affairs* 6 (1):77–93.

Dostoevsky, Fyodor. 1868. *The Idiot.* Rev. ed. 1998. New York: Oxford University Press.

Douglas, Mary. 1986. *How Institutions Think*. Syracuse, NY: Syracuse University Press.

Dower, John W. 1990. "The Useful War." *Daedalus* 119(3):49–70.

Dower, John W. 1999. *Embracing Defeat: Japan in the Wake of World War II*. New York: Norton.

Drifte, Reinhard. 1998. *Japan's Foreign Policy for the Twenty-first Century*. New York: St. Martin's Press.

Druckerman, Pamela. 2007. *Lust in Translation: The Rules of Infidelity from Tokyo to Tennessee*. New York: Penguin.

Dudden, Alexis. 2004. *Japan's Colonization of Korea: Discourse and Power*. Honolulu: University of Hawaii Press.

Dui Hua Foundation. 2007a. "China Continues Move to Lethal Injection as Executions Decline." *Dialogue* [Dui Hua Foundation] 29. www.duihua.org/work/publications/nl/dialogue/nl_txt/n129/n129_3.htm.

Dui Hua Foundation. 2007b. "Death Penalty Reform Should Bring Drop in Chinese Executions." *Dialogue* [Dui Hua Foundation] 26(Winter):1–2.

Dui Hua Foundation. 2007c. "Statistics Shed New Light on Executions in China." *Dialogue* [Dui Hua Foundation] 26(Winter):3.

Dui Hua Foundation. 2007d. "Visit Promotes Dialogue on US-China Criminal Justice." *Dialogue* [Dui Hua Foundation] 27(Spring):1–3.

Duiker, William J. 2000. *Ho Chi Minh*. New York: Hyperion.

Dunlop, Nic. 2005. *The Lost Executioner: A Journey to the Heart of the Killing Fields*. New York: Walker.

Durkheim, Emile. 1982. *The Rules of the Sociological Method and Selected Texts on Sociology and Its Method*. Ed. Steven Lukes. Trans. W. D. Halls. New York: Free Press.

Durkheim, Emile. 1983. "The Evolution of Punishment." In Steven Lukes and Andrew Scull, eds., *Durkheim and the Law*. Oxford, UK: Blackwell, 102–114.

Dutton, Michael. 1992. *Policing and Punishment in China: From Patriarchy to "the People."* Cambridge: Cambridge University Press.

Dutton, Michael. 2005a. *Policing Chinese Politics: A History*. Durham, NC: Duke University Press.

Dutton, Michael. 2005b. "Toward a Government of the Contract: Policing in the Era of Reform." In Borge Bakken, ed., *Crime, Punishment, and Policing in China*. Lanham, MD: Rowman and Littlefield, 189–233.

Duus, Peter. 1998. *The Abacus and the Sword: The Japanese Penetration of Korea, 1895–1910*. Berkeley: University of California Press.

Ebrahim, Zofeen. 2007. "Pakistan: The Trivial Difference between Life and Death." Inter Press Service. July 25.

Ebrahim, Zofeen. 2008. "'Brutalisation of State, Society behind Spurt in Executions': Interview with I.A. Rehman, Human Rights Commission of Pakistan." Inter Press Service. April 18.

Eckert, Julia. 2005. "Death and the Nation: State Killing in India." In Austin Sarat and Christian Boulanger, eds., *The Cultural Lives of Capital Punishment: Comparative Perspectives*. Stanford, CA: Stanford University Press, 195–218.

Eddyono, Lufthi Widago. 2007. "Capital Punishment Is Not the Solution." May 8. www.mahkamahkonstitusi.go.id/eng/berita.php?newscode=350.

Edelman, Murray. 1964. *The Symbolic Uses of Politics*. Urbana: University of Illinois Press.

Efron, Sonni. 2006. "Google-Earthing the Hermit Kingdom." *Los Angeles Times*. August 26.

Eiji, Takemae. 2002. *The Allied Occupation of Japan*. New York: Continuum International.

Eisenstadt, S. N. 1996. *Japanese Civilization: A Comparative Perspective*. Chicago: University of Chicago Press.

Eldridge, Philip J. 2001. *The Politics of Human Rights in Southeast Asia*. London: Routledge.

Elkins, Zachary, and Beth Simmons. 2005. "On Waves, Clusters, and Diffusion: A Conceptual Framework." *Annals of the American Academy of Political and Social Science* 598(1):33–51.

Emmott, Bill. 2007. "Rocky Road Ahead for China's Miracle Economy." www.asahi. com. May 22.

Emmott, Bill. 2008. *Rivals: How the Power Struggle between China, India, and Japan Will Shape Our Next Decade*. London: Allen Lane.

Enav, Peter. 2008. "Opposition Party Wins Big in Taiwan." *Honolulu Star Bulletin*. January 13.

Endo, Shusaku. 1966. *Silence*. Tokyo: Kodansha.

Engel, Pauline. 1977. *The Abolition of Capital Punishment in New Zealand*. Wellington: Department of Justice.

Epp, Charles R. 1998. *The Rights Revolution: Lawyers, Activists, and Supreme Courts in Comparative Perspective*. Chicago: University of Chicago Press.

Epstein, Gady. 2002. "Religious Leaders Spared Execution in China." *Baltimore Sun*. October 11.

Epstein, Gady. 2004. "Doomed, then Living to Tell Tale." *Baltimore Sun*. November 28.

Evans, Grant, and Milton Osborne. 2003. *A Short History of Laos: Land in Between*. St. Leonards, NSW: Allen and Unwin.

Evans, Richard. 1995. *Deng Xiaoping and the Making of Modern China*. New York: Penguin.

Evans, Richard J. 1996. *Rituals of Retribution: Capital Punishment in Germany, 1600–1987*. New York: Oxford University Press.

"Execution Appeals to Be Held Publicly." 2006. *South China Morning Post*. February 28.

"Execution Plans for Bali Bombers Labelled Torturous." ABC News. September 19. 2008.

"Executions Are Conducted on the Public's Behalf." 2007. asahi.com. October 5.

"Executions in the U.S. 1608–1987: The Espy File." 2007. www.deathpenaltyinfo.org/article.php?scid=8anddid=269.

"Ex-Philippine Leader 'Shocked' at Inclusion on Corruption List." 2008. Agence France-Presse. January 31.

"Face the Facts." 2008. *Times of India*. March 13.

Fackler, Martin. 2008. "Losing an Edge, Japanese Envy India's Schools." *New York Times*. January 2.

Fagan, Jeffrey. 2005. "Deterrence and the Death Penalty: A Critical Review of New Evidence." Testimony presented at the New York State Assembly's "Hearings on the Future of Capital Punishment in the State of New York." January 21.

Fagan, Jeffrey. 2007. "Deterrence and the Death Penalty." Expert opinion and testimony to the MKRI [Indonesian Constitutional Court]. May 2.

Fagan, Jeffrey, Franklin E. Zimring, and Amanda Geller. 2006. "Capital Punishment and Capital Murder: Market Share and the Deterrent Effects of the Death Penalty." *Texas Law Review* 84:1803–1867.

Fairbank, John K. 1990. "From the Ming to Deng Xiaoping." *New York Review of Books* 37(9).

Fallows, James. 1994. *Looking at the Sun: The Rise of the New East Asian Economic and Political System.* New York: Pantheon Books.

Fallows, James. 2007. "China Makes, the World Takes." *Atlantic Monthly* (July–August): 48–71.

"False Accusations." 2008. www.asahi.com. February 16.

Fang, Qiang. 2008. "The Spirit of the Rule of Law in China." *Education about Asia* 13 (Spring):36–41.

Farrell, C. 2006. "Judicial Caning in Singapore, Malaysia and Brunei." www.corpun. com. August.

Faulkner, Penelope. 2003. "The Use of the Death Penalty in the Socialist Republic of Vietnam." Report of the Vietnam Committee on Human Rights (affiliated with the International Federation of Human Rights), presented at the 59th Session of the UN Commission on Human Rights in Geneva, Switzerland. April 16.

Feldman, Eric. 2006. "The Culture of Legal Change: A Case Study of Tobacco Control in Twenty-first-century Japan." *Michigan Journal of International Law* 27(3):743–821.

Fellows, Warren. 1998. *The Damage Done: Twelve Years of Hell in a Bangkok Prison.* Edinburgh: Mainstream.

Fenby, Jonathan. 2003. *Chiang Kai-Shek: China's Generalissimo and the Nation He Lost.* New York: Carroll and Graf.

Fernandez-Armesto, Felipe. 2006. *Pathfinders: A Global History of Exploration.* New York: Norton.

Filippov, V. V. 2006. "Does Belarus Need Capital Punishment?" Occasional Papers, vol. 3, Centre for Capital Punishment Studies, University of Westminster.

"The Final Shoot: China Speeding the Use of Lethal Injection." 2008. *Nanfang Daily.* April 10.

Fingarette, Herbert. 1972. *Confucius: The Secular as Sacred.* New York: Harper and Row.

Fingleton, Eamonn. 1995. *Blindside: Why Japan Is Still on Track to Overtake the U.S. by the Year 2000.* Boston: Houghton Mifflin.

Finlay, Iain, and Trish Clark. 2006. *Good Morning Hanoi: A Year on the Airwaves in the New Vietnam.* Pymble, NSW: Simon and Schuster.

Fitzgerald, Frances. 1972. *Fire in the Lake: The Vietnamese and the Americans in Vietnam.* New York: Little, Brown.

Flybjerg, Bent. 1998. *Rationality and Power: Democracy in Practice.* Trans. Steven Sampson. Chicago: University of Chicago Press.

Flybjerg, Bent. 2001. *Making Social Science Matter: Why Social Inquiry Fails and How It Can Succeed Again.* Cambridge: Cambridge University Press.

Foote, Daniel H. 1992a. "The Benevolent Paternalism of Japanese Criminal Justice." *California Law Review* 80:317–390.

Foote, Daniel H. 1992b. "From Japan's Death Row to Freedom." *Pacific Rim Law and Policy Journal* 1(1):11–103.

Foote, Daniel H. 1993. "The Door That Never Opens: Capital Punishment and Post-conviction Review of Death Sentences in the United States and Japan." *Brooklyn Journal of International Law* 19(2):367–521.

Foote, Daniel H. 2007. *Na mo Kao mo Shiranai Shiho: Nihon no Saiban wa Kawaru no ka.* Tokyo: NTT.

Ford, Glyn. 2008. "Insurrections Push Philippines to the Brink." *Japan Times.* January 21.

Ford, Peter. 2008. "China Unchained?" *Honolulu Star-Bulletin.* April 13.

Forst, Michal. 1999. "The Abolition of the Death Penalty in France." In *The Death Penalty Abolition in Europe.* Strasbourg: Council of Europe, 105–116.

"Forty-six Sentenced to Death in 2007, Most since 1980." 2008. *Japan Times.* January 14.

Forum Asia Democracy. 2005. "The Death Penalty in Vietnam." Report. September.

Forum 90. 2007. "Saikin no Shikei Shikko." Forum 90 newsletter. January.

Foucault, Michel. 1977. *Discipline and Punish: The Birth of the Prison.* New York: Vintage Books.

Fowler, Geoffrey A., Sky Canaves, and Juliet Ye. 2008. "With New Faith in Rule of Law, More Citizens File Suits: Chinese Seek a Day in Court." *Wall Street Journal.* July 1.

Fox, Michael H. 2007. "Why I Support Executions." Interview with Justice Minister Hatoyama Kunio, with trans. and commentary. *Japan Focus.* December 19:1–8. [Originally published in *Shukan Asahi* on October 26, 2007.]

Frank, Marc. 2008. "Cuba's Raul Castro Commutes Most Death Sentences." Reuters. April 28.

Free Legal Assistance Group of the Philippines. 1994. *Free Legal Assistance Group: 1974–1994.* Quezon City: FLAG Human Rights Foundation.

Free Legal Assistance Group of the Philippines. 2003a. "Presidential Statements Lifting the Moratorium on Executions." Quezon City: FLAG. December 5–9.

Free Legal Assistance Group of the Philippines. 2003b. *Torture Philippines: Law and Practice.* Quezon City: FLAG and Foundation for Integrative and Development Studies.

Free Legal Assistance Group of the Philippines. 2004a. *Final Narrative Report.* Quezon City: FLAG.

Free Legal Assistance Group of the Philippines. 2004b. *Primer on Lethal Injection in the Philippines.* Quezon City: FLAG.

Free Legal Assistance Group of the Philippines. 2004c. *Primer on the Death Penalty.* Quezon City: FLAG.

Free Legal Assistance Group of the Philippines. 2004d. *Primer on the Innocence Project: Post-conviction DNA Testing in the Philippines.* Quezon City: FLAG.

Free Legal Assistance Group of the Philippines. 2006a. "Death Penalty Law." Unpublished notes distributed to members of Congress.

Free Legal Assistance Group of the Philippines. 2006b. *Socio-economic Profile of Capital Offenders in the Philippines.* Quezon City: FLAG.

French, Howard W. 2002. "Secrecy of Japan Executions Is Criticized as Unduly Cruel." *New York Times.* June 30.

Friedman, Benjamin M. 2005. *The Moral Consequences of Economic Growth.* New York: Vintage Books.

Friedman, Edward, and Barrett L. McCormick. 2000. *What If China Doesn't Democratize? Implications for War and Peace.* Armonk, NY: M. E. Sharpe.

Friedman, Edward, Paul G. Pickowicz, and Mark Selden. 2005. *Revolution, Resistance, and Reform in Village China.* New Haven, CT: Yale University Press.

Friend, Theodore. 2003. *Indonesian Destinies.* Cambridge, MA: Belknap Press of Harvard University Press.

Fritsch, Peter. 2004. "Thai Premier Pushes Odd Peace Gesture: An Origami Airlift." *Wall Street Journal.* December 2.

Fu, H. L. 2005. "Punishing for Profit: Profitability and Rehabilitation in a Laojiao Institution." In Neil J. Diamant, Stanley B. Lubman, and Kevin J. O'Brien, eds.,

Engaging the Law in China: State, Society, and Possibilities for Justice. Stanford, CA: Stanford University Press, 213–230.

Fu, Xin. 2005. "Review Procedure for Death Penalty in China: Last Straw or a Formality to the Defendant?" Paper presented at the Fourteenth World Congress of Criminology.

Fukada, Taku. 2007. "Introduction." In Shikei Haishi Henshu Iinkai, *Anata mo Shikei Hanketsu o Kakasareru* [*You, Too, Will Be Forced to Issue a Death Sentence*]. Tokyo: Impakuto Press, 1.

Fukuda, Masaaki. 2002. "Homu Daijin ni Shikei Shikko no Gimu wa Aru ka." In M. Fukuda, ed., *Nihon no Shakai Bunka Kozo to Jinken.* Tokyo: Akashi Shoten.

Fuller, Thomas. 2007. "No Blowing Smoke: Poppies Fade in Southeast Asia. *New York Times.* September 16.

Galanter, Marc. 1984. *Competing Equalities: Law and the Backward Classes in India.* New Delhi: Oxford University Press.

Galanter, Marc. 1989. *Law and Society in Modern India.* New Delhi: Oxford University Press.

Gall, Carlotta. 2008. "Leadership Void Seen in Pakistan." *New York Times.* June 24.

Gallagher, Mary E. 2006. "Mobilizing the Law in China: 'Informed Disenchantment' and the Development of Legal Consciousness." *Law and Society Review* 40 (4):783–816.

Gangania, Ish. 2006. "Death Penalties Mostly Awarded to Dalits and Religious Minorities." *PUCL Bulletin.*

Garland, David. 1990. *Punishment and Modern Society: A Study in Social Theory.* Chicago: University of Chicago Press.

Garland, David. 2001. *The Culture of Control: Crime and Social Order in Contemporary Society.* Chicago: University of Chicago Press.

Garland, David. 2005. "Capital Punishment and American Culture." *Punishment and Society* 7(4):347–376.

Garland, David. 2006. "Penal Excess and Surplus Meaning: Public Torture Lynchings in 20th Century America." *Law and Society Review* 39:793–833.

Garland, David. 2007a. "Death, Denial, Discourse: On the Forms and Functions of American Capital Punishment." In David Downes, Paul Rock, Christine Chinkin, and Conor Gearty, eds., *Crime, Social Control, and Human Rights: From Moral Panics to States of Denial.* Devon, UK: Willan, 136–156.

Garland, David. 2007b. "The Peculiar Forms of American Capital Punishment." *Social Research* 74:435–464.

Garrett, Brandon. 2008. "Judging Innocence." *Columbia Law Review* 108: 55–142.

Gattrell, V. A. C. 1994. *The Hanging Tree: Execution and the English People 1770–1868.* Oxford: Oxford University Press.

Gaylord, Mark S., and John F. Galliher. 1994. "Death Penalty Politics and Symbolic Law in Hong Kong." *International Journal of the Sociology of Law* 22:19–37.

Ge, Xiangwei. 2006. "The Place of Homicide in the Abolition of Chinese Capital Punishment." *Criminal Law Review* 19:1–42. [In Chinese.]

Gellately, Robert. 2007. *Lenin, Stalin, and Hitler: The Age of Social Catastrophe.* New York: Knopf.

Gelling, Peter. 2008a. "Executions for Drug Crimes Are Resumed in Indonesia." *New York Times.* July 13.

Gelling, Peter. 2008b. "Indonesia Widens Use of Death Penalty." *International Herald Tribune.* July 11.

Geum, Won-seop. 2004. "Suspected Serial Killer Charges Court Bench." *Chosun Ilbo.* September 21.

Gibson, William. 1993. "Disneyland with the Death Penalty." *Wired.* September–October. www.wired.com/wired/archive/1.04/gibson_pr.html.

Gilani, Iftikhar. 2005. *My Days in Prison.* New Delhi: Penguin.

Gilley, Bruce. 2004. *China's Democratic Future: How It Will Happen and Where It Will Lead.* New York: Columbia University Press.

Ginsburg, Tom. 2003. *Judicial Review in New Democracies: Constitutional Courts in Asian Cases.* New York: Cambridge University Press.

Ginsburg, Tom, ed. 2004. *Legal Reform in Korea.* New York: RoutledgeCurzon.

Ginsburg, Tom, and Tamir Moustafa. 2008a. "The Functions of Courts in Authoritarian Politics." In Tom Ginsburg and Tamir Moustafa, eds., *Rule by Law: The Politics of Courts in Authoritarian Regimes.* New York: Cambridge University Press.

Ginsburg, Tom, and Tamir Moustafa, eds. 2008b. *Rule by Law: The Politics of Courts in Authoritarian Regimes.* New York: Cambridge University Press.

Gitlin, Todd. 2003. *The Whole World Is Watching: Mass Media in the Making and Unmaking of the New Left.* 2nd ed. Berkeley: University of California Press.

Gladwell, Malcolm. 2000. *The Tipping Point: How Little Things Can Make a Big Difference.* New York: Little, Brown.

Glenn, H. Patrick. 2004. *Legal Traditions of the World: Sustainable Diversity in Law.* 2nd ed. Oxford: Oxford University Press.

Glionna, John M. 2008. "China Shows Caution on Executions." *Los Angeles Times.* January 6.

Glover, Jonathan. 1999. *Humanity: A Moral History of the Twentieth Century.* New Haven, CT: Yale University Press.

Gluckman, Ron. 1999a. "Divided by Death." MSNBC. www.gluckman.com/Death'Penalty2.htm.

Gluckman, Ron. 1999b. "Waiting to Go." *Asiaweek.* July 23. www.gluckman.com/Death'Penalty.htm.

Godinho, Jorge A. F. 2007. "The Regulation of Gaming and Betting Contracts in the 1999 Macau Civil Code." *Gaming Law Review* 11(3):572.

Godoy, Angelina Snodgrass. 2006. *Popular Injustice: Violence, Community, and Law in Latin America.* Stanford, CA: Stanford University Press.

Goldberg, Jonah. 2007. "A Poison Pill Deserved: Chinese Bureaucrat's Execution Little Noticed." *Boston Herald.* July 16.

Goldman, Merle. 2006. *From Comrade to Citizen: The Struggle for Political Rights in China.* Cambridge, MA: Harvard University Press.

Goodwin, Tim. 2007. Asia Death Penalty Blog. http://asiadeathpentaly.blogspot.com/.

Gordon, Andrew. 2007. "'Modern Girls' Had a Major Impact on Society." asahi.com. December 4.

Goto, Akira. 2008. "Saibanin Seido o meguru Tairitsu wa Nani o Imi Shite Iru ka." *Sekai* 779(June):90–100.

Gottschalk, Marie. 2006. *The Prison and the Gallows: The Politics of Mass Incarceration in America.* New York: Cambridge University Press.

Gourevitch, Philip. 1998. *We Wish to Inform You That Tomorrow We Will Be Killed with Our Families: Stories from Rwanda.* New York: Picador.

Gourevitch, Philip. 2003. "Alone in the Dark." *New Yorker.* September 8:55–75.

"Gov't Proposes Controversial Human Rights Roadmap." 2007. *Hankyoreh.* February 13. http://english.hani.co.kr/arti/english_edition/e_national/190645.html.

Gotoda, Masaharu. 1998. *Jo to Ri: Gotoda Masaharu no Kaikoroku.* Tokyo: Kodansha.

Greenberg, David F., and Valerie West. 2008. "Siting the Death Penalty Internationally." *Law and Social Inquiry* 33:295–343.

Greenfeld, Karl Taro. 2006. *China Syndrome: The True Story of the Twenty-first Century's First Great Epidemic.* New York: HarperCollins.

Greenlees, Donald. 2007. "A Gambling-Fueled Boom Adds to a Church's Bane." *New York Times.* December 26.

Greenlees, Donald, and Keith Bradsher. 2007. "China Pushes Back Elections in Hong Kong." *New York Times.* December 30.

Grogg, Patricia. 2006. "Death Penalty—Cuba: No Abolition in Sight." Inter Press Service. April 11. http://ipsnews.net/news.asp?idnews=32861.

Grossman, Dave. 1996. *On Killing: The Psychological Cost of Learning to Kill in War and Society.* New York: Back Bay Books.

Guha, Ramachandra. 2004. "The Sociology of Suicide." *India Together.* August.

Guha, Ramachandra. 2007. *India after Gandhi: The History of the World's Largest Democracy.* New York: HarperCollins.

Guillermo, Gilda E. 2006. *Legal Reference on Capital Cases. Volume IV: Drug Offenses.* Quezon City: Free Legal Assistance Group.

Gunn, Geoffrey, and Andre Vitchek. 2007. "Timor-Leste and Indonesia: Between a Rock and a Hard Place." *Japan Focus.* October 18:1–10.

Gunness, Christopher. 2002. "Kim Dae Jung's Tainted Legacy." BBC News. December 19.

Gupta, Subhash C. 1986. *Capital Punishment in India.* New Delhi: Deep and Deep.

Gupta, Subhash C. 2000. *Capital Punishment.* Delhi: Jnanada Prakesh.

Hadji-Ristic, Petar. 2007. "Rights: Poverty and Capital Punishment Go Hand in Hand." Inter Press Service. October 17.

Hagan, John, and Wenona Rymond-Richmond. 2008. *Darfur and the Crime of Genocide.* Cambridge: Cambridge University Press.

Hail, Henry. 2008. "Framing Processes and Identity Construction of Post-crackdown Falun Gong." Unpublished paper. Department of Sociology, University of Hawaii at Manoa.

Haines, Herbert H. 1996. *Against Capital Punishment: The Anti-death penalty Movement in America, 1972–1994.* New York: Oxford University Press.

Halperin, Rick. 2007. "Death Penalty News and Updates." http://people.smu.edu/rhalperi.

Hamai, Koichi. 2008. "Shikei to Iu 'Joshiki' no Mae ni: Deta de Miru Nihon Shakai no Jitsujo." *Ronza* (March):111–121. [Trans. as "The Death Penalty in Japan." 2008. *Japan Echo* (June):44–50.]

Hamai, Koichi, and Thomas Ellis. 2008. "Japanese Criminal Justice: Was Re-integrative Shaming a Chimera?" *Punishment and Society* 10:25–46.

Hamilton, V. Lee, and Joseph Sanders. 1992. *Everyday Justice: Responsibility and the Individual in Japan and the United States.* New Haven, CT: Yale University Press.

Hamilton-Paterson, James. 1998. *America's Boy: The Marcoses and the Philippines.* Manila: Anvil

Han, In-Sup. 2007. "Trends in Democratization and the Rule of Law in Criminal Justice and Human Rights." *Beop kwa Sahoe* [Law and Society] 32.

Han, Jane. 2007. "American Futurist Dator Says Korea Is Definition of Future." *Korea Times.* February 7.

Han, Yong-Sun. 2001. *Urinara Sahyung Jiphaeng Hyunwhanggwa Sahyung Jedo Gaesonbanganegwanhan Yeongu* [A study of the status quo of death penalty executions and schemes for improvement]. Ph.D. diss., Department of Law, Suncheon University.

Hananuntasuk, Somsri [chair, Amnesty International Thailand]. 2006. Interview. Death Penalty Thailand Blog. January 31.

Handley, Paul M. 2006. *The King Never Smiles: A Biography of Thailand's Bhumibol Adulyadej.* New Haven, CT: Yale University Press.

Hands Off Cain. Death penalty database. www.handsoffcain.info. [In addition to specific entries below, material from 1999–2008 was used.]

Hands Off Cain. 2006a. "North Korea: Three Publicly Executed." June 27.

Hands Off Cain. 2006b. "Philippines."

Hands Off Cain. 2006c. "United Nations: UN Rights Experts Urge N. Korea to Suspend Treason Execution." June 3.

Hands Off Cain. 2007. "China: More Cautious Handling of Death Penalty Cases Urged." March 11.

Hane, Mikiso, ed. 1988. *Reflections on the Way to the Gallows: Voices of Japanese Rebel Women.* New York: Pantheon Books.

Haney, Craig. 2005. *Death by Design: Capital Punishment as a Social Psychological System.* New York: Oxford University Press.

Hanley, Charles J., and Jae-Soon Chang. 2008. "Summer of Terror: At Least 100,000 Said Executed by Korean Ally of US in 1950." *Japan Focus.* July 23.

Hara, Yuji. 1997. *Korosareru tame ni Ikiru to iu koto: Shimbun Kisha to Shikei Mondai.* Tokyo: Gendaijinbunsha.

Harada, Masaharu. 2004. *Ototo o Koroshita Kare to Boku.* Tokyo: Popurasha.

Harding, John, and May Chu Harding. 2002. *Escape from Paradise (From Third World to First).* Phoenix, AZ: IDK Press.

Harrell, Steven. 1990. Introduction to Jonathan N. Lipman and Steven Harrell, eds., *Violence in China: Essays in Culture and Counterculture.* Albany: State University of New York Press.

Harring, Sid L. 1991. "Death, Drugs and Development: Malaysia's Mandatory Death Penalty for Traffickers and the International War on Drugs." *Columbia Journal of Transnational Law* 29:365ff.

Harris, Sam. 2005. *The End of Faith: Religion, Terror, and the Future of Reason.* New York: Norton.

Harrison, Dan. 2007. "PM Slams Rudd over Death Penalty." *Age.* October 9.

Harrison, Lawrence E. 2006. *The Central Liberal Truth: How Politics Can Change a Culture and Save It from Itself.* New York: Oxford University Press.

Harrison, Lawrence E., and Samuel P. Huntington, eds. 2000. *Culture Matters: How Values Shape Human Progress.* New York: Basic Books.

Hartney, Christopher. 2006. "U.S. Rates of Incarceration: A Global Perspective." *Fact Sheet: Research from the National Council on Crime and Delinquency.* November:1–8.

Harvard Law Review. 2006. "A Matter of Life and Death: The Effect of Life-without-Parole Statutes on Capital Punishment." *Harvard Law Review* 119:1838–1854.

Hasegawa, Hiroshi. 2003. "Ryogoku Keimusho ni Zenkindaisei." *AERA.* May 26:26–29.

Hashimoto, Hidetoshi. 2003. *The Prospects for a Regional Human Rights Mechanism in East Asia.* London: Routledge.

Hatoyama, Kunio. 2007. "Why I Support Executions." Interview with Hatoyama Kunio. Trans., commentary by Michael H. Fox. *Japan Focus.* December 19. [Originally published in *Shukan Asahi,* October 26, 2007.]

Hay, Douglas. 1975. "Property, Authority and the Criminal Law." In Douglas Hay, Peter Linebaugh, John G. Rule, E. P. Thompson, and Cal Winslow. *Albion's Fatal Tree: Crime and Society in Eighteenth-century England.* New York: Pantheon Books, 17–63.

Hayashi, Masahiro. 1987. "Sendai no Baishin Saiban ni Tsuite." *Hanrei Taimuzu,* 17–24.

Head, John W., and Yanping Wang. 2005. *Law Codes in Dynastic China: A Synopsis of Chinese Legal History in the Thirty Centuries from Zhou to Qing.* Durham, NC: Carolina Academic Press.

Head, Jonathan. 2008. "Bribe Case Tarnishes Thai Ex-PM." *BBC News.* June 25.

Healy, Kieran. 2007. *Last Best Gifts: Altruism and the Market for Human Blood and Organs.* Chicago: University of Chicago Press.

Hebenton, Bill. 2007. "Comparative Perspectives on 'Punitiveness.'" Unpublished paper.

Hermann, Joachim. 2002. "The Death Penalty in Japan: An Absurd Punishment." *Brooklyn Law Review* 67(Spring):827–854.

Hessler, Peter. 2006. *Oracle Bones: A Journey between China's Past and Present.* New York: HarperCollins.

Hikari-shi Jiken Bengodan. 2008. *Hikari-shi Jiken: Bengodan wa Nani o Rissho Shita no ka.* Tokyo: Impakuto.

Hilsdon, Anne-Marie. 2000. "The Contemplacion Fiasco: The Hanging of a Filipino Domestic Worker in Singapore." In A.-M. Hilsdon, M. MacIntyre, V. Mackie, and M. Stivens, eds., *Human Rights and Gender Politics: Asia-Pacific Perspectives.* London: Routledge.

Hinton, Alexander Laban. 2005. *Why Did They Kill? Cambodia in the Shadow of Genocide.* Berkeley: University of California Press.

Hiraiwa-Hasegawa, Mariko. 2005. "Homicide by Men in Japan, and Its Relationship to Age, Resources, and Risk-Taking." *Evolution and Human Behavior* 26(July 1): 332–343.

Hirano, Keiji. 2006. "Psychiatrist, 100, Fights to Clear Late Convict's Name." *Japan Times.* May 10.

Ho, Virgil K. Y. 2000. "Butchering Fish and Executing Criminals." In J. Abbink and G. Aijmer, eds., *Meanings of Violence: A Cross Cultural Perspective.* Oxford, UK: Berg.

Ho, Virgil K. Y. 2005. "What Is Wrong with Capital Punishment? Official and Unofficial Attitudes toward Capital Punishment in Modern and Contemporary China." In Austin Sarat and Christian Boulanger, eds., *The Cultural Lives of Capital Punishment: Comparative Perspectives.* Stanford, CA: Stanford University Press, 274–290.

Hoare, J. E., and Susan Pares. 2005. *North Korea in the Twenty-first Century: An Interpretive Guide.* Folkestone, UK: Global Oriental.

Hobson, John. 2004. *The Eastern Origins of Western Civilization.* New York: Cambridge University Press.

Hodgkinson, Peter, Seema Kandelia, and Simon MacKenzie. 2007. "The Recent History of Capital Punishment and Crime Rates in the Philippines: Politics, Sensibilities and the Civilizing Process." Unpublished paper.

Hodgkinson, Peter, and William A. Schabas. 2004. *Capital Punishment: Strategies for Abolition.* Cambridge: Cambridge University Press.

Hoffman, Michael. 2007a. "From Bliss to Blood." *Japan Times.* December 23.

Hoffman, Michael. 2007b. "Japan's 'Hidden Christians.'" *Japan Times.* December 23.

Hoffman, Michael. 2007c. "One Missionary's 'Swamp' Is Another's 'Religion Allergy' Challenge." *Japan Times.* December 23.

Hogg, Chris. 2007. "Secrecy of Japanese Executions." BBC News. December 7.

Holcombe, Charles. 2006. "Rethinking Early East Asian History." *Education about Asia* 11(2):9–13.

Hom, Sharon, and Stacy Mosher, eds. 2007. *Challenging China: Struggle and Hope in an Era of Change: Independent Chinese Voices on Life in Contemporary China.* New York: The New Press and Human Rights in China.

Hong, Lady. 1985. *Memoirs of a Korean Queen.* Trans. Yang-li Choe-Wall. London: Kegan Paul International.

Hongo, Jun. 2006. "New Justice Minister Ready to Sign Death Penalty Orders." *Japan Times.* October 4.

Hongo, Jun. 2007. "Three Hanged and Named in Ministry First: Disclosures End Secrecy Policy on Executions." *Japan Times.* December 8.

Hongo, Jun, Takahiro Fukada, and Akemi Nakamura. 2008. "Death Sentences on the Increase." *Japan Times.* June 18.

Hongo, Jun, and Yumi Wijers-Hasegawa. 2006. "Asahara's Execution Finalized: Aum Founder to Hang as Top Court Declares Babbling Guru Sane." *Japan Times.* September 16.

Hood, Roger. 1989. *The Death Penalty: A World-wide Perspective: A Report to the United Nations Committee on Crime Prevention and Control.* 1st ed. New York: Oxford University Press.

Hood, Roger. 1996. *The Death Penalty: A World-wide Perspective.* 2nd ed. New York: Oxford University Press.

Hood, Roger. 2001. "Capital Punishment: A Global Perspective." *Punishment and Society* 3:331–354.

Hood, Roger. 2002. *The Death Penalty: A Worldwide Perspective.* 3rd ed. New York: Oxford University Press.

Hood, Roger. 2005. "At Death's Door." *China Review* 33(Summer):10–13.

Hood, Roger. 2007. "Developments on the Road to Abolition: A Worldwide Perspective." Paper presented at Global Survey on Death Penalty Reform Workshop, Beijing. August 25–26.

Hood, Roger, and Carolyn Hoyle. 2008. *The Death Penalty: A Worldwide Perspective.* 4th ed. New York: Oxford University Press.

Hood, Roger, and Florence Seemungal. 2006. "A Rare and Arbitrary Fate: Conviction for Murder, the Mandatory Death Penalty and the Realities of Homicide in Trinidad and Tobago: A Statistical Study of Recorded Murders and Persons Indicted for Murder in 1998–2002." Report to the Death Penalty Project. www.deathpenaltyproject.org/Rare_and_arbitrary_fate_report.pdf.

Hor, Michael. 2002. "The Independence of the Criminal Justice System in Singapore." *Singapore Journal of Legal Studies* (2002):497–513.

Hor, M. 2004. "The Death Penalty in Singapore and International Law." *Singapore Yearbook of International Law* 8:105–117.

Horigan, Damien P. 1996. "Of Compassion and Capital Punishment: A Buddhist Perspective on the Death Penalty." *The American Journal of Jurisprudence* 41:271–288.

Horigan, Damien P. 2001. "An Ancient Precedent: Reflections on the Tale of Korea's Abolitionist King." *Korean Journal of International and Comparative Law* 29:87–106.

Horigan, Damien P. 2003. "Observations on the South Korean Penal Code." *Journal of Korean Law* 3(2):139–159.

Horowitz, Irving Louis. 2001. *Taking Lives: Genocide and State Power.* New Brunswick, NJ: Transaction.

Hu, Yunteng. 2002. "Application of the Death Penalty in Chinese Judicial Practice." In Chen, Li, and Otto, eds., *Implementation of Law in the People's Republic of China*. Leiden: Kluwer.

Huan, Jinting. 2006. *Wo Wei Siqiu Xie Yishu* [I write the final letters for death row]. Nanjing: Jiangsu Literature and Arts Press.

Huchet, Jean-Francois. 2002. Review of *The Chinese*, by Jasper Becker. *China Perspectives* (March–April):82–84.

Hudson, Valerie M., and Andrea M. den Boer. 2005. *Bare Branches: The Security Implications of Asia's Male Surplus Population*. Boston: MIT Press.

Hui, Wang. 2007. "The Politics of Imagining Asia: Empires, Nations, Regional and Global Orders." Trans. Matthew A. Hale. *Japan Focus*. http://japanfocus.org/products/topdf/2407.

Human Rights in China. 2006. "Setback for the Rule of Law: Lawyers under Attack in China." August. www.hrinchina.org.

Human Rights in China. 2007. "State Secrets: China's Legal Labyrinth." www.hrichina.org.

Human Rights Policy White Paper of the Republic of China. 2002. www.gio.gov.tw/taiwan-website/5-gp/2002hr/.

Human Rights Watch. 2007. *Human Rights Watch World Report 2007: Events of 2006*. New York: Seven Stories.

Human Rights Watch. 2008a. *Recurring Nightmare: State Responsibility for "Disappearances" and Abductions in Sri Lanka*. March 8. http://hrw.org/reports/2008/srilanka0308/1.htm.

Human Rights Watch. 2008b. *Walking on Thin Ice: Control, Intimidation and Harassment of Lawyers in China*. April.

Human Rights Watch. 2008c. "Getting Away with Murder: 50 Years of the Armed Forces Special Powers Act." August.

Hunt, Lynn. 2006. "For Reasons of State." *Nation*. May 29.

Hunt, Lynn. 2007. *Inventing Human Rights: A History*. New York: Norton.

Huntington, Samuel P. 1998. *The Clash of Civilizations and the Remaking of World Order*. New York: Simon and Schuster.

Hutchcroft, Paul D. 1996. "The Philippines at the Crossroads: Sustaining Economic and Political Reform." Asia Society. November. www.asiasociety.org/publications/au_philippines.html.

Hutchcroft, Paul D. 1998. *Booty Capitalism: The Politics of Banking in the Philippines*. Ithaca, NY: Cornell University Press.

Ibrahim, Anis, and V. Anbalagan. 2008. "Spotlight on Tan and Two Former Top Judges." *New Straits Times*. January 28.

"Ibuki in the Dark on Rights." 2007. www.asahi.com. February 28.

Ichikawa, Hayami. 2006. "New Report Sheds Light on N. Korea's 'Torturous' Authorities." www.asahi.com. November 15. [See esp. www.asahi.com/english/Herald-asahi/TKY200611150152.html.]

"The Illusion of Calm in Tibet." 2008. *Economist*. July 12:55–57.

"Indonesia Bucks Global Downward Trend in Executions, Killing 6 Since June." 2008. *International Herald Tribune*. July 20.

Inglehart, Ronald, and Christian Wenzel. 2005. *Modernization, Cultural Change and Democracy: The Human Development Sequence*. New York: Cambridge University Press.

Institute of Human Rights, University of the Philippines Law Center. 2005. *Symposium on the Right to Life Focusing on the Death Penalty*. [Proceedings of a symposium held

October 11–12, 2004.] Quezon City: Institute of Human Rights; Makati City: Royal
     Netherlands Embassy in the Philippines.
International Federation for Human Rights and Human Rights Commission of
     Pakistan. 2007. *Slow March to the Gallows: Death Penalty in Pakistan.* Paris: IFHR
     and Human Rights Commission of Pakistan. January.
International Federation for Human Rights and Taiwan Alliance to End the
     Death Penalty. 2006. *International Fact-Finding Mission: The Death Penalty in
     Taiwan: Towards Abolition?* Paris: IFHR and Taiwan Alliance to End the Death
     Penalty. June 2.
International Federation for Human Rights and Union for Civil Liberty. 2005.
     The Death Penalty in Thailand. Paris: IFHR and Union for Civil Liberty. March.
Ishizuka, Shinichi. 1997. "Shikei Kiroku no Etsuran to Shimin no Shiru Kenri." In
     Kikuta Koichi et al., eds., *Shikei: Sonchi to Haishi no Deai.* Tokyo: Impakuto Press,
     183–193.
Ishizuka, Shinichi. 2004. "Shushinkei Donyu to Keibatsu Seisaku no Henyo." *Gendai
     Shiso* (March):170–179.
Islam, Nazrul. 2008. "Rapid Action Battalion's (RAB) Extrajudicial Killings Under US
     Microscope." *New Age.* July 15.
Ito, Hiroyuki. 2007. "Problems Remain in Citizen Judge System." *International Herald
     Tribune.* www.asahi.com. January 10. [See esp. www.asahi.com/english/Herald-asahi/
     TKY200701100117.html.]
Ito, Masami. 2004. "Death-Row Warden: Haunted by Visions of a 'Horrifying Act.'"
     Japan Times. April 25.
Iype, George. 2004. "South India: World's Suicide Capital." *Rediff.* April 15.
Jackson, Peter A. 2003. *Buddhadasa: Theravada Buddhism and Modernist Reform in
     Thailand.* Bangkok: Silkworm Books.
Jacobs, David, and Jason T. Carmichael. 2002. "The Political Sociology of the
     Death Penalty: A Pooled Time-Series Analysis." *American Sociological Review*
     67(2):109–131.
Jacobs, David, Jason T. Carmichael, and Stephanie L. Kent. 2005. "Vigilantism,
     Current Racial Threat, and Death Sentences." *American Sociological Review*
     70:656–677.
Jamieson, Neil J. 1995. *Understanding Vietnam.* Berkeley: University of California Press.
Japan Death Penalty Information Center. Web site. www.jdpic.org.
"Japan Finally Names Three Executed." 2007. Asia Death Penalty Blog. December 9.
     http://asiadeathpentaly.blogspot.com/.
"Japan Minister Mulls 'Tranquil' Executions." 2007. Reuters. October 24.
"Japan Minister Seeks 'Peaceful' Method of Execution." 2007. ABC News. October 24.
"Japan's Death Penalty under Threat as EU Spearheads Push for Global Moratorium."
     2007. *Mainichi Daily News.* October 28.
"Japan's Grim Reaper Defends Record Executions." 2008. Agence France-Presse. July 7.
Jensen, Lionel M. 1997. *Manufacturing Confucianism: Chinese Traditions and Universal
     Civilization.* Durham, NC: Duke University Press.
Jin, Hyun-joo. 2004. "Korea: Kim's Execution Video Banned." *Asia Media.* June 24.
Jin, Ryu. 2007. "Roh Invites Pope to Visit Two Koreas." *Korea Times.* February 15.
Johnson, Andy. 2008. "TT Holds on to Death Penalty." *Trinidad and Tobago Express.*
     January 6.
Johnson, David T. 2002a. *The Japanese Way of Justice: Prosecuting Crime in Japan.* New
     York: Oxford University Press.

Johnson, David T. 2002b. "Plea Bargaining in Japan." In Malcolm M. Feeley and Setsuo Miyazawa, eds., *The Japanese Adversary System in Context: Controversies and Comparisons.* New York: Palgrave Macmillan, 140–172.

Johnson, David T. 2004a. "Nihon ni okeru Shiho Seido Kaikaku: Keisatsu no Shozai to Sono Juyosei." *Horitsu Jiho* 76(2):8–15.

Johnson, David T. 2004b. "The Prosecution of Corruption in South Korea: Achievements, Problems, and Prospects." In Tom Ginsburg, ed., *Legal Reform in Korea.* London and New York: Routledge Curzon, 47–70.

Johnson, David T. 2005. "The Death Penalty in Japan: Secrecy, Silence, and Salience." In Austin Sarat and Christian Boulanger, eds., *The Cultural Lives of Capital Punishment: Comparative Perspectives.* Stanford, CA: Stanford University Press, 251–273.

Johnson, David T. 2006a. "Japan's Secretive Death Penalty Policy: Contours, Origins, Justifications, and Meanings." *Asian-Pacific Law and Policy Journal* 7(2):62–124.

Johnson, David T. 2006b. "The Vanishing Killer: Japan's Postwar Homicide Decline." *Social Science Japan Journal* 9(1):73–90.

Johnson, David T. 2006c. "Where the State Kills in Secret: Capital Punishment in Japan." *Punishment and Society* 8:251–285.

Johnson, David T. 2007a. "Crime and Punishment in Contemporary Japan." In Michael Tonry, ed., *Crime, Punishment, and Politics in Comparative Perspective.* Crime and Justice, vol. 36. Chicago: University of Chicago Press, 371–423.

Johnson, David T. 2007b. "You Don't Need a Weather Man to Know Which Way the Wind Blows: Lessons from the United States and South Korea for Recording Interrogations in Japan." *Ritsumeikan Law Review* 24:1–34.

Johnson, David T. 2008a. "The Death Penalty in Asia." *Punishment and Society* 10:99–102.

Johnson, David T. 2008b. "The Homicide Drop in Postwar Japan." *Homicide Studies* 12(1):146–160.

Johnson, David T. 2008c. "Shikei Yokushi ni wa Chokketsu Sezu." *Asahi Shimbun.* June 20:14.

Johnson, Ian. 2004. *Wild Grass: Three Portraits of Change in Modern China.* New York: Vintage Books.

Johnson, Robert. 2003. "Life under Sentence of Death: Historical and Contemporary Perspectives." In James R. Acker, Robert M. Bohm, and Charles S. Lanier, eds., *America's Experiment with Capital Punishment: Reflections on the Past, Present, and Future of the Ultimate Penal Sanction.* 2nd ed. Durham, NC: Carolina Academic Press, 647–671.

Johnston, William. 1966. Translator's preface to Shusaku Endo, *Silence.* Tokyo: Kodansha, 1–18.

"Judiciary Disagrees on Death Penalty." 2008. *Taipei Times.* May 17.

Juergensmeyer, Mark. 2003. *Terror in the Mind of God: The Global Rise of Religious Violence.* 3rd ed. Berkeley: University of California Press.

"Justice Minister Blasts Asahi Newspaper for Calling Him 'Grim Reaper.'" 2008. *Mainichi Daily News.* June 20.

"Justice Minister Hatoyama Rejects Meeting with Kamei over Death Penalty." 2007. *Mainichi Daily News.* September 28.

"Justice Minister Sugiura Backtracks on Anti-execution Stance." 2005. *Mainichi Daily News.* November 1.

"Justice Ministry Admits Outsiders: Diet Members Tour Execution Chamber." 2003. *Japan Times.* July 24.

Kaga, Otohiko. 1980. *Shikeishu no Kiroku*. Tokyo: Chuko Shinsho.

Kahn, Joseph. 2005a. "Deep Flaws, and Little Justice, in China's Court System." *New York Times*. September 21.

Kahn, Joseph. 2005b. "Torture Still 'Widespread' in China, Says U.N. Envoy." *New York Times*. December 2.

Kahn, Joseph. 2005c. "When Chinese Sue the State, Cases Are Often Smothered." *New York Times*. December 28.

Kahn, Joseph. 2006a. "China Makes Commitment to Social Harmony." *New York Times*. October 12.

Kahn, Joseph. 2006b. "Sane Chinese Put in Asylum, Doctors Find." *New York Times*. March 17.

Kahn, Joseph. 2006c. "Where's Mao? Chinese Revise History Books." *New York Times*. September 1.

Kahn, Joseph. 2007a. "China's Elite Talk of Democracy in One-Party State." *New York Times*. April 19.

Kahn, Joseph. 2007b. "Chinese Official Warns against Independence of Courts." *New York Times*. February 3.

Kalis, Lisa, and James Brooke. 2005. "After the Tsunami, Hoping for the Balm of Tourism." *New York Times*. January 16.

Kaltman, Blaine. 2007. *Under the Heel of the Dragon: Islam, Racism, Crime, and Uighur in China*. Athens: Ohio University Press.

Kamei, Shizuka. 2002. *Shikei Haishiron*. Tokyo: Kadensha.

Kamm, Henry. 1997. *Dragon Ascending: Vietnam and the Vietnamese*. New York: Arcade.

Kamm, John. 2007. "China, the Death Penalty, and the Beijing Olympics." Third World Congress against the Death Penalty, Paris, February 1–3.

Kandelia, Seema. 2006. "Incestuous Rape and the Death Penalty in the Philippines: Psychological and Legal Implications." *Philippine Law Journal* 80(4):697–710.

Kang, Chol-Hwan, and Pierre Rigoulot. 2001. *The Aquariums of Pyongyang: Ten Years in the North Korean Gulag*. Trans. Yair Reiner. New York: Basic Books.

Kang, David C. 2002. *Crony Capitalism: Corruption and Development in South Korea and the Philippines*. Cambridge: Cambridge University Press.

Kang, David C. 2007. *China Rising: Peace, Power, and Order in East Asia*. New York: Columbia University Press.

Kaplan, David E., and Andrew Marshall. 1996. *The Cult at the End of the World: The Terrifying Story of the Aum Doomsday Cult, from the Subways of Tokyo to the Nuclear Arsenals of Russia*. New York: Crown.

Kaplan, Robert D. 2006. "When North Korea Falls." *Atlantic Monthly* (October):64–73.

Kaplan, Robert D. 2008. "Oh! Kolkata!" *Atlantic Monthly* (April):72–79.

Karnow, Stanley. 1989. *In Our Image: America's Empire in the Philippines*. New York: Ballantine Books.

Karnow, Stanley. 1997. *Vietnam: A History*. 2nd ed. New York: Penguin.

Kassymbekova, Botagoz. 2005. "Capital Punishment in Kyrgyzstan: Between the Past, 'Other' State Killings and Social Demands." In Austin Sarat and Christian Boulanger, eds., *The Cultural Lives of Capital Punishment: Comparative Perspectives*. Stanford, CA: Stanford University Press, 171–194.

Katatsumuri no Kai, ed. 1994. *Shikei no Bunka o Toinaosu*. Tokyo: Impakuto Press.

Katzenstein, Peter J. 2006. *Beyond Japan: The Dynamics of East Asian Regionalism*. Ithaca, NY: Cornell University Press.

Katzenstein, Peter J., Natasha Hamilton-Hart, Kozo Kato, and Ming Yue. 2000. *Asian Regionalism*. Ithaca, NY: Cornell University Press.

Kawai, Mikio. 2004. *Anzen Shinwa no Hokai No Paradokkusu*. Tokyo: Iwanami Shoten.

Kay, Judith W. 2005. *Murdering Myths: The Story behind the Death Penalty*. Lanham, MD: Rowman and Littlefield.

Keck, Margaret E., and Kathryn Sikkink. 1998. *Activists beyond Borders: Advocacy Networks in International Politics*. Ithaca, NY: Cornell University Press.

Keene, Donald. 2002. *Emperor of Japan: Meiji and His World, 1852–1912*. New York: Columbia University Press.

Keith, Ron. 2006. *New Crime in China: Public Order and Human Rights*. London: Routledge.

Kennedy, Brian. 2004. "Restraint and Punishment." *Taiwan Review* 54(8):24–27.

Kennedy, Brian, and Elizabeth Guo. 2006. "Eliminating Taiwan's Death Penalty." *Taiwan Review* 56(10):1–5.

Kerr, Alex. 2001. *Dogs and Demons: Tales from the Dark Side of Japan*. New York: Hill and Wang.

Kershaw, Ian. 2007. *Fateful Choices: Ten Decisions That Changed the World, 1940–1941*. New York: Penguin.

Kessler, Richard J. 1989. *Rebellion and Repression in the Philippines*. New Haven, CT: Yale University Press.

Khalik, Abdul. 2008. "Support Grows for Death Penalty for Corruption Convicts." *Jakarta Post*. July 24.

Khan, Ehtasham. 2003. "China Is the Cruelest Country in the World." *Rediff*. August 18. www.rediff.com/news/2003/aug/18spec1.htm.

Kiernan, Ben. 2002. *The Pol Pot Regime: Race, Power, and Genocide in Cambodia under the Khmer Rouge, 1975–79*. 2nd ed. New Haven, CT: Yale University Press.

Kiernan, Ben. 2005. "Barbaric Crimes of a Mystical Communism Seen through Its Own Eyes." *New York Times Higher Education Supplement*. February 25.

Kiernan, Ben. 2007. *Blood and Soil: A World History of Genocide and Extermination from Sparta to Darfur*. New Haven, CT: Yale University Press.

Kikuta, Koichi. 1993. *Shikei to Yoron*. Tokyo: Seibundo.

Kikuta, Koichi. 1999. *Shikei: Sono Kyoko to Fujori*. Tokyo: Meiseki Shoten.

Kim, Cheong-won. 2005. "Human Rights Commission Seeks to Abolish Death Penalty, Security Law." *Korea Times*. December 19.

Kim, Dae Jung. 1987. *Prison Writings*. Berkeley: University of California Press.

Kim, Dae Jung. 1994. "Is Culture Destiny? The Myth of Asia's Anti-democratic Values. *Foreign Affairs* 73 (November/December). www.foreignaffairs.org/19941101 faresponse5158/kim-dae-jung/is-culture-destiny-the-myth-of-asia-s-anti-democratic-values.html.

Kim, Dae Jung. 2007. "In Appreciation of the Announcement of Korea as a De Facto Abolitionist Country." The Press Center, Seoul. October 10.

Kim, Kwang-Tae. 2007. "Public Executions in N. Korea on the Rise." Associated Press. November 26.

Kim, Rahn. 2006. "Serial Killer Supports Death Penalty." *Korea Times*. March 22.

Kim, Rahn. 2007. "Korea to Retain Death Penalty System." *Korea Times*. February 13.

Kim, Sun-hyuk. 2000. *The Politics of Democratization in Korea: The Role of Civil Society*. Pittsburgh, PA: University of Pittsburgh Press.

Kim, Tae-jong. 2007. "Korea Recognized as Death Penalty-Free Nation." *Korea Times*. December 24.

Kim, Tong-hyung. 2007. "160 Businessmen to Be Pardoned." *Korea Times.* February 9.

Kim, Yon-se. 2008. "Lee Says Korea Can Overtake Japan in 10 Years." *Korea Times.* January 1.

Kingston, Jeff. 2004. *Japan's Quiet Transformation: Social Change and Civil Society in the Twenty-first Century.* New York: RoutledgeCurzon.

Kirk, Donald. 2005. *Philippines in Crisis: U.S. Power versus Local Revolt.* Manila: Anvil.

Kitani, Akira. 2004. *Keiji Saiban no Kokoro: Jijitsu Nintei Tekiseika no Hosaku.* Tokyo: Horitsu Bunkasha.

Kitaoka, Shinichi. 2007. "Nationalism a Running Theme in Asian History." www.asahi .com. December 28.

Klinger, David. 2004. *Into the Kill Zone: A Cop's Eye View of Deadly Force.* New York: Jossey-Bass.

Klomegah, Kester Kenn. 2007. "Russia Vacillating over Abolition of Death Penalty." Interview of Victoria Sergeyeva. *Human Rights Tribune.* May 2.

Klomegah, Kester Kenn. 2008. "Death Penalty—Belarus: Officials Hint Moratorium a Step Away." *Inter Press Service.* June 13.

Knowles, Julian B. 2004. "Capital Punishment in the Commonwealth Caribbean: Colonial Inheritance, Colonial Remedy?" In Peter Hodgkinson and William A. Schabas, eds., *Capital Punishment: Strategies for Abolition.* Cambridge: Cambridge University Press, 282–308.

Ko, Dorothy. 2005. *Cinderella's Sisters: A Revisionist History of Footbinding.* Berkeley: University of California Press.

Koh, Joseph. 2005. "Why Nguyen Must Die." *The Age.* November 30.

Kollner, Patrick. 2006. "The LDP at 50: Sources of Dominance and Changes in the Koizumi Era." *Social Science Japan Journal* 9(2):243–258.

Koo, Hagen. 2001. *Korean Workers: The Culture and Politics of Class Formation.* Ithaca, NY: Cornell University Press.

Korea Ministry of Justice. 2005. "Capital Punishment in Korea." Unpublished internal report. June 16.

Kramer, Andrew E. 2007. "New Russian History: Yes, a Lot of People Died, but . . . " *New York Times.* August 12.

Kremmer, Christopher. 1998. *Stalking the Elephant Kings.* Honolulu: University of Hawaii Press.

Kristof, Nicholas D. 1991. "Chinese Crackdown on Crime Leads to Increase in Number of Executions." *New York Times.* January 16.

Kristof, Nicholas D. 1996. "South Korean President Admits to Slush Fund." *New York Times.* January 10.

Kristof, Nicholas D. 1999. "Out at Last, Prisoner 3514 Catches Up on 40 Years." *New York Times.* April 29.

Kristof, Nicholas D. 2005. "'Mao': The Real Mao." *New York Times.* October 23.

Kumamoto, Shinichi, and Koichi Furuya. 2007. "Japan Had Good Intelligence about China's Losing Fight in Opium War." www.asahi.com. July 22. [See esp. http://www.asahi.com/english/Herald-asahi/TKY200707220231.html.]

Kumamoto, Shinichi, and Masayuki Nishi. 2008. "Painful Democratic Awakenings for South Korea, Taiwan." www.asahi.com. April 28.

Kuppusamy, Baradan. 2007a. "Death Penalty—Malaysia: Sane Voices amidst Hysteria." Inter Press Service. October 30.

Kuppusamy, Baradan. 2007b. "Death Penalty—Singapore: Stand at UN Leaves Many Angered." Inter Press Service. December 3.

Kuppusamy, Baradan. 2007c. "Malaysia—Death Penalty: Nine Years on Death Row, Denied Appeal." Inter Press Service. August 26.

Kuppusamy, Baradan. 2008a. "Death Penalty: Beijing Sentence Shakes Malaysia's Own Policy." Inter Press Service. January 23.

Kuppusamy, Baradan. 2008b. "Malaysia: Cleanup of the Judiciary Is Possible: Hearing Exposes Mahathir, His Corrupt Times." Inter Press Service. January 23.

Kurlantzick, Joshua. 2007. "China's Future: A Nation of Single Men?" Los Angeles Times. October 21.

Kynge, James. 2007. China Shakes the World: A Titan's Rise and Troubled Future—and the Challenge for America. Boston: Mariner Books.

LaFree, Gary. 1999. "Homicide: Cross-national Perspectives." In M. Dwayne Smith and Margaret A. Zahn, eds., Studying and Preventing Homicide: Issues and Challenges. Thousand Oaks, CA: Sage, 115–139.

Lagman, Edcel C. 2006. "The Days of the Death Penalty Law Are Numbered." Speech, Makati City, Philippines. May 31.

Lahiri, Tarapada. 1986. Crime and Punishment in Ancient India. New Delhi: Radiant.

Lam, Willy. 2008. "The CCP Strengthens Control over the Judiciary." China Brief 8(4).

Lambert, Eric G., Sudershan Pasupuleti, Shanhe Jiang, K. Jaishankar, and Jagadish V. Bhimarasetty. 2008. "Views on the Death Penalty among College Students in India." Punishment and Society 10(2): 207–218.

Landes, David S. 1998. The Wealth and Poverty of Nations: Why Some Are So Rich and Some So Poor. New York: Norton.

Lane, Charles. 2004. "The Death Penalty in Japan." Unpublished paper.

Lane, Charles. 2005a. "A View to a Kill." Foreign Policy (May/June):37–42.

Lane, Charles. 2005b. "Why Japan Still Has the Death Penalty." Washington Post. January 16.

Langbein, John. 1978. "Torture and Plea Bargaining." University of Chicago Law Review 46:3–22.

Lankov, Andrei. 2006. "The Natural Death of North Korean Stalinism." Asia Policy 1 (January).

Lankov, Andrei. 2007a. "The Dawn of Modern Korea: In a Class of One's Own?" Korea Times. March 1.

Lankov, Andrei. 2007b. "Golden Age of Brainwashing?" Korea Times. April 5.

Larkin, John. 2000. "Death, Be Not Proud: Opposition to Capital Punishment Grows." AsiaWeek. 26(7), February 25.

Lawoti, Mahendra. 2007. Contentious Politics and Democratization in Nepal. Thousand Oaks, CA: Sage.

"A Law unto Themselves." 2008. The Economist. April 19.

Lee, Hope. 2001. "Injustice of the Death Penalty in Taiwan: Socio-economic Aspects." In Edmund Ryden, ed., Taiwan Opposes the Death Penalty. Taipei: Fujen University John Paul II Peace Institute, 221–244.

Lee, Hyo-sik. 2005. "AI to Campaign against Death Penalty in Korea." Korea Times. December 20.

Lee, Kuan Yew. 2000. From Third World to First: The Singapore Story: 1965–2000. New York: HarperCollins.

Lee, Kuan Yew. 2007. "Excerpts from an Interview with Lee Kuan Yew." International Herald Tribune. August 29.

Lee, Lily. 2008. "Death-Sentence Judge Now Opposes Executions." *Telegraph.* April 20.

Lee, Perris, Choon Siong, Wei Yi Lim, and Jason Dean. 2008. "Kuomintang's Victory in Taiwan Seems Certain to Cheer Investors." *Wall Street Journal.* January 13.

Lee, Su-hyun. 2008. "Justice Is Swift for Novice Korean Jurors." *New York Times.* July 17.

Lee, Tahirih V. 1993. "Risky Business: Court, Culture, and the Marketplace." *University of Miami Law Review* 47:1335–1414.

Lee, Tahirih V. 1995. Review of *Order and Discipline in China: The Shanghai Mixed Court 1911–1927,* by Thomas Stephens. *Pacific Affairs* 67(Fall): 445ff.

Lee, Tahirih V. 2000. "The Future of Federalism in China." In Karen G. Turner, James V. Feinerman, and R. Kent Guy, eds., *The Limits of the Rule of Law in China.* Seattle: University of Washington Press, 271–303.

"Lee Administration Reversing Democratic Achievements." 2008. *Hankyoreh.* May 26.

Leheny, David. 2006. *Think Global, Fear Local: Sex, Violence, and Anxiety in Contemporary Japan.* Ithaca, NY: Cornell University Press.

Lenning, Emily. 2006. "Execution for Body Parts: A Case of State Crime." Paper presented at the Annual Meetings of the American Society of Criminology. Los Angeles, November 17.

Lewis, Neil A. 2006. "Death Sentences Decline, and Experts Offer Reasons." *New York Times.* December 15.

Li, Qian. 2007. "China Takes Closer Look at Death Penalties." *China Daily.* August 8.

Li, Victor H. 1977. *Law without Lawyers.* Stanford, CA: Stanford Alumni Association.

Li, Zhisui. 1994. *The Private Life of Chairman Mao: The Memoirs of Mao's Personal Physician.* Trans. Tai Hung-chao. New York: Random House.

Liang, Bin, Hong Lu, Terance D. Miethe, and Lening Zhang. 2006. "Sources of Variation in Pro-Death Penalty Attitudes in China: An Exploratory Study of Chinese Students at Home and Abroad." *British Journal of Criminology* 46(1):119–130.

Liao, Fort Fu-Te. 2001. "Plugging the Gaps: The Death Penalty, Taiwan, and International Law." In Edmund Ryden, ed., *Taiwan Opposes the Death Penalty.* Taipei: Fujen Catholic University John Paul II Peace Institute, 203–220.

Liao, Fort Fu Te. 2008. "From Seventy-Eight to Zero: Why Executions Declined after Taiwan's Democratization." *Punishment and Society* 10:153–170.

Lieberthal, Kenneth. 2003. *Governing China: From Revolution through Reform.* 2nd ed. New York: Norton.

Liebman, Benjamin L., and Timothy Wu. 2007. "China's Courts: Restricted Reform." *China Quarterly* 191(September): 620–638.

Liebman, James S., Jeffrey Fagan, and Valerie West. 2000. *A Broken System: Error Rates in Capital Cases, 1973–1995.* New York: Columbia University School of Law.

"Life and Death Difference." 2007. *China Daily.* August 9.

Lim, Audrea. 2006. "Taiwan Still Considering Whether Death Penalty Is Justifiable." *China Post.* July 3.

Lim, B. K. 2004. "China's Security Tsar Orders Fewer Executions." Reuters News. March 9.

Lim, Lydia, and Jeremy Au Yong. 2006. "Special Report: 96% of S'poreans Back the Death Penalty." *the sunday times.* February 12:8–9.

Lincoln, Edward J. 1990. "The Showa Economic Experience." *Daedalus* 119(3):191–208.

Lindsey, Tim, ed. 2006. *Law Reform in Developing and Transitional States.* London: Routledge.

Lindsey, Tim. 2007. "Sparing the Bali Bombers." *Melbourne Herald Sun.* October 15.

Lindsey, Tim. 2008. "PM Kevin Rudd Government Dilemma over Executions." *Melbourne Herald Sun.* July 18.

Lines, Rick. 2007. *The Death Penalty for Drug Offences: A Violation of International Human Rights Law.* London: International Harm Reduction Association. www.ihra.net/News#IHRALaunchDeathPenaltyReport.

Link, Perry. 2005. "An Abnormal Mind." *The Times Literary Supplement.* November 13.

Liptak, Adam. 2007. "Executions Decline Elsewhere, but Texas Holds Steady." *New York Times.* December 26.

Lithwick, Dahlia. 2007. "The Dying Death Penalty?" *Washington Post.* February 11.

Litong, Glenda B. 2006. *Legal Reference on Capital Cases. Volume III: Kidnapping.* Quezon City: Free Legal Assistance Group.

Liu, Sida. 2006. "Beyond Global Convergence: Conflicts of Legitimacy in a Chinese Lower Court." *Law and Social Inquiry* 31:75–106.

Loconte, Joseph. 2007. "British Abolition's Faith-Based Roots." *Los Angeles Times.* February 21.

"Lowest in the Rung: Bengal Deceives Itself; Bihar Accepts Reality." 2008. *Statesman.* March 21.

Lu, Hong, and Terance D. Miethe. 2003. "Confessions and Criminal Case Disposition in China." *Law and Society Review* 37:549–578.

Lu, Hong, and Terance D. Miethe. 2007. *China's Death Penalty: History, Law, and Contemporary Practices.* New York: Routledge.

Lubman, Stanley B. 1967. "Mao and Mediation: Politics and Dispute Resolution in Communist China." *California Law Review* 55:1284–1359.

Lubman, Stanley B. 1969. "Form and Function in the Chinese Criminal Process." *Columbia Law Review* 69:535–575.

Lubman, Stanley B. 1999. *Bird in a Cage: Legal Reform in China after Mao.* Stanford, CA: Stanford University Press.

Lubman, Stanley B. 2006. "Looking for Law in China." *Columbia Journal of Asian Law* 20(1):1–92.

Luce, Edward. 2007. *In Spite of the Gods: The Strange Rise of Modern India.* New York: Doubleday.

Lydgate, Chris. 2003. *Lee's Law: How Singapore Crushes Dissent.* Melbourne: Scribe.

Lynch, Colman. 2008. "Indonesia's Use of Capital Punishment for Drug-Trafficking Crimes: Legal Obligations, Extralegal Factors, and the Bali Nine Case." Unpublished paper, Columbia University School of Law.

Lynch, Daniel C. 2006. *Rising China and Asian Democratization: Socialization to "Global Culture" in the Political Transformations of Thailand, China, and Taiwan.* Stanford, CA: Stanford University Press.

Mabutas, Justice Ramon, Jr. 1995. "Philippines." In *Criminal Justice Profiles of Asia: Investigation, Prosecution, and Trial.* Tokyo: UNAFEI, 139–175.

Macan-Markar, Marwaan. 2007. "Thaksin May Yet Pay for Bloody 'War on Drugs.'" Inter Press Service. August 16.

Macbean, Nicola, and Li Qinglan. 2003. "The Death Penalty in China: A Baseline Document—Strengthening the Defence in Death Penalty Cases in the People's Republic of China." Rights Practice, European Initiative for Democracy and Human Rights. December. www.rights-practice.org.

MacCormack, Geoffrey. 1990. *Traditional Chinese Penal Law.* Edinburgh: Edinburgh University Press.

Macdonald, Peter. 1993. *Giap: The Victor in Vietnam.* New York: Norton.

MacFarquhar, Larissa. 2003. "The Devil's Accountant." *New Yorker* (March 31):64–79.

MacFarquhar, Roderick, and Michael Schoenhals. 2006. *Mao's Last Revolution.* Cambridge, MA: Belknap Press.

MacLeod, Calum. 2006. "China Makes Ultimate Punishment Mobile." *USA Today.* June 14.

Madsen, Richard. 2007. *Democracy's Dharma: Religious Renaissance and Political Development in Taiwan.* Berkeley: University of California Press.

Maga, Timothy P. 1980. *Judgment at Tokyo: The Japanese War Crimes Trials.* New York.

Magnier, Mark, and Alan Zarembo. 2006. "China Admits Transplanting Executed Prisoners' Organs." *Honolulu Advertiser.* November 18.

Magnier, Mark. 2005a. "They Can't Handle the Truth." *Los Angeles Times.* February 28.

Magnier, Mark. 2005b. "Tibetan Monk's Death Sentence Is Commuted to a Life Term." *Los Angeles Times.* January 27.

Magnier, Mark. 2007a. "Chinese Applaud Ex-official's Execution." *Los Angeles Times.* July 11.

Magnier, Mark. 2007b. "An Honest China, for All the World to See." *Los Angeles Times.* February 9.

Mahapatra, Dhananjay. 2008. " 'Where Does Common Man Go When Executive Fails.'" *Times of India.* June 13.

Mahbubani, Kishore. 2002. *Can Asians Think? Understanding the Divide between East and West.* South Royalton, VT: Steerforth Press.

Mahbubani, Kishore. 2008. *The New Asian Hemisphere: The Irresistible Shift of Global Power to the East.* New York: PublicAffairs.

Mai Elliott, Duong Van. 1999. *The Sacred Willow: Four Generations in the Life of a Vietnamese Family.* New York: Oxford University Press.

Maier, Astrid. 2005. *Die Todesstrafe in der VR China* [The Death Penalty in the People's Republic of China]. Hamburg: Institut fur Asienkunde.

Makino, Catherine. 2007. "Naming Hanged Convicts: Step towards Reform." Inter Press Service. December 11.

Malaysians against Death Penalty and Torture (MADPET). Web site. http://madpet06 .blogspot.com/.

Malia, Martin. 1999. "Foreword: The Uses of Atrocity." In Stephane Courtois, Nicolas Werth, Jean-Louis Panne, Andrzej Paczkowski, Karel Bartosek, and Jean-Louis Margolin, *The Black Book of Communism: Crime, Terror, Repression.* Cambridge, MA: Harvard University Press, ix–xx.

Mamamayang Tutol sa Bitay [Movement for Restorative Justice]. 2006. *The Criminal Justice System and the Death Penalty.* Manila: Philippine Human Rights Information Center.

Mangsatabam, Ningthi. 2004. "Indian Prisons—Rhetoric and Reality." *The Hindu.* April 20.

Mann, James. 2007. *The China Fantasy: How Our Leaders Explain away Chinese Repression.* New York: Viking.

Manthorpe, Jonathan. 2005. *Forbidden Nation: The History of Taiwan.* New York: Palgrave Macmillan.

Marcel, Cecile. 2008. "The Death Penalty Is Simply Un-American." Letter to the editor. *New York Times.* January 1.

Margolin, Jean-Louis. 1999. "Vietnam and Laos: The Impasse of War Communism." In Stephane Courtois, Nicolas Werth, Jean-Louis Panne, Andrzej Paczkowski,

Karel Bartosek, and Jean-Louis Margolin, *The Black Book of Communism: Crime, Terror, Repression*. Cambridge, MA: Harvard University Press, 565–576.

Margolin, Jean-Louis, and Pierre Rigoulot. 1999. Conclusion to pt. 4, "Communism in Asia: Between Reeducation and Massacre." In Stephane Courtois, Nicolas Werth, Jean-Louis Panne, Andrzej Paczkowski, Karel Bartosek, and Jean-Louis Margolin, *The Black Book of Communism: Crime, Terror, Repression*. Cambridge, MA: Harvard University Press, 636–641.

Markovits, Inga. 1995. *Imperfect Justice: An East-West German Diary*. Oxford: Oxford University Press.

Marks, Robert B. 2006. "Asia in the Re-making of the Modern World." *Education about Asia* 11(2):14–18.

Marks, Robert B. 2007. *The Origins of the Modern World: A Global and Ecological Narrative from the Fifteenth to the Twenty-first Century*. 2nd ed. Lanham, MD: Rowman and Littlefield.

Marquand, Robert. 2005. "S. Korea Bars Secret Video of the North." *Christian Science Monitor*. March 29.

Marshall, Joshua Micah. 2000. "Death in Venice: Europe's Death-Penalty Elitism." *New Republic* 223(5):12–14.

Marshall, Steven, Orville Schell, Elliott Sperling, and Mickey Spiegel. 2000. *Tibet since 1950: Silence, Prison or Exile*. New York: Aperture.

Marti, Michael. 2002. *China and the Legacy of Deng Xiaoping: From Communist Revolution to Capitalist Evolution*. Washington, DC: Potomac Books.

Martin, Bradley K. 2006. *Under the Loving Care of the Fatherly Leader: North Korea and the Kim Dynasty*. New York: Thomas Dunne Books.

"Martyrdoms a Tragedy for the Entire Nation." 2007. www.asahi.com. March 7.

Maruko, Eiko. 2003. "Violence in the Politics of Modern Japan." Ph.D. diss., Harvard University.

Mash. 2007. "The Death Penalty by the Numbers: The United States, Bangladesh and Texas." April 4. www.docstrangelove.com/2007/04/04/the-death-penalty-by-the-numbers-the-united-states-bangladesh-and-texas.

"Mass Defection Decimates South Korea's Ruling Party." 2007. Reuters. February 7.

Masur, Louis P. 1989. *Rites of Execution: Capital Punishment and the Transformation of American Culture, 1776–1865*. New York: Oxford University Press.

Matas, David, and David Kilgour. 2007. "Bloody Harvest: Revised Report into Allegations of Organ Harvesting of Falun Gong Practitioners in China." http://organharvestinvestigation.net/.

McCormack, Gavan. 2007. "Yokohama and Seoul: Dealing with Crimes of State in Japan and South Korea." *Japan Focus*. January 29.

McCoy, Alfred W. 1999a. *Closer Than Brothers: Manhood at the Philippine Military Academy*. New Haven, CT: Yale University Press.

McCoy, Alfred W. 1999b. "Dark Legacy: Human Rights under the Marcos Regime." Paper presented at conference "Legacies of the Marcos Dictatorship," Ateneo de Manila University, Manila, September 20. www.hartford-hwp.com/archives/54a/062.html.

McCoy, Alfred W. 2006. *A Question of Torture: CIA Interrogation, from the Cold War to the War on Terror*. New York: Metropolitan Books.

McGivering, Jill. 1999. "Cracking down on the Triads." BBC News. December 17.

McKnight, Brian E. 1981. *The Quality of Mercy: Amnesties and Traditional Chinese Justice*. Honolulu: University Press of Hawaii.

McKnight, Brian E. 2007. *Law and Order in Sung China*. Cambridge: Cambridge University Press.

McLaughlin, Kathleen E. 2008. "Woman Waits Review of Dad's Fate in China." *San Francisco Chronicle*. August 7.

McNeill, David. 2007. "Japan and the Whaling Ban." *Japan Times*. February 11.

McNeill, David, and C. M. Mason. 2007. "Dead Men Walking: Japan's Death Penalty." *Japan Times*. April 8.

McNett, Gavin. 2000. Review of *Mao: A Life*, by Philip Short, and *Mao Zedong*, by Jonathan Spence. *Salon*. January 26. http://archive.salon.com/books/review/2000/01/26/short_spence.

Mehta, Pratap Bhanu. 2003. *The Burden of Democracy*. New Delhi: Penguin.

Mehta, Suketu. 2004. *Maximum City: Bombay Lost and Found*. New York: Vintage Books.

Menand, Louis. 2005. "Everybody's an Expert." *New Yorker* (December 5):98–101.

Menda, Sakae. 2004. *Menda Sakae Gokuchu Noto: Watakushi no Miokutta Shikeishu-tachi*. Tokyo: Impakuto.

Menon, Dilip M. 2006. *The Blindness of Insight: Essays on Caste in Modern India*. Chennai: Navayana.

Meredith, Robyn. 2007. *The Elephant and the Dragon: The Rise of India and China and What It Means for All of Us*. New York: Norton.

Messner, Steven F., Robert D. Baller, and Matthew P. Zevenbergen. 2005. "The Legacy of Lynching and Southern Homicide." *American Sociological Review* 70(4):633–655.

Michelmore, Karen. 2008. "Bali Bombers Deaths 'Soon as Possible.'" *Melbourne Herald Sun*. July 21.

Michelson, Ethan. 2006a. "From 'Serving the People' to Serving Capital in the Chinese Legal System: Solidifying the Place of Politics in the Study of Lawyers." Unpublished paper.

Michelson, Ethan. 2006b. "The Practice of Law as an Obstacle to Justice: Chinese Lawyers at Work." *Law and Society Review* 40(1):1–38.

Miethe, Terance D., Hong Lu, and Gini R. Deibert. 2005. "Cross-national Variability in Capital Punishment: Exploring the Sociopolitical Sources of Its Differential Legal Status." *International Criminal Justice Review* 15(2):115–130.

Mikhlin, Alexander S. 1999. *The Death Penalty in Russia*. Berlin: Springer.

Miller, Brad. 2008. "Rights—Philippines: Death Squad 'Cleanses' Davao." *Inter Press Service*. April 16.

Milmo, Cahal. 2006a. "Hangman 'Nearly Killed Assistant by Mistake.'" *Independent*. June 1.

Milmo, Cahal. 2006b. "The Hangman's Story." *Independent*. April 7.

Milton, Giles. 2003. *Samurai William: The Englishman Who Opened Japan*. New York: Farrar, Straus and Giroux.

Minear, Richard H. 1971. *Victors' Justice: The Tokyo War Crimes Trial*. Tokyo: Tuttle.

"Minister Wants 'Tranquil' Killing: Japan." 2007. Asia Death Penalty Blog. October 29. http://asiadeathpentaly.blogspot.com/.

"Ministry Names Executed Convicts for First Time." 2007. www.asahi.com. December 8.

Mirsky, Jonathan. 1994. "Unmasking the Monster." *New York Review of Books* 41(19).

Mishima, Yukio. 1958. *Confessions of a Mask*. New York: New Directions.

Mishra, Pankaj. 2006a. "The Myth of the New India." *New York Times*. July 6.

Mishra, Pankaj. 2006b. *Temptations of the West: How to be Modern in India, Pakistan, Tibet, and Beyond*. New York: Picador.

Mitta, Manoj, and H. S. Phoolka. 2007. *When a Tree Shook Delhi: The 1984 Carnage and Its Aftermath.* New Delhi: Roli Books.

Miyazawa, Setsuo. 2008. "The Politics of Increasing Punitiveness and the Rising Populism in Japanese Criminal Justice Policy." *Punishment and Society* 10:47–77.

Mok, Ka-ho. 2006. *Education Reform and Education Policy in East Asia.* London: Routledge.

Montefiore, Simon Sebag. 2005. *Stalin: The Court of the Red Tsar.* New York: Vintage.

Moravcsik, Andrew. 2001a. *The Death Penalty: Getting Beyond "Exceptionalism."* New York: Council for European Studies at Columbia University. September.

Moravcsik, Andrew. 2001b. *The New Abolitionism: Why Does the U.S. Practice the Death Penalty While Europe Does Not?* New York: Council for European Studies at Columbia University. September.

Mori, Tatsuya. 2008. *Shikei.* Tokyo: Asahi Shuppansha.

Morris, Jan. 1997. *Hong Kong.* New York: Vintage.

Morse, H. B. 1910. *The International Relations of the Chinese Empire: The Period of Conflict, 1834–60.* London: Longmans.

Mukai, Takeko, with Masako Sato. 2004. "Shikei de Itta Musuko Shinji to tomo ni Ikita 17nen." *Chuo Koron* (March):222–232.

Mules, Warwick. 1999. "Globalizing Discourses: The Flor Contemplacion Affair." In P. G. L. Chew and A. Kramer-Dahl, eds., *Reading Culture: Textual Practices in Singapore.* Singapore: Times Academic Press.

"Mumbai Courts Top in Giving Death Penalty." 2007. *Times of India.* December 31.

Munro, Robin. 2003. *Dangerous Minds: Political Psychiatry in China Today and Its Origins in the Mao Era.* New York: Human Rights Watch.

Munsgool, Parichart. 2007. "Death Penalty in Thailand." Unpublished paper. Boalt Hall School of Law, University of California at Berkeley.

Murakami, Haruki. 2000. *Underground: The Tokyo Gas Attack and the Japanese Psyche.* Trans. Alfred Birnbaum and Philip Gabriel. New York: Vintage International.

Murakami, Mutsuko. 2007. "Embarrassing Times ahead for Retentionists." Inter Press Service. November 14.

Murakami, Ryu. 2003. *In the Miso Soup.* Trans. Ralph McCarthy. Tokyo: Kodansha.

Muralidhar, S. 1998. "Hang Them Now, Hang Them Not: India's Travails with the Death Penalty." *Journal of the Indian Law Institute* 40:143ff. www.ielrc.org/content/a9803.pdf.

Murano, Kaoru. 1990. *Nihon no Shikei.* Tokyo: Soshoku Shobo.

Murano, Kaoru. 1992. *Nihon no Shikei.* Tokyo: Soshoku Shobo.

Murano, Kaoru. 1995. *Shikei Shikko.* Tokyo: Kyoeisha.

Murphy, Kim. 2006. "Russia's Bar on Death Penalty Questioned." *Los Angeles Times.* May 18.

Mydans, Seth. 2006. "Young Singaporeans Challenge Lee." *New York Times.* May 5.

Mydans, Seth. 2007a. "From Their Nation-Turned-Bunker, Burmese Generals Peer Out, and In." *New York Times.* September 26.

Mydans, Seth. 2007b. "However Vote Goes, Tense Future Looms for Thailand." *New York Times.* December 23:A4.

Mydans, Seth. 2007c. "Myanmar's Military Is the Nation's Driving Force." *New York Times.* October 7.

Mydans, Seth. 2007d. "Two Months after Protests, Myanmar Junta's in Control." *New York Times.* December 8.

Mydans, Seth. 2008a. "Power and Tenacity Collide in Singapore: Libel Defendant Assails Lee in Court." *International Herald Tribune.* May 30:1.

Mydans, Seth. 2008b. "A Resilient Indonesia Moves beyond Suharto." *New York Times.* January 12.

Mydans, Seth, and Wayne Arnold. 2007. "Modern Singapore's Creator Is Alert to Perils." *New York Times.* September 2.

Myint-U, Thant. 2006. *The River of Lost Footsteps: Histories of Burma.* New York: Farrar, Straus and Giroux.

Nagata, Kimon. 2005. *Shikei no Susume: Sekkyoku teki Shikei Kakudairon.* Tokyo: Chuo Koron.

Nagayama, Norio. 1990. *Muchi no Namida.* Tokyo: Kawade.

"Nam Cam: Vietnam's Godfather." 2004. BBC News. June 3.

Nanjappa, Vicky. 2008. "Why Bangalore Is India's Suicide Capital." *Rediff.* February 14.

Nariman, Fali S. 2006. *India's Legal System: Can It Be Saved?* New Delhi: Penguin.

Nathan, Andrew J. 1985. *Chinese Democracy.* Berkeley: University of California Press.

Nathan, Andrew J. 2005. "Jade and Plastic." *London Review of Books.* November 17.

Nathan, Andrew J. 2006. "The Bloody Enigma." *New Republic Online.* November 17.

Nathan, Andrew J., and Bruce Gilley. 2003. *China's New Rulers: The Secret Files.* 2nd rev. ed. New York: New York Review Books.

Nathan, John. 2004. *Japan Unbound: A Volatile Nation's Quest for Pride and Purpose.* Boston: Houghton Mifflin.

Nazar, Nazia. 2008. "Relief, But for Whom?" *The Post of Pakistan.* July 9.

Neary, Ian. 2002. *Human Rights in Japan, Korea, and Taiwan.* London: Routledge.

Nelson, Paul J., and Ellen Dorsey. 2008. *New Rights Advocacy: Changing Strategies of Democracy and Human Rights NGOs.* Washington, DC: Georgetown University Press.

Neumayer, Eric. 2008. "Death Penalty: The Political Foundations of the Global Trend toward Abolition." *Human Rights Review* 9(2):241–268.

Nevins, Joseph. 2005. *A Not-so-Distant Horror: Mass Violence in East Timor.* Ithaca, NY: Cornell University Press.

Ni, Jian. 2007. "A Cold, Hard Look at the Supreme Court's 'Expansion of the Ranks' of Criminal Judges." *Dui Hua Human Rights Journal.* November 25. [Originally published in Chinese in *Beijing News,* November 21.]

"No Death Penalty Handed down So Far over Lhasa Violence." 2008. *Xinhua.* July 11.

Nomani, Asra Q. 2007. "India's New Untouchables." *Honolulu Advertiser.* November 11.

"N. Korea Resumes Public Executions." 2007. *Honolulu Advertiser.* November 27.

Nowak, Manfred. 2006. "Mission to China: Civil and Political Rights, including the Question of Torture and Detention—Report of the Special Rapporteur on Torture and Other Cruel, Inhuman or Degrading Treatment of Punishment." United Nations Commission on Human Rights. March 10.

Nussbaum, Martha C. 2007. *The Clash Within: Democracy, Religious Violence, and India's Future.* Cambridge, MA: Harvard University Presss.

Oberdorfer, Don. 2005. "Seoul Chooses Sides." *Los Angeles Times.* November 19.

Oberwittler, Dietrich, and Shenghui Qi. 2008. "Death Penalty Population Survey: Preliminary Results." Max Planck Institute, Freiburg, Germany. April (version 21).

O'Brien, Kevin J., and Lianjiang Li. 2006. *Rightful Resistance in Rural China.* New York: Cambridge University Press.

Oehlers, Alfred, and Nicole Tarulevicz. 2005. "Capital Punishment and the Culture of Developmentalism in Singapore." In Austin Sarat and Christian Boulanger, eds., *The Cultural Lives of Capital Punishment: Comparative Perspectives.* Stanford, CA: Stanford University Press, 291–307.

Oldenburg, Philip. 2007. "India's Democracy: Illusion or Reality?" *Education about Asia* 12(Winter):5–11.

Oliver, Robert T. 1951. *The Truth about Korea.* London: Unwin.

Oliveros, Benjie. 2007. "The Logic of Killers." *Cebu Daily News* and inquirer.net. March 5.

O'Neill, Tom. 2003. "Untouchable." With photographs by William Albert Allard. *National Geographic* (June):2–31.

Onishi, Norimitsu. 2006. "China's Youth Look to Seoul for Inspiration." *New York Times.* January 2.

Onishi, Norimitsu. 2007a. "The Evolution of a Man Called 'Bulldozer': Man in the News—Lee Myung-Bak." *New York Times.* December 20.

Onishi, Norimitsu. 2007b. "Lee Wins Election for Presidency in South Korea." *New York Times.* December 20.

Onishi, Norimitsu. 2007c. "Whaling: A Japanese Obsession with American Roots." *New York Times.* March 14.

Ono, Takeo. 1963. *Edo no Keibatsu Fuzokushi.* Tokyo: Tenbosha.

"Openness on Executions a Welcome Change." *Daily Yomiuri.* 2007. December 8.

"Order in the Jungle." 2008. *Economist.* March 15:83–85.

Orendain, Joan. 2008. *Not in Our Name: The Story of the Abolition of the Death Penalty in the Philippines.* Manila: Free Legal Assistance Group.

"Over 90% of Uzbeks Support Abolition of Death Penalty." 2008. *Central Asian News.* July 15.

Paddock, Richard C. 2006. "Thai Prime Minister Resigns, Hands Power to Deputy." *Honolulu Advertiser.* April 5.

"Palace: GMA Intervention Saved 24 OFWs from Execution." 2008. *Philippine Star.* July 21.

"Palace Not Keen on Zubiri's Call to Revive Death Penalty." 2008. GMA News. May 17.

Palais, James B. 1996. *Confucian Statecraft and Korean Institutions: Yu Hyongwon and the Late Choson Dynasty.* Seattle: University of Washington Press.

Pan, Philip P. 2008. *Out of Mao's Shadow: The Struggle for the Soul of a New China.* New York: Simon and Schuster.

Panagariva, Aryind. 2008. *India: The Emerging Giant.* New York: Oxford University Press.

Panganiban, Artemio V. 2003. "Judicial Globalization." Paper presented to the first Australasia Judicial Educators Forum, Makati City, Philippines. February 14.

Panganiban, Artemio V. 2006. "Abolish the Death Penalty." Address delivered at the launching of *Legal Reference of Capital Cases,* University of the Philippines, Manila, May 31.

Pape, Robert A. 2005. *Dying to Win: The Strategic Logic of Suicide Terrorism.* New York: Random House.

Park, Won-soon. 1993. *The National Security Law.* Los Angeles: Korea NGO Network for the United Nations World Conference on Human Rights.

"The Party Is Over." 2007. *Economist.* May 31.

Payne, James L. 2004. *A History of Force: Exploring the Worldwide Movement against Habits of Coercion, Bloodshed, and Mayhem.* Sandpoint, ID: Lytton.

Peerenboom, Randall, ed. 2004. *Asian Discourses of Rule of Law: Theories and Implementation of Rule of Law in Twelve Asian Countries, France and the U.S.* London: RoutledgeCurzon.

Peerenboom, Randall. 2006. "The Fire-Breathing Dragon and the Cute, Cuddly Panda: The Implications of China's Rise for Developing Countries, Human Rights, and Geopolitical Stability." Unpublished paper.

Peerenboom, Randall. 2007. *China Modernizes: Threat to the West or Model for the Rest?* New York: Oxford University Press.

Peerenboom, Randall, Carole Petersen, and Albert Chen, eds. 2006. *Human Rights in Asia: A Comparative Legal Study of Twelve Asian Jurisdictions, France, and the U.S.* London: Routledge.

Pempel, T. J., ed. 2005. *Remapping East Asia: The Construction of a Region.* Ithaca, NY: Cornell University Press.

Perry, Alex. 2003. "Urban Cowboys." *Time.* January 6.

Perry, Elizabeth J., and Mark Selden, eds. 2000. *Chinese Society: Change, Conflict and Resistance.* 2nd ed. London: RoutledgeCurzon.

Peterson, Ruth D., and William C. Bailey. 2003. "Is Capital Punishment an Effective Deterrent for Murder? An Examination of Social Science Research." In James R. Acker, Robert M. Bohm, and Charles S. Lanier, eds., *America's Experiment with Capital Punishment: Reflections on the Past, Present, and Future of the Ultimate Penal Sanction.* Durham, NC: Carolina Academic Press, 251–282.

"Philippine Rebels Waning." 2008. *Honolulu Star Bulletin.* January 13.

Pimentel, Aquilino, Jr. 2006. *Martial Law in the Philippines: My Story.* Manila: Cacho Hermanos.

Pimentel-Simbulan, Nymia. 2005. "Violence and Deception: Survival Tools of the Embattled GMA Government." *Human Rights Forum* [Philippine Human Rights Information Center] 2(3):3–7.

Pinker, Steven. 2007. "A History of Violence: We're Getting Nicer Every Day." *New Republic.* March 19:18–21.

"Poll Shows Filipinos Favor Death Penalty." 1992. *Free Press.* November 7.

Pomeranz, Kenneth. 2000. *The Great Divergence: China, Europe, and the Making of the Modern World Economy.* Princeton, NJ: Princeton University Press.

Pomfret, John. 2003. "Taiwan's Top Agitator as Bold as Ever: Popular Ex-president's Campaign for Independence Fraught with Risks." *Daily Yomiuri.* October 13. [Originally published in *Washington Post.*]

Pongsudhirak, Thitinan. 2006. "A Test for Thai Democracy." *Japan Times.* March 18.

Porter, Eduardo. 2007. "China Shrinks." *New York Times.* December 9.

Potter, Pitman B. 2001. *The Chinese Legal System: Globalization and Local Legal Culture.* London: Routledge.

Potter, Pitman B. 2004. "Legal Reform in China: Institutions, Culture, and Selective Adaptation. *Law and Social Inquiry* 29(2):465–495.

Pratirodh. 2007. "The Indian State's Killing Squads." August 9. http://pratirodh. blogspot.com/2007/08/indian-states-killing-squads.html.

"Pregnancy Saves Vietnam Convict." 2006. *Honolulu Advertiser.* October 13.

Prejean, Sister Helen. 1993. *Dead Man Walking: An Eyewitness Account of the Death Penalty in the United States.* New York: Vintage Books.

Prejean, Sister Helen. 2005. *The Death of Innocents: An Eyewitness Account of Wrongful Executions.* New York: Random House.

"Profile: Roh Moo-hyun." 2004. BBC News. May 14.

Pu, Ning. 1994. *Red in Tooth and Claw: Twenty-six Years in Communist Chinese Prisons*. New York: Grove Press.

Puhar, Eva. 2003. "The Abolition of the Death Penalty in Central and Eastern Europe: A Survey of Abolition Processes in Former Communist Countries." Master's thesis, National University of Ireland. www.wmin.ac.uk/law/pdf/Eva.pdf.

"A Punishment That Hurts Those Who Carry It Out." www.asahi.com. 2007. March 9.

"Purse-Snatching Death Penalty Introduced in China." 2006. Australian Broadcasting Corporation. March 4.

Putnam, Robert D. 1993. *Making Democracy Work: Civic Traditions in Modern Italy*. Princeton, NJ: Princeton University Press.

Pyle, Kenneth B. 1974. "Advantages of Followership: German Economics and Japanese Bureaucrats, 1890–1925." *Journal of Japanese Studies* 1(1):127–164.

Pyle, Kenneth B. 2006. "Profound Forces in the Making of Modern Japan." *Journal of Japanese Studies* 2:393–418.

Pyle, Kenneth B. 2007. *Japan Rising: The Resurgence of Japanese Power and Purpose*. New York: PublicAffairs.

Qi, Shenghui. 2005. "Strike Hard." *China Review* 33(Summer):6–9. www.gbcc.orguk/33article4.htm.

Qu, Xinjiu. 2005. "An Analysis of the Strike-Hard Criminal Policy." *Contemporary Chinese Thought* 36(3):77–88.

"A Question of Revenge." 2001. *Economist*. January 27:40.

Rabkin, April. 2008. "China's Inside Game." *New York Times*. July 2.

Radzinowicz, Leon. 1948. *A History of English Criminal Law and Its Administration from 1750*. 5 vols. London: Stevens.

Radzinowicz, Leon. 1999. *Adventures in Criminology*. London: Routledge.

Rafferty, Kevin. 2006. "Thaksin Best Underscores Fatal Flaws of His Kind of Rule." *Japan Times*. June 6.

Raghavan, R. 2004. "India." *World Factbook of Criminal Justice Systems*. http://nicic.org/Library/019426.

Ragin, Charles C. 1987. *The Comparative Method: Moving beyond Qualitative and Quantitative Strategies*. Berkeley: University of California Press.

Rahn, Kim. 2006. "Life Sentence Could Replace Death Penalty." *Korea Times*. February 21.

Ramseyer, J. Mark, and Eric B. Rasmusen. 2003. *Measuring Judicial Independence: The Political Economy of Judging in Japan*. Chicago: University of Chicago Press.

Ramzy, Austin. 2004. "Up in Arms: A Rash of Gun Crimes Strikes Taiwan." *Time Asia*. August 9.

Rayfield, Donald. 2005. *Stalin and His Hangmen: The Tyrant and Those Who Killed for Him*. New York: Random House.

Reid, T. R. 1999. *Confucius Lives Next Door: What Living in the East Teaches Us about Living in the West*. New York: Random House.

"Remove Justice Minister from Execution Process: Hatoyama." 2007. *Japan Times*. September 26.

Richards, Mike. 2002. *The Hanged Man: The Life and Death of Ronald Ryan*. Carlton North, Australia: Scribe.

Richie, Donald. 2008. "Old Royal Siam Revisited." *Japan Times*. June 1.

Rickards, Jane. 2008. "Former Taiwan Officials Face Corruption Charges." *Washington Post*. July 15.

Rigoulot, Pierre. 1999. "Crimes, Terror, and Secrecy in North Korea." In Stephane Courtois, Nicolas Werth, Jean-Louis Panne, Andrzej Paczkowski, Karel Bartosek, and

Jean-Louis Margolin, *The Black Book of Communism: Crime, Terror, Repression.* Cambridge, MA: Harvard University Press, 547–564.

Roberts, Aki, and Gary LaFree. 2004. "Explaining Japan's Postwar Violent Crime Trends." *Criminology* 42(1):179–209.

Roberts, Gregory David. 2003. *Shantaram: A Novel.* New York: St. Martin's Griffin.

Roberts, Larry. 1999. "Trinidad Executes Nine in Four Days." World Socialist Web site. June 17. www.wsws.org/articles/1999/jun1999/cari-j17.shtml.

Rohlen, Thomas P. 1992. "Learning: The Mobilization of Knowledge in the Japanese Political Economy." In Shumpei Kumon and Henry Rosovsky, eds., *The Political Economy of Japan,* vol. 3, *Cultural and Social Dynamics.* Stanford, CA: Stanford University Press.

Romero, Alexis Douglas B. 2007. "Survey Shows Arroyo Administration Facing Intense Corruption Allegation." *BusinessWorld.* December 12.

Rothman, David J., and Aryeh Neier. 1991. "India's Awful Prisons." *New York Review of Books* 28(9):53–56.

Rouwenhorst, Philip. 2007. "Death Penalty: U.N. Passes Symbolic Moratorium." Inter Press Service. December 18.

Rowe, William T. 2007. *Crimson Rain: Seven Centuries of Violence in a Chinese County.* Stanford, CA: Stanford University Press.

Rowen, Henry S. 2006. "The Predictable Consequences for Freedom of China's Economic Development." Paper presented at Conference on Democratization in Greater China: What Can We Learn from Taiwan's Past for China's Future? Stanford University, October 20–21.

Roy, Denny. 2003. *Taiwan: A Political History.* Ithaca, NY: Cornell University Press.

Rubinstein, Murray A. 2006. *Taiwan: A New History.* Armonk, NY: M. E. Sharpe.

Rummel, R. J. 1994. *Death by Government.* New Brunswick, NJ: Transaction.

Ryden, Edmund, ed. 2001. *Taiwan Opposes the Death Penalty.* Taipei: Department of Law and the John Paul II Peace Institute, Fujen Catholic University.

Safire, William. 1997. "The Misrule of Law." *New York Times.* June 1.

Safire, William. 1999. "The Dictator Speaks: A Chat with Lee Kuan Yew." *New York Times.* February 15.

Saifee, Faisal. 2005. "Dead Certain? A Critical Study of the Standard of Proof in Philippine Death Penalty Cases." Occasional Papers, vol. 2, Centre for Capital Punishment Studies, University of Westminster, 36–47.

Sainath, P. 1996. *Everybody Loves a Good Draught: Stories from India's Poorest Districts.* New Delhi: Penguin.

Sakagami, Kaori. 2008. "Futatsu no 'Shikei' Seido: Nichibei no 'Korosu' Bunka o Kangaenaosu." *Sekai* 782(September):173–181.

Sakamoto, Toshio. 2003. *Shikei wa Ika ni Shikko Sareru ka.* Tokyo: Nihon Bungeisha.

Sakamoto, Toshio. 2007. "Even Death-Row Inmates Deserve a Second Chance." www.asahi.com. January 13.

Salak, Kira. 2001. *Four Corners: One Woman's Solo Journey into the Heart of Papua New Guinea.* Washington, DC: National Geographic.

Salaverria, Leila. 2007. "Ninety-nine Special Courts to Try Political Killings." inquirer.net. March 5.

Samuels, Richard J. 2003. *Machiavelli's Children: Leaders and Their Legacies in Italy and Japan.* Ithaca, NY: Cornell University Press.

Samuels, Richard J. 2007. *Securing Japan: Tokyo's Grand Strategy and the Future of East Asia.* Ithaca, NY: Cornell University Press.

Sangara, Satyaprakasa. 1998. *Crime and Punishment in Mughal India*. New Delhi: Reliange.

Sansom, George Bailey. 1978. *Japan: A Short Cultural History*. Rev. ed. Palo Alto, CA: Stanford University Press. [Originally published 1931.]

Sarat, Austin, ed. 1999. *The Killing State: Capital Punishment in Law, Politics, and Culture*. New York: Oxford University Press.

Sarat, Austin. 2001. *When the State Kills: Capital Punishment and the American Condition*. Princeton, NJ: Princeton University Press.

Sarat, Austin. 2005. *Mercy on Trial: What It Means to Stop an Execution*. Princeton, NJ: Princeton University Press.

Sarat, Austin, and Christian Boulanger, eds. 2005. *The Cultural Lives of Capital Punishment: Comparative Perspectives*. Stanford, CA: Stanford University Press.

SarDesai, D. R. 2005. *Vietnam: Past and Present*. 4th ed. Boulder, CO: Westview Press.

Sarkar, Priyanko. 2008. "'Even Molesters Should Get the Death Penalty.'" *Times of India*. July 13.

Sarwar, Beena. 2008a. "Death Penalty—Pakistan: Reprieve Call Could Save Thousands." *Inter Press Service*. July 4.

Sarwar, Beena. 2008b. "Pakistan and the Death Penalty: Time to Call It Quits." *The Women's International Perspective*. July 22.

Sato, Iwao. 2002. "Judicial Reform in Japan in the 1990s: Increase of the Legal Profession, Reinforcement of Judicial Functions, and Expansion of the Rule of Law. *Social Science Japan Journal* 5(1):71–83.

Sato, Masako. 2001. *Gyakutai Sareta Kodomotachi no Gyakushu: Okasan no Sei Desu ka*. Tokyo: Akashi Shoten.

Sato, Tomoyuki. 1994. *Shikei no Nihonshi*. Tokyo: Sanichi Shobo.

Schabas, William A. 2000. "Life, Death and the Crime of Crimes: Supreme Penalties and the ICC Statute." *Punishment and Society* 2(3):163–285.

Schabas, William A. 2002. *The Abolition of the Death Penalty in International Law*. 3rd ed. Cambridge: Cambridge University Press.

Schabas, William A. 2004. "International Law, Politics, Diplomacy and the Abolition of the Death Penalty." *William and Mary Bill of Rights Journal* 13:417–444.

Schaede, Ulrike, and William Grimes, eds. 2003. *Japan's Managed Globalization: Adapting to the Twenty-first Century*. Armonk, NY: M. E. Sharpe.

Schell, Orville. 1996. "Unheavenly Kingdom." *New York Times*. February 4.

Schell, Orville. 2006. "History Majors." *New York Times*. August 6.

Schell, Orville. 2008. "Descendants of the Dragons." *New York Times*. July 27.

Schmidt, Petra. 2002. *Capital Punishment in Japan*. Leiden: Brill.

Schoenhals, Michael. 1996. "The Central Case Examination Group, 1966–79." *China Quarterly* 145(March):87–111.

Schoppa, Leonard. 2006. *Race for the Exits: The Unraveling of Japan's System of Social Protection*. Ithaca, NY: Cornell University Press.

Schreiber, Mark. 1996. *Shocking Crimes of Postwar Japan*. Tokyo: Yenbooks.

Schreiber, Mark. 2001. *The Dark Side: Infamous Japanese Crimes and Criminals*. Tokyo: Kodansha International.

Schwartz, Benjamin I. 1985. *The World of Thought in Ancient China*. Cambridge, MA: Harvard University Press.

Scobell, Andrew. 1990. "The Death Penalty in Post-Mao China." *China Quarterly* 123 (September):503–520.

Scobell, Andrew. 1991. "The Death Penalty under Socialism, 1917–1990: China, the Soviet Union, Cuba, and the German Democratic Republic." *Criminal Justice History: An International Annual* 12:160–234.

Scurr, Ruth. 2006. *Fatal Purity: Robespierre and the French Revolution.* New York: Metropolitan Books.

Sen, Amartya. 1992. *Inequality Reexamined.* Cambridge, MA: Harvard University Press.

Sen, Amartya. 2005. *The Argumentative Indian: Writings on Indian History, Culture, and Identity.* New York: Picador.

Sengupta, Somini. 2008. "A Daughter of India's Underclass Rises on Votes That Cross Caste Lines." *New York Times.* July 18.

Seo, Dong-shin. 2004. "Climate Ripe at Assembly for Abolition of Death Penalty." *Korea Times.* November 24.

Seo, Dong-shin. 2005. "Constitutional Justice Nominee Says Death Penalty Should Go." *Korea Times.* July 4.

Seow, Francis T. 1994. *To Catch a Tartar: A Dissident in Lee Kuan Yew's Prison.* New Haven, CT: Yale University Southeast Asian Studies.

Seow, Francis T. 2006. *Beyond Suspicion? The Singapore Judiciary.* New Haven, CT: Yale University Southeast Asian Studies.

Ser, Myo-ja. 2008. "Death Penalty Sought for Crimes against Children." *Joong Ang Daily.* April 2.

Service, Robert. 2006. *Stalin: A Biography.* Cambridge, MA: Belknap Press.

Seymour, James D. 2005. "Sizing up China's Prisons." In Borge Bakken, ed., *Crime, Punishment, and Policing in China.* Lanham, MD: Rowman and Littlefield, 141–167.

Seymour, James D., and Richard Anderson. 1998. *New Ghosts, Old Ghosts: Prisons and Labor Reform Camps in China.* Armonk, NY: M. E. Sharpe.

Shakya, Tsering. 2000. *The Dragon in the Land of Snows: A History of Modern Tibet since 1947.* New York: Penguin.

Shambaugh, David, ed. 2005. *Power Shift: China and Asia's New Dynamics.* Berkeley: University of California Press.

Shambaugh, David. 2008. *China's Communist Party: Atrophy and Adaptation.* Berkeley: University of California Press.

Shane, Scott. 2008. "China Inspired Interrogations at Guantanamo." *New York Times.* July 4.

Shankardass, Rani Dhavan, ed. 2000. *Punishment and the Prison: Indian and International Perspectives.* New Delhi: Sage.

Shapiro, Judith. 2006. "Red Guards." *New York Times.* October 8.

Shaw, Sin-Ming. 2006. "Wasted Chance as Taiwan's President." *Japan Times.* November 15.

Sherman, Lawrence W. 2004. "Evidence-based Crime Prevention: A Global View from the U.S. to Japan." *Hanzai Shakaigaku Kenkyu* [Japanese journal of sociological criminology] 29:82–93.

Shia, Ben Chang. 2001. "Survey on Abolition." In Edmund Ryden, ed., *Taiwan Opposes the Death Penalty.* Taipei: Fujen University John Paul II Peace Institute, 67–80.

Shikei Haishi Henshu Iinkai. 1996. *"Oumu ni Shikei o" ni Do Kotaeru ka.* Tokyo: Impakuto Press.

Shikei Haishi Henshu Iinkai. 1997. *Shikei Sonchi to Haishi no Deai.* Tokyo: Impakuto Press.

Shikei Haishi Henshu Iinkai. 1998. *Hanzai Higaisha to Shikei Seido.* Tokyo: Impakuto Press.

Shikei Haishi Henshu Iinkai. 1999. *Shikei to Joho Kokai*. Tokyo: Impakuto Press.
Shikei Haishi Henshu Iinkai. 2000–2001. *Shushinkei o Kangaeru*. Tokyo: Impakuto Press.
Shikei Haishi Henshu Iinkai. 2002. *Sekai no Naka no Nihon no Shikei*. Tokyo: Impakuto Press.
Shikei Haishi Henshu Iinkai. 2003. *Shikei Haishi Hoan*. Tokyo: Impakuto Press.
Shikei Haishi Henshu Iinkai. 2004. *Mujitsu no Shikeishu-tachi*. Tokyo: Impakuto Press.
Shikei Haishi Henshu Iinkai. 2005. *Oumu Jiken Ju-nen*. Tokyo: Impakuto Press.
Shikei Haishi Henshu Iinkai. 2006. *Hikari-shi Saiban: Naze Terebi wa Shikei o Motomeru no ka*. Tokyo: Impakuto Press.
Shikei Haishi Henshu Iinkai. 2007. *Anata mo Shikei Hanketsu o Kakasareru*. Tokyo: Impakuto Press.
"Shikei no Genzai." 1990. Special issue. *Hogaku Semina*. December.
Shim, Jae-yun. 2005. "Justice Minister Opposes Abolition of Death Penalty." *Korea Times*. March 29.
Shimizu, Kaho. 2002. "Time Is Ripe: Diet Group against Death Penalty to Make Its Move." *Japan Times*. October 4.
Shirk, Susan L. 2007. *China: Fragile Superpower*. New York: Oxford University Press.
Short, Philip. 2000. *Mao: A Life*. New York: Holt.
Short, Philip. 2004. *Pol Pot: Anatomy of a Nightmare*. New York: Holt.
"Shushinkei: Ze ka Hi ka." 2008. *Asahi Shimbun*. June 8.
Sidel, John T. 1999. *Capital, Coercion, and Crime: Bossism in the Philippines*. Palo Alto, CA: Stanford University Press.
Sieg, Linda. 2007. "Japan Death Row Inmates near One Hundred amid Crime Fears." Reuters. February 8.
"Silent Night: The Government Cracks Down on Bars." 2004. *Economist*. March 6:32.
Silvia, Stephen J., and Aaron Beers Sampson. 2001. "The New Abolitionism: American or European Exceptionalism Regarding the Death Penalty." New York: Council for European Studies at Columbia University. September.
Simmons, Beth A., and Zachary Elkins. 2004. "The Globalization of Liberalization: Policy Diffusion in the International Political Economy." *American Political Science Review* 98:171–189.
Simon, Jonathan. 2007. *Governing through Crime*. Chicago: University of Chicago Press.
Simon, Rita J., and Dagny A. Blaskovich. 2002. *A Comparative Analysis of Capital Punishment: Statutes, Policies, Frequencies, and Public Attitudes the World Over*. Lanham, MD: Lexington Books.
Singapore Ministry of Home Affairs. 2004. "The Singapore Government's Response to Amnesty International Report 'Singapore—The Death Penalty: A Hidden Toll of Executions.'" Government publication. January 30.
"Singapore: World Execution Capital." 1999. *Economist*. April 3–9:25.
Skinner, E. Benjamin. 2008. "Slavery's Staying Power." *Los Angeles Times*. March 23.
Smelser, Neil J. 1998. "The Rational and the Ambivalent in the Social Sciences: 1997 Presidential Address." *American Sociological Review* 63(1):1–16.
Sommer, Matthew H. 2000. *Sex, Law, and Society in Late Imperial China*. Stanford, CA: Stanford University Press.
"Soryushi." 2008. *Asahi Shimbun* (evening edition). June 18.
Sotooka, Hidetoshi. 2006. "Interview: Kim Dae Jung: For Peace in Asia, Japan Must Switch Course." www.asahi.com.
"South Korea Close to Ending Death Penalty." 2006. *Korea Times*. February 21.

"South Korea Man Sentenced to Life for Subway Arson." 2003. *Daily Yomiuri.* August 7.

"S. Korea Marks Ten-year Moratorium on Death Penalty." 2007. Agence France-Presse. December 31.

Spence, Jonathan D. 1974. *Emperor of China: Self-Portrait of K'ang-hsi.* New York: Vintage Books.

Spence, Jonathan D. 1990. *The Search for Modern China.* New York: Norton.

Spence, Jonathan D. 1995. "In China's Gulag." *New York Review of Books* 42(13).

Spence, Jonathan D. 1996. *God's Chinese Son: The Taiping Heavenly Kingdom of Hong Xiuquan.* New York: Norton.

Spence, Jonathan D. 2005. "Portrait of a Monster." *New York Review of Books* 52(17).

Spence, Jonathan D. 2006. "China's Great Terror." *New York Review of Books* 53(14).

Spierenburg, Pieter. 1995. "The Body and the State: Early Modern Europe." In Norval Morris and David J. Rothman, eds., *The Oxford History of the Prison: The Practice of Punishment in Western Society.* New York: Oxford University Press, 48–77.

Stamatel, Janet P. 2006. "Incorporating Socio-historical Context into Quantitative Cross-national Criminology." *International Journal of Comparative and Applied Criminal Justice* 30(2): 177–207.

Stark, Rodney. 2005. *The Victory of Reason: How Christianity Led to Freedom, Capitalism, and Western Success.* New York: Random House.

"State of Education: Making It up in Volume?" 2007. *Atlantic Monthly* (January/February):101.

"State without Pity." 2007. *New York Times.* December 27.

Steiker, Carol S. 2002. "Capital Punishment and American Exceptionalism." *Oregon Law Review* 81:97–130.

Steinberg, David Joel. 2000. *The Philippines: A Singular and Plural Place.* 4th ed. Boulder, CO: Westview Press.

Stephens, Thomas B. 1992. *Order and Discipline in China: The Shanghai Mixed Court 1911–1927.* Seattle: University of Washington Press.

Stille, Alexander. 2006. *The Sack of Rome: How a Beautiful European Country with a Fabled History and a Storied Culture Was Taken over by a Man Named Silvio Berlusconi.* New York: Penguin.

Struck, Doug. 2001. "On Japan's Death Row, Uncertainty by Design." *Washington Post.* May 3.

Studwell, Joe. 2007. *Asian Godfathers: Money and Power in Hong Kong and Southeast Asia.* New York: Atlantic Monthly Press.

Subramanian, K. S. 2007. *Political Violence and the Police in India.* Thousand Oaks, CA: Sage.

Subramanian, Nirupama. 2008. "Commutation Will Benefit 7,000 Prisoners on Death Row: Gilani." *The Hindu.* June 22.

Sullivan, Tim. 2008. "In India, Young University Caters to Masses." *Honolulu Advertiser.* January 3.

Sun, Lena H. 1994. "China's Social Changes Spur More Executions: Families Don't See the Body, but They Pay for the Bullet." *Washington Post.* March 27.

Sundby, Scott E. 2007. *A Life and Death Decision: A Jury Weighs the Death Penalty.* New York: Palgrave Macmillan.

Sung, Hung-En. 2006. "Democracy and Criminal Justice in Cross-national Perspective: From Crime Control to Due Process." In Suzanne Karstedt and Gary LaFree, eds., *The ANNALS of the American Academy of Political and Social Science* 605(1):311–337.

Sunga, Ricardo A., III. 2006. *Legal Reference on Capital Cases. Volume II: Murder and Parricide*. Quezon City: Free Legal Assistance Group.

"Support for Death Penalty Passes 80% for First Time." 2005. *Japan Times*. February 20.

"Suspected Serial Killer Charges Court Bench." 2004. *Chosun Ilbo*. September 21.

"Suspended Death Sentences Exceed Immediate Executions for First Time." 2007. *Xinhua*. November 23.

Suzuki, Izumi. 2007. "'Guilty until Proven Innocent' Unjust to Accused." www.asahi .com. February 14.

Suzuki, Keio, ed. 2007. *Toajia no Shikei Haishi Ronko*. Tokyo: Seibundo.

Svensson, Marina. 2001. "State Coercion, Deterrence, and the Death Penalty in the PRC." Paper presented at the annual meeting of the Association for Asian Studies, Chicago, March 22–25.

Tagayuna, Arlie. 2004. "Capital Punishment in the Philippines." *Explorations in Southeast Asian Studies* 5(1):1–27. www.hawaii.edu/cseas/pubs/explore/v5/v015n01.html.

Taiwan Alliance to End the Death Penalty. 2004. Report prepared for the 2nd World Congress against the Death Penalty, Montreal.

"Taiwan Must Not Abolish Its Death Penalty." 2008. *The China Post*. April 25.

Takano, Takashi. 2004. "Jiken Kiroku: Shinri Igai no Katsuyo mo Mitomeyo." *Asahi Shimbun*. May 18.

Takamura, Kaoru. 2008. "Death Sentence for Itoh Slaying Highly Suspect." www.asahi .com. June 18.

Takayama, Shunkichi. 2006. *Saibanin Seido wa Iranai*. Tokyo: Kodansha.

"Takuma Hangs for Massacre of Eight Kids at Osaka School." 2004. *Japan Times*. September 15.

Taleb, Nassim Nicholas. 2007. *The Black Swan: The Impact of the Highly Improbable*. New York: Random House.

Tamil Nation. 2007. www.tamilnation.org/indictment/disappearances/index.htm.

Tan, Amy. 2002. "Singapore Death Penalty Shrouded in Silence." Reuters. April 12. www.singapore-window.org/sw02/020412re.htm.

Tanaka, Fumio. 2006. "Lay Judge Rulings Need Debate: Court Survey Shows Opinions Vary on Type, Length of Sentence." *Daily Yomiuri Online*. December 26. www.yomiuri.co.jp/dy/national/20061226TDY03001.htm.

Tanaka, Fumio, and Tsukasa Kinoshita. 2008. "Miyazaki Case Puts Death Penalty in Spotlight." *Daily Yomiuri*. June 19.

Tanner, Harold M. 1999. *Strike Hard! Anti-Crime Campaigns and Chinese Criminal Justice, 1979–1985*. Ithaca, NY: Cornell University East Asia Program.

Tanner, Harold M. 2007. "China's Law and Government in the Mao Years (1949–1976)." *Education about Asia* 12(3):18–24.

Tanner, Murray Scot. 2000. "State Coercion and the Balance of Awe: The 1983–1986 'Stern Blows' Anti-crime Campaign." *China Journal* (July):93–125.

Tanner, Murray Scot. 2005. "Campaign-Style Policing in China and Its Critics." In Borge Bakken, ed., *Crime, Punishment, and Policing in China*. Lanham, MD: Rowman and Littlefield, 171–188.

Tanner, Murray Scot, and Eric Green. 2007. "Principals and Secret Agents: Central versus Local Controls over Policing and Obstacles to 'Rule of Law' in China." *China Quarterly* 191(September):644–670.

Tate, C. Neal, and Stacia L. Haynie. 1993. "Authoritarianism and the Functions of the Courts: A Time Series Analysis of the Philippine Supreme Court, 1961–1981." *Law and Society Review* 27:707–740.

Tavernise, Sabrina. 2008. "For West, No Good Answer to Uzbekistan." *International Herald Tribune.* May 30.

Te, Theodore O. 1999. "Words Will Never Be Enough: Eyewitness Accounts of the Executions of Leo Echegaray and Pablito Andan." In Free Legal Assistance Group of the Philippines, 2004, *Primer on Lethal Injection in the Philippines.* Quezon City: Free Legal Assistance Group, 5–6.

Te, Theodore O. 2006. *Legal Reference on Capital Cases*, vol. 1, *Rape.* Quezon City: Free Legal Assistance Group, 1–83.

Templer, Robert. 1998. *Shadows and Wind: A View of Modern Vietnam.* New York: Penguin.

Terwiel, Barend Jan. 2008. *Traveler in Siam in the Year 1655: Extracts from the Journal of Gijsbert Heeck.* Chiang Mai: Silkworm Books.

Tetlock, Philip E. 2005. *Expert Political Judgment: How Good Is It? How Can We Know?* Princeton, NJ: Princeton University Press.

Thacher, David. 2006. "The Normative Case Study." *American Journal of Sociology* 111(May):1631–1676.

"Thailand Fears More Attacks after Dubious 'Ceasefire.'" 2008. *New York Times.* July 18.

Tharoor, Shashi. 2007a. *The Elephant, the Tiger, and the Cellphone.* New Delhi: Penguin.

Tharoor, Shashi. 2007b. *India: From Midnight to the Millennium and Beyond.* Rev. and updated. New Delhi: Penguin.

Thomas, Cullen. 2007. *Brother One Cell: An American Coming of Age in South Korea's Prisons.* New York: Viking.

Thompson, Michael, Richard Ellis, and Aaron Wildavsky. 1990. *Cultural Theory.* Boulder, CO: Westview Press.

"Three Japanese Prisoners Executed." 2008. BBC News. February 1.

"Three Murderers Executed." 2007. www.asahi.com. April 27.

Thurow, Lester. 2007. "A Chinese Century? Maybe It's the Next One." *New York Times.* August 19.

"Time Is Ripe for Open Debate on Abolition." 2008. Editorial. *Korea Times.* January 1.

Timmons, Patrick. 2005. "Seed of Abolition: Experience and Culture in the Desire to End Capital Punishment in Mexico, 1841–1857." In Austin Sarat and Christian Boulanger, eds., *The Cultural Lives of Capital Punishment: Comparative Perspectives.* Stanford, CA: Stanford University Press, 69–91.

Tokyo Bengoshikai Jinken Hogo Iinkai—Keiho "Kaisei" Mondai Taisaku Tokubetsu Iinkai. 1994. *Shikei Sompai Mondai ni kan suru Tokyo Bengoshikai Kaain Anketo Chosa Hokokusho.* Tokyo: Tokyo Bar Association.

Tomiya, Itaru, ed. 2008. *Toajia no Shikei.* Kyoto: Kyoto Daigaku Gakujutsu Shuppankai.

Toms, Sarah. 2006a. "Philippines' Death Penalty Debate." BBC News. June 26.

Toms, Sarah. 2006b. "Philippines Stops Death Penalty." BBC News. June 24.

Tonry, Michael. 2007. "Determinants of Penal Policies." In Michael Tonry, ed., *Crime and Justice.* Chicago: University of Chicago Press, 1–34.

Toobin, Jeffrey. 2007. *The Nine: Inside the Secret World of the Supreme Court.* New York: Doubleday.

Totani, Yuma. 2008. *The Tokyo War Crimes Trial: The Pursuit of Justice in the Wake of World War II.* Cambridge, MA: Harvard University Asia Center.

Tran Dinh Thanh Lam. 2006. "In Capitalist Vietnam, Death to Bankers." *Asia Times.* August 24.

Tretiak, Daniel. 1970. "Political Assassinations in China, 1600–1968." In *Assassination and Political Violence*. Report to the National Commission on the Causes and Prevention of Violence. New York: Praeger.

Trevaskes, Susan. 2002. "Courts on the Campaign Path in China: Criminal Court Work in the 'Yanda' 2001 Anti-crime Campaign." *Asian Survey* 42(5):673–693.

Trevaskes, Susan. 2004. "Propaganda Work in Chinese Courts: Public Trials and Sentencing Rallies as Sites of Expressive Punishment and Public Education in the People's Republic of China." *Punishment and Society* 6(1):5–21.

Trevaskes, Susan. 2007. *Courts and Criminal Justice in Contemporary China*. Lanham, MD: Lexington Books.

Trevaskes, Susan. 2008. "The Death Penalty in China Today: Kill Fewer, Kill Cautiously." *Asian Survey* 48:393–413.

Trocki, Carl. 2006. *Singapore: Wealth, Power and the Culture of Control*. London: Routledge.

"The True State of C.S.I. Justice." 2007. Editorial. *New York Times*. January 29.

Truong, Nhu Tang. 1986. *A Vietcong Memoir: An Inside Account of the Vietnam War and Its Aftermath*. New York: Vintage.

Tsujimoto, Yoshio, and Isa Tsujimoto. 1993. *Ajia no Shikei*. Tokyo: Seibundo.

Turner, Karen G., James V. Feinerman, and R. Kent Guy, eds. 2000. *The Limits of the Rule of Law in China*. Seattle: University of Washington Press.

Turrell, Robert. 2004. *White Mercy: A Study of the Death Penalty in South Africa*. Westport, CT: Praeger.

Turow, Scott. 2003. *Ultimate Punishment: A Lawyer's Reflections on Dealing with the Death Penalty*. New York: Picador.

"229 Executed for Drug Trafficking in Past 30 Years." 2005. *Malaysiakini*. April 13. www.malaysiakini.com/news/35303.

Tyler, Patrick E. 1997. "Deng Xiaoping: A Political Wizard Who Put China on the Capitalist Road." *New York Times*. February 20.

"UN Condemns Japan's Execution of Three Prisoners." 2007. *Mainichi Daily News*. December 10.

"U.N. Death Penalty Moratorium Snubbed." 2007. www.asahi.com. December 20.

Upadhyaya, S. 1982. "Capital Punishment in a Changing Society." *Indian Journal of Criminology and Criminalistics* 2:197–201.

Upham, Frank K. 1987. *Law and Social Change in Postwar Japan*. Cambridge, MA: Harvard University Press.

U.S. Census Bureau. 2001. Census data for 2000.

U.S. Department of Justice, Bureau of Justice Statistics. 2006. Information on executions, 1930–2006. www.ojp.gov/bjs/correct.htm.

U.S. State Department, Bureau of International Narcotics and Law Enforcement Affairs. 2003. *International Narcotics Control Strategy Report*. Washington, DC: Government Printing Office.

Uy, Veronica. 2007. "Spanish King Lauds RP for Junking Death Penalty, Thanks OFWs." inquirer.net. December 4.

"Uzbekistan to End Death Penalty in 2008." 2005. Reuters. August 1.

"Uzbek Senate Votes to Abolish Death Penalty." 2007. Radio Free Europe. June 29.

Vagg, Jon. 1997. "Robbery, Death, and Irony: How an Armed Robbery Wave in Hong Kong Led to the Abolition of the Death Penalty." *Howard Journal of Criminal Justice* 34(4):393–405.

van der Sprenkel, S. 1971. *Legal Institutions in Manchu China: A Sociological Analysis.* London: Athlone Press.

van Wolferen, Karel. 1989. *The Enigma of Japanese Power: People and Politics in a Stateless Nation.* New York: Knopf.

Victoria, Brian Daizen. 2006. *Zen at War.* 2nd ed. Blue Ridge Summit, PA: Rowman and Littlefield.

Vieira, Constanza. 2007. "The 'Other' Death Penalty." Inter Press Service. October 12.

"Vietnam Buddhist Monk Speaks Out after Years in Prison." 2005. Alliance for Reform and Democracy in Asia. February 7.

"Vietnam Considers Dropping Death Penalty for Twelve Crimes." 2008. Associated Press. July 15. [From the *Vietnam News* of July 15, 2008.]

"Vietnam Officials Sacked for Mob Links." 2002. BBC News. July 16.

Vijayan, K. C. 2007. "Law Society: Give Judges Leeway to Set Aside Death Penalty." *Straits Times.* April 5.

Villamor, Ignacio. 1909. *Criminality in the Philippine Islands 1903–1908.* Manila: Bureau of Printing.

Vo, Nghia M. 2004. *The Bamboo Gulag: Political Imprisonment in Communist Vietnam.* Jefferson, NC: McFarland.

Vo, Van Ai. 2007. "Land Reform in North Vietnam." Research report by the president of the Vietnam Committee on Human Rights (affiliated with the International Federation of Human Rights in Paris).

Vogel, Ezra F. 1991. *The Four Little Dragons: The Spread of Industrialization in East Asia.* Cambridge, MA: Harvard University Press.

Vogel, Steven Kent. 2006. *Japan Remodeled: How Government and Industry Are Reforming Japanese Capitalism.* Ithaca, NY: Cornell University Press.

Vornic, Andre. 2008. "Japan MPs Moot Halt to Executions." BBC News. February 10.

Wakakuwa, Midori. 2005. *Kuatoro Ragattsui: Tensho Shonen Shisetsu to Sekai Teikoku* [Quattro Ragazzi: The Tensho Juvenile Mission and the Global Empire]. Tokyo: Shueisha.

Wakeman, Frederic, Jr. 1995. *Policing Shanghai, 1927–1937.* Berkeley: University of California Press.

Wakeman, Frederic, Jr. 2003. *Spymaster: Dai Li and the Chinese Secret Service.* Berkeley: University of California Press.

Waley, Arthur. 1958. *The Opium War through Chinese Eyes.* Stanford, CA: Stanford University Press.

Walmsley, Roy. 2004. *World Prison Population List.* 5th ed. Research finding no. 86. Home Office Research, Development and Statistics, Directorate.

Wang, Tay-sheng. 2000. *Legal Reform in Taiwan under Japanese Colonial Rule, 1895–1945.* Seattle: University of Washington Press.

Wang, Youquin. 2007. "The Past Is Not Another Country: An Interview with Wang Youquin." In Sharon Hom and Stacy Mosher, eds., *Challenging China: Struggle and Hope in an Era of Change.* New York and London: New Press, 175–182.

Wang, Yunhai. 2005. *Shikei no Hikaku Kenkyu: Chugoku, Beikoku, Nihon.* Tokyo: Seibundo.

Wang, Yunhai. 2008. "The Death Penalty and Society in Contemporary China." *Punishment and Society* 10:137–151.

Warrier, Shashi. 2000. *Hangman's Journal.* New Delhi: Penguin.

Waters, David M. 1997. "Korean Constitutionalism and the 'Special Act' to Prosecute Former Presidents Chun Doo-Hwan and Roh Tae-Woo." *Columbia Journal of Asian Law* 10(2):461–488.

Watson, James L. 2006. *Golden Arches East: McDonald's in East Asia.* 2nd ed. Stanford, CA: Stanford University Press.

Wehrfritz, George, and Joe Cochran. 2006. "A 'Fragile Foundation.'" *Newsweek.* April 3:22–23.

Weil, Elizabeth. 2007. "The Needle and the Damage Done." *New York Times Magazine.* February 11:46–51.

West, James M. 1997. "Martial Lawlessness: The Legal Aftermath of Kwangju." *Pacific Rim Law and Policy Journal* 6(1):85–168.

Westney, D. Eleanor. 1987. *Imitation and Innovation: The Transfer of Western Organizational Patterns to Meiji Japan.* Cambridge, MA: Harvard University Press.

Whaley, Joachim. 1996. "The Rise and Fall of the Axe: Fluctuations of Capital Punishment in Germany." *Times Literary Supplement.* October 11:8–9.

Whitman, James Q. 2003. *Harsh Justice: Criminal Punishment and the Widening Divide between America and Europe.* New York: Oxford University Press.

Wickramasinghe, Arjuna. 2004. "Sri Lanka Reactivates Dormant Death Penalty." Reuters. November 20.

Wilkinson, Earl K., with Alan C. Atkins. 2000. "... *Sentenced to Death": The Truth about Englishman Albert Wilson's Sentence and Eventual Acquittal in the Philippines.* Zirndorf-Weiherhof, Germany: Book of Dreams.

Williams, Yoko. 2003. *Tsumi—Offence and Retribution in Early Japan.* London: RoutledgeCurzon.

Wilson, Richard L., and Hong Wang. 2008. "Teaching China's Legal and Political System: Culture and Revolution." *Education about Asia* 13(Spring): 45–47.

Wonacott, Peter. 2007. "Lawless Legislators Thwart Social Progress in India." *Wall Street Journal.* May 4.

World Health Organization. 2002. *World Report on Violence and Health.* Geneva: WHO. www.who.int.

Xie, Chuanjiao. 2008. "Top Court Overturns 15% Death Sentences in 1st Half Year." *China Daily.* June 27.

Xin, Ren. 1997. *Tradition of the Law and Law of the Tradition: Law, State, and Social Control in China.* Westport, CT: Greenwood.

Xu, Xiaoqun. 2008. *Trial of Modernity: Judicial Reform in Early Twentieth-century China, 1901–1937.* Stanford, CA: Stanford University Press.

Yamaguchi, Masanori. 2004. "Death Penalty and the Media." Trans. Nobuko Adachi. *Japan Focus.* http://japanfocus.org/161.html. [Originally published in *Shukan Kinyobi,* December 12, 2003.]

Yang, Anand A. 1985. *Crime and Criminality in British India.* Tucson: University of Arizona Press.

Yang, Benjamin. 1997. *Deng: A Political Biography.* East Gate Books. Armonk, NY: M. E. Sharpe.

Yang, Xi. 2008. "Expert: China Is Fit for Lethal Injections." Interview with Liu Renwen. *Beijing News.* January 3. [English trans.: www.china.org.cn/english/GS-e/237842. htm.]

Yardley, Jim. 2005a. "Desperate Search for Justice: One Man vs. China." *New York Times.* November 12.

Yardley, Jim. 2005b. "In Workers' Death, View of China's Harsh Justice." *New York Times*. December 31.

Yardley, Jim. 2005c. "A Judge Tests China's Courts, Making History." *New York Times*. November 28.

Yardley, Jim. 2006a. "The Chinese Go after Corruption, Corruptly." *New York Times*. October 22.

Yardley, Jim. 2006b. "Corruption Scandal at Top Tests Taiwan's Democracy." *New York Times*. November 25.

Yardley, Jim. 2006c. "Three Deaths in China Reveal Disparity in Price of Lives." *New York Times*. April 14.

Yardley, Jim. 2007. "With New Law, China Reports Drop in Executions." *New York Times*. June 9.

Yasuda, Yoshihiro. 2004. "Kokka to Shikei: Oumu to Iu Tenkanten." *Gendai Shiso* (March):44–55.

Yasuda, Yoshihiro. 2005. *"Ikiru" to Iu Kenri: Asahara Shoko Shunin Bengonin no Shuki*. Tokyo: Kodansha.

Yatsko, Pamela. 2001. *New Shanghai: The Rocky Rebirth of China's Legendary City*. New York: Wiley.

Ye, Juliet, and Geoffrey A. Fowler. 2008. "Chinese Bloggers Scale the 'Great Firewall' in Riot's Aftermath. *Wall Street Journal*. July 2.

Ye, Sang. 2006. *China Candid: The People on the People's Republic*. Ed. Geremie R. Barme and Miriam Lang. Berkeley: University of California Press.

Yi, Mun-yol. 2001. *The Poet*. Trans. Ching Chong-wha and Brother Anthony of Taize. London: Harvill Press.

Yi, Yanyou. 2008. "Arrest as Punishment: The Abuse of Arrest in the People's Republic of China." *Punishment and Society* 10:9–24.

Yoon, Sanghyun. 1996. "South Korea's Kim Young Sam Government: Political Agendas." *Asian Survey* 36(5):511–522.

Yorke, Jon. 2003. "The Death Penalty in Africa." *Amicus Journal* 8:12ff.

Yorke, Jon. 2005. "Extradition, Terrorism and the Death Penalty in Africa: Charting through the Labyrinth." *Amicus Journal* 15:25–34.

Yorke, Jon. 2006–2007. "The Evolving European Union Strategy against the Death Penalty: From Internal Renunciation to a Global Ideology." *Amicus Journal* 16:23–28 and 17:26–33.

Yoshida, Reiji, and Masami Ito. 2006. "Lasting Impact: Aum's Crimes Marked Start of Growing Public Safety Fear." *Japan Times*. September 18.

Yoshimura, Akira. 1989. "Kyuka." In *Hotaru*. Tokyo: Chuo Koronsha.

Zaide, Gregorio. 1983. *History of the Republic of the Philippines*. Manila: National Book Store.

Zakaria, Rafia. 2007. "The Death of Compassion." *Daily Times*. September 1.

Zeisel, Hans. 1985. *Say It with Figures*. 6th ed. New York: Harper and Row.

Zhang, Lening, Steven F. Messner, and Jianhong Liu. 2007. "An Exploration of the Determinants of Reporting Crime to the Police in the City of Tianjin, China." *Criminology* 45(4):959–983.

Zhang, Ning. 2005a. "The Debate over the Death Penalty in Today's China." *China Perspectives* 62:2–10.

Zhang, Ning. 2005b. Guest editor's introduction to special issue, "The Debate over the Death Penalty in China Today." *Contemporary Chinese Thought* 36(3):3–8.

Zhang, Ning. 2008. "The Political Origins of Death Penalty Exceptionalism: Mao Zedong and the Practice of Capital Punishment in Contemporary China." *Punishment and Society* 10:117–136.

Zhao, Suisheng, ed. 2006. *Debating Political Reform in China: The Rule of Law vs. Democratization.* Armonk, NY: M. E. Sharpe.

Zi, Yue. 2007. "Why China Favors the Death Penalty." UPI Asia Online. November 22.

Zimring, Franklin E. 2003. *The Contradictions of American Capital Punishment.* New York: Oxford University Press.

Zimring, Franklin E. 2007. *The Great American Crime Decline.* New York: Oxford University Press.

Zimring, Franklin E. 2008. "Criminology and Its Discontents: The American Society of Criminology Sutherland Address." *Criminology* 46:255–266.

Zimring, Franklin E., and Gordon Hawkins. 1986. *Capital Punishment and the American Agenda.* Cambridge: Cambridge University Press.

Zimring, Franklin E., and David T. Johnson. 2006. "Public Opinion and the Governance of Punishment in Democratic Political Systems." In Suzanne Karstedt and Gary LaFree, eds. *The ANNALS of the American Academy of Political and Social Science* 605(1):265–280.

Zimring, Franklin E., and David T. Johnson. 2008. "Law, Society, and Capital Punishment in Asia." *Punishment and Society* 10:103–115.

Zimring, Franklin E., David T. Johnson, and Jeffrey Fagan. 2008. "Executions and Homicides: A Tale of Two Cities." Unpublished paper.

Zin, Min. 2008. "All of Burma Is a Prison." *Wall Street Journal Asia.* June 29.

Zoellick, Robert. 2006. "Japan Is Ready for Revolution and Reform." *Financial Times.* November 28.

Zwartz, Barney. 2008. "Spare the Bali Bombers, Says Catholic Church." *Age.* January 3.

Index

capital offenses
  high-execution nations, 307–311
  North Korea, 360
  Philippines, 111, 118
  Thailand, 400–401
capital punishment
  communism and, 320–322
  declining importance for crime
    control, 299–300
  expenses and "super due process,"
    19n.10
  India, 428–439
  judicial vs. extrajudicial executions,
    27n.19
  Kim Young Sam's decision for South
    Korea, 170–172
  North-South Korean conflict,
    157–158
  politics and, in authoritarian
    regimes, 351–355
  politics of, in postwar Japan, 48–49
capital punishment categories, Amnesty
  International, 15–16
capital statute revisions, Taiwan's
  execution drop, 215
Caribbean countries, death row and
  executions, 32n.22
carnapping, crimes of death row
  inmates in Philippines, 121
cash, clemency in China, 277
caste system and class, India, 425–426,
  428
Catholic Church
  ambivalence in Philippines, 139, 141
  campaign to end capital punishment,
    211
  high profile in Philippines, 347
  pillar of South Korea's anti–death
    penalty movement, 175n.32
"censored democracy"
  capital punishment in Japan, 85
  U.S. occupation of Japan, 63, 79
Central Asia, definition, 16
Changxing, Lai, China's outlaw
  entrepreneur, 335
Chatterjee, Dhananjoy, Indian
  execution, 429, 429n.4, 431n.4
child-rape cases, "witch-hunt hysteria,"
  120

China. *See also* Taiwan
  cash for clemency, 277
  communism and capital punishment,
    320–322
  direct vs. indirect effects of policy shift,
    278
  early reports on impact of reform,
    280–282
  economic diversity of death row
    persons, 309–310
  estimating executions, 10, 231–243
  execution estimates by Amnesty
    International, 236
  execution estimates since 1998, 237
  execution rate of Meiji Japan vs., 58
  Hong Kong and Macao, 365–366
  hosting 2008 Olympics, 280–281, 285
  imprisonment rate, 230
  incidence of executions, 28–29
  influence on Japan, 98–99
  "kill less and kill carefully"
    policy, 18–19
  lethal injection, 275–276
  organ seizures from Falun Gong
    members, 232–233n.5
  outlaw entrepreneur Lai Changxing,
    335
  predicting impacts of reform, 277–280
  public support for death penalty, 302
  reform or reinstatement of Supreme
    People's Court (SPC), 273–274
  "retentionist" in Amnesty
    International sense, 18
  secrecy of execution data, 225–226
  selection in research plan, 41–42
  similarity of North Korea to,
    363–364
  size of prison system, 229–231
  Stalin's influence on Mao,
    253–257
  Strike Hard initiative, 227, 242
  "super due process," 271
Chinese Communist Party (CCP), 169,
  237–238
Chinese concepts of punishment,
  influencing Japan, 50, 78–79
Chinese economy, "purchasing power
  parity" measure, 231n.3
Ching-kuo, Chiang, ruler of Taiwan, 198